THE HOUSE OF DUDLEY

Joanne Paul is an Honorary Senior Lecturer and BBC/AHRC New Generation Thinker. Her research focuses on the intellectual and cultural history of the Renaissance and Early Modern periods. She has written for the Cambridge University Press 'Ideas in Context' series, and been widely praised for her work on Thomas More, William Shakespeare, Machiavelli and Thomas Hobbes. *The House of Dudley* is her first book.

JOANNE PAUL

The House of Dudley

A New History of Tudor England

PENGUIN BOOKS

PENGUIN BOOKS

UK | USA | Canada | Ireland | Australia
India | New Zealand | South Africa

Penguin Books is part of the Penguin Random House group of companies
whose addresses can be found at global.penguinrandomhouse.com

First published by Penguin Michael Joseph 2022
Published in Penguin Books 2023
002

Set in 9.25/12.5pt Sabon LT Std
Typeset by Jouve (UK), Milton Keynes
Printed and bound in Great Britain by Clays Ltd, Elcograf S.p.A.

The authorized representative in the EEA is Penguin Random House Ireland,
Morrison Chambers, 32 Nassau Street, Dublin D02 YH68

A CIP catalogue record for this book is available from the British Library

ISBN: 978-1-405-93719-1

www.greenpenguin.co.uk

To my family, by blood, by law and by love.

Contents

List of Illustrations

1. Tortington Church, Sussex © 2018 Joanne Paul

2. Funeral Mask of Henry VII, 1509 © 2021 Dean and Chapter of Westminster

3. Edmund Dudley's account book fol. 46, 1507, with the pardon of Thomas Sunnyff for £500 and the king's signature. Seventeenth-century copy © British Library

4. Henry VII on his deathbed, 1509, from Wriothesley, Garter King of Arms, Add 45131, fol. 54. Richard Fox is to the left of the king's bed and Hugh Denys stands fourth from the left on the right of the bed. © British Library

5. Tower of London, 1597. Eighteenth-century copy. © The National Archives

6. Portrait of John Dudley at Knole, Kent. Early seventeenth century. © Wikipedia

7. Siege of Boulogne, 1544. Eighteenth-century engraving after sixteenth-century painting. The destruction of the wall of the town can be seen in the centre of the image. © Wikipedia

8. Battle of the Solent, 1545. Sixteenth century. Charles Brandon, Duke of Suffolk, follows the king at the centre of the painting. In the water just above them the *Mary Rose* has sunk and John Dudley's *Henri Grâce à Dieu* leads the fleet. © Mary Rose Museum

9. Family of Henry VIII, c. 1545. From the left, Mary I, Edward VI, Henry VIII, Jane Seymour and Elizabeth I. The figures in the archways are two of the household fools. © Royal Collection Trust

Note on Conventions

Spelling

There was no standardization of spelling, including for proper names, in the sixteenth century. Quotations from sixteenth-century texts have been modernized, but an effort has been made to preserve punctuation and archaic vocabulary, with definitions provided in the footnotes and glossary. Where necessary, I have attempted to use spellings to make distinctions between individuals (for instance, the elder Katherine and younger Catherine Dudley, elder Henry and younger Harry Dudley, as well as Catherine of Aragon, Katherine Howard and Catherine Parr). I have largely modernized place names, except in a few cases so as to preserve the original sense of the name. Non-English place names have been Anglicized.

Dates

Much of Europe adopted the Gregorian calendar in October 1582, but England persisted with the Julian calendar until 1751, meaning there was a difference of ten days between countries of continental Europe and England from the latter part of the sixteenth century. Dates here have been given in Old Style (according to the Julian calendar), but with the presumption that the new year begins on 1 January, not 25 March.

Money

All values have been given in contemporary terms. One pound in 1500 was worth about £665.96 in 2017, one pound in 1550 about £274.70 in 2017, and one pound in 1600 about £137.88 in 2017. These values and the purchasing power of the amount have been taken from https://www.nationalarchives.gov.uk/currency-converter/. More detailed and slightly different conversions can also be found at https://measuringworth.com/.

Houses of Tudor & Stuart

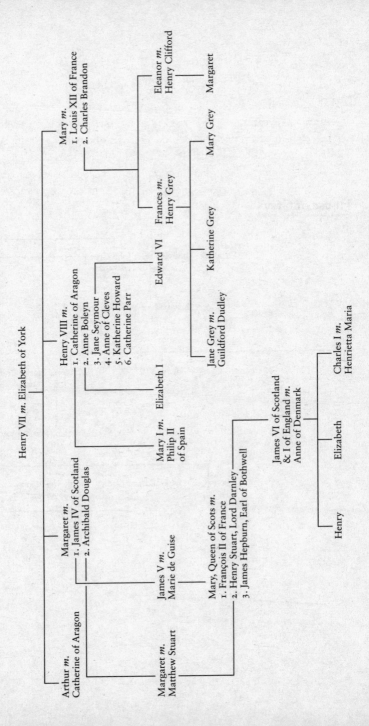

House of Grey

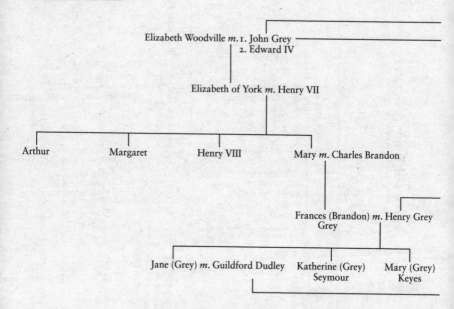

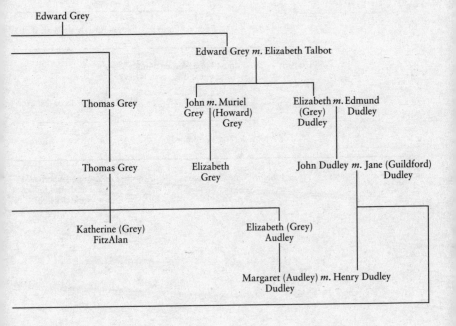

Edward Grey

Edward Grey *m.* Elizabeth Talbot

Thomas Grey

John *m.* Muriel
Grey (Howard)
Grey

Elizabeth *m.* Edmund
(Grey) Dudley
Dudley

Thomas Grey

Elizabeth
Grey

John Dudley *m.* Jane (Guildford)
Dudley

Katherine (Grey)
FitzAlan

Elizabeth (Grey)
Audley

Margaret (Audley) *m.* Henry Dudley
Dudley

House of Dudley

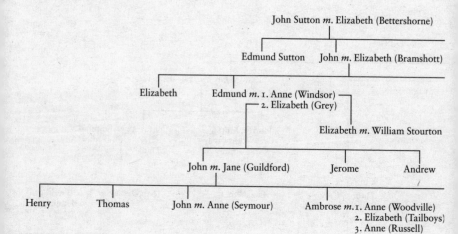

John Sutton *m.* Elizabeth (Bettershorne)

Edmund Sutton   John *m.* Elizabeth (Bramshott)

Elizabeth   Edmund *m.* 1. Anne (Windsor)
    2. Elizabeth (Grey)

Elizabeth *m.* William Stourton

John *m.* Jane (Guildford)   Jerome   Andrew

Henry   Thomas   John *m.* Anne (Seymour)   Ambrose *m.* 1. Anne (Woodville)
    2. Elizabeth (Tailboys)
    3. Anne (Russell)

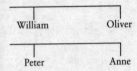

William   Oliver

Peter   Anne

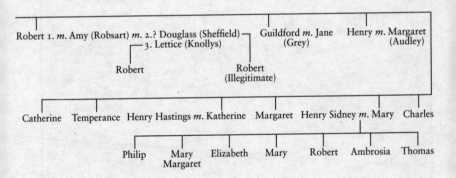

Robert 1. *m.* Amy (Robsart) *m.* 2.? Douglass (Sheffield)   Guildford *m.* Jane   Henry *m.* Margaret
       3. Lettice (Knollys)   (Grey)   (Audley)

Robert   Robert
                       (Illegitimate)

Catherine   Temperance   Henry Hastings *m.* Katherine   Margaret   Henry Sidney *m.* Mary   Charles

Philip   Mary   Elizabeth   Mary   Robert   Ambrosia   Thomas
       Margaret

England c. 1500

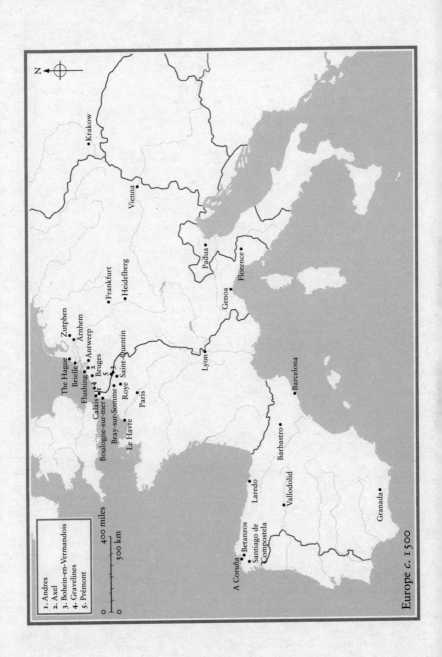

N

• Krakow

• Vienna

• Frankfurt
• Heidelberg

Zutphen •
The Hague • • Arnhem
Brielle • • Antwerp
Flushing • • Bruges
Calais • 4 1 2
Boulogne-sur-mer • 5 3 Saint-Quentin
Bray-sur-Somme • • Roye
Le Havre • • Paris

• Padua
• Florence
• Genoa

• Lyon

• Barcelona

• Barbastro

Laredo •
• Valladolid

A Coruña •
Betanzos •
Santiago de
Compostela •

• Granada

1. Andres
2. Axel
3. Bohein-en-Vermandois
4. Gravelines
5. Prémont

0   400 miles
0   500 km

Europe c. 1500

Prologue
A tribe of traitors

'For it is a settled rule of Machiavel which the Dudleys do observe, that where you have once done a great injury, there must you never forgive.'

The forbidden book circulated the Elizabethan court in the summer of 1584.

Clutched at by greedy fingers, laughed over by jealous tongues, it had a modest title: *The Copy of a Letter Written by a Master of Arts at Cambridge*. What it contained, however, was enough to have the author – whoever they were – punished with public mutilation. As the clandestine work spread like a wildfire across the court and beyond, while the queen's spymaster intimidated and interrogated to uncover the author, the work acquired a new title: *Leicester's Commonwealth*.

Robert Dudley, Earl of Leicester, was one of the most powerful men in the English court. One did not reach such heights without making enemies and, perhaps, deserving them. The little book rehearsed a litany of crimes committed by the earl – 'plots, treasons, murders, falsehoods, poisonings, lusts, incitements and evil stratagems' – all of which endangered crown and country.[1] Robert Dudley had killed husbands to acquire their wives, killed his own wife to marry the queen and discarded women who bore him children. He was forever ruled by his lust and ambition, neither of which could be fully sated.

But it was not just Robert who suffered in this short book. For generations, its author proclaimed, the House of Dudley had raised its children to challenge England's monarchs for the throne. Robert had been 'nuzzled in treason from his infancy'.[2] 'From his ancestors,' the pamphlet asserted, 'this lord receiveth neither honour nor honesty, but only succession of treason and infamy.'[3]

For decades the Dudley family and its emblem, the bear chained to the ragged staff, had become linked with ruthless and bloody ambition. Violent riot, rebellion and warfare could all be traced back to this single family, who had risen from political irrelevance within living memory. From this unimportant beginning, three generations of Dudleys had stood at the right hand of monarchs. Three generations of Dudleys had been revealed as traitorous vipers, stained by treason, and faced the executioner's blade. Vanity and vainglory, desire and deadly purpose – these defined the name of Dudley as the little pamphlet circulated the court.

Readers from either side of the religious and political divides that rent Queen Elizabeth's England began to wonder: was it true? Were the children of the House of Dudley raised to conspire against the ruling house of England? Was the Dudley family scheming to the highest ambition in the land?

Were the Dudleys out to steal the throne?

PART ONE
1500–1510

I
Remember that you must die

The priest stood outside his humble church just before dawn, in the shadow of the forests and meadows of the rolling South Downs in Tortington, Sussex.[1] Wearing his alb and stole, he thrust a spade into the damp earth, carving a large cross into the soil: 'This is the gate of the Lord,' he intoned, 'the just shall enter into it.'[2]

He was marking a grave for the body of a young mother. The corpse of Anne Dudley, born Anne Windsor, had been prepared and watched since her passing, to be sure that life would not return to it.[3] Her soul was already suffering in Purgatory; the priest's arrangements would begin the long process of lifting it to Heaven and scaring off the demons who might seek to seize her.[4]

The priest's parish of Tortington was a place of little national importance. Just north of the church was Tortington Priory, a small monastic community. The Priory had been founded at the end of the twelfth century by a former mistress of King Henry I, Alice de Corbet, who dedicated both church and priory to Mary Magdalene; perhaps de Corbet saw something of herself in the repentant harlot who dedicated her life to God.[5]

The church itself had been cobbled together with flint and chalk rubble scavenged from various other buildings.[6] Some of the stones had a bright green moss growing on them; others had had some part of them chipped off, exposing their bright white interior, like a flash of light across the murky surface of a pond. The effect was of a mosaic that never quite resolved itself into a clear picture.

Not long after the priest's preparations were complete, the ringing of a small bell heralded the arrival of the wrapped body to the church.

Dressed in solemn black, her lead mourners were women – family and friends – who were expected to precede the arrival of the rest of her family, such as her brother and sisters, and her husband, Edmund Dudley. The procession was of a decent size; Edmund and Anne were notables in the area and able to afford a modestly elaborate ceremony. They had been well matched; both were children of the violent civil war which had devastated the country in the last century and both were members of families who had risen up in the vacuum of power left by slaughtered noble houses.

Edmund's grandfather had been Sir John Sutton Dudley, a noted courtier and diplomat. Before Edmund was born, Sir John had fought beside the legendary King Henry V on the battlefields of France and travelled as far as Prussia and Mantua on behalf of the Crown. With the accession of Henry VI and the outbreak of war, Sutton Dudley clung to favour, and was wounded and captured fighting against the opposing forces of Richard, Duke of York. He switched sides, however, when the king himself was captured in 1460, and joined the court of the new Yorkist king Edward IV, becoming Constable of the Tower of London. There he oversaw the imprisonment of the warrior queen whom he had formerly served, Margaret of Anjou.

Edmund had been in his youth when he watched his grandfather dextrously and repeatedly switch loyalties, welcoming the reigns of Edward V, Richard III and Henry VII in quick succession in the years 1483 to 1485. John Sutton Dudley died two years into the reign of Henry VII, and the title of Lord Dudley followed the line of his eldest son. Edmund was the child of Sir John's second son, also called John. This younger John had not had such an illustrious career, but through his marriage to Elizabeth Bramshott he had secured a reliable amount of wealth and security with which to raise his family.

Edmund Dudley had, thus, received a gentleman's education. Thanks to his time at Oxford, Edmund was trained in the classics – authors such as Aristotle, Cicero and Augustine – as well as in the power of rhetoric and persuasion. He had left before finishing his degree, a fairly traditional move, in order to train in the law at the Inns of Court. There he joined other young men as they pored over legal texts by day and caroused about London by night.

It was not long after passing the bar in London that Edmund had married the young Anne Windsor. Anne's father had been appointed Constable of Windsor Castle by Richard III and died shortly after the accession of Henry VII. Her mother, Lady Elizabeth Windsor, remarried, and took as her new husband Sir Robert Lytton, the Keeper of the Wardrobe to Henry VII. Lytton's position put him in powerful proximity to the king, as overseer of all transactions of the royal household. Anne was the youngest of the Windsor daughters and the last to be married; her father had left her 100 marks, or just over £66, a skilled tradesman's salary for several years, in his will for her dowry.[7] It was not just the modest dowry, however, that Anne Windsor brought to her marriage with Edmund Dudley, but a growing proximity to power, an even more valuable asset.

Such a marriage was not just the joining of two people, but of two families. In the time since their wedding, Edmund Dudley and Anne's eldest brother, Andrew Windsor, had become staunch allies, working together securing lands in Sussex for both the Dudleys and the Windsors.[8] Andrew, his younger brothers, Anthony and John, and their two sisters had married into some of the most influential families in Sussex. Edmund also had siblings, two younger brothers and two sisters. Together, they had become one of the best-connected families in the county. All might have been expected to attend the burial service of Anne Dudley.

Anne's procession passed through an ornate archway supported by two columned pillars. The corpse was placed upon a bier under the chancel arch, which separated the nave – containing the laypeople – from the area around the altar, which was reserved for the clergy. Anne's body, like her soul, hovered in a place between this world and the next. Her mourners' prayers, and those that would be said in her honour in the coming months and years, would help ensure that her soul entered Heaven and escaped the torments of Purgatory. Those who prayed for her, however, still had to face the tortures of this world. Above the bier, decorating the chancel arch were grotesque stone birds, with tongues protruding and wide, saucer-like eyes. They stared down at Anne's mourners. Faith was not meant to be a comfortable experience. Religion sought to unsettle even as it consoled.

This world, with its pestilence, violence and various temptations, was a prison. Remembering that would help lift one to the ultimate escape of Heaven.

Much of the church was draped in black. Gone was the colourful altar cloth that Anne's father-in-law, John Dudley, had donated to the church on his death, embroidered with the Dudley arms. John had dearly loved his daughter-in-law. In his will he had left her gold from which to design a chain in whatever fashion she so chose. When she died, the chain would pass to her daughter, his granddaughter, the 'little Elizabeth' as he affectionately called her.[9] John might not have predicted that this would happen so soon after his own death; Elizabeth was still an infant at her mother's burial. She was unlikely to remember anything about her mother as she grew up.

The members of the procession took their places as the priest called on the mercy of God. At the appointed time, the deacon advanced with his censer of incense, wafting billowing smoke on either side of Anne's body, which dispersed into the nave and filled the church. When those present retired home, after the burial feast, they would be reminded of the ceremony by the thick smell of incense on their clothes as they undressed.

The first reading was offered to comfort those who mourned Anne's early and unexpected death: 'But I would not have you to be ignorant, brethren, concerning them which are asleep, that ye sorrow not, even as others which have no hope', a theme repeated by the three clerks standing at the head of the wrapped body: 'Yea, though I walk through the valley of the shadow of death, I will fear no evil: for thou art with me, O Lord. Thy rod and thy staff comfort me.'[10]

Saint Augustine, whose works Edmund had scoured as a youth, had written that funerals were more for the living than for the dead. Anne's death was early and unexpected, and her husband, for all his education and noble lineage, found himself in a precarious situation. He was approaching forty and he had no wife or male heir, just a daughter who was still young enough to succumb to the many ailments and illnesses common to that time of life. It was true that he had represented the Sussex town of Lewes in the king's parliament and was undersheriff of London, a deputy performing some of the legal duties of the sheriff, including hearing cases in London's courts.[11] He had also won modest renown amongst his academically inclined friends for his ability to debate the nuances and intricacies of the law, including the Crown's right to challenge private authorities and jurisdictions.[12] He was becoming an established local landowner, and agent of the Crown in his own county, but was still far from a source of any real political power.

As the service ended, the assembly proceeded into the churchyard to where the priest had marked the grave that morning, now a rectangular wound in the earth several feet deep. They watched as Anne's body was lowered into the fresh grave. The priest gathered a handful of earth, throwing it on her corpse in the shape of the cross, like that he had drawn hours before: 'Earth to earth, ashes to ashes, dust to dust'.[13] The ritual was one of the many reminders surrounding Edmund that he too would meet this fate, sooner or later. The only way to overcome death in this world was through family or fame. Standing by the open grave of his wife, Edmund Dudley had neither.

*

Sixty-five miles to the north, in the sprawling city of London, King Henry VII's worries were much like those of Edmund Dudley. He too had recently buried his wife, though Queen Elizabeth's funeral was substantially grander than that of Anne Dudley. Hundreds of common folk and nobles had witnessed the procession along torch-lined streets from the Tower of London to Westminster Abbey to mark the death of the White Rose of England.[14] By her marriage almost twenty years before to Henry of Richmond, the Lancastrian heir, Elizabeth of York had smoothed the path to a peaceful resolution of the civil war. The grandeur of her funeral, however, did not change the worrying position in which her death had put the family.

Less than a year before, on the morning of 4 April 1502, Henry had been woken earlier than usual in his palace at Greenwich. Greenwich – or the Palace of Placentia – was one of Henry VII's building projects, and he had worked to modernize the residence over the previous five years. Although he spent much of his time elsewhere, Greenwich was the official royal residence.

Standing before the king was his grey-robed confessor, who delivered the heart-breaking news. Henry and Elizabeth's eldest son had died, the culmination of an eight-week illness which had struck down the youth as he approached his sixteenth year. Arthur, with a name more legendary than the sickly adolescent had been able to carry, was meant to be the living manifestation of the peace brokered by his parents' marriage. Henry VII had come to the throne not long before his son's birth. He had been forced to conquer his country, winning it in battle against the previous king, Richard III, who Henry saw as a usurper. Richard had died on the battlefield, and Henry had been crowned not long after. He had quickly married Richard's niece, Elizabeth, whose father and brother had also been kings (Edward IV and the short-lived Edward V). Her claim was infinitely stronger than Henry's, except for the fact of her sex, of course. Henry's great-great-great-grandfather was King Edward III, though one had to overlook an illegitimate birth in order to draw the connection to the new king of England. For the three decades before Henry took the crown, the country had been in turmoil, as blood was spilled between the Houses of Lancaster – of which Henry VII was the heir – and that of York – to which Elizabeth his wife belonged. Their first child, Arthur, was the fulfilment of a promise of unity and peace. On him had rested the hope for the nascent dynasty, and the country.

Now Arthur was dead. On hearing the news, Henry had sent for his wife, who consoled him with the reminder of their remaining children and the possibility that they might yet have more, before collapsing in grief herself.[15] As if by prophecy, Elizabeth became pregnant not long after, but it was not the reversal of fortune for which Henry had hoped. Following a long and difficult labour, both Queen Elizabeth and her newborn daughter died. Henry was left with only three living children – and importantly, just one son, Henry– and no wife. He shut himself away from his duties and his closest advisers, disappearing into the depths of his private chambers at Richmond Palace for over a month.[16]

Locked away, he did battle with death. It was not unheard of for grief to kill a man, the heart going cold and drying out, eventually breaking.[17] It was a slow process and aged the body prematurely. The remedies were fresh air, exercise and good counsel, all of which Henry pushed away. He was cast into a deep fever and robbed of his ability even to speak or cry out.[18] To the public, the king was 'in mourning'. Those closest to him, however, knew that the king was near death, and his heir just a little boy who was still distraught over the loss of his mother. The king, perhaps aware of the necessity of his recovery, rallied as spring broke.

When Henry emerged, he was a changed man. The king had always been close, secretive and suspicious, but heavy loss made him paranoid and obsessive. Henry had snatched the crown in bloody battle not two decades before from a king, Richard III, who had seized it from the hands of a murdered boy, Edward V, whose own father, Edward IV, had wrenched it from another slaughtered king, Henry VI, who had come to the throne as an infant. Henry had endured multiple threats against his throne, most significantly in the form of 'pretenders': frauds who claimed to be heirs to the throne with better claims than Henry's own. He had always put them down, but the unexpected deaths of his wife and daughter would weaken any man's sense of security. Officers of the king whispered that not only was their master 'weak and sickly' and 'not likely to be a long-lived man', but also that if any 'knew King Harry' as they did, they would be wise to tread carefully, for he was likely to assume that bad news 'came of envy, ill-will, and malice', turning on those who delivered it.[19]

And it was about to get worse. Throughout his reign Henry strategically refused to promote the nobles who might look to supplant him, instead elevating educated men from middling backgrounds who he could raise – and destroy – as needed.[20] One of the first and the most important was Sir Reginald Bray, whom Henry had known as a boy and relied on as a king. Bray had begun his career in the service of Henry's mother, Margaret Beaufort, gifting her young son with a bow and quiver of arrows. Bray had worked tirelessly to support Henry's invasion against Richard III and had always found ways – not always beneficent ones – to ensure the Crown was well supported financially.[21] Bray's lack of scruples made him perfect to oversee Henry's 'Council Learned in the Law', a conciliar court with no fixed membership, location or mandate, which operated outside of the official judicial system without any statutory authority.[22] Henry counted on Bray to execute his justice as he needed and, at times, even to sell it: for instance, the £200 extracted from the widowed sister of the Queen of England to provide 'indifferent justice', something she might have hoped to receive from the courts without needing to pay for it.[23] By means of his spies and enforcers, Bray gathered information to enforce the king's prerogative, keep wayward subjects obligated to him and ensure a steady stream of revenue – with a cut off the top for himself, of course.[24] Only six months after the death of Queen Elizabeth, however, Henry lost him too.[25]

With Bray's death, Henry faced a hole in the various and wide-ranging networks protecting his reign.[26] The Earl of Suffolk, Edmund de la Pole, was threatening to invade, with the support of the Holy Roman Emperor, Maximilian I. Pole's elder brother, John, had been the designated heir of Richard III, but had died in the midst of a rebellion two years after Henry VII's conquest, leaving his younger brother as a competing claimant to the throne. Styling himself the 'duke' rather than 'earl' of Suffolk, Pole had fled to the continent and into the waiting arms of Maximilian in 1501. A month before Bray's death in August 1503, seven men had been hanged, drawn and quartered for conspiring with Pole.[27] Bray's death, on the heels of the deaths of the queen and heir to the throne, was yet another disaster in what was surely an unravelling and vulnerable regime.

Bray had not left Henry entirely bereft, however. One of his last acts was to introduce the king to a man who – though he lacked Bray's experience – was perhaps even more knowledgeable in the skills and connections Henry needed: a wide-ranging legal knowledge of the king's prerogatives alongside connections to London informants and the city's officials.[28] If Henry could not rely on a plenitude of sons on which to establish his dynasty and avoid civil war, he would need to fortify his crown another way.[29] If his nobles would not respect his claim to the throne by claim of blood, they would need to be faithful to him through forced financial obligation.[30] What Henry needed was someone versed in the laws which would allow him to bind his subjects to him – and his son – in the incontrovertible language of coin. What – or who – the king needed was Edmund Dudley.[31]

*

On Thursday, 25 January 1504, the nineteenth year of the reign of King Henry VII, the king's seventh parliament was called. The opening of parliament was always a majestic affair, and the people braved the cold of a January morning to take to the streets of London to watch the king and his lords arrive at Westminster Palace.[32] The Palace of Westminster had been used as a royal residence since before the conquest of 1066, thanks to its strategic position on the Thames. It sat to the west of the City of London, requiring travel by boat from a home in the centre of the city. Parliament, the representative assembly of lords and nobles who gave their counsel and consent to the king's laws and taxes, had met at this grand palace since the thirteenth century.

The Lords, attired in their traditional red and ermine robes and crowns of nobility, processed into the chamber where the first session would be held, while the king prepared in an adjacent room.[33] They were joined there by the bishops, abbots and prelates, another twenty to thirty solemn robed men. At last, the king entered, golden sceptre in hand, and sat enthroned under a grand cloth of state. Once settled, he summoned the Commons to join them.

The House of Commons had only recently begun to take on similar power to that of the Lords. Nevertheless, refusing requests for taxation remained one of the Commons' most effective checks on monarchical power.[34] With very few exceptions (which Edmund knew well), Henry VII could not impose taxes on his subjects without the assent of the Commons. It was also an excellent place to test the temperature of public opinion.[35] If Henry wanted to shore up financial reserves, he would either have to go via the House of Commons, or cleverly circumvent it.

Amongst the cluster of the three hundred or so men who made up the Commons was Edmund Dudley.[36] It was not his first time as a member of parliament, and he recognized many of the men swarming about him. This time, however, he had a new sense of purpose, of privilege. He was to be set apart from his peers.

At the king's summons, the knights, citizens and burgesses walked into the great hall to join their monarch and the Lords. This was the Chamber of the Holy Cross, also called the Painted Chamber; the former because it was the supposed death-place of the hallowed saint and king, Edward the Confessor, the latter because of the ornate paintings that covered every inch of the walls.[37] It was huge: standing shoulder to shoulder about 1,000 men would fit inside its walls, and still have space to manoeuvre, and it would take at least five tall men standing one on top of the other to come anywhere near the height of the ceiling.

Each wall had been divided into horizontal sections of painted scenes, about the height of a man, so that the people in them were brilliantly life-sized. Entering from the ornate doorway on the south-west side of the room, you were faced with the beginning of the story on the north wall, which you followed east to your right, and turning around, ended the story just above the door through which you'd entered.[38] As you did, you noticed that the painted story did not just evolve as you turned around the room, but from the uppermost strip to the lower as well. The stories at the highest level, the ones you strained your neck to see, were of virtuous kings, like Judas Maccabeus, the great Old Testament king. He was portrayed immediately across from the entrance, leading his troops into a walled city, slaughtering its inhabitants and the enemy underfoot. Those at the lowest level, beside the entrance, presented a clear warning about the death and perpetual humiliation of tyrannical rulers, like Antiochus IV, who after condemning the seven 'Maccabean martyrs' to brutal torture and death by boiling in oil was himself tortured by God with crippling bowel pain and a fatal fall from a speeding chariot.[39]

Death and destruction – especially in battle – was the dominant theme: men and boys killed in combat, the faithful cruelly tortured, citizens violently slaughtered. Such scenes formed an odd juxaposition with the other paintings in the room, which portrayed scenes of quiet victory, even piety. The Virtues were gloriously illustrated on the tall window splays that punctuated the room. Depicted as women in medieval suits of armour, they serenely vanquished their opposing Vices, writhing defeated beneath them. Even more holy was the scene portrayed in the bottom right corner, just right of the large hearth and next to the king's throne. There St Edward the Confessor, in a gilded purple robe, was crowned by the bishops of the Church, holding bright gold mitres. Edward, at the centre, was clearly the pivotal figure in the scene, but he was vastly outnumbered by the eighteen bishops, who seemed to speak and gesture approvingly amongst themselves, and the centre-most of whom placed the gilded crown upon the saintly ruler's head. On either side painted soldiers stood guard over the royal presence.

Regal piety and virtue, fierce war-like violence and the cruel punishment of the vicious, these were the scenes that met the eyes of the gathered members of parliament as they entered the presence of the king.[40]

King Henry, sat on his throne amongst the painted scenes, looked like a living manifestation of these opposed regal burdens. Painted to his left was the great Judas Maccabeus. In his youth Henry had not been unlike the young biblical king, taking back his realm by righteous force of arms. Since the death of Richard III at Bosworth, however, Henry avoided war whenever possible. Neither, though, did Henry have the pure piety of Edward the Confessor, staring at him from the wall on his right. Henry's religious policy was orthodox – heretics were burnt and the pope's authority in England upheld – though he had also placed increasingly intense financial burdens on Church institutions in order to line his own coffers.[41]

There was an observable difference between this Henry and the one who had presided over parliament seven years before.[42] Then, Henry had been triumphant and conquering, secure in his throne and his dynasty. Now – thanks particularly to the deaths of his wife and son – he teetered on the precipice of insignificance. One more tragedy could render this new and feeble dynasty nothing more than a strange and inexplicable aberration in the line of English kings. This difficult reality showed in every part of the king's person. Henry had always been slender, but now he looked drawn. This was heightened by the fact that he stood taller than most of those around him, making him seem even leaner. Grey eyes that could appear kind, or cheerful, now took on the appearance of weariness and wariness. Thin lips concealed worn teeth. He had a sallow complexion and protruding high cheekbones that gave an air of alertness and cunning. The hair that fell from under his heavy crown and brushed the shoulders of his robes was white. He would soon be fifty, but his pinched face showed the strain of greater years.

As Edmund and the other members took their places in the Painted Chamber, a solemn-looking stout man in his early fifties, with intelligent dark eyes and long brows, stood to give his speech. This was the newly appointed Lord Chancellor and Archbishop of Canterbury, William Warham. Born of humble if not obscure stock, the law-educated Warham had been in royal service for well over a decade but had risen quickly in the previous few years, and indeed the last few days.[43] Warham was not an obvious choice for high promotion – he was not known for his charisma or brilliance, but he had the experience and loyalty that Henry had clearly found to be useful.[44] Appointed Lord Chancellor only days before parliament opened, Warham had become, almost overnight, the most politically powerful man in England under the king, presiding over the King's Council and the Chancery.[45] Such was a world ruled by a precarious king: fortune's wheel could turn very quickly indeed.

'Love justice, you who judge the land,' Warham proclaimed to those assembled.[46] This line of scripture was the theme of Warham's speech, the content of which was so banal as to verge on boring; Edmund would have heard many other sermons like it in his time. 'As Augustine says,' Warham continued, 'when justice has been taken away, what are kingdoms but great bands of robbers?' He then exhorted those assembled to scorn not only pleasures in the pursuit of justice, but pains as well, not letting fear of prisons, chains, banishment, torture or death get in the way of the just path in the service of their country. Did a few men nervously eye the chamber's painted image of the martyrs, tongues violently ripped from their mouths before they were boiled alive?

At long last, Warham finished his speech and shifted to the first order of business. The commons had been brought together to choose from their ranks a man to speak for them, their 'Speaker'. The Speaker controlled in what order bills were read and thus could prioritize those proposals from the Crown over private bills – or vice versa – in the short period allotted to the meeting of parliament. It was an important role, and thus had to be chosen from and by the ranks of the members themselves. Those assembled knew this for a charade, however; the Speaker had already been chosen – and not by the people.[47] The recently widowed Edmund Dudley, standing in that crowd of men before the throne, knew this powerful position was already his.

*

On his formal appointment four days later, Edmund walked in procession into the Commons' chamber in the chapter house at Westminster Abbey. The chapter house was octagonal in shape, with dramatic scenes from the apocalypse played out on the walls within the grand sweeping arches.[48] Edmund's feet passed over the ornate tile floor, on which was inscribed '*Ut rosa flos florum sic est domus ista domorum*'. The inscription was centuries old, but its meaning – 'As the rose is the flower of flowers, so is this house the house of houses' – was apt for the royal dynasty brought in under Henry VII, with its symbol of the combined red and white roses.

Edmund was flanked by two of the most powerful councillors of the reign: the Treasurer, Sir John Heron, was on his right side, and the Comptroller, Sir Richard Guildford, was on his left.[49] John Heron was of an age with Edmund, though he had been in royal service since Henry VII's accession and had held the powerful post of Treasurer for over a decade. Richard Guildford, on the other hand, was approaching old age and already had an adult heir. He had been a long-time friend of Bray's, working with him to facilitate Henry VII's conquest. He had known Edmund's father, and may have also played a role in manoeuvring Edmund into his current position.[50] It was only right he stood at his side now.

Edmund approached the throne and made three deep bows to the seated king. Henry announced he was 'well satisfied' with the choice of Speaker (given it was his own) and indicated to Edmund to speak. Edmund knew what he had to say, though it may have felt a risk to say it. He forced himself to lie to the king, begging to be relieved of the heavy burden of the proffered office. Such a grand speech belied the fact that Edmund had gambled his whole legal career on this position, boldly and expensively turning down a promotion the previous autumn to serjeant-at-law, the step before becoming a judge.[51] This was the performance every Speaker was required to make – he must not appear eager for promotion, even if desperate for it. Every king, upon hearing this speech, had always refused the request, but this precedent did not mean that the prospect of being publicly demoted was not terrifying. Fortunately for Edmund, the king confirmed his appointment – Edmund Dudley now presided over the House of Commons and was trusted by the King of England to do so in his name.[52]

Once officially recognized in his office, Edmund was seated in the Speaker's chair at the head of the room.[53] Before him was the clerks' table, where votes would be decided, picked out from the din of shouted assent or dissent. Arranged around this core were the members of the Commons, sitting on benches in no particular arrangement, though one might suspect allies and factions found each other for support. Members of the Commons, all 296 of them, were elected from their respective regions, and were there to represent the interest of their constituency.[54] Of course, Edmund knew well that it did not always work this way. Many poorer boroughs welcomed outsider representation, if they didn't have to pay them, and members of the court frequently ensured their own men were elected to the Commons, in order to have more control over what went on in the Lower House.

Most of the statutes passed were customary and of little national significance – legislating that those who did not accompany the king into war suffered financial penalties or that apprentices played at dice and cards only during the twelve days of Christmas – but Edmund needed to introduce two crucial pieces of business for the Crown during this session of parliament.[55] The first was straightforward and uncontroversial, though significant. The heir to the throne, Prince Arthur, was dead. This made his twelve-year-old brother, Henry, next-in-line, but Prince Henry had not yet been officially invested with the proper titles. Henry had grown up as Duke of York to his elder brother's Prince of Wales; his first public appearance, as a ten-year-old, was in his brother's wedding procession when Arthur married the Spanish princess, Catherine of Aragon. Prince Henry had been well educated and had a genuine interest in scholarly matters. He had been devastated – 'wounded' as the young prince put it – by his mother's death, and now had to take on the mantle of heir to the English throne.[56] There was no Duke of York to succeed him. The entire Tudor dynasty rested on this twelve-year-old's shoulders. The Commons were happy to approve the investiture of Henry as Prince of Wales: 'it hath pleased Almighty God to call the King's dearest son Henry Duke of York to be now the King's heir apparent and Prince of Wales'.[57]

The second request from the king was trickier. Prince Henry would need to be bolstered financially if the dynasty was to survive. Parliament needed to be called on to provide much of this revenue. This was always a difficult subject and could lead to all-out revolt if handled badly, as the king knew well. In 1497, Henry had sought £120,000 from parliament and had faced a nearly devastating rebellion. Tens of thousands had marched on the capital, and Henry had to recall his soldiers marching towards Scotland to deal with the peasants' army.[58] Raising funds, though necessary, was a dangerous business.

Perhaps on the advice of a certain clever lawyer well versed in the king's feudal rights and prerogatives, Henry put before the parliament his medieval right to 'reasonable aids' in paying for major royal events in an attempt to dredge up extra coin.[59] As announced to those assembled, these events were the 'making Knight of the right noble Prince his first begotten son Arthur late Prince of Wales deceased', an event which had occurred almost two decades earlier in 1489, and the marriage of Henry's daughter, Margaret, to the King of Scots, which had occurred the previous year.[60] Though it was also added that 'his Highness hath sustained and borne great and inestimable charges for the defence of this his Realm', it was a blatant attempt on the king's part to revive his regal rights as feudal overlord and squeeze money out of his subjects.[61] Henry perhaps hoped that the members would be too sensitive to Arthur's recent death to raise objections to the request. They had no such qualms.

No matter how much the request was phrased in the language of the king's ancient rights and the protection of the realm, it was exorbitant and unwelcome. Edmund presided over a ferocious debate. In the end, the Commons agreed to hand over £40,000, less than half of what the king seemed to expect.[62] Edmund had done well to get the king even this much, but it was clear that parliament would not be providing the extra coin the king sought to protect his young son's reign.[63] Henry stated clearly that he did not intend to call another parliament for as long as he could manage without. Both Edmund Dudley and Andrew Windsor were named as commissioners to collect the funds, allowing them to take money from the collection to pay for their own 'costs, expenses and charge'.[64] It was becoming increasingly clear to Edmund how to serve the king and oneself – including one's family – in the same stroke.

As rumours of the debate and the king's attempt to shake coin out of parliament were whispered around the city, it was reported that the king – and Edmund – were defeated by the arguments of a 'beardless boy', a city lawyer in his mid-twenties by the name of Thomas More.[65] The gossips of London were seldom kind, but Edmund was not particularly inclined to ingratiate himself. Let tongues wag. He was the king's man.

*

Elizabeth Grey, recently Elizabeth Dudley, screamed in the Great Parlour of her grand London home. She was in labour, her pregnancy coming not long after her marriage to the rising lawyer, Edmund Dudley. The daughter of a late Viscount and descended from a host of noble families, including Lisle, Beauchamp, Talbot and Grey, Elizabeth was above Edmund in social standing.[66] His recent elevation in the king's favour, however, had made him a viable suitor for a young heiress.[67] Now Elizabeth, in her early twenties, needed to safely deliver a male heir to the Dudleys' rising good fortune and favour. Another daughter, like the motherless 'Little Elizabeth', would not be enough. Though Edmund's first wife had been buried sixty miles away, reminders of her and Edmund's roots in Sussex were all around Elizabeth Dudley. Her new home at Candlewick Street, just east of St Paul's Cathedral, was adjacent to a parish church under the control of the prior of Tortington, where Anne had been buried.[68] Elizabeth, straining and crying, needed to pray she would not soon join her predecessor.

Of all the rooms in their large home at Candlewick Street, the Great Parlour was the only one that met all the requirements for a

birthing room.[69] There was a fireplace to heat water and the chamber –
the mother must not be allowed to get cold – and it was large enough
to house all the women who needed to be present, Elizabeth's friends
and kinswomen and her midwife, who shouted orders and encouragement.[70] Childbirth was terrifying; both mother and child could die in
a state of unconfessed sin and agonizing pain. For Elizabeth's comfort
and safety, there were prayers, especially to the Virgin Mary, whose
sinless condition resulted in the painless delivery of the Messiah.
There were also prayers to St Margaret, who was eaten by a dragon
but spat back out, in the hopes that the newborn would emerge as
effortlessly as Margaret went hurtling out of the dragon. Elizabeth
could also take comfort in various talismans and relics brought to her
by the women who surrounded her. Prayer rolls could be wrapped
girdle-like around her belly or encased in amulets at her ankle or
knee.[71] The Flemish printer Wynkyn de Worde sold birthing girdles
with printed prayers on them at his shop on Fleet Street, a short walk
away. These prayers, 'Christ calls you child + come out + come out +
Christ conquers + Christ rules + Christ is lord', could also be chanted
rhythmically as Elizabeth panted and strained.[72]

There was other help for Elizabeth as well. Books like the medieval
Trotula advised herbal remedies for the pains of childbirth, such as a
concentrated liquor of fenugreek, laurel, flax and fleawort.[73] Sweet-
smelling smoke – of aloewood, mint, oregano – could be produced,
but was not for the mother's nose; instead it was fanned between her
open legs. For reasons unknown to midwives, it seemed to help if the
mother held a magnet in her right hand, drank ivory shavings, or had
coral around her neck. Potions could also be made from the white
excrement of a hawk, or water which had been used to wash dissected
parts of a firstborn swallow. It might be God's will whether mother
and child survived this ordeal, but Elizabeth had copious instructions
for what, nevertheless, might help things along.

At last, Elizabeth's screams subsided. In the silence, another's took
her place. Edmund's wife had given birth to a healthy son. Quickly,
the baby's ears were pressed, ensuring that nothing foul entered them.
The umbilical cord was tied, ideally at a distance of three fingers
from the belly; a practice said to ensure a well-sized male member

(it was never too early for such precautions). To be certain that the child would speak at a young age, his palate would be anointed with honey and his little nose with warm water from the pot by the fire. He was wrapped in tight cloths to straighten and massage his limbs. As the doors and windows were at last opened, welcoming in light and air from outside, his eyes would be covered to protect him from the harsh light.[74] The baby boy was to be christened John, sharing his name with Edmund's father and grandfather, as well as Elizabeth's own grandfather, through whom her child might one day inherit her family's title of Viscount Lisle.

Walking through the long gallery of Candlewick, overlooking the garden he shared with the prior of Tortington, Edmund could begin to feel the security he was building for himself and his growing family. Edmund had a son, and the promise of more to follow. What's more, the king's increasing insecurity provided opportunity for Edmund to step in, applying his talents, experience and contacts to meet the king's needs and desires. As faithful instrument of the king's will, enforcer of the king's laws and prerogatives, Edmund could hope to rise. The only way to overcome death in this world was through family or fame. Standing by the cradle of his newborn son, Edmund Dudley had his sights on both.

2

Two ravening wolves

Sir William Clopton approached the entryway at Candlewick Street nervously, his shallow breath appearing like smoke in the air before him.[1] He was in his fifties and entering a colder time of life; it was no wonder that the chill made him ache in ways it had not when he was young. It was not his first time at the large home on Candlewick Street, dealing with the king's newly made royal councillor.[2] Previously, he had left cornered but hopeful. Today, he just wanted the whole ordeal over with. He had brought a simple property arbitration to the Exchequer of Pleas, a court designed to settle issues of equity presided over by the Barons of the Exchequer. He had been close to being awarded restitution when Edmund Dudley had suddenly intervened, interrupting proceedings. Dudley, a full decade younger than the knight, told him that he would not receive a penny, not even enough to cover the costs of the case, unless he promised that a full half of it would be paid directly to the king. Dudley had put a steep price on justice, but Clopton had seen no way out. He agreed.

He had returned to the Exchequer the next day, and called for immediate judgement, assured he had bought an outcome in his favour. His opponent in the case, Thomas Stanley, the Earl of Derby, however, was not interested in being a pawn in Dudley's plan. A young man with a protruding chin and sharp glance, Stanley had inherited his title only a few months before. He moved quickly. Interrupting proceedings and pulling Clopton aside, Stanley offered the value of 200 marks, or £132, if Clopton settled the case immediately.

Clopton once again agreed. Now, he just needed to convince Edmund to take the settlement. And so he journeyed to Candlewick Street, Stanley's agreement in hand.

He was joined by his friend and neighbour, Sir Robert Drury, a royal councillor and experienced lawyer, to back him up. Drury, of an age with Clopton, had been a Speaker in Parliament, like Edmund, and his career, though not progressing as rapidly, was not dissimilar. If anyone could speak reason to Edmund Dudley, surely it would be Drury.

Dudley's home was a large two-storey merchant's house, located just two streets north of the busy River Thames, at the corner of Walbrook and Candlewick Streets. Across the street from his home stood the legendary London Stone, a block of limestone about the size of a large chest, said to date back to the first kings of England. 'Candlewick' was one of the first homes in London to contain a long gallery, designed to allow one to take recreation in inclement weather; its size also facilitated private whispered conversation.[3] The hangings on the wall were of red and green vertical stripes, called 'paly', and the two windows were curtained with green say, a delicate twilled woollen fabric. On the wall opposite the windows stood the fireplace, which warmed the gallery against the chill outside. The room was furnished simply, but as necessary, with a table, bench and chair, the last clearly meant for Edmund himself. There was also a coffer, a strong box, in which Edmund kept the bills and evidence he needed to do his work.

Edmund Dudley dressed plainly but fashionably: black with hints of crimson, a flash of gold or silver woven through the cloth. The black reminded those around him that he was a trained man of law. The expensive fur that lined his gowns was a reminder of his wealth. It was sombre yet expensive and painted a picture of quiet ambition.

Edmund watched the two men approach. He had been given strict instructions in this case to get at least 300 marks for the king. This could be easily done; he had full control of the court and the promise of payment from Clopton. If Clopton didn't cooperate, he was sure that the young, presumably malleable, Stanley would. The king required the money, and he would get it.

Clopton approached Edmund and showed him the agreement he

had struck. A settlement of 200 marks meant only 100 marks for the king. This was not enough. Dudley offered Clopton a choice: 'If you take fifty marks and go on your way, and let me continue the suit in the Exchequer, you can have your fifty marks, or else you'll have never a penny.' It was not a good deal, at least not if you were Sir William Clopton.

Drury stepped forward to intercede on his friend's behalf. 'Considering the king's grace had no right but by the grant of William,' he interjected, 'the end that William has taken with the Earl of Derby should stand.'

Edmund was taken aback. The king had 'no right'? Who was Drury to lecture him on the king's rights? 'Are you of the king's council,' he retorted, 'and will argue against the king's advantage?' Drury was indeed a member of the king's council, a knight and chief steward to the Earl of Oxford. An upstart lawyer with no title should have afforded him more respect. Edmund did not.

Ignoring Drury, Edmund returned to Clopton once again. 'Be not so hardy,' he cautioned, 'that you make any end but continue your said suit in the Exchequer, as you will eschew the king's displeasure.' The stark warning ended any further conversation. The two men left Candlewick, walking back out into the cold, bustling streets of London, outmanoeuvred by Dudley. As long as Edmund wielded the weapon of the king's pleasure, no man or men could defeat him.

Edmund wasted little time in going directly to the Earl of Derby. With Stanley he privately negotiated the settlement of 300 marks, all of which went straight to the king. As he had threatened, not a penny went to Clopton. Dudley later went on to fine Clopton a further £200, without recording a reason. Neither Drury nor Clopton would forget the encounter, or its lessons. The black-robed lawyer was a force to be reckoned with.

*

Clopton and Drury were not the only such visitors Edmund saw at Candlewick. Almost overnight his home had become a hub of activity. Parliament had ended in April of 1504, and on 9 September, shortly before the Clopton case, Edmund had begun his account books on behalf of the king. Two days later he officially became a royal councillor. He was tasked with collecting money on the king's behalf, through whatever means the law – or Edmund's dexterous interpretation of it – allowed. So it was that there was a steady stream of people in and out of Candlewick. Like so many of the London shops, marketplaces and alehouses, for Edmund his house was both a home and a workplace.

There, Edmund met those who had been summoned to enter into 'bonds' to the king, committing money they might never pay in a financial expression of binding loyalty, as well as those whose bonds needed paying. It was also where he met with his 'informers' or 'promoters'. These men were royal agents, who walked the streets of London, sat in its law courts and listened for gossip on the wind, hoping to sniff out cases that could be exploited to the king's benefit and – more specifically – profit. One's bond to keep the peace might mean the forfeiture of hundreds of pounds to the king, if a promoter discovered that the person in question was implicated in a crime and passed that knowledge on to Dudley. Some, like the Italian John Baptist Grimaldi, had been at it for decades, and were highly skilled.

Grimaldi, a Genoan merchant who had arrived in London under King Richard III, had long been called a 'wretch' by London citizens for his willingness to inform upon them. Londoners knew well that Genoans were cheaters; the trick was to avoid looking them directly in the eyes; if you did, they had you.[4] Among Grimaldi's victims was none other than the respected draper and Sheriff of London, William Capel, who in 1496 had been fined nearly £3,000 thanks to information passed on by Grimaldi.[5] Also long-active and reviled in the city was John Camby, a grocer and officer of the Sheriff, who almost lost his job when it was rumoured that he conducted a 'wayward' second life, running a brothel by the Thames. Dudley, however, secured him a position in the London customs house, as well as running the Poultry Yard Prison, ironically where those convicted of offences related to prostitution often ended up.[6] Such men as Grimaldi and Camby could be frequently seen at Candlewick, passing on any news they had gleaned to Edmund. These associations did not endear Edmund Dudley to the people of London, nor to the court, but they did help him perform his office for the king.

Once the business of meeting with petitioners, penitents and promoters had ended for the day, Edmund moved his books and coin purses safely into the closet within the great chamber of the house. Through his hands moved sovereigns, groats, angels and other coins, with the king's head hammered on one side. In minting his coins, Henry VII had ensured that not only was he represented, but that the image was a clear likeness. As his reign had worn on, he had changed the nature of the image, so that it was just his profile that appeared. Rather than staring directly at the owner of the coin, Henry VII simply glanced at them sidelong.[7]

Most of the money that flowed through Dudley's account books was in pounds and marks. A 'mark' was not a coin, but a weighted measure that came to a value of two thirds of a pound. Not long before Dudley began his collections, Henry had issued a new coin – the 'sovereign' – a large gold coin worth the value of one silver pound. A pound was made up of twenty shillings or one hundred and twenty pennies. The carpenters, bricklayers and other skilled craftsmen of London could expect about eight pennies a day for their labours, maybe a bit more if they weren't given meals, quite a bit less if they happened to be women.[8] Servants and labourers would look for about five pennies a day. A golden sovereign was worth at least three weeks' work for most of the labouring population of London; they would be unlikely to take home more than £20 in a year. Dudley's bonds and debts for hundreds of pounds were thus each a small fortune, all passing through Candlewick before making their way to the king's coffers.

That was not to say that Dudley and the king did not deal in small change. On one day in February 1509, Henry VII made £5,000 worth of payments to eleven different individuals in over one million pennies, in an attempt to rid his treasury of all the small change he had accumulated over the years, much of it having passed through Edmund Dudley's chamber closet.[9]

Edmund's work life was relegated to the small closet in the grand chamber; the rest of the room was much more intimate. In the large bedroom, he and Elizabeth shared a grand featherbed. When it was cold, as it was the day Clopton came to visit, they could pull their beautifully embroidered quilt from the large, two-lidded coffer in the chamber, to keep them warm in the night.

In this large featherbed Edmund and Elizabeth engaged in the 'chamber game', as a popular poem called it (it was no accident that the woman in the poem referred to it instead as 'chamber work').[10] As the daughter of a noble house, Elizabeth would have been expected to be a virgin on the marriage market, and Edmund to teach her all she needed to know about the goings-on of the bedroom. She knew that women were expected to be the passive recipients of their husbands' sexual affections, all in the hopes of producing children. Sex within marriage should be purposeful and practical, as well as regulated by the festivals of the Church.[11] It was to be avoided during Lent, all holy days, as well as when the wife was ill, menstruating, pregnant and before she was 'churched'.* Days when the Church actually approved of the sexual activities of married couples were few and far between and needed to be taken advantage of. 'Excessive' marital sex had been condemned by the Church Father St Jerome as equivalent to adultery.[12] This not only included the frequency of sexual activity, but the positions used and the ardour involved. Even engaging in sexual activity outside of the bed itself could have dire consequences.[13] Transgression could result in harm to the child, not only death but also deformation.

That all being said, it was common knowledge that a woman's enjoyment of the chamber game aided conception. Since women's privy parts were the inversion of men's, it followed that their climax would be just as important for conception.[14] Husbands like Edmund ought to tickle, tease and stoke the flame of their wives' desire if they wanted children. It was only 'chamber work' when husbands neglected to do so.

Edmund and Elizabeth did well at the chamber game; Elizabeth became pregnant again not long after she had given birth to their eldest, John. When the second child was born, Edmund and Elizabeth chose the uncommon name of Jerome for him. Jerome was less physically

---

* Churching was a ceremony taking place after childbirth, blessing the new mother and giving thanks for her survival.

capable than his brother and needed assistance in meeting the needs of life. Edmund decided he was best suited for a career in the Church.[15] His name certainly alluded to the life of a scholarly saint, but might also make one think of St Jerome's precautions against excessive or untraditional sexual activity and its consequences.

Edmund and Elizabeth could speak freely, openly and even equally to each other within their private room.[16] Elizabeth could offer advice to her husband about his political trajectory, the cases before him, or the men he'd surrounded himself with. Although Edmund's grandfather had experience of court circles, Elizabeth's family could claim even more intimate connections, and thus her family's experience might be of use to Edmund. Elizabeth's uncle had been Sir John Grey, whose wife had been Elizabeth Woodville, later Edward IV's queen. The royal couple had married secretly; one of the few in attendance was Elizabeth Dudley's grandmother. The Grey family had remained close – scandalously close – to the reins of power throughout Edward's reign. On her mother's side, Elizabeth carried noble blood. Her mother had been heir to the Viscount Lisle. Through her, Elizabeth's great-great-great-grandfather was Richard Beauchamp, the Earl of Warwick. His son's position had been elevated to Duke of Warwick, and his granddaughter had reached even further, briefly becoming Queen of England, thanks to her marriage to King Richard III. As Elizabeth Dudley's eldest son, John would need to understand his place in this proud family history, tracing names and lines on parchment, and the claim he could one day make to titles such as Viscount Lisle and, even more impressive, that of Earl of Warwick, with its symbol of the bear, chained to a ragged staff.

There were other chambers in the house, on the other side of the courtyard, two of which were perfectly sized for nurseries. 'Little Elizabeth' was approaching the age at which she would move from the loose gowns of childhood to the bodices, sleeves and skirts of adulthood. Her stepmother would teach her the necessary skills and virtues of a young lady – the love of children and husband, discretion, chastity, obedience, as well as the knowledge of tasks around the household, such as washing, brewing, baking and dressing meat.[17] Her father had already arranged a marriage for her, to be solemnized when she was of a proper age. Elizabeth's small hand had been exchanged for the return of land which Dudley had seized from the nobleman, Lord Stourton. To get his land back, the childless lord was persuaded to affiance his eldest nephew to Edmund Dudley's daughter. If she were very lucky, and her future husband inherited the lordship, one day she could style herself 'Elizabeth, Lady Stourton'. Until then, she helped her new mother with the running of the house and practised the art of being a lady.

The day at Candlewick began a little before dawn and – following morning prayers – the work of the household began with it. Although urban life meant avoiding the farm-work associated with rural living, there was still much to be done in the household, most of it by the handful of servants they employed, overseen by the higher-ranking servants, such as Elizabeth's serving-woman, Lettice Brownd, and Edmund's clerk, Thomas Mitchell.[18] Daily tasks included sweeping the rushes, which protected the floor from dirt and spills, waking and caring for the children, ensuring that bread was baked, ale was brewed, butter and cheese were made, clothing was stitched and hemmed, and that there were meals available for the household. The most important meal was dinner, served just before midday. This would be held in the great hall, a room downstairs near the entryway. Here little Elizabeth would sit with her stepmother and father, when he was not away on business, other members of the family and honoured guests, on the dais at the far end of the rectangular room, backed by a great tapestry. On either side of the table on the dais were two more long tables with benches on either side, where the rest of the household could sit to eat.

Often joining them on the dais was little Elizabeth's grandmother, Lady Elizabeth Lytton, who held a simple room in Candlewick. After the death of young Elizabeth's grandfather in 1485, her grandmother had married Sir Robert Lytton, the Keeper of the Wardrobe. He too had died, and Lady Lytton had found herself a home, at least on occasion, with the Dudley family. This meant that Elizabeth's uncles, Andrew and Anthony, could also be expected to visit. Andrew Windsor and Edmund Dudley continued to make a formidable pair; Andrew had been given his stepfather's position of Keeper of the

Wardrobe after his death. While Edmund filled in his account books with obligations, bonds and payments to the king, Andrew likewise populated the wardrobe accounts with various expenditures and gifts.

This extended family and its household were served grand dinners from the kitchen and buttery, where servants worked at no fewer than eleven spits – seven large and four small – cooking every variety of meat and fish. They prepared smaller victuals in the nine pans of various sizes, and stews and soups in the two large pots, stirred by large brass ladles. Another eight smaller pots were used for sauces and gravies. The wine which they poured with dinner was kept in the buttery: several hogsheads each containing 300 litres of wine.

The house was perfectly positioned to make the most of the diverse foodstuffs that came into London daily. If you exited the house and headed north up Walbrook, you would first pass Bucklersbury, the home of Thomas More, before finding yourself on the eastern end of Cheapside. It was in Cheapside that you could locate all the essentials – and a few luxuries – necessary for running a household such as Candlewick. Cheapside had got its name from the Old English 'ceapan', or 'to buy', and had retained its function for hundreds of years. Heading west, shopping basket in hand, you passed Ironmonger Lane, Bread Street, Milk Street, Wood Street and so on, all named after the provisions you could purchase from the sellers peddling their wares loudly from the house-fronts. It wasn't long before you could see the great St Paul's Cathedral looming before you. Beyond that was the limit of the city, marked by the long wall that encircled it.

Edmund was often required to continue this journey west, usually by boat, to the palace of Westminster, where parliament was held, and even further along the Thames, about ten miles, to Richmond, Henry VII's preferred royal residence. Though the court was itinerant, King Henry and his court spent much of their time at Richmond. The palace had begun as a manor house, which had become a royal residence in the fourteenth century and had been granted, more recently, to Queen Elizabeth Woodville – Elizabeth Dudley's royal kinswoman – during the reign of Edward IV. While Henry's family celebrated Christmas at Richmond in 1497, a violent fire had ripped through the building, originating in the king's private apartments. It brought down the large roofbeams and tapestries that decorated the halls and chambers, as well as destroying the clothing and many of the jewels that were kept there. It had, as well, almost been the end of the king's reign. The king and his family had been forced to rapidly escape the fire as it burned through their home. Nursemaids frantically grabbed Prince Henry and his two sisters and pulled them through the smoke to safety. The king, however, took the disaster in his stride, and decided to turn it into an opportunity to build a grander and far more modern palace on the site.

When the new palace was completed in 1501 it was a marvel. Built of brick and white stone, it shone in the summer sun next to the Thames. It was studded with near-countless octagonal towers and decorated with ornate brickwork chimneys. It was entirely in line with the architectural fashions of the time, and significantly less flammable than the manor house that had preceded it. There were long galleries to display not only tapestries, but the sculpture and portraiture of the Renaissance as well. Henry had had the opportunity to show off his new palace in 1501 when his heir, Prince Arthur, had wed Catherine of Aragon, daughter of the powerful Spanish monarchs King Ferdinand and Queen Isabella. Now, following the death of her husband, Catherine was trapped at glistening Richmond, a prisoner of unfortunate circumstance in one of its immaculate modern towers overlooking the Thames.[19]

Edmund Dudley was not a part of the inner workings of the court, though he would have heard every word of the gossip that made its way from Richmond Palace, largely because he had men amongst the king's servants; Hugh Denys, the groom of the stool, increasingly in charge of the king's quotidian financial matters, was Dudley's man.[20] Edmund would have been aware of the prince's rejection of any marriage contract with Catherine of Aragon in 1505, and the fire that started up in the king's chamber at Richmond – yet again – in January. Through the harsh winter, he would have been informed of the – quite accidental – visit of Archduke Philip, and the festivities that came with it, and heard the whisperings of Londoners when the golden eagle fell from the weathervane of St Paul's on to the Inn of the Black Eagle; it was surely an ill omen.[21] By July 1506 Edmund had been made

President of the King's Council, joining the ranks of the king's closest advisers in an institution that had grown in importance over the course of Henry's reign, and where the most crucial matters to the Crown were discussed.[22] The President of the Council oversaw the judicial sessions of the Council, including that of the Star Chamber, a role to which Dudley was well suited.[23]

Dudley's promotion fell closely on the heels of yet another near disaster at Richmond, when the king and the prince were almost killed by the collapse of the gallery as they walked along it. The king had his carpenter imprisoned, but the gossip of malevolent portents continued. Perhaps this new reign was destined for failure after all. Perhaps God was displeased with the king's closeness to men such as Edmund Dudley and, through him, promoters like Grimaldi and Camby. Dudley had become a grim spectre to the inhabitants of London, his agents haunting the streets, seeking out information that could add coin to the king's coffers, even if it meant the destruction of entire families. Little could be done to keep these spirits at bay: secrets always resurfaced in Henry VII's London, exacting fierce and often blind revenge.

*

Above the rolling Thames, the small body of a newborn infant fell quickly and silently through the air. When it collided with the murky waters, it made such a small noise that one might have thought it had not hit the water at all, but remained floating forever above the waves, weightless as well as lifeless.

Before long, the case was before the courts. Agnes Sunnyff, wife of the wealthy merchant haberdasher Thomas Sunnyff, was accused of the death of the child, though quickly acquitted.[24] There was little reason for a respected merchant's wife to dispose of the body of a child without a proper Christian burial. Some wondered why anyone had turned to the esteemed Sunnyffs at all in relation to the case, which clearly had more to do with the sordid world of prostitution and crime on the banks of the Thames than that of respected merchants.

By March 1507, it was clear to all those with an eye on this particularly juicy tale that the much-reviled promoter John Camby had more than just a peripheral role to play. Camby had taken and imprisoned Alice Damston, the Sunnyffs' servant, forcing her into further accusations against her master and mistress, and his servant had been tasked with continuing to spread the rumour that it was the Sunnyffs who were behind it all. When Thomas Sunnyff, catching wind of it, had confronted the promoter, Camby refused outright to end his campaign against him. Instead, he demanded £500 from the merchant.

Sunnyff had signed a bond for that amount a year before, promising to keep the peace in London.[25] The accusations against his wife – which Camby himself had fuelled – potentially represented a transgression of that promise. Camby had come, as one of Dudley's men, to retrieve the money. The people of London saw it for the 'facing' (brow-beating) and 'polling' (extortion) that it was, but this did not stop Camby from continuing to hunt down his prey in the hopes of a £500 prize for Dudley and his king.

Sunnyff was not so easily faced, however, and so took his case to Sir Richard Empson. A lawyer in his fifties, Empson also had a reputation for sniffing out money that could be collected for the king. He too had followed the well-trod path of studying the law and acting as Speaker of the Commons, though this had been over a decade before Edmund held the post. Empson had begun his political career under Edward IV, and by the 1490s had a reputation as one of Henry VII's 'low-born and evil counsellors', as named by the pretender to the throne, Perkin Warbeck in 1497 in a move that was surely intended to accrue popularity amongst Londoners.[26] It was well known in London that the court composer himself, William Cornysh, had written a satire aimed at Empson and his attempts to use the law in his favour.[27]

Sunnyff explained his predicament to Empson. Unfortunately for Sunnyff, Dudley had got to Empson first. 'You must go to prison,' Empson calmly informed him, 'for the certain matter that was laid to your wife's charge.' Rather than granting his appeal, Empson had Sunnyff committed to the Fleet for his perceived transgression of the law and his bond.

Fleet Prison was located by the city wall, just to the east of Sunnyff's home at Lud Gate, on the banks of the River Fleet. First built in the twelfth century, the Fleet was largely a debtor's prison; its prisoners either found means to gather the money to pay their debts from inside its walls, or died there. The prison was under the wardship of the Babington family, to whom the prisoners were forced to pay rent as well as small fees for various other services.[28] If one arrived already in dire financial straits, a visit to the Fleet Prison would not solve anything.

Sunnyff had six weeks to stew in the Fleet; surely he would now agree to pay the money to the king. Edmund had him summoned to the palace at Greenwich, where he was attending to business for the king.

Sunnyff was taken by the Warden of Fleet Prison along the Thames to meet Edmund in one of the chambers he used for such purposes. When he arrived, Edmund immediately enquired whether Camby had accompanied him. Realizing that he had not, Dudley refused to see him, and so Sunnyff waited. When Camby at last arrived, he was quick to ask Sunnyff if he had spoken to Dudley. Sunnyff denied it, and Camby gave him another chance to pay the £500 and be done with it. Sunnyff refused. Camby left him waiting there and went in to speak with Edmund alone.

When they emerged back into the hall, Edmund spoke to Sunnyff. The situation was very clear: 'Sunnyff,' he told him, 'agree with the king, or else you must go to the Tower.'

The merchant held his ground, though it was slipping beneath him. 'It was not the king's will,' he boldly retorted, 'that I should yield myself guilty of the thing that I was never guilty of.'

Sunnyff was in an even lesser position to dictate the nature of the king's will to Edmund Dudley than Drury had been. Edmund turned to Camby and commanded him to make good on his threat: to take the haberdasher directly to the Tower of London. The pair left Edmund's presence and walked back to the boat, still floating on the Thames. When they went to board, Camby ordered the Fleet Prison Warden out of the boat; he would take Sunnyff himself. The warden, wary, replied that he required a discharge for a man still his prisoner. 'My word shall be sufficient discharge,' Camby answered with cool authority, and the warden stepped back.

Camby took the oars. Before long they reached the Tower of

London, looming over the Thames. Sunnyff steeled himself for entry into a place where so few left alive. To his shock, but not necessarily his relief, Camby continued rowing, gliding right past it. When he asked Camby why they had not gone in, Camby responded that the gates had already shut. Sunnyff glanced at the imposing gate through which a small boat like theirs could slide. It was very clearly open. But Camby stood firm; he would take Sunnyff back to his own home for the evening and take him to the Tower in the morning. Camby locked Sunnyff in a chamber. He did not let him out for almost a month.

While Sunnyff lay imprisoned in Camby's home, the court proceedings with regard to the death of the child continued. Alice Damston had remained in her own imprisonment, but without Camby there to intimidate her, she was ready to come forward and admit that she had slandered the Sunnyffs. 'My master nor my mastress never knew of the birth nor the death of the child, but it was dead born,' she declared publicly. It was a bombshell.

When news of this reached Camby, he exploded with rage at those he blamed for empowering Alice Damston in this way, screaming that they were harlots.[29] He immediately sought Alice out, and demanded that she testify that Agnes Sunnyff was the one who killed the child. She was to announce that she had been coerced into her previous recantation.

Appearing once again in court, Alice Damston repeated Camby's words: Agnes Sunnyff had killed the young child. Edmund Dudley was present that day, to see if Camby's efforts would yield fruit. Under questioning, however, Alice's story broke down. Camby had not prepared her sufficiently, and her account wandered and contradicted itself. Edmund was unconvinced, as were the judges. Agnes Sunnyff was acquitted of the murder. Camby was failing.

Yet he would not release Thomas Sunnyff, not without the £500 that he had evidently committed himself to retrieving for Dudley. When Sunnyff demanded to know why he and his wife had been made to suffer in this way, Camby informed him simply that the king desired the money. Sunnyff protested, 'If the King's good grace knew the truth of my matter, he would not take a penny of me.' Frustrated with his stubborn prisoner, Camby had Sunnyff and his wife transferred to

King's Bench Prison in Southwark.[30] South of London Bridge, the prison was far from the hub of the city. This was a fate like death; it took years off the Sunnyffs' lives and ruined their names and reputations in the city. As Sunnyff was crushed by fear and suffering in prison, Camby and a band of other men broke into his home in Tower Row and retrieved goods to pay off the original obligation.

Fearing that Camby would kill them both while they waited in prison, Sunnyff at last acquiesced, and agreed to pay £500 to the king. He would pay £100 to Dudley now, and owe him £400, and in return he would gain a pardon. Dudley, likely while sitting in his little room beside his chamber in Candlewick, was thus able to record the debt on 21 July 1507: £500 for a pardon 'for the murdering of the child', a crime he very well knew Sunnyff did not commit. Five months later, however, the Sunnyffs were still in prison, Sunnyff having failed to produce the remaining £400. As more and more of his friends demanded his release, Dudley agreed to free him from prison, on the promise of a further £260.

Sunnyff at last left the King's Bench Prison in November 1507, less than a year after the whole affair had begun. He had spent almost all of the previous seven months in various prisons, narrowly avoiding the Tower itself. For refusing to pay the king £500, he had lost that amount in the break-in by Camby, paid another £100 and was in debt a further £400, with the penalty of even more exactions to come pouring down at the slightest provocation. Over half a year in prison had also taken a toll on his business. Agnes Sunnyff had done what she could to keep it going, but this had ended when she joined him in prison. A wealthy merchant like Sunnyff could expect to make almost £500 in a year, and he would have lost almost all of that in 1507. Dudley had nearly destroyed him, and he was not free yet.

In November 1508, almost exactly a year after he left prison, Sunnyff received a knock at his door. He opened it to a messenger. 'You must come and speak with Master Dudley in all haste,' he told Sunnyff.

'I have recently come from Master Dudley,' Sunnyff objected, 'even now from his place.' However, the messenger was insistent. Sunnyff was to meet Dudley, not at Candlewick, but at a tavern just to the east of Dudley's home, on the corner of Eastcheap and Fish Street to the north of London Bridge, known as the Boar's Head.

Sunnyff entered the darkness of the public house and searched for Dudley, but instead he found himself looking at one of the last faces in the world he wanted to see: that of John Camby. Beside him was Sir John Digby, the Lieutenant of the Tower of London. He grabbed Sunnyff by the arm and dragged him from the tavern, taking him immediately to the Tower, where Camby had promised Sunnyff would one day find himself. As he entered its dark confines, Sunnyff had no reason to hope he would ever be free again.

The list of those suffering like Sunnyff under Dudley's regime grew with every line in his meticulous account book. Thomasine Percyvale, in the midst of running her late husband's trading business and founding a grammar school, found herself imprisoned and forced to 'loan' £1,000 to the king, in the same month that Sunnyff had been dragged to the Tower. Sir William Capel, who had been hounded by the promoters on other occasions, was framed by Grimaldi and imprisoned after refusing to pay a £2,000 fine. Justice was also for sale. In 1507, Dudley ensured the pardon of a Sussex gentleman, indicted for murder, for £200 paid to the king; Dudley ended up with his lands and manor. Dudley certainly enriched himself as he worked for the king. He offered to pay a Cheshire landowner's debt in 1507 in exchange for his two manors; perhaps a fair deal, except that Dudley had imposed the debt to begin with.[31] His work did not discriminate between the most obscure of London merchants and the noblest of king's servants; he just might demand more of the latter. The son of Sir John Mordaunt, another former Speaker and ally of Bray, found himself subject to what he called 'the hard dealing' of Dudley after a dispute about his inheritance. Dudley demanded £1,200, and Mordaunt agreed £1,000 in five annual payments. Dudley took out the balance in the deed to a manor. Bray's own executors faced a payment of nearly £4,000 for a pardon for Bray's perceived offences.[32] Dudley's victims high and low bemoaned the 'sorrow throughout the land', as he and his informers hunted out cash for the king's coffers.

By May 1508, Dudley had filled in the last page of the account book he had begun in September 1504. In it, he had managed to raise almost £220,000 for the Crown, single-handedly increasing the income of the Crown by well over half.[33] Thousands were now bound by financial debts to the king. Dudley had woven an ornate financial web, with the king sitting proudly at the centre, feeding off the blood of those unfortunate enough to become trapped in it.

*

In the depths of winter 1508–9, the king rode with his retinue to Chertsey Abbey in Surrey, about twelve miles from Richmond Palace.[34] Here Henry's Lancastrian predecessor, Henry VI, had been buried with little pomp under the Lady Chapel. Henry VI had been slain while imprisoned in the Tower of London, his son in battle three weeks before, and his wife in exile in France a decade later. Henry VII had done better, but the dynasty he had built from the ashes of the conflict was by no means assured. Henry VI's remains were no longer present at Chertsey – Richard III, often accused of his murder, had moved them to Windsor in 1484, where the former King of England was given a grander tomb and even a little box for pilgrims' offerings.[35] Many had come to see him as both a martyr and even a saint, a cult that the king encouraged. Henry hoped to one day lay his bones near those of his saintly martyred predecessor.

As he entered Chertsey Abbey that cold day, Henry VII knew that time was coming soon.

The king was dying. As if his life was entwined with the turning of the seasons, he had fallen ill in February of every year since the death of his wife. He would disappear into Richmond, lying weakened, voiceless and delusional for weeks, before rallying once again for the summer months, when he would process proudly amongst his people once more.[36] This February, six years since the queen's death, he was sure he would not make it to another summer. His son, Prince Henry, was approaching eighteen years. Although the king might have wished for another five to fully secure his son's reign, the prince was old enough to carry the throne in his own right, without the oversight of a Lord Protector who might try to snatch it from him.[37] The prince was tall, strong and confident. He towered over his ageing father and was by all accounts straining at the restrictions that the king had imposed on him, limiting his movements and contact with the court.[38] He would have to be ready.

Chertsey was a place of reflection and prayer for the king. The Benedictine monks who kept it wandered the grounds in their black habits, compiling and making use of vast libraries for holy reading. The Abbey was split into inner and outer precincts, with the inner containing the church and cloister and the outer the more menial necessities of the abbey: gardens, fishponds and the like. Within the Abbey were gorgeously decorated medieval floors, displaying the triumph of Richard the Lionheart over the infidel Saladin, and the tale of Tristan and Isolde.[39] There were also tiles showing the labours of the months and the signs of the zodiac.[40] Henry was a patron both of religion and of astrology, and saw no particular conflict between the two, though the latter had let him down. His court astrologer had failed to predict Prince Arthur's death and foretold that the king's wife would live to eighty or ninety. She had died only a few months later.[41] The astrologer had not remained at court much longer after that.

From Chertsey, Henry made an unprecedented trip. Travelling on a Sunday, which was unusual for him, he made the eight-mile journey to Esher Place, the home of the Bishop of Winchester, Richard Fox. Henry approached the large brick residence with its slender tower gatehouse and entered to speak with the bishop. Fox had been by Henry's side since the beginning. He had joined the young Henry in exile in Paris, sailed with him to conquer England, and even joined him on the battlefield as he defeated Richard III. Such youthful exploits were long past them now, and they spoke on that bitter winter Sunday as sickly old men, days of glory firmly behind them.

With a long, drawn face, Fox had the censorious countenance of a clergyman, though it was unclear whether he had been predisposed to such a role by God's design, or whether the knit brows and pinched cheeks had been chiselled there by decades of executing God's judgement. His most recent disapproving looks had been reserved for Henry's reliance on men such as Edmund Dudley.

If Henry was dying, he had much to discuss with Fox, and Fox had much he needed to say to him in return. Fox had known better than to directly challenge the king on his choice of ministers, but this was an opportunity for change, now that the king's soul was truly in danger. The king must turn aside from any wickedness and pursue the righteous path if he were to secure salvation, a good legacy and a secure dynasty. Edmund Dudley and his work were a certain danger to all three.

From Esher Place, Henry travelled back to Hanworth Manor, a property recently acquired by the king.[42] He had equipped Hanworth with a pleasure garden, hunting lodge and aviary, though he would not make much use of them in the cold months of late winter.[43] Hanworth, like Chertsey and Esher, had become a place where Henry could rest and hide as his illness took hold.

Henry had chosen his time well; Lent was the ideal Christian time to be dying. The whole season was a rumination on death and suffering, and the dangerous temptations of life. At the end was promised salvation, thanks to the sacrifice of Christ, and eternal life. Mass on the first Sunday of the Lenten season came with a sermon preached by one of Fox's allies, John Fisher. Fisher was a decade or two younger than Fox and the king, with a round face, kind eyes and a soft, small mouth. He had served as the spiritual director and confessor to the king's mother, the formidable Margaret Beaufort, for over a decade, which had brought him into court circles, and particularly into the group which increasingly stood opposed to Dudley and his ilk. Margaret Beaufort too had reason to dislike Dudley; she, like many others, had been forced to pay into his pocket when he acted as intermediary for a financial transaction, though she had also benefitted from his legal guidance.[44] More pressing than any financial resentments, however, Fox, Beaufort, Fisher and others also might whisper angrily about Dudley's place in Henry's government.[45] Few were allowed to see the king while he was suffering with his annual illness, yet Dudley's name cropped up everywhere on letters and account books. Harassing the pesky citizens of London was one thing, but Edmund Dudley had not earned the right to manage the king and court as well. He wasn't even a knight. Edmund may have entered the king's favour thanks to the recommendation and protection of some of the king's oldest friends and companions – Reginald Bray, Richard Guildford, Robert Lytton – but by 1507 these men had all died, and Dudley had not invested the requisite time or energies in making new allies.[46] Dudley had only the king to protect him. And that king was dying.

On 25 February, the church at Hanworth was veiled and solemn for Lent; there were no crucifixes or statues visible. All signs of Christian triumph and consolation had been hidden away. There was just stark death, reinforced by Fisher's tendency to preach with a human skull beside him on the altar. On this day, Fisher could not miss how closely the king and the skull were beginning to resemble each other.

A few days later, Henry returned to Richmond. He would not leave it again.

*

Henry's condition was not as apparent to those outside the inner circle. As Henry visited Chertsey, Esher and Hanworth, Edmund Dudley was occupied with other business, still solidly entrenched in the affairs of the city, as well as pressing family matters. He and Elizabeth had welcomed a third son, Andrew, into their home at Candlewick Street. Their youngest shared his name with Edmund's former brother-in-law, who had, in turn, named his own third son Edmund. Edmund Dudley's relations with the Windsors continued to be strong, and he did what he could to advance them as he continued to rise in wealth and position.[47]

Candlewick was now an opulent home, and as little John Dudley, approaching five years old, explored its corridors and rooms, he was confronted with ornate and expensive tapestries and carpets, silver pots, spoons and flagons, gilded candlesticks and goblets. Two large gilded cups were particularly impressive: one with the images of kings enamelled upon it, another adorned with Dudley's arms. Increasingly, John might also find fierce-looking men-at-arms at Candlewick, and piles of weapons were mounting up in the bow-house and armoury chamber – hundreds of bows, over two dozen sheaves of arrows, a handful of crossbows and other martial equipment.

Amongst the thirty sets of armour were two plate metal jackets that Edmund had commissioned for himself: one of black velvet, the other of crimson.[48] Edmund might have been outside court circles, but he was aware of how exposed the king's death could leave him.

Fox made his first move to distance the king and his heir from

Dudley and his kind not long after the king had visited him at Esher. Like capturing a knight on a chessboard, Fox had slid his man, Sir Richard Weston, into the space previously occupied by Dudley's ally, Sir Hugh Denys. Denys had succumbed to the sweating sickness that had ravaged the city in the summer of 1508. Both Denys and Fox took to their beds, with little hope that either would emerge. Miraculously, both did, though both were weakened. The king, in his panic, had decreed that no one from the city would be allowed to enter the court until the epidemic had passed, effectively barring Dudley and his men from personal communications with their colleagues near the king. It was into this space that Weston had been moved. Weston was at least two decades younger than the bishop and had been a member of the court for some years. Although he had worked with Edmund Dudley, he was not his friend, and had gained the trust of several of Henry's nobles in opposing Dudley's attempts to squeeze yet more coin from them.[49] By February he had all but displaced the recovering Denys, doing what he could to galvanize opposition to Dudley, all while outwardly working alongside him.

The tide, controlled by Henry's movement towards the heavens, did certainly seem to be turning against Dudley and his work. The king seemed sincere in his last-ditch reformation, distancing himself from practices which might endanger his vulnerable soul and paying out significant sums of money to have thousands of masses said for his recovery. These were to be led by Fisher, by the Observant Franciscan Friars, and by one of Henry VII's chaplains, Thomas Wolsey, a young priest in his thirties. Wolsey's father had been a tavern owner and butcher, though with enough connections to provide his son with a modest education in the city, followed by Oxford. After holding a variety of positions across the country, Wolsey had manoeuvred himself into the household of the Archbishop of Canterbury, and then the treasurer of Calais. When the latter died, Wolsey was awarded a post as a royal chaplain, where he quickly became an ally and protégé of Fox. He was sent on diplomatic missions, the speed and success of which amazed the king. By Lent 1509, Wolsey had been awarded the deanship of Lincoln Cathedral, though he remained at the king's side, one of a few remaining intimates, and resolutely one of Fox's men.

Even while those around him began to conspire against Dudley, the king had not forgotten him, and sought to include him in his mission of reform and renewal. The weekend of Palm Sunday – marking Jesus' triumphant entry into Jerusalem to shouts of Hosanna just days before that same crowd demanded his crucifixion – Henry VII drew up his final will.[50] He had collapsed a week before and been bedridden ever since. Propped up by numerous expensive pillows and bolsters, he and his scribe worked out the final preparations necessary for his legacy. He offered up prayers and supplications to God and the Virgin Mary, along with all the saints, angels, archangels and prophets for the salvation of his soul: 'I am a sinful creature, in sin conceived, and in sin I have lived.'[51] Only their mercy would save him. 'If any man can for any cause reasonable,' Henry dictated, 'show that we have wronged him in any manner of ways, that might or shall charge our conscience . . . to be readily heard and answered, as reason and conscience shall require.'[52] Henry was prepared to ensure that all his wrongs were righted, by financial means if necessary. This was left to a group of men, which included not only Fox, but also Richard Empson and 'Edmund Dudley, Squire, our Attorney', included amongst the king's executors.[53] Henry had not excluded Dudley from his new mission, but he had made him vulnerable by acknowledging that he – through Edmund – might have done significant harm to his subjects.

Two weeks later, this acknowledgement went public. On Monday, 16 April, a general pardon was read out, and citizens were invited to make their way to the Chancery offices in order to record their names and grievances. Dudley had reason to observe the mobs of indignant Londoners with trepidation.

By this point, the king had been suffering for months. With his last will completed, and the means of his redemption underway, there was nothing to do but to await death. It did not come quickly for the suffering monarch. He faced fierce bouts of pain for hours on end, unable to eat or speak, and struggling for breath. He was said to suffer with quinsy, an infection of the throat that, if not helped, could strangle a man from within. The remedies were blood-letting: of the large vein on the arm, and – much more painfully – the vein of the tongue as well.[54]

As the sun set on Friday, 20 April, the king suffered like never before. He reeked with the infection that was slowly asphyxiating him and entered a feverish otherworld as the pus leaked into his bloodstream. So he remained as the sun rose, reached its zenith, and set once again. He would not see it rise. Before him had been raised a crucifix, on which he was to keep his eyes fixed as he prepared to enter the next life. At last, unable to breathe and overcome with pain, the king met his end.

Ten miles away in their home at Candlewick, Edmund, Elizabeth and the children were oblivious to the interregnum that had just fallen on them. Succession had not been peaceful in England for a hundred years, and Dudley knew his unpopularity meant that he would be one of the first cut down if bloody civil war broke out afresh around them.

Edmund Dudley had risen in less than a decade from obscure country gentleman and middling city official to one of the king's closest ministers. He had acted with the trust of the king and within the scope of the law, giving no ear to those who grumbled about injustice. The king's will had been Edmund's lodestar, but it had also been his only defence. Now the king was dead. Had Edmund done enough to protect himself, and his family?

3

A dead man by the King's laws

It was not long before they came for him. Amid the heralds' cries announcing the reign of 'Henry VIII, by the Grace of God, King of England and France and Lord of Ireland', Edmund was taken from his home and led through the streets of London to the Tower. News of the king's death had not made it outside the court, and Edmund Dudley was caught unprepared. His home had been readied to defend against an angry, anarchic mob. However, it was not such a horde that confronted him as the sun rose on the morning of 24 April 1509, but an official arrest from the new, uncrowned king. Dudley had been outfoxed, and it took some time to piece together precisely what had happened.

As the soul of Henry VII had left his pain-wracked body late in the evening of 21 April 1509, the thoughts of those who surrounded him went immediately to what would come next.[1] The heir to the throne was seventeen and vulnerable. If they did not handle this masterfully, it could mean civil war. The safest route would be to proceed as if the king were still alive, while they put their plans in place to secure the succession. So it was that on the next morning, the second Sunday of Easter, prayers at mass were given up as usual for the continued long life and reign of King Henry VII, with very few of those in attendance aware that his corpse was growing cold not far away.

It was Fox, Bishop of Winchester, who played director during the strange secret interregnum that followed Henry's death. Fox had been with the king when he died, and immediately took control. God had smiled on him and his plans; like the king's Lenten illness, his death could not have been better timed. The 23 April was St George's Day, and many of the leading nobles of the land – the members of the exclusive order of the Knights of the Garter – had gathered for a large feast in celebration of their patron saint with Fox as prelate. He had the perfect excuse to act like an interim king.

Following the grand banquet, Fox's man Weston approached the Archbishop of Canterbury, William Warham. Warham had aged somewhat since he had made his debut in the parliament of 1504 and was now comfortable in his role as the right hand of the king. Smiling, Weston invited him – along with some other leading lords – to speak to the king in his privy chamber. Not knowing what awaited them, Warham and the lords proceeded into the king's chambers for a royal audience. There they found not only the king's stiff corpse, but also Fox, who informed them of what had taken place. Together, they laid plans for how the following days would play out.

Before leaving the king's private chambers, the lords and bishops prepared their faces for the outside world. No one must know of the king's death or their plans. Like play-actors, they emerged from conference smiling and cheerful. Even the prince, now king, participated in the charade. In his attendance at evensong and supper, the seventeen-year-old continued to be addressed as Prince, not as King. The play did not have to last long. After supper, as evening fell and candles were lit, the king's death was revealed to the court. Prince Henry, now Henry VIII, took his place amongst his councillors and ministers. Top in their minds was what was to be done with Edmund Dudley and Richard Empson. Cleverly, they realized that Dudley's defences could be made to be his downfall. Dudley was accused of summoning troops to London and stockpiling weapons in an attempt to seize the throne from Prince Henry, now king. Circumstance lent kindling to the accusation, and resentment gave it fire. All could be counted on to support a move against the dead king's wolves.

It was in the early hours of the next morning that a closed fist knocked on the thick wooden door of Candlewick Street. Edmund had little time to say goodbye to his wife, daughter, and three young sons – John was still only five – before he was taken from his home to the Tower of London, at the easternmost edge of the city.

The medieval Tower, built almost five hundred years before, was a royal palace, an armed stronghold and a fearsome prison. It had become even more impressive under Henry's building programme; the king had improved the royal lodgings of the palace by adding impressive Renaissance galleries.[2] At the centre of the large, moated complex of the Tower was its oldest building, the White Tower, the keep of the original Tower. Just to the south of that were the buildings making up the royal residences, where English monarchs were expected to spend the eve of their coronation. Joining these buildings within the inner ward was the Chapel of Peter ad Vincula. The walls of the inner ward were punctuated with thirteen tall towers, which dominated the skyline and housed prisoners, such as Edmund Dudley.

Edmund's status did not demand that he be given the amenities and consideration a nobleman would have received upon his imprisonment. He was, however, allowed servants and materials with which to write. His clerk, Thomas Mitchell, was with him, as well as another of his servants, William Frank.[3] It was unclear how long he would have to remain there, or in precisely what condition he was to leave.

The same day Edmund was taken into the Tower, the new adolescent king also rode confidently into its precincts. As he did so, proclamations were made in the streets, a restatement of Henry VII's pardon two weeks before, but 'more ample, gracious and beneficial'.[4] Surely Edmund might hope to fall under such a pardon? Imprisoning him for a short time would let tempers cool, before he resumed his vital part in the machinery of government. Edmund had built the financial foundation of the new king's reign; surely there would be little reason for Henry to permanently cast aside such a valuable tool?

Less than a week later, on the last day of April, Henry VIII was once again at the Tower, not far from where Edmund was imprisoned. He was composing – via his scribe, Henry did not like putting pen to paper much himself – a note to William Warham, still one of the most powerful men in the country. 'We of our especial grace,' he proclaimed as the scribe quickly jotted down his words, 'have granted unto all our true subjects a general pardon.' Nearing the end, the tone changed: 'reserving and excepting only such persons whose names be specified in a bill signed with our hand and here unto annexed'. The list of names had been prepared, and Henry himself looked it over, adding to it as he saw necessary before putting his signature to it. Not far under his signature, eleventh from the top, was the name of Edmund Dudley, along with a number of his servants and informers, including Mitchell, Grimaldi and Camby.[5]

Edmund was not to be included in the king's fresh slate. That hope of salvation would not be his. His enemies had closed around him, and the new king would not protect him.

*

The displeasure of the citizens of London continued to rise up from the city like sickly vapours from an unhealed wound:

'Every time the king got £200 he and his had £300 to themselves.'

'Or the king got not a penny!'

'He was so proud, it was easier to speak to the highest duke in the land than get an audience with Edmund Dudley.'

'He forgot himself, rising so high.'

'Whatever shameful condition he comes to, it will not be without cause.'[6]

Andrew Windsor was well aware of his former brother-in-law's predicament. As the new reign began, it was increasingly Edmund Dudley who carried the sins of the one just passed.

But Andrew, and the citizens of London, were quickly gripped in a fury of activity that distracted them from much concern over the fate of Edmund Dudley. Preparations were being made for the funeral of Henry VII. Arrangements had begun the very day that the king's death had been announced – the same day that Edmund had been taken to the Tower. If Andrew had given thought to intervening on Edmund's behalf, there would be little time for it now.

Provided with £1,000 by Sir John Heron, the treasurer who had worked so closely with Edmund, Andrew searched London for enough black cloth to clothe the court and chapel, eventually going to fifty-six different merchants to acquire a sufficient amount.[7] Goldsmiths, tailors and carpenters were employed to make the hearse and its covering and the various hangings for the procession; £500 went on torches, another £500 on banners and escutcheons, upon which the heraldry of the crown and court was depicted. A troupe of painters had been employed to decorate the escutcheons, coats of arms, banners, borders and pennons. As the receipts piled up, and the day of the funeral approached, it became too difficult to itemize every expense; one hastily scribbled receipt on 1 May simply noted a £2,000 payment to Andrew Windsor for 'diverse things'.[8]

The preparations to move the corpse of the king from where it lay in his privy chamber to its final resting place in Westminster were complex. The body was taken in stages from the king's private-most chambers to gradually more public sites: spending three days each in the king's great chamber, his hall and the chapel, where masses and dirges were sung over it. The body reached the chapel on the fourth Sunday of Easter and the funeral itself began three days later, on 9 May.[9] People lined the streets with torches as the king's corpse was placed in a chariot that wound through the streets of London.

The procession was massive, well over two thousand black-robed lords, ladies and other high-ranking participants slowly making their way through the spectator-lined streets of London. It was led by a sword bearer and officers of London, followed by the king's messengers and his trumpeters and minstrels.[10] Ambassadors and foreign officials walked behind, from Florence, Venice, Portugal, Spain, France and Germany. A group of ushers, squires and chaplains processed behind this group, followed by the aldermen and sheriffs. As this company passed, bystanders at last came closer to the royal presence. Two heralds came riding up on large horses, in full coat armour, joined by a knight mourner, Sir Edward Darrell, on a courser trapped with black velvet and bearing the king's standard. Darrell had been accused of joining Edmund Dudley in his plot to seize power, but this had been quickly dismissed, a fact demonstrated by his prominent role in the funeral procession.

Behind Darrell and his large courser were the rest of the King's Council, Knights and Justices. As they passed, bystanders could already hear the voices of the friars and canons who walked, singing, behind them. The remainder of the lords and barons together with the abbots and bishops followed the robed singers. At long last, headed by knights carrying Henry's crowned helmet, battle-axe and armour, was the chariot with the king's corpse.

Those who gathered to watch the procession came face to face with the dead king, by means of the life-like effigy placed upon his coffin. It showed the king in his grand parliament robes, with sceptre in his right hand and orb in his left. The effigy lay under a cloth of gold, with all the regal dignity Henry had held in life. Those who were able to get close enough to the image, torch in hand, also saw the weariness in the lines captured by the death-mask effigy.

The rest of the funeral took several days, and Andrew Windsor had his work cut out for him in ensuring that both St Paul's and Westminster were draped in black, that all the courtiers in attendance, including the Spanish princess, were properly clothed, and that the entire retinue were fed and housed over the three-day event. As the sun rose on the final day of the funeral, the court once again put on their black robes and settled in the church for an early morning mass. From there, the corpse was at last interred to the strains of *Libera me*: 'Deliver me, O Lord, from death eternal on that fearful day, When the heavens and the earth shall be moved, When thou shalt come to judge the world by fire.' At a sign, the leading members of the king's household broke their staves and threw them on to the coffin in the grave. With that, the old king's reign was over. The heralds cried 'The noble King Henry the Seventh is dead. God send the noble King Henry the Eighth long life. Amen!' and the company departed to partake in the great feast that had been prepared for them.

It had all gone as planned. But Andrew – and the merchants and craftspeople of London – did not have long to rest once the old king was interred. They still had to crown the new one. On 11 June, Henry VIII finally married the Spanish princess he had repudiated four years earlier, Catherine of Aragon, in a – mercifully – quiet ceremony at Greenwich Palace. The grandeur would be saved for their double coronation. With only a month between the royal funeral and the coronation, the tailors and smiths of London had been working tirelessly all summer, only now they were producing brilliant red and scarlet robes, cloth of gold, sparkling harnesses and glittering jewellery. The sombre atmosphere that had closed the previous reign was behind them.

On the evening of 22 June, two days before the coronation, Andrew attended a grand banquet at the Tower of London, just yards from where Edmund was imprisoned. Andrew was one of twenty-six men who served the king an elaborate dinner, signifying that they would thereafter never have to serve a dish again. The next day Andrew, along with the others, was made a Knight of the Bath.[11] On the day of the coronation, he took a prestigious place in the long procession.[12] The king, dressed in ermine and velvet, and glittering with jewels, rode on his gold-trapped courser through London with all the exuberance of charismatic youth, and Londoners echoed his enthusiasm with cries of celebration and loyalty. His new wife, Catherine, was also a vision; dressed in white satin and borne in a litter by horses trapped in white cloth of gold. She wore her auburn hair loose, encircled by a pearl band.[13] They were both young, healthy and exuded the promise of a golden age.

Thomas More, the aspiring lawyer and scholar, and the Dudleys' neighbour, wrote a coronation poem in honour of the day, marking it as 'the end of our slavery, the beginning of our freedom, the end of sadness, the source of joy'.[14] In it, he levelled a side-long critique of Dudley and his promoters:

> Now each man happily does not hesitate to show the possessions which in the past his fear kept hidden in dark seclusion.
>
> Now there is enjoyment in any profit which managed to escape the many sly clutching hands of the many thieves.
>
> No longer is it a criminal offense to own property which was honestly acquired (formerly it was a serious offense).
>
> No longer does fear hiss whispered secrets in one's ear, for no one has secrets either to keep or to whisper.
>
> Now it is a delight to ignore informers. Only ex-informers fear informers now.

The joy of the new reign was simultaneously a condemnation of the evils of the one that had come before, and particularly of the role that Edmund Dudley had played in it.

To a boy of five, such as John Dudley, the grand parades and songs, and the glittering king and queen, were the stuff of dreams and legends. Enjoyment of the spectacle was marred by the absence of his father, the sorrow and strain he saw in the face of his mother, and the strange resentful glances from those who saw them in the streets. It was not easy to understand why such a cloud had so abruptly come over his young life, but it was clear enough that it had coincided with being told that he must now pray not for Henry VII, who was dead and with God, but for a new king, Henry VIII. Perhaps this new king did not like his father as much as the last one had? That fact seemed to matter a very great deal.

*

As the city celebrated, Edmund Dudley waited. It wasn't until after the burial of Henry VII (and his mother, Margaret Beaufort), and the wedding and coronation of Henry VIII, that the attention of king and council could once again turn to the task of what to do with that unpopular remnant of the previous reign, Edmund Dudley.

At last, in the middle of July, Edmund was taken from the Tower to the Guildhall, just north of the market streets and lanes of Cheapside. The Guildhall was a familiar site to Edmund; it was where he had worked as an undersheriff of London, just before his rapid rise to power. The great hall had been built in the first half of the fifteenth century and contained the grey stone beams and pointed arches which were hallmarks of that time.

Edmund was led into this great room by Sir Richard Chomley, deputy-constable of the Tower.[15] A company of some of the highest-ranking peers and knights of the realm, including the Duke of Buckingham and George Talbot, Earl of Shrewsbury, had been assembled to oversee the arraignment of the former king's minister. The imposing ranks of stern-faced men also included Sir Robert Drury, who had accompanied William Clopton to Dudley's home five years before, and Sir Henry Marney, who also owned a home on Candlewick Street.[16]

The charges against him were read out. Until now the exact nature of the accusations he faced were unknown, and Edmund might have thought to face a substantial fine or a significant demotion. Few could have predicted the magnitude of the indictment that was read out to him. Edmund was accused of being a 'false traitor' for 'falsely, feloniously, and traitorously conspiring, imagining and compassing how and in what manner he, with a great force of men and armed power,

53

might hold, guide, and govern the King and his Council against the wishes of the King'. He was charged with plotting to 'totally deprive the King of his Royal liberty', and if the councillors of the king would not assent to his power, of planning to 'completely destroy the King, and to depose, remove, and deprive him of his Royal authority'. Edmund Dudley, it was proclaimed, had plotted a total overthrow of the government, and even considered regicide, so that he might hold sovereign power himself. The penalty for such crimes could only be death.

As a lawyer, Edmund knew how weak the case against him was, but as an experienced member of the king's council, he knew how little that mattered. If he protested the charges, he was unlikely to win; if he confessed, there might be mercy. The only certainty was that his life hung in the balance.

Defiantly, he pled not guilty to the charges.

It was two days before Edmund was brought back to the great hall in the Guildhall to hear the verdict made against him. The implications of the accusations hung heavy in the room. Treason was one of the worst crimes imaginable; an attack on the sovereign was an attack on the whole body of the people, and for this reason carried one of the worst punishments. No one had been convicted of high treason in England since 1502, when Sir James Tyrrell, a former servant of Richard III, had been executed for throwing his support behind one of Henry VII's Yorkist rivals. The case against Edmund was flimsy, even fanciful, by comparison,[17] but he had packed, persuaded, bullied and bribed juries before. The question was, did his enemies hate him enough to go so far as to condemn him to a violent death?

The jury delivered their verdict. Edmund Dudley was found guilty of treason. He would be drawn through the streets of London on a hurdle – subject to everything that the angry inhabitants of London could throw at him, verbal and otherwise. Once he arrived at the scaffold he would be hanged by the neck until nearly dead, taken down, his privy parts and bowels cut out and burned before him. In the midst of this torture he would die, and his head would be removed from his neck and his body cut into four pieces to be sent to various parts of the realm as a warning against those who might attempt the same crime. It was one of the worst deaths that could be imagined, and on that July day in the Guildhall, Edmund Dudley was coolly told that he would leave this earth in the perfect expression of public agony.

*

When James Tyrrell had been found guilty of treason seven years before, he had been executed within days. Eyeing the door to his cell, Edmund waited for the Constable of the Tower, or his deputy, to walk through it, and tell him the time that he had been appointed to die, but no such message came.

Instead, he was delivered messages from men empowered by the pardon and the new reign to seek recompense for the action Dudley had taken against them.[18] John Spencer, a merchant and landowner in Northamptonshire, asked Edmund to write to the king and his council, to help him obtain a manor that Edmund's dealings had interfered with. A Justice of the Peace also wrote to him, seeking remuneration for the £20 which Edmund had taken. He asked Edmund to 'cause the king's most honourable council to be moved that I may be restored to my money again'. Neither of these men seemed to understand the situation that Edmund himself was in.

Not only did Edmund have the threat of the axe hanging over him, but the attainder meant that all of his possessions, wealth and lands were forfeit to the Crown. Edmund did not have a penny to his name, and what was worse, there was nothing he could pass on to his young children. John, who would have been his heir, was disinherited by the law and banned from asking for or laying claim to any of his father's lands, or those which had belonged to Edmund's ancestors.[19] His family was entirely destroyed by the attainder.

Edmund responded with sympathy but defensiveness to the letters. To the Justice of the Peace he acknowledged that he had taken the money, but that he 'paid it to the kings grace'.[20] There was no way, he scribbled hastily, he could have lessened the fine. It was true, he admitted, that the man ought to have the money back, in conscience he had been wronged, but there was nothing Edmund could do. He signed off with his own request: 'pray for me, if I were of power I would restore you myself'.

He also responded to the complaints of Thomas Sunnyff, still likewise imprisoned in the Tower for his refusal to bend to the
manipulations of Dudley and Camby. There was no matter, he stated,
that caused him more remorse, than Sunnyff's. It was the king, however, who took all of Sunnyff's money, Edmund was just the 'executor
of the wrong', not the cause of it. Once again, he regretted not being
in a position to recompense him, for a 'great wrong' had been done to
him.[21] Sunnyff may have found this expression of sympathy cold comfort indeed.

Such accusations of wrongdoing weigh heavily on the soul of a
man condemned to die, and as Edmund waited in the Tower for the
axe to fall, he became increasingly frightened of his fate. He tried to
petition the King's Council, to make note of all those wronged by the
king's policies, and his own actions, in the hopes that the victims
might be compensated. After all, that was the promise behind the new
king's pardon. He also had a residual duty to the king he had served,
who too had attempted to cleanse his soul before death. If it was truly
Henry VII who was the cause of these men's unhappiness, then there
was work to be done to release the late king of the consequences of
these sins, as he suffered in Purgatory.

Edmund called for his account books to be brought to him, and
carefully went through them, attempting to pull out all the names of
those who had been treated unjustly.[22] This included the Bishop of
London, Richard FitzJames, who had protested to Edmund that 'by
the priesthood, the matter laid against me was not true!' and yet had
been forced into an obligation for £500. The Lord Abergavenny had
been fined £70,000, a 'very sore end' Edmund wrote, for having a private army, despite insufficient proof. Others included Sir John Digby,
Thomas Sunnyff, Clopton, and a host more who had been imprisoned
lengths of time for light causes or fined for accusations which had
been entirely untrue. If those listed were given some recompense they
would be, he wrote, 'very well and reasonably contented'. Pausing
and considering the anger of men like FitzJames, Edmund crossed out
the word 'very'. They would be contented enough.

Perhaps prompted by these letters, and with long days stretching
before him, Edmund began to reflect on the nature of rule and service

to the Crown, penning a lengthy treatise for the new king: *The Tree of Commonwealth*. In it, he warned Henry VIII against the practices of his father, to eschew 'extraordinary' legal powers, such as the king's prerogative.[23] 'Oftentimes,' he wrote, 'the prince shall have councillors and servants that in his own causes will do further than conscience requireth', whether this be for favour, advancement or malice. 'Let these servants or councillors take heed that they do the party no wrong, for the rod of punishment dieth not.'[24]

It was impossible not to imbue the treatise with an awareness of his own situation: 'death cometh and tarrieth not', he wrote, and when it comes, 'all the treasure in the tower cannot entreat him for one day.'[25] Men might expect 'to die in their beds in good prosperity' but instead 'die by execution and not worth a penny'.[26] As he wrote, Edmund could not escape the knowledge that this was the fate which also awaited him.

*

It wasn't long after hearing that her husband had been condemned to a traitor's death that Elizabeth gathered up the children, along with any ready money and important papers, and fled Candlewick.[27] She was forced to leave behind not only the expensive cloth and precious plate, but more sentimental items as well; such as the rich tapestries with her and Edmund's arms intertwined. She took, however, her own clothing, as well as the children's clothes and toys. Her stepdaughter, 'the little Elizabeth', was of an age to be under her tutelage, and would now find out how a household ran when the male head was removed from the picture. It was not easy, but all over the country women made do when their husbands were killed, ran off, or – like Edmund – were arrested.

Elizabeth had been right to leave; a month after Edmund's trial, the King's Marshal, Sir John Digby, entered the Dudley home at Candlewick.[28] Sir John Digby was an experienced courtier and had suffered at Edmund Dudley's hands. As Knight Marshal, Digby was responsible for the Marshalsea Prison, and in 1505 the king – through Edmund – had fined him for escapes at the prison.[29] Digby had handed over £100 and promised £500, and another £625 at the king's pleasure. He had also been pulled before The Council Learned, led by

Empson and Dudley, and promised a further eight biannual payments of £100. In short, through Edmund Dudley John Digby had entered into agreements to pay the king a small fortune. By May 1509, when Henry VIII came to the throne, he had been forgiven £825 of this vast sum. Providing a condemnatory list of Dudley's possessions would not have been an unwelcome prospect.

Digby entered through the hall, and from there scrutinized the entire house, prying open coffers and pulling out robes and bed-clothes, riffling through them to add to his list for the king. Edmund's doublets of black, crimson, green and purple satin spoke to his expensive tastes. Edmund had not broken any laws in wearing purple, sable fur, velvet or 'tinselled' satin, but only a few months later Henry VIII's first parliament would place fines on those below the rank of baron who wore tinsel satin, below the rank of earl who wore sable and below the rank of knight of the Garter who wore crimson velvet.[30] Edmund Dudley had no such status, and his possession of such fabrics might have been part of the reason that the king and parliament were so keen to generate a clear visual distinction between ranks.

Candlewick was not Dudley's only property, and in fact it was one of the few he didn't own outright. Dudley had acquired land in Surrey, Sussex, Dorset, Wiltshire and beyond. The king had a list made of all these as well, with their values attached. Edmund Dudley possessed over £333 in landed income and more than £5,000 in goods; all of it went to the Crown, though Londoners murmured that he was worth four times that, more than £20,000.[31] All of the items that Digby had recorded eventually went to another rising man of the court, Sir Henry Marney, who also had a house in St Swithin's parish and had been present at Dudley's trial.[32] He had brokered connections with William Capel, more than once a victim of Edmund's fiercest collections, though he himself had only had to hand over an obligation for £12. Marney was a favourite of Henry VIII's and replaced Richard Empson as Chancellor of the Duchy of Lancaster, in addition to taking all of Edmund's goods. To Marney these were impressive spoils. To Elizabeth Dudley they had been the makings of a home. Now she left it all behind. It would be up to her to protect her children now.

*

Over the winter of 1509–1510, Edmund Dudley continued to wait. The new parliament would be called in January – would it confirm his attainder and at last sentence him to death? Or would he be released? Perhaps he would remain in the Tower till he died of some illness, a prisoner of the king's pleasure. The constant presence of death haunted him, and he was weighed down with the heaviness of his fate.

As the days wore on and the terror set in, Edmund's mind began to grasp for ways of escaping this end. The king could change his mind, parliament might never confirm the attainder, but if the order did come down for Edmund's execution, he would be entirely trapped. He hunted around for an option if it all went wrong. Desperately, he asked his brother-in-law, Andrew Windsor, to offer sums of money to powerful men of the court, to help secure him a pardon. Andrew had licence to sell off lands if he needed to, in order to deliver on these promises, if the pleas and bribes were successful.

Such attempts yielded no fruit, however, and he searched for another way out. Could he, to save his own life, escape the Tower of London?

There had been escapes in the past. In the twelfth century, the bishop Ranulf Flambard had escaped by getting his guards drunk and climbing out of his window with a rope he'd smuggled in inside a casket of wine. A similar technique had been employed by Roger Mortimer in the thirteenth century; he had drugged his guard's wine. Others had not been so lucky. The Welshman Gruffydd ap Llywelyn Fawr had died while trying to escape, falling from the makeshift rope he had made from sheets and cloths. More recently, the pretender and rebel Perkin Warbeck had planned an escape, but when it was discovered, it had only served to expedite his execution.

For a successful escape, Edmund would need support both inside and outside the Tower. He solicited the help of his younger brother, Peter, and kinsman, James Beamond, as well as his servants, William Frank and Thomas Mitchell, imprisoned with him.[33] All were dedicated to saving his life, if the worst should happen. Yet no plans were to be put in motion unless his attainder was confirmed by both Houses of Parliament and the king. Edmund refused to make a move to preserve himself until the last possible moment.

The first parliament of Henry VIII opened on 21 January, in the same decorated chamber in which Edmund had presided as Speaker six years before. Amongst its other business were bills against commissioners and promoters, as well as a discussion of Edmund's lands. By the end of February, the Bill of Attainder was in the House of Lords.[34] If it passed and the king signed it, Dudley's fate would be sealed.

As the time to act drew nearer, Edmund's servants were forced to face what they had agreed to do – and its consequences – and balked. James Beamond wrote that Edmund would need to find some other help, for he would not assist him in such a daring escape. This last-minute abortion did not help avoid adverse consequences, however. Edmund's letters had been watched, and a man by the name of Brymely caught wind of the plot in one of Edmund's missives to Beamond and revealed it. Dudley's collaborators were apprehended. With this, his final hope to escape his fate disappeared. In planning an escape Edmund had risked the safety of his family, abandoning them to face the anger of the king and his ministers alone.

With resignation and perhaps some regret, on 12 March 1510 Dudley turned to composing his Last Will and Testament, which he wrote in his own hand.[35] Resigned he may have been, but submissive he was not. He once again protested the 'false and untrue verdict' which had been passed against him, he who was 'clear and innocent of that treason'.[36] He even went so far as to assert that the king 'at his departing' should 'clearly know that I was his true subject and no traitor'.

Leaving various bequests, Edmund prayed that his executors 'be helping and friendly to my wife and children'.[37] He reinforced in his will that his daughter, Elizabeth, should marry the eldest nephew of Baron Stourton, or any nephew if the eldest should die. He also asked the Lord Steward, George Talbot, Earl of Shrewsbury, and the Lord Treasurer, Sir John Heron, to help in the arrangement of a marriage of his eldest son, John, only five, as well as to 'see him up in virtue and learning'. After all, Shrewsbury was a kinsman of John's mother and Edmund had worked very closely with Heron. He asked Shrewsbury and the other lords named in his will to protect his 'loving wife' from harm and give her good counsel after he had died.[38] Even with these provisions, she and their young children would be left vulnerable should he be executed. In his will, his thoughts went to them, accepting that this was almost certainly to be their fate.

*

There was no way of knowing in which direction the king's will would turn, and, like her husband, all Elizabeth Dudley could do was wait.[39] Perhaps this was what Purgatory was like, waiting on the mercy of a divine ruler for your salvation, or damnation. She knew the verdict that had been passed at the Guildhall and had heard the celebratory reaction from the merchants and craftspeople of London. Edmund had written to her, as well, of the plan to escape from the Tower, and she had waited with terror to see what would come of it. There would likely be no mercy on his family if Edmund Dudley escaped justice.

As spring came, there was still nothing from the court on the fate of Edmund Dudley. The queen, Catherine of Aragon, had become pregnant not long after the wedding, but this had ended in miscarriage. Some of the debts Edmund had established had been cancelled, but others were still being collected by the new king, a fact that must have seemed morosely ironic to Elizabeth. The king also began selling or handing off the lands he had confiscated from Dudley. Henry was making profits on all sides from the fallen minister.

By summer, the queen was pregnant again, and the king was off on progress, to see his new lands and to let his new subjects see him. All the more reason, one might be tempted to think, for Henry to forget about the problems he left behind in the city, problems like what to do with Edmund Dudley. His reticence to punish his father's minister up to this point indicated that he probably did not believe the charges against him, despite the guilty verdicts. Away from London, any ill-feeling he continued to have might dissipate. Elizabeth could at last, it seemed, begin to breathe.

Such optimism, however, overlooked that it was not just in London that Dudley, and the likewise imprisoned Richard Empson, had cultivated resentment. It was reported that as Henry VIII travelled, he was handed bills and complaints against the imprisoned ministers.

These areas, west of London, were prone to rebellion, and measures had to be taken to satisfy them. They demanded a sacrifice for their loyalty. Henry had a decision to make.

The order came to John de Vere, Earl of Oxford and Constable of the Tower, at the height of an excessively hot summer. He made the arrangements and sent out the pronouncements. The news spread west from the Tower like a wave. On Saturday, 17 August, those ravening wolves, Richard Empson and Edmund Dudley, were at last to be executed for treason. In the king's mercy, he had commuted the sentence to beheading. There might have been some disappointment at this from angry Londoners, but with a laudatory acknowledgement of the merciful nature of a powerful king.

Scores of Londoners woke early on the morning of the execution, packed up a crust of bread or an apple, and headed east towards the looming walls of the Tower of London. As they went, they met with other small pockets of people, until they were a great mass, standing as near as they could to the scaffold which had been erected on Tower Hill, to watch the execution. For many, this was God's justice, communicated through the body of the king and the laws of the realm of England. Perhaps if they repented, these men might find Heaven, but their punishment here on earth was just and godly. Some in the crowd, those who had known the men, benefitted from some of their kinder acts, or simply had a charitable nature, would spend the time praying for the souls of the convicted men, and perhaps even shed a tear as the axe came down. Such souls prayed the axe fell true. The more inclined to violence in the crowd might have hoped for a botched job, and the butchery that would result.

It wasn't long after dawn that the men were taken out of their rooms and led under guard from the middle gate of the Tower of London, to where the crowd was assembled around the scaffold at Tower Hill. Neither Empson nor Dudley was young, and the strain of imprisonment through the months of winter and the sweltering summer – no matter how comfortable their lodgings – had left a mark. Richard Empson was sixty and had several adult children. His eldest son, Thomas, had shared his imprisonment with him, though not his final fate.[40] As the more senior – Empson was a knight – it was expected that he would be executed first. His standing would save him the indignity and the terror of seeing his fate performed on another man and having to lay his head on a block warm and wet with his colleague's blood.[41]

The crowd knew and watched the routine, as if it were a well-worn dance or stage-play. It was customary for the condemned man to give some alms on the way to the scaffold, as well as to pay and forgive the executioner. There would be a short speech, in which the guilty man admitted to living a sinful life and reasserted his loyalty to the king and laws which killed him. He would beg prayers of those assembled as he prepared to offer up his soul to God. Then he knelt. Blink, and you might miss the executioner's long axe falling, and the moment between a living man, desperately praying, and nothing but a bloody corpse, in two pieces. And so it was that Richard Empson met his end.

With this death before him, it was Edmund Dudley's turn. The scaffold was slippery with the older man's blood. It was getting hotter, especially in the tightly packed crowd, which was growing rank with sweat. The executioner's axe dripped with russet-coloured blood. It was a much different experience of death than the tranquil funeral of his wife, not that many years before. 'Yea, though I walk through the valley of the shadow of death, I will fear no evil: for thou art with me, O Lord. Thy rod and thy staff comfort me.'

The second scaffold performance was much the same. The executioner accepted Edmund's pardon; the crowd jeered over his speech. He knelt in the blood, barely absorbed by the rushes. It soaked through his hose and stained his skin. He had investigated every avenue, but there was no way out now. His cheek met the bloody block. It smelled woody and metallic, like a coffer full of coins.

PART TWO
1510–1547

4
My Lord the Bastard

Sparks erupted on the surface of the ornate polished plate as metal struck metal. The tiny fires reflected on the smooth blade of the massive two-handed sword before vanishing into the air, almost as quickly as they'd appeared. The two men grunted as they heaved their swords up to strike again. It was the end of May, the Thursday of Pentecost week, and it was already clear it was going to be a hot summer.[1] Straining under their heavy armour in the park outside Greenwich Palace, it wasn't long before heavy drops of sweat appeared on both men's brows.

Pentecost, or Whitsunday, was the festival that marked when the Lord sent down his Spirit as drops of flame – like sparks – to his apostles, uniting them in their mission to spread his Holy Word. It also signalled the end of the Easter season, with its Lenten fasts and Easter renewal. This year Pentecost had fallen only a few weeks after Mayday, which marked the beginning of the summer months, as well as the anniversary of the new king's reign. May 1510 was thus a month of celebrations, and what better way to celebrate than with ceremonial combat.

One of the two men had the advantage of height over the other. His armour was more ornately – and expensively – made, and he had an air of superiority about him. The shorter man was older than his opponent, a fact that became clear as the fight went on. They faced each other over a wooden barrier that reached their torsos, about three feet high, meant to ensure the fight did not become lethal. As they struck, the heralds standing by the supported ends of the barrier counted and kept score. They were allowed twelve strikes each with their swords, and then the battle was declared to be over. They had begun by casting their four-foot capped spears at each other, before moving on to the sword-play. Wearing armour that could weigh almost a hundred pounds, and hefting swords of five pounds or more in heavy locking gauntlets, by the time the twelfth stroke hit, the men, especially the smaller, older man, were happy to lay down their weapons and remove their helmets from their sweat-soaked heads.

No one was surprised when one of the combatants was revealed to be the king himself. When Henry VIII had appeared earlier that year in a tournament at Richmond Palace, his first tournament as king, he had done so in disguise, though had had to quickly reveal himself when his opponent became injured. It was the king who had issued the challenge for Whitsuntide. He invited gentlemen to meet him and his aids – Sir Thomas Knyvet, Sir Edward Howard and Charles Brandon – fighting at barriers at Greenwich Palace for the next several weeks. The first to answer the king's challenge in battle had been Sir Thomas Boleyn, who managed a fight with the king without incident. The watching crowd, secured behind railings, cheered for the men and the fight.

Between the spectators and the combatants stood a company of men in their twenties and thirties, all companions of the king who joined him in his martial exercises. A number of these men were linked to the Howard family, a house in the midst of climbing its way back into favour and power. The family had been disgraced when the Duke of Norfolk had died fighting against Henry VII at Bosworth in 1485. His son, Thomas Howard, had been imprisoned in the Tower of London, though demonstrated his loyalty to the new regime when, unlike Edmund Dudley, he had refused an opportunity to escape. He had been released and began the work of restoring himself and his family, many of whom joined the new king at his Whitsuntide tournament.

Boleyn, the king's first opponent, was one of Thomas Howard's sons-in-law, married to his eldest daughter, Elizabeth. The son of a Norfolk landowner, Thomas Boleyn had joined Andrew Windsor in becoming a Knight of the Bath at the king's coronation. In his early thirties, he and Elizabeth already had three young children, two daughters, Anne and Mary, and a son, George. Thomas Boleyn had the honour of fighting the king first on that morning of 23 May, while the crowds were at their most enthused, attentive and sober. Having secured the highest-profile spot, he didn't pick up another sword during the tournament.

His Howard kinsmen were much more deeply involved. The eldest Howard brother, named Thomas like his father, was also one of the challengers fighting the king in the afternoon of the opening day of the tournament. In his late-thirties, Thomas already had almost two decades of battle experience, having accompanied his (newly released) father and other noblemen to battle against the Scots in the 1490s. Thomas had married one of the daughters of Edward IV, Anne of York, meaning that by marriage he was the young king's uncle. From treasonous disgrace, the Howards had married their way into becoming companions and kin of the king. His younger brother, Edward Howard, was one of the challengers of the tournament, fighting alongside the king, while the youngest and least-experienced brother, Edmund, joined the group of answerers to the royal challenge.

Rounding out the Howard contingent at these events was Thomas Knyvet, a Howard brother-in-law like Boleyn, who had served the king at his coronation banquet and was another of the king's challengers. In his mid-twenties, he had married a younger daughter of the Howard house, Muriel, some years before, becoming stepfather to her young daughter, Elizabeth Grey. Muriel's first husband had been John Grey, the Viscount Lisle, brother-in-law to the disgraced and imprisoned Edmund Dudley.[2] Knyvet's stepdaughter, Elizabeth, as her late father's only heir, carried the grand title of Lady Lisle on her little five-year-old shoulders. With the title of Viscount Lisle on offer to her husband, she was already attractive property on the marriage market. Any potential suitors would have to go through her stepfather, Knyvet, and though official sanction from the king was only needed for those in the succession, it still would do well to select someone from the king's coterie.

One of the men who may have been eying her as a potential bride was Charles Brandon, an athletic man in his twenties, one of the few who could keep up physically with the king, and the final of the king's aides at the tournament. Although the tournament took place over a week and a half, from 23 May to 3 June, there were only four days of events, and both Brandon and the king competed ten times over those four days, fighting at barriers as many as five times over the course of a single day. Charles Brandon's uncle, Thomas Brandon, had been a trusted servant of Henry VII, which had allowed the orphaned Charles to enter royal circles, impressing the court with his athletic and martial abilities. Charles, however, had not gained much in material terms at his uncle's death; the lands and properties went to the widow of Thomas Brandon's former colleague, Sir Richard Guildford, who rented it to the young Charles.[3] Charles Brandon had many connections, but little wealth. He had a lot to prove on the tournament ground.

On 1 June, the third day of events, another of the king's companions joined the group, fighting the youngest Howard brother. Arthur Plantagenet had a few extra years on the Howard brothers, and came from much more illustrious stock, albeit contaminated by bastardy. Arthur Plantagenet was an illegitimate son of Edward IV, making him the king's half-uncle, as well as related, by marriage, to the eldest Howard.[4] Plantagenet had spent time in his half-sister Elizabeth's household while she was queen, as well as in the household of Henry VII. This had made him a companion of the new king, though he was not as keen to participate in these sorts of displays as some of the younger men. He fought only the once over the Whitsuntide tournament, though this still marked him as part of this masculine inner circle.

Plantagenet was one of the fifty or so gentlemen making up the king's 'Spears of Honour', along with Charles Brandon, Edward Howard, Thomas Knyvet and others.[5] Well paid – four weeks of Spears' services was costing the king almost £150 – to defend the king and participate with him in tournaments, the 'Spears' were marked out as an elite company close to the king, both companions and champions.

Not seen carousing and combating with the king were the ministers upon whom he relied to run the government. This included his father's men, Richard Fox and William Warham, still in possession of the highest offices in the land. These men didn't feel the need to whack each other about the head with pointed sticks to prove their worth, though they might have wanted to. The relationship between Warham and Fox was breaking down, with Fox emerging as the clearly more powerful. Keeper of the privy seal, Fox had transitioned from self-appointed chief executor of Henry VII's will to head amongst Henry VIII's ministers, and there was talk of him becoming a cardinal of the Church. That April, the Spanish ambassador, after meeting with Fox, identified him as '*alter rex*' – the other king – though Henry himself viewed him with suspicion. 'Here in England they think he is a fox,' the king was heard to say, 'and such is his name.'[6]

Henry, instead, seemed to prefer Fox's protégé, the former chaplain of the old king, Thomas Wolsey. Much younger than Fox, Wolsey appealed to the king's preference for youth and vitality and did not chide the king for his activities outside of government; on the contrary, he encouraged them. All of this was fine by Fox. Wolsey was after all his man, and he was grooming him as his replacement in the management of government and king.

Henry might have packed his council with wise elder statesmen, but his company were these younger, boisterous and adventurous men, and despite the appearance of frivolity and waste, these events were important to the wellbeing of the country. Displays of chivalry such as these primed a country for warfare. They presented the glamour and fame of combat, without the blood, guts and dysentery that came with real military campaigns. It kept knights' training up and introduced the untried to the basics of combat. Most importantly, it stirred pride in king and country, a desire to follow and defend the mighty king against all comers. As much as he enjoyed these events, and there were few months in the first years of his reign without some sort of tournament, Henry craved real combat against England's real enemies. This was all just practice for something much bigger.

As the event drew to a close on 3 June, the king prepared himself for progress. While he was away he would send back the order for the death of Edmund Dudley. Such a man, with his reputation for rapacity and injustice, was not a part of this new world with its shining young king and his strong, loyal companions.

*

It might have been difficult for John Dudley to remember his father, and it was rarely wise for him to do so. With Candlewick fading from his mind, John got to know his new home and new family at Halden Manor, Kent. Halden Manor was a reasonably sized country home for middling nobility; Henry VII had even visited in 1504. The manor lands consisted of a number of adjacent buildings and lands, known as messuages and tofts, a dove house or 'dovecote', a garden, and thousands of acres of land, including arable land, meadow, pasture, woodland, heath and marshland.[7] The manor itself had crenellated battlements, a medieval moat and far larger and grander rooms than John had known at Candlewick. It was also a very different life. John's guardian, Sir Edward Guildford, did not meet with shady informers and distressed knights, but with farmers, millers and families who made up the community which he oversaw. They treated Guildford not with fear or resentment, but with respect and a sense of solidarity.

Sir Edward Guildford had been granted John's wardship. As John understood it, this meant that Edward would take care of him, educate him and bring him up until he was ready to take his place in the world, whatever that might mean. At Halden John would become part of Guildford's family, though he would remain a Dudley.

The Guildfords had long been friends of the Dudleys; Edward's father, Richard, had supported Edmund's initial climb to power, and Edmund's position at court had been weakened by Richard's death in 1506. Richard Guildford had been dogged by debt in the years up to his death. Imprisoned for a time in the Fleet, he was pardoned in April 1506 but did not return to his position in Henry VII's service. Instead, he went on pilgrimage to Jerusalem. Forced to spend a night in a cave, Guildford fell ill, and died shortly after arriving at the holy city. He left his manor of Halden to his eldest son, Edward. Much of the rest of Richard Guildford's belongings were left to his widow, Jane, who had served Margaret Beaufort and Elizabeth of York, as well as acting as a governess to Henry VIII's sisters, Margaret and Mary (who affectionately referred to her as 'Mother Guildford').[8]

Edward's children, Richard and Jane, shared their names with their grandparents.[9] Richard was of an age with John, Jane a few years younger. The three children were tutored in the country manor. The boys learned how to read and write – in English, Latin and French – the art of chivalry and the ornaments of a courtier, such as music and dance. Rhetoric was also essential, as was instruction in how to run an estate. John was not a particularly keen student, especially of Latin; he did not have the concentrated dedication to the written word that his father had possessed.

There was some debate about how girls like Jane should be educated. Many members of the burgeoning humanist movement maintained that women's wit was no less capable than men's, even if it was naturally and rightly geared towards different tasks and virtues. If she were to be taught, it was in order to learn good manners and Holy Scripture, inculcating obedience and chastity.[10] Whereas a humanist education might encourage its male pupils to assert their own authority and become active citizens in the commonwealth, female students were to learn silence and humble subjection.[11]

Jane learned how to read and write, as the boys did, and there were some lessons for which it made sense to educate all the young children of the household together, such as dance. Dance was one of the most essential skills for rising in the court, as well as being an enjoyable one for many young men and women, as John, Jane and Richard were becoming. It allowed men and women to be physically close, touching hands, and moving in rhythm. It also allowed them to exchange heated whispers without the adults overhearing.

Whereas it was primarily the mother's task to educate girls in the practical skills of household management, the boys of the household would be tutored by a graduate of Oxford or Cambridge. The boys were introduced to more martial skills, joining Edward for archery practice on Sundays, learning the use of the axe and sword, and how to dress a man in armour. Edward Guildford was one of the best men in England from which to learn such lessons. He had joined his father as master of the royal armoury from the age of fourteen and then succeeded him upon his death.

John's mother did not join him at Halden. Whereas his wardship had gone to Edward Guildford, his mother had been married by the king's permission to Arthur Plantagenet, the king's illegitimate uncle.

As would undoubtedly have been explained to John, this was a brilliant step for his mother, who was now related to the king himself, though it was harder to discern his mother's feelings on her new marriage. From what he could gather, Arthur Plantagenet had thought he would get both mother and son, and resented Edward Guildford for winning John's lucrative wardship.[12]

John was told that his father's attainder had been reversed, thanks to his guardian's petition to parliament, and he would be – upon reaching the age of majority – in possession of those lands his father had left for him, of about £200 in value. John was 'restored as son and heir of the said Edmund Dudley in name, blood and degree' and the indictment was to be 'utterly anietised,* evoided,† repelled frustrate and of none effect as never none such . . . had never be had nor done.'[13] It was easy to wonder why the king, who had seemed to have forgiven his father so quickly after his death, couldn't have done that before he'd killed him, but perhaps that was the sort of thing best understood when one was older; in 1512 John was not yet eight and these things were beyond his understanding, and certainly his control.

Despite his youth, both his guardian and his king expected great things of him. Guildford's petition noted John's 'tender age', but also 'the faithful and true service that the said John Dudley hereafter may and intendeth to do unto your Highness and to your heirs'. John would be given back his lands and his place in the world. In return, he must live his life in service of the Crown: whatever that might entail.

*

England was at war. Sir Edward Howard, the second Howard son, had been made Lord Admiral in April, and his crews and ships had been harassing any ship they came across, seizing and plundering like pirates and causing panic across the continent.[14] They then turned to raiding the coast of Brittany and established dominance across the English Channel, Howard commanding from the English flagship, the *Mary Rose*. But the French had caught up by the end of the summer

* Anietised: annulled.
† Evoided: removed.

and had assembled a fleet at Brest, a port town on the eastern tip of Brittany.

Edward Howard, fresh off his numerous naval victories and keen for a fight, took the formation of the French fleet as a challenge and sailed in the *Mary Rose* from Portsmouth, on the southern coast of England, towards Brest. In all there were twenty-five ships, ranging from smaller ships like the *Jennet* at 70 tons, up to the *Regent* at 1,000 tons.[15] The *Mary Rose* was a middling-sized ship, about 600 tons, but it was by far the most modern. With Edward Howard on the *Mary Rose*, the *Regent* had been given to Sir Thomas Knyvet, his brother-in-law. Henry had given commands to many of his closest companions. Knyvet's brother, James, was captain of the *Margaret of Topsham*; Edward Guildford's half-brother Henry commanded the *Catherine Pomegranate*, aided by Charles Brandon.[16]

Edward Howard's impetuosity had mixed results. The French had not expected his attack, and he had caught the French commanders off guard while their ships were at anchor. The Breton flagship, *Marie la Cordelière*, even had 300 guests celebrating the Feast of St Lawrence aboard when the English attacked, including some women who did not have time to disembark before the battle began. Swept up in the midst of the attack, the civilians did their best to pitch in, especially as many of the crew of the ship were still ashore.

After some initial gunplay – Howard's *Mary Rose* blew the mast off the *Grand Louise* – it was clear that the centre of the battle could be found in the engagement between the *Regent*, commanded by Knyvet, and the *Marie la Cordelière*. The ships were at close range, the English archers on the *Regent* and the French crossbowmen on the *Cordelière* firing incessantly at each other. Before long the ships had been tied together with grappling hooks, allowing the Englishmen to board the *Cordelière* and engage in close-range and hand-to-hand combat. The English had the upper hand, massacring the French, and were close to taking the ship entirely.

Amidst the sounds of gunfire and shouting, the smells of blood and gunpowder, it is no surprise that the fire at the heart of the *Cordelière* at first went unnoticed. Before long it had spread up the sides and rigging of the ship. Whereas moments before the English and French had been at each other's throats, now they were united in an effort to escape the fire. Some scrambled up the rigging, others rushed back to the *Regent*. The luckiest jumped right off the ship into the saltwater, for soon the fire had reached the *Cordelière*'s powder magazine, filled with sixty barrels of gunpowder.[17] They ignited. The resulting explosion blew both the *Cordelière* and the *Regent* to pieces. Whether in the initial attack, the blast, through drowning or later from their wounds, of the 1,600 people aboard the two ships only 140 survived the encounter. This did not include Sir Thomas Knyvet.

Charles Brandon and Edward Howard were forced to watch as their friend's ship burned, and him along with it. Faced with this tragedy, Howard made an oath not to look the king in the face again until he'd had his revenge for the death of his brother-in-law. He went on a campaign of burning and destruction all along the Breton coast, until winter forced him back home, where he was welcomed as a hero for the destruction of the *Cordelière*.[18] Rather than teaching him caution, the events of August 1512 had inspired in Edward Howard a desire to cast more French blood into the salty sea.

Six months later, in April 1513, Edward Howard returned to the waters around Brest, chasing his opportunity for revenge. Many of his ships had received refits, including new guns, and eight more ships had been added to his force. He was keen to hunt the enemy, bragging about his *Mary Rose*, 'the noblest ship of sail in Christendom', which could outrace any ship in the fleet, even starting some four miles behind them.[19] Hearing news that the French had a hundred ships of war waiting for him, he eagerly set out to meet them.

The winds were unfriendly this year, however, and Howard had trouble keeping his fleet supplied. The French had also learned from the battle the year before. They sealed off the harbour near Brest, forcing Howard and his fleet to sail along the coast in unfamiliar waters. They did their best, nevertheless, to keep up their harassment of the French and to keep their men fed.

As the English pulled away from a land battle in early April, fought in part to keep the hungry and impatient men satisfied, Howard was alerted to a problem – the *Nicholas of Hampton*, captained by Arthur Plantagenet, had struck a rock. At only 200 tons and inexplicably under full sail, such damage was likely to tear the *Nicholas* to pieces.

As the ship broke apart and water rushed in, Plantagenet could be heard calling out to Our Lady of Walsingham, the incarnation of the Virgin Mary associated with Walsingham, Norfolk, for help and comfort. He promised her that if she delivered him out of his peril, he would never eat flesh nor fish till he had seen her.[20]

His prayers were answered. Miraculously Plantagenet and his men were rescued from the wreck, and Howard was able to find places for them in the army, in vacancies left by the deaths of their comrades. Plantagenet, however, remained inconsolable. He was aware of the need to complete his solemn vow, as well as the duty he had promised to the king. They had sailed for only a month, and all Plantagenet had done was annoy a few Frenchmen and sink his own ship. Unsure of what would await him, but with a letter from Howard encouraging the king to 'give him comfortable words', Plantagenet set off home to his wife, his Holy Lady and his king.

Within a week of Plantagenet's departure, the French had found Howard and his fleet. The French galleys sailed into a nearby bay and waited.[21] With gun batteries on the cliffs overlooking the bay and their own armaments pointed towards the sea, any enemy ships which attacked would be sailing into an artillery bombardment. Their proximity to land also meant that, whereas the English were down to their last supplies and struggling to care for the injured and sick men who lay in the lower decks of the ships, the French were well supplied and easily able to replenish their troops as needed.

As Edward Howard assessed the situation, he knew he only had two options: he could play into the Frenchmen's hands, hoping for another miracle, or he could sail home. The second option would not satisfy his need for revenge, and so he was forced to work with the situation as it was. If he could not sail his ships into the bay to attack the French galleys, perhaps he could take them by land. He landed 6,000 troops, but they were repulsed by the French, and had to retreat back to the ships. There was no option but a frontal assault. He would not return to England with his tail between his legs like Plantagenet.

Rather than sail the fleet into the bay, he selected five shallower ships, crammed with men and weapons, to enter the bay, with the intention not of gunning down the French ships, but of boarding and taking them. Crossbow and gun fire fell upon them like hailstones as they approached the lead French galley, and threw a grappling iron hook on to the ship.

Howard was one of the first to board, heavily armoured for hand-to-hand combat, not unlike the fighting he had done over the barriers at Greenwich two years before. Soon after he had begun his attack aboard the ship, however, a cunning Frenchman cut the line connecting the two ships. Howard, surrounded by the enemy, turned to see his ship drifting away. Desperately he called out to his men, 'Come aboard again! Come aboard again!' Having lost the advantage, and perhaps a fair measure of their nerve, they did not.

Howard fought as long as he could until, pinned against the side of the enemy's ship, he knew the fight was lost. Rather than surrender, he pulled out the chain upon which hung his badge of office – a long boatswain's whistle – and cast it into the sea. He lasted only a few breaths longer before he too was forced into the sea by the French onslaught. Any life left in him when he hit the water quickly faded as his armour pulled him under.

*

The news of the death of the Lord Admiral came fast on the heels of Arthur Plantagenet's return, and may have contributed to the king's leniency with him. Before long, Plantagenet was back in command of another ship, one he managed to keep afloat. There were other frustrations for him, however. It was galling that Edward Guildford continued in his wardship of Arthur's stepson, John Dudley, and was making revenue off his lands.[22] And although Plantagenet's wife, Elizabeth, was tantalizingly close to inheriting the Viscountcy of Lisle, which would make him Viscount Lisle, here too there were obstacles.

The Viscountcy currently rested, as it had for almost a decade, in his wife's young niece, Elizabeth Grey. This little girl, only eight in 1513, had been Lady Lisle since her birth. She was now, in addition, an orphan. Her stepfather had been Sir Thomas Knyvet; Plantagenet himself had seen the destruction of the *Regent* which had killed the young knight. Knyvet's wife and Lady Lisle's mother, Muriel Howard, had been devastated by the death of her second husband and predicted her death within five months of his demise. She had died two days late, on 12 January 1513, leaving her young daughter without a guardian.

Elizabeth Grey's wardship was quickly granted to Charles Brandon – 'Sir' Charles Brandon as of March 1512 – who jumped at the opportunity presented by the eight-year-old heiress. She had not been in his care long before the two were betrothed. On 15 May 1513 he was confirmed as Viscount Lisle, in anticipation of nuptials once the bride was of age. Brandon was rapidly emerging as the man who swept up much of what Thomas Knyvet, and especially Edward Howard, had left behind on their deaths. Howard had named only one executor, aside from his widow, in his will, and that was 'his special trusty friend', Brandon. He also left Brandon the chain upon which his Admiral's whistle hung, and one of his two bastard sons – whichever of the two was left after the king had claimed one.[23] With Henry's friends rapidly falling to the French, it was clear that Brandon was becoming the foremost favourite. Entering the nobility as Viscount Lisle was only the overt declaration of what the court had already come to realize about this upstart young man.

By the time of his engagement to the Lady Lisle, Brandon had already been married twice.[24] Rumour abounded about what precisely had happened in both cases. In about 1503, Brandon had courted, contracted to marry and impregnated Anne Browne, a gentlewoman to the queen – though in what order he had gone about this no one was quite sure. What was certain was that he had professed to be madly in love with her and Browne had ended up pregnant. Before she came to term, however, Brandon had already left her to marry her much older aunt, Dame Margaret Mortimer, who carried with her a hefty inheritance. By 1507 he had made a healthy sum selling the lands he had acquired through the marriage. He then had it annulled on the grounds of consanguinity (closeness of blood). He had, after all, slept with her niece.

By the end of 1507 he had taken up with Anne Browne once again, and they had married secretly, with his friends Edward Guildford and Edward Howard among the few in attendance.[25] She gave birth to a second child – this one irrefutably legitimate – but died only two weeks later. This left Brandon unattached in 1513, and thus able once again to contract an advantageous marriage, this time to Grey. This did not stop him from looking around, however, and by 1514 it was rumoured – falsely – that he was engaged to Margaret of Austria, the regent of the Netherlands, with whom he had shared a heated flirtation. Until he managed to charm his way into a more profitable arrangement, he retained the Viscountcy of Lisle through his engagement to Elizabeth Grey.

And so Arthur remained on the periphery of any real position of privilege, though he was in favour and a part of the circle of young men who surrounded Henry VIII. By the summer of 1513, many of these young men, with the Viscount Lisle at their head and the King of England amongst them, made for France to go to war. They included Arthur Plantagenet, Edward Guildford's half-brother Sir Henry Guildford, Sir Thomas Boleyn, recently returned from a year with Margaret of Austria – to whose court in the Netherlands he sent his daughter, Anne – Sir John Seymour of Wulfhall, an experienced knight, who had a whole brood of children of his own back home, and Sir Thomas Parr, whose wife had just given birth to their first daughter, named for the queen. Sir Andrew Windsor was also among the company, though increasingly a part of the old guard, rather than the group of young men who the king obviously favoured. Edward Guildford, as master of the armoury, had received the order to outfit all these men, and especially the king himself. In all, the king led a force of more than 28,000 into France.[26]

By the end of August news came back that the king had achieved a grand victory at Guinegate, known as the 'Battle of the Spurs' for the way the fleeing French spurs glinted in the summer sunlight. Before long they had also taken the nearby towns of Therouanne and Tournai.

Guildford had his hands full that summer, as the English were also fighting in the north with the Scots. Scotland had revived the 'auld alliance' with France and attempted to invade while Henry and his best knights and soldiers were fighting on the continent, never mind that the Scottish King, James IV, was married to Henry VIII's sister, Margaret. The English army, led by the two Howard brothers, Thomas and Edmund, and their father, met the Scottish army at Flodden Field on 9 September 1513. At 34,000 men, it was the largest Scottish army ever to attempt an invasion of England and they had found substantial success in taking the major fortresses across Northumberland. Bogged down, however, by inclement weather and cut down by the superior weaponry of the English, the Scots were slaughtered. About a third of the Scottish army was killed, including most of the Scottish nobility and their king.[27] Thanks to their work, the Howards were fully restored, and the title of Duke of Norfolk, lost when they had supported Richard III, returned to their family. The Howards were climbing back into power at an impressive speed, with Brandon at their heels.

Honours were also given out on the battlefields of France. On 25 September the English army entered the great city of Tournai, and Edward Guildford was knighted for his service. The next day he oversaw a grand tournament to celebrate the king's great victory. The king and Charles Brandon were singled out, wearing silver damask and white satin, with crimson crosses on the borders. Soon after his return to England Brandon would be made Duke of Suffolk, on a par with the Howard's duchy of Norfolk. Other men, including Henry Guildford, were provided with green velvet and cloth of silver coats.[28] Arthur Plantagenet, too, was given a knighthood for his service on the battlefield. The English army, and its king, were back in England by the end of October, though Edward Guildford continued to make trips to the continent on behalf of the Crown over the following years, leaving his two young children and ward at home in Halden. Soon it would be their turn to enter the tempestuous world of warfare and diplomacy.

Whereas the two Guildford children were sure to prosper – their family was well regarded and on the rise – for John Dudley, there were no guarantees. Guildford could do his best for him, but it would be up to John to carve himself a place in the world, demonstrating to all that the taint of his father's treason had well and truly been removed. He was the master of his own fate: a prospect that was both empowering and terrifying.

5
Some fit exercise for war

The journey across the narrow sea could be a treacherous one, albeit short, and the vista of the English city of Calais, as it grew on the horizon, a welcome sight. First to appear would be the general outline of the land itself, white cliffs like the ones the traveller had lately left behind in Kent. Then the skyline of the city would emerge, punctuated by four imposing towers. Beginning on the left, on the eastern edge of the city, was the tall steeple of the Church of Our Lady.[1] The other church, towards the west, St Nicholas, was the spiritual centre of the town, where the king went to hear mass when he was visiting, as he had in 1513.[2] To the east of it was the Staple Hall with its own impressive tower. In the centre of the city, dominating the skyline, was the Day Watch Tower, the newest of these buildings, built by Henry VII. By now, the city's walls had also come into view, with their six round towers and four gates, and the castle on the western edge of the wall. Towns and mills could also be seen, dotted around the green landscape that made up the Pale of Calais.[3] John Dudley's guardian, Edward Guildford, had made this trip numerous times before, and by 1521 had been Knight Marshall of Calais for two years. John himself, at seventeen, arriving in Calais that day in August 1521, was not so well travelled.

The ship carefully entered the harbour, guarded by Rysbank Tower, and was met with the shot of cannon from the walls and from the other ships. The moats, waterworks and sluices surrounding the town were essential to the protection of the city, whose castle and walls provided little defence against the bombardment of modern gunpowder weapons, and were frequently damaged by tempestuous weather and the marshy ground upon which they stood. Such elements provided their own natural fortification, however, as an advancing army struggled to make it through such soft terrain.[4]

These defences were essential; the English needed Calais. It was their gateway to the continent and their foothold in France. Without it, the English had only one eye on the narrow sea that separated them from the continent and the formidable powers of France, Spain and the Holy Roman Empire.[5]

As the ship docked, and John and the other passengers disembarked, it was now possible to see the many royal emblems that Henry VII had commissioned to be placed about the town. On Lantern Gate, the main entrance to the town, was a red rose adorned with a crown, and there were two 'king's beasts' – a dragon and a greyhound – on the quayside by the gate.[6] The town itself was not very large – around 4,000 inhabitants within its quarter of a square mile limestone walls.[7] Despite its size, Calais was certainly not sleepy, and was a stark contrast from the rural existence John had known at Halden. Its population was diverse; John could pick up French, Flemish and other languages as he walked through the busy commercial streets.[8]

Entering through the Lantern Gate, visitors would first find themselves in the area belonging to fishermen and their families, providing for the twenty or so herring hangs in the city.[9] The houses were for the most part half-timbered – strong wooden beams, visible from the outside, supported the house, with infill between them – and had courtyards and gardens.[10] Other homes were owned by traders and artisans, many of whom were members of the powerful Company of the Staple.[11] Controlling wool exports from England, the Company brought in significant money to the Crown, as well as funding the Calais garrison.[12] Towards the east, and the parish of Our Lady, were the commercial buildings, including the marketplace, where smells of fresh-caught fish mixed with spices, such as cinnamon and ginger, and the always abundant smells of beer, ale and wine.[13] Around the large market square were the Company of the Staple headquarters and the town hall. Nearby were also the large houses of the merchants, over fifty such houses in Calais in total, many of which had names, such as the 'Rose', the 'Woolsack' and the unappealingly named 'Nettlebed'.[14] These merchants made their fortunes in the nearly one hundred wool stores dotted around the commercial area. The poorer residents were aided by about two dozen almshouses and the Trinity tables* supported by the two parishes within the town walls. The wealthy families of the town were also generous; both churches were richly furnished with precious plate, ready money and vestments with gold detailing.[15]

Calais, positioned on the knife-edge between England and the continent, was the perfect place for a young man to gain experience in war, diplomacy and politics.[16] Despite its commercial importance, it was, as was often said, a 'town of war', and held the largest permanent military presence in England.[17] There were around five hundred troops in the Calais garrison, seven hundred in the pale as a whole and that number could go to well over a thousand when the town was threatened.[18] A large number of these were archers. By the fifteenth century the crossbow had joined the longbow as one of the essential weapons of the English soldier, especially in defensive castles such as the one at Calais.[19] There were also bills – a kind of broadsword – long battle axes, spears and pikes. Alongside these were the newer hand-held firearms, part of the Calais arsenal since the 1460s.[20]

John Dudley was in Calais as part of the retinue of Cardinal Thomas Wolsey, who had taken Richard Fox's place as the *'alter rex'* after the older man, alongside William Warham, had resigned in 1515, in protest against the king's desire to curb clerical authority in England.[21] Wolsey was now a Catholic cardinal, Lord Chancellor and the king's lead minister. He was also one of the wealthiest men in the country, bringing in about £9,500 per year, more than what a skilled labourer might hope to make in ten centuries.

Calais had been especially busy with royal business of late. Not only had the king passed through on his way to and from the battlefields in 1513, but when peace was made with France a year later with the Treaty of London, Henry's sister, Mary, had been part of the bargain. She had made the journey to Calais, losing one of the ships of her entourage to a storm on the way, and been married to the aged

---

* Trinity tables: 'charities for the relief of poverty', Rose, *Calais*, 140.

King of France, Louis XII. She had been accompanied by her ladies, but these were largely dismissed by the king, saving a few, including the daughters of Sir Thomas Boleyn: Anne and Mary. Most upsettingly, the new French queen had been deprived of her 'mother Guildford', Edward Guildford's stepmother Jane. The marriage, as it was, did not last very long, as the King of France died, apparently 'danced to death' by his eighteen-year-old English bride. Sir Charles Brandon was charged with bringing her back. This he did, as his new (and third) wife.

With Charles Brandon married to the king's sister, his proposed marriage to the young Elizabeth Grey was very clearly off, and the Lady Lisle was shifted into the household of Catherine Courtenay, Arthur Plantagenet's legitimate half-sister.[22] After a short-lived marriage to Catherine's son, Henry Courtenay, at the age of only fourteen the young Lady Lisle died, making Elizabeth Grey, once Elizabeth Dudley and now Elizabeth Plantagenet, Viscountess of Lisle. Her husband was granted the title Viscount Lisle in May 1519, at about the same time that Edward Guildford was dispatched to Calais. John Dudley was now in line to inherit the title of Viscount Lisle. He needed an education to match the title he might yet inherit.

Both John and his guardian's son Richard were of an age to move beyond the schoolroom and gain more practical instruction. With the king's endorsement, Richard joined the court of the sixteen-year-old Ferdinand, whose brother, Charles, had recently become King of Spain, Holy Roman Emperor, Duke of Burgundy, Archduke of Austria and a real threat to the balance of European power. Ferdinand was sent to govern the Austrian lands controlled by their Habsburg family, and it was decided that Richard Guildford, of a similar age, would go with him.

John Dudley would get his education ever so slightly closer to home in Calais, though he had arrived a year too late for the grand events that had taken place just outside it the summer before, when Henry VIII had met the new French king, Francis I, at 'The Field of the Cloth of Gold', designed to cement the peace between the two powers. John's guardian had been responsible for arranging the lodgings for the more than a thousand Englishmen and women who had arrived in the company of the king and queen. This had included leading men such as Cardinal Wolsey and the Duke of Buckingham, as well as those well known to John, including his guardian, Edward Guildford, and his 'uncle', Andrew Windsor, along with his stepfather and mother – who joined in the dancing. It had been an event on a truly legendary scale, followed by a visit by the emperor, Charles V to Calais, which Guildford had also been partly responsible for arranging. He evidently had the trust of the king, albeit for the sort of bureaucratic work others might seek to avoid.

The trip that John was a part of was not nearly so grand, though it had important ramifications. Francis I and Charles V were at war, and Wolsey's attempts to negotiate between them had proved unsuccessful, although his manoeuvrings had left England out of any further military engagements. In July 1521, Francis I had been backed into a corner by the threat of an English–imperial alliance and reached out to Wolsey to arbitrate between him and the Habsburg emperor according to the terms of the Treaty of London's non-aggression pact. In the balance hung the peace of Europe, and Wolsey had the power to decide where England would place its allegiance if this peace was not agreed. Anyone paying attention, however, might begin to question whether Wolsey's role of peacemaker of Europe was simply a façade.[23] Months before it had been suggested to English ambassadors by a councillor of Charles V that a peace conference in Calais would be an excellent opportunity to acquire intelligence and secure the imperial alliance, right under French noses.[24] It was a masterful performance of political craft – and craftiness – and John Dudley had a front-row seat.

John was one of fifty gentlemen who had been selected to accompany the cardinal, along with scores of yeomen, grooms, clerks, footmen and other servants.[25] Each of the fifty gentlemen, John included, were given ten yards of black velvet to clothe themselves. John was also given an ornate slashed Milan bonnet, a hat very much in vogue, with an upturned brim and decorated with stones. The gentlemen's uniform attire, followed by the yeomen in scarlet and the grooms in red, generated an air of dignity even as they sweated under black velvet gowns in the hot August sun.

Though much smaller than the delegation for the Field of the Cloth of Gold, Wolsey's troupe was not insignificant. In just two meals at Dover, before they had sailed to Calais, John had joined feasts consisting of – among other things – four muttons, two veals, four capons,* thirty rabbits, four roasted herons, three dozen chickens, four dozen pigeons, two dozen quails, two pheasants and two hundred eggs, all washed down with a hogshead of ale and wine, and two barrels of beer.[26] The dessert used up four pounds of sugar, two hundred pears and a peck of hazelnuts, and all of it costing almost £10 – just for the two meals. Sitting with him while he ate were the other gentlemen who had been selected for the mission and other young men of middling rank. The higher-ranking nobles and gentlemen, seated elsewhere, included Edward Guildford's half-brother, Henry, and Sir Thomas Boleyn, now well known as ambassador to the French.[27]

The English delegation arrived in Calais on 2 August.[28] Their welcome was a warm one, but the negotiations were fierce, and despite the heat it was impossible not to feel the icy chill between the French and imperial ambassadors. News of a Spanish victory over the French on day two of negotiations did not help matters, and Wolsey had his hands full hearing the complaints of the ambassadors every day as he banqueted them.[29] By the middle of August, Wolsey had accepted an invitation to visit the emperor himself, Charles V, at Bruges, seventy miles up the coast. The large entourage packed up and made the four-day trip, the cardinal wining and dining eminent personages along the way. The company, John Dudley included, were especially well ordered – bonnets on and harnesses shining – for the approach into Bruges, where the emperor and his own entourage met them just outside the city.

Charles V, Holy Roman Emperor, King of the Romans, King of Italy, King of Spain, Duke of Burgundy, Lord of the Netherlands and Archduke of Austria was twenty-one years old and rather unattractive, though he was dressed magnificently. He had a protruding triangular lower jaw which made it difficult for the emperor to keep his mouth from hanging open. His brown hair was cut just below his

* Capon: a castrated rooster.

ears and across his forehead, like the short fringe of a Turkish carpet. Nevertheless, he had a commanding air, and the look of one you were better not to cross. He and the cardinal greeted each other warmly, if formally, before at last they proceeded into the city itself.

The days were filled with processions and feasting and meetings in beautiful gardens over great bowls of wine and fruit. John Dudley participated in the official events as was needed and the less formal evenings of flowing beer and wine as he desired. Bruges was a city of beautiful buildings and winding streets, kept impressively clean, all surrounded by a circular double moat, walled on the south-western side. Its position on the tidal inlet meant that it had central importance to the Flemish trade in the area, reflected in the diversity of wares for sale in the marketplace. There were well over a hundred thousand inhabitants, including, it was said, some of the best spinners and weavers in Europe, and certainly some of the best artists and printers. To top it all off, the women of Bruges, one of John's companions noted, were also 'marvellous fair' with the 'best hair in the world'.[30]

They remained there only two weeks, before returning to Calais, where the negotiations continued, with added suspicious glances from the French contingent for the cardinal's time spent with their sworn enemy. The actual terms of the negotiations were not terribly thrilling – money and marriages – but Wolsey argued them with passion and a steely nerve. The royal hand at stake this time was another Princess Mary, Henry VIII's five-year-old daughter. She had been born in February 1516 at Greenwich Palace. By the age of two she had been betrothed to the French dauphin. Now, if there was an alliance with the emperor, she would be betrothed to Charles V himself, never mind that he was her first cousin (by way of her mother, Catherine of Aragon, Charles V's aunt) and sixteen years her elder.

Mary was the only living child of Henry VIII and Catherine of Aragon after twelve years of marriage; Catherine's numerous other pregnancies had ended in miscarriages, stillbirths, and one son who lived only seven weeks. This was the cause of much distress and frustration; after all, Henry's mother – whom he had adored – had given birth to five children in the first ten years of her marriage to his father, beginning with a male heir within the first year. Henry was sure he was not to blame for the couple's inability to produce living sons. His mistress, Elizabeth Blount, had borne him a son in 1519, whom he claimed as his own, and his new mistress, Mary, the daughter of Sir Thomas Boleyn, bore a daughter, Catherine, with questionable paternity. As it was, Princess Mary was Henry's only legitimate child and thus his only bargaining chip, the only heir to the English throne. It was a position far more precarious than the one that had so worried Henry's father almost two decades before.

John watched as Wolsey got almost everything he asked for, including a delay on England's entering the continental war, allowing time to prepare for England's 'Great Enterprise' against the French. Right timing was everything, in diplomacy and in war. Despite having arrived as a peacemaker, Wolsey left with England once again at war. John Dudley saw all the plans, machinations and deceptions take place before his eyes, controlled by the mastermind of all three, Cardinal Thomas Wolsey. Wolsey had successfully deceived the French, delayed the Spanish and defended England's interests from a position of relative weakness. His politic flexibility came from an awareness that alliances changed quickly: better to be in control of these shifts, rather than at their mercy.[31] Had John heard tell on his travels of the manuscript written by the Italian Niccolò Machiavelli, he might have seen some resemblance to its principles, as he gazed upon the man in red at work.[32] Great men, Machiavelli wrote, 'owed nothing to fortune except the opportunity to shape the material into the form that seemed best to them'; such a man 'must be prepared to vary his conduct as the winds of fortune and changing circumstances constrain him and,' he went on, 'not deviate from right conduct if possible, but be capable of entering upon the path of wrongdoing when this becomes necessary.'[33] It was a far cry from what his father had written to the king when imprisoned in the Tower – 'of all worldly losses', Edmund had instructed, 'honour and credence is the most.'[34] But his father was gone; John would have to make his own lessons.

*

'War is a great consumer of treasure and riches,' John's father had written before his death, 'therefore let every man beware what counsel he giveth his sovereign to enter or to begin war. There are many ways to enter into it, and the beginning seemeth a great pleasure, but the way is very narrow to come honourably out thereof, and then oftentimes full painful.'[35] King Henry VIII had entirely disregarded Edmund Dudley's counsel, if he had even read it. The war in 1513, which had claimed the lives of Thomas Knyvet, Edward Howard and countless others, had cost the Crown £1,000,000 – ten years of Crown revenue.[36] In a few short years, Henry VIII had definitively emptied the coffers his father had filled with the help of Edmund Dudley. Now, ten years later, England was at war again.

John Dudley, a member of the army led by Charles Brandon, now Duke of Suffolk, awoke in the early hours on 19 September 1523. Working out the cramps caused by sleeping in a makeshift bed, John emerged into a vast forest of tents and pavilions. To the north he could see the walled city of Calais; to the south, the small parish church of St Peter's. The camp lay between the two, in the green fields directly south of Calais.

The army had entered Calais at the end of August, thousands on a mission to make war with the French: Welshmen with their spears and clubs, Cornishmen – many of them expert miners – with slings, and Englishmen, raised to the bow.[37] Once at Calais, they had joined with the Dutch and Italian gunners, men from the Calais garrison – including John Dudley – and the 'adventurers': a troop of a thousand mercenaries out for plunder and adventure.[38] All in all, about 11,000 had combined forces to take on the French. It was the most impressive force to attempt to penetrate France since the reign of Henry V, which was precisely what Henry VIII had in mind.[39]

Almost a month later, however, the army still had not begun their march into France. At first, it had been bureaucracy which had slowed them down – complex negotiations between rulers with their own agendas – Henry VIII, Margaret of Austria, Charles V – and the practical difficulty of providing food and munitions to such vast numbers. In some ways, it was a miracle that the expedition had got even this far. Henry VIII had called a parliament earlier that year in order to demand funds for the enterprise against the French but had encountered resistance. Even the great negotiator, Thomas Wolsey, could not convince them. Appearing before the Commons, and their chosen speaker, Sir Thomas More, Wolsey eloquently declared to them: 'The French king, Francis I, called "the most Christian king", has so often broken promise with the King of England, and his well-beloved nephew Charles the emperor, that the king of his honour can no longer suffer it. Wherefore the king of necessity is driven to war and defence, which in no ways can be maintained without great sums of money. With this, the king and the emperor will make such war in France as hath never been seen.'[40] Thomas More had reinforced Wolsey's plea with talk of duty, but the Commons had resisted, proclaiming that he had asked too much of them. Wolsey's own man, a London lawyer named Thomas Cromwell, composed a speech predicting that such an enterprise was doomed to failure, due to bad weather and poor supplies. When a commission was sent from the parliament to suggest a lower sum, Wolsey replied, 'I would rather have my tongue plucked out of my head with a pair of pincers, than to move the king to take a lesser sum.'[41] With some resistance, the cardinal succeeded in getting a substantial amount from the parliament, though still not as much as he would have liked. His tongue, all the same, remained securely in his mouth.

Once provisioned and in Calais, the problems did not end. Less than two weeks after arriving in the town, finding lodging and enjoying the food and the women, some of the men began to suffer a fever, muscle pain and nausea. A few days later, they awoke to find the first tell-tale small, reddish spots around their mouth and throat. Soon the spots had spread all over their face and body. By this point, it was easy enough to identify the cause: smallpox. Some would emerge from their illness to be horribly pock-marked for the rest of their lives. Others would not emerge at all. Without a single encounter with the enemy, Suffolk's troops were already dying. It was for this reason that he moved his troops into the field outside the town, in the hope of escaping further infection from the bustling town and its travellers.

As much as the army sought to get out of Calais, the town's citizens were keen to get rid of the army. The Welshmen had all but begun a riot and refused to disperse even when the Holy Sacrament had been held before them. They had been stewing too long and needed action to sate them.

At last, the army, with men like Charles Brandon, Henry and Edward Guildford and Andrew Windsor at its head, and John Dudley somewhere in the upper middle ranks, rode south. They met their allies, the Dutch forces sent by Margaret of Austria, at Andres and by 1 October began the campaign in earnest, just as the first signs of winter appeared.[42] They made impressive progress. As they approached Bray, a fortified town on the River Somme, on 20 October, they made camp. Under the cover of darkness, a team of strong men pulled the heavy guns into place around the walls. As the first light trickled over the horizon, the bombardment began, targeting weak areas in the stone walls. By the time the sun had risen, the guns had punched holes into the once mighty walls, and streams of men poured into the now vulnerable French town. Plunder was on almost everyone's minds, but the Duke of Suffolk did his best to keep his men under control. They were there for conquest, not destruction. French townspeople were to be herded together after their surrender, to swear allegiance to the true king of France: Henry VIII.

As Suffolk went about his work claiming subjects for the Crown, the soldiers revelled in their loot – honey, leather, pewter, salt, grain, fat pigs and especially the wine – more than some of them had ever seen. What they could not carry, they drank. Hangovers were worsened by the state of the weather. By the middle of October it was clear it was going to be a wet autumn. This not only sank the moods of the men but also pulled down the food and munitions carts. They had not left the pestilence behind in Calais either, and more succumbed to the pox as they made their way deeper into the heart of France, while others snickered and accused them of making their illness appear worse in a bid to return home.

This was not John Dudley's first experience of warfare, though he had never participated in an extended campaign such as this one. He had faced the consequences of the cardinal's 'negotiations' not long after Wolsey had left, by joining the Calais garrison. Their mission had been one of destruction, burning their way around the countryside outside Calais. Edward Guildford, with a firebrand on his coat of arms, had lived up to this device, setting fire to towns near the French army's camps. In those days, their problem had been heat and thirst;

men died for lack of water in the countryside outside Guines that September. A year later, John Dudley was heartily aware of the opposite problem as his boots sank into the mud and cold rain struck his face like a cruel slap.

On All Saints Day, 1 November, the army at last rested, in the small town of Roye. Battered by the wind and rain, the troops were glad to take respite in the town, which had surrendered a week before. There, on All Saints' Day, Brandon presided over a ceremony in the town's main church of St Pierre, in which he knighted fourteen men. Amongst them were those who had served him and his wife in the past: William Stourton – John Dudley's brother-in-law by his half-sister Elizabeth – along with the son of John Seymour, Edward, who had been a page to Brandon's wife. These men proceeded into the church in great honour, with a herald before them. The herald introduced each man to Brandon, as 'showing himself valiant in the field, and in so doing deserving to be advanced to the degree of knight'.[43] Laying a sword upon their shoulders, with a gesture and a word, the men were suddenly of a higher rank than those who had moments ago been their peers.

They stayed in Roye only a day, before moving on again, causing intense resentment amongst soldiers exhausted by the relentless weather. The mood was decidedly sour as many became convinced that they would be led ceaselessly around Northern France all winter, until they had all been picked off by the cruel weather and the pox. Such men were mocked by the more stoic types, who retorted that all they'd done was stroll around the French countryside, eating bread and fish and drinking wine.

Crossing the gentle-flowing Somme River, they reached Beauvois, a small town less than ten miles from the bigger fortress of Saint-Quentin. Before camping, Brandon, in front of the rest of the men, including Edward Guildford (who might have had a few words with his friend Brandon for leaving his charge out of the ceremony a week before) and Andrew Windsor, knighted John Dudley for his service and valiance in the campaign. A knighthood was John's entry into chivalry and – quite possibly – the world of the court. And it was more than his father had achieved, for all his intimacy with the king.

Sir John Dudley, with the help of those watching over him, had done very well for his nineteen years.

A few days after John was knighted, disaster struck. They had reached the town of Prémont, to the east of the Somme, and directly south of Bruges, by 11 November. There was plenty of food and drink, but the company continued to grumble and to begrudge the continental soldiers, who could easily send their plunder back home. Considering payment for the troops hadn't come in for some time, securing plunder was more than a matter of greed.

As the sun set, the temperature plummeted. Holding their hands close to their bodies for warmth, the men muttered amongst themselves that they had never felt such a cold night; not even the oldest nor most experienced man could recall one colder, and there were several men of sixty years or more amongst the troops. The wet ground into which they had spent weeks sinking suddenly became solid and unyielding beneath them, and the remaining crops froze in the fields. The men traded stories of warm beds at home, next to their obliging wives. John might dream of a hearth and a fire in Halden Hall, but the recollection of what it actually was to be warm escaped like smoke through fingertips. That just over a year before he had watched men die from the heat seemed unimaginable. But whereas heat had made it difficult to sleep, the cold often made it all too easy, and frequently those who drank away the pain of frozen fingers and toes slipped into a peaceful, but final, rest.

As morning broke, the sun's rays teasing them with light but little warmth, groans and cries erupted from the camp. Many men had lost fingernails overnight, some entire fingers or toes, and some could not be woken. The cold had not broken with the dawn, but still Suffolk ordered that they continue, perhaps hoping that movement might at least keep them warm. But it did no good. On the second night of freezing temperatures, the men kept themselves warm with talk of mutiny and desertion. A group of Suffolk's men swore they would be gone by first light. When it was pointed out to them that this was treason, they retorted brazenly that 'it was no worse being hanged in England than dying of the cold in France.'[44]

A crowd of shouting soldiers greeted the dawn on the next day. Standing outside the duke's tent, the men chanted an endless refrain of 'home! home!'. Before long a new competing chant echoed theirs: 'hang! hang!', shouted the hardened adventurers, mocking their companions for their weakness and cowardice. With some persuasion, the men were silenced. It was at that moment that Edward Guildford stepped in with an enticing distraction.

Nearby stood the castle of Bohain, which had long been thought to be impregnable because of the deep and impassable marshes that surrounded it. Edward had noticed, however, that these marshes had become entirely frozen, allowing a man – or a whole army – to walk right across them. The freezing temperatures might be a weapon that could be used to their advantage, if they seized the occasion. The company waited until nightfall, to see if the temperature would drop enough. It was as cold as the nights that had preceded it, and Brandon gave Guildford permission to take his men across the dangerous marshes to attack Bohain.

Quietly and cautiously they dragged the heavy guns across the frozen land, attentive to the sounds the ice made beneath them as they moved. Once they were in position, the gunners made ready to start the assault, and the men on horse and foot prepared themselves to follow. Before the first shot was fired, however, the captain of Bohain castle approached the English troops, to offer a full surrender. Speaking with Edward Guildford, the captain gave over the castle to Charles V and Henry VIII, along with all its weapons. Triumphantly, the men entered the castle, but there were few provisions to be found. Disappointed, frustrated and dying from cold, the men were at their wits' end.

At last, with his grand plans for a great conquest of France dissolving before him, the duke gave the order. They could wait no longer for help from their allies or their countrymen. Leaving men frozen to death on the road behind them, the company at last marched north, headed for Calais, and home. It took no time at all for the French, trailing behind them, to recover the towns and castles that the English had sacrificed so much to capture. John's father had warned that war was 'very dangerous for the soul and body'; now he knew it to be true. John was learning, however, that war could also bring certain advantages, if you managed to survive it.

*

The fifty-foot castle looked like it had emerged from a tale of King Arthur. From a distance – across the great tiltyard of Greenwich Palace – you might think it was the real thing, complete with ditches and steep ramparts. Approach closer, and you would be reminded of a castle in an illuminated manuscript: convincing but somehow not quite right. Come within a few feet, however, and you would begin to notice that the ancient-looking stones were simply painted on canvas that was laid across timber walls, and the great height was out of proportion with the width of the base for any building that was meant to stand for long.[45] This masquerading and impermanent structure had been named the 'Castle of Loyalty' and was constructed over six weeks for the Christmas celebrations of the court of Henry VIII in the sixteenth year of his reign.

Although the king had thrown his full support behind the tournament and its trappings, the initiative lay with a group of young knights. They included John Dudley, now twenty and back from his adventures in France, Edward Seymour, his comrade from the wars, William Carey, husband of the king's mistress, Mary Boleyn, and a tall, attractive young man, also from Kent, named Thomas Wyatt. Most of the company, including John, had been made Esquires of the Body, personal attendants and bodyguards to the king. John now operated in close proximity to the king who had ordered the death of his father. If he held any resentment on this score, it was vital that he did not express it.

The carpenters and painters had been busy on the preparations since November. Four days before Christmas the challenge was read out before the king and queen in her great chamber. The herald, wearing arms of red silk embroidered with a castle of silver turrets, each with a maiden upon it, stood before the king and queen. 'Whereas your most noble grace hath most abundantly given unto four maidens of your most honourable court the castle called "Loyal" to dispose according to their pleasures, they have most liberally given the guard and custody of the same unto a captain and with him fifteen gentlemen.'[46] This was, of course, no news to the king and queen, but the pageantry of it was delightful. 'They have undertaken the defence of the same, and defend and keep the same against all comers.'[47]

At thirty-three, Henry VIII was no longer the energetic youth who had come to the throne a decade and a half before. He had not ridden in a tournament since March, when a raised visor on his helmet had almost cost him his life and threatened the stability of the entire realm. It was an open question whether the king would compete in such tournaments again. This certainly presented a tempting opportunity to take up the lance, however.

The queen, with her ladies, was also expected to participate in the charade of chivalry. Queen Catherine was now almost forty. She had been pregnant no fewer than seven times in the first decade of her marriage to Henry, miscarrying twice, giving birth to two stillborn boys and three living children, two boys and a girl, of which only Mary had survived beyond two months. This had all ended, however, some years before, and the queen was now unlikely to be pregnant again, creating a palpable tension in their marriage, to say the least.

The tournament continued through the Christmas season and into February. Alongside the Castle of Loyalty a large white unicorn had been constructed, holding four differently coloured shields, indicating the different sports of the tournament: jousting, sword-fighting, fighting at barriers, and the assault of the castle. On each day of the tournament, men approached and struck a shield, held by the mythical beast, to indicate their combat of choice, while the ladies of the court looked on, some taking positions within the castle itself, feigning fear of being assaulted and 'taken' by the brave warriors. Those 'defending' it, John Dudley included, were expected to combat the answerers to their challenge, demonstrating their ability before the whole court. It was an exhausting prospect, but essential to making a name for oneself. John joined the other defenders as they took to the barriers and the field, fighting the king, who had in the end decided to risk his health and realm to participate.

To get close enough to serve the king was one thing, to get close enough to fight him quite another, and John had to be aware of the importance of being a part of this band, fighting before the Castle of Loyalty. This new year, John would turn twenty-one, reaching the age at which he would no longer be the ward of Edward Guildford, but his own man, with his own properties to manage and standing to acquire.[48] The same year he turned twenty-one, Guildford's daughter Jane would be sixteen, likewise old enough to marry and establish her own home and family. The children of Halden were growing up.

*

Jane Guildford stood at the entrance to the church where she would be married, wearing one of her best gowns.[49] At sixteen, she was a younger bride, compared to her servants or the local craftspeople and farmers, but as a member of the gentry her life would be dedicated to providing sons to her new husband, and for this it was best to begin early. Standing next to her, on her right hand, with a priest between them, was the man who was about to become her husband.

Strong and self-assured, John Dudley was turning into an attractive man, with dark hair and deep-set eyes. A slight underbite gave him a forward chin, but this only added to the air of confidence and strength. Long arched eyebrows gave a look of contemplation, to balance the appearance of physical strength.[50] Jane stood on his left, in remembrance of the story of Genesis, when woman was formed out of the left rib of Adam, created as his helpmate and companion.

They were an ideal match. John had been a part of Jane's life since she could remember. Her childhood memories were filled with John and her brother Richard, tearing around Halden. She knew everything about John and his treasonous family background, and they had grown up together, sharing in lessons, the games of childhood and letters from Edward Guildford's travels abroad. Her father, approaching fifty, had watched over and cultivated the career of her future husband.

'Brethren,' the priest proclaimed, 'we are gathered together here, in the sight of God, and his angels, and all the saints and in the face of the Church, to join together two bodies, to wit, those of this man,' he indicated John, 'and this woman,' he glanced at Jane, 'that henceforth they may be one body.'[51] John vowed to love, honour, keep and guard Jane, in both sickness and health, as long as they both lived, and Jane did the same, vowing also to serve her husband.

Then Jane's father stepped forward and, taking her uncovered right hand – signifying her maidenhood – he gave over his custody of Jane to her new husband, placing it in John's right hand, and they plighted their troths to each other.

John took out a ring, and gold and silver coins, placing them before the priest. The priest blessed the little ring, praying with the sign of the cross, 'O Lord, send thy blessing upon this ring, that she who shall wear it may be armed with the strength of heavenly defence, and that it may be profitable unto her eternal salvation.'

John took up the ring in his right hand, and held Jane's right hand with his left, 'With this ring I thee wed and this gold and silver I thee give, and with my body I thee worship, and with all my worldly chattel I thee honour.' He moved the ring to Jane's thumb, 'in the name of the Father', to her index finger, 'and of the Son', to her middle finger, 'and of the Holy Ghost' and finally to her ring finger, 'Amen', sliding it into place on this finger, which Jane knew contained a vein leading directly to her heart.

After the reading of a Psalm to give the couple strength for the trials that would come, the priest turned once again to the assembly, praying together and making the sign of the Cross, 'God the Father bless you; Jesus Christ keep you, the Holy Ghost enlighten you; the Lord make his face to shine upon you, and be merciful unto you; may he turn his countenance upon you, and give you peace.'

Kneeling before the altar, the whole congregation prayed for them. 'Save thy servant, and thy handmaid,' the priest intoned, 'O Lord, send them help from thy holy place. Be unto them, O Lord, a tower of strength.'

'From the face of their enemy,' the assembly replied. Every new couple would face challenges for which they would need God's protection, strength and intervention. John and Jane Dudley would be no exception.

The service went on, with various prayers and blessings interwoven into the usual parts of the mass. John and Jane went through each part, prostrating themselves under a pall before the altar and kneeling before the Sacrament. Throughout, Jane was reminded of her new role as helper to her husband, 'O God, by whom woman is joined to man,' the priest read out, 'look graciously, we beseech thee, on this handmaiden, who now to be joined in wedlock, seeketh to be guarded by thy protection. May the yoke of love and peace be upon her; may she be a faithful and chaste wife in Christ.' Calling on biblical exemplars such as Rachel, Rebecca and Sara, the priest prayed that she might be 'bashful and grave, reverential and modest' as well as, of course, 'fruitful in child-bearing', hoping that she might see 'her children's children unto the third and fourth generation'.

As John and Jane, now husband and wife, exited the church, there were celebrations and congratulations, and feasting for the friends and family who joined them. John's was not the first wedding in his family. His half-sister, Elizabeth, had married some years before, to the heir of Baron Stourton, as their father had intended. In 1524 her husband, William, who had been with John in France, had become Baron Stourton himself, and Elizabeth had at last become Lady Stourton, with a son, Charles, born not long after. Charles would ensure the continuance of the family's arms and accompanying motto: '*Loyal je serai durant ma vie*', 'I will be loyal throughout my life'.[52]

Jane's brother, Richard, with whom John had grown up, was noticeably absent from the festivities, but they had assurances that he would return to them soon, perhaps to make his own happy and advantageous marriage.

*

Richard Guildford's face was covered with sweat as he burned from within. Cries ripped through him, but he was only dimly aware of them. Perhaps he had not cried out at all? The pain radiated from an open wound on the outside of his left leg, just under the knee. Despite being over two years old, the wound had reopened, and streams of blood spilt out of it, with no end in sight.[53]

Richard had been suffering from an intense fever for almost a month. The emperor himself, Charles V, had sent his best physicians and surgeons, who treated him with the care they would have afforded their royal master, but they could not stop the bleeding or the fever. They made it clear to the English ambassadors who were responsible for him that young Richard Guildford was not expected to live.[54]

The heat of the city in which he lay worsened the sweat that poured out of him. He was in Granada, a city at the foot of the Sierra Nevada mountains in southern Spain, almost a thousand miles from home. Until recently, the city had been held by the Moors, who had been driven out by the parents of Catherine of Aragon, Ferdinand II and Isabella I; the city still bore the marks of Moorish architecture and culture. Catherine herself had lived in the Moorish-built Alhambra Palace in Granada before her journey to England to marry the heir to the throne, Prince Arthur. The queen's illustrious parents, as well as her sister and brother-in-law, had been entombed in the nearby Royal Chapel of Granada, built by Charles V.

Richard had served the brother of Charles V, Ferdinand, before entering into the service of the Prince of Orange, Philibert of Chalon. Burgundian-born, Philibert had become Prince of Orange, a principality in southern France, before he was a month old. At not-yet twenty, he had broken ties with King Francis I, who sought to annex his lands, and instead allied with Charles V, who made him general of the Spanish infantry. It was about this time, when Philibert was twenty-one and Richard Guildford about the same age, that the young Englishman had joined his service.

Not everyone wanted him serving the young prince, however. In the summer of 1524, letters were sent from his father and the king, giving Richard licence to return to England and asking him to do so with all speed. Richard, with the prince's company, was in Barcelona, making preparations to join the imperial army in Italy. The servant carrying the king's and his father's letters took an extra three days in his journey to find Richard. When he arrived, he was informed that the prince's company had sailed only a half-day before.[55] He had just missed them. Had the letter reached the company in time, young Richard would probably have been home for his sister's wedding, rather than slowly dying amongst strangers in Granada.

The prince, with Richard, had left Barcelona in a company of three ships, sailing east past southern France towards Italy. As they passed Villafranca, Philibert caught sight of a fleet that he presumed to be the emperor's navy. Thinking them allies, he sailed his ship, with Richard aboard, deep amongst them. Too late, they recognized not imperial but French colours flying on the ships that surrounded them. In the desperate fight that ensued, Prince Philibert and ten of his men, including Richard, were captured, and Richard badly injured.[56]

The men were brought to Lyon, in the south-east of France, and held in a stone cell. Letters crossed the continent for the return of the prince and his men. Philibert even attempted an escape, by cutting a hole in the rocks under his cell, but it was discovered when a guard fell into it during a game of cards, and they were moved to a more secure location.[57]

The prince and his retinue were at last released, according to the terms of the Treaty of Madrid in early 1526.[58] Charles V wrote eagerly from Toledo that he expected the Prince of Orange, along with Guildford, returned to his household.[59] It wasn't until September, however, that they joined his court at Granada.[60]

As soon as there was news that Richard would be freed, his father sent more letters for his son's return. By autumn 1526, plans were in motion to send Richard Guildford back to his home and family, carrying important diplomatic correspondence. By this point, however, it was clear that he was not well enough to travel, and by the end of September, Henry VIII had to be informed that Edward Guildford's son was not likely to live. The letter assured him that Richard was one of the best young men of England and had a 'good whole mind, and no worse stomach', and prayed the Lord be his comfort.

If Richard had been told of his sister's wedding to the boy he had grown up with in Halden, such knowledge was almost certainly beyond him now, as his mind conjured images both real and imagined, memories, dreams and nightmares, all indistinguishable from each other. At last, his breathing slowed and stopped. Young Richard Guildford died a thousand miles from home in agony, serving his king, country and family.

By the time news of Richard's death reached England, Jane and John had already welcomed a son, whom they dutifully named Henry. The king himself, however, was to have no more children – and importantly no male children – from Catherine of Aragon. The court reverberated with whispers about what he would do. To simply discard his Spanish queen would threaten European alliances, angering the powerful emperor in his palace in Granada, but without a male heir, the dynasty would end with its second king. At Greenwich the Castle of Loyalty had been replaced by a tournament that took as its theme unrequited love. The king's eye fell on his former mistress's sister, Anne, who had served Margaret of Austria and Queen Claude of France, and now served as one of Catherine's ladies.

In the summer of 1527, John Dudley, now a married man with a growing son, and a newborn he had named Thomas, once again left for the continent with Cardinal Thomas Wolsey. Just as six years before, a more secretive mission had been assigned to the cardinal, though this time it was not an alliance with the emperor. Instead, Wolsey was tasked with gaining expert opinion on a delicate matter concerning the king. Henry VIII wanted an annulment to his marriage with Catherine of Aragon, the emperor's aunt, and the cardinal needed to find a way to secure it.

Wolsey would fail; Wolsey would fall and Wolsey would die disgraced, and neither duplicitous scheming nor dedicated service would save him.

But John had taken what he'd needed from his education in the company of the cardinal, as well as from Charles Brandon, who, despite his secret marriage to the king's sister and his objections to the king's desires, remained in his good graces.[61] It was becoming clear: John needed allies at court. He could not be the lone reviled wolf, dependent only on the grace of a fickle and mortal king, as his father and the cardinal had been. Wolsey's demise was a reminder that such a path led to death and dishonour. And John now had a family to look after. He would need something his father, for all his coin, had never managed to retain: powerful friends.

John had survived battle in scorching heat and freezing cold, but he knew all too well that it was the illusory comforts of the court that could prove truly fatal, not just to the man, but to his family and his legacy.

6

And the Queen herself
shall be condemned

'God of his infinite goodness,' the Garter King of Arms proclaimed, 'send prosperous life and long, to the high and mighty Princess of England.'[1] Thomas Wriothesley had held the position of Garter King of Arms, the senior herald in the College of Arms, for almost thirty years, inheriting it from his father, who had held the position for the thirty years before that. Wriothesley had been with Henry VII in Brittany and had participated in major events of the late king's reign, as well as those of the reign of his son. Recently, these had become increasingly unusual.

In 1525 he had performed his role when Henry VIII made his illegitimate son the Duke of Richmond, a title created especially for the bastard child, based on the earldom held by the king's father before coming to the throne. In 1529 Wriothesley was asked to give evidence at the divorce proceedings against the Queen of England, Catherine of Aragon. In the end the marriage had been annulled – legally it had never happened – making their child, Mary, a bastard. In 1532, he had presided over the ceremony making the king's mistress, Anne Boleyn, Marquess of Pembroke, and then, in 1533, he had participated in her coronation. Today, 10 September 1533, just three months later, he was announcing the christening of Queen Anne's child with the king. Henry VIII had counted on this child being a boy, but when the delivery had taken place three days prior, Anne produced a girl. So it was, on that afternoon in September, in the Church of the Observant Friars at the west end of Greenwich Palace, Thomas Wriothesley presented the new princess to the world: 'the high and mighty Princess of England, Elizabeth'.

The walls of the church had been hung with decorative arras, and the way strewn with fresh green rushes.[2] Usually the Church of the Observant Friars was a humble building, befitting the friars' dedication to poverty. Built by Henry VII, the church was a simple rectangle without aisles and with a single steeple where the nave met the chancel.[3] The roof was steep, allowing for tall windows which brought light inside the church. One such window, of stained glass, had been commissioned by Henry VII, showing him in his robes of state surrounded by his family, arms and badges. Positioned to the east of the church, it would catch the morning sun, filling the late king with brilliance as shards of light seemed to beam from his body. The friars might have dedicated their lives to poverty and humility, but kings did not make such vows.

Henry VIII had once praised the friars for their devotion and sincerity, but recently a battle of words had broken out between the Order and the king. The friars had remained loyal to Catherine of Aragon – the king had not. It began when Henry VIII had heard mass at the Friars' Church at Easter eighteen months before, on 31 March 1532. The Provincial of the friars had preached a sermon which spoke truth to the crowned power before him. Deviating significantly from the theme of Christ's resurrection, the Provincial instead spoke on the Old Testament king, Ahab, who had married Queen Jezebel, a temptress who led him away from the true faith.

'This King Ahab would needs give ear to the false prophets,' he told the congregation and king, 'which did circumvent and deceive him, and would not harken to God's own prophet Micheas.' Speaking directly to the king, he told him, 'Sir, I am the Micheas that you deadly hate for prophesying and telling you the truth; and, albeit I know that I shall be fed with the bread of tribulation, yet that which God putteth in my heart I will frankly speak.' Going even further, he warned the king, 'If you will needs follow Ahab in his doings, you incur his unhappy end also, and that the dogs lick your blood as they did his.'[4]

When Henry took the man, William Peto, into the garden to express his displeasure with the sermon, Peto was even clearer in his meaning, telling the king that 'he could have no other wife' while Catherine was still alive, for the king's whole case against her rested on whether the marriage to Henry's brother Arthur had been consummated, and only she could say whether or not that was the case. Catherine had sworn before the Sacrament that she and Arthur had not consummated their union. The king, in Peto's view, had no legal justification to divorce her. Henry was 'endangering his crown, for both great and little were murmuring at this marriage' planned to Anne Boleyn, including that the king had 'meddled' with her sister, Mary, as well as her mother.[5]

The divorce and planned remarriage had indeed proved to be extremely controversial, as had the measures taken to procure them, namely the establishment of an independent English Church with not the Pope, but Henry VIII himself at its head. In the face of such opposition, Henry had first responded with persuasion, then propaganda. By the time Peto came to him with his counsel, Henry was beginning to take a more hardline approach. Peto was forced to leave the country.

The battle between the Observant Friars and the king had not ended there, however. Thomas Cromwell, now the king's leading minister after the fall of his master, Wolsey, had placed spies amongst the friars to keep tabs on the situation. He arrested two of them in the summer of 1533, months before Princess Elizabeth's christening. They would be prompted to speak, he told Henry, if they were 'examined as they ought to be, that is to say by pains'.[6]

Normally, life went on as if this silent war were not taking place. Several times each day and night, the grey-robed friars streamed from their cloisters – with dormitory, refectory and chapter house – through a passage between the nave and presbytery, under the bell tower and into the church, to kneel on the black and white tiled floor and present their prayers to God.[7]

Yet on 10 September 1533, the procession was very different. In the place of humble, chaste friars in their simple grey robes, some of the highest nobles in the land paraded into the small church wearing their finery. Once the christening was done, the three-day-old princess was also confirmed, and then presented with extravagant gifts: cups of gold and bowls, elaborately gilt and engraved. The food was brought in: light, crisp cakes, sweetmeats of fruit and sugar and a sweetened wine flavoured with spices.

Once the esteemed party had eaten their fill, they processed back through the arras-lined gallery into the palace. Five hundred torches, held by the king's guard and other servants, lit their way. They were guided into the queen's chamber, where Queen Anne lay ready to receive them. Leading the procession of the gifts, carrying three standing bowls given by one of the princess's godmothers, was Sir John Dudley.

John was the only man who ranked as low as a humble knight to be given such a role; the other gifts were carried by lords and earls. It was a remarkable sign of his rising favour in this transformed court. Attaching himself to the circle around the king's new paramour, John had accompanied the king and Anne when they had travelled to Calais to meet with the French king, who was once again an ally.[8] Henry and Anne had married very soon after their return, and she had given birth eight months later. John, along with his stepfather, Arthur Plantagenet, had also been present at Anne's coronation.[9] At the coronation feast, John had served the new Archbishop of Canterbury, Thomas Cranmer, who had replaced William Warham in the role after his death in 1532, at the age of more than eighty. Arthur, as Viscount Lisle, had been given the role of Panter, supplying the food for the sumptuous banquet. He must have done well, for the event was a success, but he would not have relished the task. Plantagenet was a conservative, clinging to the old queen and the old Church. Very soon after the coronation, he had been packed off to Calais. His daughter, Elizabeth, had remained in England, to live in her much more flexible half-brother's household.

Elizabeth Plantagenet, who shared her name with her and John's mother, as well as her aunt – Henry VII's queen – was just on the cusp of womanhood when she joined the Dudley household. She was the second of three daughters born to Elizabeth and Arthur Plantagenet. The eldest, Frances, shared her name with the eldest daughter of Charles Brandon and the king's sister. The youngest, Bridget, had probably been named for another of Arthur's royal half-sisters, Bridget of York. Their mother, and John's, had not lived to see the childhood of this youngest Plantagenet daughter. Elizabeth Plantagenet had lived fifteen years after the death of her first husband,

Edmund Dudley, long enough to oversee her eldest son's happy marriage. But she did not live to see her grandchildren.

Little Henry Dudley had been born shortly after John and Jane's wedding and was quickly followed by a brother, Thomas. Thomas had died at the tender age of two. He had probably been named for the king's leading minister at the time of his birth, Cardinal Thomas Wolsey. Wolsey's dramatic fall from favour – caused by his inability to produce the king's desired divorce – had occurred at about the same time that his Dudley namesake had died. Not long after Thomas's death, Jane gave birth again, to another son. Rather than attempting to curry favour with the naming of this Dudley, he was named John, for his father. By the time of Princess Elizabeth's christening in 1533, two more sons, first Ambrose and then – most recently – Robert, had also joined the expanding household, along with Elizabeth Plantagenet, and John's ward, Anthony Norton.

As John entered the queen's presence at Greenwich, holding the precious gifts for the infant princess, he was a man unquestionably on the ascendant. His participation at court had been facilitated by his guardian, now father-in-law, and supported by his military performance. Now, the vacuum left by those who had expressed opposition to the new direction of the regime projected him into the inner circles around the monarch. Queen Anne had produced one healthy child. Next time it would just have to be a son, and then both she and those, like John, whom she had carried into the court on her train could enjoy their favour and position with security.

*

Henry VIII loved the thrill of the hunt. Like jousting, it gave him the opportunity to exercise his martial skills and, as an added advantage, ended in actual bloodshed.[10] In his youth, Henry would spend entire summer days in the saddle, from sun-up to sun-down, chasing his quarry and leaving the business of ruling to Cardinal Wolsey. Wielding crossbows with forked arrows, hunting swords and boar spears, Henry and his companions raced through the forests of England, chasing the hart. When a terrified and battered deer was at last caught, either brought down by arrows or driven into a net, the king would be presented with a hoof, before stabbing the already-dead animal through the heart with his long hunting dagger. That was, of course, unless it was to be given to the dogs, who – to ensure obedience – must be allowed to tear an animal apart from time to time.[11]

There were fewer opportunities for such exercises now, and if asked the forty-four-year-old king would have certainly insisted that shortness of time was the only thing barring him from day-long hunting excursions.

In the summer of 1535, Henry had been invited to hunt in the grounds at Painswick Lodge, Gloucestershire by one of his knights, and his new master of the Tower armoury, after the death of Sir Edward Guildford the year before.[12] Sir John Dudley had caught wind of the plans for the progress two months before and had written to his stepfather to acquire the use of one of the Lisle properties for this purpose. 'In case you would be so good lord and father-in-law unto me,' he wrote, 'as to depute me with your letters and give me your authority, if his Grace come nigh Painswick or Kingston Lisle, to welcome him in your absence, I were much beholding to your lordship.' He signed the letter, 'your assured son during his life, John Dudley'.[13]

Contrary to his sign-off, John had not always been on the best of terms with his stepfather, and Painswick in particular had become a sore spot. The medieval hunting lodge was a part of his late mother's lands, which he would receive upon Arthur Plantagenet's death.[14] John, however, had already begun to sell some of these lands, including to his friend Edward Seymour, son of John Seymour of Wulfhall.[15] Seymour and Plantagenet had disputed the details of the deals and properties, and John had sided with Seymour against his stepfather. Arthur was also in the midst of a dispute with William Kingston, the Constable of the Tower, over trees at Painswick, which Plantagenet wanted to sell off as timber. Kingston, the owner of a nearby property, as well as Warden of the Hunts in the county, was against felling the four hundred trees, which would significantly damage the quality of the hunt. It was probable that he also had an eye to acquiring Painswick, once it had passed into John Dudley's hands.

Despite all of this, John Dudley acquired the licence he needed to welcome the king and queen, and they arrived on 5 August 1535 to enjoy the hospitality – and the trees – of Painswick Lodge.[16] The king was now a far cry from the jubilant youth that John had seen riding through the streets of London when he was a boy. Whereas then his hair had shone like fire, now the colour had dimmed somewhat, and one might suspect that under his jewelled bonnet there was significantly less of it. Always a tall man, the king had broadened out significantly, making him an even more imposing figure than he had been as a youth, if a slightly less athletic one. He had his mother's broad face and small drawn lips. In fact, there was very little of his father in him at all, at least not in appearance.

Henry and Anne arrived later than originally planned. The king had been forced to delay the progress to take care of a matter in London. John had assumed, when writing to his stepfather, that the company would ride out on 6 July. On that day, instead, Sir Thomas More, the man who had taken up the mantle of Lord Chancellor following Cardinal Wolsey's demise, had been executed for treason. He had, according to the court, 'maliciously denied the king's supremacy' as head of the church in England, and thus was sentenced to hanging, drawing and quartering, though this was commuted to beheading.

John had sat in the parliament which enacted the 'Treasons Act', the piece of legislation which had condemned More, as well as Bishop John Fisher, by making it treason to deny the king's supremacy of the Church. Many claimed that these were holy men and ought not to have been executed for their defence of the Catholic Church. Both More and Fisher, however, had also had a hand in the condemnation and defamation of John's father, and they clung to a superstitious religion that John had himself denounced. He had little reason to wring his hands over their demise. It was, nevertheless, hard not to miss the parallels with his father's execution: the king on progress, a former servant sacrificed. Although Henry seemed a very different man to the young king who had executed his father, perhaps he had not changed so much, or at least not for the better. It was a lesson to keep in mind.

The king and queen had travelled south from Gloucester in the morning, entering the forests of the Cotswolds on their hour-long ride, before coming at last to Painswick Lodge. The Lodge was to the north-east of the town of Painswick itself, and had originally been built, some century and a half before, as nothing more than a hunting lodge, adjacent to a deer park; a place where the lords and ladies partaking of the hunt might plan their chase and take their respite.[17] Over time, it had taken the place of the main manor and been transformed into a building fit for a king's visit. A four-sided stone house, with a paved courtyard in the centre, the Lodge had recently been refurbished to include a large hall, where Dudley could host his royal guests for dinner. Several smaller rooms, with wood-panelled walls and large stone fireplaces, served as chambers where the monarchs and their company might retire for a time between the events of the day.

Queen Anne, as had her predecessor, often joined the king in his hunting exertions.[18] Their hunting parties were small, meaning that there was some opportunity for intimacy between Anne and Henry, a fact which had been especially luring in their prolonged courtship. Henry had bought her French saddles, bows, arrows and gloves, and at times she would share a saddle with him as he rode, their bodies separated only by their riding clothes.

These were different times, however, and the connection between Henry and Anne had noticeably cooled.

Anne had never been a traditionally beautiful woman; she was considered darker than the accepted requirements of beauty, but even her enemies struggled to deny that she was captivating.[19] Raised in the courts of France, she had adopted a more continental way of speaking and moving which communicated grace and wit. Her most winning features had always been her pretty mouth and alluring dark eyes. John Dudley had seen her at her height: speaking with the King of France in Calais, during her coronation and at Elizabeth's christening.

She had lost some of the sheen of triumph she had worn in those days. It had been almost two years since the christening of her daughter, and no son – indeed no second living child – had followed. Rumour had it that Henry had already become enamoured with another woman, or possibly more than one, and that he grew tired of their passionate fights. Still, the performance of happy royal couple was necessary, especially when he had gone to such great lengths to secure this marriage. There were those who still wanted him to return to the 'dowager princess' Catherine, exiled to Kimbolton Castle,

Cambridgeshire. Henry and Anne might disagree on an increasingly many things, but they were a united front on the question of Henry reuniting with his first wife. And in this John Dudley stood with them.

The Dudleys had ingratiated themselves amongst the reformist group around Anne Boleyn. On the queen's recommendation, a sign of their place within her circle, they had placed their ten-year-old son under the tutelage of Nicholas Bourbon, a scholar–refugee from France whose religious views had landed him in prison on the continent.[20] Bourbon expressed his gratitude in a poem to the boy's father: 'you have always loved me / Hence, I will love you in return, if I do not, I shall die'.[21] (It was not his best work.) Henry joined a class of other young boys of the court, including Henry Norris, the son of the king's Groom of the Stool, and Henry Carey, the son of Mary Boleyn and her husband William Carey (or so it was maintained): Henry Carey was thus the nephew of the queen (if not also the son of the king).[22] It was an elite bunch of mostly Henrys (though there was also a Thomas), and Henry Dudley, given his lower status, was fortunate to be amongst them.

Henry and his peers gathered in a small room, transformed into a schoolroom, to hear their tutor lecture. Quietly taking notes in his book with ink and pen, Henry was instructed to record Bourbon's words carefully, asking his friends if he missed something.[23] When he was called on, he knew he was to close his book and recite back what he had been told in a clear, loud voice: 'With,' Master Bourbon instructed, 'a cheerful brow, direct eyes, modulated speech, steady foot, clean nose, quiet hands.'[24] Bourbon also took it upon himself to teach Henry and the other ten-year-old boys how to act in the world: everything from hygiene to doffing caps. Henry was lucky to have a schoolmaster who preferred rewarding good behaviour (with cakes, no less) to punishing bad.[25] Henry's learning was filled with lessons focused on pacificism and virtue: 'God Himself and your parents,' Bourbon instructed his pupils, 'gave you to me, not just to learn grammar and rhetoric, but also so that you should learn honest behaviour from me.'[26] He attempted to deter Henry and the other boys from blood-sports of any kind, 'Feeding horses and fierce dogs, competing in wrestling and with spears and swords: these things please the strong,' he told them; 'Do not accustom your minds to any grim warfare: depart from the harsh work of bloodthirsty Mars.'[27]

The king himself had a different philosophy. While the company enjoyed some rather bloodthirsty activities at Painswick that August day, Henry VIII 'asked' (commanded) to speak to his host. As John later reported to his stepfather, the conversation remained entirely on the topic of timber. Henry objected strongly to the proposed sale of trees that Arthur Plantagenet had been pursuing, for, he told him, 'the lordship were utterly destroyed if it should so be spoiled, which were too much pity'.[28] It was no surprise that Henry had sided against his half-uncle, Arthur; not only had he clearly enjoyed the hunting at Painswick, but Arthur Plantagenet was decidedly not in favour, thanks to his religious conservatism and refusal to promote the men Cromwell instructed him to. If John and the king's conversation had gone beyond a discussion of the foliage, John did not tell his stepfather.

The company stayed until dusk, when they made the journey back to Gloucester, arriving after sun-down. The following day, the monarchs graced Arthur Plantagenet's opponent in the timber case with a visit. William Kingston had also been with Henry and Anne in Calais in 1532 and present at her coronation. He had been Constable of the Tower since 1524. In that time he had overseen the arrest of a string of enemies to the Crown, including Cardinal Wolsey and, more recently, Thomas More. A month after More's execution, he, along with his wife, welcomed Henry and Anne to Miserden Park, where once again king and queen enjoyed a day of hunting.

From there, the royal couple continued their progress, heading south through Gloucestershire, before veering east, and arriving by early September in Wiltshire, where they spent almost a week – including the princess Elizabeth's second birthday – with the family of Dudley's friend, Edward Seymour, at Wulfhall. By the end of the year, when they had returned to London, Anne Boleyn knew she was once again pregnant, with a child conceived while they were on progress. The adventure of the hunt seems to have, once again, added fire to their relationship.

*

'Right honourable and my very good Lady,' John Dudley scribbled in a note to his stepmother, Arthur Plantagenet's second wife, Honour, Lady Lisle, 'in my most hearty wise I recommend me unto you.'[29] It was 10 May 1536, a Wednesday, just nine months after the king and queen had visited him at the Lisle property in Painswick. John was at the court of the king, though few had seen Henry VIII since the May Day tournaments over a week before.

Henry had not been riding that day, after a near-fatal fall he had taken four months earlier in January. He had recovered, but the accident had been cited as the reason why, just five days later, Anne Boleyn had miscarried the child conceived during the couple's progress the summer before. The miscarriage occurred on the same day that Henry's first wife, Catherine of Aragon, was buried, having died three weeks earlier. Any relief that the royal couple had felt upon Catherine's death was fleeting. Anne's miscarriage was seen as the final straw in the mounting movement against her by members of the court, including the powerful Thomas Cromwell, with whom she had recently quarrelled.[30] Additionally, with Catherine gone Henry would not be forced to reconcile with the former queen if he cast off his current wife. He had options, and had already decided on one. Within days of the miscarriage, Henry began sending elaborate gifts to one of Anne's ladies, Jane, the sister of John Dudley's friend Edward Seymour.

In Jane Seymour, it seemed, the king had reverted to type. A quieter, paler, more solemn-looking woman than Anne, Jane was far more like his mother. She had – coyly – rejected his advances at first, citing her honour; she was a 'well-born damsel' who was 'without blame or reproach of any kind; there was no treasure in this world she valued as much as her honour'. If the king wanted to give her gifts, she 'requested him to reserve it for such a time as God would be pleased to send her some advantageous marriage'.[31] The king ate it up. He would be the one to marry her.

Edward Seymour had already done well from this new courtship. He was made a gentleman of the privy chamber, giving him intimate access to the king, and he and his wife were given apartments at Greenwich next to the king's, reached via a private passage. John had chosen his friends well indeed.

Of course, for Henry and Jane to be married, the king had to do something about his current wife. That was the topic of John's letter to Lady Lisle. 'As touching the news that are here, I am sure it needeth not to write to you nor my lord of them, for all the world knoweth them by this time.' Queen Anne had been arrested the day after the May Day tournament, along with five men: a musician and four gentlemen of the court, including her own brother, all of them accused of having committed adultery with the king's wife. The charges were difficult to substantiate, though the queen's unpopularity and the pressure of the king's will gave them a power beyond truth. Though he had been young at the time of his father's downfall, John Dudley had personal experience of how these factors could produce choruses of shaking heads and reproachful glances, no matter how fantastic the charges.

The fear that anyone might be next also fuelled acceptance of the accusations against the queen. In an attempt to mitigate at least some of the anxiety buzzing through the court, Thomas Cromwell, the orchestrator of the arrests and accusations, held a meeting with twenty-two members of the court, including John, to set the record straight on what had happened and what was going to happen next. It was more shocking than any could have imagined. The next day, John sat to write some of this news to his stepmother. 'This day,' he wrote, 'was indicted Mr Norris,' – father to one of John's son's school-companions – 'Mr Weston,' – the son of the man whom Fox had slid into place to oppose Edmund Dudley – 'William a Brereton, Marks,' – Mark Smeaton, a musician – 'and my Lord of Rochford' – Anne's brother George. The Constable of the Tower, Sir William Kingston, had on 10 May been commanded 'to bring up the bodies of Sir Francis Weston, knight, Henry Norris, esquire, William Brereton, esquire and Mark Smeaton, gentleman at Westminster' to be tried on 12 May. George Boleyn, Lord Rochford, was to go on trial three days later. Dudley had more news, however; 'And the Queen herself,' he scribbled, 'upon' – he crossed it out; he needed to gather his thoughts to write the monumental news – 'shall be condemned by Parliament.'[32]

Anne Boleyn was tried by a panel of her peers, including her uncle, Thomas Howard, the Duke of Norfolk,[33] who represented the king as

Lord High Steward, as well as Charles Brandon, Duke of Suffolk, and Andrew Windsor, now Lord Windsor, who had continued to be a central member of the court since the execution of his former brother-in-law twenty-six years before.[34] There were also some two thousand spectators and little reason for John and his wife not to attend.

John had been right; the Queen was found guilty and condemned to death (though not by parliament). Instead, her own uncle proclaimed: 'Because thou hast offended against our sovereign the King's Grace in committing treason against his person, and here attainted of the same, the law of the realm is this, that thou hast deserved death, and thy judgment is this: that thou shalt be burned here within the Tower of London on the Green, else to have thy head smitten off, as the King's pleasure shall be further known of the same.'[35] She was led from the King's Hall in the Tower by the constable, Kingston, the man she had spent the day with the August before.

The king's pleasure was that she be beheaded by an expert swordsman brought in from Calais. On the morning of 19 May, she was led from her room at the Tower by Kingston, through the Tower grounds, and up the scaffold that had been prepared. A large crowd had gathered to witness the first crowned queen of England ever to be executed. One of the men recording the event was Charles Wriothesley, son of the former Garter King of Arms who had proclaimed the christening of Anne's daughter, Elizabeth. Charles had been with his father at Anne's coronation; it had been the first event he had recorded in full. Now, he wrote the details of Anne's execution. Wriothesley noted that in attendance at the execution was the king's son, the Duke of Richmond, along with Charles Brandon and most of the King's Council, earls, lords and other nobles.[36] Wriothesley did not record whether or not Sir John Dudley came to see the death of the queen who had bestowed such favour upon his family.

Despite the charges of adultery which led to her execution, Anne's marriage to Henry had already been annulled – he had been no more married to her than he had been to Catherine of Aragon – on the grounds of, once again, consanguinity; Henry had had a sexual relationship with her sister. When Henry married Jane Seymour on 30 May 1536, less than two weeks after Anne's execution, legally, she was his first wife. Despite their associations with the disgraced former queen, switching allegiance to the sister of Edward Seymour would be simple enough for the Dudleys, thanks to their friendship with Edward Seymour and his wife, Anne. They might be even closer to the Crown – that ultimate source of power – under Queen Jane than they had under the condemned Queen Anne.

*

Dozens of young boys stood solemnly, dressed in black gowns, clasping small wax candles in their hands. The flames flickered in the dying light of the day. It was mid-November, and night came earlier and earlier. It had been a very wet summer and the biting chill of a cold winter would settle in soon. Jane Dudley had been travelling all day on horseback. She looked down at the gathered children, some of them the same age as her own sons. Were there tears in their eyes? Did they think the death of a queen terribly significant? Or were they simply enduring the spectacle, dreaming of the moment they would be released back into their own rooms to warm up and gossip with their friends? After all, Queen Jane Seymour had only reigned seventeen months and had never been crowned. Even boys younger than ten had seen two other queens in their lifetimes. One could forgive a lack of genuine emotion.

Before Jane was a great winding sea of black silks and velvets.[37] She rode her black-trapped horse in the company of seven other ladies, all dressed in gowns of black, behind a chariot, likewise covered in black cloth, and garnished with coats of arms and fine gold. Within the chariot were four ladies, including the Lady Rochford, the widow of George Boleyn, whose father-in-law, Thomas Boleyn, was also amongst the procession. It was hard to say how comfortable the chariot would be after a full day of riding, but there was a good chance it was more comfortable than a side-saddle. Each stop along the way– at a parish church to censor and bless the body of the queen – was an opportunity for a short rest, but it also prolonged the journey. They had left shortly after breakfast from Hampton Court, where the queen had lain in state since her death there on 24 October 1537. They were headed to Windsor, where the king had decided that his wife would be buried. It was a fifteen-mile journey or more, but this – at Eton – was mercifully one of the last stops along the way.

Just beyond the chariot in front of Jane rode Queen Jane's chief mourner, the Lady Mary, daughter to the king. Mary, now twenty, had been reintroduced to her father's favour by Jane Seymour and now sincerely mourned the death of her stepmother. She had been so overcome by emotion shortly after Jane's death that she had been unable to fulfil her role, but now, three weeks later, she performed it with the grace and poise expected of a woman raised from birth as a princess of England. Despite their differences in religion – Mary clung steadfastly to the Catholic Church – Mary and Jane Dudley shared good relations; Jane was good at making powerful friends, perhaps even better at it than her husband.[38] Mary had stood as god-mother to their eldest daughter, who shared her name, and another son, Guildford, who also had the honour of the visiting Spaniard Don Diego de Mendoza as his godfather.[39] Having served the queen, Jane Dudley would serve the Lady Mary once the late queen was interred.[40]

Directly before the chief mourner went the chariot carrying the queen's corpse. Covered in black velvet decorated with arms, the chariot was pulled by six horses also trapped in black velvet. Over the chariot was a canopy of black velvet with a white satin cross and a fringe of black silk, fixed into the four corners of the chariot with large black staffs. Banners of arms belonging to the king and queen, as well as Henry's father and mother, sat at each of the corners of the chariot, marking Jane's place as successor to Queen Elizabeth, wife of Henry VII.

At the centre of the chariot was the body, covered with a rich dark pall. Upon it lay an effigy of the queen, dressed as if for the coronation she never had, with robes of estate and a golden crown upon her head. The effigy carried a sceptre of gold in a right hand covered with ornate rings. Beneath its head was a pillow of cloth of gold tissue. Had Queen Jane been crowned, Jane Dudley would have probably ridden along in that procession as well, following a living queen through the cheering streets of London. Instead, it was a dark, sombre and quiet parade, following the lifeless wooden queen.

Walking alongside the chariot were barons carrying fringed banners of fine white silk and gold, illustrating moments in the life of the

Virgin Mary, including the birth of Jesus and her assumption into Heaven. Perhaps the most poignant was that of the Mother holding her infant child in her arms. Jane had died less than a fortnight after giving birth to her son, Edward, the long-awaited male heir to King Henry VIII. Any chance she had had to hold her young son in her arms had been fleeting, as she had quickly succumbed to the fever which had killed her.

The arrival of Prince Edward had come as a great relief to King Henry, even as he watched his wife decline and die. He had annulled his first two marriages, invalidating the children born of them; they were both daughters in any case. His bastard son, whom he had made Duke of Richmond, had sickened and died in July 1536 without producing any heirs. Henry's sister Mary, who had married Charles Brandon, had died in 1533 and also left only daughters, the eldest of which had borne another girl, named Jane for the Queen. His other sister, Margaret, had borne sons, but the eldest of these was the King of Scotland, whose father had died at the hands of English troops. It was a branch of the family better ignored in making plans for the succession. In short, without Edward, the dynasty would very likely end with Henry. Everything must be done to protect this infant, especially as the Queen's death meant no brothers would follow.

Knights and messengers had been sent off to the courts of Europe to announce the prince's birth, amongst them Jane's husband, Sir John Dudley. On 20 October, just eight days after Edward's birth and five days after his christening, John had been dispatched by Thomas Cromwell to the court of Emperor Charles V in Barbastro. Jane had to face the tragedy that followed without her husband.

The court John returned home to in November was very different from the one he had left, though the mourning king commended him for his work in Spain. It was not long after that the letters went out from London informing Europe of the queen's death. With three queens dead and buried, Henry VIII was looking to marry again. Having served Queen Jane, Lady Jane Dudley could hope to be in the household of another Queen of England. Assuming, of course, that there was a woman in Europe willing to take the job.

*

It was difficult to work out what the king thought he was doing, or indeed if he was thinking at all. News from England was met with incredulity by Charles V and a deep sigh by Francis I. Among the members of the Protestant League of the Holy Roman Empire, Henry VIII was becoming known as that 'crazy man'.[41]

Henry VIII's new (and fourth) wife had arrived in London on 3 January in the thirty-first year of his reign. As with his first marriage, this was a diplomatic union; the king was welcoming a foreign princess to England's shores. Anne of Cleves was the twenty-four-year-old daughter of the duke of Juliers-Cleves, a small duchy in the north of Germany, ostensibly under the control of the Holy Roman Empire, but run independently. Positioned on the joining of the River Lippe and the Rhine, the duchy held a position of economic, military and political significance, as well as being home to a host of musicians and scholars.

Politically and religiously the match was an ideal one. With Francis I and Charles V surprising the continent by making overtures of peace and friendship, the balance of power in Europe was teetering, and England was losing its footing. Henry VIII needed new allies, and so his ministers looked to Germany. By marrying Anne of Cleves, Henry ensured that her brother, duke of several states in the Holy Roman Empire, did not ally, instead, with the King of France. The duchy remained Catholic, though Anne's father, Duke Johann, had – like Henry – rejected the authority of the pope, thus pleasing reformers on both sides of the Channel. Anne carried this diplomatic importance as well as an impressive lineage, as had Catherine of Aragon, but also had the continental upbringing of Anne Boleyn (albeit more sheltered) and the attractive modesty of Jane Seymour.[42] Thomas Cromwell had masterminded the match, and the court painter Hans Holbein had been dispatched to produce a portrait of the princess, which captured the combined elements of wealth, culture and humility, united with a direct gaze and tantalizing half-smile. The English ambassador, Nicholas Wotton, declared it an accurate likeness of the attractive princess.[43]

Anne's arrival would usher in a revitalized spirit to Henry's court, lacking a queen since Jane Seymour's death more than two years before. A new queen represented fresh opportunities for office and advancement, and the Dudleys were in a position to take advantage. Their continued friendship with reformers such as Thomas Cromwell, still the king's right-hand man and 'special counsellor of the match' with Anne of Cleves, was essential to such placements.[44] John Dudley had recently engaged in a colossal land sale with Cromwell; for £3,500, Dudley had sold his childhood home of Halden and associated lands in Kent and Sussex to the Lord Privy Seal, ostensibly to pay off debts but also to curry favour with the powerful man.[45] Cromwell quickly went to work establishing them as profitable holdings for his son, Gregory, and his new Seymour wife.[46] Continuing to ride in the wake of Cromwell, the fortunes of the Dudley family were tied up with the success of the king's new marriage.

Anne of Cleves, travelling since November, finally arrived in London on 3 January.[47] The whole event had been marvellously set out. It was a Saturday, and despite the midwinter date, the weather was fair enough to allow for a grand spectacle. Blackheath Plain, a stretch of ground next to Greenwich Palace, had been selected for the reception, and trees felled to create even more space for the attendees. Much like the Field of the Cloth of Gold twenty years before, the open space had been littered with pavilions. Lines of richly dressed merchants, London officials, gentlemen, knights and nobles stood waiting in the cold January morning air. They had been ordered to arrive there by eight of the clock, just as the sun was rising. They waited, shivering, for their soon-to-be queen to appear.

As the sun reached its height around noon, the princess and her entourage at last emerged, a golden trickle slowly streaming over the hill towards the tents and pavilions. Anne was accompanied by a hundred of her countrymen and women on horseback, as well as some of the leading nobles of England who had met her on her journey. Anne retired momentarily in a gilded tent to refresh, where a banquet of sweets and spiced wine waited for her. She had been travelling since 26 November, when her horse-drawn chariot had left Cleves. She had reached Calais on 11 December, where she and her company were forced to wait out the bad weather until two days after Christmas. She landed in Dover and rested at Rochester.

It was there that the vision of an idyllic royal union was shattered. Henry, forty-eight but attempting to revive his youthful playfulness, had dressed in disguise to enter Anne's chamber and sneak a look at his new bride. While she was distracted by the bull-baiting outside her window, the amorous king had approached with kisses, embraces and presents, but she – apparently not recognizing him – had been far more interested in the contest on the other side of her window.[48] It took his assumption of his royal purple cloak to provoke interest – and reverence – in the young woman and her attendants, but the damage, it seemed, had been done, in particular to the king's not insignificant and rather insecure sense of pride.

Despite this awkwardness, on 3 January, the affianced couple put on a show of great warmth and affection. Trumpets blew as the king approached in a large company of noblemen, gentlemen and ambassadors. He was an impressive sight: his coat of purple velvet was covered in gem-stone buttons and so heavily embroidered with gold that the velvet could barely be seen. His sword was likewise adorned with jewels, especially emeralds, and his cap was so gem-encrusted that those who wondered upon its value could not come up with the total sum. Upon a courser trapped in latticed cloth of gold, he made his way across the field to his intended bride. His arrival prompted Anne's exit from her tent, upon which she mounted a richly trapped horse, and rode towards the king. The two met at the designated spot near the centre of the field. The king doffed his cap and welcomed her with an embrace, and she responded with fulsome thanks. Together, the apparent lovebirds made their way back to the palace. Directly behind Anne, leading her spare horse – a palfrey, trapped in tissue from head to hooves – was her newly selected Master of Horse: Sir John Dudley. John had travelled to the continent to help fetch back the new queen, and was as aware as any of the rumours that were already circulating of the king's displeasure. Master of Horse was an important and intimate role, which gave John privileged access to the new queen few others would have. If Cromwell had wanted an ally to keep an eye on the new queen and report back, he could do worse than John Dudley, though of course John would not be able to enter the closest confines of her confidence; for that a woman was needed.

Fortunately – as if fortune had anything to do with it – Jane Dudley had been chosen to be one of the ladies attendant upon the queen, whom Anne had greeted and kissed as she arrived at Blackheath. The French ambassador had reported Anne of Cleves of 'middling beauty'. On this day she shone. She too was dressed in cloth of gold, wearing a gown of it, without a train, in the Dutch fashion. Her long blond hair was secure under a headdress covered with a round bonnet set with orient pearls. Her usually serious countenance was enlivened by a glistening collar of rich gemstones, which caught the noon-day sun and cast dancing light across the field as she rode. Apparelled as she was, and amongst this great procession, it was difficult not to think her very fair indeed.

The king did not agree. He had berated Cromwell for his choice, yet he knew a great deal was riding on the marriage – telling Cromwell that he feared 'making a ruffle* in the world that is the mean to drive her brother into the hands of the emperor and French king's hands'. He was powerless to stop the match, and so they married on 6 January, three days after her arrival.[49] Anyone who had believed that the king might be brought around, as he often was, within the confines of the chamber bed was to be sorely disappointed. The king claimed to be unable to consummate this marriage, not because of any lack of power in himself – that particular rumour had been circulating since the Boleyn trials and needed quashing – but because of his dislike for his bride. There was no evidence that the new royal couple had properly – physically – coupled, and along with the king's inability swirled rumours about the queen's sexual naivety. Jane Dudley, mother seven times over, might have reason to laugh with the other queen's ladies about both partners in the royal embarrassment.

There was also reason, however, to pity the young queen, far from home, rejected on flimsy grounds by an increasingly aged and corpulent husband with a reputation for casting off wives. And Jane might well worry for her own standing, should Anne fall from grace. Or even worse, should the architect of their good fortune and the king's unwanted marriage, Thomas Cromwell, follow in the bloody footsteps of More, Wolsey and Jane's own father-in-law.

* Ruffle: disturbance.

7

A mortal breakfast if he were the king's enemy

Dudley Castle had stood since the Norman Conquest, if not before.[1] With a large oval curtain wall at least nine feet thick and impressive fortifications – including a drawbridge, two portcullises and three sets of heavy doors within its two-storey gatehouse – it had been designed to withstand the bellicose turmoil of the English Middle Ages. A turreted keep had been added in the fourteenth century; standing to the west of the gatehouse, it was a well-fortified manor house, consisting of ten-foot-thick walls, as well as chambers, pantry, buttery and kitchen. To the other side of the gatehouse was the chapel, with its large, pointed window, which loomed over visitors as they entered. Next to the chapel was the great chamber, and below it, various cellars and smaller rooms.

Dudley Castle had given its name to John's family; to take possession of it was to claim lordship over the family itself. The family seat had typically resided, of course, with the elder branch of the family, of which John was not a member. John's grandfather and namesake, John Sutton Dudley of Atherington, had been the younger son of John Sutton, Baron Dudley, and so the castle and the barony had been inherited by his elder brother, Edward, and then Edward's son, John Sutton, Baron Dudley. John Sutton, however, had fallen on hard times, and was forced to sell many of his lands; John Dudley, in the glow of Cromwell's and the king's favour, was more than happy to scoop them up.[2] John's cousin quickly became known as 'Lord Quondam' or 'Lord Has-Been' as John became the Dudley on the ascendant. By the spring, following the arrival of the new Queen Anne, John Dudley had taken possession of the family castle and was calling it home.

Soon, Baron Dudley was in debt to his cousin, and writing to Cromwell in hopes of funds, even offering to sell off the lordship when his eighty-six-year-old mother died. He would come to Cromwell himself to plead his case, he wrote, but 'I am informed that Sir John Dudley doth lay in a wait in all places in the City of London to keep me afore the days of payment to the intent that he may obtain his purpose.'[3]

His cousin's protestations were not the first criticisms John Dudley had heard about his financial transactions. His stepfather had complained that he had connived with Edward Seymour to wrangle him out of money as Dudley and Seymour bought up the estates Plantagenet had inherited from John's mother. Another man, Thomas Pope, had reported to Thomas Cromwell that, although he 'had made sundry requests to Sir John Dudley for payment' of the money owed him, Dudley 'has not hitherto paid me one penny thereof', treating him as one would treat 'the lewdest fellow in a country'.[4] John had his father's aptitude for shrugging off such complaints in the acquisition of wealth, and it was beginning to become known. Arrogant negligence towards his reputation had, in many ways, been the downfall of his father. As resilient as he was becoming, John would have to ensure he did not fall into the same fatal trap.

With his place at court balanced precariously on the axe-edge of Cromwell's power and thus the king's affections, it would be wise to turn his attention to establishing a local base, from which he could build a more secure foundation of land and stone. The Boleyns, for instance, had Hever Castle in Kent, to which Anne Boleyn's father had been able to return when disgraced by his children's apparent sordid affairs. Members of the peerage established themselves not only by seeing to the king's whims at court, but also by building up offices and holdings in the country, which could be extremely lucrative in ways that service to the king frequently was not. John was next-in-line to inherit the title of Viscount Lisle, after all, and his stepfather had yet to re-enter the king's good graces; in fact, rumour had it that the king was every day turning further away from his half-uncle in Calais, as Arthur Plantagenet emerged even more clearly as a religious conservative and enemy of Cromwell. Dudley Castle represented a base from which Sir John Dudley, the next Viscount Lisle, could establish himself as a local lord and his family as legitimate claimants to ancestral titles.

Following spring in the uncomfortable court of King Henry and the new, precarious Queen Anne, in the weeks before Easter 1540, John travelled the 120 miles home to Dudley, on the border of Staffordshire and Worcestershire. Although well-secured, the castle was lacking in luxury, refinement and, indeed, space. With civil war long past, a knight's castle needed to be more fashionable than fortified – an unexpected and very expensive visit from the king was a more likely threat than an attack – and John had ambitious plans for the renovation of Dudley.

Within a few days of his return, in the middle of March 1540, John was notified of visitors. Sir Andrew Flammock, one of the king's standard bearers, and his son had arrived, hoping to find hospitality for the night.[5] John, in line with Christian teachings and societal expectations, granted it.[6] Flammock had a reputation as a jovial fellow, and tales circulated of his brash but witty humour. On one occasion, it was said, he had accompanied the king on a hunting expedition at Greenwich Park. When the king had blown his horn, Flammock, with a belly full from dinner, had responded with some wind of his own. Responding to the king's shocked questioning, Flammock retorted, 'If it please you, your Majesty blew one blast for the keeper, and I another for his man.'[7] The king was so amused Flammock escaped reproach. On another occasion, the king – lusting after some woman or another – had asked Flammock to finish a rhyme for him. The king began, 'Within this tower / There lieth a flower / That hath my heart.' Flammock responded, 'Within this hour / She will . . .' and rhyming, he echoed his earlier interjection.[8]

Did Flammock look less merry as John Dudley welcomed him? Perhaps a little too pale, even for March? He and his son had arrived from Gloucestershire to the south, not a terribly long ride, and yet it seemed perhaps they were more tired than such a journey warranted.

By the next day it was clear – the Flammocks were suffering with the plague. Plague had first reached England in 1348, killing almost a third of the population. Although it had subsided significantly, periodic and local breakouts were still terrifying. While the king and his first Queen Anne were hunting at Painswick, the plague had erupted in London, violently in some areas, killing around a hundred people.[9] The intervening years had seen a number of outbreaks across the country.[10] And now it had arrived in Dudley's home. Where the Flammocks had picked it up, Dudley could not tell; Staffordshire had been free of it until they arrived. Both men were covered in plague marks – large pustules containing blood and pus – and sickened quickly. By the second night, the night before Palm Sunday, the Flammock son died. Those treating them confirmed that the father would soon follow.

In the morning, before the strains of the Palm Sunday hosannas that marked the arrival of Jesus at Jerusalem, where he would be betrayed and put to death, John Dudley took up his quill to write a hurried letter to Thomas Cromwell. Skipping the formalities, he immediately informed the Lord Secretary of events, and the sad prognosis of the elder Flammock, dying nearby. He then got to the crux of the matter. He hoped Cromwell might intervene with the king for the office of keeper of Kenilworth Castle, the position currently held by the plague-ridden Sir Andrew. It was a difficult request, and made far too soon, with the current office holder still breathing, and under John's care and hospitality.[11]

A year previously John had written to Cromwell for the position of commission of the Marches, joining the Council to help control lands on the border with Wales, just west of Dudley.[12] Telling Cromwell that 'I have spent a great deal of my life and my youth in the court about my master' he felt himself 'drawing homewards where I trust to make an end of my life in God's service'. As such, 'it would be a great comfort to me and to all my poor friends in these parts' if he would be given the commission.[13] This letter was in the same vein. Seeing his position of Master of the Queen's Horse likely drawing to a close, he might have calculated that an office thirty miles from Dudley would not be too far and would still allow him to keep other local positions and landholdings.

Dudley's hastily written letter proved in vain. Perhaps to the chagrin of his host, the merrily breezy Sir Andrew Flammock made a full recovery. If John Dudley was displeased by his guest's return from death's doorstep, it would be indecorous to show it. Flammock had escaped the grip of plague, but Dudley had not managed to escape the even more powerful pull of the court by finding himself a lucrative, and perhaps safer, post elsewhere.

An outside observer, such as Cromwell, reading these various letters of complaint about Dudley's methods, and the opportunist letters from Dudley himself, might be forgiven for thinking him grasping. A man and his son were dying in Dudley's newly acquired castle, and all he could think about was seizing the man's position. Cromwell himself, however, would be unlikely to pass such judgement. His own reputation for ruthlessness, and an undue accumulation of land and position, were by now widely acknowledged, if not openly discussed. In April this had become even more offensive to Cromwell's enemies, as he was ennobled – given the ancient earldom of Essex – as well as the office of Lord Great Chamberlain, a role which had been held by three generations of earls of Oxford, and a series of estates and incomes, largely taken from the monasteries he had helped to bring down.

Cromwell's current attention, however, was focused on much more troubling matters. The new Earl of Essex had been largely responsible for the king's latest unhappy marriage, arguing passionately against his friend and ally Thomas Cranmer, the now well-established Archbishop of Canterbury, who had advocated for a domestic match.[14] Cromwell – aided by the unbalanced state of European affairs and the pleasing portrait of Anne – had convinced the king of the merits of the union, though reminding Henry that he had been a consenting agent would be unwise now. Instead, Cromwell set to work to free his master from the marriage in which he had entangled him, though to little avail. Unless they publicly declared that the king had been unable to consummate the marriage, he would have to see it through. Neither option brought relief to the king, and Cromwell had been suffering for some months under the weight of royal frustration. Eventually, as it always did, something would have to give. It was unlikely to be the king.

*

John Dudley fell to the earth hard. His heavy armour, designed to protect him, impeded the natural commands of his reflexes as he tumbled from his rebelling horse. He was like an insect flicked off a windowsill, struggling to right himself again. At the age of thirty-six, this was a harder task than it had been a decade or so earlier. Eventually, white velvet trappings soiled by the dirt from which he rose, Dudley got back to his feet. There was relief in the reaction from the crowd, though it might have been tinged with disappointment, even judgement. This was, in many ways, Dudley's tournament; his name had seniority atop the list of challengers who had arranged the May Day events, the others likewise leading knights in the king's court, including Sir Thomas Seymour, Edward Seymour's younger, charismatic brother.[15]

This was the first day of the tournament, the joust, and Dudley had been running courses* against a series of answerers. Before him, perfectly well and untouched, was his opponent, Richard Breme, a middling servant of the king with the much lower rank of esquire. It wasn't much of a consolation that Breme had not been responsible for Dudley's unhorsing, as it was his horse who had sent John flying.

The crowd assembled at Westminster for the tournament was significant, with dozens of knights and gentlemen answering the challenge. Despite the possibility of embarrassment, participation in a tournament remained an important way to please and appeal to the king. The king himself, along with his queen, was in attendance, though despite the new armour he'd commissioned for himself that year (complete with a fifty-inch waistline), he did not ride in the lists. Chief among the answerers was the poet-knight Henry Howard, Earl of Surrey, and Thomas Cromwell's son, Gregory Cromwell, now Lord Cromwell thanks to his father's elevation to the position of Earl of Essex a fortnight before. At the bottom of the list was John's own younger brother, Andrew, entering court life as an officer of the exchequer. The previous year, John had granted his younger brother, now in his early thirties, lands and manors in Worcestershire and Staffordshire, all within a short ride of Dudley Castle.[16]

---

* Course: the rush together of two combatants in battle or tournament.

The fall was hard, but John managed to recover his position – and dignity – over the course of the day, breaking a number of lances against opponents. The painstaking removal of armour and sweat-soaked underclothes did not signal the end of the day's festivities, however. Following the jousting, John and his challengers led the way out of Westminster and past Whitehall Palace, processing through the large, imposing gatehouse that spanned the road.[17] Covered in terra-cotta roundels of busts of past Roman emperors, the gatehouse contained Henry VIII's private study, where he had married Anne Boleyn.[18] From there the parade of knights, ladies, gentlemen, king and queen followed the road east, to Charing Cross, marked by the large stone cross erected by Edward I to the memory of his wife, Elea-nor of Castile, at the bend, or *cerring*, of the Thames. At last they reached the gates of Durham House. Previously in the possession of the Bishop of Durham, Cuthbert Tunstall, it had been granted to the king four years previous, adding to the king's growing monopoly on Thameside property.

Entering via the gate on the Strand, John and the rest of the courtly entourage arrived in a large yard, big enough to host tournaments of its own, before making their way through the gate of the house itself and into its central courtyard. Durham House was best appreciated from the water, where its impressive turreted walls could be seen, framed by three-storey towers. Catherine of Aragon had lived within its walls immediately following Arthur's death, trapped and uncertain as to her future.[19] Henry's new queen, as she entered, might have empathised.

Little had improved for Anne of Cleves, though it remained pos-sible that she was ignorant of the true danger of her situation. It was not just that Henry VIII was uninterested in her as a wife, but that he had found someone else towards whom to direct his affections. This was, rather predictably, one of Anne's own ladies, the young Kather-ine Howard, described as 'a lady of great beauty' by the French ambassador, even if she was rather short.[20] Not yet twenty, Katherine was the recently orphaned daughter of Edmund Howard, the third of the Howard brothers, and a cousin of Anne Boleyn.[21] She had joined Anne of Cleves' ladies at the start of the year, and by the end of April was the recipient of significant gifts from the king, including lands in Sussex, confiscated from a father and son who stood accused of murder and had fled.[22] If the queen was cognisant of her husband's excessive flirting, she had not commented on it yet, but much of the court was aware of what was happening under the queen's nose. Katherine, constantly in attendance, was expected to join the queen for major events, such as the May Day tournament and the feasting that followed.

Dudley and his compatriots wined and dined the king and court. Cupboards overflowing with rich plate, meat and drink were freely available, accompanied by the sweet melody of minstrels. For the whole week of the tournament, Dudley and his friends played host to the court, along with members of the Common House of Parliament and the mayor and aldermen of London.

Dudley also continued to compete as the week wore on, battling with swords on horseback against the Earl of Surrey, Henry Howard, a religious conservative and cousin to Katherine Howard, on the Monday and again fighting at barriers on the final day of the tournament on Wednesday. That day also saw one of the stars of the tournament, Richard Cromwell, in combat. The nephew of Thomas Cromwell, Richard had been knighted on the Sunday of the tournament and continued to demonstrate his skills all week, far outshining Cromwell's son and heir, Gregory. The final day of the tournament was no exception. The thirty-year-old faced off at barriers against an opponent a dozen or so years younger, Thomas Culpeper. Culpeper was no match for the older man, who decidedly overthrew him – Culpeper was better known for his ability to overpower women than men, whether through persuasion or force. While in the service of Dudley's stepfather, he had worked his way into the affections of Honour, Lady Lisle, and she had sent him bracelets with her colours for him to wear.[23] There were further demands. Another Lisle servant, while writing a letter to his mistress, had been forced to add to the bottom – evidently surrendering to persistent badgering – 'there is no remedy, Culpeper must have a hawk'.[24]

As the tournament drew to a close, the household at Durham House was dismantled. It was to be Anne's last major function as

Queen of England. At the end of June, Anne was moved to Richmond and by July, with Anne's desperate cooperation – she wrote to the king that 'the pretended Matrimony between us is void and of none effect, whereby I neither can nor will repute myself your grace's wife' – the marriage was declared invalid.[25] Henry had been forced to admit publicly his inability to consummate the union, though it was Cromwell who paid the price for this indignity.

On the same day that Henry married his fifth (or second, by his measure) wife, Katherine Howard, Cromwell was taken to Tower Hill and executed. Henry had already turned his back on his erstwhile minister, as he had on Edmund Dudley in the first year of his reign, and was preoccupied with his delightful new young wife.

The fall of Anne of Cleves and Thomas Cromwell was disastrous news to John and Jane. Cromwell had seen them through the deaths of Anne Boleyn and Jane Seymour, helping them to their highest positions yet under this most recent queen. Now he was gone, and the new queen's circle, dominated by Howards, were no friends to reformers like Seymour and Dudley. To make matters worse, John's stepfather Arthur Plantagenet had been arrested and thrown into the Tower of London just two weeks after the end of the May Day tournament. His traditionalist and conservative religious leanings had put him on the wrong side of Cromwell and, despite the Earl of Essex's demise, he remained imprisoned and under threat of execution. Cast out by the new Howard-led regime at court, who looked down on the Dudleys' humbler ancestry, John and Jane were without position or power. As the country suffered a summer of extreme drought and sickness, the Dudleys returned to their castle, unsure if their one opportunity for position at court had passed them by. Anne of Cleves had been praised for showing 'patience in affliction' and it was clear she would survive the end of her marriage.[26] Would the Dudleys?

*

In his hands John Dudley carried a piece of paper with the power to destroy the Queen of England. It was 7 November 1541, just over a year since the execution of Cromwell and the king's marriage to Katherine Howard.[27] Dudley had received the letter from the hand of Thomas Cranmer, Archbishop of Canterbury. Though he had clashed with Cromwell at times, Cranmer had defended his former friend and ally to the end. That could make him an important friend to John Dudley as well. The letter Cranmer handed John was a single double-sided page of Cranmer's small, meticulous script, addressed simply 'To the King'.

John had met with Cranmer at Hampton Court, the former home of Wolsey, which had become one of the king's preferred residences. To the south-west of London, the majestic red-bricked Hampton Court rose over the north bank of the Thames, amongst sprawling parks and woodland. Topped by intricate chimneys and decorated with roundels of ancient heroes and leaders, including the tyrant Emperor Nero, Hampton Court was a monument to the Renaissance might of the age. After taking the building from Wolsey, Henry had added significantly to the palace; work had still been ongoing in 1536 on Anne Boleyn's apartments when she was executed.[28] A year later Hampton Court had seen the birth of Henry's son and the death of his favourite queen.

Jane Seymour's was one of the souls that Henry VIII would have been expected to call to mind at Hampton Court a week earlier, on All Souls, a day of remembrance for those who had passed. There was reason for their son, his only heir, to have also been in his prayers. The king had recently received news that Edward was suffering from a recurring fever, which could be deadly.[29] Much, therefore, rested on the success of his current marriage to the young Katherine Howard – a child from that union might have been another entreaty sent heavenward by Henry as he sat in the Chapel Royal, listening to the All Souls service.

It was not uncommon for the king to read letters while listening to the liturgy in his private pew. It was separated from the congregation by floor-to-ceiling glass windows and from the queen and her ladies by a decorated timber wall, which meant that it provided a rare opportunity to catch the king alone.[30] This serene, sacred space, under a ceiling of golden stars and angels, also meant that it was unlikely the king would unleash his famous temper on a minister delivering unwelcome news. Cranmer wisely chose this moment to convey to the king the intelligence he'd been collecting for almost a month about Queen Katherine.

It had all begun with John Lassells, a servant of Cromwell's whom Cranmer occasionally still used as a messenger. Lassells was an ardent evangelical and Lutheran, and in September of that year had declared that men like Bishop Gardiner and Thomas Howard, Duke of Norfolk and the queen's great-uncle, were standing in the way of the evangelical cause in England.[31] Howard in particular had been no friend of Cromwell, and was still enjoying the victory that had come with the demise of the king's minister, as well as the gratitude of the king for his youthful new wife. With Cromwell dead and Katherine in power, Howard's power might seem unassailable. When Lassells visited his sister, Mary, in Sussex in autumn 1540, however, he unexpectedly found the means to bring them all down.

Mary had once served in the household of the Dowager Duchess of Norfolk at Chesworth House, Sussex, the same household in which Katherine Howard had grown up. Every noble household had the potential for gossip, but Chesworth House was fertile ground for scandal indeed. The Dowager Duchess was one of the richest women in the kingdom, with a large household of servants. Katherine's position in the household was little more than servant herself, and so she shared a room in the evenings with a range of women and girls in the Duchess's service and care, such as Mary.[32] When, however, John suggested his sister use this connection to gain a post from the queen, Mary was surprisingly opposed.

'I would not do so,' she had responded strongly, 'but I am very sorry for the queen.'[33]

'Why?' John had asked.

'For she is light both in living and in conditions,' she had said vaguely. John pressed his sister further, sensing a powerful secret. 'There is one Francis Dereham,' Mary went on, 'who was servant also in my Lady of Norfolk's house, who hath lied in bed with her.' There had been 'such puffing and blowing between them' that a maid had objected that Katherine surely 'knew not what matrimony meant'. And this was not all. 'One Mannox, sometime also servant to the said Duchess, knew a privy mark of Catherine's body'; as far as Lassells was concerned, there was only one way the servant could have discovered something like that.[34]

Lassells wasted no time in relaying this conversation to Cranmer. The archbishop, now in his early fifties, had already witnessed the downfalls of friends and patrons, not least Anne Boleyn and Thomas Cromwell. In each of these cases, Cranmer had made attempts to intervene with the king on their behalf. He had failed. Now he had information that, if proved correct, might bring death to a young queen and, along with her, the entire Howard faction and their conservative religious stance. This could pave the way to a reformist England, and the final end of the heathen superstitions he associated with the Catholic Church.

If Cranmer's 'intelligence' could not be substantiated, however, it would undoubtedly lead to his own destruction.

After some hand-wringing, Cranmer decided that this information needed to be delivered to the king himself. And so, on All Souls Day, Cranmer passed his missive to Henry.

The king, shocked and disbelieving, demanded further investigations. He could not, he said, 'believe it until the certainty was known'.[35] From Hampton Court went William FitzWilliam, Earl of Southampton, to speak to John Lassells.[36] Lassells declared boldly – and dramatically – that 'he would rather die in declaration of the truth than live with the concealment of the same.' Next the king sent Fitz-William to Sussex to interrogate Lassells' sister. When he arrived he told her husband that he was there for the hunt, but once he had Mary alone, pressed her on her testimony. She remained firm. At the same time, Sir Thomas Wriothesley, who had only the year before betrayed his former master Thomas Cromwell, was sent to find Francis Dereham and Henry Mannox.[37] Both men confessed under Wriothesley's interrogations. Mannox professed that he 'commonly used to feel the secret and other parts of her body' and Dereham told Wriothesley that he 'had known her carnally many times'.[38] Dereham even provided witnesses to corroborate his scandalous story.

On 6 November, these findings were reported to the king, who, by all accounts, wept bitterly. A cloud of anxiety and tension settled over Hampton Court, as nobles and clergy were swiftly summoned. Katherine was instructed that she must remain in her richly decorated apartments, where musicians were solemnly informed 'it is no more the time to dance.'³⁹ The king, as he was like to do, exited the situation entirely, riding to Whitehall and leaving his queen behind. It was Cranmer who led the delegation to the queen's apartments, finally informing her of the accusations that had been made against her, not only of unvirtuous living, but of – potentially – having contracted marriage to Francis Dereham, making her marriage to the king illegal and illegitimate. In front of many dignitaries, including her great-uncle the Duke of Norfolk, she was firm in her denial. Later that night, however, Cranmer returned to her apartments to find her in deep distress. The result of that meeting was contained in the letter held by Sir John Dudley.⁴⁰

Cranmer had found the queen, he wrote, in 'such lamentation and heaviness, as I never saw no creature'. According to her servants, she had been in this state since he had left her earlier that day. Although he'd been tasked by the king to inform her of the laws under which she was poised to suffer, he began instead by reiterating to her the king's mercy, for fear that the former might have 'driven her unto some dangerous ecstasy, and else into a very frenzy'. Hearing of the king's mercy, Cranmer reported that she threw up her hands and thanked the king, 'who had showed unto her more grace and mercy, than she herself thought meet to sue for or could have hoped of'. After that, Cranmer wrote, she sobbed quietly again, before 'she suddenly fell into a new rage, much worse than she was before.'

Presented with this new frenzy, Cranmer sought to discover its cause, asking her what 'new fantasy' had come into her head. Regaining her composure enough to speak, the young queen cried and said, 'Alas, my lord, that I am alive, that fear of death grieved me not so much before, as doth now the remembrance of the King's goodness.' The offer of the king's mercy, she told the archbishop, 'maketh mine offences so appear before mine eyes much more heinous than they did before', and she once again was lost to her paroxysm of mania.⁴¹

And so the middle-aged archbishop and the young queen spent the evening: she falling into sporadic fits of madness and he attempting to calm and interrogate her in equal measure. When at last he exited, Cranmer had little time to jot down the notes of what he'd gleaned, though it was enough, he said, to prove both a contract and 'carnal copulation following'. She herself claimed that it was all done through Dereham's 'forcement, and, in a manner, violence, rather than of her free consent and will'. As he handed Dudley the letter, he informed him of the details he did not have time to put down on paper, details Dudley was to relate to the king himself.

John Dudley, with this monumental letter in his possession, rode through the rear court of Hampton Court and over the bridged moat, under the gaze of Nero, travelling the fourteen miles from the palace south-west of London to where the king had secluded himself at Whitehall. John had been given a unique but dangerous opportunity in delivering the news from Cranmer. He would either be rewarded as an essential go-between, or the king would shoot the messenger – as it were – and exclude him on account of the private and embarrassing knowledge that John now possessed about his monarch.

The king received the news and consulted with his Privy Council, of which John was not a part.

When orders went out, John could heave a sigh of relief: he had avoided the king's rage. In fact, he was to be given an important and honoured task. It was the 'king's pleasure' that his daughter, the Lady Mary, 'be conveyed to my Lord Prince's house by Sir John Dudley', along with 'a convenient number of the queen's servants', as the queen's household was to be severely stripped down.[42] Dudley would be a part of the king's offensive against the queen, rather than caught in the cross-fire. It was a lucky escape.

Dudley was an appropriate choice for this commission. His family had continued a friendly relationship with the twenty-five-year-old former princess, despite holding different opinions in regard to religion. Small and slight, the Lady Mary appeared delicate at first glance, but her spare frame hid a deeper strength, which many members of the court knew well, as she had resisted her father's attempts to bring her to heel during the course of his second marriage. With piercing dark eyes and a deep voice, Mary had her father's commanding air. She was also beautiful, well-read, polylingual and deeply passionate.[43] The Lady Mary had remained staunchly dedicated to the pope since the break with Rome some years before. This had not stopped her cultivating positive relationships with more evangelical members of the king's court and indeed with her own half-siblings. She had particularly welcomed the birth of her young brother and lavished him with gifts. The Dudleys too benefitted from Mary's generosity, receiving a small gift of coin each time she stood as godmother to one of their children.[44] Sir John Dudley, son of a traitor and a reformer, and the Lady Mary, daughter to the King of England and a devout Catholic, might have seemed an odd pair, but Mary looked favourably on the Dudley family. Once Mary had been delivered to her younger brother's household, John returned to the court at Westminster, where the scandal continued to unfold and deepen.

'These things which be revealed – I dare say –' Dudley confessed to Thomas Manners, the Earl of Rutland, another former member of the household of Anne of Cleves, 'are far out of your expectation and mine.'[45] It was 26 November, the day before the first Sunday of Advent 1541, less than four weeks after Cranmer's delivery of the bad news to Henry on All Souls Day. John remained at the court, which would have little festive cheer this Christmas and remained torn by fear and suspicion. 'All that are the King's true servants and subjects,' he went on, 'are bound to thank God that these sudden miseries were so soon revealed, for the dangers that might have ensued to our sovereign lord our master's person.' Those who wished the king ill, he ended, 'short life, with due reward of their merits I pray our Lord send them.'[46]

There had been rumblings around the court that there was some greater abomination to be uncovered surrounding the queen's behaviour. When Dereham had been interrogated in early November, he had suggested that another man had replaced him in the queen's affections: the notorious Thomas Culpeper.[47] Katherine had been confronted with this accusation on 12 November while still at Hampton Court. She confessed to several secret nocturnal meetings with Culpeper, though placed the blame on her lady, Jane Boleyn, Lady Rochford, the widowed sister-in-law of Anne Boleyn, for coaxing the pair to speak. By the end of November, it was quite clear that the queen had at least had the opportunity to commit adultery with Culpeper on several occasions, and so it was assumed that she had indeed done so. This was treason; Katherine and Culpeper endangered the royal bloodline through their liaisons.

Dudley's prayer for a short life and due reward to those who threatened the person of the king was answered. On Saturday, 10 December, Dereham and Culpeper were publicly executed at Tyburn in London. Dereham, having already endured weeks of torture, suffered the full sentence for treason. He was hung by the neck until his body began to spasm for the lack of air, then he was cut down and mutilated while he was still alive; his genitals cut off and his intestines and bowels removed and burnt before him. Culpeper was only beheaded.

With this bloodletting hanging in the air, the court was ruthlessly searched for those who might have been involved in this affair and cover-up. Katherine's ladies were subjected to days of interrogations and the dowager duchess was forced to take to her bed to avoid questions.[48] The Howards, unsurprisingly, were especially under suspicion, which suited Cranmer, Dudley and the other evangelicals just fine. In the end, fourteen people were sent to the Tower for suspicion of involvement in the queen's treason, including several members of the Howard family and household, as well as the dowager duchess.[49] For the Dudleys, rather than missing an opportunity for promotion by being outside Queen Katherine's household, they effectively dodged a bullet, and could now step forward as the cloud of suspicion fell on leading members of the court.[50]

A new parliament began following a sombre Christmas, and John Dudley sat in the Commons as a knight of Staffordshire. Sir Thomas Audley, a man almost twenty years Dudley's senior, had been Lord Chancellor since Thomas More resigned the office less than a decade before in protest of the king's break with Rome. That was four queens ago. On 16 January Audley opened parliament before the king with an exaggerated speech outlining the current queen's various 'misdeeds'.[51] By the end of the month Katherine Howard had been declared guilty of high treason by both houses of parliament. Two weeks later, the queen having been moved to the Tower, Dudley and the other Members of the Common House gathered in their grand parliament robes to hear her sentence read out. Katherine was beheaded on 13 February. The next day, St Valentine's Day, Henry VIII held a grand feast for the ladies of the court, who passed the night in Whitehall. Unlike his rapid marriages on the execution of Anne Boleyn and the annulment of his marriage to Anne of Cleves, this time the king did not have an immediate alternative to hand. 'Besides,' the Spanish ambassador noted slyly, 'there are few, if any, ladies at Court now-a-days likely to aspire to the honour of becoming one of the King's wives.'[52]

*

All eyes were on John Dudley as he entered the King's Great Chamber at Whitehall on 12 March 1542. The Great Chamber was a series of rooms occupied by the king, which included his presence chamber and privy chamber, with a small closet between them.[53] Beyond this was the withdrawing chamber and the even more private rooms, including the king's bedchamber. The presence chamber was one of the oldest rooms in the palace, dating back to the days when the palace had been occupied by medieval bishops of York. It was, on this day, very clearly Henry VIII's; it was his cloth of estate that hung over the dais and throne, and his coats of arms carved into the ancient fireplace. Tapestries covered the walls. A door at the east end of the room led to the Queen's presence chamber and lodgings beyond. Whitehall had not originally had queen's apartments, which had made it a perfect get-away for Henry while seeking to distance himself from Catherine of Aragon. He had then converted Wolsey's apartments into lodgings for Anne Boleyn. As the court was currently without a queen, there would be no need to enter those rooms that day.

John Dudley made ready in the pages' chamber near the Great Chamber, putting on his surcoat and hood.[54] From there, he processed into the Chamber before king and court. On his right was his friend Sir Edward Seymour, now Earl of Hereford, wearing his robe of estate. On his left, in his parliament robes, was Sir John Russell, Baron Russell, a politician twenty years Dudley's senior and Lord High Admiral of the king's navy. John's mantle, the long, sleeveless cloak that demonstrated his new status, was carried into the chamber by Thomas West, Lord De La Warr, an even older member of the court, approaching seventy, whose brother-in-law had been Sir Edward Guildford, John's late guardian and father-in-law. De La Warr had also been a friend and ally to John Dudley's stepfather, Arthur

Plantagenet, Viscount Lisle. Lisle was the reason that Dudley was the centre of attention today.

Plantagenet had remained in the Tower, even after his political enemy Thomas Cromwell had been executed. With both Cromwell and the Howards on the out, however, Henry VIII had looked to rehabilitate his half-uncle. On 3 March Plantagenet was told that he would be released and restored. Unfortunately, the excitement of this release proved too much for the seventy-year-old bastard of Edward IV, and he died just two days later. John Dudley, by the right of his mother, was heir to the Viscountcy Plantagenet had held. On 12 March 1542 he received his birthright.

Coming before Henry VIII, the Garter King of Arms presented the letters patent to the king, who passed them on to his secretary, who read them to the whole assembly. As he announced John Dudley's new title, John bent so that the king could place the mantle over his shoulders, officially creating him Viscount Lisle. He received from the king his official letters patent, proving the legitimacy of his new status to the world and, bowing, thanked Henry for the great honour done to him. Then the whole company, to the sound of trumpets, paraded out of the room and to dinner, where Dudley was given pre-eminence, with all other lords and nobles at his pleasure.

John Dudley, son of the executed traitor Edmund Dudley, was now Viscount Lisle, a member of the nobility, ranking even above barons such as De La Warr and Russell. His wife was Lady Lisle, and his son, Henry, could expect to inherit the family title.

It was time to see to the eldest Dudley son's education; not in the schoolroom, but as John himself had been educated – in the theatre of politics and war.

8

Envious Nemesis

John Dudley, Viscount Lisle, at the head of five hundred men, finally arrived at the heavily fortified Alnwick Castle the last day of November 1542. Dudley had ridden the 300 miles from London, watching as the land around him became colder, wetter and less familiar. John was entering the Borderlands, a place of intense violence and disorder. The people there were thought to be 'wild and unruly', 'savage' and 'barbarous', compared to the civilized English.[1] Governing the area was difficult, even when all-out warfare didn't break out. Like a flint and steel, where England and Scotland met there were often sparks and, provided there was enough kindling, fire as well.

As he approached the imposing castle, thirty miles to the north the small village of Coldstream was being put to the flame.[2] Tensions between England and Scotland were once again at a height, caused in large part by the refusal on the part of the King of Scots, James V, to join Henry VIII in breaking with Rome. The night before Dudley's arrival at Alnwick, Edward Seymour, Earl of Hertford and Warden of the Scottish Marches, had sent a raid of a thousand men into Scotland, though more to harry, annoy and impoverish than to invade.[3] As the sun rose, the company descended on the little town. They set alight the fields and buildings, as well as the four-century-old abbey, dedicated to the Virgin Mary.[4] It was unclear whether Seymour knew that the former Prioress of Coldstream, Isabella Hoppringle, had been a spy for the Scots; if he had, this was sure retribution.[5] The men returned with 80 prisoners, 60 horses, 20 heads of wheat and 3,000 sheep in tow. Seymour claimed it was the most impressive loot ever acquired in the area, and it came pouring into Alnwick just as Dudley and his men settled into the castle.

The base of the English Middle March command, Alnwick Castle had withstood waves of ill-fated assaults for four centuries or more.* The town in which it sat was situated on the south bank of the River Aln, in a valley bounded by hills: natural fortifications that matched the artificial ones built up over the generations. The castle had been erected in piecemeal fashion, with the primary goal of strength and defence rather than any aesthetic aspirations. It was sprawling and asymmetrical, but it was sturdy. An expansive curtain wall, dotted with turreted semi-circle towers and small, square guerites, surrounded two baileys, which stretched out from the central keep like misshapen butterfly wings. For reasons no one could remember, the central keep was not square, as most were; in fact, it was not any recognizable shape. On one side of the keep there were the beginnings of an octagon, but the other side had refused to cooperate, and although one might make out four sections of inner wall, they were of varying lengths. At home, John Dudley was working on the perfect Renaissance symmetry of his own castle; Alnwick stood in stark contrast, but it had a different purpose. For that its hodgepodge nature was impressively well suited.

Alnwick Castle was the traditional home of the Percy family, the Earls of Northumberland. The Earls had for generations been loyal guardians of the North, though when Dudley arrived at Alnwick there was no Earl of Northumberland to greet him. Henry Percy, the last earl, had died without issue, sinking into depression and obscurity after being ensnared by the Anne Boleyn affair. His nephew, Thomas, would have been heir apparent, but his father had been executed in the aftermath of the 1536 religious rebellion against the Crown known as the Pilgrimage of Grace, and Thomas, just shy of his majority, remained

---

* The 'marches' were the protected strips of territory at England's frontiers with Scotland, Ireland and Wales. The boundary with Scotland was separated into three such 'marches' – East, Middle and West, though East and Middle were often taken together (with Alnwick sat between them). Soldiers of the marches were the king's subjects in the region; Ellis, *Tudor Frontiers*, 7.

stained by his father's treason. Therefore, the properties and titles had reverted to the king, and it became the residence of the Lord Warden of the Marches, now John Dudley.

The office of Lord Warden of the Marches had been established in the thirteenth century, to fulfil three central roles. First, to ensure the defence of the kingdom against northern encroachment; wardens such as Dudley were required to swear to uphold the truce between England and Scotland, 'without any deceit, fraud, or evil intention', but also to engage in warfare when required.[6] Second, the Lord Warden was responsible for the punishment of murderers, thieves, fugitives and felons in the Borderlands, frequently with death. Finally, the warden was required to govern the area in times of peace, according to the sparse 'Border Laws'.[7]

This, however, was not a time of peace. A week earlier, while he was somewhere between Newcastle and Berwick, Dudley had received news of a great battle between the English and Scots some seventy miles west, at Solway Moss, on the River Esk. James V, incensed by recent English incursions and raids, had assembled a massive force, more than 15,000, to invade England. The English were unprepared, most of their forces being in the East, at Berwick. Whereas Dudley was en route to take over as Lord Warden of the Marches in the East, there was currently no equivalent in the West. Only a few thousand English men met a force at least five times their size at Solway Moss. Nevertheless, they prevailed, losing only a handful, while the Scots were cut down and captured by the hundreds. While it was a great victory for the English, they had come very close to a devastating defeat.

After briefing John Dudley about the situation upon his arrival, the current Warden, Edward Seymour, was to return to London to attend on the king. Like Dudley, Seymour was in his early forties, and always appeared to be one step ahead of the new Viscount Lisle in promotion. There was no reason for them to be on equal footing, of course. Seymour was the uncle of the heir to the throne; Dudley was the son of a traitor. Despite Dudley's humble beginnings, he and Seymour had maintained a firm friendship through the years.[8] Now it was incumbent upon Seymour to show John the ropes and introduce him to life on the Marches – soggy as it was – before leaving him to his difficult post.

There was little need to sugar-coat the reality of the situation in the North; Seymour had struggled in his position, one he had not wanted to begin with.[9] There were not enough provisions for those already garrisoned at Alnwick, and Dudley's new scores of soldiers would only make things worse. Horses were dropping dead daily, Seymour reported, sick from the musty wet straw they were being fed. How the garrison, surrounded by snow and scorched land, would support another five hundred people was anyone's guess, and John Dudley's problem.

They would need to keep numbers in the garrison down until March, Seymour and Dudley decided, when the Scots were able to sow corn once again, or else they risked starvation.[10] They also had to take decisions on further instructions from the king. Henry VIII had ordered that Scots captured in the raids should be sent to be slaves in the king's galleys – a living death for those reprieved of execution. Henry VIII had built his first galleys in the 1510s, after a French galley had pushed its way through Sir Edward Howard's fleet that fateful day in 1512. For the most part, these were oared by free men, though clearly the creation of an organized slave force for the galleys had crossed Henry's mind.[11] Both Seymour and Dudley saw certain 'inconveniences' with the harsh plan set out by the king, and decided that they would not proceed as commanded until Seymour had relayed these issues to him directly. Until then, Dudley would keep the condemned men at Alnwick, a stock of Scottish prisoners – including great numbers captured at the Battle of Solway Moss – to feed alongside the fighting men, servants and spies.[12]

Day and night the March Watch kept an eye over the tempestuous border lands, while John went through account books and sifted intelligence. Though the Warden of the Marches was tasked with the defence of the Borderlands in battle, he also sat at the centre of a web of spies that stretched between the two realms. John had been at Alnwick only a week when a particular piece of intelligence brought by one of his spies captured his full attention. The Scottish Queen, Marie de Guise, had delivered a son, an heir to the childless King of Scots.[13]

If the report delivered to John were true, if James V had an heir – especially a male heir – it would change the face of European politics. James was the son of Henry VIII's sister, Margaret; his son would have a claim not only to the Scottish throne, but to the English one as well should anything happen to Henry's only male heir, Edward. This was a risk that Henry VII had taken in marrying his daughter to James IV of Scotland. The goal of his Treaty of Perpetual Peace of 1502 had been for England to eventually subsume the increasingly bothersome Scotland under a dual crown, not the other way around.

The 'perpetual peace' had, of course, been anything but long-lasting. The birth of a Scottish heir would only fuel the flames. Not only would the child carry royal English blood through his father, but through his mother would also be a Guise, one of the most influential families at the French court, who could muster support for Scotland in a war against England.[14] This would not be a difficult task: the 'Auld Alliance' between Scotland and France had lasted for centuries. Scotland was a back door for a French invasion of England, and France was a powerful supporter of Scottish attempts to advance into, and thus weaken, England. With a male French-Scots-English heir, Scotland would be perhaps the strongest position it had been for centuries, and thus a frightening threat to England. It was imperative that John Dudley verify these reports before sending them on to the king.

John questioned the prisoners that had been brought to Alnwick, to see if any could confirm his spy's report. One professed that on the Saturday before, 2 December, he had heard proclaimed that the Scottish queen had given birth to a son. The king himself, it was reported, had come very close to invading England, but had retreated to Linlithgow in order to see the arrival of his child.[15]

By the middle of December, the rumours about a Scottish heir were swirling around with as much celerity as the snow, and John struggled to sort truth from falsehood.[16] Some spies reported that it was a daughter, not a son, who had been born to the Scottish royal couple. Another suggested that the queen had delivered the child prematurely, and it would not live long, regardless of its sex.[17] John had also heard that the Scottish king had not rushed home to be with his wife and child, but instead to be with his mistress, whom he preferred before the queen.

John was keen to act. He had men at his disposal, and the Scots were weakened by the winter and poor victualling. An heir would rally the Scots by springtime. Now was the chance to finally take control of the Borderlands. He just had to convince the king. As the watch called midnight on 12 December, John wrote passionately to Henry: 'Oh!' he exclaimed in ink, 'what godly act should it be to your excellent Highness to bring such a sort of people to the knowledge of God's laws.' To conquer more lands would be divine work, 'considering how brutely and beastly the people now be governed'.[18] The moon above the castle was waxing as he wrote, casting little light on the surrounding lands and making the paths through the marches even more treacherous than usual. John feared that when it was next full, just before Christmas, there would be more Scottish raiding. They had to act now.

Five days later, on 17 December, he was finalizing his preparations with two of his commanders, poring over maps and musters.[19] Ten miles north of Coldstream was the small town of Duns. Dudley planned to send 2,500 men pulled from the Alnwick garrison and Northumberland pensioners to seize the town on 21 December. It would be a triumphant and decisive battle on the darkest day of the year; a victory not just for England, of course, but also for John himself.

His planning was interrupted by the arrival of Sir George Douglas, brother and heir to the Scottish Earl of Angus. Known for his deep knowledge and experience of politics, the fifty-year-old Douglas had been in exile in England since James V reached his majority in 1529, following a failed attempt on the part of the Douglases to control the young king, but had kept an effective network of spies in Scotland.[20] Dudley had called for Douglas to join their planning, and when he was told that the Scotsman came with news, might have assumed it was further clarification of the new heir; no one could seem to confirm anything to him as regards the sex or health of the child, or even its very existence.[21] Douglas, however, brought far more shocking news. The King of Scots, only thirty years old, had died. Stunned and disbelieving, by the mid-afternoon Dudley had abandoned his planning and penned a letter to the king relaying the news, sending it off with one of Douglas's servants.[22]

George Douglas was sent back to Berwick, from whence he'd come, to confirm the news with his source. The two-hour journey was more perilous in the dark, and he arrived at eight o'clock. He had not even removed his wet boots when he called his spy, Simon of Penanghawe, a servant of James V's, to give him the full account, which he wrote for Dudley at two o'clock that morning. The king had sickened, Douglas wrote, on 6 December, two days before his child had been born, and died on 14 December. 'All this time,' Douglas informed Dudley, 'he did rage and cry out, and spoke few wise words, and so,' he added, with no shortage of dry Scottish wit, 'departed much according to the life that he lived.'[23] His daughter, for indeed it was a daughter, was now Queen of Scots at only six days old. A regency council had been established, which, Douglas told John, was keen for war. After signing off, Douglas added to the end of the letter: 'The Princess of Scotland, as I am informed, is a very weak child.'[24]

Surely the sickly newborn would not hold the throne of Scotland for long, albeit the competitors were all simpletons and fools, best John could tell. The strongest, not the smartest, would win out. Any plans for a conquest of Scottish lands must be stalled. As John wrote to the Privy Council with resignation, it would not do well for the King of England to make war against a dead body, a grieving widow, or an infant girl.[25] Though Dudley had at first reported her named 'Elizabeth', the infant queen had in fact been named Mary, presumably for her mother. The Scottish lords were in a mess about what to do with their squalling sovereign.[26] Although they were used to young monarchs – an adult monarch had not come to the Scottish throne since 1371 – six days old was a new extreme. And as in England, which had seen the tenuous rule of Matilda in the twelfth century, in Scotland there was only one example of a female ruler – Margaret of Norway in the thirteenth century – and, like the Empress Matilda, there was debate over whether she had indeed been queen. Disputes over who had control of the new royal infant began immediately. Her accession to the throne posed a problem for England, but it threatened to tear apart Scotland as well.

John Dudley had only been at Alnwick a month, and it had seen some of the most shocking news to come out of the Borderlands in decades. It made the English court look calm and stable by comparison. Well, almost.

*

Henry VIII's sixth bride had been named after his first. Catherine, born Catherine Parr to Sir Thomas Parr and his wife Maud in 1512, was better known as the Lady Latimer. She was the widow of John Neville, third Baron Latimer, a member of an old and powerful family. He had died in March 1543, only four months before her new marriage. As Lady Latimer she had entered the household of the Lady Mary and from there been a regular presence at court. Catherine was fiercely intelligent, having received a wide-ranging education after her father's death. She joined a circle of courtly ladies of evangelical leanings, which included Jane Dudley, now Lady Lisle.

Henry VIII had broken with the Roman Catholic Church, and its pope, in order to annul his marriage to his first wife, Catherine of Aragon, and marry his second, Anne Boleyn. Although the king was still opposed to Lutheranism, or indeed any heterodox views departing from the teachings of the Catholic Church, by rejecting the authority of the pope within his kingdom, Henry had opened the door to reformist beliefs and those who held them, men such as Cromwell and Cranmer. There were women, too, who held the value of God's word over the authority of the Church, and studied it accordingly, rejecting the need for mediation from priest or bishop. The king's new wife was one such woman; Jane Dudley was another.

The two women had become close, and it would be no surprise if Catherine had confided in Jane when she, with her husband dying, turned her affections to the younger brother of Edward Seymour, Thomas. From Jane Dudley's point of view this was a perfect match: friends of the family united in marriage. It was not to be, however, and it was almost certainly with mixed feelings that Jane's friend instead became the sixth queen England had seen in just over a decade. As Queen of England, Catherine could accomplish much more by way of God's plan than as the wife of Thomas Seymour, and she might be able to lend a hand to the Dudley family as well.

John had returned to London with the spring, escaping the lawless violence and bitter cold of the North, undoubtedly to the great relief of his family. On 8 January he had been named Lord Admiral of the Navy, once again a step behind Edward Seymour, who had recently relinquished the post and was now Lord Chamberlain. As Lord Admiral, John was sworn into the Privy Council and made a Knight of the Garter. He was unquestionably a member of the king's inner circle now and one of the great officers of state.[27] Jane's fortunes rose with his. When John wrote in June to William Parr, Marquess of Northampton, that the Lady Latimer was at court in the company of Henry's daughters, the Lady Mary and Lady Elizabeth, it was because Jane was also associated with such company.

Jane joined these other women for Catherine's intimate wedding to the king in the Queen's Closet at Hampton Court on 12 July 1543. At thirty-one, Catherine was only a few years younger than Jane. She was of a middling height and slight build, with red hair and grey eyes, which she liked to pair with crimson gowns and fine jewellery.[28] She was a stark contrast to the man she was about to marry. At fifty-two, the king was not well. Always tall and commanding, the king now weighed almost three hundred pounds, his waist and chest measuring well above fifty inches each. It was said that three large men could easily fit inside his doublet.[29] He had a wound in his leg which would not heal and which resulted in bouts of fever and a limp. The infected leg excreted pus and unpleasant odours and Henry's eating habits caused stomach upset and persistent constipation.[30] It was no small sacrifice Catherine was making in fulfilling God's will.

Jane was amongst a company of fewer than twenty gathered to witness the marriage. Among the men was Edward Seymour, though his younger brother was not present, perhaps for good reason. In the company of the seven ladies was Edward's wife, Anne Seymour, mother to five children not that much younger than Jane's own. The Lady Mary was also in attendance, along with her half-sister Elizabeth. Nearing the age of ten, Elizabeth had her mother's dark eyes and her father's fiery hair. She was already extremely well educated, learning Latin, Italian and French, and seemed drawn to the cultivated intelligence of her latest stepmother.

The sixty-year-old Bishop of Winchester, Stephen Gardiner, performed the ceremony. Gardiner was a religious conservative and stood in the way of many of the reforms that the evangelicals such as the Seymours, Dudleys and the Lady Latimer – about to become queen – would have liked to see in England. The break with Rome had created a fissure within the court itself. Conservatives such as Gardiner and his ally Thomas Howard, Duke of Norfolk, refused to let the king's rejection of the pope be a slippery slope into Lutheranism, stripping the church – albeit the Church of England rather than the Roman Catholic Church – of trappings as well as spiritual power. If Gardiner knew of the new queen's leanings, he performed his duties admirably all the same.

'If anyone knows of any impediment to the marriage,' Gardiner intoned, 'he should declare it.' There was silence – previously existing 'impediments' had put an end to all but one of the king's last five marriages – followed by relieved applause. As he went through the questions of the wedding ceremony, the corpulent king responded with an assenting 'yea' to each. Catherine too gave her consent, though perhaps with less obvious enthusiasm.

Henry then took Catherine's right hand and, repeating after Gardiner (though surely the king knew the words by now), 'I, Henry, take thee, Catherine, to my wedded wife, to have and to hold from this day forward, for better for worse, for richer for poorer, in sickness and in health, till death us depart, and thereto I plight thee my troth.'

He released her hand, and Catherine took his up again, repeating the words spoken by Gardiner, 'I, Catherine, take thee Henry to my wedded husband, to have and to hold from this day forward, for better for worse, for richer for poorer, in sickness and in health, to be bonny and buxom in bed and at board, till death us depart, and thereto I plight unto thee my troth.' As John had with Jane all those years ago, the king slipped the wedding ring on to the fourth finger of Catherine's left hand. Henry had a new wife, and England a new queen. And Jane Dudley could count her as one of her friends. She and her family could do very well from this new marriage. That was as long as they all managed to survive it.

*

The sound of guns that had pounded day in and day out, from morning until mid-afternoon, across the wounds and lesions the king's army had made in the soil of France, was nothing compared to the great noise that cracked through the early evening air on 12 September 1544.[31] Turning at the cacophony, the tired men watched stones and dust shooting into the sky. Large sections of what was once castle wall, weighing as much as sixty pounds, fell for a hundred metres around, crushing those unfortunate enough to be in their path. Smaller debris was just as deadly, shooting from the sky with as much force and discrimination as a rain of arrows. When the dust settled and the cries from the injured men faded to the background, the damage was evident. There was a sizeable breach in the walls of the city, large enough to fit an army through. An army with John Dudley, Viscount Lisle, at its head.

Henry VIII's army had been beating against the walls of Boulogne since the height of summer, caught up in the pan-European war initiated by Frances I and Charles V. Part of a much longer conflict which had been raging in Europe for almost fifty years, for some two decades it had largely centred around a personal animosity between Henry VIII's French and Spanish counterparts. Renewing his allegiance with the emperor, Henry had agreed to an invasion of France the previous December, having been reliably informed that the raids on Scotland – led by Edward Seymour and John Dudley – had weakened the country sufficiently to avoid a Scottish invasion while the English were in France (as had occurred thirty years before). John and Edward Seymour had burned their way around Edinburgh through the spring of 1544, doing all they could to ensure that the enemy should not recover.[32] This had impressed the king no end, and as he made plans to invade France once again, he wanted his fierce Lord Admiral at the front of it all.[33]

The English had been able to sail their ships right into Boulogne's port, situated on the edge of the Channel and the mouth of the River Liane. Men, weapons, armour and animals poured out into the French countryside around it. Two camps were made, one to the north of the city, the other to the east. From there they faced the eastern wall of the city, bordered on the south corner by the Château de Boulogne and just to the north of it, within the city walls, the large church of Notre-Dame, whose spire dominated the skyline. To the south of the city was

the 'Basse Ville' and the River Liane. To the east was more open countryside. The large medieval lighthouse tower to the north of the town,
known as 'Tour d'Ordre' or colloquially as 'the Old Man' had fallen
to the English already. The thick walls of the 'Haute Ville', with their
massive towers, had held strong, however.

The city had withstood English siege before – in 1492, when Henry
VII had brought a force of 12,000 against Boulogne. Peace was concluded before either side had yielded. Henry VIII's force was three
times that of his father's; the largest expedition ever led by an English
monarch. The approximately 36,000 troops were divided into three
armies: one led by the Duke of Norfolk, laying siege to Montreuil, a
small town twenty miles to the south of Boulogne; one led by the
Duke of Suffolk, assaulting Boulogne; and one led by the king himself,
which had combined with Suffolk's army at Boulogne at the end of
July.[34] Boulogne's position on the coast made it not only accessible to
the English invaders, but of strategic importance. Boulogne was a port
city, a channel for material in and out of northern France, and was
also the centre of a rich agricultural region. If Henry VIII could capture Boulogne, it would weaken the French, yes, but it would also give
Henry a valuable foothold in France, like Calais, until it might serve
his purpose to use it as a bargaining chip in the constantly shifting
game of European power politics.

Dudley had arrived in the camps around Boulogne in the middle of
July, upon which reports of the 'hot work' the men had had to endure
in order to approach the city were relayed to him.[35] Riding out beside
Charles Brandon, Duke of Suffolk, he visited the north wall, near the
lower city. Conferring, they agreed that ordinance placed there would
greatly 'annoy' the town and beat down the barrier. Brandon's strategy, as John observed, was to besiege the town from three angles,
forcing the French away from their gates and safe havens. John had
been particularly struck by Brandon's willingness to put himself in the
line of fire to lead and inspire his men. On one after-supper walk, the
two knights toured the trenches, including one in which three men
had been shot down not long before. Nearby shots of artillery caused
so little reaction in the battle-hardened duke that the other men took
strength and courage from his example, John noted. Brandon had

been his commander in France all those years ago and had knighted him on the field. Now they discussed battle tactics and exchanged advice as near-equals: the commander of the King's Forces and the Lord Admiral of his Navy. The Duke of Suffolk would have reason to remark on Dudley's impressive rise in the time since they had last been in France together; John had not achieved the status of duke, like Brandon, but then again Brandon had not had to recover from the stain of treason. Steadfastly executing the king's will had ensured that they had survived the tumults of the two decades, when so many others had fallen.

After his meetings with Suffolk, John had ridden out from Boulogne to meet the king at Calais, returning with him at the end of July. Six weeks later, however, little progress had been made. The walls held strong as raids continued in the areas surrounding the town, bringing in cattle and prisoners to strengthen the English and starve out the French. The roads were dotted with beleaguered and starving French families who had been forced to leave their homes in the wake of the English stranglehold. They stopped friendly-looking soldiers, begging for a piece of bread to keep their dying children alive, but refused money, for fear it would be beaten out of them later.

Beneath this air of stagnation and starvation, however, the English had been hard at work. By 8 September, they had struck on a new strategy. The sappers – soldiers expert in building and repairing the fortifications of war – were sent out to dig under the foundations of the castle on the eastern corner of the town. By the fourth day the holes the sappers had made were filled with gun powder. John Dudley prepared his light guns and moved them towards the castle wall. At six o'clock the order was given and the powder was set alight, blasting a hole in the side of the castle wall and killing and maiming many of the men who stood nearby. The assault was vicious, artillery pounding the French who tried to defend the breach and repulse the invaders. There was loss on both sides, but the French were falling faster than the English. A week later the siege was over; the English had taken Boulogne.

The eastern wall of the city was little more than rubble, as were the towers which had stood at its two ends. Both the castle and church had lost most of their roofs, open to the rain that now fell in torrents, their bare wood beams sticking into the sky like the naked ribs of a stripped corpse. The proud church steeple was gone, battered down by English artillery. Many inhabitants left the city, carrying belongings and children in their arms and on their backs, fainting in the wet and the mud along the roads. They rested in the scorched church of a nearby village, abandoned after the raid that had burned it. The weather had decidedly turned, and the cold, wet conditions after weeks of siege proved fatal to many of the former inhabitants of Boulogne.

With the city emptied of any who might challenge the regime, and the new council – John Dudley included – firmly established, Henry VIII entered Boulogne as its king. There was feasting and celebration, despite the tempestuous weather. The king rode forward as a triumphant conqueror, the sword borne before him by Henry Grey, the Marquess of Dorset and husband to Henry VIII's niece and Charles Brandon's daughter, Frances. Trumpeters sounded from the walls where a week before soldiers had fought and fallen. The Duke of Suffolk met the king as he entered, handing him the keys to the town. Not long after, Sir John Dudley, High Admiral of the Seas, was publicly declared to be the king's deputy in Boulogne. Like many gifts from the king, a position such as this was a poisoned chalice – as John knew from his uncle's experience as Lord Deputy of Calais – bringing honour but also distance from the court and more than a few challenges. Henry FitzAlan, Earl of Arundel, who had taken over from Arthur Plantagenet as Lord Deputy of Calais, was among the Duke of Suffolk's officers at Boulogne and could easily – with characteristic melancholia – report to John the various struggles of such a post, having just escaped them, along with a bout of smallpox. John himself had only just returned from an under-supported outpost on the border of enemy territory; there would be little reason for him to rejoice at an even more remote and difficult assignment.

There were, however, other reasons to celebrate. Before the king left, there was one more matter to attend to. Several young men had sufficiently proven their worth (and their connections) to be knighted. They would receive their knighthood from the king's own hand. Amongst them was John Dudley's eldest son, Henry.

'Our God is a lover of peace,' Henry's boyhood tutor Nicholas Bourbon had taught; 'let us then cultivate peace, we who follow Him.'[36] These were the ways to achieve true nobility, not the nobility of long blood lines or patents handed out by the king: 'Noble is he, and of high lineage,' Bourbon instructed, 'whose name is written in heaven.'[37] This was all well and good to be preached by a timid scholar, but Henry Dudley's family history had taught him very different lessons. He could compare his scholarly grandfather's dire fate with the brilliant ascendance of his father, built on the foundations of the battlefield. John Dudley's reputation was going from strength to strength, and there was no reason for Henry not to admire and seek to emulate his path. Maps of John's campaigns were prominently displayed in the family home, and the year before John had written to the king, 'I mean nothing less than the sparing of my pore body in anything wherein I may do his majesty service to his honour and pleasure.'[38] Nicholas Bourbon may have taught Henry pacifism, but his father's example taught him to offer all in the service of the king, and to reap the rewards. From almost nothing – less than nothing – his father was now Viscount Lisle, Lord Admiral of the King's Navy and one of the king's closest confidants.

Henry Dudley, at nineteen, had joined his father on the battlefields of France, just as John had joined his guardian, Sir Edward Guildford, when he was a young man. John had returned home with a knighthood, the first step in his increasingly illustrious career. Henry would do the same. Just shy of his twentieth birthday, Henry Dudley was lauded as a shining example of youth: a 'splendid jewel', a 'shining morning star', 'Castor to be seen upon a Spanish horse'. He was attractive, with 'an outstandingly noble body', as well as possessing 'a keen intelligence' and, by the way, 'also modest'.[39]

This attractive Dudley youth, along with the other young men who had proven their worth and connections, processed to the king's pavilion behind the heralds, carrying their pennons, painted with the men's arms.[40] When they reached the king's pavilion, the heralds introduced the men as 'valiant in the field' and thus 'deserving to be advanced to the degree of Knight Banneret' – similar to the words that had been spoken over John Dudley all those years ago. Then the king performed the ceremony, inviting them to be 'true knights'.[41] In Henry's company were the lords of Fitzwalter, Nevell and Braye, as well as the eldest son of a Lincolnshire knight, Francis Askew. Charles Brandon's own illegitimate son was also knighted, as were the Lords John and Edward Grey, younger brothers of Brandon's son-in-law, Henry Grey. Both Greys were also Henry Dudley's kinsmen, as their grandfather was the cousin of Henry's grandmother, Elizabeth. Another young man with Dudley connections was also knighted, Thomas Cawarden, whose father had done business with Elizabeth Dudley after Edmund's death. It appears this had not been forgotten, as another Cawarden had married one of Elizabeth's daughters by Arthur Plantagenet.

There were several other Dudley kinsmen in attendance on the king in Boulogne, able to share in Henry Dudley's triumph. This included John's younger brother Andrew, who had recently risen through the Exchequer and joined the king's company in France. Also present was Edward Clinton, the son-in-law of John's half-sister, Elizabeth. Elizabeth, the daughter of Edmund Dudley and Anne Windsor, had married Lord Stourton, as Edmund had arranged, and together they had had nine children. The marriage, however, was not a happy one. Stourton had left Elizabeth and kept a household with his mistress, Agnes Rice, a niece of Anne Boleyn.

Despite family turmoil, Henry's shining moment was one to be shared amongst the entire, extended Dudley family. He would be the first Dudley son to benefit from his father's advancement and seek fame and glory of his own. With a number of brothers and sisters, and parents in the inner circles of power, Henry's was a powerful generation of the house, ready to cement the Dudley name in history.

*

The ancients had worshipped a goddess of divine retribution, called Nemesis. She was familiar to scholars such as Nicholas Bourbon, Henry Dudley's childhood tutor, as the goddess of 'taking vengeance on such as are proud and disdainful in time of their prosperity'.[42] In books, woodcuts and tapestries, she was usually figured as a naked winged woman, holding a rich cup to reward the deserving and a bridle to punish the hubristic. She was often associated with Fortune, whose wheel ensured that those who rose high would also come crashing down.

Henry Dudley was an ideal target for a jealous goddess such as Nemesis, despite all the talk of his modesty. In the prime of his youth, and with opportunity and favour piled before him, Henry – Sir Henry – was certainly high on fortune's wheel.

Shortly after Henry VIII had handed over the keys and governance of Boulogne to John Dudley and sailed back to England, his Dudley namesake fell ill. It was a decidedly inglorious illness, as Henry's guts cramped and stabbed, and he voided his bowels with frequency and pain. Such illness was a reality in every military camp; agonizing and humiliating disease was waiting for many who survived the field, and it was far more deadly than any battle. It struck indiscriminately, felling young and old, injured and strong, common and knighted. There was no grandeur in this fate: a painful death of sweat, blood and shit.

Those like Henry who fell ill to the bloody flux were usually given little by way of remedy. The bodily evacuation associated with the flux could be a way of nature taking its course, clearing the body of harmful humours.[43] As the attractive young knight clutched his belly in pain and expelled blood, mucus and excrement day and night, those attending to him could do little but hope his condition would improve. When at last, however, the expulsion became truly violent, taking the patient's life-force with it, remedies might be tried to stem the flow, anything from a marmalade and wine dinner to an opium and honey-soaked cloth to the penis.[44] If none of these worked, the patient died in agony, often having expelled not only their bodily fluids, but at times pieces of their own bowels. It was a death that seemed to mock all the talk of the glories of battle, chivalry and ambition. It was a perfect tool for laughing Nemesis, who exacted her revenge on the eldest Dudley son, as his father watched him slowly, painfully and ingloriously die.

Such a fate awaited many of those in Boulogne and its surrounding areas following the English invasion. Piles of corpses, massive rainshowers and crowds of exhausted soldiers created conditions perfect for the spread of dysentery, alongside other illnesses. The plague erupted in Boulogne with such force that the city became known as a lifeless tomb, and soldiers feared to enter it.[45] There was talk that well over 50,000 had been killed as a result of famine, plague and poverty in the area. Villages of hundreds were reduced to handfuls of five and ten people, sheltering in hollowed-out churches or makeshift huts. From a prosperous and lively area, dotted with villages, the countryside around Boulogne began to resemble a desert, devoid of life, but full of misery.

Henry Dudley's stinking corpse would need to be bathed and prepared for burial, a funeral which took place in Boulogne. His mother and siblings would not get the opportunity to say their goodbyes to the eldest Dudley child, and they would be forced to pray for his soul from afar.

Henry's father, perhaps masking grief, threw himself immediately into his work. Boulogne was a mess: under-supplied, flooded and constantly under threat. Keeping it was harder work than winning it, and John was given little support in doing so, though supplies provided by Thomas Seymour by the end of November helped.[46] John was concerned that he would lose his naval position while Captain of Boulogne. So far from the court, it was difficult to exert the personal influence required to advance or defend oneself, as John knew his stepfather had experienced in Calais, to his downfall.[47] It can only have been with great relief that he arrived home in London for Christmas 1544, though he did so without his eldest son.

John would not need to worry much longer about Boulogne, as there was a more pressing threat to deal with: the invasion of England. The European war had not ended with the fall of Boulogne, far from it, but now England was the primary focus of the French king's bellicosity. Charles V, short on funds, had made peace with France while Henry was celebrating his victory in Boulogne, leaving the English alone and vulnerable. King Francis I was determined to invade England as France had been invaded, which would mean a significant naval force. By January, the French king was writing of his plan to other European leaders, suggesting that England's forces had been depleted by years of warfare. He assembled a mighty armada near Le Havre, directly across the Channel from Portsmouth, the home of Henry's navy. The French had gathered hundreds of ships, including twenty-five galleys, four times the number that had devastated the

English forces in 1512. Dudley went to work attacking the armada while it was still in port, but had little luck engaging the galleys directly or with the fire-ships he sent across the Channel. He gathered his forces at Portsmouth, where on 15 July the king and his council joined him.[48]

John Dudley was no veteran soldier or sailor, but over the previous few years, first in the North and then in France, he had learned quickly and developed a reputation which had impressed the king. His old ally, Edward Seymour, had recommended John's abilities to the king in the months before the French campaign, 'as one that hath served you hardly, wisely, diligently, painfully and as obediently as any that I have seen'.[49] As Lord Admiral, John seemed to have found an office that kept him close to the court, in a position of power and favour, but which also suited him well. Like his guardian and father-in-law, from whom he had learned, John was a firebrand, raiding and razing as the king needed. He also had enough administrative ability to organize the complex affairs of the king's navy, in desperate need of someone with talent and passion, and not just noble blood.

It quickly became clear to John and the rest of the Council that the French force would cross the Channel, though their plans to land precisely where the king and his forces lay in an attempt to embarrass him demonstrated some combination of bravery and folly. They set sail on 12 July, led by the experienced French Admiral Claude d'Annebault, and arrived at the Sussex coast six days later, attacking the small fishing town of Brighton.[50] From there, they advanced towards Portsmouth, where Dudley's vastly outnumbered fleet of eighty ships hastened a retreat into the harbour.

The two sides eyed each other warily across the waters of the Solent. The English boasted two large flagships, the *Mary Rose* and the *Henri Grâce à Dieu*. The *Mary Rose* was the smaller of the two, commissioned at the start of Henry's reign and on the water during the first conflict with the French three decades before. Originally a 400-ton ship, it was now some 700 tons, and stretched over 130 feet from stem to stern, though at only 39 feet across, it was a longer and thinner ship than most on the continent.[51] The *Henri Grâce à Dieu*, or *Great Harry*, was much larger at 1,000 tons and 165 feet long.[52] The

Mary Rose was the cutting-edge warship, the *Henry Grâce à Dieu* the impressive diplomatic vessel. It was on the *Great Harry* that Dudley and the king dined on 18 July, eating from golden plates emblazoned with the Lisle coat of arms as they discussed tactics. The alarm was sounded during their conference, and the king retreated onshore, safe from the naval battle that would fill the waters with smoke, fire and blood.[53] Before he did, he awarded Sir George Carew with the vice-admiralty. Carew, of an age with John, had served under him some eight years before, when John had been vice-admiral and Carew just a newly made knight. Sharing religious sympathies, the two men had worked together since the spring, preparing England against the threatened invasion. Along with his new position, Carew was also given the command of the *Mary Rose*. In the forthcoming battle, it was decided that Dudley would be on the *Henri Grâce à Dieu*, Carew would be on the *Mary Rose*.

After some cautious back-and-forth between the two sides, in which Dudley demonstrated his restraint in response to the French baiting, the battle commenced in earnest on 19 July.[54] The French gathered in three lines of thirty-six ships each, with their magnificent galleys ahead to pull the English into battle. The morning wind favoured the French, allowing them to advance on the motionless English ships in harbour. Shot fired at the trapped English ships, but still Dudley waited, holding for a better wind despite the persistent drum of cannon fire.

His patience was rewarded. As morning shifted into afternoon, a new wind began to shake and fill the English sails. The ships navigated out at last to meet their assailants. This sudden advance of the English ships caught the French unprepared and they struggled to turn their ships about to avoid complete devastation under the bombardment of the English guns. The English ships pursued the French, with the *Great Harry* and the *Mary Rose* leading the way.

They had travelled only two miles when, suddenly, there were shouts from the *Mary Rose*. It was taking on water, slowly capsizing in the midst of the battle. The seas rushed through its gunports, dragging the ship to one side. As it tilted, the heavy munitions and men it was carrying began to tumble downwards, increasing the pull into the sea. The crew was in a panic, desperately trying to escape from the lower levels of the ship by any means necessary. Most were trapped. The net which had been spread across the upper decks to prevent the French from boarding and taking the ship now prevented its men from escaping. Those already above the netting were dressed for battle, wearing thick leather and chainmail. Their protections too would be their doom. Men who could both manage to jump from the ship and avoid immediately sinking had little to grab hold of to keep themselves above the water. The *Mary Rose* had not broken apart, leaving shards of itself as flotsam bobbing above the waves; the only thing to hold on to was the ship itself, as it continued its journey into the depths. In the end, only about thirty men managed to make it to another ship. Another four hundred or so vanished beneath the waters, including the vice-admiral, George Carew.

Those watching were forced to turn their eyes away as the *Mary Rose* and its crew sank beneath the waves. The battle was not yet over; it had not even truly begun. The *Great Harry* was still on the water with John Dudley in command. The two sides resumed their cautious stand-off. The French, however, were doing more than just facing down the English. Their ships were also preoccupied with landing men on the Isle of Wight, and ferrying reinforcements and supplies to them. The French had invaded.

Terrifying as that prospect was, however, it was also an advantage, as Dudley came to realize. As he mulled over the stalemate upon the *Henri Grâce à Dieu* on the evening of 20 July, the day after the sinking of the *Mary Rose*, a small gale rose up.[55] Suddenly, he was struck by a thought. He gathered the shipmasters on the *Great Harry* to him and asked, should the same gale come again another night and remain stable, would there be a suitable opportunity to attack the French? The masters agreed; the French would be fools to remain in anchor under an English attack, supported by such a wind. Dudley pressed them further; if they did raise anchor and turn to face the English attack, was there any way they could hold their position on the Isle of Wight? Not possible, the masters responded; the attack and the wind would force them into the high seas, and into a dangerous patch of rock and shoal to the east known as the Owers. This was it. John now turned to Henry Howard, Earl of Surrey, the king's Lieutenant General and emissary to the Lord Admiral on the *Henri Grâce à Dieu*. Dudley communicated his plan to him, telling him that if the Frenchmen landed, 'They may happen find such a blast that they shall never see their own country again.' Surrey reminded him that he could do no such thing without the king's approval and so, as he had in the North, John was forced to rein in his enthusiasm for conquest and ask the king's permission first. For his own part, he wrote passionately to the king, he would 'little pass to shed the best blood in my body to remove the Frenchmen out of your sight'. Dudley was ready to risk all to defeat the French; he just needed the king to let him.

As in the North, no such approval came. The end of the stand-off was anti-climactic. The French were repelled on land, by both troops and villagers. On 22 July they set sail again, with Dudley and his fleet following close behind, to ensure they truly exited English waters. The French ships returned across the Channel and landed at Boulogne, where they joined the siege to retake the city. If John had had his way, the French troops would have been destroyed in England, leaving none available to reinforce the siege of the city he had once commanded, and his son had died taking.

Rather than sinking the French, John Dudley turned his attention to raising the *Mary Rose*. The tops of its masts were still visible on the water, the ship having sunk only thirty-six feet.[56] There was still almost £2,000 worth of ordinance on the ship to be reclaimed.[57] Charles Brandon, Duke of Suffolk joined him in this enterprise, and the two men set about to pull the ship back up from the depths. They employed two Venetians named Petre de Andreas and Symonde de Maryne with the task. The plan was straightforward enough. Two large ships, the *Samson* and the *Jesus of Lubeck*, each 700 tons, would sail up alongside the wreck of the *Mary Rose*. Having set the *Mary Rose* upright by pulling on her masts, cables would then be run underneath her sunken hull and between the two ships at low tide. When the tide rose, the cables would cause the *Mary Rose* to rise along with the two ships, which would then pull it to shallower waters. That was step one. It would require, among other things, some ninety men along with the two warships. They began on 3 August and two days later had the *Mary Rose*'s sails and yards ashore, and cables secured to her masts to begin the process of righting it. A few days after that, however, their efforts had broken the foremast. The Italians reported this to Dudley, asking for another six days to try instead to pull the great ship to shallower waters and then to right her. This new plan did not work either, and eventually divers were sent down to at least try to retrieve some of the ordinance. This was yet more disappointment for John.

And there were other issues to attend to. By the time the first attempts were made to raise the *Mary Rose*, a severe sickness was making its way through the sailors on almost every ship: dysentery and a strange swelling of their heads, faces and legs. It was a swelteringly hot summer, and the sailors were forced to remain on board the ships at port, eating increasingly questionable food. John, too, felt trapped, imprisoned at Portsmouth, unable to chase the French and feeling he was doing little good for anyone.

It didn't get better as the summer wore on. At the end of August the man who had made John Dudley a knight, led him into battle and, in the end, become something of a friend, Charles Brandon, Duke of Suffolk, died. He was sixty-one, some two decades older than John, and had achieved wonders over the course of his life, thanks in large part to his close friendship with the king. He left several children behind him, including a male heir, named for the king, and – more importantly – two nieces to the king through his marriage to Henry's sister: Frances and Eleanor.

Each death of an ally brought danger, but also the potential for gain. With Brandon gone, there was the opportunity to take his place as a favourite of the king, and observers certainly thought John Dudley might do so. John had sharpened his skills as a warrior, commander and conqueror, though his martial reputation had cost him his eldest son. John could, of course, retire from the court to Dudley Castle, focus on building his legacy of stone and live out the rest of his life as a country gentleman, ensuring his new heir and namesake would live in peace and plenty, inheriting the modest noble title John had inherited from his mother. Ambition, however, was in the Dudley blood.

9

Flesh, blood and bone

In 1546, at the age of only fifteen, Ambrose became the first of Jane and John Dudley's sons to be married.[1] As his father had married the daughter of his guardian, so too Ambrose married one of John's wards, Anne Whorwood. She had joined the Dudley household after the death of her father, William Whorwood, the king's Attorney General, a year before.[2] Ambrose's marriage to Anne would ensure her inheritance remained within the Dudley fold as she came of age. As they were both young, there was little expectation that they immediately fulfil their roles as husband and wife. There was not yet any pressure to produce a new generation of Dudleys; after all, Ambrose's parents were not done producing this one. Ambrose had acquired a new baby sister the autumn before. Like her elder sister, she had the king's daughter, Mary, as a godmother, though not as a namesake. Instead, she was named for her other godmother, Katherine, Duchess of Suffolk, the widow of Charles Brandon.[3] Ambrose, following his elder brother's death in France, was now the second-eldest Dudley son after his father's namesake, John, one year his senior. As the heir to the great fortunes and offices that his father was amassing, John the younger might be expected to do better than the daughter of an attorney general. Ambrose, however, had every reason to be content with his bride and with the path his father was laying out for him.

Like the fallen Henry, Ambrose and his brothers had received a skilled education at the hands of humanist scholars. One of these was their kinsman, Sir Francis Jobson, who had married Elizabeth Plantagenet, the half-sister of John Dudley, by John's arrangement. Ambrose and his brothers knew their aunt Elizabeth well, as she had lived with them through the 1530s. His father had taken it upon himself to ensure she made a good marriage, promising to Jobson a manor owned by Sir Andrew Windsor, Ambrose's great-uncle by his grandfather Edmund's first marriage.[4] The manor never reached Jobson; nevertheless he did well from his association with the Dudley family as secretary and tutor to the children.[5]

Ambrose and his brothers had also been introduced to even more esteemed scholars, including Roger Ascham, Thomas Wilson and John Dee, and were given a more intensive education than their father had received.[6] They were instructed in Latin, and also picked up French and Italian. Ambrose's younger brother Robert especially professed a preference for mathematics – the key to engineering and navigation. Ambrose's sisters were also very well educated. The eldest, Mary, about thirteen at the time her brother was married, was equally proficient in Latin, Italian and French.[7] It was a large and busy family, and with the children reaching an age for marriage, and Ambrose having already taken a bride, his parents could confidently hope that soon it would get even bigger. Edmund Dudley had not lived to see his grandchildren; John had every reason to expect that he might die secure in the knowledge that he was head of a line that would persist past his own demise.

For that was the ambition of any man of even moderate name, from merchants to kings, and certainly viscounts. No one was wise to say it, but the king himself was unlikely to ever gaze into the face of his own grandchild, or even see his children married. The reign might soon end, and the king's heir was a child. Regime changes brought bloodshed, but also opportunity. Ambrose's marriage to a well-connected heiress would not protect the family, but it was an important step in providing the security to survive the death of the king, and all that came with it. They would all have to tread carefully, as the king's health failed.

*

Jane Dudley, Lady Lisle, teetered on the edge of a political scourge bloodier than that which had brought down Anne Boleyn and her five reported lovers. The scandal this time was far worse than Boleyn's betrayal, greater even than the treason that it had entailed. This was treason against both king and God. It was heresy. And it was punishable by a more painful, prolonged and public death than Queen Anne or any of her supposed lovers had suffered: death by fire.

When Jane was a child, heretics known as Lollards had been the subject of such painful executions, often burned in groups of half a dozen or so. By the time she had become a mother, it was Lutherans who were put to the flame; the first such execution was carried out in 1529, under the Lord Chancellorship of Thomas More. Shortly thereafter, Henry VIII had broken with Rome and established an independent English Church, thanks in large part to the work of the Dudleys' ally, Thomas Cromwell. The structure of that Church, however, was still being fought over: would the soul of England be fundamentally Catholic (albeit *sans* Pope), essentially Lutheran or something else entirely? The Henrician Church had rejected the pope and turned to the king for guidance, but he was nothing if not changeable. As a result, while the law on heresy was clear, what defined it often required interpretation and caution. The Bible was in English, but not everyone was meant to read it. Catholic images were smashed, but Protestant 'heretics' burned. In 1539 parliament had passed the 'Act Abolishing Diversity in Opinions' or 'Act of Six Articles', which set out that many of the fundamental aspects of the Catholic Church, including the belief in 'transubstantiation' – that the bread and wine of the Sacrament materially transformed into the body and blood of Christ – would remain essential to the English Church. Contravention of them constituted heresy, punishable by death. Four years later it was enacted that the reading of the English Bible, which had been supported and commissioned by Henry VIII to appear in every parish church in the land, would be restricted, barring it especially and specifically from women, among others of low social standing.[8] In 1543, the musician Robert Testwood was burned to death for averting his eyes while the Sacrament was elevated during the mass, a gesture held to be a denial of transubstantiation. Protestants maintained that to believe such a thing was superstition and idol-worship. As the king's faith swung once more towards Catholic tenets, men such as Testwood died for their reformist beliefs and courtiers such as John and Jane had reason to worry for their fortunes, if not their lives.

If only by association with families like the Seymours, the Dudleys were ranged against the religious conservatives in Henry's court, men like Stephen Gardiner, still Bishop of Winchester.[9] To Gardiner's allies, the queen's reformist tendencies, growing group of powerful supporters and especially their influence on the young heir to the throne, were a danger. The conservatives just needed a spark to light a fire at the queen's feet that would sweep away all around her.

They found it in a young Lincolnshire woman who had fled to London to escape an unhappy marriage. Anne Askew was seeking a divorce from her husband, Thomas Kymes. Their marriage had produced two children, but the couple had parted ways – it was reported that he had violently thrown her out of the house – after she had come under some scrutiny for her reformist beliefs. Anne was welcomed in London, as her family was well connected and her cause viewed sympathetically. One of her brothers, Edward, was the king's cupbearer and another, Francis, had been knighted by the king alongside Henry Dudley at Boulogne.[10] Anne's cause, beliefs, piety and standing gave the circle of reformers around the queen, including Jane, reason to be interested in Anne's case. These powerful connections harboured Askew on her arrival in London, but they also made her a target.

Before long, Askew was being spied on. Sir Thomas Wriothesley, the wily son of a herald who had risen to the position of Lord Chancellor, and long-time enemy of Edward Seymour, installed one of his men in a nearby lodging, to spy on her and report back. First brought before the Lord Mayor of London under suspicion of heresy, it wasn't long before her case was being elevated to the highest levels. In summer 1546, Anne was called before the Privy Council at Greenwich – a Council which included John Dudley.

John had spent the spring in Europe, negotiating with French commissioners. It had been hard work, but a treaty, the Treaty of Camp, was on the table. Once again, to claim victory, he just needed approval from the king, though he had been disappointed on that front before.[11] He arrived home in June in the midst of a political maelstrom. Anne Askew had been called to Greenwich, alongside her estranged husband, on 19 June. There, she was interrogated for five long hours by a council led by the Bishop of Winchester on everything from her relationship with her husband to the nature of the Sacrament. On the second day, she was questioned again, before being approached by a smaller three-person delegation. This once again included Stephen Gardiner, alongside the queen's brother, William Parr, Earl of Essex, and John Dudley. As both Parr and Dudley were known reformers and close to the queen, Winchester may have hoped their presence would make Askew more amenable. Or perhaps he hoped that he might catch them both out in the process of interrogating Anne. Either way, it was a trap.

John and his companions pressed Anne to confess that the Sacrament was 'flesh, blood and bone', not just bread and wine. She refused. Turning specifically to Parr and Dudley, Anne rebuked them: 'It is a great shame,' she declared, 'for you to counsel contrary to your knowledge.'[12] It was a comment designed to strike at the core of John's conscience. He was part of a machine condemning a woman for beliefs he also held, that his family supported. What's more, it was a pointed reminder of how much he stood to lose. It was an impossible situation. Fail to bring Anne Askew down, and he invited the king's disfavour, putting himself next in line for persecution. Execute the king's will and see her destroyed, and he could very well implicate himself and his wife in her crime, as well as condemn his soul.

The interrogations continued, with the threat of death at the stake ever present. At last, sick and exhausted, Anne was sent to Newgate Prison. Remaining there for just over a week, on 29 June, Anne arrived at the Tower of London. At three o'clock, she was joined by two of Gardiner's supporters, Thomas Wriothesley and Richard Rich. The questions changed. No longer pressed to answer questions about the Sacrament, these men wanted to know if there were others of her sect. Anne resolutely responded that she knew none. Then the questions grew more specific, asking about her knowledge of ladies of the court, including Jane Dudley's friends, Katherine Brandon, Duchess of Suffolk, and Anne Seymour, Lady Hertford. Anne retorted that even if she did pronounce anything against them, there would be no proof to back it up. But how, they responded, had she been supported while in prison, if not by such beneficent hands? She had received various presents of money, she admitted, but they came by her maid, and so she had no idea of their source. Feeling they were closing in, the councillors pressed further: gentlewomen of the court must have given her this money; all she had to do was name them. At first, Anne claimed ignorance. Finally, she admitted that two men had visited, delivering money that they claimed came from Lady Hertford and Lady Denny, but the men might have been lying.

Her interrogators moved on to an even more important question: were there members of the King's Council who had supported her? Were there traitors and heretics among the king's closest and most trusted advisers? She answered no, and at this point her questioners lost their patience; after all, she had all but named John Dudley and William Parr the week before. If she would not bend to niceties or pressure, it was time to see how she would stand up to pain. She was led to a large mechanistic frame of iron and wood, not unlike a bed-frame, with axles at the top and bottom. Her interrogators, desperate to identify her friends near the king and queen, were threatening her with the rack.

By all rights it should never have come to this. Torture was not expressly legal, though could it be used in extreme cases of treason. This was not such a case. Furthermore, as a gentle-born woman, Anne Askew should have been exempt. Nevertheless, Anne was forced to lie down on the device and spread her arms and legs, which were then tied with coarse ropes. Wooden poles were inserted into the axles, which turned beneath the frame, causing the ropes around her limbs to wrench, and slowly pulling her arms and legs from their sockets. As the device operated, she was questioned about whether there were any ladies of the court who shared her beliefs. She refused to name any, causing those working the rack to wrench her limbs further. Her near-complete silence caused Wriothesley and Rich even to work the rack with their own hands. Still, she did not answer. At last, the Lieu-tenant of the Tower, Sir Anthony Knyvett, released her from the bonds that held her to the device, and she fainted. This did not stop Wrioth-esley, who spent another two hours speaking to her as she lay on the hard floor, trying to persuade her to change her mind. She refused. Her fate was clear; she would burn, but she had not implicated any of the ladies of the court or members of the King's Council. John and Jane Dudley would be safe.

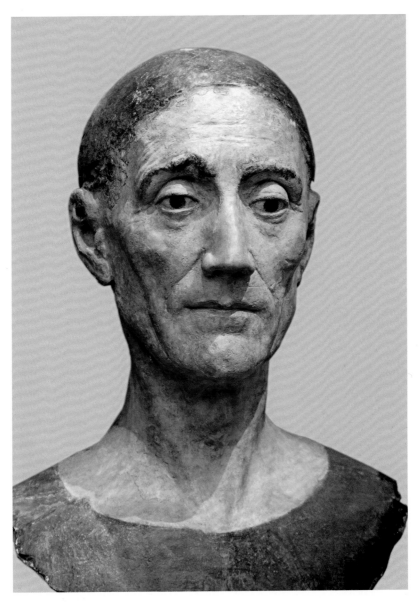

Funeral Mask of Henry VII, 1509.

Edmund Dudley's account book, with the pardon of Thomas Sunnyff for £500 and the king's signature.

Tortington Church, Sussex.

Henry VII on his deathbed, 1509. Richard Fox is to the left of the king's bed and Hugh Denys stands fourth from the left on the right of the bed.

Portrait of John Dudley at Knole, Kent.

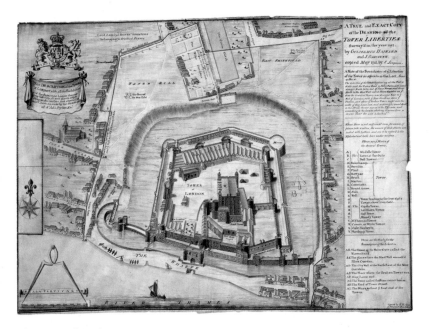

The Tower of London, 1597.

Siege of Boulogne, 1544. The destruction of the wall of the town can be seen in the centre of the image.

Battle of the Solent, 1545. Charles Brandon, duke of Suffolk, follows the king at the centre of the painting. In the water just above them the *Mary Rose* has sunk and John Dudley's *Henri a Grace a Dieu* leads the fleet.

Family of Henry VIII, *c*.1545. From the left, Mary I, Edward VI, Henry VIII, Jane Seymour and Elizabeth I. The figures in the archways are two of the household fools.

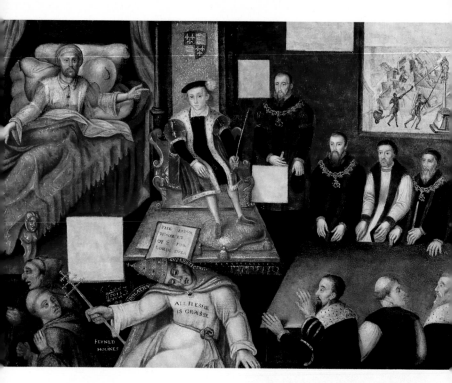

Henry VIII, Edward VI and the Pope.
Immediately to the left of Edward VI are
Edward Seymour, John Dudley, Thomas
Cranmer and John Russell.

Edward VI's Device for the Succession,
1553.

On 16 July, less than a month later, Anne Askew was brought to West Smithfield Marketplace to die. Just north of the city walls, a stone's throw from Newgate Prison, Smithfield Market was large enough for both the executions themselves and the crowd that they would draw. Smithfield had been a site of execution for over four hundred years; in 1305 the Scottish rebel William Wallace had been hanged, drawn and quartered there. No one seemed to mind that the market was also known for its excellent butchers. On the day that Anne Askew was to die, four stakes had been erected on a wooden platform, about three feet off the ground.[13] Each was surrounded by the sort of small faggots of brushwood, rods and sticks used in hearths, bakeries and brew-houses across the city. Eyewitnesses claimed that Anne's stake had been altered slightly, including a small seat, as she could no longer stand following her torture. One of the other stakes was for John Lassells, the man who had passed on the information that had condemned Katherine Howard only a few years before, and was now also convicted for heresy. A special viewing scaffold had been erected nearby for the occasion, where Wriothesley and other members of the Council could watch the twenty-five-year-old woman who had so challenged them meet her end. John Dudley was not among them.

Instead, John was rushing to meet the French king to ratify the treaty between him and Henry VIII. Desperate letters had been crossing the Channel through the first half of July, wondering why the Lord Admiral was not yet on his way. He had received his passport on 2 July and was reported to be departing on 4 July, but this turned out to be false.[14] The king, it was said, was deep in melancholy, dressing for mass but then not attending, staying indoors when he was usually like to enjoy his gardens in the summer.[15] He had ordered John to stay, suspicious that his counterpart, the French admiral Claude d'Annebault, had also been delayed. It would be a diplomatic disaster if John travelled all that way, and the French did not make a showing. Henry made clear that he would not dissolve his forces until the French revoked theirs; it was a dangerous stalemate.[16] John's delay threatened the peace he had worked so hard to secure.[17] On Thursday, 8 July, there was finally a list compiled of who would attend the mission alongside the admiral, including his younger brother, Andrew. At last, Dudley left on 12 July, almost too late to save the peace.[18] He set sail for France just four days before Anne Askew's execution. He would be royally banqueted in Paris while the embers cooled.

*

The little boy, not yet nine years old, sat nervously on his horse. He was dressed magnificently for such a small child, light auburn hair and dark eyes peeking out beneath his ornamented hat. Around and behind him were nearly eight hundred men on horseback; the lords and gentlemen in velvet coats, their yeomen in new liveries for the occasion.[19] They all looked to him. He was the centre of attention today and was required to perform his role properly. For Prince Edward, it was his first chance to prove himself, to show to the world what kind of a king he might one day be. The young prince was tasked with meeting the Admiral of France, Claude d'Annebault, as he travelled south from his welcome in London towards his meeting with Edward's father, the king. Upon his arrival at Greenwich, d'Annebault had been greeted by the king's brother-in-law, William Parr, Earl of Essex. The next day he sailed his galleys up the Thames and was formally greeted by the mayor and other London officials while shot rang out from the Tower of London. After a day parading through London, he travelled along the Thames to Hampton Court, where Edward awaited him. He had brought a train of well over a thousand Frenchmen with him.

Edward had been anxious about this moment. He had written to his stepmother, Queen Catherine, almost a fortnight before, asking her to find out for him if the admiral knew Latin, so that he could greet him formally in the shared European language of scholars and diplomats.[20] He would have needed to work hard with his tutors to write and practise such a greeting. At last the moment came, as the thousand-strong company settled before him with the admiral at its head. The eight-year-old prince greeted and embraced the hardened French admiral as he'd practised, before leading him towards Hampton Court. It was an impressive performance, and those in attendance carried tales of the young prince's wit and audacity back to the palace; news that could only delight his doting father. When the combined company reached Hampton Court, led by Prince Edward, the Council greeted d'Annebault, but it was John Dudley, his English counterpart, who led the fifty-year-old French admiral to his specially prepared chambers. Dudley might have been a decade or so d'Annebault's junior, but the two were counterparts on either side of the Channel. They had faced off at the Battle of the Solent and worked together to bring a peace between their masters. There was animosity between the two men, but there was also an understanding.

The next day, St Bartholomew's Day, the French admiral was led into the chapel at Hampton Court, where the king was waiting. Together they ratified the treaty that John Dudley had raced across the Channel to secure. It was not, however, all celebrations and pleasantries; Dudley still had more negotiating to do. By the terms of the treaty, Henry would be allowed to keep the hard-won Boulogne for another nine years, when the French would pay 2 million écus (about half a million pounds) to get it back, a colossal sum.[21] D'Annebault wanted this number reduced, but the English refused to budge.[22] They fired back that the French had been building fortifications in contradiction to the terms of the treaty. Then it was d'Annebault's turn again, demanding that the galley and galley-slaves captured by the English fleet be returned to him. The king happily returned his galley but could not return the slaves. On the day that Dudley had left London for France to ratify the treaty, he had been accompanied by the captured French galley, noting that the slaves were in poor condition, with hardly a stitch on them.[23] As such, he advised the king to grant them their liberty, not for mercy, but to demonstrate to the French and others that they ought not to bring their galleys near English shores, for fear of losing their enslaved workforce. It was a coy and clever trick to play on the French, though at the time he might not have thought that he would have to answer for it in such circumstances. When the admiral demanded to be compensated for the loss, Dudley refused, and the argument became heated. With the king and Council looking on, the two men reined in their animosity, and put on a show of friendliness for the sake of peace.

After the treaty was signed at last, the court feasted and feted for days, including rich banquets, costly masques and liberal hunting.[24]

Jane Dudley joined her husband at the centre of the court for the festivities, in the company of the king's daughters, Mary and Elizabeth, and his former queen, Anne of Cleves, who had been given special status as 'the king's sister'. Jane was joined by other leading ladies of the court, including her friends, Anne Seymour, Lady Hertford and Katherine Brandon, Duchess of Suffolk.[25]

As the festivities came to a close and the French admiral returned home, John made a bold decision. At the height of his power and with other courtiers closing in as the king's health failed, John was leaving the court. He was drained both physically and financially and was in no condition to work. When Wriothesley and Gardiner met with him to get his advice on a naval matter only a few weeks after the French admiral's departure, they found him in too great pain to even read the letter they had brought him.[26] With the king's permission, he retired to the country. It was unclear whether he would return.

*

In the cold weeks of January 1547, after nearly four decades on the throne, the longest continuous reign of an adult monarch in England since Edward III in the fourteenth century, Henry VIII was about to breathe his last. He gestured wordlessly and desperately to his archbishop, Thomas Cranmer, to indicate his dedication to the true religion, a commitment that had underpinned the great decisions of his life and reign, spilling streams of blood and sending great plumes of smoke, thick with the smell of charred flesh, into the air. The king was fifty-five and had been in bad health for some time. Those who could remember the shining youth riding through the streets of London would struggle to recognize him in the dying man before them. As with the death of his father, those closest to the king had been quietly waiting for this moment for months and were ready to take control of the situation, turning it to their advantage. Those who acted quickly and well would be able to shape the reign to come, especially as Henry's heir was still only nine years old. Those who did not could face ostracism, imprisonment or worse. The start of a new reign was a scramble for power, a frantic feeding frenzy hidden behind mourning robes and peels of triumphant bells. This was a lesson the six-year-old John Dudley had learned tragically on the day that the youthful

Henry VIII had been declared king and his father had been taken from him, and one the adult John Dudley would hold close to his heart on the day that pitiful king died.

John had returned from his retreat to the countryside by November, retaking his place on the Privy Council. At the beginning of December, Henry Howard, Earl of Surrey, was arrested – Henry feared he planned to usurp the throne – and imprisoned at the Lord Chancellor Thomas Wriothesley's home at Ely Place, Holborn. It was there that the Privy Council conducted their meetings for the rest of the month. On 12 December, both Henry Howard and his father, Thomas Howard, Duke of Norfolk, were conducted to the Tower. The Howards were no friends of the Dudleys, nor the Seymours. Proud of their noble lineage, they had a reputation for sneering at the rise of the 'new men', like Dudley and his father before him. The elder, Thomas Howard, well into his seventies, had been made a Knight of the Garter just a few months before Edmund Dudley was executed. His first wife had been Henry VIII's aunt, his nieces queens Anne Boleyn and Katherine Howard. He had been just as opposed to the rise of Wolsey and Cromwell as he was to Dudley and Seymour, and in both the former cases had emerged triumphant while the other men fell. A religious conservative, Thomas Howard had been part of a failed attempt to arrest Archbishop Thomas Cranmer in 1543. Now that it was clear that the Seymours would be pre-eminent in a court ruled by their nephew, Prince Edward, Thomas Howard had suggested a marriage to unite the families and put any differences aside.

His son was not so ready to capitulate. Instead, the aggressively forthright Earl of Surrey went so far as to include the royal arms on his heraldry, seeming to imply a right to rule.[27] Both father and son were arrested and imprisoned in the Tower. Many expected that they would die.[28] The Duke of Norfolk wrote a conciliatory letter to the king, while his son wrote to the Council demanding that he be given an audience with four members of the Council, including Wriothesley, but notably excluding both Seymour and Dudley.[29] Dudley had been the recipient of some 'parables' from the poet-earl during the summer, as he set off to France, which he had thought suspicious enough to forward to the king.[30] Now it was made explicit that Surrey had held Dudley an enemy.[31]

It was a tense Christmas season. While the queen oversaw the festivities at Greenwich, Dudley and the rest of the Privy Council remained in business at Whitehall, alongside an increasingly ailing king. This illness was not new. In March, it had been reported that he had suffered a fever, but had spent his time while afflicted playing cards with John Dudley and other intimate friends.[32] He had fallen ill again over the summer, suffered a bout of fever again in November, and fallen into an especially severe fever shortly before Christmas.[33] When he recovered, he was visibly weakened, though no one would have dared tell him. As it was, he largely shut himself away, seen only by his councillors and a few select gentlemen. His ailment was so concerning that the imperial ambassador, François Van der Delft, wrote to Dudley to ask if the arrests of the Howards had been contrived as a way to distract from the severity of the king's illness.[34] Secretly, Van der Delft was more concerned that the Howards may have been the victims of a new regime headed by Seymour and Dudley.

The idea of a Seymour–Dudley supremacy especially worried the Catholics and conservatives at court. Seymour and Dudley had recently managed to forestall any great enquiries or prosecutions of the 'heretics'.[35] They may have lost the fight for Anne Askew's life, but they could prevent the same fate befalling others. John's support of reformers and growing enmity with Bishop Gardiner meant that he was seen to be no friend to the emperor's subjects. Van der Delft looked on his rise with trepidation.

Henry made it through Christmas, as did the Howards, imprisoned in the Tower of London. Evidence had been rapidly compiled over the previous weeks, but the case against them remained weak. On 12 January, John joined seven other members of the Council, including Wriothesley and Seymour, in meeting with the elder Howard, Thomas Howard, Duke of Norfolk. They emerged triumphant with a signed confession, written, it (unconvincingly) claimed, 'without compulsion or counsel'. Thomas Howard, Duke of Norfolk, admitted to having committed 'high treason and, although I do not deserve it, humbly begs his Highness to have pity upon me'.[36] What's more, he also confessed to having 'concealed high treason in keeping secret the false acts of my son, Henry Earl of Surrey'. It was enough to condemn his son, though he may have been told that it would save him.

The next day, John Dudley arrived at the Guildhall for the trial of Henry Howard, Earl of Surrey. He sat on a panel of judges which once again included Wriothesley and Seymour. Wriothesley read out the indictment: that Henry Howard had committed high treason by quartering the royal arms. Howard himself was brought forward, led by the Constable of the Tower, and pleaded not guilty, probably unaware of his father's condemnatory confession. Howard put up a spirited fight against the charges laid against him, especially attacking the low-born status of those assembled to judge him.[37] He reserved his most cutting comments for John Dudley. When John pressed him, the earl shot back, 'You, my lord, know well that however right a man may be, they always find the fallen one guilty.'[38] It was a reminder not only of Dudley's treasonous family background, but an attempt to draw parallels between the Howards' demise and that of Empson and Dudley at the close of the last reign. If this was intended to save him, it did not work. The jury of knights and gentlemen returned a verdict instantly. The earl was guilty of high treason, and was to be taken back to the Tower and thence led through the City of London to the gallows at Tyburn to be hanged, disembowelled and quartered.[39]

The bill of attainder against the two Howards came before parliament on 18 January, just four days into the new session. Both were said to have committed high treason, based on Norfolk's confession and Surrey's trial. The next day, before it had even been passed by parliament, Henry Howard, Earl of Surrey, was executed, beheaded at Tower Hill. The Council had gone from the confession of the father to the execution of the son in a week. The Act of Attainder, finally passed five days after Surrey's execution, was the only statute passed by this session of parliament, which had been assembled in November 1545.[40] Parliament could not continue without the king who had called it.

Henry VIII died at about two o'clock in the morning on 28 January, precisely ninety years after the birth of his father, the founder of the dynasty. As with the death of Henry VII, the king's death was attended by leading courtiers, but now there was nothing to bar a Dudley from being there. This time, as the king's death was kept a secret, and clandestine plans were made, John Dudley was a part of it all. He had been only a child when the last king had died, but he had learned quickly the importance of reputation and proximity to power. His father's enemies had plotted the destruction of his family over the deathbed of the last king. It had taken decades of persistence through bloody battles, anxious negotiations, dangerous scandals and agonizing losses but, as the king breathed his last, John Dudley had not only endured, but was now in a position to take control of his fate and that of the country. With the death of Henry VIII, and the accession of a malleable child in his place, the Dudleys were poised to become one of the most powerful families in England.

PART THREE
1547–1555

10

The bear and ragged staff

The young boy, barely nine years old, lay prostrate before the altar at Westminster Abbey. His little knees in their crimson hose were separated from the cold, hard floor by a cushion of black velvet, embroidered with gold thread.[1] He wore a surcoat furred with pure white miniver, its collar and sleeves garnished with gold ribbon, and two short, sleeveless, hooded tabards, furred with powdered ermine. It was near midday on 20 February 1547, Shrove Sunday, the day which had been selected for the new king's coronation.

Over the boy stood Thomas Cranmer, the Archbishop of Canterbury. Now almost sixty, Cranmer looked well for his age and the turmoil he had seen. He had dark hair and eyes in a long but full face. He had mastered the look of a solemn churchman, though from time to time a slight playful arch found its way to his left eyebrow. The shadow of a beard lay across his cheeks and chin. Cranmer had now been Archbishop for fifteen years. He would be the senior official in a Church whose head was the young boy before him.

Cranmer intoned, 'Oh God, which dost visit those that are humble, and dost comfort us by the Holy Spirit, send down thy grace upon this thy servant Edward that by him we may feel thy presence among us, through Jesus Christ. Amen.'[2] At this, the boy rose and sat on a large chair which faced the altar, St Edward's Chair, the traditional seat for English monarchs during their coronation. Covered in white embroidered silk with flowers of gold, the chair was backed with two pillars, each with a lion of gold upon it, and a turret of gold *fleur de lis*.[3]

The chair sat upon a large scaffold built in front of the altar, which had been covered in red cloth, the stairs leading up and down it covered in rich silks and ornate carpets.⁴ Four gentlemen stood around the scaffold, ready with another, lighter chair, garnished with rich cloth, for when the boy was required to descend to the altar or be shown to the watching crowds. Around the scaffold were rows of finely dressed people – nobles, knights, gentlemen – their eyes fixed on what was happening between the archbishop and the boy before the altar.

'Will ye grant,' Archbishop Cranmer asked him, 'to keep to the people of England and other your realms and dominions the laws and liberties of this realm, and other your realms and dominions?'

The boy answered, 'I grant and promise.'

By tradition, the promises taken by the new king were essential to his accession. However, despite all the performance of the ceremony, the new king had been king when he entered, his accession directly following his father's death and not dependent, as his predecessors' had been, on the acceptance of the people, the oaths taken or the ceremony of the coronation.⁵ Edward VI had been proclaimed King of England, France and Ireland, Supreme Head on earth of the Church on the morning of 1 February, nearly three weeks before, at which time it was recognized that he was invested and established with the crown imperial. Today's ceremony was important, but Edward VI was already King of England.

Cranmer continued, 'You shall keep to your strength and power to the Church of God and to all the people holy peace and concord.'

Again, Edward replied, 'I shall keep.'

Edward as the new monarch had been resident in the Tower of London in the days before the coronation, having been hastily fetched by his uncle, Edward Seymour, and brought to London in the hours after his father's death. Henry VIII's death, like his father's before him, had been kept a secret for three days, during which plans were made and the heir secured. The leader during this secret contrived interregnum was undoubtedly Seymour, who not only secured his nephew, but whose right-hand man, William Paget, also safeguarded the late king's will. Together they planned to expand upon the form of regency government set out by Henry for the reign of his young son.

'You shall make to be done,' Cranmer continued, 'after your

strength and power, equal and right justice in all your laws and judgements, with mercy and truth.'

'I shall do,' Edward replied.

As he was only a boy, the new king could not rule in his own right, so his father had envisaged a regency council to govern in his name until he was eighteen. Recent history had warned against allowing a single Lord Protector to rule. Henry VII's predecessor, Richard III, had been Lord Protector in the minority of his own nephew, Edward V. The boy and his younger brother had ended up dead and Richard had seized the throne for himself, a twist of history that had benefitted the current dynasty, but which Henry VIII had been keen not to see repeated. As such, he had selected sixteen of his most trusted councillors to oversee the governance of Edward VI while he was yet a child. None was given pre-eminence in Henry's will, to guard against the rise of one who might try to take royal power for himself. Nevertheless, within a week of Henry's death, Edward Seymour had been declared Lord Protector as well as Duke of Somerset, the leading noble in England. Seymour had processed into Westminster Abbey on the morning of the coronation directly before Edward himself, holding the crown to be placed on the young king's head and wearing furs taken from gowns formerly belonging to Henry VIII.[6]

Cranmer had come to the final promise the boy would be asked to make: 'Do ye grant to make no new laws but such as shall be to the honour and glory of God, and to the good of the common wealth and that the same shall be made by the consent of your people as hath been accustomed?'

'I grant and promise,' Edward replied.

This last oath was a notable alteration from the one his father had taken, in which he had promised to strengthen and defend the laws chosen by his people, not make his own.[7] Edward was Supreme Head in England, though within some limits. He could not override all laws, nor make any that contravened the good of the commonwealth and the glory of God. Notably the definition of these limits might be open for debate.

Promises done, Edward arose from his chair and was assisted by the gentlemen ushers to the altar, where the Sacrament lay. Placing his hand on a Bible, Edward recited, 'The things which I have before promised I shall observe and keep, so God help me and these holy Evangelists by me bodily touched upon this holy Altar.' He fell to the ground again, and above him Cranmer, in a loud voice, called down the Holy Spirit to be upon him.

Following some further kneeling and invocations, Edward was led to a small compartment to the left of the high altar, screened off from the watching crowds. There he was joined by his Lord Chamberlain, who had immediately followed the king on his procession into the abbey, bearing the train of his long, furred robe of crimson velvet, and who had stood with him on the mounted platform, handing him items as he needed them. The Lord Chamberlain was the newly made Earl of Warwick, John Dudley.

John had received his new title just three days before, in a grand ceremony at the Tower of London. After his letters patent were read to the assembled nobles, the boy-king had girt John's sword upon him and placed a small crown on his head. John had also received from the king the white staff of his new office, Great Lord Chamberlain. First instituted in the twelfth century, it had been held for four hundred years by the Earls of Oxford, until Henry VIII reclaimed the office for the Crown, awarding it to Thomas Cromwell. The post had most recently been held by Edward Seymour, the Lord Protector; Dudley continued to follow in his old friend's footsteps. Becoming Lord Chamberlain made John one of the three principal officers of the King's Household and today, on the day of the new king's coronation, one of the central players.

It was John's duty to un-dress and re-dress Edward, preparing him for one of the most sacred elements of the coronation: the anointing. Out of the grand robes that he wore into Westminster, John helped Edward change into two shirts of fine silk – one brown, the other crimson – with wide collars, exposing his small shoulders.[8] Over his crimson hose, Edward was given a short breech of fine white linen, reaching from his waist to his thighs and secured with a belt of crimson velvet tied with silk and gold.[9] His sleeveless surcoat of crimson cotton, decorated with ermine and miniver furs, was open at the front and secured loosely around the shoulders with small ribbons and garnished with ribbons of gold at the collar and sleeves. On his head was placed a small coif of crimson satin.[10] As John helped him dress, they could hear Thomas Wriothesley, Lord Chancellor and now Earl of Southampton (thanks to the old king's will and certainly not the Lord Protector's favour), reading a general pardon to all of Edward's people, excluding those few excepted, as John's father had been after the accession of Henry VIII.

The old king had been buried only four days before in a temporary tomb at Windsor, next to his third wife and Edward's mother, Jane Seymour. The funeral procession had begun at Westminster, resting overnight at Syon, and then continuing to Windsor for a grand funeral on 16 February. Most of the leading members of the court had been in attendance, except for – as custom dictated – the new king himself. The former king's two other children, the ladies Mary and Elizabeth, both rode along in the procession, on saddles covered in black velvet.[11] The late king's corpse was carried in a chariot covered in cloth of gold tissue, lined with tawny satin. The chariot was fringed with gold and purple, and black ribbon adorned the shafts. The inner part of the chariot, where the king's coffin lay, was garnished with purple velvet.[12] Over the coffin was a life-sized and life-like effigy of the king, with cloth of gold, silk sabaton and crimson velvet shoes, lying beneath a cloth of state.[13] The chariot was pulled by seven black-trapped horses, ridden by seven black-robed children of honour.[14] Around the chariot were banners and standards of coats of arms and saints.[15] In his final role as Lord Admiral, John had ridden alongside other members of the King's Privy Chamber in the procession. Jane, likewise, joined members of the Queen's Chamber, and their son rode alongside other knights' and lords' sons. At Windsor, after the prayers and ceremonies, Henry VIII had been lowered into his temporary tomb, and the officers of his household broke their white staffs of office, signifying the end of their tenure and the end of his reign. The next day John Dudley received his new white staff as Lord Chamberlain.

When John had finished preparing the boy in his rich robes, Edward emerged once again and was brought before the altar. A crimson and gold pall was lifted over him, to shield him during the sacred ceremony, and the choir of young boys began to sing Psalm 21: 'Lord, The king shall be glad in thy virtue'.[16] Archbishop Cranmer dipped his fingers in the holy oil and anointed Edward's boyish hands, his chest, the middle of his back, the bend of his arms and his head, making a cross, speaking quiet prayers as he placed the unction on the small King of England.

At last, this done, Cranmer gently wiped off the oil with a cotton and linen cloth, to be burned after the ceremony, and laced up the king's coat and shirt. John Dudley handed Edward a pair of linen gloves and a small linen coif, which had been carefully prepared for this moment, for the king to put on.

Edward was brought to his small private compartment to change once again. He had performed well during this ceremony. The gravity of his role was not something that would have to be pressed upon the boy. There was a seriousness about Edward, born perhaps of his schooling, the constant reminders of his importance as his father's son, and the deep religiosity that had been impressed upon him in his nine years. In another child this might have been shrugged off in favour of the pleasurable privileges that came with his station; Edward's own father could at times have been accused of such tendency to distraction. King Edward VI, however, was a boy-king filled with a sense of divine purpose, or most of the time at least. Riding just ahead of the king in his grand procession to Westminster, it would have been hard for John Dudley to have missed the way Edward hurried past the various solemn pageants and speeches, as they droned on about the virtues required of a king, but paused for some length watching the impressive tumbler on the tightrope suspended from the steeple at St Paul's. For all his regal standing, solemn scholarliness and divine vocation, Edward was at times, rather endearingly, a nine-year-old boy.

When he emerged, Edward was once again in his parliament robe of crimson velvet and ermine, his surcoat of miniver fur and golden ribbons and his hooded tabards, with a sword girt around his waist. He was brought to the altar, where he placed the sword upon it, to demonstrate that the great power he had received came first from God. This done, he sat back in his great chair and Archbishop Cranmer and his uncle, the Duke of Somerset, brought three crowns before him. Together, they crowned him with each one in turn, as trumpets rang out. First was the crown of King Edward, the boy's sainted namesake, then the crown imperial of England, and finally a crown which had been made for the occasion, small enough to fit the young boy's head. Edward would be the first king to be crowned in this way with three crowns, echoing the pope's three-tiered tiara, and demonstrating that his imperial power was given by God.[17] The power was also, importantly, given by his uncle, Edward and England's Protector, who along with the archbishop placed these crowns on the young king's head. With the final, smaller crown placed, the echo of the trumpets quieted, and the choir struck up, singing 'We praise thee, oh God'. A small ring of gold was placed on Edward's fourth finger. Edward was now married to the realm of England.

In sequence, Edward's nobles brought him other symbols of his reign: the staff of St Edward, the royal spurs, the orb and his sceptre. This last was too heavy for the boy, and so the Earl of Shrewsbury, Francis Talbot, had to stand alongside him, helping to hold the heavy golden staff. The king was now fully anointed and adorned, and sat on his throne in his robes, with the crown imperial on his head, the orb in his left hand and the sceptre in his right. The image was only slightly marred by the fact that the crown was significantly smaller than one might expect, the orb would barely fit in his hand and he couldn't manage the staff unaided.

All that was left to do was to pay homage to this new King of England. His uncle did so first, then Archbishop Cranmer. John Dudley was not long after. Standing before his new king Dudley declared, 'I, John, Earl of Warwick, become your liegeman of life and limb, and of earthly worship, and faith and truth I shall bear unto you, to live and die against all manner of folks. So help me God and All Hallows.' This done, he approached the young king and kissed his left cheek, cementing his loyalty.[18]

When all the nobles had so pledged their allegiance, John joined his peers in kneeling before the king, hands in the air, and loudly proclaiming, 'We offer to sustain and defend you and your Crown with our lives, hands and goods against all the world. GOD SAVE KING EDWARD VI!' The cry was taken up and echoed by the others congregated in the great church. England's new monarch had been crowned.

*

The king's forces, led by John Dudley, Earl of Warwick, were outnumbered two to one by the rebels they had been sent to put down. Having driven them out of the city of Norwich, Dudley was forced to pursue them into a valley to the east. There, the rebels controlled the roads and were well protected by enclosed fields and the River Yare.[19] Dudley's army was thus forced to mount a difficult frontal assault through hills and hedges, funnelled through a third-of-a-mile or so gap between two enclosed fields. The rebels had augmented these natural defences with trenches, bulwarks and other barricades, making it nearly impossible to launch the sort of attack necessary to even the odds. To this the rebels had added another fearsome defence. As Dudley's forces approached, they were repulsed by the wall the rebels had constructed, not of wood or of earth, but of men. Before their front line the rebels had placed gentleman-prisoners taken in their previous attacks, chained together as a human shield.

The rebels, led by a local landowner and tanner by trade, Robert Kett, had occupied the nearby city of Norwich for about a month before Dudley's army had driven them out. The rebels had congregated in the summer of 1549 against the enclosure of lands and Edward Seymour's unpopular agrarian policies. Kett had ripped his own fences down in response to the initial rioting, which had begun in the market town of Wymondham, where Kett had held the manor from John Dudley himself.[20] Under Kett's leadership, they decided to march to Norwich, adding supporters as they went, until they were more than ten thousand strong.

In Norwich the rebels had withstood the attack of William Parr, now the Marquess of Northampton, which, although it had weakened their forces somewhat, had also had the unfortunate outcome of leaving them with eleven more pieces of artillery than they had started with. Dudley had arrived with his forces on 24 August, having travelled from London via Cambridge. His troops consisted of his own and other nobles' men, local militia loyal to the Crown as well as a significant number of paid mercenaries. This included the German *landsknechts*, known for their fearsome battle style and willingness to fight for whosoever paid them.

Dudley had first attempted to talk the rebels into surrendering

Norwich from where he was staying just outside the city, at Intwood, the home of Thomas Gresham. When they had refused, he and his men forced their way in, cutting down and executing any they found. Many had hidden themselves in the lanes on the outskirts of the city, however, and drew Dudley and his men into a skirmish, letting down arrows like snowflakes in a storm. The royal army responded with a hail of gunfire. The rebels ran, leaving hundreds slain in the streets behind them. Having lost control of the city, the rebels resorted to more cunning tactics. While Dudley and his men were attending to other matters, the enemy's most skilled shooter took down the king's master gunner, unleashing a wave of rebels, some armed only with pitchforks, who surprised a band of Welshmen guarding carriages and carts of ordinance and gunpowder. Shocked by the surprise and the noise, they ran, leaving behind the valuable and dangerous weaponry. Beating the rebels would be a lot easier if the king's forces could stop accidentally arming them.

Battles raged all through the Sunday after Dudley's arrival. There were fires in the city and shot rang against the walls and sailed over the tops of houses. Small bands attacked without warning where they saw opportunity. It was a dangerous situation; Dudley was counselled by the leaders of the Norwich citizenry to withdraw for his safety, but refused, swearing not to leave the city until he had either destroyed the enemy, or died trying. At last, under the cover of darkness, the rebels abandoned the city and headed east, to the valley of Dussin's Dale. Rumour had it the choice of this location had been inspired by whispers of prophecy and dark magic. The tactics of the choice, however, were undeniable. They would be protected by the fields and hills and were well supplied by the roads. It was an ideal place for a final stand.

When the enemy's movement was reported to him by the sentry he had posted on the steeple of a local church, John Dudley led an elite portion of his army after them. Approaching what would soon become a battlefield on the morning of 27 August, he sent some of his knights to try to convince the rebels to stand down and surrender, knowing full well this was unlikely. It was worthwhile all the same: not only did the offer demonstrate the king's willingness to show mercy, but he could use the time to scope out the position of the rebel army and their leader, Kett. The picture he put together was not an encouraging one. They had chosen their position well and taken steps to improve upon it further. Though they had a number of weaknesses against Dudley's forces – lack of cavalry and command experience amongst them – they knew the land and were using it to their full advantage. And they still had superior numbers. Although some of the rebels were landless labourers and urban poor, others were wealthier farmers and yeomen, and all would have some level of military training. All able-bodied men between the ages of sixteen and sixty were expected to form part of the Crown's militia, and were trained appropriately, especially with the bow. Many were also armed with swords and spears and had even acquired pieces of armour. This was not a rag-tag band of revolting peasants, but a well-armed and semi-professional militia.

In the end, the four thousand or so troops representing the Crown, largely well-trained professional fighters under the command of the experienced commander John Dudley, faced off against the determined, organized and still sufficiently trained rebels, numbering nearly ten thousand. Before the battle commenced, Dudley addressed his troops. They were to attack with no doubt in their minds that the men they fought were not men, but cruel, brute beasts. They were not there to fight them, but to dole out punishment against these mad animals who sought to overthrow Crown and Church. It was a rousing oration, though potentially a hubristic one.

Among the knights, militia and mercenaries listening to this merciless speech were two of John's children, Ambrose and Robert Dudley. At seventeen and sixteen, these two middle sons were at the right age to begin their battlefield training, as had their late elder brother. The experience of losing Henry in France had not dissuaded John from the surety that this was an essential part of his sons' upbringing. Illness had killed Henry, and this was less a threat on a campaign such as this than in the horrible conditions around Boulogne five summers past. His eldest son, John, did not join them. Despite having been knighted at Edward's coronation, John, a year older than Ambrose, seemed to take after his grandfather more than his father, and had begun amassing an impressive library whilst enjoying the life of a courtier. Perhaps, as well, having lost his eldest on the battlefield once before, the Earl of Warwick was simply not willing to take such a risk again; Ambrose and Robert were more expendable.

The rebels attacked first, opening fire on Dudley's forces. Casualties followed quickly. The standard bearer received a bullet to the leg which entered the skin with such force and speed that it ripped through his thigh and into the shoulder of the horse on which he rode. Delay now could risk more bodies. It was imperative that Dudley's forces move quickly, with their own artillery clearing the way before them.

It was true that the guns that Dudley had distributed amongst his troops were effective, but so were the longbows wielded by the rebels. His troops' advantage largely lay in their mounted cavalry, but this did little good in the face of the longbow's efficient dispatch of their unarmed horses. John's horse went down from underneath him in a volley of arrows, as did that of his son, Ambrose. Both men recovered, but their mounted advantage was gone.

Despite these losses in the royal forces' cavalry, the rebels' ranks and courage began to waver under the fire and assault, and they let the prisoners who were shielding them run free. Now Dudley's footmen could attack with harquebuses and pikes, the firearms being used at short range to ensure accuracy and maximum damage, with the pikes to finish the job. The rebels scattered. Many turned to put up a last fight, preferring to die as men fighting, rather than sheep before the slaughter, but they were decidedly cut down by Dudley's now unquestionably superior forces. Their remaining resilience was lost once they knew their leader had abandoned them. Amid the fighting and bloodshed Kett had fled. Handfuls of retreating men became mobs, whom the royalist cavalry cut down in heaps. The rebels' location had been chosen for defence, not for retreat; it was open field with nowhere for the terrified men to hide. Those rebels at the back of the company, who had withstood the onslaught until the end, shielded by ordinance, trenches, stakes and carts, were at last convinced to surrender by the promise of pardon from Dudley. The abject but grateful rebels ended the day by proclaiming 'God save King Edward!' in the field strewn with their co-insurgents' bodies.

The battle was over by four o'clock. In the end, thousands of bodies were scattered across the valley. These were largely those of the rebels, though Dudley had lost more than he would like to admit. Importantly, his sons were both intact, and now had the opportunity to learn first-hand about the other, less glorious side of battle, staring across the Norfolk countryside, littered with the bodies of their countrymen, traitors though some of them were. It was direct experience of the swift and terrible justice awaiting those who opposed the Crown, not that Ambrose and Robert had lived their lives unaware of that reality.

This massacre was the result of goings-on in London, towards which John Dudley now marched his army. The king's uncle, Edward Seymour, Duke of Somerset, had badly mismanaged affairs. He had not, of course, murdered his nephew or – overtly at least – tried to steal his crown like his predecessor Richard III, which was to his credit, but two years in, the reign was not going well. Whereas Henry VIII had taken up his crown with the assurance that there was plenty of coin to spend – most of it amassed by the work of Edmund Dudley – Edward VI and his Protector had to deal with staggering debt. Henry had spent £1.3 million in the war years of 1544 and 1545, a full million over what he could afford.[21] He had responded by taking out loans, selling monastic lands and debasing the coinage, replacing some of the precious metal in the coin with a cheaper alloy, effectively halving the value of his currency. None of these were effective long-term solutions – in fact, they stood to make the problem much worse – but there were few other suggestions to be had. In the face of increasing deficits in the new reign, Seymour followed the same strategy. Within months of the coronation, Seymour was selling off lands and within a year he had begun a further round of coinage debasement.[22]

In the midst of this, he had also executed his brother, Thomas Seymour, Baron Sudeley. This had been difficult to avoid. Thomas Seymour was not an endearing fellow and had made colossal missteps, apparently convinced that his position as uncle of the king should not only protect him, but against all contrary expectations, elevate him. He had married the king's widowed stepmother very quickly – too quickly – after the death of the old king, to the great frustration of his brother.[23] When she died in September 1548, he made overtures towards his late wife's stepdaughter, the Lady Elizabeth, who had lived in his household while the former queen Catherine was alive. Rumours circulated that he had even laid hands on the fourteen-year-old princess. The Baron Sudeley had also done everything possible to get closer to his nephew, the King of England, in an attempt to wrest some power away from his older brother.

John Dudley also had reason not to like him. On Edward's accession, the younger Seymour had been given Dudley's treasured position of Lord Admiral. Whereas Dudley as Lord Admiral had instituted a dramatic reorganization of the navy, fought intense battles at the helm of flagships and negotiated a peace between France and England, Thomas Seymour seemed uninterested in doing much with the post, even avoiding the warfare with Scotland which had broken out in the summer of 1547. While his older brother and John Dudley went to battle, Thomas Seymour stayed in London, taking the opportunity to further ingratiate himself with the king. Thomas was determined to be a thorn in Dudley's paw, advising his friends to keep their property in Warwickshire, so as to curb Dudley's control of the area.[24] The two men had even quarrelled, according to reports, and Dudley had chastised him for his lack of loyalty to his brother, telling him, 'Be content therefore, with the honour done to you for your brother's sake, and with the office of Lord Admiral, which I gave up to you for the same motive.' He continued with a warning, 'for neither the king nor I will be governed by you, nor would we be governed by your brother were it not that his virtues and loyalty towards the king and country made him the man fittest to administer the affairs of the country during the king's minority.'[25] John's loyalty was linked to the elder Seymour's virtues and abilities, which the younger did not have.

Thomas had been arrested in January 1549. The investigations by the Privy Council were wide-ranging and took a month to collect. When he was examined in February, he refused to talk to any councillors until he could face his accusers. This was not a wise move. The day after a particularly unfruitful interview with the prisoner, a bill of attainder was introduced to parliament, which passed unopposed in the Lords (his elder brother being excused) and caused much debate in the Commons. It was at last passed in the first week of March. Within a week the king had assented to the execution of his uncle, though it was clear that this had taken some persuading. Thomas Seymour had been executed on 20 March 1549.

It was largely the Privy Council who had urged the arrest and execution of the Lord Protector's brother; the elder Seymour may have protected himself for a time by acquiescing to their demands. Perhaps it was this crisis that had caused a furthering of the rift between the Protector and the Council, with whom Edward Seymour met seldom in the spring and summer of 1549. As rebellions arose and the economy plummeted, Seymour was quickly losing support from his councillors. The primary objectors were Thomas Wriothesley, Earl of Southampton – long an enemy – and Henry FitzAlan, Earl of Arundel, a man just below Dudley in age and experience, having served as deputy of Calais, in the troops at Boulogne and now as Lord High Constable under Edward VI. Notably, both Wriothesley and FitzAlan were religious conservatives, just as against Seymour's reformist policies as they were against his failed management of the realm.

By the time that John Dudley had routed the rebels at Dussin's Dale and was heading back to London, he too had had enough of Edward Seymour's failed leadership. His policies had driven thousands to rebellion, a rebellion which Seymour had not taken seriously until it had almost been too late. Dudley had urged early action, but was rebuffed by Seymour's unwillingness to heed advice, even from him.[26] Every day Seymour was acting less the virtuous and loyal servant and more the ambitious tyrant. Having put down the rebellion that Seymour's poor governance had stirred up, John marched with his own men and the mercenaries who had joined him, failing – or refusing – to disband them when they reached London in early September. By mid-September, he joined former enemies Wriothesley and FitzAlan in making overtures to the Lady Mary for her support, and he himself met with the imperial ambassador, Van der Delft, to see if he would support a coup against the Protector. To win their support, Dudley would have to compromise on any reformist religious sensibilities he held, feigning that his own religious views were closer to those of his co-conspirators. Mary refused to help but Van der Delft gave cautious support.

By 30 September, Seymour had at last caught wind of the plot against him. He ordered Dudley's soldiers to disband and to leave the city. When that failed, on 5 October, he panicked. A public letter went out from Hampton Court, where he and the king were residing, condemning the wicked conspiracy against them, and demanding that others band together to defend them.[27] The next day, the Council met in the home that John Dudley had received from Wriothesley, Ely Place, and set out a letter of their own to the people, decrying the falsehoods spread abroad by the Lord Protector, who presented a danger to the preservation of the king.[28] Rather than repairing to his side, people ought to come to them to prepare to fight. These were the first volleys of a potential civil war.

Later that day, having failed to secure Hampton Court, Seymour rode with the king to Windsor, a desperate trip that Edward resented. From their positions, Seymour with the king at Windsor and the Council meeting at John's London home, the two parties attempted to negotiate. Seymour would not be tempted back. Rumours were spreading – being spread – that he had not only kidnapped the king (which was at least partly true), but also that he was purchasing support from France and planning on taking the king out of the country (which was unlikely). Seymour needed assurances that his actions would be defended and his life and property secure. At last, having received these, Seymour surrendered himself, and on 14 October he was taken to the Tower, along with a number of his servants and advisers. His fate, despite promises, was uncertain. No less certain was that of his old friend, John Dudley, who, unless he played his cards right, could soon join him. John's temporary allies in the coup, men such as FitzAlan and Wriothesley, were just as willing to become his enemies once again. Now that their primary target had been removed, John Dudley would surely be next.

*

It might have seemed impossible at the outset of the year to imagine the scene which took place at the chapel at Richmond on 3 June 1550. Standing before the communion table, where once a gold-sheathed and gem-encrusted altar had stood, was the twenty-year-old John Dudley, Viscount Lisle, son of the Earl of Warwick.[29] Large clerestory windows brought light into the 250-square-foot chapel, illuminating the precious stones worn by the many guests in attendance. Between the windows were painted murals of saintly kings of history, including Edward VI's namesake, and beneath them hung devotional tapestries.[30] On the ceiling were wooden lozenges containing red roses and portcullises, symbols of the king's ancestry. Richmond, still occasionally known by its ancient name of Sheen, had burned in 1497, almost taking the dynasty with it. Henry VII had rebuilt it as a monument to his family line, before it had been all but abandoned by his son. His twelve-year-old grandchild and heir, Edward VI, now sat in the chapel closet beside the altar, observing events.

Beside the young John stood his soon-to-be wife, Anne, the eldest daughter of Edward Seymour, still Duke of Somerset despite his arrest. Little more than a child, Anne was only twelve, born a year after the king her cousin, and a full eight years younger than her groom. The young John Dudley had agreed to the wedding knowing full well that it was a politically efficacious match and not one born of any romantic motivation.[31] He did this for his father and his family; if he was lucky in a few years he would have a wife with whom he could build a happy marriage, but that was hardly the point.

After the fall of the bride's father, John Dudley, Earl of Warwick, had been forced to fend off attacks from Wriothesley and his fellow conservatives. They had him in an impressive trap over the affair with Seymour. Should he join in their demands to have Seymour executed, he was in danger of alienating men like Cranmer, who had promised Seymour clemency. If he did not, he risked exposing himself as an ally of Seymour's and would perhaps be forced to share his fate. In the end, John cut through their carefully constructed net with all the subtlety of a broadsword.

Having spent some time away, once again claiming illness, upon hearing of Wriothesley's fervent speeches calling for the death of Seymour, John stormed into a Council meeting, wearing the face he reserved for the battlefield. Laying his hand on the long sword which hung by his side, he confronted Wriothesley. 'My lord,' he growled, 'you seek his blood and he that seeketh his blood would have mine also.'[32] In one passionate fell swoop, Dudley ended discussion about the execution of the former Lord Protector and frightened his enemies off from attempting anything against himself either. At least for the moment.

Dudley's position in Council had been bolstered by the admission of Henry Grey, Marquis of Dorset – husband of the daughter of Charles Brandon (and granddaughter of Henry VII) – in November 1549, providing John Dudley with another reformist ally. As always, John could also count on the support of his brother, Andrew, who too was on the Council. Two conservatives had also thrown their support behind Dudley: John Russell and William Paulet; they were rewarded with earldoms.

By Candlemas on Sunday, 2 February, John Dudley was Lord President of the Council, and Wriothesley and FitzAlan, his two co-conspirators in the coup against Seymour, had been removed. Four days later, Seymour was released from the Tower, following an interview with Dudley and the Council.[33] By April Seymour had been rehabilitated, rejoining the Council and dining with the king. Seymour's reform had involved bowing to the authority of Dudley and the Council, literally. Seymour had been brought before the Council, meeting at the home of the Sheriff of London, a stone's throw from the home where John had spent his youngest years, and forced to remove his cap and bow to them, before the letters securing his pardon were placed before him.[34] Seymour was bowing to the whole Council, but it was John Dudley who was Lord President and leader of that Council. The imperial ambassador described him as 'absolute master here and the Lords of the Council are under his orders. They go daily to his house to learn his pleasure; nothing is done except by his command.'[35]

For Dudley, as he watched his friend-turned-enemy bow before him, allowing Seymour to return to even limited power was a gamble, and another man might have sought to have his competitor permanently out of the way at the first opportunity. John did not pursue Wriothesley and FitzAlan to their deaths either, though Wriothesley was well on that path anyway, having fallen ill shortly after his removal. Of course, there was enough to do in just managing the realm, a task that now fell largely to him. Seymour could be useful in that, especially when it came to religious reforms, though perhaps Dudley would keep him away from anything to do with the finances.

Dudley had negotiated a new treaty with France in the spring, one that involved the sale of Boulogne for over £150,000, to be paid in two instalments, an agreement that would go a long way to helping England out of a difficult financial situation, even if John was all too aware of the price that had been paid to claim Boulogne in the first place.[36] Though he was the force behind the treaty, much of the negotiation had taken place while John was away, apparently ill. There were murmurings that his frequent ailments were a political tactic; by withdrawing himself from the court at opportune moments or forcing the Council to meet at his own home, he controlled the situation without putting himself at undue risk and avoided awkward or dangerous confrontations.

Whatever the reason, he was also not at Sheen on the day of his eldest son's wedding.[37] He had finalized the negotiations a week before, granting the couple various lands and manors. Edward Seymour had also contributed a manor in Warwickshire. John and Anne would be a powerful couple, combining Seymour and Dudley inheritances and kinship networks. It was also a symbolic marriage, a burying of any remaining hatchets between the two fathers. This would have been more convincing, of course, had the groom's father actually been in attendance.

Nevertheless, the celebration was a magnificent one. Marriage was no longer a sacrament in the Church, as it had been when John's parents had been married, and so the ceremony was somewhat different, based on the Book of Common Prayer, instituted by the Council the year before.[38] In the grand setting of the chapel at Richmond, first John and then Anne said their vows.

When the ceremony was complete, the company proceeded along the gallery at the south end of the chapel, past the courtyard, and into the hall for dinner and dancing. The hall ran parallel to the chapel, both in placement and design. It too had large clerestory windows underneath which hung ornate tapestries, though these were of more secular themes. Between the windows, raised on large corbels were life-sized statues of Edward VI's predecessors, including King Arthur,

Henry V and Henry VII, who watched over the proceedings with solemn stone eyes. When the air in the hall became too warm – it was, after all, June – attendees could slip out of the hall and into the courtyard between the two buildings and enjoy the spray from the large fountain. Water poured from a specially crafted bush of red roses, at the centre of which were red dragons and lions, more symbols of royal power.

In the afternoon there was a joust, led by the bride's elder half-brother, Lord Edward Seymour, followed by a supper. The king retired to his lodgings at Westminster, having had, by all estimations, a thoroughly enjoyable time. This, however, was not the end of the week's festivities. The following day there was a second wedding, though one of lesser political significance. The groom was the newly wed John's younger brother, Robert, who was to marry Amy Robsart, the daughter of a Norfolk squire. Unlike John and his young bride, these two were of an age, both approaching their eighteenth birthdays. They could thus be husband and wife in the full sense without the delay that awaited John, and there was every reason to believe they looked forward to such a life with great anticipation. This marriage too had strategic significance for the Dudley family; Robert's father was shoring up support and lands in Norfolk following the rebellions that summer. The bride was heir to several large manors in Norfolk; when her father died, she and her husband would become the wealthiest landowners in the county. That said, Robert was still only a lesser son, and the wedding was nothing like the Seymour–Dudley union of the day before.[39]

The ceremony was much the same. Robert was asked, 'Wilt thou have this woman to thy wedded wife, to live together after God's ordinance in the holy estate of matrimony? Wilt thou love her, comfort her, honour and keep her, in sickness and in health? And forsaking all other, keep thee only to her so long as you both shall live?'

Robert replied, 'I will.'

Amy answered the same question, with the addition that she would also obey Robert. They then exchanged their vows, promising to love and cherish (and, again, in Amy's case, obey) until death.

Robert placed the ring on Amy's hand, and the minister said the prayer over it, asking God to bless the couple: 'So these persons may surely perform and keep the vow and covenant betwixt them made; whereof this ring given, and received, is a token and pledge, and may ever remain in perfect love and peace together, and live according to thy laws, through Jesus Christ our Lord. Amen.' That done, he warned, 'Those whom God hath joined together, let no man put asunder.' He declared them married and blessed them, making the sign of the cross.

The activities following the ceremony were less vigorous than the day before, though they still seemed to amuse the king, who was once again in attendance. A live goose was hung from two cross posts, and various gentlemen in attendance competed to see who could first remove its head. As blood sports went, it was somewhat crude, but it seemed to satisfy those in attendance. The real tournament began again on the day following Robert and Amy's wedding, with men fighting with large staves.

Through it all, the grooms' father remained distant. By the end of June, there were reports that John Dudley, Earl of Warwick, had reason once again to mistrust his son's father-in-law, the Duke of Somerset, fearing that he was working to regain his former position. Meanwhile, John also had the intransigent Lady Mary to contend with. Mary had been told that, should she support the coup against Somerset, she would be allowed to celebrate the Catholic mass. When Dudley emerged as Lord President, however, he redoubled efforts to impose religious – Protestant – uniformity, in line with the king's wishes. After many decades of alliance and friendship between Mary and the Dudley family, she was resentful, to say the least, suggesting that John's proceedings against the former Lord Protector were motivated by 'envy and ambition' and that 'no good will come of this move, but that it is punishment from Heaven, and may be only the beginning of our misfortunes.'[40] Mary planned an escape from England, 'I would willingly stay,' she wrote, 'were I able to live and serve God as I have done in the past; which is what I have always said. But these men,' by which she meant John Dudley and his allies, 'are so changeable that I know not what to say.' Mary was desperate to get away from the person she now held to be the 'most unstable man in England'.[41] John Dudley had a new enemy, and she was next in line to the throne.

11

I will serve without fear

Edward Seymour, Duke of Somerset, had plotted to kill his erstwhile friend – and now kinsman – John Dudley, Earl of Warwick. He had planned to invite Dudley, along with his allies, to a banquet at William Paget's London home and, while they feasted and celebrated, he would attack, cutting off their heads.[1] This, at least, was the accusation made against him as he stood on trial in the hall at Westminster on 1 December 1551. It was eighteen months since the marriage of the Dudley and Seymour families at Sheen, and it had become increasingly clear that only one of the two former friends would hold the king's trust and favour. The other would have to die.

'The whole Council,' Dudley had complained of Seymour to Seymour's steward, Richard Whalley, in July, 'doth much dislike his late attempts herein.'[2] Seymour had objected strongly to John's hard-earned alliance with France, which had also worried the Lady Mary and her imperial supporters, and had intervened in the matter of religious conservatives who were imprisoned in the Tower, including Stephen Gardiner, Bishop of Winchester. 'His Grace hath brought the whole Council in suspicion that he taketh and aspireth to have the self and same order and authority to the despatch and direction of the proceedings therein as his grace had being Protector.' Though there had been rumours throughout 1551 that Seymour was gathering his power for a counter-attack on the Earl of Warwick, this was largely hopeful thinking on the part of Catholics and conservatives, who objected to Dudley's reformist religious policies. The rumours remained concerning: surely Seymour *could* draw on the conservative support base who had once abandoned him to turn on Dudley. After all, Dudley had not endeared himself to the conservatives.[3]

'Alas,' John cried to Whalley, 'what meaneth my Lord in this ways to discredit himself, and why will he not see his own decay herein? Thinks he,' he continued, 'to rule and direct the whole Council as he will considering how his late governance is yet misliked?'

Edward Seymour was becoming to John Dudley as Thomas Seymour had been to Edward: a liability. His blood-link to the throne was stronger than any relationship that John could try to cultivate with the young, though maturing, king. If Dudley's position was to survive Edward's majority, when the king could make his own decisions unfettered by Dudley and his council, Edward Seymour could not be allowed to live.

Whalley had relayed Dudley's complaints to Seymour's former secretary, William Cecil – recently made Sir William Cecil. Three months later it was to Cecil that Seymour had written, expressing his fears of a plot against him. Cecil replied with coldness: if Seymour had nothing to hide then he had nothing to fear; if he did have something to hide, Cecil wanted nothing to do with him.[4] Dudley had clearly already got to Cecil, along with Whalley. Seymour was arrested two days later, followed by his wife and other accused co-conspirators. This included the cunning and popular – if melancholic and taciturn – Henry FitzAlan, the Earl of Arundel. After FitzAlan's turn against Dudley following the initial overthrow of Seymour, Dudley, as Lord President of the Council, had fined him the astronomical fee of £12,000 for his scheming, though had not enforced its payment, accepting instead FitzAlan's quiet retirement to Sussex. This did not last long, however, and the earl was back at court, this time to plot against Dudley with Seymour.[5] When confronted with his machinations, FitzAlan apparently barked back at Dudley that he had none in his family who had ever been traitors, but all knew who had.[6] FitzAlan was imprisoned.

It took only six weeks for the Council to put together the case against Edward Seymour, and so on 1 December, two days into Advent, he was brought before the lords at Westminster Hall.

The scant winter light crept in through the high, deep window.

Hanging over them all was the impressive and imposing hammer-beam roof.[7] The two-metre thick stone walls of Westminster Hall reverberated with ancient royal power. The entrance to the hall was so grand, it looked like the doorway to a medieval cathedral, but its use was purely secular, and undoubtedly political.[8] It had been built almost five hundred years before by the son of William the Conqueror to be as large and imposing as possible; seventy-three metres long and twenty metres wide, it was the largest of its kind on its conception, and remained the model for subsequent halls.[9]

Not five years before, Edward Seymour had sat in a place of honour and power in this very hall, overseeing the coronation feast of his nephew. Now, he was forced to answer multiple charges of treason, including conspiracy to raise men against the king, resisting arrest, planning to attack the Council and, of course, plotting to kill John Dudley.[10]

At the forefront of the hall, where the king had sat at his coronation feast, was William Paulet, the Marquess of Winchester and Lord High Treasurer, who oversaw proceedings. Approaching seventy, Paulet had been born under Richard III, and had served as a judge for other doomed members of the court through the years, including Thomas More and Anne Boleyn. Paulet had sided with Dudley against the Duke of Somerset in the coup two years before and not faltered since; he would not be favourable to the accused. Paulet was sitting on a large platform under a cloth of estate, representing the power of the king himself. One step down from him were placed the other twenty-seven lords who would be judging the Duke of Somerset's case, including two newly created English dukes. The first was Henry Grey, the Duke of Suffolk, who had been given the same title as his late father-in-law, Charles Brandon. The other was an entirely new ducal creation, the Duke of Northumberland, awarded to none other than the President of the Council, formally the Earl of Warwick: John Dudley.

Dudley had received his title, along with the gold, fur-lined coronet, at the beginning of October, just five days before Seymour's arrest. As a duke, John Dudley held the highest noble rank under the king, one often possessed by members of the royal family. The title had been created especially for Dudley, a variation on the title of Earl of Northumberland, which had formerly been held by the members of the Percy family, resident at Alnwick Castle. The two young heirs to the earldom, however, had been tainted by their father's treason after his involvement in the Pilgrimage of Grace, and thus had not received the title. So it was that John Dudley, son of an executed traitor, became the Duke of Northumberland, one of only three dukes in England.

And it might soon be only two, though the Duke of Somerset was doing an admirable job of defending himself against the accusations made against him. He argued that his assembly of men had always been for defensive purposes and that the testimonies against him were untrue. When it came to a plot to kill John Dudley, however, his denial was less categorical. He told the assembled lords, Dudley amongst them, that he had not determined to kill the Duke of Northumberland, though he had considered it.

The trial lasted all day. In the end, despite Dudley's and the Council's best efforts, there was little evidence of treason. Seymour had almost certainly been plotting to overthrow, and perhaps even execute, Dudley, but this was his only crime, and it was not enough to convict him of treason.[11] It was enough, however, to convict him of a felony, for having planned an illicit assembly for nefarious purposes, namely arresting and possibly killing several Privy Council members. Though Seymour would not be found guilty of treason, the sentence was still death by hanging.

His conviction read out, Seymour begged the Council – his former colleagues and friends – to intercede with the king. He might have expected little agreement to this request, but John answered him. Seeing as Edward Seymour had not been convicted of treason, he would do all he could to obtain a pardon for him from the king.[12] No one could be sure if the new Duke of Northumberland meant it or not, though Seymour's pleas did reach Edward, who recorded his uncle's cries for mercy – dispassionately – in his journal.[13]

Edward VI seemed content to be distracted from his uncle's fate. In this, John Dudley employed the help of his sons, who participated in a series of tournaments and jousts to amuse the fourteen-year-old king. On 17 December, two weeks after the trial, the younger John

Dudley, now in his father's relinquished position of Earl of Warwick and still, rather awkwardly, married to Edward Seymour's daughter, issued a challenge to all comers for a tournament, which was held at Greenwich on 3 January as part of the Christmas celebrations.

Alongside John and among the defenders was his brother-in-law, Sir Henry Sidney, who had married the eldest Dudley daughter, Mary, in the spring. It was a good match; the two were close in age and shared an interest in literature. Among the challengers were also John's two younger brothers, Ambrose and Robert. Four days later, Ambrose participated in fighting-at-barriers before the king, and on Sunday, 17 January all three were at the tilt again.[14]

The day after the festivities, the Council met, along with the king.[15] On the agenda, prepared by the young king, was the matter of Edward Seymour's confederates. This was altered to include a consideration of Seymour's fate as well, and the subject of his execution. The king seemed to believe all the stories about his uncle, writing in his journal that the Duke of Somerset had made a plan 'to call the Earl of Warwick to a banquet with the Marquis of Northampton and divers others and to cut off their heads.'[16] By Tuesday, it was decided: the former Lord Protector would have to die.

The day was chosen as 22 January, that Saturday, perhaps in the hopes that the streets would be quieter and the quick action would lessen the crowds. Nevertheless, as a precaution, the king's guard along with a thousand other men from across the city gathered at Tower Hill, to ensure there would be no rioting or uprising in response to the execution. As the sun rose, Edward Seymour was led out to the scaffold. He gave an appropriately pious speech, and the executioner struck his head from his body. The Council met that very day, and commissioners were sent out to Syon House, once an abbey and – thanks to Seymour's efforts – now a grand three-storey mansion, to make an inventory of the executed duke's belongings.[17] Before long, Syon was in the possession of the Duke of Northumberland.

With the execution of his former friend, John Dudley was undeniably the most powerful man in England, at the head of a Council consisting almost entirely of men loyal to him, and in the service of a king who looked to him for guidance. Not only was John Dudley

Lord Protector in all but name, he was just shy of being king himself.

*

When the axe fell that killed his father, on that warm August day, John Dudley had been only six. Now at almost fifty, resting at his newly acquired manor at Chelsea over the harsh winter of 1552, his memories of his father were scattered and shaped by what he had been told since that moment.[18] His father had been so busy in John's early years: a black-robed figure with ink-stained fingers bowed over account books. The explanation, however, was always clear: his father had served the king. His late nights, his anxieties, his desire to get it all right, had all been in service of the Crown. For this service, he had been reviled and ridiculed, even hated. John had not escaped the residual resentment four decades later, hurled at him like spit by men indignant of his rise from such tainted beginnings. For his service John's father had been taken from him, and John cast into an uncertain world. 'Though my poor father,' John reflected, 'suffered death for doing his master's commandment, who was the wisest prince of the world living in those days, and yet could not his commandment be my father's discharge after he was departed this life.'[19]

Now, John Dudley was also in service to the king, though his role was different from that of his father. His hands were more likely to be stained with blood than ink, and he had accrued the reverence of titles far beyond his father's grasp. In contrast to Edmund's subtle expressions of superiority and favour – the hints of crimson and flashes of gold – John had licence to proclaim his standing loudly with every inch of fabric he wore: gowns of cloth of silver, of purple velvet, of white satin embroidered with gold.[20] The dangers, however, remained. John, too, had become unpopular. In October the Privy Council had dealt with a rumour that coins were being minted not with the king's head and emblem on them, but with John Dudley's symbol of the bear and ragged staff.[21] The renowned preacher John Knox had accused him of dissembling his religion.[22] And the common folk, fickle and ignorant as they were, had made their sentiments very clear during the Seymour affair a year before, when they had shouted their support for the former Lord Protector, John's former friend, at his trial.[23]

John, at the time, had emerged as the preferred option to Seymour amongst those in power. Seymour had mismanaged affairs, revealed himself to be ambitious for power and neglected the advice of those who had been appointed to offer it. Dudley had not taken the position of Lord Protector and, perhaps most importantly, he worked *with* the Council, not in spite of it. Given the choice between them – and it was a choice, the Council had proven itself too small for the both of them – Dudley had piled up supporters while Seymour had been left in the cold to die. Even his regal nephew had turned his back on him. With Edward VI past his fourteenth birthday, he was approaching the age at which he could rule independently. Rather than avoiding this seeming inevitability, Dudley did what he could to support it, relinquishing his own power in favour of Edward's.

In late 1551, Edward began attending Council sessions, and by November that year the Council was no longer signing commissions alongside the king. In fact, there had been no formal restatement of a regency since the Protector's fall two years before.[24] Edward was beginning to form his own mind on matters and John knew that it was best not to get in the way. When in 1552 Edward wanted to directly intervene in the creation of the Book of Common Prayer, despite it being approved, completed and under the jurisdiction of Thomas Cranmer, Archbishop of Canterbury, Dudley was blamed by Cranmer for the intrusion, but facilitated the king's will all the same.[25]

One could guide the king, but for this John Dudley was ill-equipped. He was not a well-educated scholar like his father, who had written a treatise on good kingship. This work, of course, was severely behind the times. Since Edmund Dudley composed his *Tree of Commonwealth* in the Tower, there had been a noticeable revolution in political thinking, led by an Italian named Niccolò Machiavelli. His work, *Il Principe*, had reached England some twenty years before, when it had been recommended to men like Thomas Cromwell as being relevant to those who served so near the prince.[26] Machiavelli's teachings were also, at the same time, frequently condemned. Whereas previous writers, like John's own father, had argued that virtue was the key to good government, Machiavelli suggested that this was not always the case. At times, in order to protect the state, a king would have to act in ways that were decidedly *not* virtuous: 'that man,' Machiavelli wrote, 'who will possess honesty in all his actions, must needs go to ruin, among so many that are dishonest. Whereupon,' the Italian continued, 'it is necessary for a Prince, desiring to preserve himself, to be able to make use of that honesty, and lay it aside again, as need shall require.'[27] There was merit in Machiavelli's writing, and John himself had abandoned honesty in some matters; everyone knew many of the claims against Seymour had been fabricated. In the summer of 1551, William Thomas, a clerk of the Council whom John Dudley had promoted, had begun to send short Machiavellian essays to Edward VI.[28] These made clear that the ultimate end for every prince is to maintain his state, even if this means acting in a devious fashion: lying to foreign powers and casting off friends when they are no longer necessary.

Machiavelli and Thomas both stressed, as well, the importance of biding one's time and seizing the right moment. John had learned that lesson long ago, watching Wolsey's expert opportunistic negotiations and before the frozen marshes at Bohain. Had John's own time passed? Over the winter of 1552, Dudley retreated from the court, despite his high position, to Chelsea, claiming illness. He complained of a fever hot as fire and a pain in his lower abdomen. He sank into a melancholic mood, welcoming death as an escape from it all, and holding his children among the few things in life which made it all worth it.[29]

On this count, there had been recent tragedies. The previous summer had seen an intense bout of the sweating sickness in London, which had reached the Dudley home in Otford, Kent, south-east of London. Ambrose's wife, Anne, had died, as had Anne and Ambrose's child, John and Jane's first grandchild.[30] John had also lost his own young daughter, taken by the illness with devastating speed; merry one evening and dead the next. Her bout with measles a month before must have weakened her, leaving her with a cough, though she had seemed largely recovered. Such tragedies delayed John's assignment in the north and his son's attendance on the king before the summer's progress. John was absent from the court most of the summer checking the northern border. He was back over the autumn, before retreating again over the Christmas season, slipping into this melancholic, reflective mood.

Would he follow his father along his duty-bound but deadly path? Was it better to seek admiration, or to serve the king and risk fatal unpopularity? As far as John could tell, one couldn't have both. He reflected on this to Cecil as he rested at Chelsea, 'I would wish therefore as it is most decent in the service of all kings and in the commonwealth, that there were always a difference between such as sought their own before their master's, and such as for conscience sake seeketh the advancement of their master and country before their own.'[31] Seymour, for instance, had gained popularity in the end, but the means – it seemed – had been self-serving. No, John was determined to follow his father's example. This meant serving the king, no matter the scorn and threat of death. Penning his letter to Cecil, he had first written it as an encouragement to them both, to serve the king without concern for what might become of them, but in looking it over, he turned it into a personal manifesto: '*For my own part*,' he added, 'with all earnestness and duty *I will* serve without fear, seeking nothing but the true glory of God, and his highness's surety, so shall ~~you~~' (he crossed it out and added), '*I* most please god and have ~~one's~~' (again, he changed his writing to reflect his own thoughts) '*my* conscience upright, and then not fear what man doth to ~~us~~ *me* for' (he began a new page) 'they cannot kill the body, but he that seeketh to save that with an unpure conscience killeth the soul.'[32]

John had made his decision. He would need to face the court, with all its critics and cravers, once again. And he was under no illusions: to serve the king was to risk one's own life. But not to do so was to risk one's soul. And that he was not willing to do.

*

The boy, not yet sixteen, lay prostrate on his bed as the minister before him spoke of death: 'Verily I say unto you, he that heareth my word, and believeth in him that sent me, hath everlasting life, and shall not come into damnation, but he passeth from death into life.'[33] Covered in sweat and shaking, the boy bore every sign of the illness that he had suffered for months.[34] Ulcers and scabs covered his swollen torso, and his breath was ragged and weak from months of continual coughing caused by the illness in his lungs. Although his face, stomach and legs had swollen, the rest of him was emaciated from lack of food. He could barely move. His nails had fallen off and his hair was gone; it had come off in patches until at last the physicians had it shaved, covering his head in a wrapping of bandages. Intense fevers wracked his body at intervals. These left him too weak to expel the foul humours which caused him so much pain and discomfort. When he worked up the energy to rid himself of them, they gave off a foul stench, stinking up the private chamber where he lay at Greenwich.

The king had first appeared to be ill in March, when he was forced to open parliament at Whitehall, rather than Westminster. By the end of parliament at the beginning of April, he showed signs of improving. This did not last, however, and by the end of April there were reports that he was wasting away, coughing up yellow and black phlegm lined with blood. By the beginning of May, the king's physicians were desperate, and three more doctors were sought, including John Dudley's own.[35] John had suspended the treatment he had been taking for his own ailment when the severity of the king's illness became known.[36] The king's physicians were required to take a solemn oath, in front of leading members of the Council, including Dudley, not to share details of the king's condition.[37] This, of course, did not stop the whispers.

There were so many rumours circulating the court it was hard to keep track of them.[38] No one could find out exactly what the Duke of Northumberland was planning. Despite earlier tensions over religion, he seemed keen to retain good relations with the Lady Mary, sending her updates on the king's health, offering his services and even sending her the coat of arms she bore as Princess of England when her mother was still queen.[39] When the Lady Mary arrived to visit the king in February, Dudley's eldest son, John, Earl of Warwick, led the procession, and she was received and entertained as if she were already the queen of England.[40] She was met in a similar manner when she arrived at court by the Duke of Northumberland himself, and when she withdrew following her audience with the king, she was accompanied by Jane, Duchess of Northumberland.[41]

The imperial ambassador, Jean Scheyfve, adviser to and advocate for the Lady Mary, remained mistrustful of these overtures, suspicious at first that Dudley would try to supplant Mary with her younger sister and thus himself: 'The Duke's and his party's designs to deprive the Lady Mary of the succession to the Crown are only too plain,' Scheyfve wrote to the Emperor Charles V. 'It is said that if the Duke of Northumberland felt himself well supported, he would find means to marry his eldest son, the Earl of Warwick, to the Lady Elizabeth, after causing him to divorce his wife, daughter of the late Duke of Somerset; or else that he might find it expedient to get rid of his own wife and marry the said Elizabeth himself, and claim the Crown for the house of Warwick as descendants of the House of Lancaster.'[42]

In mid-June the ambassador's opinion changed. It was neither Mary nor Elizabeth who it was said would inherit Edward's throne, but their cousin, Jane, along with her new husband, Northumberland's son, Guildford Dudley: 'Their main object will be to make shift to exclude the Princess and the Lady Elizabeth, and declare the true heir to be the Duke of Suffolk's eldest daughter, who was lately married to the Duke of Northumberland's son.'[43] Scheyfve wasn't entirely sure how this would take place, but concluded: 'No one is able to find out exactly what Northumberland is planning to do; and it seems he will be guided by events, though there is no doubt that he is aspiring to the Crown.'[44]

Guildford, now the fourth eldest son of John and Jane, was sixteen, and ready to enter public life as his elder brothers all had done. Guildford had at first expected to marry another of the grandchildren of Mary and Charles Brandon, Margaret Clifford.[45] John's friendship with Henry Grey, the Duke of Suffolk, went some way to helping smooth the path to a bride of even higher standing. Henry Grey had not always been the most popular man at court; Henry VIII had overlooked him for the honour of Knight of the Garter repeatedly, despite nominations from Grey's father-in-law, Charles Brandon, and he had also bypassed him and his wife in his will. Grey had fallen in with the plans of Thomas Seymour in the early years of Edward's reign, encouraged by promises that the younger Seymour would marry Grey's eldest daughter to the king. At Thomas Seymour's fall, however, Grey entered instead the circle around John Dudley, who awarded him with the dukedom of Suffolk following the fall of Edward Seymour. Grey was ambitious and opportunistic, if not terribly cunning. But he was not especially important himself; his greatest value lay in his daughter, Jane.

According to the will of the late king, Henry VIII, Guildford's new bride was third in line to the throne, following Edward's two sisters, Mary and Elizabeth. This already involved skipping the rights of Henry's elder sister, Margaret, who had married the Scottish king, and whose young granddaughter, Mary, was now Queen of Scots as well as being betrothed to the Dauphin of France. It also meant bypassing Jane's mother, Frances, the daughter of Charles Brandon and Henry VIII's sister, Mary; probably because Frances's husband, Henry Grey, had not endeared himself to his uncle-in-law and sovereign.[46] Jane's place in that succession also relied on Edward, Mary and Elizabeth not producing any heirs, which Henry might have expected they would in the time it would take for the Crown to pass anywhere near her. Had her mother produced a son, he would have also pushed her further down the line by right of being male. It was a strange twist of fate, and Henry VIII's nightmare, that there were so many women in the succession. Not only were women unsuitable for sole rule by virtue of their nature, but their necessary submission to their husbands threw a dangerous variable into the practice of royal sovereignty; as Henry VIII himself had put it: 'if the female heir shall chance to rule, she cannot continue long without an husband, which, by God's law, must then be her governor and head.'[47] After Jane and her sisters were yet more women: her aunt Eleanor Clifford and her daughter Margaret, Guildford's original intended bride. After that Henry VIII had given up trying to name heirs; the idea that not one of these would produce a child – ideally a male child – was unfathomable.

Jane and Guildford's engagement had been agreed at the end of April, in the midst of the king's illness, but with his and the Council's approval and support. The date was set for Whitsuntide, the festival of Pentecost, Thursday, 25 May. The king's St George's Day and May Day tournaments, ceremonies and celebrations had also been moved to this week, when he would – presumably – be well enough to enjoy them. It was a triple wedding; Guildford's younger sister, Katherine, would also be married that day, to Lord Henry Hastings, the son of the Earl of Huntingdon, and Jane's younger sister, also named Catherine, would marry the son of the Earl of Pembroke, Henry Herbert. They were all children; the eldest of them, Henry Hastings, was approaching eighteen, the youngest, Katherine Dudley, was not yet ten. Securing alliances through marriage was the aim of every noble parent and the age of the child mattered little; these particular marriages only gained significance if observers – such as Scheyfve – connected them to the wider goings-on in the court.

Guildford Dudley had entered the chapel at Durham Place, the princely home his father had acquired of the Lady Elizabeth earlier in the year (though not without her 'conceiving some displeasure before against' the duke, for having sought it without checking her thoughts on the matter), with his bride and the two other couples.[48] The large windows let in the early summer light and faint lapping of the Thames nearby. Wearing rich cloth of silver and gold in black, crimson and purple, embroidered with roses and branches, Guildford and Jane looked decidedly royal.[49] They were bejewelled with rubies, emeralds, roses made of pearls, and large diamonds. Jane wore a girdle of agate and gold, with a long hanging pendant ornamented with pearls around her slim waist, and her hood was decorated with diamonds and enamelled gold. Both bride and groom were attractive young people, adorned in the best the royal wardrobe could offer them. Behind them were Guildford's younger sister, Katherine, and her groom, Henry. They wore silver and crimson, in cloths of gold and silver, as well as rich velvet.

Although the audience consisted of nobles and ambassadors, the king himself was not able to attend this wedding, as he had that of Guildford's elder brother. Edward was improving; he had appeared at his window in Greenwich and received the French ambassador the week before, but the wedding was perhaps a bit much. As a wedding gift, delivered by Guildford's uncle Andrew, he had sent the rich clothes the couples wore. He also sent presents to Guildford's mother, including purple and black velvet, a clock and a unicorn horn. The fact that much of his offering had been previously owned by the executed Duke of Somerset and his wife, the latter still in the Tower, did not take away from the sincerity of the gesture.

For the festivities, Guildford's father had turned to an old contact, Thomas Cawarden, whose father had done business with John's mother. Cawarden had held a variety of posts under Henry VIII and Edward VI, including master of the revels, which made him the perfect person to arrange masques to entertain the esteemed guests at the wedding.[50] Preparations were also made for games and jousts to mark the important occasion, along with a fine banquet.

Guildford was not the only Dudley son to be married that spring. His elder brother, Ambrose, lately a widower, remarried, this time to Elizabeth Tailboys. Elizabeth was the eldest daughter of Gilbert Tailboys and his wife, Elizabeth, also known as Bessie. Bessie had been Henry VIII's mistress in the early decades of his reign and had borne him a son, Henry Fitzroy. The king had never acknowledged his mistress's next child, Elizabeth Tailboys, as his own, but the closeness of their ages and the favour shown to her during his reign indicated it was a possibility. As Baroness Tailboys of Kyme in her own right, it was a good match, even if Elizabeth was a decade Ambrose's senior.

Guildford's younger brother, Harry, had also been married. His bride was the thirteen-year-old Margaret Audley. A cousin of Guildford's new wife, Margaret was also a distant cousin of Harry's through his grandmother, Elizabeth Grey. As the only surviving child of Thomas Audley, 1st Baron Audley, who had died a decade before with some £800 per year in lands, Margaret was a fortunate match for the younger son of a duke, as well as further securing the ties between the Grey and Dudley families.

Even Andrew Dudley, Guildford's uncle, was said to be engaged: to Margaret Clifford, the woman originally intended for Guildford himself, despite the thirty-year gap in their ages. Guildford's father seemed driven to marry off every relative as strategically as he could. It was as if he were preparing for something, ensuring he could draw on some of the most powerful and well-connected families in the realm for support, if he should need it. Or perhaps preparing a legacy that would ensure the continuation of the Dudley family line, should its patriarch depart this life. Or, to another observer, it might appear that John Dudley was manoeuvring his family as close to the line of succession as he could.

All eyes were focused on the inheritance of the dying King of England. Across Europe, the powers held their breath to see whether the crown would pass, as willed, to the Lady Mary. The Holy Roman Emperor, as a relation to Mary through her mother, was prepared to do whatever it took to ensure she came to the throne; as he wrote to his ambassadors, 'you must deliberate among yourselves according to the turn events take, and decide on the wisest course to be adopted for the safety of our cousin, the Princess.' Furthermore, they were to 'take such steps as you shall consider necessary to defeat the machinations of the French and keep them out of England'.[51] The French, it was rumoured, were allied with the Duke of Northumberland, ready to support him if the imperial powers should invade.[52] They were also, perhaps, keen to see it all come tumbling down, in case they could advance the claim of Mary, Queen of Scots, who was living in France as the Dauphin's betrothed. In England, the Lady Mary remained popular as the eldest daughter of Henry VIII, as a victim of his unpopular marriage to Anne Boleyn and as a gracious and wealthy landowner in her own right.

All the rumours were in accord about one thing: the Duke of Northumberland would decide the fate of the throne and the country; all rested on what course he took when the king died. John Dudley had not risen any higher in the popular estimation, nor made any attempt to, and was seen by some as a 'great tyrant', ruling over a young, dying king.[53]

It wasn't until the beginning of June, a few weeks after the weddings at Durham Place, that Edward was forced to truly confront the possibility that he might never recover. He shared his father's nightmare: all his successors were female, and not one had produced a son. He needed a plan. The search needed to be for a woman in the succession who could, in the shortest possible time, produce a male heir. Mary and Elizabeth were not married, and thus unlikely to produce a legitimate male heir any time soon. Frances Grey had not produced a child in some time; at the age of thirty-six the likelihood was low that she would have a son. Her eldest daughter, however, was married and of child-bearing years. She could already be pregnant with the male heir Edward desired and England needed. It just so happened that heir would also be a Dudley.

Edward would have to admit the fact, though, that even if Jane did carry the much-desired male successor, he would not live long enough to see it born. He needed an interim solution for the succession, and he needed it quickly.

In the first weeks of June, Edward revised his plan for the succession, and he gathered his justices and lawyers to make his will, enforced by the Privy Council's reminder that to refuse the king's bidding in this matter would be treason.[54] When the seventy-year-old judge, Sir Edward Montagu, objected to the plan, he reported that Dudley flew into a rage before the entire Privy Council. 'Traitor!' Dudley hurled at him, as the other councillors looked on. 'In the quarrel of that matter,' Dudley was reported to have said, 'I would fight in my shirt with any man living.'[55] Likewise, the next day the king himself also angrily commanded Montagu to do as he had been commanded. Sickly and not yet sixteen, Edward nonetheless had an impressive sense of his authority and purpose. By 21 June, justices, lawyers, councillors and peers of the realm had sworn to the new order that Edward had imposed. When word of it reached the court, it seemed obvious to everyone that the ambitious Duke of Northumberland must be behind it, ventriloquizing a dying king to his own advantage.

Dudley, reflecting in the peace of Chelsea six months earlier, had sworn to enforce the king's will, even if it meant his own death, and he had decried those who served their own interests above that of king and country. What if the king's will was to one's own advantage, however, so much so that everyone took one for the other? The fact that Dudley might benefit from the king's revised succession had the potential to be a poisoned chalice. John's father had known the dangers of being protected only by the favour of a dying king, and John had reflected long and hard on how little this had gained him in the end. When Henry VIII had died, John had been in the centre of it all – not excluded like his father – but he had also been surrounded by allies. Now John was above the parapet, exposed. Seymour had sought to control the king, to rule over him; Dudley had done what he could to avoid the same mistake, but it could not be denied that Dudley's own wishes and those of the king had blurred sufficiently to provoke suspicion. It might not matter that Edward had penned his device for the succession himself, or even whether the duke had been in the room when he did; the line between serving his king and moulding him was a difficult one to make out. Edward's will could be a more difficult – and more dangerous – burden to carry out when it was so clearly in Dudley's own benefit to do so. It was a difficult situation to be in, and at least in part of his own making. It could, of course, also be turned to his own advantage if he was cunning and mindful of opportunity: the frozen marshes of Bohain once again.

As word went out as to the revised succession, it was clear that Edward had entered the final stage of his illness. On his deathbed, Edward was urged to repent of his sins, forgiving those who had wronged him and seeking forgiveness from those he had mistreated. He was comforted that God had already forgiven him, and that he would find a place beside Him as one of his elect. As evening fell on 6 July 1553, Edward grew even weaker. Around him were his physicians and members of his privy chamber, including Sir Henry Sidney, Guildford Dudley's brother-in-law. As the sun dipped into the twilight of a July evening, Edward VI died. He was just fifteen and had never attained the majority allowing him to rule in his own right. But he had chosen his heir.

Once again, the machinery of a secret interregnum sprang into action; this time it was unmistakably Guildford's father who was working the gears. A message went out to the Lady Mary summoning her to London to see her brother. She had, however, the day before her brother's death, travelled the seventy miles from nearby Hunsdon to Kenninghall near the Norwich coast. The daughter of Catherine of Aragon was wiser than to fall into so obvious a trap.

Guildford himself had been resident in Durham House since his wedding, and Jane had joined him there, where they had consummated their marriage and begun living as man and wife. This had taken some time, as Guildford, along with other members of his wedding party, had been poisoned at the wedding feast. This had apparently been accidental: one of the cooks had mistaken one leaf for another more dangerous one while making the salad. Guildford had been ill for almost a month. Shortly after he recovered it was

Jane's turn to fall ill, and she was sent to Chelsea to recover. Guildford had barely had any opportunity to become acquainted with his new wife.

Guildford was informed of the succession by his father three days before the official proclamation of the king's death went out. Without a male heir apparent, Edward VI had indeed decided to exclude his two half-sisters, Mary and Elizabeth, from inheriting the Crown, as well as the eldest daughter of Mary and Charles Brandon, Frances Grey. Despite the lack of legal precedent or justification, the Council and John Dudley had sworn to uphold the monarch upon whom Edward had settled the Crown.

Lady Jane Dudley was Queen of England.

12

Blood can wash away the spots

Mary Sidney – formerly Mary Dudley – eyed the young woman sharing the barge with her as it moved slowly but steadily westward along the Thames. The young woman was only a few years younger than Mary herself, sixteen to Mary's eighteen, and looked pale, ill and distressed.[1] They were both dressed in fine clothes, though only Mary knew that they ought to be in mourning black. Both women wore wedding bands. Mary had been a wife for about two years now, though she was yet to have any living children. As a wife, Mary was expected to rule through obedience, as the handbook of the humanist Juan Luis Vives, written for the education of the then Princess Mary, had put it.[2] Although her primary virtues were meant to be modesty, obedience and chastity, even in marriage, she was encouraged as well to be graceful, witty and to cultivate the virtues of the mind. She was also responsible for looking after her and her husband's household, which in the case of the Sidneys was a significant one. Her father-in-law was Sir William Sidney, a courtier in his seventies whose kinship to Sir Charles Brandon and dedicated service to the Crown had helped him to accrue significant land holdings, most recently and most notably the manor of Penshurst in Kent, though that may have had as much to do with the intervention of Mary's own father. This elder Sidney was not long for this world, and Mary would soon have to take charge of Penshurst. The lot of the wife was rule through obedience indeed.

The woman across from her, Jane, had been married to Mary's younger brother Guildford for only a few months, and they had been together little of that time. Jane had not adapted well to married life, and had especially struggled to get along with her new family. It seemed that Jane had even exchanged harsh words with her mother-in-law, who had threatened to keep Guildford from her.[3] There were, of course, other factors at play, and it was probable that in other circumstances a smart young woman like Jane would have made a perfect addition to the Dudley family. As it was, however, she seemed to view them all with suspicion and seek to distance herself from them whenever possible. She had retreated to Chelsea, from which Mary had had to fetch her on this tense day in July.

After a journey of about an hour, the barge docked at Syon, one of the Dudley family's homes, some fifteen miles west of London. Once an abbey, Syon had been taken over by the old king only a few years after Mary was born and had been granted to the late Lord Protector, Edward Seymour, the old friend and enemy of Mary's father, at the accession of Edward VI. His efforts had produced the grand three-storey mansion before the two young women, with its turrets and battlements. Disembarking and entering at the south end of the house, they stepped on to the red and yellow foot carpet in the narrow entry chamber.[4] Another carpet of yellow and blue was draped over a walnut table and a third, red and yellow like the one at their feet, hung from the windowsill. There was a fireplace and a small chair with a cushion of crimson satin, embroidered with silver. On the walls hung tapestries of the story of Diana, the Roman goddess of the hunt, who, when seen while bathing by a spying man, turned him into a deer so that his own hunting dogs could rip him to shreds.

After her journey, Mary could retire to her own chamber at Syon. Her down bed was covered with a canopy of yellow damask and blue satin, with curtains of fine soft silk.[5] Two wool quilts, two pillows and a bolster of down lay on the bed. On the walls hung tapestries of peaceful shepherds, and carpets were draped over her oak table and windowsill. She could recline on an old chair adorned with gold, made more comfortable by the addition of a long cushion of silver and silk needlework. Her close chair, covered in green cloth and concealing her pewter chamber pot, sat in an adjoining room, along with a featherbed for her gentlewoman. Similar suites were occupied by her brothers Ambrose and Harry, and her sister Margaret.[6] The Lady

Jane also had a chamber at Syon, in which she would spend the night, containing a small featherbed, coverlets and stools.

The grandest chambers, with windows looking on to the courtyard and grounds, were of course reserved for Mary's parents, the Duke and Duchess of Northumberland. Mary's father had both an outer chamber, for receiving guests – such as the Council lords with whom he was in conference when Mary arrived – and a private chamber. The more public room was hung with tapestries of the story of the prodigal son and a window carpet ornamented with trees and greenery.[7] Entering his private chamber, the duke was immediately reminded of his duty by four pairs of scarlet hangings, embroidered with the king's arms. The frame of his bed was painted green and silver and the canopy hung with gold silk embroidered with green and fringed with gold and silk. On the wool mattress lay a green Turkish quilt and down pillows. His chair was of white rich tissue with a matching square cushion. Tucked out of the way was a close chair covered in red cloth, discreetly hiding a pewter chamber pot. Mary's father did not have ample time to relax at home, but when he did, it was in style and comfort.

There was a traditional hall, on the west range of the building, with large plank tables and cupboards, in addition to a more modern dining room for the family, with hangings, carpets and a crimson velvet chair with a matching cushion, covered in small pearls. Beyond these chambers used by the family were the whole series of rooms needed to support their fashionable life – the armoury, kitchen, scullery, ewery, wine cellar, buttery, spicery – as well as the rooms used by the hundreds of servants – steward, treasurer, marshal, porters, chamberlain, apothecary, grooms, footmen, ushers, drummers, riders, gardeners, armourers, brewers, bakers, butchers, launderers, gentlemen and gentlewomen.

Another of Mary's brothers, Robert, was not at Syon and did not keep a room there. He and his wife, Amy, had lands in Norfolk, and he kept many of his goods at the home of his kinsman and former tutor, Sir Francis Jobson.[8] Robert had left two days before Mary's arrival at the head of three hundred men, tasked with bringing the Lady Mary to London. He was one of the first to hear the secret that was being whispered within the corridors of power: the king was dead and, furthermore, his heir was not to be his eldest half-sister, Lady Mary, but the young woman with whom Mary Sidney had travelled to Syon, the Lady Jane Dudley. Jane was Queen of England; she just didn't know it yet.

No one expected much resistance from either woman, Lady Mary or Lady Jane. Lady Mary was stubborn and resilient, that much the Dudley family knew well, having battled with her for years over the issue of religion. They had, however, also enjoyed something like a friendship through the decades as well. Mary Sidney, after all, was named for the Lady Mary, having had her as a godmother. Stubbornness aside, the Lady Mary had never shown herself to be a power to be much concerned with, and she certainly could not boast the military experience and expertise of the battle-worn Duke of Northumberland. Perhaps that is why Mary Sidney's twenty-one-year-old brother had been sent out with only three hundred men to bring her in. Worst-case, Lady Mary would flee to the continent and the protection of her Habsburg kin. Such a move would be beneficial to the Dudley cause in the end, as it would be tantamount to an abdication of any claim to the English throne. It was also a possibility the duke may have prepared for; it was rumoured that the French would be ready to stand with the English should the Holy Roman Empire come to the aid of the Lady Mary. It was doubtful, however, that it would come to this, and even the imperial ambassadors questioned both Mary's ability to resist and the emperor's desire to come to her rescue. Far more likely was that Robert would bring the defiant yet defeated woman to London, where she would have to be forced to acknowledge Jane as queen, as per her brother's command. Mary Sidney's namesake would never forgive the Dudley family, but it was a small price to pay to serve the Crown and true religion. And this frail young woman who Mary led through her home at Syon, her sister-in-law, Jane Dudley, would rule England.

*

As Jane remembered it, she had burst into tears the moment she had been told of her cousin's death and her new position.[9]

The long gallery at Syon, on the east range of the house opposite the great hall, was sumptuously decorated. Along its length of over one hundred feet were displayed more than two dozen hangings, a red Turkish carpet, a long oak trestle table, a low cupboard for exhibiting plate and a walnut chair, covered in purple velvet and fringed with silk and gold.[10] It was elaborate enough to host the scene that took place as Jane was informed of the new regime.

After a short wait upon arriving at Syon, Jane had been greeted by several members of the Council, including her father-in-law, John Dudley, Duke of Northumberland, along with William Parr, Marquess of Northampton, and Henry FitzAlan, Earl of Arundel. With them were Francis Hastings, Earl of Huntingdon, and William Herbert, Earl of Pembroke, whose sons – both named Henry – had married the two young Catherines on Jane's wedding day. The two men paid her deep homage, far beyond her station, or so it seemed to Jane. At last, her mother, Frances Grey, Duchess of Suffolk, arrived, along with Jane's mother-in-law, Jane Dudley, Duchess of Northumberland, and Elisabeth Parr, Marchioness of Northampton. Once they were assembled, John Dudley proceeded to explain why they were all there.

The king, his majesty Edward VI, had died. He had led a virtuous life and met death admirably. In the final hours of his life, the late king had shown great care for his realm, praying to God to defend it from the popish faith and from his sisters, who would do it ill. For this reason, he had approved by Act of Parliament a law by which any who acknowledged the king's sisters, the Ladies Mary and Elizabeth, as heirs to the Crown were guilty of treason. Both were illegitimate issue, and the Lady Mary had been undutiful, an arch enemy of God's word. It had been the king's will that in no case were they to succeed to the Crown. They were both disinherited and the Council had been sworn to do his will in this matter.

John Dudley now turned to Jane. It was she who had been chosen by the king to be his heir. It was she who would be Queen of England. At this, the assembled lords bowed to her as their monarch and pledged their loyalty to their new sovereign, a girl awash in salty tears.

*

The sun rose over Durham Place, light striking the helmets, swords, stirrups and bridles of the thousands of men who waited there, armed and ready to depart. At their head was a black-robed duke.[11] He was riding north, and he had almost certainly never left London with more reluctance.

Durham Place was John's London residence, though at the moment the furnishings were quite bare, the family being at Syon.[12] The house was filled with chests of the family's belongings, to be opened and used when they returned. The rooms still had their bare furnishings – tables, stools and benches – but lacked the carpets and linens that adorned them when they were in use. Amongst the various belongings were some of great personal value to John and his family, including a pedigree of his family, his duke's coronet and robes, and his order of the garter. There were also two paintings of Henry VIII, one of queen Jane Seymour and maps of Scotland and England from John's days as a military commander. He would need to call on that experience now.

The Lady Mary was proving more of an obstacle than expected, and John Dudley would have to deal with her himself. The day that Jane had taken up residence in the Tower of London, the proclamations ringing out of her accession to the throne, the Council had received a letter from the Lady Mary – who was regrettably not in the custody of John's son Robert – in which she asserted her right to the throne. She had moved, in the days before the late king's death, from her house at Hunsdon, just twenty-five miles north of London, to Kenninghall, a full ninety miles away. By the time Robert Dudley had left to retrieve her, she was already several days, and several dozen miles, ahead of him. In the days that followed, several local lords had pledged their allegiance and their men to her. It seemed she was not intent on fleeing, but on fighting. Robert's three hundred men would be woefully insufficient. The Lady Mary was now a rebel to the Crown.

John had resisted going after her himself.[13] There was little reason to trust many of the lords who surrounded him; he had imprisoned so many of them in the past. If he abandoned the centre of power, they could quickly seize it and turn against him. The regime had already faced opposition in London; a local barman named Gilbert Potter had openly declared that Mary should be queen instead. He was put in the pillory and his ears cut off.[14] The Council had first lighted on the Duke of Suffolk, the queen's father, to lead a force against Mary. This, however, had met with disagreement, especially from the queen herself, who feared being separated from her father. The queen's father-in-law was suggested in his stead. After all, John Dudley was the duke with the superior military experience, and in that area of the country no less, his reputation built on the fierceness of the battle of Dussin's Dale. Men in the north-east would fear him so much that none would lift a weapon against him. He was the realm's best commander. No man in England was better suited to the task of quelling this rebellion in the making.

With the queen and Council in accord, there was little John could do to resist. He met with the Council over dinner as preparations were made and impressed on them the importance of fidelity in his absence. God would be watching and would hold them to account for any betrayal. Having done so, he met with the queen to receive her commission. On leaving, he found himself before Henry FitzAlan, the Earl of Arundel, whom he had arrested in the wake of the Edward Seymour affair, before having him rehabilitated and placed back in power. FitzAlan pledged his allegiance as the others had, confessing his regret that he could not go and spill his blood in his service. It was quite the show from the man who had spat venom at Dudley's rise from treasonous roots only a few years before. If John was suspicious, there was little he could do about it now.

John joined forces with his sons, John, Ambrose and Harry, as well as his brother, Andrew. Their company would be several thousand strong, including some dozen pieces of artillery and thirty cartloads of ammunition. Robert would continue to raise support in the area around Kenninghall and Framlingham and join them if needed. John could also rely on more troops sent from London as well as other allies, including his stalwart friend, Sir William Cecil.[15] From a surety that the Lady Mary would make much fuss but little trouble, it was clear she had become a threat to reckon with. Not one the duke could not handle, but certainly a nuisance, and one that could weaken his position in London by drawing him away. Even her strongest supporters in London banked on the Duke of Northumberland's success in subduing her meagre resistance.[16]

*

There was good reason to think some of his enemies, William Paget and Henry FitzAlan, had this planned all along. Sent off because he was the greatest man of war in the country, the Council that he had left in London had surrendered without a shot fired. By sending him away and crawling on their knees to the Lady Mary, they had left him isolated as the sole architect of the stunted regime she sought to raze. What was more hurtful was the betrayal by those who claimed to be friends, men like Cecil and Jane's own father, who seems to have crumpled under the pressure of the sudden change. John and his family were now rebels.

The Council had folded within a week of his departure. The same day that John had reached Cambridge, waiting for the reinforcements to be sent from London, rewards were issued for his arrest, up to £1,000 in lands to be given to a noble who apprehended him and brought him before the (true) queen.[17] Mary had clearly decided that John Dudley, Duke of Northumberland, was the leading figure in this rebellion. She issued a proclamation, stating that he had sought to make himself king through the marriage of his son to the false queen he promoted, Jane.[18] With John identified as the key traitor and target of Mary's wrath, the rest of the Council were free to renounce him as well. Over the course of 19 July, the Council speedily shifted allegiance, writing against supporters of the Lady Mary in the morning and proclaiming the accession of Mary I at the cross in Cheapside in the afternoon.[19] By the evening, the Duke of Suffolk, the not-Queen Jane's father, had surrendered the Tower of London, and FitzAlan and Paget were on their way to the now-Queen Mary's residence at Framlingham to deliver the Great Seal and pledge their allegiance, in the hopes that this sudden reversal and the sacrifice of the House of Dudley would save their necks.

John and his family were not beaten yet, however. Having received the official proclamation of the accession of Mary, John was faced with a choice. He had a significant army at his disposal, though it had diminished somewhat as men deserted the cause. He could attempt a military coup, but with London lost and forces flocking to Mary, it seemed foolhardy. He had received letters from the Council warning him against such a move, letters which Mary had intercepted on their way to him. If the Council was hoping for a reprieve in exchange for their support, there was no reason why he might not expect the same.

Cambridge's market hill – not an actual hill but a meeting place – had been in operation for hundreds of years, a perfect middling point between the River Cam and the highways leading to other parts of the country, including London. In the shadow of the medieval church of St Mary, it was also positioned adjacent to the large and growing university colleges. The market cross stood on the western edge of the marketplace, near the entrance to the church passage, and it was here that public announcements were made, such as the one that John was about to authorize. When he had arrived in Cambridge, having retreated from Bury St Edmunds, he had declared for Queen Jane, just as his son Robert had done in King's Lynn to the north. Now he would have to decide whether to stand by that declaration, or proclaim for Queen Mary, as his fellow councillors had done.

With the sun curving towards its descent, casting the shadow of the church over the assembled crowd, the proclamation authorized by Dudley was read: 'Mary by the Grace of God Queen of England, France, and Ireland, defender of the faith, and in the earth supreme head of the Church of England and Ireland: to all our most loving, faithful, and obedient subjects, greeting.

'Forasmuch as it hath pleased Almighty God to call unto his mercy the most excellent Prince, King Edward VI, our late brother of most worthy memory, whereby the crown imperial of the realms of England and Ireland, with the title France and all other things appertaining unto the same, do most rightfully and lawfully belong unto us:

'We do signify unto you that according to our said right and title we do take upon us and be in the just and lawful possession of the same; not doubting but that all our true and faithful subjects will so accept us, take us, and obey us as their natural and liege sovereign lady and Queen, according to the duties of their allegiance; assuring all our good and faithful subjects that in their so doing they shall find us their benign and gracious sovereign lady, as others our most noble progenitors have heretofore been.'[20]

In the end, there was little choice to make. John had forged his career and protected his life by shifting with the changing winds while remaining anchored to the Crown. He had served Henry VIII despite the hardship wrought on his family by him. When Edward had come to the throne, he had supported the rise of Edward Seymour, until it was clear he was a threat to the throne itself. And at Edward's death, he had sought to fulfil his final will, no matter how unconventional. But it was to be Mary on the throne, and so John must serve her too. The alternative was unthinkable, and lethal.

All John could do now that the proclamation had been read was wait. If he moved towards London it could be seen as a sign of aggression. Any other move would be seen as flight. His remaining men disbanded, heading south towards London or back to the neighbouring towns and villages from whence they'd come. Some perhaps answered the musters issued by the new queen. To a local servant John gave one of the two nightgowns he had brought with him: a gown of damask decorated with scallop shells and trimmed with marten's fur.[21]

Mary I had been proclaimed in London on the Wednesday. John was still in Cambridge on the Sunday, as the residents of Cambridge went to their local churches, most of which had been stripped of their grand altars and golden images, wondering if everything would change once again now that a Catholic queen was on the throne. He couldn't have known that men were already entering his homes at Syon and Durham Place, making inventories of his family's goods to be given away and sold to the highest bidders, many of whom were his enemies and only too keen to get their hands on those items in which he took most pride.[22]

They came for him the next day, Monday, 24 July. He was arrested by none other than Henry FitzAlan, the Earl of Arundel, who no doubt took immense pleasure in doing so. At the head of the troops as they brought John into London, FitzAlan paused at its outer gates to force John to remove his velvet cape and hat, so that all of the city could see the traitorous and disgraced Dudley.[23] If that were not enough, he commanded the trumpeters to sound as they marched, prompting the people to shout 'traitor, traitor' at John as he passed. John's son Robert had been apprehended at King's Lynn some days before, and sent to Framlingham to appear in front of the queen, and then sent onwards towards London.[24] Less than a fortnight after he had left it, John Dudley was returned to the Tower of London, his worst nightmares upon leaving having been realized. His brother and four sons – John, Ambrose, Robert and Harry – joined him there. His wife, remaining son, Guildford, and daughter-in-law had not left, their palace having been abruptly transformed into their prison.

A week later deafening cannon shot fired from the Tower over the Thames as the queen, Mary I, entered the Tower in triumph and took over the royal apartments so recently occupied by the Royal House of Dudley. At the age of thirty-seven, the new queen was one of the oldest monarchs to have taken the throne and the only woman to do so since the Empress Matilda in the twelfth century, unless you counted Jane, which was unwise. Mary had always been small and slim, but had a commanding air about her, a legacy no doubt of the proud royal lines that she had inherited from both her parents. Her sense of purpose and righteousness could have only been increased by the events of the past weeks. At the beginning of the month, anyone would have said that only a miracle would have seen the Lady Mary, who for the past two decades had been bullied and sidelined, overcome the forces of the mighty Duke of Northumberland, who had spent those years growing in influence and authority. And yet there they were. The Lady Mary was entering the Tower in triumph, and John and his entire family were imprisoned within its walls. If Mary and her supporters – or indeed her defeated enemies – wished to see the outcome as the result of divine intervention, one could hardly blame them.

All those years ago John's father had been forced to abide the sound of victorious gunshot from within the thick walls of the Tower prison when the new queen's father had entered. Now, after decades of fighting, hardship, sacrifice, pain and great cost, all to win back what had been lost that fateful day, John had ended up in the same position his father had been, feeling the rumble of jubilant cannon fire through stone walls. Only unlike his father, John could not look out of his window to London beyond, and imagine his sons, free to pursue a better life. There was no guarantee that a single one of his children would escape the pain and terror of a traitor's death. Certainly, he was unlikely to.

*

It fell to Jane Dudley, Duchess of Northumberland, to save her family. She had been released from the Tower, where she had witnessed the stripping of the Crown from Queen Jane, shortly after her husband and sons were marched into their prison. Immediately following her release, orders went out to prepare her horses: she was to travel the twenty-eight miles to where the new queen lay at Beaulieu Castle.[25] She would petition Mary in person to have mercy on her husband and sons. It took almost half a day but at last, as the day turned to night on 28 July, she was only five miles away, approaching the town of Chelmsford, to the north-east of which lay Beaulieu. Suddenly, she saw a messenger approaching, from the queen. Mary had been informed of her progress and, Jane was told, would not grant her an audience. Jane was to turn around and return to London immediately. There would be no hope of begging for her children's lives directly. The new queen refused to hear her pleas for mercy.

Jane, however, was not so easily cowed. Her husband's networks and contacts may have betrayed and failed him, but Jane too had powerful friends to whom she could appeal. The work of protecting and promoting the family was not done only by her husband and the other men of the family. It was as much up to Jane and her daughters, and they had spent years cultivating connections.[26] In this, Jane was advantaged by the fact that there was a woman on the throne, with a Privy Chamber made up of women, women that Jane knew and might be able to rely upon.

Returning to London, Jane was unable to sleep, getting up several times in the night to be sick, her stomach churning.[27] Nevertheless, she set to work. She wrote an appeal to Lady Anne Paget, the wife of William, Lord Paget. William Paget had been one of John Dudley's fellow councillors; he had been Henry VIII's Secretary of State, corresponding frequently with John towards the end of Henry VIII's reign. He had also been Edward Seymour's right-hand man in the transition to Edward's reign, and his position had fallen with Seymour's execution. He was thus yet another man who had it in for

John, and he had joined FitzAlan in defecting to Mary once John was safely in Cambridge. It was clear that he would be navigating the transition to Mary's reign with ease.

He and Anne had been married for some twenty years and had almost as many children as the Dudleys. Theirs had been a close marriage, and Anne had been allowed to visit her husband while he was imprisoned during the Seymour affair.[28] She had also been granted his goods while he was imprisoned, to meet her needs and those of their children.[29] These concessions were, no doubt, granted thanks to her own petitioning and appeals to the intercessions of women such as Jane herself. Might she now be inclined to return the favour?

For all her husband's position, Jane knew that Anne Paget herself was not close enough to power to intercede. She could, however, appeal to women who were. Jane's request to Anne was thus that she, in turn, pass on her plea to other women in positions of greater authority. These were Gertrude Courtenay, the Marchioness of Exeter, and Susan Clarencius, the widow of a herald. Both women had been close to the queen since she was a young woman, suffering under the annulment of Mary's parents' marriage and the trials that followed. Courtenay might even become the queen's mother-in-law, as it was rumoured that Mary might marry her son, Edward. Clarencius had taken the role of Mary's mistress of the robes and was effectively the chief gentlewoman of her Privy Chamber. If one wanted to reach the queen, these were the women to appeal to.

With her heart full and heavy, Jane poured out her pleas to Anne Paget to encourage these women to save her husband. It was becoming increasingly clear that he would bear the brunt of the queen's revenge. She was less anxious about her children; it was John who was clearly in the most pressing danger.[30] On 1 August a pamphlet was published in London, detailing the suffering of poor, earless Gilbert Potter at the hands of 'the ragged bear most rank' who had neither 'mercy, pity, nor compassion'.[31] London was turning against the disgraced duke.

But John had been a loving, constant husband to Jane, and she could barely remember a world without him, before he was brought home to Halden some forty years before, just a boy who had so recently lost his father. Long before they had been duke and duchess, before they had even been husband and wife, they had been children together at Halden. Their bond was decades old and strong. These women must do all they could to save him. She sent off the letter to Anne Paget, and waited.

Commissioners from the queen were already rummaging through the Dudleys' possessions at Syon and Durham Place, selling off the family's belongings, or simply passing them on to the queen to use as she pleased. Tapestries were torn down, boxes and cases unlocked and spilled open, paintings and mirrors uncovered and shipped off as the commissioners coldly calculated the value of those things which had made up Jane's life. Under the gatehouse at Syon, the commissioners discovered a hidden chest, red, bound with iron and covered in leather.[32] In it they found hangings of Jane's father's badge, perfectly symbolizing her union with John – fire burning atop a ragged staff – which were delivered to the queen.[33] They would be torn apart, and the remnants of valuable silk repurposed, perhaps to make hangings or banners for the queen's upcoming coronation.

Jane received back many of her belongings – gowns, sleeves, kirtles and waistcoats. She would even be granted many of the furnishings from her and her husband's rooms – the tapestries portraying Diana, David, and the story of Hester, the interceding queen, which hung in her husband's chamber in the old lodging at Syon.[34] She was given a place to live and materials with which to furnish it. These were the concessions granted to her by the queen and the women around her. But all of this was empty without assurances that she would hold her husband and children once again.

*

In the early morning hours of 21 August, crowds of Londoners made their way to the Tower of London. They were there to witness a rare sight: a triple execution. In many ways, it was a morning much like the one precisely forty-three years and five days before, when Edmund Dudley had been executed. Everyone could expect August heat to make an uncomfortable experience for those standing in the crowds, as the axe fell and the blood spattered. It was worth it, however, for today John Dudley, Duke of Northumberland, was to die: the tyrant who had manipulated and poisoned the young king, married his son to the young Lady Jane and raised an army to oppose the forces of the true claimant, Queen Mary; all of this done to appease his unquenchable thirst for power. He was a true rebel and traitor, a villain like Herod or Richard III. No one would want to miss seeing him meet his rightful end.

The executioner stood upon the large wooden scaffold, ready to perform his duty. The people waited, eager to see the duke brought out, to hear what he would have to say for himself, to witness his final breaths and behold the severed head of the traitor's son who would be king. But he did not emerge. Instead, the order was given for the crowds to disperse. There would be no execution this day. Had the duke been forgiven? Would he be allowed to live? Surely the queen could not be so merciful? When the execution of Anne Boleyn had been delayed, it had been for want of the executioner, yet here one was. So where was the duke?

John had been condemned at Westminster Hall three days before, on 18 August, less than a month after his arrival into the Tower. He was to avoid the long, agonizing wait and the terrible hope his father had endured. Leading his trial was another of his enemies, one he might have thought he'd been well rid of, Thomas Howard, Duke of Norfolk. Howard had remained in the Tower following his own delayed execution after the death of Henry VIII and been released by Mary I just in time to preside over John's trial. Despite being eighty years old, he would not have forgotten that his son had seen John as one of the leading architects in his downfall and death, nor the role that John had played in the rise of the reformed religion in the country, which the Howards had opposed. The Duke of Norfolk would receive some of John's most valuable possessions: his collar of the Order of the Garter, his duke's coronet and cape, as well as his parliamentary and ducal robes, signs that he had earned a position on a level with the Howards.[35] Thomas Howard would have been only too glad to have taken them from him.

The Duke of Norfolk sat on a chair with an ornamental cloth covering the back, upon a high scaffolding under a pall and royal mantle.[36] He was not, however, the only enemy John was to be faced with that day. To the right of Thomas Howard sat Henry FitzAlan, the Earl of Arundel, undoubtedly inwardly beaming to be at such an occasion. Even harder to bear was William Paulet, Marquess of Winchester, sat beside FitzAlan, who was not an old enemy, but an old friend. On the left of the duke were other members of the Privy Council, who had also proclaimed Queen Jane and ordered John out of London to arrest the Lady Mary. They sat in judgement over John Dudley, as if he were the only one to have acted against the queen.

John's composure at his trial had drawn respect even from his detractors, the picture of both humility and gravity. To the Tower he had brought with him a gown of black satin, with a matching cape furred with sable and decorated with two dozen ornamental aglets.[37] His charges were as expected, and difficult to contest: he had raised troops against the queen, and declared Queen Jane in her stead. In John's home at Durham Place, in the ewery, where commissioners might have only expected to find linens and towels, they had found chests full of John's papers, letters and a book covered in velvet, with silver clasps, lock and key.[38] If his enemies did not have all the evidence they needed from those who testified, surely the papers hidden away in the ewery would have provided them with something to use against him. His father's charges had been fabricated with circumstantial evidence; John on the other hand had done precisely as he was accused, but did this make him guilty?

Faced with a wealth of evidence, John did not argue the charges. He did, however, raise questions about the validity of the proceedings, and especially the men who sat before him, in such a way as would have made his lawyer father proud. First he asked them 'whether any man doing any deed by authority of the Prince's Council and by warrant of the great seal of England, and doing nothing without the same, might be charged with treason?'[39] Everything he had done over the past weeks had been done with the Council's authority; it was they who had shifted position without informing him of the change.

To this, it was answered by the court that 'the great seal which he pretended for his warrant was not the seal of the lawful Queen of the realm, but the seal of a usurper, who had no authority, and therefore could not warrant him.' If the queen was not legitimate, then anything he had done in her name was equally invalid. It was a frustrating technicality.

Second, and much more controversially, he asked, 'whether any such persons as were equally culpable in the crime, and those by whose letters and commandment he was directed in all his doings, might sit as judges and pass upon trial as peers?' This was a very pointed question. Before him sat members of Queen Jane's own Council, who had in recent weeks become members of Queen Mary's Council. John was determined to avoid being the sole scapegoat in all the previous reign's misdemeanours, as his father had been. Surely it was not right that those who had stood beside him, had persuaded him to lead men into the field against Mary, now stood ready to condemn him for treason against her?

The answer to this question was no more satisfactory. 'If any were as deeply to be touched in the case as himself, yet so long as no attainder was on record against them, they were looked upon by law as persons capable of passing any trial.' This was followed by a warning, 'they were not to be challenged by any in that respect, but only at the Prince's pleasure.' John had lost that argument as well.

The Duke of Norfolk proclaimed the sentence. John Dudley was to be hanged, his heart and entrails taken from his body and burned before him, and his body quartered. Thanks to the noble status he had accrued, this was commuted to beheading by axe. He was returned to the Tower. Later that day, his eldest son, John, was given the same death sentence, and on the next, Andrew, the younger son of Edmund Dudley, was also sentenced to die for treason against the Crown. The remaining Dudley men, Ambrose, Robert, Guildford and Harry, remained in the Tower, with their fates uncertain.

And yet, on the date appointed, John Dudley had not been executed. Not long after the disappointed crowds had dispersed on 21 August, John Dudley appeared in the Chapel at the Tower of London, where the bodies of executed traitors were laid to rest. It was a sacred and yet threatening place, sitting in the north-west corner of the Tower complex, within view of the large Beauchamp Tower, in which John's sons were lodged. The small chapel, St Peter ad Vincula – 'St Peter in Chains' – had been destroyed by fire in 1512 and restored by

Henry VIII by 1520, who at the time was unlikely to have realized how much he was going to use it. The entrance was along the west end of the chapel, closest to the Tower walls and the church's own modest bell-tower. John passed through the arched doorway and into the cool darkness of the chapel.[40]

For John, this modest chapel was the resting place of people he had served, admired, even loved. The queen who had so favoured him, and whom he had witnessed triumphant in childbed, Anne Boleyn, lay here, as did Thomas Cromwell, the man who had orchestrated her downfall, and who too had helped John to rise. Both the Seymour brothers lay here, Thomas and, of course, Edward, whom John had counted as a friend for so many years – from his time as a young man on the battlefields of France – but in the end, he himself had seen killed.

John was indeed scheduled to have entered the chapel at about this time on 21 August; he just wasn't supposed to have been alive. His execution had been postponed in order to accommodate the ceremony that was about to take place, though whether John would remain above ground for much longer remained to be seen. The chapel was filled with officials from the City of London, and John was joined by his brother, Andrew, William Parr, Marquess of Northampton, and two other men condemned to die, Henry Gates and Thomas Palmer, who had also supported Jane's rise.[41] Some twenty years before, the scene would have been so commonplace as to be entirely unremarkable. John Dudley was there to receive Holy Communion, as he had as a child, and as had been performed in that chapel for five centuries or more. This meant receiving the Sacrament in the old form of the mass, which he himself had worked to eliminate. The Blessed Sacrament, the body and blood of Christ, was elevated before them, and he worshipped it. Before partaking of it, he turned to those assembled and proclaimed his belief in the Catholic mass as the true way, from which he and those assembled had been seduced for sixteen years. This waywardness was the cause of all the realm's misfortunes, as well as his own. He knelt before them and begged their forgiveness. In front of all those in attendance, John Dudley publicly renounced his own religion, in favour of the religion of the new queen, which he had spent years attempting to persuade her to abandon.

Would it save him? If it saved his body, would it condemn his soul? Or perhaps it was the other way around, and he sacrificed his body to the queen's pleasure, but saved his soul from damnation. He had once decried the preacher who had suggested he was untrue in his beliefs, and yet here he had forsaken them with shocking alacrity. He had, in the same vehement objection, also condemned those men who served themselves before the realm to hellfire. Was he serving himself or the new queen by bowing before the Sacrament he had once held to be no more than bread? Only she – or perhaps it was God? – could save him now. By renouncing his reformed faith, he was abandoning all hope of help from the reformers, who would condemn him for his disloyalty. The Catholics, of course, already hated him, for having put a usurper on the throne, instead of their own Catholic Mary. The country could now unite in their shared loathing of the man who had betrayed them all. The new queen could establish her reign as the victor over the most hated man in England, who in the end had acknowledged her religion as the true religion. Would this sacrifice be enough to save John? Would it be enough to save his family?

*

'Good people,' he began, 'hither I am come this day to die, as ye know.'[42] John Dudley stood upon the scaffold erected in the grounds of the Tower of London, upon which the day before the London crowds had so eagerly gazed, only to be met with disappointment. This morning, however, the crowd – perhaps as many as fifty thousand strong – was not to leave so unsatisfied.[43] John had been led out of his room in the Tower and up the stairs of the scaffold, where he now stood, addressing those who had been willing to make the journey a second time. With him, in addition to the necessary officers, were the two other men who would be executed that morning, Thomas Palmer and John Gates. His brother, with him the day before in the chapel, was not to die that day, nor were any of his sons, still locked away in the nearby Beauchamp Tower. That was a mercy. There was one last thing, however, he needed to do.

'Indeed, I confess to you,' John continued, 'I have lived an evil life, and have done wickedly all the days of my life, and of all, most against the queen's highness, who I here openly ask forgiveness.' At this he dropped to his knees on the wood of the scaffold. He had spent time working out what he would say with his confessor, the Catholic Bishop Nicholas Heath.[44] His speech would be published and circulated after his death, a sign of Mary's complete triumph over the man who had opposed her. He did, however, have a few things he wanted to say himself. He stood: 'But not I alone was the original doer thereof, I assure you, for there were some other which procured the same,' those who had been at his trial might have remembered his similarly pointed comments towards his judges, 'but I will not name them;' he added, 'for I will hurt now no man.' John had given up the thought that others might share his fate, but he would die protesting the accusation that he had been the sole cause of the treason against Queen Mary.

'I have erred from the Catholic faith,' he continued, 'and true doctrines of Christ. The doctrine I mean which hath continued through all Christendom since Christ.' Those who had not got wind of the duke's conversion the day before were in for a shock now, as he renounced the faith he had spent years writing into the laws that governed them: 'For, good people, there is and hath been, ever since Christ, one Catholic Church, which Church hath continued from Him to His disciples in one unity and concord, and so hath always continued from time to time until this day, and yet do throughout all Christendom, only us excepted.' The true reformers in the crowd would despise what came next, a reiteration of the Catholic argument against Lutheranism and the break with Rome as old as the break itself, 'whereas all holy fathers and all other saints, throughout all Christendom since Christ and His disciples, have ever agreed in one unity, faith and doctrine, we alone dissent from their opinions and follow our own private interpretation of Scriptures.' Sounding very much like Thomas More, who had died two decades before for similar beliefs, he continued, 'Do you think, good people, that we, being one spark[45] in comparison, be wiser than all the world besides, and ever since Christ? No, I assure you, you are far deceived.' As the summer sun continued to heat the crowds, John continued as he had been instructed, lecturing the crowds as to the many miseries that had come as a result of straying from the path of true religion.

At last, the time came. 'I exhort you all, good people, take you all example of me, and forsake this new doctrine in good time, defer it not long, lest God plague you, as he hath me, which now suffer this vile death most worthily.'[46] The headsman waited. 'I have no more to say, good people; but all those which I have offended I ask forgiveness, and they which have offended me I forgive them, as I would God forgive me.' The royal palace within the Tower of London lay to the south-east, casting a shadow upon the Tower Hill grounds on which he stood. 'I trust the queen's highness hath forgiven me, whereas I was with force and arms against her in the field, I might have been rent in pieces without law; here grace hath given me time and respect to have judgement.'

He appealed to the crowd, 'I beseech you all most heartily to pray for me.' He knelt, and prayed, ending, 'into thy hands, Oh Lord, I commend my spirit.' At this, the waiting executioner stepped forward and asked his forgiveness for what he was about to do. John responded as expected, 'I forgive thee with all my heart; do thy part without fear.' He was given a small piece of cloth. Covering his eyes with it, he could still hear the Thames washing against the wharf. Beyond he could recognize the bustling sounds of London, his London, less than a mile from the room in which he'd been born. His hands found the block. Then his head. The block was fresh, no different from the newly sanded wood of a ship.

13

The ragged staff and firebrand

Guildford Dudley was led out from the Tower that he had entered in triumph some four months before. Then it had been a season of warmth, sunshine and grand hopes. The crowds had stood by in wonder – some had cheered – as he had processed through the stone gates into the palace of the Tower of London. For a few short days Guildford Dudley had been King of England. He had been addressed as 'grace' and 'excellence' and sat at the head of Council meetings.[1] He had been recognized by others abroad as the next King of England.[2] Despite Jane's apparent reluctance, there was little reason to think that he would not be crowned alongside her, as Catherine of Aragon had been when Henry VIII had come to the throne. As Jane's husband, he had the rule of her as well; thus, although she would be queen by right of her inheritance, he would be king over her by right of his sex.

Now all was grey and dour, with a chill that never quite left the bones. He was leaving not a palace but a prison. The people who had congregated to watch his slow march leered at him – he was a traitor, not a king. Walking in front of him was Thomas Cranmer, who had welcomed him into the Tower those few months ago. The man who had crowned the last king of England was now in his mid-sixties and likewise implicated in the Jane Grey affair. It did not help, of course, that he had also been so involved in the annulment of the marriage of Queen Mary's parents, as well as being such a pivotal figure in the reformed religion instituted under Edward VI. It was not a good sign that Guildford was sharing a trial with him. Immediately behind Guildford walked his black-clothed wife, clutching a book in her hands as she walked, the perfect picture of Protestant piety.[3] She was probably pleased to be on trial with one such as Cranmer, doomed as he was. With them were also two of Guildford's brothers, Ambrose and the young Harry.

Unlike Queen Jane, Mary did not, as of yet, have a king, though there were numerous rumours. The most worrying was that she might take a foreign prince, such as her cousin Philip of Spain. Just as Guildford would have expected to rule over Jane, so too Philip would expect to rule over Mary and thus, effectively, Spain would rule over England. As far as the Dudleys knew, nothing had yet been confirmed, but they were reliant on report and rumour, communicated to them by servants, visitors and officers at the Tower. It had been a long time since the Dudleys had been this far from the workings of power.

When Guildford and the others entered the Guildhall, he – as his father had been – was faced with the elderly figure of Thomas Howard, the restored Duke of Norfolk.[4] Surrounding Howard were other leading members of the Council and court, including Edward Stanley, Earl of Derby, Norfolk's brother-in-law, whose daughter had married Guildford's cousin, Edward Sutton, recently Baron Dudley. This new Baron Dudley had taken back Dudley Castle, the property which Guildford's father had gone to such great lengths to improve and modernize.[5] Also present was Henry Radclyffe, Earl of Sussex, who had recently been knighted by Henry FitzAlan, the Earl of Arundel, and was a nephew of the Duke of Norfolk. Guildford, his wife and Cranmer would find little friendliness or sympathy amongst this group.

Their inquests had revealed that Thomas Cranmer, along with Guildford's father and other 'false traitors and rebels against the most illustrious ruler Mary' were 'seduced by diabolical instigation' and so entered the Tower of London 'with force and arms' and 'took possession of it'. It was a very different account of the events of 10 July than Guildford would have remembered, entering the Tower in state on a summer's day, with the full support of the Council. Further, the inquest reiterated the crimes of Guildford's father in Cambridge, who 'falsely and treacherously prepared and ordained a cruel war against the said Queen', supported, they said, by Cranmer, and participated in by

Andrew, Ambrose and Harry Dudley. Guildford and Jane were declared 'traitors and rebels' for likewise 'forcibly' holding the Tower of London. Jane was accused of proclaiming herself queen, and Guildford of 'abetting and assisting' her.

Cranmer, at first, resisted the charges of treason, but could not deny that he had supported the efforts to put Jane on the throne, and thus in the end pled guilty, throwing himself on the mercy of a queen who was unlikely to grant him any. Guildford, his wife and two brothers all likewise pled guilty; there was no denying the truth of the accusations, even if the account of events seemed almost unrecognizable. Cranmer, Guildford, Ambrose and young Harry were all given the fullest sentence for treason: 'dragged through the middle of the city of London to the gallows of Tyburn, and there hung, and laid out rotting on the ground, and their interior organs should be brought outside of their stomachs, and as these rot they should be burned. And their heads should be cut off, and their bodies should be divided into four quarters, and their heads and quarters should be placed where the Queen wishes them to be assigned.'6 Jane was to be burned or decapitated, 'as it will then please the Queen'.

This was not surprising, though it was hard not to be affected hearing it. Guildford was still only sixteen, after all, and Harry even younger. Then again, Guildford's older brother John had survived four months with such a sentence hanging over him. As they left the Guildhall, the edge of the axe turned towards them, the sign that they were condemned traitors. Now they would just have to wait to see if that axe's edge would fall.

*

Mary Sidney's young brother stood on a scaffold in Tower Hill, the same on which their father had died just six months before. It was a cold February morning; no one could have faulted the youth for trembling. With no priest beside him to guide him in his prayers, Guildford made his own. This done, he asked the people assembled to pray for him. The boy knelt and placed his head on the block. The sharp, heavy axe fell, cutting through skin, muscle, bone, and finally finding the wood of the block beneath, and he was dead. They threw her brother's body in a cart, wrapping his discorporated head in a cloth, and brought it back to the Tower for burial in full sight of any other prisoners within, including his wife and brothers. It was small consolation that his sentence had been commuted to beheading. Guildford was the first of the Dudley children to suffer beneath the axe that had been hanging over them.

Both Mary and Guildford had been born in the tumultuous years of Henry VIII's break with the Catholic Church. Mary had been two years old when Guildford had been born, just shortly after the large-scale rebellion known as the Pilgrimage of Grace, mounted in protest against the changes wrought to the Church. Mary and Guildford had never known another world, another faith. Despite this, they had both had overtly Catholic godparents, and shared a godmother – the Lady Mary, now Queen Mary of England.

About a month before, around the same time that Mary's brother Robert had also been tried for treason, another rebellion had broken out – this time against the queen's planned marriage to Philip of Spain. It had been disorganized, rushed and panicked. The rebels had planned for Eastertide, but the queen's councillors had got wind of it, and they had been forced to move earlier than planned. Nevertheless, one of the conspirators, Thomas Wyatt, had reached London with a large force of men, after overcoming the queen's forces, led by the octogenarian Duke of Norfolk. The duke had been sent to oppose the rebellion and stop it reaching London, but he had failed spectacularly, mounting a doomed frontal assault and then running when more than half his army defected to the other side.[7] He was a pitiful replacement for the cool military leadership of the former Duke of Northumberland. Had Howard succeeded in routing the rebels at Rochester, they might have never reached London, and the threat posed by them nervously laughed off. As it was, the rebels had entered London, and there was skirmishing in the streets. The queen's faithful Londoners had defended her, however, and it was all over in a couple of days. By Ash Wednesday, on 7 February, Wyatt had been led to the Tower. Queen Mary had accomplished another miracle in defence of her divinely appointed reign, and just in time for Lent.

It was then that Mary Sidney's namesake had condemned her godchild to die. Guildford's father-in-law, Henry Grey, Duke of Suffolk, had played a role in the rebellion, albeit a disappointingly weak one. Report had it he had even proclaimed his daughter queen again, perhaps attempting to make up for his refusal to ride out in her defence the summer before. Despite the queen's inclination to grant life to the Dudley youths, they were sure to continue to be the focus of such rebellions in the future. They were too dangerous to let live, especially with the queen's new husband arriving. The sentence passed against Guildford and his wife would have to be acted upon, and quickly.

Their executions were originally planned to immediately follow the end of the rebellion, the day after Ash Wednesday, but they were given a short remission in the hopes that they might convert. Neither agreed to do so. They would die in the reform faith, the faith in which they had been brought up; they had known no other. Jane was executed later the same day as her husband, within the Tower precincts themselves. People said she had met her death bravely, though in the end had panicked; blindfolded, she could not find the block, and her hands had grasped about in the cold air before she was directed to it and could lay herself down to die. Or perhaps the scene was just a tale, an allegory for the way in which others, chiefly Mary Sidney's father, were thought to be the cause of this innocent's demise. She had been led blindly to the block, indeed.

It was clear now that no one was safe. The verdicts of treason, with their devastating sentences, could be carried out at any point, against any of the Dudley children. The axe's edge which had been facing them for months had become devastatingly real, coated in their brother's blood.

Mary, along with her younger sister, Katherine, still only a child, had escaped imprisonment. Mary's husband, Sir Henry Sidney, had ridden alongside her father to Cambridge, and thus was as culpable as the rest of them. He had been saved, however, thanks to his connections with some of the regime's most powerful women. His niece was Jane Dormer, one of the queen's closest friends and confidantes, and his sisters were in the queen's household. Mary too benefitted from her husband's speedy rehabilitation, though it was not without its difficulties. Just a month after Guildford's execution, Mary was forced to bid farewell to her husband; he would be travelling to Spain, an agent of the Spanish marriage which had resulted in her brother's death.

Mary, nineteen, and Henry, twenty-five, were still both in the flush of youth, despite the tragedy they'd survived, and showed every appearance of sharing a firm bond of love, companionship and affection, not unlike that which had existed between Mary's parents. On their marriage three years before, the couple had inscribed verses to each other in a book of history. Mary had written 'Of all things the newest is the best, save of love and friendship, which the elder it waxeth is ever the better.'[8] Three years into their marriage her aphorism had a ring of truth to it, though their marriage still lacked what many took to be its primary object: a child.[9] Perhaps a warm and heartfelt farewell in their chamber before his departure would remedy that, now that Lent was passed. It would be some months before they would have another such opportunity.

Although his official mission was to secure the queen's marriage to Philip, Henry Sidney might also make overtures to the new king on behalf of the Dudley family.[10] He was following in the train of John Russell, the Earl of Bedford, a veteran courtier approaching seventy, who, like Henry's late father-in-law, had spent time as Lord High Admiral. Unlike John Dudley, however, John Russell had managed to both support Queen Jane and survive Queen Mary, and he had held the position of Privy Seal through the tumults of the previous decade, under three – or arguably four – monarchs. The betrothal of Queen Mary and Prince Philip had already taken place, a full week before his departure, and Bedford's expedition would not only put the final seal on the contract between the two monarchs but would – hopefully – also bring Philip to England so that the marriage could actually take place.

Henry's outward journey was delayed by contrary winds, which had sent the ships, sailing from Plymouth, to Coruña instead of Laredo, some three hundred miles east along the northern coast of Spain, and a hundred miles further from the court at Valladolid.[11] They arrived after a difficult trip of six days, landing in Coruña to a great welcome from the officials of the town. There they remained until the following Tuesday, waiting for the necessary supplies to support the hundreds of men and almost two hundred horse.[12] In two days the entourage had only travelled 15 miles of the 250-mile journey, to Betanzos, but it was for the best, as Philip had decided against hosting the entourage at the court in Valladolid, and instead would meet them at Santiago, just 35 miles to the south-west.[13] Philip's original estimate of eight days until his arrival had been wildly off target: it was three weeks until he even left Valladolid.[14] In the meantime, the queen had sent the English navy to the coast of Spain, to attend Philip's journey.

Philip and his extensive retinue arrived at Santiago, where Henry Sidney and the other English representatives waited, on 23 June.[15] Two years older than Henry, Philip was the picture of a young Renaissance prince. The son of Charles V, whom Henry's father-in-law had met a number of times over the course of his diplomatic career, he had, unfortunately, inherited his father's famous chin, but it was nowhere near as prominent, and was hidden beneath a closely groomed beard. He had also inherited his father's deep-set eyes, serious-looking brows and full lips, though these might also have come from his mother, Isabella of Portugal. He was accompanied by thousands of Spanish courtiers, many of whom would also be making the journey to England and populating the court. Among them was Don Diego de Mendoza, who had been Guildford Dudley's godfather some seventeen years before and had welcomed his reign as king.[16] Watching them arrive in hordes into the city of Santiago, Henry and the other English ambassadors might finally have had an idea of what change would be wrought by a foreign marriage.

After mass at the great cathedral at Compostela, Philip at last signed the marriage treaty.[17] It would still be another three weeks before they set sail back to England.[18] There was plenty of time for Henry to take the prince aside and, perhaps in their shared Latin or French, to explain the situation that the Dudley family were in and how Philip's mercy might win their loyalty.[19] Despite his long train of Spanish courtiers, or perhaps because of them, Philip would need the support of Englishmen at court, and the hispanophile faction was sparse at best. A ready supply of young, connected, cultured Englishmen who owed him their lives might come in handy.

Back in England, there were other reasons to be hopeful for the House of Dudley. Not long after Henry's arrival in Spain, his wife had begun to notice changes – rounded breasts, strange cravings and the lessening of monthly bleeding.[20] Mary Sidney was pregnant. Of course, it might take months between these first signs and her quickening, when the child was ensouled and moved for the first time.[21] She would need to wait anxiously for those first small shifts that confirmed she was truly carrying a child within her, and then excitedly for those more significant movements that others might feel, vindicating her condition. Without such motions, there remained the chance that Mary was not actually with child, and had experienced a false conception, or was carrying some other growth inside her. It was important, despite these anxieties, that she stay calm, avoid exertion and ensure she did not take a fall. If she feared miscarriage, there were remedies available. For a womb that would not shut properly, she could take baths, apply fumigations or ointments.[22] If she was weak, and concerned for the health of the child, she was advised to feast on kid, lamb, veal and other rich meats.[23] Her health, and thus the well-being of the infant she carried, was of utmost importance, especially as none of her siblings had yet had any living children.

Maintaining a temperate state of mind was made more difficult by the absence of her husband, whose journey abroad was not without its risks. There had been rumours that the French might lie in wait for Philip's ships and entourage, and there was the ever-present threat of a sudden ship-toppling storm.[24] The fleet of almost a hundred ships set sail for England on 13 July, just as Mary would have been experiencing the first movements of her unborn child. Thankfully, they caught a fair wind on the return journey. This was especially good news for the Spanish prince, who was prone to seasickness; letters had gone ahead of him, warning the English that he might have to land at Plymouth rather than Southampton if he found himself desperate to make port.[25] Nevertheless, they laid anchor just outside rain-sodden Southampton a week later and by 23 July, Philip had entered Winchester and met his bride. Their marriage would be solemnized two days later, at Winchester Cathedral, still in the pouring rain, and consummated immediately afterwards in the hope of producing an heir.

Henry Sidney, however, would be keen to get home to see his wife, who had wonderful news for him.

*

The young John Dudley, Earl of Warwick, had left his masterpiece, his tribute to his brothers and his family, unfinished in their prison in the Beauchamp Tower. He had employed the skills of a gifted stonemason to create a coat of arms, of sorts, on their chamber wall. In the centre rose the ragged staff of their house, with the bear and lion grasping it on either side, and his name beneath. Around the crest were four flowers of different types, one in each corner, riddles revealing his brother's names: roses for Ambrose, oak (or *robur*) leaves for Robert, gillyflowers for Guildford and honeysuckle for Harry. Beneath the image were seven lines of text, though only four had been completed: 'You that these beasts do well behold and see / may deem with ease wherefore here made they be / with borders eke wherein are to be found / 4 brothers names who list to search the ground.'[26]

A scholar and student of rhetoric such as John – keen to make allusions and leave clues – might well have been thinking of the verse from the Old Testament, 'Seek not out the things that are above thy capacity, and search not the ground of such things as are too mighty for thee'.[27] The carving thus would be a sign of their penitence, an acknowledgement of their sin of reaching beyond themselves, or perhaps it was an explicit rejection of precisely such modesty. Those who would understand the reference might be prompted to remember the rest of the chapter, encouraging children to honour both their father and their mother. Especially relevant for the Dudley sons was the passage that encouraged children to 'rejoice not when thy father is reproved, for it is not honour unto thee but a shame. For the worship of a man's father is his own worship, & where the father is without honour, it is the dishonesty of the son.' John, named for his father, would have felt this verse keenly.

As the male head of the family, at twenty-three John was responsible for looking after his brothers, though he was not far above most of them in age and – in his younger days – had lacked the responsibility required to do so, causing his parents to lovingly reprimand him.[28] His marriage to Anne Seymour had endured the execution of both their fathers, and she had been allowed to visit him in the Tower, though it had not yet resulted in a child.[29] She, after all, was still only sixteen.

His younger brother, Robert, two years his junior, also seemed to have a flair for the artistic and intellectual. He joined John in carving his name on the wall in their prison, accompanied by oak leaves, as in John's grander design. The two also composed metrical psalms together, a poetical form much in vogue, especially amongst the imprisoned elite.[30] Employing the same metre, the brothers took psalms from the Old Testament and transformed them into poetry, expressing at the same time their own feelings and desires, which for the most part bent upon divine revenge.

'Give ear unto me my God,' John wrote, 'and hear my mourning voice / break down the wicked swarming flocks that at my fall rejoice.' He ended with a vengeful prayer: 'I appeal to thee that will when fit time is / Discharge my fraught breast of woe and pour in heaps of bliss / And send consuming plagues for their deserts most due / That thirst so sore my guiltless blood their tyrants hands to imbrue.'[31]

His younger brother infused his poem with an even greater desire for revenge: 'Oh mighty Lord to whom all vengeance doth belong', Robert wrote, 'and just revenge for their deserts which do oppress by wrong.' He issued a warning to all that had harmed him: 'But yet in time beware you forward bloody band / What things against the Lord your God you seek to take in hand,' for 'sure the Lord my God mine aid and only strength / Will them reward and sharply scourge with endless pain at length.'[32] The young men would be only too happy to exact a cruel revenge on certain false friends, should they be released.

These former friends might, therefore, have had some cause for concern when John was released from the Tower in the autumn of 1554, having been imprisoned for over a year.[33] There was little opportunity for revenge, however. Upon his release, he travelled the thirty miles south-east to Penshurst Place, the home of his sister Mary and her husband. Henry had inherited the manor at his father's death in February of that year. A medieval fortified house, Penshurst was built around a central courtyard, on one side of which was the great hall. Extensive lodgings had been added some decades before.

This was not a joyous reunion between brother and sister. John was dangerously ill, which – combined with his brother-in-law's appeal to the new king and his mother's work amongst the network of courtiers – had probably secured his release. Mary, now eight months pregnant, was not to go near anyone ill, let alone to visit someone near death.[34] The distress alone could kill both mother and child. If she said a final goodbye to her elder brother, she risked killing her unborn child.

John lived only three days in freedom at his sister's home. His verses inscribed in stone at the Tower remained unfinished. Rather than a clear allusion to a verse of Scripture, the remaining words left the impression of five young men, restless to find meaning, revenge, or simply to escape the confines which held them. John died at twenty-three, the second of Mary's brothers to have died in as many years.

Mary entered her lying-in not long after her brother's death. Her chamber was hung with curtains and tapestries to keep out light and draft, and the evil spirits that might come with them. It was a place of birth, not death, and yet fit the requirements of mourning just as well. The reformed religion did not countenance the prayers to saints or use of stones or girdles to help during childbirth, but Mary did still have recourse to other aids during her delivery.[35] Prayers were still important, though addressed directly to God, none of this nonsense about saints hurtling out of dragons. Henry, too, was expected to pray for the safety of his wife and child, though he would have to do so away from the event itself; husbands were not allowed into the birthing chamber. Instead, Mary was to be surrounded by female friends and relatives. This included her mother – who reassuringly had been through the ordeal herself some thirteen times; her sister Katherine – who at the age of nine might have found it all a bit terrifying; and her sisters-in-law, Elizabeth and Amy, who would hope to be in such condition soon, despite the blood and screams.[36] Her other sister-in-law, Anne, had only recently become a young widow; it would have been a lot to have asked her to be there as well.

Despite the relentless tragedy, Mary brought her child to term. Her son – for it was a son – was born a month after John's death, in her dark and closed-off chamber in Penshurst Place. The midwife cut the umbilical cord, bathed, anointed and swaddled the babe, before handing him to his waiting father and mother. Mary certainly had reason to hope and pray, as she held her child in her arms, that he would live a fuller, safer life than the ones that she and her siblings had seen. His family would do what they could to ensure this from the moment he took his first breaths. When the infant was baptised, he – like his mother – was given the blessing of a royal godparent and namesake. He was named for the new king, Philip. The baby's godmother, however, was his grandmother, Jane Dudley, still Duchess of Northumberland, who after so recently losing two sons could at last welcome a grandson.[37] Philip Sidney might carry his father's name, along with that of a Spanish prince, but he was also a Dudley, and even as a swaddled infant, was doing his work for the good of the family.

*

In a dark room within Chelsea Manor, Jane Dudley, armed with a quill, was scratching out lines of text with purpose. Although not yet fifty, she carried the lines and heaviness of too many pregnancies with too few surviving children. Around her, the room was decorated in black, with glimmers of gold trim.[38] Even the bed was of black velvet, like a coffin covered in a dark pall. This was fitting. The document she was writing was her final will and testament. The Duchess of Northumberland did not think she would live much longer.

As she wrote, her thoughts were focused on her family. Of thirteen children born, only five remained alive. Three of them still lay under the shadow of death sentence. She was desperate with every act and breath she had left to save them from the fate of their brother, father and grandfather.

Through the window Jane could see the grand gardens of Chelsea Manor, lifeless and barren in the depths of winter. Jane had chosen the location of her last stand well; Chelsea Manor was a property fit for the death of a queen. With tall stone columns and large chimneys, the building proclaimed wealth and power.[39] Part of the estate had been built for the late Queen Catherine Parr, whom Jane had served and even called a friend. The former queen, too, had spent her last years there, along with the Princess Elizabeth and the girl who would become Jane's daughter-in-law and for a short time her queen. By the time Jane and her husband were given Chelsea by Edward VI, it was as quasi-royalty themselves.

Those times were gone now, and Jane had been forced to humbly petition Queen Mary I – the woman who had ordered the deaths of Jane's husband and son – to have Chelsea returned to her. She cannot have cherished the thought. That she had succeeded in her request was a sign of her return to favour, despite the treason that clung to the family like a disease. Now, once again, she had to make supplication to the monarch in the hopes of restoring her family.

She had spent the previous months building up networks of people to help her. As she wrote, she went through a mental list of those she could count on to help her family. The Dudleys had few friends and many enemies. The arrival of Philip and his Spanish court in the wake of the royal wedding had presented a unique opportunity for the Dudleys: a fresh slate in the form of powerful nobles who did not have reason to distrust and despise them. And so, as Jane wrote her will in her dark chamber at Chelsea Manor, their names became interspersed with those of her family and servants. A gift to Don Diego de Acevedo[40] came with the request that he continue to show 'himself like a father and brother to my sons' and reminded him of the many friends that he had secured around Philip for the family. A green parrot went to the Duchess of Alva, once again requesting she continue her support of the Dudley children. Jane also bequeathed gifts to other high-profile members of the court, all of whom had supported the Spanish marriage, and thus formed part of a particular faction at court. These included her late husband's half-sister, Elizabeth Jobson, who received a black gown of wrought velvet with furred squares, and both the Lord and Lady Paget, whom she still hoped might intervene on her family's behalf; Anne Paget received a gown and her husband a black enamelled ring.

Jane was not content, though, to just work through intermediaries. In her will, she made an impassioned plea directly to Mary and her new husband Philip, requesting that they grant pardon to her condemned sons. None of her attempts to pass on property to them would be worth much unless Mary restored them. The queen had taken so much from Jane Dudley, and Jane must have sensed that Mary's heart was beginning to soften towards the family as the death toll rose. Jane's own death might just be the final means by which the restoration of the Dudleys would be achieved.

As she wrote, she ensured her will was filled not only with the sort of strategic gift-giving that might secure her children's pardon, but sentimental gifts as well. She decided on gowns of black velvet for her daughters and daughters-in-law. They also received large coffers with Jane's husband's badge on them, a reminder of the family of which they would always remain a part. Her eldest son, Ambrose, received the furnishings and hangings of the chamber in which she lay. To Harry, her youngest, she gave the furnishings and hangings from the gallery: his parents' arms in gold and green, a Turkish carpet, a chair and cushion.[41] Her eldest daughter, Mary, was given one of Jane's most prized possessions, a clock which had belonged to John. She asked Mary to continue to treasure it as she had, as a precious jewel.

With these last efforts to keep her family loved and safe dispensed with, Jane Dudley sank into her bed of black velvet. She died in the weeks following Christmas, less than two months after the birth of her grandson. Her funeral was held a week later in Chelsea Old Church. Although in her will Jane had requested that her corpse, no more than 'meat of worms', would be unceremoniously wrapped in ashes and deposited in a coffin of wood, the funeral was a much grander affair. The church, like the room in which she'd died, was hung elaborately in black, with the heraldic arms of Jane's family and six dozen burning torches honouring the daughter of the firebrand. Her body was processed in with two banners of arms, four banners of holy images, two heralds of arms and a great many mourners.[42] Her coffin was topped with a wax effigy, pennons and heraldic devices, and covered with a rich canopy. She was also given an elaborate entombment in a chapel of the church, which immortalized her dedication to her family. There, captured for ever in brass, on either side of Jane knelt her thirteen children. It would live as an eternal testimony to Jane's legacy: the next generation of the Dudley family.

PART FOUR
1555–1588

14
Restored in blood

The Lady Day joust of 1555 was one of the grandest and largest tournaments ever seen at Whitehall.[1] The event attracted thousands – perhaps even tens of thousands – of spectators, packed into double-tiered stands. Approaching the yard at the height of the tournament, it would be difficult to make out anything but floating heads in the stands: seemingly disembodied faces frozen with excitement and rapture at the spectacle.[2] By the time the festivities began around midday, the nobility would have arrived, walking up the long staircase and taking their places in the sumptuous viewing gallery purpose-built for such occasions.[3] The gallery walls were decorated with paintings, the floor ornamented with mats, and the ceiling covered in gilt. One of the paintings to be found in the gallery was the anamorphic portrait of Edward VI, which required the viewer to stand in a particular place and look through a hole in order to see the otherwise-distorted portrait properly. The work astonished visitors; from one perspective the late king looked barely human, from another, sheer perfection.[4] Tapestries separated the gallery into viewing boxes, the most privileged nobles sitting closest to the royals. From the gallery, they had a perfect view of the tiltyard before them, covered in gravel and sand to make it easier for the galloping horses. The tilt-barrier, about the height of a very tall man (such as Henry VIII himself), ran through the centre, and the whole yard was surrounded by painted fencing and guards. In the shadow of the monumental Holbein gate, the crowds watched the young men compete.

Held to mark the celebration of the Annunciation – when the Virgin Mary was told she was to carry the son of God – and the beginning of the new year, this March tournament had a particular resonance. Mary I had announced her own pregnancy in November: the Catholic saviour was on his way and England was to enter a new age, emerging from the heresy of the decades before. Coming at the end of a carnival of events to mark the start of the year, the tournament was the ultimate public spectacle.[5]

It was also a significant moment for the Dudley brothers, who after more than a year of imprisonment were all there to witness it. Ambrose, now the eldest at twenty-four, had been released shortly following their mother's death at the end of January. He became head of the Dudley family, and responsible for the wellbeing of his younger brothers, Robert and Harry. When they had entered the Tower, there had been five of them and both their parents were alive. Now they were just three, and both their mother and father were also gone. Despite their release, they were still stained with treason, and would have to find a way to climb back into favour.

In this, they followed their mother's lead: the key lay in the opportunity provided by Philip's Spanish court. Fortunately for them, the new king needed the Dudleys as much as they needed him. The Spanish and English were not mixing well, to say the least. Many English courtiers saw the arrival of the Spanish as an invasion that threatened every element of English life.[6] The imperial ambassador reported that many of the nobles had ridden to their homes in the country to raise troops in fear of a military invasion.[7] At the court, Philip was stuck between a rock and a hard place. If he let himself be served by Englishmen, as he was required to by the pesky marriage contract he'd barely bothered to read, the Spanish nobles who had accompanied him felt snubbed and, admittedly, bored. But if he was served by his Spanish friends, he risked outright rebellion. The two groups – English and Spanish – kept far apart from each other at court. As one Spanish gentleman in Philip's company put it, 'We Spaniards move among the English as if they were animals, trying not to notice them; and they do the same to us.'[8] When they did interact, violence erupted. One of the Spanish noblemen wrote home in October 1554 that not a day passed at the court without some 'knife-work' between the two nations, often with blood spilled.[9] The situation was not helped by the fact that the twenty-eight-year-old king consort of England had never actually learned English.

For those willing to make the effort to ingratiate themselves with the new king and his retinue the rewards could be substantial.[10] Being seen as hispanophiles could make a family unpopular, but on this count the Dudleys had little to lose and quite a lot to gain. Philip was notoriously paranoid and his Spanish court was known for its factionalism, yet in his few years in London he seems to have taken a shine to the traitorous Dudleys, especially the charming Robert, and made genuine attempts to repair the growing rifts. Nothing seemed to please the English better than a good old joust and the young, athletic Dudley brothers could provide on this count.

So it was that on 25 March 1555, the Dudley brothers arrived to take their places in the tournament. Like their fellows, the two elder Dudleys mounted destriers, bred for their ability to carry the heavy load of knight, armour and lance, and took to the lists. Over their armour they wore elaborate costumes. The king's men wore blue trimmed with yellow, with great tufts of blue and yellow feathers sprouting from their helmets.[11] Other groups that day wore white or green, and one was even dressed in exotic Turkish dress: crimson satin gowns and capes with curved swords and small round shields. Each prepared themselves at one end of the tiltyard, before – at the sound of a trumpet blast – thundering down the lists against their opponents. Carrying lances over three metres long, they reached speeds of over thirty-five miles per hour as they charged towards the centre of the yard. Robert rode against William Howard, Baron Howard of Effingham, striking him in one course in the chest with his lance.[12] Baron Howard too was suspected of treason. The event was a tournament of traitors, a desperate attempt on the part of Philip to hold his conflict-ridden court together.

The young king, in his fine blue and yellow, was amongst the twenty-odd jousters riding that day. With fair hair and blue eyes, and reportedly very attractive legs, the king must have inspired at least some confidence in even the most dubious English nobles. He did find himself, however, caught up in a rather dramatic scene that disrupted the revelry. His wife the queen, not bothering to hide her 'fear and disquietude' about the possible dangers of jousting, begged Philip never to run the lists again.[13] After all, there were many in England who wished Philip ill, and might use the veil of chivalric competition to rid England of the foreign usurper. Doing all he could to be amicable to his new wife, and considering her pregnancy, Philip agreed. About twenty years before, Henry VIII had taken a near-fatal fall during a joust, and Anne Boleyn had claimed that the shock had caused her to miscarry their child. Philip would have been keen to avoid the same. He would leave such events until their young son could ride himself.[14]

Ambrose and Robert, too, must have been a sight to behold as they entered the lists. Both in their early twenties, they were in their prime, and undoubtedly bursting with the pent-up energies of young men imprisoned for far too long. Robert was especially able on horseback and seemed to possess a flair for the courtly arts: display, flattery and machination. Dudley's motto at the tournament, embroidered on a large cloth banner so it could be seen from the galleries, was 'Te stante virebo' – 'With you standing, I shall flourish', accompanied by the image of a pyramid encircled by ivy.[15] In 1555, the pyramid might have been Philip, the ivy most certainly Robert.

Whereas Robert must have inherited his thick lips and soft features from his mother, Ambrose seems to have resembled his father – he shared the long nose and deep-set eyes, though his was a sterner gaze. Ambrose's motto at the tournament was 'Spiritus durissima coquit' – 'A noble mind digests even the most painful injuries', an apt saying for Robert's more pensive – even sullen – older brother. While younger Robert could be free to enjoy the festivities, Ambrose had much more on his mind. Fortunately, his wife, Elizabeth, was heavily pregnant, with an heir expected soon. That would help alleviate the pressure on the remaining Dudley children.

Two months after the Lady Day tournament, however, it was clear that Elizabeth Dudley, Countess of Warwick, was in fact not pregnant, never mind her swollen belly and breasts. At the age of thirty-five, Elizabeth suffered under the burden of the Dudley family expectations. Jane Dudley's thirteen effigy children must have haunted her, alongside her own mother's fortuitous fertility with the king. Elizabeth's pregnancy had ended in neither a living nor a dead child; there had never been a child at all.[16] She was not the only one, however; a week after Elizabeth's false pregnancy was revealed, hope that the queen was carrying a child had also begun to dissipate.[17] She too had suffered a phantom pregnancy, born of the overwhelming desire to produce an heir to the throne. What's more, her husband, now King of Spain, left in August, taking with him any chance that they could produce another. As Elizabeth and Ambrose's marriage showed its cracks, and a Dudley heir remained simply a hope, the royal marriage also was rumoured to have been a disaster, and lacked its essential successor.

*

The English were late, very late. If they did not arrive in time, Philip's continental war would be in tatters, and all his efforts to ingratiate himself with the bothersome English for naught. For all his apparent confidence, and very fine legs, Philip was riddled with anxiety and indecision, and the pressure of one of his first military ventures, years in the making, was taking its toll. As he sat in his tent in the north of France he despatched a series of desperate missives. He was 'greatly distressed' and rendered 'quite desperate' by the lateness of the English troops; they had better 'hurry up'.[18]

The new King of England was in the midst of a complex war on the continent. He, like his Dudley allies, also had the burden of family pressure on him. His father, Charles V, had amassed one of the greatest empires ever seen. In Europe, Charles's holdings surrounded an increasingly nervous France, and included Spain, Germany and large parts of Italy, as well as territory in the west of France. In 1555, the French king, Henry II, allied with the Ottoman Suleiman the Magnificent, had declared war on Charles in an attempt to place Italy under French, rather than Habsburg, control. Only a year later, Charles abdicated his throne, splitting the empire between his brother, Ferdinand I, Holy Roman Emperor, and Philip, who became King of Spain and the Netherlands. It was now up to Philip to continue his father's fight against France.

The king's attention was focused on a single small French city: Saint-Quentin. At one time home to booming textile and wine industries, the city had declined in numbers since the fourteenth century thanks to the plague and a misfortune of geography. Saint-Quentin was strategically located between France and Burgundy, thus becoming a point of contention during the Hundred Years' War and now essential to Philip's war against France. His imperial troops established a long siege against the city, and – with the arrival of the English – would be in a position to finally take it.

To say that the citizens of Saint-Quentin were long-suffering would be an understatement, but Philip's anxieties meant hope for them. On the way to Saint-Quentin was the experienced French Constable Anne de Montmorency, a veteran of battles against the English since the first decade of the reign of Henry VIII. He had ridden out with 22,000 troops to relieve the siege at Saint-Quentin. If the French forces arrived before the English, Montmorency would attack the Spanish and imperial troops before they had the chance to try to take the city. The citizens of Saint-Quentin prayed for salvation. Philip predicted disaster.

It was a wonder that the English were coming at all. Philip's marriage agreement promised that he could not involve the English in his war, and there were few nobles willing to support him.[19] He had left England in September 1555, just five months after the Lady Day joust, in order to attend to affairs on the continent. He soon realized that he would need the help of his new kingdom. A year and a half later, in March 1557, Robert Dudley had travelled to Calais, to meet with Philip upon his return to England.[20] The two men appear to have struck a deal of sorts. Ambrose and Robert were granted access to lands gifted to them by their mother's will, a brief respite from the attainder under which they still suffered. They would use these properties to raise troops and funds to support Philip's dangerous and controversial war.[21] Once again, an alliance would need to be formed between the Spanish king and the treasonous Dudleys, but this one would be of a much riskier nature. All Philip had to do was to convince his wife, and the rest of the country.

At some point it must have been pointed out to Philip that there was a loophole in the marriage treaty. Philip could not embroil England in his war against France, but there was nothing stopping England declaring its own separate war against the French and allying with Philip to fight them. After weeks of intense political deliberation, and a timely French-supported attack on Scarborough, this was exactly what transpired. England was to go to war with France, and Philip would have the support he so desperately needed. The war was announced with great fanfare – and to mixed response – in the streets of Cheapside on 7 June 1557, and three days later the list of commanders was drawn up, including the names of all three Dudley brothers.[22] They left their wives quite suddenly and joined a force of over seven thousand, sailing across the Channel in the first weeks of July.[23] It was young Harry's first trip out of England, as well as his first opportunity to prove himself in battle. His older brothers had reason to be more sullen about the expedition. Both had sold and leased lands in order to cover the costs of joining Philip and his war, though there were whispers that Robert's finances might also be directed elsewhere, supporting Philip's young, fair sister-in-law Elizabeth, next in line for the throne.[24]

It appeared to all be for nothing in the early days of August 1557. Montmorency was coming, and the English would not be there to reinforce the tired imperial troops. As the English made their achingly slow way across northern France, and Philip wrung his hands in his tent, the French reached Saint-Quentin. Their arrival, however, was bogged down by the mud surrounding the river. Draughts the summer before had yielded to intense rains and floods across France. The imperial troops attacked as the French fought through the mud. Seeing a massacre in the making, Montmorency called for a retreat, but the Spanish troops caught up to his too quickly, and the French were cut down as they attempted to make it back to the river where their mired boats waited for them.[25] The imperial troops secured their victory. It was one of the most important and decisive battles of the Italian Wars, and the English missed it.

Ambrose, Robert and Harry arrived alongside their countrymen two days later, in time to see the aftermath of the dramatic battle. The French lost over five thousand men, with thousands taken prisoner, including Montmorency and three of his sons. The Spanish saw the victory as a miracle, and celebrated accordingly. Not far away, the battlefield was strewn with bodies for half a league around. Identifying family members or friends amongst the dead was nearly impossible as the corpses putrefied under the hot August sun. The French could scarcely remain in the area because of the cadaverous stench.[26] Those who had survived the battle and been dragged into tents continued to suffer, as their injuries filled with worms and rotted, forcing the French surgeon Ambroise Paré to remove countless limbs in an attempt to save as many soldiers as he could. Though they had fared better, the view – and smell – from the Spanish side cannot have been much different, and it was said that the sight of the carnage turned even the king off any taste for further war. Young Harry may have missed the crucial battle, but he became well acquainted with its aftermath.

He would also get his chance at warfare, however, and Ambrose and Robert their chance to make good on their promise of support to Philip. Two weeks after this dramatic battle, Philip led his combined force, with the English troops – and the Dudleys – behind him, to at last take Saint-Quentin.[27] The combined imperial forces had occupied the land to the east, and surrounded it with large cannons. Centipede-like formations of pikemen wound their way around the city, taking on whatever French forces remained as they streamed towards its walls. Knights on horseback clashed just outside the city, chivalric ceremony long forgotten in the pitched battle.

Young and eager, Harry was one of the first to attempt to scale the wall of Saint-Quentin. Robert watched through the chaos of the battle as his young brother raced forward toward a ladder, stopping before ascending to rip his tight hose, which otherwise might restrict his climb. In the moment that Harry paused, distracted, there was a blast from a large gun.[28] Robert watched as his brother fell, lifeless. Young Harry, Robert's last younger brother, was gone in a spray of gunsmoke and blood. Amongst the tears of his companions, Harry's corpse was brought back to the camp in a shroud.[29] The image of his younger brother's death would remain seared on his memory for the rest of Robert's life.[30]

As the imperial troops successfully routed the French and took the city, the two remaining Dudley brothers were unlikely to have joined in the celebrations, or the carnage, that followed. The German mercenaries who had joined Philip's army sacked Saint-Quentin, causing more bloodshed than the battle itself. Women grabbed their children as the men broke through the walls and attacked the city, hiding themselves in cellars to avoid being raped or killed. From their hiding places, they could hear the screams of those who had not managed to find a place to hide, and smell the sickly combined odour of blood, gunpowder and corpses. Then, another smell reached them. It was smoke. The whole city was on fire. Those who had hidden in cellars to save their lives now had no escape. Across the battlefield, the English could hear their screams as survivors both of the battle and the sacking of the city slowly burned alive.[31] Covered in the sweat and dirt of battle, and watching the great plumes of smoke and flame rise around the city's proud basilica, Robert and Ambrose mourned.

Both Philip and the Dudley sons had achieved what they had set out to in journeying to France, but it had come at a high cost. Once the flames died and the smoke cleared, Saint-Quentin was a city of ghosts.

*

London was awash in fanfare and celebration. Despite the late November weather, people flocked from their houses to watch the procession move through the newly gravelled streets.[32] It began at the Charterhouse, just north of Smithfield. The Charterhouse had once been the home of Carthusian monks; when the monastery was dissolved, its resisting prior had been hanged, drawn and quartered at Tyburn, the other monks left to starve at Newgate. Now it was the home of Edward North, Baron North, a former supporter of Jane Grey who had survived and even thrived under Queen Mary. From there – rather than turning south and to Smithfield Market, the site of countless burnings – the procession headed east, along the Barbican. It entered the city at Cripplegate and travelled eastwards along the south side of the stone-built London Wall, past Austin Friars, to Bishopsgate. From there, it proceeded south, passing by the Leadenhall Market, and at last arrived at Tower Street, where it passed through the southern-most part of Tower Hill, just in sight of the scaffold, and through the gate into the Tower of London itself.

Watching the procession pass, excited onlookers were first met with the sight of countless gentlemen, knights and the lords on horseback, in fine array. Following them were the trumpeters, blowing their salute in the cold November air. After they passed, the heralds processed by, in their respective liveries. Finally, William Herbert, Earl of Pembroke rode past. In his fifties, Herbert was one of the Crown's great military commanders, and had overseen the engagement at Saint-Quentin the year before. Once an ally of John Dudley, Herbert's son had married Catherine Grey in the same ceremony that had also seen the wedding of Jane Grey and Guildford Dudley, and Katherine Dudley and Henry Hastings. He had been one of the first, however, to throw in his lot with Henry FitzAlan, and had had his son's marriage annulled. This had been enough to convince Mary of his loyalty. Now he rode behind the heralds in the procession, carrying before him the queen's sword. But the weapon did not belong to Mary.

As the Earl of Pembroke passed, all heads turned to see the figure around whom the procession had been formed, like links around a great diamond. A young woman, about twenty-five, rode on horseback through the streets of London, in profile against the might of the London Wall. She was dressed simply but finely, in a gown of purple velvet, with a scarf around her neck. Sergeants-at-arms surrounded her as she rode, but the keen-eyed would still be able to see her, the flash of purple and the glimpse of red hair. This young woman was Elizabeth, the new Queen of England.

Elizabeth had entered the Tower before, as a prisoner, spending two months behind its walls in the spring of 1554, the same time at which the Dudley sons were imprisoned there, suspected for her role in the rebellion which had resulted in Guildford Dudley's death. She had spent much of the remainder of her sister's reign at Hatfield House, in Hertfordshire, gathering support should her sister die without giving birth to a child of her own.

This had at first seemed unlikely, given Mary's symptoms soon after her marriage, but the queen who had been so triumphantly pregnant at the tournament in March 1555 had not delivered a child then or in the subsequent years. To make matters worse, Philip's short return to raise troops in 1557 for his war against France was his last trip to England and to his wife. Frequently unwell throughout her life, Mary had once again fallen ill in the months that followed Saint-Quentin, and by September 1558 she was suffering frequent bouts of fever from which she never made a full recovery.[33] A month later, Philip was informed of his wife's decline. He sent his physician but did not travel to her himself. By early November Mary had had to face the truth: she would die without a child to replace her, and the crown would pass to her still-Protestant half-sister, the child of Anne Boleyn, Elizabeth.

Elizabeth had been prepared for this. She had already been assembling a shadow council at Hatfield.[34] At its helm was Sir William Cecil, the man with whom John Dudley had worked so closely under Edward VI. Cecil, too, had survived Mary, and taken up a position as surveyor in Elizabeth's household. When the news reached Hatfield that Mary had died, Cecil put together lists of all the important and urgent tasks that would need to be done in the coming days in order to secure her accession.[35] Near the top of the list was the need to send messengers to some of the princes of Europe, notifying them that Elizabeth was now Queen of England. Whereas in the first draft of this memorandum Cecil had included the pope, the emperor, the King of Spain and the King of Denmark, his final draft was expanded to include a handful of English courtiers, who had suffered under Mary and could be trusted to support the new order.[36]

A letter also went to her new Master of the Horse, who appeared directly behind Elizabeth as the procession continued past and the queen rode slowly but surely out of view. In his mid-twenties, the Master of the Horse was certainly handsome, with a certain swarthiness to him.[37] Of middling stature, with dark hair and eyes, the young man sat proudly and expertly on the horse behind his new queen as they entered the Tower. He too had entered the Tower of London before as a prisoner. It had robbed him of a father, two brothers, and years of his life. That was a whole reign ago now, however. Following closely behind the young queen in purple velvet, Robert Dudley, along with what remained of his family, might indeed hope to flourish once again.

15
Carnal marriages

The Lady Mary Sidney, still not twenty-five, stood before the much elder Álvaro de la Quadra, Bishop of Aquila, the Spanish ambassador. She assured him that the new queen, Elizabeth I, would definitely marry, never mind protestations to the contrary. It is the 'custom among ladies here', she confidently assured him, 'not to give their consent in such matters until they are teased into it'.[1] Between them an Italian man translated her words, somewhat unnecessarily; Sidney was proficient in a variety of languages. It would only be a matter of days, she went on, and the Council would press the queen into marrying. De la Quadra need not worry about his master's chosen suitor, Charles II, Archduke of Austria; Elizabeth would come around.

It was the eve of the queen's twenty-sixth birthday, which she would spend at Hampton Court Palace, the splendid home once belonging to Cardinal Wolsey, which had been significantly expanded for the enjoyment of the queen's mother, Anne Boleyn, before her downfall. Outside the ground was wet, and the evidence of the fierce storm that had raged the day before was strewn across the surrounding gardens and forests. The summer of celebrations had come to a decided end.

Having been made a Gentlewoman of the Household at the time of Elizabeth's coronation that January, Mary Sidney was at the heart of power, closer to Elizabeth than any man could hope to get, as long as he wasn't sharing her bed, of course. Continually accompanying the queen, Mary and the other ladies, glittering smaller gems, were there to accentuate the brilliance of the central stone. For this reason, Mary was given clothes of only white or black, setting off and highlighting Elizabeth's brilliant purples, reds and blues.[2] Such women, however, were far more than decorative counterpoints to the shining queen; they performed important domestic duties within the queen's chamber, including participating in the time-consuming and complex affair of dressing the queen each morning, and had a pivotal, though informal, role in the political functioning of the court.[3] It was an exhausting and demanding position, without any hope of privacy or solitude, but one that was fiercely sought after.[4] There were only a handful of these women, Elizabeth having decreased the size of the queen's Privy Chamber and Bed Chamber significantly.[5] It was for this reason that these esteemed envoys such as de la Quadra were so interested in what Mary Sidney could tell them. The fate of England's foreign affairs with the Habsburg nations rested on the information she could relay. The question remained, however, was Mary Sidney to be trusted?

Mary had accompanied her husband to Ireland when he had been appointed Vice-Treasurer in 1556 but had returned shortly before Elizabeth's accession, leaving her husband in Ireland.[6] Ireland, to the Sidneys, was an uncivilized place filled with a near-barbaric people. The island had been divided into three distinct parts according to the statutes of Kilkenny in 1366: the English-controlled 'Pale' around Dublin, the area controlled by the Gaelic lords, much of it around Ulster, and, between them, lands ruled by descendants of the original English settlers. They had sworn loyalty to the Crown in 1558, but still bristled under the control of the London lords assigned to rule from Dublin, a worrying threat given their continued possession of feudal retainers, essentially their own private armies.[7]

Henry's position of Vice-Treasurer lay just below that of Lord Deputy, a position held by his brother-in-law, Sir Thomas Radcliffe, Earl of Sussex. Their time there was marked by simmering tension and fear: Radcliffe quickly lost the loyalty of the Palesmen and was bent on a conquest of Ulster.[8] It was in this context that Mary gave birth to their second child, Mary Margaret, though she had died in Ireland, not long before Mary's return to England. Philip remained in Ireland while Mary made the dangerous crossing back to English shores in order to welcome their new queen.

Mary's initial absence, as well as the Sidneys' success under Mary I, did not stop her from benefitting as her brother had from the new queen. Almost a year into the reign, and Mary was at the centre of the intense negotiations and machinations centred around attaining the queen's hand. Elizabeth had spent the weeks before Mary's meeting with the ambassador in fever and melancholy, barely sleeping, apparently exhausted by the persistent badgering about her marriage. At such a time, it was only her women who would have access to her.[9] Mary Sidney carried extremely privileged information.

Frustratingly inscrutable, Elizabeth's stubborn indecision on the matter of her marriage had already been the occasion of angry missives on both sides of the Channel. The last of the legitimate children of Henry VIII, Elizabeth's claim was considered tenuous by many. For the Catholics, Henry VIII's marriage to Elizabeth's mother, Anne Boleyn, could not have been legitimate as it had taken place during the lifetime of his first queen, Catherine of Aragon. Henry VIII had broken with Rome to declare that first marriage invalid, and as such the Catholics could not recognize the annulment. Henry himself had subsequently disavowed his marriage to Anne Boleyn, bastardizing Elizabeth (though he'd later gone back on that too). Although Elizabeth had not had to overcome a usurpation of her throne, as Mary had with Queen Jane, there was ample reason to question her claim.

After Elizabeth, the already complex line of succession became even more of a tangle. Technically speaking, her successor ought to be drawn from the lineage of Henry VII's eldest daughter, Margaret, who had married James IV of Scotland. This made Margaret's granddaughter, Mary, heir to the English throne. There were, however, three problems with this scenario. First, Mary was Catholic. Second, Mary was already Queen of Scots. And third, Mary was also the Queen of France, her father-in-law, Henry II, having died suddenly in a jousting accident two months before. If Elizabeth was truly a bastard, then Mary, Queen of Scots, was already Queen of England, Scotland and France. Her arms indicated these overlapping claims, as Robert Dudley had heard first-hand from his contacts in Paris.[10] Protestants and francophobes quivered at the thought.

Excepting this line, the next option would be to take the route that Edward VI had, following the children of Mary and Charles Brandon, to the Greys. Of course, the eldest Grey daughter was dead for having pressed this claim (or having the claim pressed for her), along with Mary Sidney 's brother Guildford, but she had sisters. Catherine Grey, the elder, had been married to Henry Herbert, but it had been quickly dissolved. Now a part of the new queen's household, Catherine was heir presumptive according to the terms of Henry VIII's will, though she too was a young woman, and without the superior claim of Mary, Queen of Scots. She had also expressed an interest in marrying the eldest son of the late Duke of Somerset: a controversial choice to say the least, and one to which it was unlikely the queen would agree.

All the more pressing it was, then, that Elizabeth be married, and to the right husband. Suitors circled like birds of prey. There were domestic and foreign matches, Catholic and Protestant. First to make an attempt was Philip II of Spain, Elizabeth's erstwhile brother-in-law. Ambassadors were dispatched and entreaties made. Philip's representatives tried various tactics with Elizabeth, both political and personal. They emphasized her geopolitical isolation, should Mary, Queen of Scots, seek to make her claim to the English throne with the force of the French army behind her. They also, taking a different tack, suggested that Elizabeth's hardships under Mary had been caused by jealousy, a fear on Mary's part that Philip would look to marry Elizabeth once Mary died – an odd sort of flattery indeed. Two months after Elizabeth's coronation, however, the negotiations came to an end. Having witnessed the public resistance to her sister's marriage to the King of Spain, and the difficulties Mary had suffered as a result, it was little wonder that Elizabeth dismissed this offer, though she did draw the refusal out.

As the negotiations with Philip II came to an end over Easter 1559, they were soon replaced by those on behalf of Prince Erik of Sweden, a young man of Elizabeth's age, who courted her against his ageing father's wishes. The Habsburgs also replaced Philip with another, perhaps more suitable, candidate, Philip's cousin, the Archduke of Austria, son of the Holy Roman Emperor. Within weeks, however, court observers began to consider another possibility. The Spanish ambassadors noticed an increasing closeness between the queen and her Master of the Horse: the young son of a traitor, Robert Dudley. By the middle of April it was reported that not only did Robert have access to the queen's chamber day and night, but this level of access had given him a startling level of control over royal affairs.[11] On her first St George's Day as queen, Elizabeth made Robert a Knight of the Garter. That same month she travelled to Chelsea, where Mary and Robert's mother had died, and Robert gifted her with a pair of gloves, set with gilt buttons.[12] Even Robert's illness in May, and the queen's brief attentions on the unmarried and elder Sir William Pickering, a former ally of Robert's father, did not seem much of an interruption to the closeness between the pair, who it was reported were very much in love and very intimate.[13] As summer began, Robert was once again courting the queen at suppers in St James's Park and present as she went on her summer progress in July and August, dining on suppers of fresh sturgeon and Rhenish wine.[14]

The matter reached such a head, that it was reported that Kat Ashley, former governess of Elizabeth and one of her most trusted friends, had fallen to her knees before the queen, imploring her to marry, in order to put an end to the rumours that Elizabeth had been living a disreputable life with her Master of the Horse.[15] Elizabeth's rumoured affair with Dudley would cause, Ashley was reported to have said, much bloodshed in the realm, and it would have been better if the governess had strangled the infant Elizabeth in the cradle than it had come to that. As the emperor's special ambassador, Caspar Breuner, reported the conversation, Elizabeth took this imagined treason kindly, defending her choice to be gracious towards Robert Dudley, who was deserving of it. From there, her defence began to fall apart, as she both protested that, as she was always surrounded by her ladies, Mary included, she could never have engaged in anything illicit with her Master of the Horse, and, furthermore, that if she wanted to live a dishonourable life, no one could forbid it to her. Nothing about these protestations was particularly reassuring, and the certainty that something untoward was going on between the young queen and the dashing Robert Dudley only grew.

This rumoured intervention within Elizabeth's household had taken place just days before the court arrived at the home of another reported rival suitor, and an old Dudley enemy, Henry FitzAlan, Earl of Arundel, who put on almost a full week's worth of events for the queen, spending

£1,500 on banquets, masques, tournaments and other entertainments to try to woo her.[16] The court had gathered at Nonsuch, a former palace built by Henry VIII after the birth of his son Edward. Henry had chosen the name to demonstrate the palace's exceptionalism – there was to be none such like it in the world – a fitting palace for his son, who would surpass even his father in virtue and glory.[17] Nonsuch, like Edward, however, never realized its greatness, remaining unfinished into the reign of Mary I. She had sold it to Henry FitzAlan, Earl of Arundel, the man who had brought her the traitorous Duke of Northumberland. Now approaching fifty, FitzAlan was putting on an impressive show at his home in the former palace, sixteen miles south-west of London.[18] From the nearby banqueting house, guests gossiped, supped and circled as they were treated to a steady stream of spiced wines and sugared delicacies, brought up by servants from an underground cellar. Perched on the highest point in a sweeping park in Surrey, the banqueting house had impressive views of London to the north and the Sussex Downs to the south.

Swirling around the queen as they sipped their spiced wine, her courtiers issued rumours like the hiss of shots from a bow, striving to strike down their opponents. Courteous smiles masked gritted teeth and unuttered insults. The only security was in greater status, to climb higher, and avoid the common barbs. This, of course, also meant a higher fall, should one find its mark. But with the greatest prize of all – the crown itself – set before them, no gamble was too risky. The key strategy was to see and be seen, and to control the stories being whispered. As Robert wrote to a friend the day before arriving at Nonsuch, 'the trade of court you know is such as presence with diligence helpeth much'.[19]

Unfortunately for their host, Henry FitzAlan was considered by most to be a pretty poor contender for Elizabeth's hand, as much as he might try. Nearly thirty years older than the queen and her other suitors, he was a bit of a laughing stock, not only 'loutish' but silly and strikingly unhandsome.[20] The progress came to an end not long after, and the court returned to Hampton Court early, citing the queen's illness. Feeling harangued as her rather flirtatious summer came to an end, Elizabeth had told the imperial ambassador that she was 'daily pestered with petitions' about her marriage.[21] Two weeks later, the ambassador met with Mary Sidney.

The queen, Mary reported, had changed her mind in regard to the question of her marriage, due in large part to the events of that summer. The queen had been informed of a plot to murder Robert Dudley, as well as poison her, as they dined as guests of the Earl of Arundel at Nonsuch.[22] This, along with talk of a French war, had alarmed her to such an extent that she had decided to marry after all. As such, they ought to write to the emperor to send the Archduke at once. With de la Quadra once again suspicious, Mary reassured him that she risked her life if what she said were not true and communicated with the queen's consent.[23] Not entirely reassured, de la Quadra went to Mary's brother, Robert, who promised that in all things he served the Spanish king, to whom he owed his life.[24] The Dudleys owed Philip II a debt of gratitude, and Robert reassured the Spanish bishop that it would be paid in full. Both Mary and Robert seemed entirely happy to support the Habsburg match. Surely by Christmas the whole matter would be settled; the new year promised a wedding and, if all was well, an heir.

*

'It is not a small grief,' the passionate letter read, 'to be severed from my lord as I am.'[25] Scratched out in a woman's inexpert hand, and addressed to Robert Dudley, the letter told a woeful tale of spousal abandonment. It was April, the second Eastertide of the reign, and the court was busy. The queen had spent the Easter season at Whitehall, occupying the chamber in which her father had died.[26] From the royal apartments, Elizabeth, like her father before her, could descend a private stair directly into the expansive walled hunting park.[27] From there, she could walk directly into a privy gallery, which then connected to a tiltyard gallery. The gallery and tiltyard had been commissioned by Henry VIII as part of a series of buildings known as Parkside.[28] These were designed as a centre for recreation, first used for the coronation of Elizabeth's mother.

On the day after Palm Sunday, Elizabeth made her way to Parkside, and passing the tiltyard gallery, entered one of the two great tennis courts adjacent to it.[29] From the outside, the great close court resembled a majestic hall or chapel more than a centre for recreation, with windows twenty feet high and buttresses topped by stone beasts clutching gilded vanes. Inside, the court stretched ninety feet, bordered on the southern end with another gallery. From this gallery, protected by a red-painted wire mesh, spectators could watch the game. The queen's mother had been watching a game at Parkside when she had received news of her arrest. On this particular Monday, Elizabeth herself had come to spectate, playing truant to the official meetings she was meant to have that day.

On the court, two men in light, loose-fitting shirts faced each other across a net, holding stitched wooden rackets. They ran to hit the leather ball which moved swiftly between them, hitting the floor and walls as it did so. It was an athletic contest, and the men shone with sweat and exertion through their fine shirts. That, of course, was part of the draw of spectating. Elizabeth had attended that day to watch Robert Dudley as he raced across the court.

Robert had continued to reign supreme, despite his many detractors and threats against his life. He had had a special coat of chainmail made that he could wear under his clothes, in case of an ambush or a knife drawn in a darkened corner.[30] His pre-eminence was based in large part on his dexterous ability to manage the balance of power and the sources of rumour within the court. In October, despite the confidence he had nurtured in the emperor's ambassadors, and the suspicions that he too sought the queen's hand, he had hosted a lavish banquet for the proxy of Erik XIV.[31]

Even though the eyes of the court were permanently fixed on the royal bed, no one had yet been able to determine for certain whether a certain traitor's son had access to the queen's most private – to put it delicately – chambers. The imperial ambassador had even hired a spy to find out if there had been any transgression on this count.[32] His report, drawn from the observations of ladies of the bedchamber like Mary Sidney, was that the queen had not forgotten her honour in her relations with Robert. Even the doomed Queen Katherine Howard had needed to let one of her ladies in on her rendezvous with Thomas Culpepper; it was unlikely that Elizabeth and Robert could have conducted a physical affair without anyone knowing, or betraying that knowledge, though rumours persisted of a secret stair between their chambers. At the New Year exchange of gifts that January, Robert had given a few pennies to members of the Queen's household, from the Buttery to the Porters to the Bake-House, as well as to members of the Queen's Chamber.[33] Whether he was greasing the wheels of access, rewarding access already given, or simply being a gentleman remained unclear.

It was even said that Robert and the queen had a secret agreement between them regarding their marriage.[34] This was of great concern to the imperial ambassador, Caspar Breuner, still trying to arrange an imperial match, as it was to many of the court. As Breuner wrote to Archduke Maximilian, another of the sons of the Holy Roman Emperor, if the queen 'marry the said Mylord Robert, she will incur so much enmity that she may one evening lay herself down as Queen of England and rise the next morning as plain Mistress Elizabeth', such was the hatred of Robert and his family. No one should assume, he continued, 'that the other lords and gentry would quietly accept as their King a man whose grandfather had plotted so villainously against the English Crown that his head was struck off in public'. And it was not just Robert's grandfather, 'His father, too, rebelled against the late Queen Mary, and wished to make his son, Mylord Robert's brother, King and his son's wife Queen; wherefore all of them were beheaded.' He added that it was only at the 'King of Spain's earnest intercession' that Robert and his brothers gained their liberty. 'I really do believe,' he continued with vehemence, 'that he will follow in the footsteps of his parents, and may the Devil be his companion, for he causes me and all those who are active on behalf of His Princely Highness, a world of trouble.' There was no stopping Breuner's pen now, 'He is so hated,' he went on, 'that it is a marvel that he has not been slain long ere this.' One of Robert's own countrymen, Breuner reported, 'once asked if England was so poor that none could be found to stab him.'

Of course, as Breuner knew well, in any secret betrothal between Robert and Elizabeth there remained the obstacle of Robert's wife. Amy Dudley had visited London over the summer, shortly before the progress which had ended at Nonsuch. Husband and wife had spent some weeks together, after Robert's illness and before Kat Ashley's rumoured appeal to her mistress about Elizabeth's closeness with her Master of Horse. It was not much time in the midst of circling rumours about Robert's affair with the queen.

The letter sent to Robert in April, however, was not from his own somewhat estranged wife, but from his sister-in-law, Ambrose's wife, Elizabeth. It was not the first such letter Elizabeth had addressed to her brother-in-law, though she promised that she would stop troubling him, if only her husband returned to her. Despite her possible (though illegitimate) regal parentage, Ambrose had abandoned Elizabeth. Her phantom pregnancy two years before had been the last sign of a child, and Elizabeth was approaching the end of her child-bearing years. All the same, Elizabeth could think of no reason for her husband to leave her. 'My conscience,' she told Robert, 'doth bear me witness I have well deserved to have me a loving husband.'[35] Elizabeth had stood by Ambrose when he was imprisoned for treason, even petitioning Mary and Philip for his liberty. Now he had left her. She may not have produced a child, but she did 'her duty to him' and thus asked Robert to 'remember to send my lord home.'

As Elizabeth suggested to Robert, Ambrose did 'lie in one place' and she 'in another'. Ambrose, like his brother, was in London, staying in Holborn.[36] He, too, was firmly attached to the court. On Good Friday he had been named Master of the Ordinance for life, having performed the role since the queen's accession some eighteen months before. It was a military position and suited Ambrose well, who like his father was not a charmer or politicker but had a military mind. The art of the courtier he could leave to his younger brother. Not long after receiving his sister-in-law's letter, in early May, Robert visited Ambrose at his home in Holborn, where his elder brother was recovering from an illness.[37] Whether Robert broached the subject or not, Ambrose did not reconcile with his wife.

Like Ambrose, Robert had not lain by his wife's side for some time and instead was constantly by the hand of the queen. Although some thought that Robert would find reason to seek an annulment of his marriage to Amy, as Elizabeth's father had done in order to marry Elizabeth's mother, rumours suggested another path to freedom. As Breuner put it, 'Although he is married to a beautiful wife he is not living with her, and, as I have been told by many persons, is trying to do away with her by poison.' Given Robert's treacherous family history, 'It is just like him to protract this marriage' with the Queen, 'until he has sent his wife into Eternity.'[38]

*

The traveller rode into the small town of Abingdon, Berkshire. Situated between the Thames and the Ock rivers, some sixty miles north-west of London, Abingdon had once been dominated by the medieval abbey, which had stood there for almost a thousand years, through the ninth-century attacks by the Danes and fourteenth-century plagues, to finally be dissolved by an edict of Henry VIII in 1538. By the time of this man's arrival in 1560, the town was – slowly – beginning to find its feet again, independent of the rule of the Abbey.[39]

Fortunately for the traveller, who had already covered some forty miles that day, there were plenty of inns and alehouses in Abingdon at which he could break his journey. Most convenient for him, arriving from the south, were the handful of inns on Bridge Street, where he crossed the Thames, and those scattered around the large market square; if he was feeling particularly ironic, he could choose to rest himself at the Bear, just east of the square on Ock Street.

Once decided on his lodgings, dismounted and settled, he called for his evening meal. As he ate, the traveller, a man of middling age named Thomas Blount, asked to speak with his host, the innkeeper. Blount informed him that he was passing through Abingdon on his way to Gloucestershire and was eager for any local news he could share with him. The innkeeper was only too happy to oblige. There had indeed been some news of late, and more scandalous, though tragic, than he'd heard in a long while.

'There is fallen a great misfortune,' the innkeeper informed Blount, 'within three or four miles of the town.' Was there a pause for dramatic effect? 'My Lord Robert Dudley's wife is dead.'[40]

'How?' Blount asked curtly.

'By a misfortune as I heard,' the innkeeper reported, 'by a fall from a pair of stairs.'*

---

* 'a pair of stairs': a staircase.

'By what chance?' Blount asked, but the landlord couldn't say for certain. Blount continued to press: 'What is your judgement and the judgement of the people?'

Cautiously and diplomatically, the landlord responded, 'Some are disposed to say well, and some evil.'

Still unsatisfied, Blount tried again, 'What is your judgement?'

'By my troth,' he said at last, 'I judge it a misfortune, because it happened in that honest gentleman's house,' they both knew him to mean the house of Sir Anthony Forster, some four miles away at Cumnor. 'His great honesty,' the landlord continued, 'doth much curb the evil thoughts of the people.' Notably, the innkeeper did not suggest that the reputation of the dead woman's husband, Robert Dudley, might have also played a role in stemming the flow of evil rumour.

Abandoning this tack, Blount tried another: 'Methinks,' he said, 'that some of her people that waited on her should have something to say about this?'

'No, sir,' the innkeeper responded respectfully but firmly, 'but little: for it is said that they were all here,' by which he meant Abingdon itself, 'at the fair, and none left with her.'

'How might that chance?' Blount asked him.

'It is said that she rose that day very early,' the landlord told him, 'and commanded all her sort to go to the fair, and would suffer none to tarry at home.'

At this, Blount returned to his dinner, and the landlord to his work. It was unlikely to be the only time the innkeeper shared this particularly juicy bit of gossip with a stranger, though later, as the smoke and the din cleared, he might have remarked to himself how very inquisitive this particular guest had been. And if he'd been especially astute, he might have noted the lack of surprise when he'd told Blount the news, almost as if the man had already known.

Thomas Blount, turning in for the night, had indeed already been acquainted with this information. The Lady Amy Dudley was the lady he was in Berkshire to serve. The trip to Gloucestershire was simply a ruse to hide his identity. Thomas Blount was one of the loyal servants, and a distant cousin, of the lady's husband, Robert Dudley. His family had served the Dudley family for at least a generation, and he had been with Robert's father almost right to the end.[41]

Blount had been sent to Cumnor to see the Lady Amy that very morning, with no idea of what awaited him. On his way, not long after his departure from Windsor, he had run into another family servant, Mr Bowes, rushing from Cumnor.[42] He carried the news of the death of Amy Dudley to her unwitting widower but had paused to inform Blount of the circumstances. Bowes had told Blount of Amy's odd request – insistence even – that her servants attend the fair in Abingdon on the day of her death. When it was suggested to Amy that the servants go the next day instead, she had become unexpectedly angry. When the servants returned, their mistress was dead. Not long after Bowes had continued on, Blount was halted in his journey once again, this time by Mr Bryse, another servant of Robert Dudley's, carrying a letter from their master for him. Bowes had reached Dudley at Windsor and passed on the news. Robert wrote to Blount via Bryse that he was deeply troubled by what Bowes had told him and needed him to investigate further.[43] Dudley could not rest, knowing how the world would spin malicious talk about the event. Blount was to use all means at his disposal to get to the bottom of it and find out the truth. This included lying to innocent innkeepers.

It was essential that Blount get a sense of the talk of the town, which is why he had interrogated the innkeeper, despite already having been in possession of the information the man had given him. Blount wasn't interested solely in the bare facts: he wanted to know people's thoughts about what had happened. Thomas Blount, and Robert Dudley back in London, knew well that justice did not run a straight course from event to judgement to sentence. Rather, it was a winding, often diverging path, muddied by the intervention of others' half-formed opinions and prejudices. The men charged with investigating a mysterious death such as Amy Dudley's depended strongly on the views and sentiments of the community, and were also frequently subject to corruption, from above and from below.[44] No coroner wanted trouble from a local lord, neither would he welcome becoming a pariah in his own community. The investigation of a death was a community affair, the results of which could be published to the country at large, as had the murder of poor Thomas Arden, which had been such a source of gossip just ten years before.[45] Public opinion was everything, and it was Blount's task to ensure that it did not turn against the family he served. Or, if it did, he could at least give them fair warning.

The next day Blount made his way the remaining few miles to the small village of Cumnor, due north of Abingdon. In the centre of the village, immediately south of the medieval churchyard of St Michael's and connected by an arch in the partition wall, was the manor, where Amy Dudley had been living.[46] Of largely fourteenth-century construction, the manor had once belonged to the monks at Abingdon Abbey, but had come to the possession of Sir Anthony Forster, who had altered it significantly in line with the style of the time. The main entrance to the manor was from the north, via Abingdon Road. From there, travellers like Blount would approach the grand quadrangle building through the vaulted gatehouse at the centre of the north range.[47] This opened into a large courtyard, seventy-two feet by fifty-two feet. On the right as one entered, the west side, was a large medieval hall, where Blount might hope to eat with the members of the household, and perhaps overhear some gossip beneath the high timber roof and impressive windows of painted glass. In the north range, on an upper floor, was a long gallery; an ideal location for conducting interviews.

The members of the household that he met confirmed, wittingly or unwittingly, that there had been something very strange going on the day that their mistress had been found dead. Most notable, perhaps, was his interview with Amy Dudley's attendant, Mrs Picto. The woman's love and admiration for her mistress was undeniable, which lent an emotional desperation to the story she told Blount.[48]

'What think you of this matter,' Blount asked her openly, 'be it chance or villainy?'

'By my faith,' she responded earnestly, 'I do judge it very chance, and neither done by man nor by herself.' This was a surprising denial; Blount had not suggested the Lady Amy had played a role in her own death. 'For herself,' the maid went on, 'she was a good, virtuous gentlewoman, and daily would pray upon her knees, and diverse times,' she was all but rambling now, 'I hath heard her pray to God to deliver her from desperation.'

Blount seized on the implication that Picto seemed to be making, 'She might have had an evil toy* in her mind?' Did Amy Dudley kill herself?

'No, good Mr Blount,' Picto replied, 'do not judge so of my words; if you should so gather, I am sorry I said so much.'

It was no wonder the woman was afraid of Blount's deduction. To have a suicide in the family was a cause of intense shame.[49] Hiding it was a matter of honour, and many went to great lengths to do so. Self-murder was a crime, not just against the Crown, but against God and Nature. If the coroner found the death to be a suicide, Amy Dudley could posthumously be declared a felon.[50]

Amy Dudley's death seemed to fit the accepted narrative of a woman's suicide perfectly: a wife, abandoned by her husband, despairingly takes her own life. It was a story at least as old as Virgil's *Aeneid*, written in the decades before Christ and widely popular in the Renaissance.[51] Dido, the Queen of Carthage, falls in love with the hero Aeneas, who leaves her to carry out a divine quest. Dido, abandoned, commits suicide: 'But Dido quaking fierce with frantick mode and grisly hue, / With trembling spotted cheeks, her huge attemptings to pursue, / Besides her self for rage, and towards death her visage wan, / Her eyes about she rolled, as red as blood they looked then' – so too could those imagining the death of Amy Dudley see her, poised hysterically at the top of the stairs.[52] Of course, aside from cases where a queen had publicly stabbed herself on a funeral pyre, as had Dido, it could be incredibly difficult to prove a death was a suicide, and 'misadventure' could just as likely mean an accident as it could a suspected but impossible to prove suicide.[53] Throwing oneself down a set of stairs was not a common way to commit suicide, but that didn't rule it out.[54]

There was another possibility beyond accident and suicide, and it cannot have failed to occur to Blount or those whose watched the affairs at Cumnor. In fact, three days after Amy had been found dead,

* Toy: fancy or notion.

back in London, Cecil had suggested this conclusion to de la Quadra, who still had not heard the news.[55] 'They intend to kill the wife of Robert Dudley,' Cecil had told him without prelude. 'It is now published that she is ill, although she is not, but on the contrary is very well and has protected herself carefully from being poisoned.'[56] Later that day, de la Quadra was informed that – as Cecil had seemed to predict – Amy Dudley was dead. Cecil's insinuation was either impressively prescient or very well informed. Seemingly already aware that Robert Dudley's wife was dead, Cecil had spun the story to suit his needs, which were to bring down the ascendant Dudley, son of the man he had once served.[57] As he had also told de la Quadra that day (twice, for good effect), 'Lord Robert would be better in paradise than here.'[58]

And if he were found guilty of his wife's murder, that might indeed be his fate. Robert's own cousin, Charles Stourton, Baron Stourton, the son of John Dudley's half-sister Elizabeth, had been hanged for murder just three years before.[59] Just like those who might be suspected in the death of Amy Dudley, Stourton had not committed the murder himself, but had ordered it, and thus swung for it. His baronial status had not saved him from this fate, or from threats of torture during his interrogation. Robert Dudley, close to the queen though he may be, was not even a baron. It was not more than seven years since the executions of his father and brother, either. Murder was not the same crime as treason, but they were not wholly distinct, and the threats that had been made to Stourton were not empty: the Privy Council had decreed some two decades before that murder suspects could be tortured like traitors: murder too was a crime against the entire body politic, not just the singular victim.[60] It was, perhaps relatedly, fairly uncommon, at least in conviction, and only very rarely involved a woman.[61] The suggestion that Amy Dudley had been murdered, then, was more than rare; it was positively titillating.

The coroner, a man from the nearby village of Slipton named John Pudsey, had arrived at the scene before Blount and had begun his investigation, gathering a jury of local men who would determine the cause of death, headed by a burgess of Abingdon named Sir Richard Smythe.[62] Pudsey needed twelve jurors to agree, so picked fifteen, to better the odds of success.[63] All were of middling standing and from the local area. Despite what the innkeeper had told Blount, not everyone thought well of Anthony Forster, including some of the jurors, who may have been selected precisely for that reason. Blount met with these men, and – as Robert Dudley requested – asked them to proceed without respect of the standing of those involved.[64] They seemed well chosen, he determined, and would seek the truth above all else. The fact that some held some animosity towards Forster only made it more likely that they would declare wrongdoing in his home if there was any to be found. Joining the group at Cumnor was Amy's brother, John Appleyard, summoned by Robert himself.[65] Blount noted that his presence served to counter fears that Robert sought to cover up some element of Amy's death.

Amy's cold, broken body was stripped, laid out and examined by this group of men, who could poke and prod at it as they thought necessary.[66] She had only been twenty-eight at her death, and the injuries she had suffered – fatal though they might have been – had not done much to mar her appearance. The most obvious injury was her broken neck, which the jurors determined was the immediate cause of death.[67] Running eyes and fingers over her body, they found two more injuries, both on her head, causing her hair to be matted with dried blood. One was more serious than the other, a full two thumbs deep, the other just a quarter of a thumb deep. Below the neck, they could not find a single further injury. No more in-depth examination was conducted. Autopsies were only commonly done on the continent, though it would have been helpful for the male jurors to consult with a local trained female surgeon; she might have even performed the examination, inserting her thumbs or instruments into the lesions in Amy Dudley's skull.[68] The jurors could also put Amy's body up for wider display and comment; transparency was more important than decorum.[69] Ultimately, however, it was this group of fifteen men, reporting to the coroner, who would determine the cause of her death.

As the jurors deliberated, meeting daily, Blount waited anxiously. He could get no direct information from the coroner's jury, but overheard whispers suggested to him that they could find no evidence of evil doings, even though some of them might like to. The inquest could take weeks, or more, and the jurors would not just examine the body, but conduct a more wide-ranging investigation as they pleased.

Meanwhile, Robert Dudley, now a widower, retired from the court to his house at Kew. The site had been granted to him a few weeks after Elizabeth's coronation, returning land to him once owned by his father.[70] The building was small, though impressive, of brick with high-vaulted ceilings, and had also become another home for Mary Sidney, who was once again pregnant and very near to giving birth.[71] As always, it was advised to keep a pregnant woman away from talk of death, but by now Mary was used to it. Robert's brother-in-law, Henry Hastings, recently made Earl of Huntingdon, also wrote with his condolences. 'I doubt not,' he wrote, 'but long before this time you have considered what a happy hour it is which bringeth man from sorrow to Joy, from mortality to Immortality, from care and trouble to rest and quietness.'[72] Life was a prison of struggle to be escaped in death. Though if he meant that Amy had particular troubles that she was now free from, he did not clarify.

Robert's fate lay almost entirely in the hands of those unknown jurors, along with the Privy Councillors over whom he had lorded not long before. Fortune's wheel had well and truly turned on him again, and Robert found himself in a familiar position of desperation. Dressed in elaborate mourning black satins and silks, Robert was visited by his brother Ambrose, the elder's marital woes now paling in significance to those his younger brother now faced.[73] More surprisingly, perhaps, Robert also received a visit from Sir William Cecil.[74] Robert was unlikely to have known that just a short while before Cecil had been crying for his death to the Spanish ambassador. If he had known, it didn't matter now. Cecil, his father's erstwhile secretary, now reigned supreme, and Robert recognized him as one of his few paths back to favour. If Cecil would plead Robert's case to queen and court, this sad event might not end his career entirely. It all seemed like a dream, he told Cecil, and he was desperate to return to the court. He was in bondage, trapped and imprisoned – albeit in a gilded cage – and terrified of being forgotten where he could not be seen.

Robert had, however, already received reassurances directly from the foreman of the jury, Richard Smythe, before he had left Windsor.[75] Though they continued their investigation, under Blount's anxious gaze, Amy's death was to all their minds a 'misfortune', Smythe assured Robert. They were not inclined to rule it a murder or a suicide, and Robert encouraged them to dig as deeply as possible into the case before declaring their final verdict. Within a month, it was reported abroad that Amy Dudley had broken her neck falling down a flight of stairs. No one would be held accountable for Amy Dudley's death but the hand of God himself.

Rumour held otherwise, and in the French court the English ambassador, Sir Nicholas Throckmorton, shuddered to even recall and record the allegations that he heard, at his wits' end to try to defend his queen and country.[76] The treason that lay in Robert's family line was at the centre of these whispers. Could the queen forget he was the son and grandson of traitors? Would she really marry one so marred by treason, and now by the suspicious fate of his late wife? The French were reportedly convinced she would do just that.[77]

*

Just four months after the death of Amy Dudley, de la Quadra found himself once more discussing the queen's marriage with a Sidney. This time it was Sir Henry Sidney, recently a father once again, to a daughter named for the queen.[78] De la Quadra had not long ago been informed that a marriage had already taken place between Robert Dudley and the queen, which Henry assured him was not so.[79] Nevertheless, Henry told him, 'as the matter is now public property, and you know how much inclined her majesty is to the marriage, I wonder that you have not suggested to his majesty, King Philip, this opportunity for gaining over Lord Robert by extending a hand to him now. He would thereafter serve and obey his Majesty like one of his own vassals.'

Rather than seeking Robert's support for a Spanish marriage, Henry was suggesting that the King of Spain ought to support Robert's suit, in exchange for Robert's fealty. 'What I have so far heard of this matter,' de la Quadra rejoined, 'was of such a character that I had hardly ventured to write two lines to his Majesty about it, nor had either the Queen or Lord Robert ever said a word to me that I could write.' De la Quadra found Henry an amicable man to talk to, and better behaved, he thought, than most English courtiers. Nevertheless, all the rumours he had heard pointed to a scandalous physical relationship between the queen and her Master of the Horse, not to mention a plot to do away with Robert's wife, which by all appearances had been successful. He could not suggest Philip support such a union. Henry tried to reassure him on both counts.

'If you are satisfied with the death of Robert's wife,' Henry told him, 'I see no other reason why you should hesitate to write the purport of this conversation to his Majesty, as, after all, although it is a love affair,' he continued, 'yet the object of it is marriage, and there is nothing illicit about it or such as could not be set right by his Majesty's authority.' Was de la Quadra to take from this that there had been some illicit relation between the two parties, 'a love affair', that his king would have to justify? Henry went on, 'As regards the death of the wife, I am certain that it is accidental, and I have never been able to learn otherwise, although I have inquired with great care and I know that public opinion holds to the contrary.'

'If what you say is true, the evil is less,' de la Quadra replied, 'for, if murder had been committed, God would never help nor fail to punish so abominable a crime, whatever men might do to mend it, but it will be difficult for Lord Robert to make things appear as you represent them.'

'It is quite true,' Henry acknowledged, 'no one believes it.' Nevertheless, Henry was at pains to explain, if Philip II would support Robert's controversial marriage to the queen, Robert would support the realm's return to Catholicism. He solemnly swore to de la Quadra that 'the Queen and Lord Robert were determined to restore religion'.

'You know,' de la Quadra responded, 'what happened with your wife in the matter of the Archduke, when the Queen had deceived both of us.' Mary Sidney's promises that the queen would marry, and would marry the archduke, had turned out to be lies, and de la Quadra had felt thoroughly betrayed.[80] He would not write to his master without explicit authorization from the queen herself on this matter. The ambassador had learned his lesson in dealing with the Dudleys.

Three weeks later, having also met with Robert himself, who according to de la Quadra, 'repeated all that Sidney had told me' and promised the 'service that his brother-in-law had told me, and very much more', de la Quadra at last had the opportunity to broach the topic with the queen.[81] Requesting that she speak to the bishop as a confessor, which should have meant confidentially, though de la Quadra happily reported it to Philip, Elizabeth told the ambassador, 'I do not deny that I have some affection for Lord Robert for the many good qualities he possesses, but I certainly have never decided to marry him or anyone else, though I daily see more clearly the necessity for my marriage. What would his Majesty think,' she asked, 'if I married one of my servitors?'

'I could not say what his Majesty would think,' de la Quadra replied carefully, 'but I promise I will use all diligence to learn.' Sure to encourage her towards a husband of any kind, he continued, 'I quite believe that his Majesty would be pleased to hear of your Majesty's marriage with whomever it might be as was so important to your Majesty and your Majesty's kingdom, and I also know that his Majesty would be happy to hear of the advancement and aggrandizement of Lord Robert, as I understand that his Majesty has great affection for him and holds him in high esteem.'

Appearing pleased by this, the queen replied, 'When the time comes, I will speak to you, and promise to do nothing without the advice and countenance of his Majesty.'

It took a month, but de la Quadra received his reply from Philip: he was to support the marriage to Dudley, as long as they got in writing that he and the queen would return the realm to Catholicism. 'In the conversations you may have with Sidney and Lord Robert,' Philip instructed his ambassador, 'you had better give them to understand that I have the same good will towards the latter as I ever had, and take every opportunity you may see to express affection and attachment to him, so as to forward the affair by this means'.[82] De la Quadra had little reason to doubt: despite the vicious rumours that still circulated, the queen's marriage to Lord Robert Dudley, suddenly wifeless, was not only the best course for the realm, but was also the most likely eventuality. A Dudley was sure to be king consort once again.

16
Hide thee from the bear

Catherine Grey was desperate. Nothing else would have brought her, shrouded in darkness and silence, to Robert Dudley's bedside that night.[1] It was August, and the weather had been a mix of oppressive heat and fierce storms.[2] The moon, had she been able to see it, was directly above the rooftops of Ipswich, a waning crescent, barely more than a sliver. The dark night was her ally.

Hiding had become an art born of necessity for Catherine. She had worked hard to conceal her growing bump under loose-flowing gowns and resisted the urge to put a hand to calm or cradle the baby inside while others, including the queen and entire court, were watching. Eight months she had hidden not just the facts but also the effects of her pregnancy: the nausea, fatigue and pain. Darkness was on her side, but time was not, and soon all her efforts at concealment would be for nothing.

She had also successfully disguised her emotions. Catherine Grey was carrying the child of the man she loved but had lost. Though secretly married, the only witness was her husband's sister, who had died unexpectedly at the age of nineteen. A few weeks later Catherine's secret husband had left for the French court, from which letters to his wife were scarce and unsafe. Secrecy was of the utmost importance. Not just because of her husband's identity, though it did bring with it some complications. Catherine Grey – now secretly Catherine Seymour – was carrying the child of Edward Seymour, the Earl of Hertford. He was the son of the former Lord Protector, the executed Edward Seymour, Duke of Somerset, erstwhile friend-cum-enemy of the Dudley family. Young Seymour had once been cousin to the king, his aunt being Queen Jane, mother to Edward VI. This line, however, had ended, and his children were of no import to the succession.

It was Catherine herself who bore the vital royal blood, blood that had begun to pump in the veins of the child she carried. This blood was also why she approached Robert Dudley's chamber by the weak light of a waning August moon. Robert was Catherine's brother-in-law. Catherine, just a child at the time, had been married at the same ceremony which had also witnessed the marriage of her sister and two of Robert's siblings, including her elder sister, Jane, to Robert's younger brother, Guildford. Of course, this had been an ill-fated union, and Catherine's own marriage to Henry Herbert, son of the Earl of Pembroke, had been dissolved in the aftermath of the triumph of Mary I over Jane Grey Dudley. With her elder sister dead, Catherine was now the heir to that line, drawn from her grandmother, Mary, the daughter of Henry VII. Henry VIII's will had stated clearly that, should his children all die without legitimate issue, and two had already done so, the Crown would skip the stronger claims of his elder sister's line, now represented in the person of the Queen of Scots, and instead proceed through the issue of Mary, manifest in Catherine and, now, her child.

A member of royal blood was by law required to seek the approval of the monarch before marrying. Catherine and Edward had done no such thing. Young and in love, they had wed before Christmas and Catherine was pregnant by the new year. She had spent most of the spring and summer in a state of panic. She had even attempted to renew her marriage to Henry Herbert. He had, however, become suspicious and rebuked her fiercely for her 'whoredom', which he threatened to expose.[3] Whether by Herbert's doing, or the child's arrival, Catherine's summer of desperate secrecy would soon come to an end, and she would be forced to face the full wrath of the queen. She needed a champion. She needed a shield. She needed Robert Dudley.

The court was coming to the end of its summer progress and was residing for much of the week at Ipswich, in the home of Edmund Withipole, a successful merchant whose father had purchased the lands formerly belonging to the local priory of Christchurch to build a grand red-brick family home that he called Withipole House. To have attracted the interest of the queen was both an honour and a burden; supporting the queen and court for the better part of the week was a difficult task. It was perhaps with some irony then that the engraving on one of the stones of the house read *frugalitatem sic servas, ut dissipationem non incurras*: 'embrace frugality in order to avoid squandering one's wealth'.[4]

Among other preparations, the visit of the monarch could involve building works, such as the expansion of the west wing of the mansion to house her and her ladies, who included the Lady Catherine Grey. It also housed the queen's closest servants, including Robert Dudley, her Master of the Horse. His room was conveniently adjacent to the queen's, which made it easy for Catherine to slip unseen from one to the other while the court slept.

Robert was shocked and frightened to see her there, a young woman, heavily pregnant, pleading with him at his bedside. As if the rumours about him were not bad enough. And the stakes could not be higher. He was still spoken of as a prospective husband for the queen, another reason that Catherine might try to appeal to him, but he had fierce competition. The King of Sweden, Erik XIV, had been courting the queen from afar, and that summer souvenirs of a not-yet-accomplished royal wedding between the monarchs had circulated the capital.[5] The same age as the queen, Erik was young and by all accounts attractive. What's more, he shared many interests and experiences with Elizabeth. A Protestant monarch, he had lost his mother as a child and his father had quickly remarried. Like Elizabeth, too, he had been given a comprehensive humanist education and was a bright and interested student. He had risked much in entering into marriage negotiations for Elizabeth's hand; his father had disapproved, and it was his father's death in September 1560, not long after Amy Dudley's death, that had prevented his arrival in England, at one of the weakest moments in Robert Dudley's standing. His arrival in London was considered imminent, however, to be followed closely by the announcement of a wedding. Of course, Robert was well aware that the queen might have been favouring the Swedish match just to tease him, but there was also the possibility he was the tease to Erik's sincere suit. Or perhaps they were all being successfully played by the queen in a game entirely of her own devising.

Catherine explained the situation to her brother-in-law, asking him to intercede with the queen on behalf of her and her unborn child. Robert, keen to end the incriminating situation, agreed, and rushed her out of his chambers.[6] It would now fall to him to tell the queen of this news. It could only serve to anger her. It didn't necessarily, however, have to kill the messenger, and it could even work to his advantage. Catherine's claim was a strong one, and she was a Protestant, but it was not the only claim Robert might support. For almost a year, he had been working on a meeting between Mary, Queen of Scots, and Elizabeth I, which might serve as a form of reconciliation between the two monarchs.[7] Mary, having returned from France following the death of her husband the king, was not only a potential heir for Elizabeth, but at times had even made claims that she was the rightful queen ahead of Elizabeth, as Elizabeth's parentage could be held in doubt. This had not endeared her to the Queen of England. Nevertheless, there was a chance that the two could be brought together, and the Catholic faction in particular hoped that Mary would be named Elizabeth's heir, even if she could not supplant her. Robert, as the architect of this solution, would stand to benefit.

There was another claimant even closer to Robert than Catherine Grey. This was the third bridegroom married in the triple wedding at Durham House not ten years before: Henry Hastings, recently made Earl of Huntingdon, and married to Robert's younger sister, Katherine. Katherine had written to her brother just that February, reminding him of his familial duty towards her husband, who would need his help on his arrival in London.[8] Hastings was the descendant of George, Duke of Clarence, the brother of Kings Edward IV and Richard III. As such, he carried legitimate Plantagenet blood and could also be put forward as a claimant to the English throne, and one of use to Robert Dudley.

In short, almost everywhere one looked for an heir to Elizabeth I, there one found Robert Dudley in some shape or another, a position he could further secure by making himself of use to Catherine Grey.

Of course, all of this could become immaterial if Robert himself married Elizabeth and together they produced an unquestionable, incontestable heir to the throne. The fate of Catherine Grey would matter little to this.

As it was, Robert faced the fury of the queen the next morning, though it remained directed at its primary target: Catherine Grey herself. Eight months pregnant, she was ordered to the Tower to be imprisoned and interrogated. Catherine's plea to Robert, and his intervention, did little to mitigate the queen's rage and revenge. One could easily wonder if he'd intended it to.

*

Robert Dudley made a resplendent prince, basking in adoration and cheer. He rode through London two days after Christmas, the light reflecting off the gilt of his harness, as a hundred gentlemen followed, proudly wearing their chains of gold.[9] It was a procession for a coronation, though for now merely a shadow of the real thing. Robert had been chosen as the Christmas Prince for the Inner Temple revels over Christmas 1561. He had defended their interests, and the lawyers of the Temple made a solemn oath never to litigate against him, as well as honouring him as their prince.[10]

The members of the Inner Temple also took the opportunity to reinforce Robert Dudley's candidacy to be a king. Robert was presented to the lawyers and their guests, including members of the queen's council, not just as the Christmas Prince, their Lord of Misrule, but as a far more impressive figure: Prince Pallaphilos, literally 'lover of Pallas'.[11] Pallas Athena, as the goddess of Wisdom and War, was the ideal deity for the lawyers of the inner temple to worship, as well as standing in for their own queen, Elizabeth.

Elizabeth had not married Robert, but she still clearly favoured him. That day Robert had written with happy news to his friend George Talbot, Earl of Shrewsbury: 'it hath pleased the Queens Majesty,' he told him with delight, 'to restore our house to the name of Warwick, and as yesterday hath created my said brother Earl thereof.'[12] Robert's elder brother Ambrose had been restored to the title of Earl of Warwick, the position that had been held by his father and brother before their deaths. Robert himself had not been ennobled, but his family was once again in the peerage. Recently, there had even been an offer to write a defence of Robert's executed father and grandfather, to prove that their unjust, innocent deaths were caused by naught but envy and malice.[13] Robert could celebrate the revival of his family in style at the Inner Temple in a court that mirrored the one at Whitehall.[14]

The members of the Inner Temple created a grand narrative and spectacle to honour Robert Dudley in the role of champion and lover of Pallas.[15] On their way to the great hall of the Inner Temple, the revellers were treated to a masque: actors in elaborate costumes acting the parts of characters who were also the personification of a virtue or vice.[16] These allegorical plays were entertaining, but also had specific and often political messages. On that day, they were treated to a masque of Beauty and Desire, and the lessons were not difficult to interpret.[17]

Catching a glimpse of the character of Beauty, the young gentleman Desire was enraptured, and must have her. His way was blocked, however, by the figures of Danger and Fortune. Distraught, he turned to Counsel to guide him, who encouraged him on.

'Whoso will pleasure win,' Counsel proclaimed to Desire (and the audience), 'let him with wisdom first begin.'

'Alas,' Desire responded, sorrowfully, 'she' (meaning Beauty, but perhaps someone else as well) 'is besides all ornaments of Nature, of noble parentage, Rich in possessions, and large of dominion.'

'Yield not although she say nay,' Counsel told Desire. 'The woman & wife is evermore to delay. But none so strong, that is invincible.'

Aided by a host of virtues and skills, including Truth, Speed, Audacity and Honour, Desire battled on, overcoming a serpent with nine heads, each with its own vice: Dissimulation, Delay, Shame, Misreport, Discomfort, Variance, Envy, Detraction and Doubleness. Having defeated the serpent, Desire offered it up to the goddess Pallas, who gave him the lady Beauty in return for his service. He was remembered, in the final act, by Eternity.

As shot rang out, the audience digested the message. Desire, a virtuous young gentleman, blocked by Danger and Fortune, wins his rich and ennobled love, Beauty, through persistence and triumph over obstacles synonymous with a bad reputation. Desire could only be one man, and Beauty only one woman.

Those assembled were then brought along the gallery to the decorated hall for a meal, led by the sound of drum and fife. Sitting at the head of the hall was Dudley himself, adorned as Prince Pallaphilos. Served tender meats, sweet fruits and dainty delicacies, each course was accompanied by music: trumpets, drum, fife, violin, sackbuts, recorders and cornets.[18]

As the lavish meal came to an end, the herald of Pallaphilos proclaimed the creation of the Knights of the Order of Pegasus.[19] Just as other knights, the herald proclaimed, were to be recognized for their power, policy or fortune in the field of battle, so too ought these knights to be honoured for their wisdom. These knights were true servants of Pallas, he declared: 'where as she is daughter to the Mighty Jove, nothing is Inferior to her father, so policy to her is proper, that the rather these natural powers (armed wisdom) working in you her knights, ye may like soldiers of so mighty a patroness, continue and advance the glory already gained.'[20]

The twenty-four men selected to be members of the Order of Pegasus stepped forward. Each was dressed in symbolic clothing: the helmet of fortitude, the breastplate of courage, the sword of justice, the spurs of speed. He was further given the shield of Pallas, with its intertwined dragons under an imperial crown, the Mantle of Pallas, in silver, gold and purple, and the collar: a chain of interlocking 'PPs' on which hung a pendant depicting Pegasus surrounded by the motto: *VIRTUS VOLAT ALTA AD SIDERA* : 'virtue flies to the stars'.[21]

The knights then repeated their oath, dedicating themselves to the pursuit not just of wisdom, but of fame: 'Wisdom the Guide of Armed strength, up raise your Knightly name,' they intoned, 'By force of Prowess hot, to climb the lofty tower of Fame. Advance your honours by your deeds, to live for evermore. As Pallas knights, by Pallas's help, Pallas serve ye therefore.'[22]

That night and subsequent nights were spent in jousting, banqueting, masquing and general revelry. The event was a coronation in miniature, complete with a knighting ceremony, and many – including Robert himself – might hope that it was a precursor to the event itself.

Robert and his supporters did more than hope, however. There was another performance in store for the revellers. A crowd of spectators – lawyers, students, courtiers, ambassadors and councillors – gathered in the great hall of the Inner Temple to watch the play, sitting in scaffolding seats around a raised platform.[23] In the middle of the hall raged a great fire, illuminating the faces of the actors as they performed.

Written by two members of the Inner Temple, Thomas Norton and Thomas Sackville, and overseen by Robert himself, their play *Gorboduc* was full of deceit, murder and drama, and like the masque carried a clear message. The play told the tale of King Gorboduc, an early king of Britain, who foolishly follows the advice of flatterers, and rather than passing on his realm to the appointed heir, splits it between his two sons. A bloody civil war inevitably erupts, in which the members of the royal family are killed. With no clear successor, the realm is left vulnerable to attack from the north. The parallels to England's current situation were not difficult to grasp for any who witnessed *Gorboduc*, but all the same they were spelled out for any not paying sufficient attention (or already too drunk to work it out).

'Lo,' the character of Eubulus (literally 'the good counsellor') cried out to those assembled in the fifth and final act, 'Britain realm is left an open prey, / A present spoil by conquest to ensue.'[24]

'And this doth grow when lo unto the prince,' Eubulus declaimed, 'Whom death or sudden hap of life bereaves, / No certain heir remains, such certain heir, / As not only is the rightful heir, / But to the realm is made known to be, / And truth thereby vested in subjects' hearts, / To owe faith there where right is known to rest.'[25]

'Parliament should have been holden, /' Eubulus concluded, 'And certain heirs appointed to the crown, / To stay the title of established right, / And in the people plant obedience, / While yet the prince did live.'[26]

The playwrights could not have forced the words 'certain heirs' more times in fewer lines if they had tried. There was a clear argument in the conclusion of the play: Elizabeth needed to call a parliament and declare an heir to the throne. It was, thus, incumbent upon her councillors to give this good advice and her to listen to it.[27] If not, they faced a situation like that of the play: England bloodied and anarchic and under threat from a foreign power.

It was not just the succession, however, that the councillors in attendance needed to move the queen to address. It was also her marriage. In the midst of the play, between the acts, an actor dressed as a king appeared to the sound of cornets, surrounded by his court.[28] As the audience watched, he mutely took his seat on his chair of estate. Once seated, he was silently handed two glasses filled with wine by his kneeling gentlemen. The first was plain and clear, the second was an elaborate gold cup with a matching lid. The sound of breaking glass reverberated through the hall, cutting through the silence of the dumb-show, as the king emphatically took the clear glass cup and smashed it on the ground, crushing it with his foot. Instead, he took a drink from the golden cup. Drinking, he fell dead, to be carried away by the members of his play court.

The audience absorbed the double meaning. The clear cup signified truthful counsel, the gold cup flattery – anyone with even the barest education would understand that, and this audience, worshippers of Pallas Athena, esteemed themselves the wisest. There was a second meaning, however, which was also grasped by at least some of those assembled. The clear glass was what was known and certain, though perhaps not as grand. The gold cup was an uncertain and enticing prospect, but one that was ultimately dangerous and deadly. In other words, the gold cup was King Erik of Sweden, who had still not presented himself to the queen. The clear cup was Robert Dudley. The queen rejected his suit at her peril.

The play was a success and was performed before the queen in the chess-board hall at Whitehall on 18 January. By then any advice about marriage may have been superfluous. It was rumoured that not three days before there had been a secret ceremony following a banquet and masque at the Earl of Pembroke's home.[29] The queen, it was said, had chosen the safe, clear glass after all; she had at last married Robert Dudley, the lover of Pallas.

*

Lying in her chamber at Hampton Court, wrapped in red cloth, the queen was in the clutches of a raging fever and unable to speak. She had always been small, but now she was frail, unable to eat or even drink. The message went out: Sir William Cecil must be fetched from London. Mary Sidney watched over the queen as her condition worsened.[30] There was only one disease this was likely to be, and it was extremely deadly.

Mary had watched the illness progress day by day as she served the queen. Elizabeth had first shown signs of feeling unwell five days before, on 10 October, and had sought to ease her pains in the bath. The next day, she felt well enough to dictate letters of state, largely to do with affairs in Scotland and France. By the next morning, however, her condition had worsened, and by 13 October she was cancelling meetings with ambassadors, too unwell to see them. She still persisted in her work, facing this challenge with the determination for which she was becoming known. That very day she had penned a letter to her cousin, Mary, Queen of Scots. It was poetic, emotional and yet firm: 'I would sooner pass over in silence the murders on land than tell in writing of the burials in water,' Elizabeth wrote to her cousin, 'and would say nothing of men cut in pieces, if the cries of pregnant women strangled with the wails of infants at their mothers' breasts did not stir me.'[31]

The meeting which Mary Sidney's brother Robert had put so much personal effort into arranging that summer had not occurred. All the details had been in place by early July.[32] The two queens would meet in Nottingham on 3 September. The tilt grounds were being prepared and the safe passage for the Queen of Scots and her entourage had been secured. Not everyone was as enthusiastic about the project as Robert Dudley, however; the Council had concerns about the cost as well as the message it would send to the Protestants who had been recently and viciously attacked in France. Three days after Robert had notice that all was in place, Mary Sidney's husband, not long returned from France, had been dispatched to Scotland to inform the Scottish queen that the meeting would be postponed.[33] Henry Sidney for one was not surprised; he had suspected the meeting would not happen for more than a month already.[34]

It was a significant blow to Robert's standing, which appeared to be on a downward spiral in any case. Some suspected he had been pushing the meeting as an opportunity to bring the marriage question to a head. The support for Robert's suit was beginning to wane. The rumours of a secret marriage had not only turned out to be unfounded, but those responsible for spreading them were being fiercely interrogated.[35]

At the April meeting of the Order of the Garter, the Dudley bear and ragged staff heraldry had been returned to Robert, and Thomas Howard, Duke of Norfolk, son of the executed poet Henry Howard, Earl of Surrey, and once an enemy to Robert's cause, had spearheaded the effort to stamp the Order's support on Robert's suit.[36] Henry Fitz-Alan Earl of Arundel, however, was more constant in his enmity, and stormed out in the company of Thomas Percy, Earl of Northumberland. By the end of July, it was said that the queen had publicly humiliated Robert, railing against him in front of the court and proudly proclaiming that she would never marry one from as mean a stock as he.[37] In more private quarters, one of her closest friends, and long opponent of the Dudley marriage, Kat Ashley was telling interested parties that the queen had reached a decision on the question of marriage to Robert Dudley; it was not one he would like.[38]

Nevertheless, she kept him close. There was to be a military campaign into France, and rather than Robert, Elizabeth chose to send his elder brother, Ambrose, the Earl of Warwick. The affairs in France had complicated the relationship with Scotland, which was why Elizabeth, struggling against her fever, had penned her emotional missive to the Queen of Scots: 'Although I am sending a naval force to Havre, I have in that no other thought, except that there they should do every good office to the king and to all others.' At last, she was forced to stop, 'The burning fever, which now holds me entirely in its grasp, prevents me from writing more'. Elizabeth, stubborn and fierce, could no longer hold this fever at bay. She retired to her bed, attended by Mary Sidney.

The queen's doctors conferred and concluded: Elizabeth had smallpox. Highly contagious, the disease began as a fever, often followed by vomiting, and in the final stages manifested in tell-tale red lesions, which frequently ruptured, leaving the victim scarred for life. That was assuming they lived, of course. Every year, smallpox was responsible for the deaths of thousands, if not hundreds of thousands, across Europe.[39] The epidemic had swept London at the highest point in the summer, and Lady Margaret Russell, Countess of Bedford, the wife of one of Elizabeth's Privy Councillors, had died not six weeks before of the disease. It was entirely conceivable that the queen of England could be added to this number, though it remained treason to utter it.

Elizabeth's councillors, nevertheless, had no choice but to speak of the queen's death. Elizabeth had still not named an heir. The spectre of *Gorboduc* loomed over them, now seeming more prophecy than counsel. The list of prospective heirs had not changed, though Catherine Grey remained in the Tower with her one-year-old son. This child was a bastard, Catherine's marriage to Edward Seymour (who had also been imprisoned) having been declared void. Despite this, Catherine was pregnant again by her not-husband, as sympathetic guards had taken pity on the young lovers, allowing them a few nights together. Her shaming and imprisonment had damaged her case, just as affairs in France had undermined that of Mary, Queen of Scots. Out of the wreckage, Mary Sidney's brother-in-law, Henry Hastings, emerged as a strong candidate, despite his weaker claim. It was presumed that, in the case of the queen's death, Robert Dudley would support his brother-in-law, with military force if needs be.[40] Although his elder brother had been made Lieutenant General of the queen's army, bad weather had conveniently delayed his departure, so Ambrose remained in the country as a potential force to be called to action as well.[41] The Jane Grey affair remained fresh in everyone's minds, not a decade gone. Robert and Ambrose Dudley had ridden with the troops to defend their sister-in-law's claim then; why would they not do the same for their brother-in-law, especially in the absence of a further legitimate child of Henry VIII?

As the queen suffered in the depths of her fever over the night of 15 October, Robert Dudley, Francis Russell, Earl of Bedford – whose wife had recently been carried away by the disease – William Herbert, Earl of Pembroke, and the Duke of Norfolk passionately made arguments for the cause of Henry Hastings, the Earl of Huntingdon.[42] Like Catherine, Hastings was Protestant and English-born, but unlike

Catherine, he had entered into a legal marriage to a faultless wife. William Herbert was particularly touched by this point; it was his son whom Catherine had tried to persuade into taking her back, pregnant by another man. True, there were no children of the Hastings marriage yet, but Robert's sister was still young, and children might yet follow. Henry was also a member of the peerage, his father having received his title from Henry VIII for his efforts in the French campaigns. He also had the potential, though a Protestant, to appeal to some members of the Catholic faction. He had been much favoured by Mary I because of his kinship with the Catholic Pole family. Henry Hastings as – though it was wiser not to utter it – King Henry IX, had greater potential to unite the country than the daughter of Anne Boleyn. Not to mention, of course, he was a man, and thus in that respect far more qualified to rule than the current queen or any of the other contenders.

Against them were those who still supported Henry VIII's own will, and thus the claim of Catherine Grey, despite her bastard child, imprisonment and gender. Finally, there was a third faction, whose moderate arguments well suited the caution of men such as William Cecil, suggesting that no decision could be made without calling jurists and deeply pondering the matter.

As the men argued over the fate of the country, Mary Sidney cared for its queen. Elizabeth had been wrapped in red cloth and fed a potion to combat the illness raging through her. It was essential that the sickness exit her body through its characteristic lesions, or it would continue to torment and poison her, but these were slow to manifest on the queen's pale skin. After hours of unconsciousness, the queen at last woke. Members of the Council were called to her bedside, where Mary had watched over her.[43]

This was an extremely private meeting: this conference between queen and Council was likely to decide the fate of the country in the case of the queen's death. But, as always, whispers trickled out. The queen, it was said, had immediately called on her council to appoint a regent in the case of her death. This suited the moderate party well; they had preferred an interregnum solution to the immediate declaration of an heir. Others, however, would be less enthusiastic. The last

Lord Protector had been Edward Seymour and before that the usurper, Richard III. A regency council would be far superior to a single Protector, as Henry VIII had set out for the minority of Edward VI. Lord Protectors were a dangerous notion, especially if they had any ambition at all.

For this reason, the person it was rumoured Elizabeth I had in mind was a terrifying prospect. Elizabeth wanted Lord Robert Dudley named Lord Protector, with a salary of £20,000 a year, about ten percent of the entire annual income of the Crown.[44] This could not have helped but raise a few eyebrows, as well as a few shouts. Elizabeth protested, perhaps too much, that though she loved and had always loved Lord Robert dearly, nothing improper had ever passed between them. She, quite conflictingly, then went on to insist that Robert's groom, who slept in his chamber, be given £500 a year, for what services those who heard the tale could only guess. Unwilling to argue with a dying monarch, those assembled agreed to her wishes. Plans were put into motion to admit Robert to the Privy Council. It was no good to have a Lord Protector who was not even a member of the Council.

The next day, as Mary watched, the lesions at last began to appear on Elizabeth's skin, prompting a mixture of relief and horror. It was a good sign for her recovery; the lesions would ensure that the ill humours of the pox would escape her body. As they spread, however, they threatened to leave her permanently disfigured, perhaps even blind. And she was not free of the disease yet. Death tended to come to sufferers ten days after the first symptoms; the queen had only been ill for a week.

On that all-important tenth day, Lord Robert Dudley was made a privy councillor.[45] Along with the Duke of Norfolk, he now controlled much of the business of the Crown as the queen remained shut away in her chamber. Mary could see that she was improving. It seemed there would be no need for her brother to become acting king after all. Ambrose at last left for France, along with Mary's husband, the weather having improved alongside the queen's condition.

Mary herself, however, began to feel tired and unwell. Soon, she too was experiencing shivers and sweats, as her mistress had done.

Rather than risk any further contagions in the palace, Mary was quickly sent away, to her home at Penshurst, where it was imperative that she keep away from her three young children. Exposure to smallpox could easily kill Philip, now eight, and the two infants, Elizabeth and Mary. It could also, of course, kill her. As Ambrose landed in France to wage war and Robert sought to tame the forces against him in the court, Mary too had risked her life for the Crown. If she survived, she too would bear the scars of service.

17

Being now the last of our house

The young woman entered the queen's great chapel at Whitehall. These rooms had once been occupied by Henry VIII, a king this woman had never known.[1] She had not yet been born when that great king had breathed his last in a room not far from where she now stood. At sixteen, Anne Russell's first prayers for her monarch had been for Edward VI, then briefly Queen Jane, before being corrected to Queen Mary, each of whose names she had formed as a child, but fleetingly. It was Queen Elizabeth with whom Anne Russell had grown up. Ten years old at Elizabeth's accession, Anne knew well the advancement her father had been graced with in Elizabeth's reign. This had not saved them from hardship, of course, and Anne's mother had been carried away by smallpox in the weeks before Elizabeth had first shown signs of the disease, just three years ago.

Before Anne as she entered the chapel was a crowd of lords and gentlemen, finely attired.[2] Behind her walked the gentlewomen of the court, along with the queen's maids of honour, all dressed in yellow satin, trimmed with green velvet and silver lace. Anne was led by two young earls, Edward de Vere, the Earl of Oxford, and Edward Manners, the Earl of Rutland. Both were of an age with Anne herself, having only recently been made earls at the deaths of their fathers. The trio of young people represented a new generation, a new age and new promise.

Anne's own father, Francis, was not there to witness this, her wedding day. He was instrumental in the ongoing negotiations in the North with the Queen of Scots. This had included, the previous year, proposing a husband for the Scottish queen. Elizabeth was concerned about who the Queen of Scots might marry, given her claim on the English throne. Anne's father had been one of the English agents sent to Scotland to relay the English queen's choice for Mary's marriage-bed. Elizabeth had proposed none other than Robert Dudley, whom she had recently made Earl of Leicester.[3] This noble veneer had not impressed the rival queen, however, who it appeared did not want Elizabeth's cast-off. Whether the English queen had ever seriously considered parting with Dudley was a matter of much debate, but a year later that question no longer mattered. Queen Mary had married someone else, Henry Stuart, Lord Darnley, grandson of Henry VIII's sister Margaret by a Scottish nobleman, whom she had married after the death of James IV. Robert Dudley, however, had remained Earl of Leicester, a step higher on the noble ladder. This mightn't have mattered very much to the young Anne, except she was about to become a Dudley herself.

Anne, taking her place for the ceremony, shone in her brilliant attire, light sparkling in the silver embroidery that decorated her gown of purple velvet and kirtle of cloth of silver and blue. Over her auburn hair she wore a caul of gold. Her velvet train was carried by the six-year-old Catherine Knollys, the daughter of the Vice Chamberlain, Sir Francis Knollys. Through her mother, Catherine Carey, and grandmother, Mary Boleyn, Catherine Knollys was a cousin (one generation removed) of the queen herself. It remained possible, as well, that her mother had been born while Mary Boleyn was still a mistress of the queen's father, Henry VIII, making them twice related. Little Catherine had become an aunt (not for the first time) only the day before, when her elder sister, Lettice, Countess of Essex, had given birth to her first son. Despite – or perhaps to dispel – rumours of a flirtation between Lettice and Robert Dudley, the infant was to be named Robert, with the Earl of Leicester to stand as his godfather.

Once Anne was settled, a contingent of lords left the chapel, to bring her bridegroom to stand before her. Dressed in a matching gown of purple velvet, with an edging of sables and embroidered with gold, the Earl of Warwick entered the chapel. Ambrose Dudley was almost twenty years Anne's senior, and had been married twice before, though had no heirs to show for it. A child by his first wife had not survived, and she had died not long after. His second wife had died while Ambrose was on campaign in France, some two and a half years before. He had returned from France a widower, with a nasty leg wound that still plagued him (the wound may have caused him more grief than the loss of his wife, with whom he had never reconciled). In Anne, Ambrose had the chance for a new life, and God willing, an heir. Though he had been the fourth Dudley son born, he had carried the weight of being the eldest for almost a decade and knew his responsibility. Anne was the eldest of seven surviving children, including four boys. There was every reason to hope she might at last produce the longed-for Dudley heir.

Behind Ambrose followed his younger brother. Dressed in purple satin with a wide trim of embroidered gold, Robert's fine, swarthy features were set off by his clipped moustache and beard. Robert, too, had no child to inherit. It had been five years since the death of his wife, and despite intermittent whispers of flirtations with countesses or persistent rumours that he remained on the cusp of marriage to the queen, Robert had not remarried. Now ennobled, he certainly had received the queen's favour, and the two remained close, to the point that he had felt the need to apologize for his absence from court on his wounded brother's return from France two years before.[4] But they had not married.

Where the two Dudley brothers had failed, their sister Mary had triumphed, becoming the mother to a growing brood. Mary Sidney, among the ladies of the court at her brother's wedding, had given birth twice in the previous two years, aided by the more frequent attentions of her husband, returned from abroad. Little Robert Sidney was on the cusp of celebrating his second birthday, and Ambrosia Sidney had followed not long after. Both named for their uncles, they were nevertheless no substitute for a Dudley heir.

With Ambrose and Robert in the chapel, the lords exited again, this time to accompany the queen into the chapel, surrounded by the nobility. Now thirty-two, Elizabeth was about to celebrate seven years on the throne, surpassing the reigns of her brother and sister, but nowhere near the longevity of her father's almost four-decade reign. Her bout of smallpox three years previous had left its marks, not only on her skin, but on the minds of the court and Council, terrified of the lessons of *Gorboduc*. Parliament had begged her to marry, the nobles had rallied behind candidates and suitors both within and without the realm continued to press their suits, but nothing thus far had convinced the queen to take a bridegroom, including a Dudley one, as Anne was about to.

'Dearly beloved friends . . .' the minister began. The ceremony ran according to the Book of Common Prayer, which had been issued some six years before.[5] The liturgy harkened back to the prayer book of 1552, when the Dudleys had been in the ascendant under Edward VI, the same liturgy that had been used at Ambrose's last wedding in 1553.

'. . . Which holy state,' the minister continued, 'is not to be enterprised, nor taken in hand, unadvisedly, lightly, or wantonly, to satisfy men's carnal lusts and appetites, like brute beasts that have no understanding: but reverently, discreetly, advisedly, soberly, and in the fear of God, duly considering the causes for the which matrimony was ordained.

'One,' he continued, 'was the procreation of children, to be brought up in the fear and nurture of the Lord, and praise of God.' This was certainly what Ambrose was hoping for from the marriage, and if anyone looked side-long at Elizabeth at this point, they had better have done so discreetly. 'Secondly,' he went on, 'it was ordained for a remedy against sin, and to avoid fornication.' It was wise to keep eyes firmly on shoes.

He went on through the prescribed lines, asking if anyone knew of any impediment to the marriage, and then turning to Ambrose and Anne for the customary vows, which they made. After Anne had responded 'I will,' the minister turned to face the crowd again, declaring, 'Who giveth this woman to be married unto this man?' Traditionally, of course, this role would have been fulfilled by her father, but in his absence, Robert stepped forward to take his place. Taking Anne's hands, he passed them to the minister, who in turn placed them in Ambrose's. More vows, and Ambrose placed the ring on Anne's fourth finger, before the minister gave a blessing, and pronounced their married state to all those high and mighty who were assembled. The mass continued, with various prayers, blessings and the receiving of Communion.

'Oh, merciful Lord,' the minister intoned, 'and heavenly Father, by whose gracious gift mankind is increased, we beseech thee assist with thy blessing these two persons, that they may both be fruitful in procreation of children, also live together so long in Godly love and honesty, that they may see their children's children, unto the third and fourth generation, unto thy praise and honour, through Jesus Christ our Lord. Amen.' Anne Russell was a Dudley, and Countess of Warwick. As wife to the eldest son, she was now also the matriarch of the Dudley family.

After the ceremony, Anne processed out of the chapel behind her husband. From there, she made the short trip from the chapel to the Council Chamber, located between the queen's private lodgings and the privy gallery. Continuing within the gallery, as many of the assembly did, led to the gardens and tiltyards, which were being carefully prepared for the afternoon's festivities. The Council Chamber had been built under Edward VI, when it was recognized that the daily governance of the realm would not rest with the monarch, but with his council.[6] Through the large central window, the room had views of – and could be viewed from – the privy gardens, bordered to the west by the courtier lodgings, where Anne had spent her last night as an unmarried maid. The Council Chamber was governance on display, though today the display was all about Anne Dudley. Entering, she took her seat at the long table. The room had been hung with rich arras, surrounding the large fireplace, which warmed the room against the November chill. Anne would preside over this meal, surrounded by the lords and ladies of the court.

Once Anne rose, sated, from her place at the board, the celebrations began in earnest. Walking through the gallery, past the entrance to the courtier lodgings, and through the elaborate gate, the most esteemed of the wedding party entered the tiltyard gallery, from which they could view the events. Beneath the elaborate gilded ceiling, and resting against the cushions as needed, they observed the festivities.

The four challengers entered first. These included Henry Knollys, brother to Catherine and Lettice. Twenty-three, Henry had recently become an MP for Shoreham in Sussex, and just months ago had celebrated his own wedding, to the daughter of the Chancellor of the Duchy of Lancaster. Knollys was trapped in red, white and black, and his horse covered in steel over the breast and flanks. Following not far behind Knollys was another young up-and-comer of the court, Christopher Hatton. A member of the Inner Temple, he had been a part of the Christmas celebrations over which Robert Dudley had presided some five years before. Nimble, strong and some might say attractive, he had caught the eye of the queen, and was now a gentleman pensioner. Keen observers might comment that he was one to watch, and not just on the tiltyard. He entered trapped in crimson satin, decorated with wreaths of white and black fine silk in lozenges.

Behind each of the challengers entered a mythical figure. Wearing a long gown with sleeves of crimson satin, she rode a horse trapped in white silk laid with black wreaths and red roses. At her side was a sword, and she wore a visor over her face, underneath which was long black hair that fell to her boots. In her hand she carried her challenger's arms on a small shield. The challengers had each been accompanied by an Amazon, warrior-women from the classical world, ruled over by a great queen.

Taking a circuit of the tiltyard, the challengers at last came to a halt under the viewing gallery, where the queen stood watching. Their shields were fastened to four posts underneath the queen's window, marking their challenge to all comers. At this, the trumpets sounded for the entrance of the defendants. From each trumpet, and from the gentlemen assembled, hung a scarf of fine yellow silk. At last, the first defendant entered: Robert Dudley, Earl of Leicester, his horse trapped in rich purple cloth of tissue. The games could begin.

The jousters made the most of the waning November light, before withdrawing for the evening. As night fell, the small guns were fired over the bank of the Thames nearby at Westminster to salute the new couple. The Master Gunner of England himself was there, Robert Thomas, honouring the feast and marriage day of the Earl of Warwick. As he went to fire the second gun, it exploded, impaling him with a piece of the chamber, and killing him. The unknowing crowds at Whitehall marvelled at the peal of the guns, ignorant of the blood being spilled by them.

The celebrations lasted for three days. On the third day, the bridegroom himself took to the tiltyard, before his brother – and Anne's new brother-in-law – Robert hosted a great dinner to mark the end of the festivities at his home in Durham Place, the same house which had seen the ill-fated triple wedding some dozen years before. Neither this legacy, nor the funeral of poor Robert Thomas taking place the same day, could fully overshadow the display of joy put on by the Dudleys for the court. In all, over a hundred and fifty lances were broken between challengers and defenders, not to mention the fine silks and feathers beaten into the mud. The queen was there to oversee and enjoy it all, prompting comment that Elizabeth was celebrating as if it were her own brother's wedding. Anne Dudley would have to get used to such crowds and salacious talk as the new Countess of Warwick, as well as perhaps adjusting herself to the occasional shedding of blood.

*

The mob was at their door, determined to slaughter them all. It was impossible to block out the angry shouts and screams as they tried to enter the house. The bodies of two servants lay at their feet, dead or dying in the blistering August sun.[7] Philip Sidney, just seventeen, had fled to the house in the suburb at Saint Marceau, on the south-east edge of Paris, in fear of his life.[8] Bodies were already piling up within the walls of Paris, hundreds already dead, as the sun reached its height on St Bartholomew's Day, 24 August 1572.

Philip was one of a handful of English noblemen in Paris who had escaped to the English embassy house at Saint Marceau in a desperate bid to keep themselves alive. Francis Walsingham, the English ambassador, had opened his doors to them all, to join him, his wife and his five-year-old daughter Frances. Walsingham had arrived in France on New Year's Day almost two years before, following a Christmas spent in conference over important matters with the likes of Philip's uncle, Robert Dudley, Earl of Leicester.[9] At forty, Walsingham was of an age with Leicester, though his connections to the centres of power were more tenuous. After his father's death, his mother had married Sir John Carey, the younger brother of the husband of Mary Boleyn, from whom were descended the Knollys and Carey families, giving Walsingham a loose kinship to both. Beyond that, his rather slow rise had been founded on his skills and self-made connections. He had already spent several years on the continent before his embassy to France, while Mary I was on the throne, joining other English exiles including Sir Francis Russell, father of Philip's aunt, Anne Dudley, the Countess of Warwick.

Walsingham's own wife, Ursula, had joined him in France not long after his arrival the previous year, along with their young daughter, Frances. Ursula, too, had some connections to the court, and was distantly related to Philip and his mother's family through Elizabeth Grey Dudley, Philip's great-grandmother. Ursula and Francis's marriage was the second for both, though the two sons from Ursula's first marriage had been killed just five years before in an accidental explosion, leaving Frances as her only child. Fortune appeared to be shining on the couple now, however, as Ursula Walsingham was pregnant again, about five months along. Perhaps this would be a son for the Walsingham line. First, though, Walsingham would have to keep them all alive.

As the mob advanced on the embassy, determined to attack them with knives and throw their bodies into the nearby Seine, hoofbeats could be heard on the street outside. The grand-looking duc de Nevers was approaching the embassy with a contingent of the French royal guard. Walsingham had made the acquaintance of Louis Gonzaga, duc de Nevers, already, having dined at his home some five weeks before.[10] Gonzaga, an Italian-born Frenchman in his early thirties, was an experienced soldier, having fought against the English and Spanish at Saint-Quentin, where Philip's uncle, Harry, had been killed. In all the confusion and bloodshed, it would not be immediately clear which side he was on now. Was he there to save them, or to kill them?

Philip too had encountered Gonzaga before, albeit from afar, dining with the ambassadors in the gardens of his estate. His journey to France had been to make precisely these sorts of connections. Philip's uncle, Lord Robert, had charged Francis Walsingham with keeping an eye on his nephew before he had departed England, asking his friend to take 'a special care' with Philip, as he was still 'young and raw'.[11]

'His father and I,' Robert informed Francis, 'do intend his further travel if the world be quiet and you shall think it convenient for him.' If either the world or Philip was running amok, he was to be sent home. Not even Robert Dudley, experienced as he was with the bloody rise and fall of political fortune, could have predicted that Philip would have found himself at the centre of – indeed the target of – a massacre.

Philip knew well his role within the Dudley family and its various enterprises. When he was eleven, at school in Shrewsbury, his father had sent him a lengthy letter over the Easter weekend, instructing him in his duties to his family, his Dudley family. 'Remember my son,' Henry had told him, 'the noble blood you are descended of by your mother's side, and think that only by virtuous life and good action, you may be an ornament to that illustrious family.[12]

'Otherwise,' he warned, 'through vice and sloth you may be accompted *Labes generis*, a spot on your kin, one of the greatest curses that can happen to man.' Young Philip was required to understand what it meant to be a Dudley son and, moreover, the eldest Dudley son, or bring disgrace to his family. His mother added her hand to the letter. She endorsed the lessons Henry had imparted to Philip, encouraging him to read them repeatedly, at least once every four or five days. 'Farewell my little Philip,' she had signed off, 'and once again the Lord bless you.'

That summer, his uncle, Robert, had begun Philip's political education. Philip had travelled to Robert's home at Kenilworth, and then together on to Oxford, where Robert Dudley had been appointed Chancellor of the University two years prior. Robert was thus partly responsible for the entertainments for the queen, who would be arriving two days later, though as Robert and Philip rode into Oxford in the pouring rain it seemed an inauspicious start.[13] Philip had the opportunity to watch as his grand uncle sent out orders, organized teams of workmen, and met with the country's great men, men like William Cecil, the Secretary of State (and Chancellor of rival Cambridge).

Two days later, as the sun began to set, the queen had entered Oxford in a glorious open chariot, to shouts of '*Vivat Regina*' to which she responded gratefully, '*Gratias ago*'. The queen and court had remained for six days of disputations on topics such as 'It is not lawful for a private individual to take up arms against a prince, even if he is unjust,' and 'A prince should be declared by succession, not by election.' In the evening had been plays, including an adaptation of Geoffrey Chaucer's *Knight's Tale*, in which two knights, Palamon and Arcite, fight over the love of the beautiful Emily. Before the tournament which will decide her hand, Palamon prays to marry Emily, Arcite prays for victory, and Emily prays to remain unmarried. Arcite wins the tournament for her hand, but is thrown off his horse, dying, and Palamon marries Emily. In the end, all have their prayers answered, except for Emily, who wished to remain a maid. Elizabeth had given a generous gift to the boy who played the unfortunate Emily.

During the festivities, both of Philip's uncles, Ambrose and Robert, had lodged at Christ Church College, along with men like William Cecil and Francis Knollys. While staying with them, Philip had also met Walter Devereux, husband to Lettice Knollys and father of the nearly one-year-old Robert – named for Philip's uncle – as well as the three-year-old Penelope. Walter had gifted the young lad with a red horse, currying favour with both Philip's father and uncle. Philip also returned from Oxford with a fine chest, filled with a host of new clothes provided by his uncle – doublets in crimson satin and green taffeta, hose of crimson velvet and a white leather jerkin, trimmed with gold lace – and marked with the bear and ragged staff.[14]

The trip to Paris, in the entourage of the Earl of Lincoln, had been the perfect opportunity for Philip, now a young man, to continue his education and to represent the Dudley family abroad. At sixty, the Earl of Lincoln, Edward Fiennes de Clinton, was a veteran of the court. He too was related to Philip and his Dudley kin, largely through his wives. The first had been Elizabeth Blount, the former mistress of Henry VIII and the mother of Ambrose Dudley's second wife. His second, Ursula Stourton, was a Dudley cousin, the granddaughter of Edmund Dudley through his eldest daughter, Elizabeth. His third and current wife, Elizabeth FitzGerald, was, like Ursula Walsingham, related to the Dudleys through Elizabeth Grey Dudley, Philip's great-grandmother. Fiennes had known Elizabeth Dudley's son John Dudley well, serving under him in France, following him as Governor of Boulogne as well as Lord High Admiral, and helping him seize the Tower in support of Lady Jane Grey. Despite this, he had suffered only a short imprisonment before being well rewarded by Queen Mary during her reign. Philip could learn a lot from this experienced near-kinsman.

Philip's rigorous education at Shrewsbury also served him well on this trip. His French was near-impeccable, having been raised on the grisly yet moralizing tales of Matteo Bandello's *Histoires Tragiques*, translated into French by François de Belleforest. He was accompanied by a handful of his own servants, Harry White, John Fisher and the Welshman Griffin Maddox, as well as an older companion, Lodowick Bryskett, an experienced and well-educated clerk with powerful Italian connections. Once in Paris, he had made the acquaintance of a number of continental intellectuals. This included the German-born ambassador Gaspard de Schomberg, whom Philip found to be eager in his king's service, the German student Johann Conrad Brüning and the Strasburg jurist Dr Jean Lobbett.[15] Perhaps the most notable of his new acquaintances was the French humanist Petrus Ramus. Some forty years older, Ramus had been debating in front of the French king Francis I before Philip was born. He was best known for his controversial positions and more recently for his conversion to the Protestant religion. For this he had faced violent opposition; his house in Paris had been sacked and his library burned while he took refuge in the palace at Fontainebleau. Like many other French Protestants, he had returned to the city in the hope of a peace. This hope had also brought Philip to Paris.

Philip had spent most of his life in smaller towns, as well as in the country. Shrewsbury could boast about six thousand people, and Oxford, where he had been resident on and off for the previous four years, was about half of that. On his few trips to London, he had seen what a bustling city could be – with a population over the 200,000 mark – but Paris was more densely populated still, boasting almost 300,000 people in its winding medieval streets.[16] Like London, it was walled – though the city had since outgrown its original walls several times over – and cut through by a central river, the Seine. At the centre was a large island, reached by bridges lined with houses, and the city's grand cathedral, Notre-Dame de Paris.

West of the cathedral, on the north bank of the Seine, was the palace of the Louvre, where Philip had the great honour and pleasure of being lodged in his first two weeks in Paris. In the train of the Earl of Lincoln, Philip and his companions had arrived into Paris on 8 June and proceeded to their lodgings at the Louvre. Once a fortress, much of the medieval structure had been demolished by King Francis I in order to build a grand new palace, a Renaissance royal residence in the centre of Paris. Retaining some of the sense of a medieval fortress in its grand towers, the newly designed wings of the palace reflected the Renaissance emphasis on symmetry, with columns, roundels and classical figures decorating its large arched windows.

The English visitors had been given a few days to rest in these grand settings before their first audience with the court. In part, this was to help them recover from their journey. More pressing, however, was that their arrival had been followed almost immediately by a death in the royal family.[17] Jeanne d'Albret, the queen regnant of Navarre, had died the day after the English arrival in Paris. Situated between France and Spain, the small kingdom of Navarre had already suffered a loss of its southern territory to the Spanish earlier in the century and now faced encroachment by the French. Jeanne d'Albret had ruled Navarre for almost two decades, converting the entire kingdom to the Calvinist Protestant religion. She had died in Paris, not long after negotiating the marriage contract which would bring together her son, the Protestant Navarrese heir, Henry, with Marguerite, sister to the Catholic French king, Charles IX. With d'Albret's death, this marriage became even more important, as nineteen-year-old Henry was now King of Navarre. Niece of Francis I, Charles IX's grandfather, Jeanne d'Albret was close enough to the French royal family that her death had necessitated a period of mourning, regardless of the inconvenience this might cause to their visitors.

At last, on the Friday following their arrival, a host of fine coaches were sent to the Louvre to bring the Earl of Lincoln and his coterie to the court at Château de Madrid, six kilometres west from the Louvre.[18] The Château had also been a building project of Francis I who, after returning from imprisonment in Madrid, had sought a new, smaller, palace than the Louvre. Richly decorated, the Château de Madrid did not have to battle any medieval foundations, and thus was a proudly Renaissance building, covered in high relief and maiolica pottery. There, the highest-ranking members of the company, the Earl of Lincoln and Francis Walsingham, met and dined with the French royal family: the twenty-two-year-old king and his two brothers, Henry, duc d'Anjou, and Francis, duc d'Alençon. On the surface, the English assembly were there to see signed the Treaty of Blois, a promise of alliance and friendship between the French and English against the Spanish. They were also there, however, to advance a potential marriage between Elizabeth and the duc d'Anjou.[19] Though she was now approaching forty, and he just twenty, scarcely older than Philip himself, the marriage had support, especially from his mother, Catherine de Medici.

The ratification of the treaty had taken place at the Church of Saint-Germain, a grand building a stone's throw from the Louvre palace. To avoid offending their Protestant visitors, the signing was held at the evening ceremony of vespers rather than the mass. The English nobles and gentlemen waited in specially prepared side chapels, hung with tapestries and provided with seats covered with cloth of gold. As the impressive choral music ended, the English, led by the Earl of Lincoln, were brought into the church, which was packed with spectators. To strains of the *Te Deum*, the King of France signed the document, cementing – once again – a promise of perpetual alliance between the French and the English. From there, the company processed out of the church and into the streets, so full of people, it seemed, that the king and his parade of French and English notables would struggle to make it past. At various points the king paused, looking on his people as they looked on him, blessing their king.

Whereas then the streets of Paris had been had filled with joyous shouts, now they were full of terrified and angry screams, as well as animalistic whistles and hoots.[20] As the duc de Nevers approached Walsingham's embassy, it soon became clear to the relief of those within that he had been sent to protect them, and he made quick work of the mob.

It was, in fact, Elizabeth's continuing marriage negotiations which had saved them. Philip, as a member of the Earl of Lincoln's train, had been merely peripheral to the ceremonies and dinners which accompanied the signing of the treaty, but he was becoming well acquainted with the moves and motives of international politics. Charles IX and his mother, Catherine de Medici, could not risk the prospective marriage between Elizabeth and the duc d'Anjou by allowing the English ambassadors, including the nephew of Elizabeth's favourite, to be murdered in the streets. To do so would cast a pall over the courtship, to say the least. Had Philip's uncle already been the king consort of England, as so many had predicted he would be by now, it might have ended very differently for the English Protestants in Paris, and the duc de Nevers might not have minded slaughtering a contingent of them, or at least allowing it to happen. As it was, a royal guard was set up to protect the embassy; they could all breathe a cautious sigh of relief.[21]

Not that the bloodshed was over. They would have to remain in the embassy for the time being; who knew how long. Walsingham's stores were not infinite, and he had struggled to maintain his household in a city choked by a series of poor harvests and almost continuous warfare.[22]

Walsingham had become an important contact for Philip in his time in Paris. The official visit had not lasted long after the signing of the treaty, but Philip had remained in the city, suffering under the intense heat, but also enjoying stimulating conversation with the resident intellectuals. His education in international political machinations only increased after the end of official proceedings and the departure of Lincoln. Philip could explore the city himself, and become closer to Walsingham, giving him the opportunity to acquaint himself with Walsingham's approach to affairs back home.

These affairs were largely concerned with the persistent problem of the Queen of Scots. Mary had wed the charming Henry Stuart, Lord Darnley, in the spring of 1565, though rumours suggested the love-match had soured fast. By the time of the birth of their child, James, the summer of the following year, it appeared the Scottish court was in violent uproar. These rumours were confirmed when in

February 1567, not two years after their wedding, Henry Stuart, king consort of Scotland, was killed. The case was as mysterious as the death of Amy Dudley, though Darnley's death was unquestionably murder. He was recovering from an illness that was almost certainly syphilis at a house a short walk from Mary's Holyrood Castle, when two explosions were heard in the cold early hours of the morning. Darnley's half-naked corpse, along with that of his servant, was found outside the house, along with a cloak, a dagger, a chair and a coat. How these strange circumstances came about, no one could be quite sure.

That didn't stop people guessing, however, and Mary was certainly a prime suspect, along with James Hepburn, Earl Bothwell, with whom she was suspected of having an affair. Three months later, Bothwell had abducted Mary and apparently raped her, though the reports to London suggested that she had been a willing accomplice. In May the two were married, but by July the queen was forced to abdicate in favour of her one-year-old son, now the infant James VI.

It was at this point that the gossip of Scotland had become very much the problem of the Queen of England and her court, as the Queen of Scots had fled to England. She was imprisoned, first at Bolton Castle, supervised by Sir Francis Knollys, and then at Tutbury Castle, under the care of George and Elizabeth Talbot, the Earl and Countess of Shrewsbury. From there, she had been plotting, primarily to marry Thomas Howard, Duke of Norfolk, the grandson of the Duke of Norfolk who had condemned Philip's grandfather. Philip's uncle, Robert, had played his part in notifying the queen, who arrested and imprisoned the duke. This, however, did not stop any of them, and when it was revealed, largely through the work of Walsingham and Cecil, that Mary and the duke not only planned to marry, but hoped to overthrow Elizabeth, the duke had been executed, the last of the House of Howard to pester the Dudleys.

Now the question which faced the queen, and thus her advisers, was what to do with the Queen of Scots. Walsingham's opinion on the matter was clear: as long as the Queen of Scots lived, not only would there be no peace in England, and no strong relations with Scotland, but it was also damaging to the friendship just agreed with France.[23]

There had always been an alliance to be called upon between France and Scotland to harry England, and this was embodied in Mary herself. She was the daughter of Marie de Guise, a member of one of the most important families in France, and had been married to Francis II, elder brother of Charles IX, albeit both their marriage and his reign had been brief. As sister-in-law, then, to the French king (brother to Elizabeth's potential spouse), her continued presence, in Walsingham's view, could only exacerbate tensions between the two countries at a time when peace was essential. Convincing the queen to execute an anointed sovereign and cousin, however, was not easy and had not, as yet, been successful.

Philip's time in Paris had not been all heated intellectual dialogue and political frustration, however. His trip had also coincided with another event, far more important than the signing of the treaty: the marriage of Henry – now the King of Navarre – and Marguerite – sister to the king – on 18 August, a month after Lincoln's departure. A week before the wedding, Philip had been made a gentleman of Charles IX's bedchamber and a French baron, Baron de Sidenay, granting him access to a better vantage point for the wedding ceremony and a greater excuse to join in the revelry that followed.

Paris had been packed with people for the wedding; at the end of June permission had been granted to allow Protestants from all over the country to witness the marriage ceremony of one of their leaders, the King of Navarre. Crammed into a Paris already suffering from lack of food and boiling under an unrelenting heat, the Catholics and Protestants of France maintained an uneasy peace. Walsingham had not been unaware of the high-pressure situation that Paris was in. Unless God Himself intervened, he had dreaded a fearful outcome.[24]

The ceremony itself had taken place at the spectacular medieval cathedral of Notre-Dame de Paris. As it was a Catholic ceremony, the Protestant lords and gentlemen, such as Philip himself, waited outside the Cathedral for the bride and groom to exit. The Cathedral had been the subject of violence between Protestants and Catholics some twenty-five years before, when rioting Protestants had destroyed some of the statues of Notre-Dame, attacking the Catholics' worship of false idols. On that day in August, however, this could be forgotten in the celebration of what many hoped would be a new peaceful beginning for France, represented in the young couple. For the second time in as many months, the streets were ringed with people, shouting their joy and blessings.

That had been less than a week before. The wedding festivities had come to an end in the bloodshed now filling the streets of Paris. On the fourth day of celebration following the wedding, shots had been fired at one of the leaders of the Protestant cause, the Admiral de Coligny, almost killing him. The king had sent his surgeon, the same who had been at the devastating siege of Saint-Quentin almost two decades before, Ambroise Paré, to attend to Coligny's injuries. The Count of Montgomery had rushed to Walsingham's home, to inform him of the attack, and assure him that the king was taking good care of the admiral.[25] There was no reason for concern. Walsingham cautiously believed him.

But two days later, in the early hours of the morning, the church bells of Saint-Germain had rung out, the same church in which Philip had witnessed the signing of the treaty just over a month before. Soon, bells across the city were ringing. It was a signal. The attack on the Protestants sheltered in the city for the wedding had begun. Panicked, Philip and others fled to Walsingham's embassy. With the arrival of each terrified Protestant, seeking refuge in the embassy, came a new flood of distressing news. Before dawn had even broken, the recovering Admiral de Coligny had been brutally stabbed to death and his body thrown out of the window, all under the supervision of Henri de Guise, cousin to Mary, Queen of Scots. The hundreds of Protestants housed in the Louvre, in suites of rooms that Philip and the English entourage had only recently inhabited themselves, had been murdered, their bodies stacked high in the courtyard under the gaze of Charles IX. With the gates closed and boats secured in their docks, Protestants fled to the countryside, willing to face the dangers of the wilderness rather than the violence that filled their city.[26] As they fled, it was said that they were hunted for sport by pursuing Catholics.[27] Young girls were baptised in their parents' blood, women were mutilated and impaled on spits, and no one was safe from such rites of violence.[28]

Philip and the other Protestants of Paris spent an uneasy night, hiding themselves in fear of their lives. The next day, some began to cautiously emerge from where they had sheltered, but it was not over. For days the violence raged on. On the third day, one of Philip's friends and mentors fell victim to the massacre. Having spent the first day and night hidden in the cellar of a bookshop, as looters sacked the contents above, on the second day, Petrus Ramus felt secure enough to return to his accommodation at the college around the corner. This was a mistake. He was attacked in his rooms and, like Coligny before him, stabbed before being thrown out of his window. Catholic students attacked and cut up his corpse, dragging it through the streets to the Seine, where it joined countless others in a morbid, mutilated baptism beneath the shadow of the great Cathedral.

It was starkly clear that this was not just disordered mob violence. The order for the elimination of French Protestants had come from the highest levels, from the king and queen mother themselves. Philip would never forgive any of the French royal family for their part in the butchery he was forced to witness of his own religious brethren. 'He is the son of the Jezebel of our age,' Philip later wrote to Elizabeth of the duc, 'his brother made oblation of his own sister's marriage, the easier to make massacres of all sexes.'[29] How could a young Catholic duc, soaked in the blood of the martyrs of Christ, ever compare to his uncle, a shining champion of the true religion?

*

The large bear strained against his chains, desperately fending off attacks that came from every side, his pink eyes rolling in his head, trying to see in every direction at once.[30] He was already bleeding in several places, his blood dripping from the greedy mouths and paws of the large, powerful mastiffs who surrounded him. The bear was not a passive victim, however, to the attacking dogs. As they cornered and covered him, and the watching crowd was sure that the dogs had triumphed, suddenly from beneath the pile of broad-shouldered canines the bear would emerge, roaring and taking his revenge by swiping and biting at his attackers. It was amazing with what nimbleness this large, burly creature could move, tossing and tumbling to free himself as the dogs attacked. Having been fended off mid-assault, the dogs drew back, as if silently formulating a new plan, taking account of the injuries they had suffered as well as the new weaknesses they could smell on their victim. For a moment or two there was quiet as the animals eyed each other up. The crowd looked on. The bear shook blood and saliva from his ears. And then, the last attack. As the lifeblood trickled onto the rushes and stones, the crowd dispersed, this bloodletting having provided a sense of relief and a means to forget, for a few moments, their own heavy concerns.

There had been thirteen bears chained to stakes in the outer court of Kenilworth – also called Killingworth – Castle that Tuesday afternoon in July.[31] The keen-eyed might have noticed their reflection in the stonework and decoration of the courtyard and castle – on windows, carpets, bed linens, chairs and cushions – they were in Warwickshire, after all, and at the home of Robert Dudley, who was not subtle in his use of the heraldic symbol he shared with his elder brother.[32] There was not much, it had to be said, that was subtle about Robert Dudley, from his expensive clothing to his elaborate castle to his choice of entertainments. Here, at Kenilworth, Robert Dudley ruled supreme, and he let you know.

The court had arrived at Robert's home at Kenilworth five days earlier, in the company of the queen's summer progress. Arriving from the manor house of Fawsley, some twenty-five miles to the south-east, the court had stopped for dinner at Long Itchington. There, Robert had hosted the queen and her court in a large tent, containing several rooms and with all the grandness of a palace of its own. Finishing dinner, they had continued along the road to Kenilworth. At last, the sun making its descent behind the westernmost edge of its walls, they had seen Kenilworth itself. Appearing to float on the glassy lake that surrounded it, it was a medieval vision emerging from the verdant wood. With fortified walls and crenellated parapets, the dying sunlight illuminated its red sandstone walls and gleamed off its many large windows, to be replaced by the twinkling light of candles and torches.[33]

As they approached, the company was stopped before reaching the south gate. Sitting in a tree bordering the highway, was a sibyl – a prophetess – dressed in a robe of white silk, who had spoken to the queen and those around her, prophesying the queen's long, prosperous and peaceful reign: 'The rage of war,' she had declared, 'bound fast in chains, / shall never stir ne move:/ But peace shall govern all your days, / Increasing Subjects' love.' It was a pretty sentiment, but those among the court knew very well how shaky relations remained with a number of England's allies and enemies.

'And whilest your highness here abides, /' she meant at Kenilworth, 'nothing shall rest unsought, / That may bring pleasure to your mind, / or quiet to your thought.'[34] The time at Kenilworth was to be a retreat for Elizabeth, a holiday from the cares of the crown.

Despite any cynicism she might have felt at this particular prophecy, the queen had benevolently accepted the sibyl's words, and the company had moved on to the south gate. There they had been met by a man dressed in silks as the mighty hero Hercules, who on his knees presented the castle keys to the queen, hers to use while she remained at Kenilworth. On the battlements stood six large men, eight foot tall at least, all likewise robed in silk and each with a silver five-foot-long trumpet, who appeared to herald the queen's entry.

Moving through the Gallery Tower, the queen and her company came over the long dam that separated the waters of the mere – an artificial pool created as part of the castle's defences – from the lower pool – a smaller, quieter body of water to the east. Some four hundred feet long, the dam served a second purpose as the castle's majestic tiltyard, recalling scenes from romantic tales of chivalric knights doing battle in the shadow of grand medieval castles. The idea to put the tiltyard on the dam had not been Robert's, but rather had been his father's project. John Dudley had widened the dam as part of building projects at the Castle in the few months before his downfall and death. Robert had perfected the plan, adding the Gallery Tower through which the court had just moved, and from which spectators could observe the sport on the tiltyard below.

Emerging from the tiltyard, through Mortimer's Tower at its northern end, and into the outer court, queen and company had been hailed by another silk-clad lady, attended by two nymphs. Rather than being poised atop a tree, this lady called to the queen from a floating artificial island in the midst of the pool, ringed with torches and moving steadily towards them. 'I am the Lady of this pleasant Lake,' she had told the queen, 'Who since the time of great king Arthur's reign, / That here with royal Court abode did make, / Have led a lowering* life in restless pain. / Til now that this your third arrival here / Doth cause me come abroad and boldly thus appear.' Elizabeth had visited Kenilworth twice before, including on the eve of the St Bartholomew's Day Massacre, when she had assured the French ambassadors of her conviction to take a husband.[35]

There could be no mistaking the intended identity of the lady flocked with nymphs: the Lady of the Lake, a mystical figure who aided Arthur and his knights in the tales of old. Combined with the giants at the gate, it was clear that Kenilworth was being recast as Camelot, and both Elizabeth and Robert Dudley as heirs to Arthur's crown and glory.

'Pass on Madame,' the Lady finished, 'you need no longer stand, / The Lake, the Lodge, the Lord, are yours for to command.'[36]

The queen graciously thanked the Lady, before adding, 'We had thought indeed the Lake had been ours, and do you call it yours now? Well, we will herein commune more with you hereafter.' As always, it was difficult to tell if the queen was joking or not, and perhaps it was Kenilworth's lord she was more concerned with being in possession of.

At the Lady's invitation and to the sound of music, the queen and her entourage had continued towards the inner court, passing over a twenty-foot land bridge bordered with offerings on posts: caged birds, silver bowls of fruit, grains and grapes, staves of arms and bay branches decorated with musical instruments, further signs of the queen's mastery of the castle. To the sound of sweet music, the queen and those with her at last entered the inner court, where she had dismounted her palfrey after her long ride, slowed by the progress of these various scenes and entertainments. From there, she had entered her lodging, at the south end of the inner court.

Three storeys high, not counting the basement at its foundation, the queen's lodgings had been built especially for her visit, much

---

* Lowering: gloomy, sullen.

improved from the last time she had been at Kenilworth. The size of a small country manor, the lodging was large enough to house both the queen and her ladies, with withdrawing chambers, a privy chamber and bedroom on the principal floor. It was on the top floor, in the dancing chamber overlooking the waters of the mere, that the queen had the best view of the expensive and extravagant fireworks planned for the rest of the evening: burning darts, flashes of glittering stars, streams of fiery sparks, lightnings of wildfire and flight and shot of thunderbolts which shook the earth and tossed the waters below.[37]

The days since the queen's arrival had been spent in music, dancing, entertainment and – when the heat of the day had retreated somewhat – hunting in the Chase north-west of the castle. The woods there had been cultivated to present the perfect balance between wild woodland and calm countryside, with seats, walks and a host of red deer for hunting.[38] Like her father and mother before her, the queen enjoyed the thrill of the hunt; the yearning of the hounds, the swiftness of the deer, the running of the footmen, the galloping of horses, the blasting of horns and the shouting of the huntsmen, echoing from the woods and waters in the nearby valleys.[39]

Between the castle and the Chase lay the magnificent gardens, perhaps the most impressive in the country, laid out so that court, queen and favourite could spend hours walking their paths, enjoying the sweet smells of herbs, flowers and fruits.[40] Entering via the State Chamber in Cesare's Tower, Robert could lead his queen through the well-lit loggia arcades and out into the garden. It was Robert's father who had first introduced the Italian loggia to English architecture at Dudley Castle, and Robert would have remembered well the brilliant effect that this neo-classical exterior gallery could have on the architecture of a building.

From the loggia, the queen could walk along the raised terrace of fresh grass, dotted with obelisks, spheres and white bears made to appear as if hewn from solid stone, though they were in fact convincingly painted wood. Having taken in a view of the garden from above, she could then descend the nearby stairs and enter the garden's paradise.[41] The garden was set in quarters, with alleys of grass and fine, tightly packed sand, like sand by the seashore when the tide has gone out.[42] In the centre of each rectangular quarter were more obelisks, rising fifteen feet high, on a two-foot base and topped by an orb ten inches thick. Made to look as if they were carved from porphyry, the reddish-purple stone quarried from the deserts of Egypt, it was only up close that one realized that they, like the terrace ornaments, were just painted wood.[43] Hearing the sound of birdsong, the ear and eye were drawn to the aviary, set against the northern wall.[44] Painted gems caught the light of the sun, over flat columns and two levels of arched windows.[45] Soaring twenty feet high, it was a pleasant and engaging pastime to walk the aviary's full thirty-foot width, seeking to pick out the various species of birds which Robert had acquired from around the globe: France, Spain, the Canary Islands and even North Africa, as well as a few native English species.[46]

The true glory of the garden was at its centre, where the trickle and glimmer of water drew the viewer to a magnificent marble fountain. The eight-square basin, carved with aquatic – and rather titillating – scenes from Ovid's *Metamorphoses*, stood almost as high as the queen's shoulder. Peering over the side, one could catch the gleam of fish – carp, tench, bream, perch and eel – playfully intertwining in the waters. Emerging from the basin was a column of marble, atop which stood two sculpted men, back-to-back, hoisting a three-foot wide orb between them, like a pair of mighty Atlases.[47] Anyone finding themselves a little too heated from looking at the naked Ovidian figures on the sides of the basin was quickly cooled by the water which fell from pipes emerging from the ball they held. Atop the orb that they supported between them was a single marble-hewn ragged staff.

Robert Dudley was at the centre of it all, orchestrating the events, and ensuring that his queen and guests were treated to an experience beyond their most romantic fantasies. As a pageant given to the queen on her return from the hunt on the third day reminded her: Robert Dudley 'gave him self and all, / A worthy gift to be received, / and so I trust it shall.' The queen was in possession of the worthy lord of Kenilworth and should be glad of it.

Robert was also able to ensure that while he kept the court captivated, he also remained closest to the queen. The lodgings he had built for her, at the south-east corner of the castle range, bordered the east range, where his own chambers lay. In order for the queen to quietly access the gardens, the Chase and the State Chamber housed in the Great Tower, especially in the heat of the day, she would need to traverse that eastern range, or else would have to wade through the guests who awaited her in her great and presence chambers along the southern range. As host, Robert had first pick of lodgings, and many guests were not even housed at Kenilworth itself but nearly six miles south, at Warwick Castle, in the possession of Robert's elder brother, Ambrose.

It was thus convenient for Ambrose to play an important part in the festivities, as did their sister, Mary, attendant upon the queen and with her own chamber at Kenilworth.[48] Her husband, Henry, who had been installed as a Knight of the Garter that May, was also there for the revels, as well as the business which could not be – contrary to the sibyl's suggestion – set aside. Neither Mary nor Henry had been particularly pleased with the queen of late. Both had suffered from ill health, caused in part by Henry's difficult task in Ireland, as well as the death of their daughter, Elizabeth, in Dublin in 1567. They had returned to England that year, Henry suffering an attack of the stone, one of which he claimed was the size of a nutmeg (though he was prone to exaggeration). Two years later Mary had given birth to a third son, Thomas, before returning to serve the queen, while Henry was posted in Wales. Neither Sidney was content with the rewards for their difficult service, and the previous year Mary had refused to work unless she was able to retain the chambers she had come to regard as her own. Any ill will between Mary and the queen she served – with increasing resentment – was overshadowed by the death of Henry and Mary's ten-year-old daughter, Ambrosia, the February before the Kenilworth celebrations. This was the third daughter the pair had lost over the course of their marriage, and the queen shared in their grief.[49]

At Kenilworth Mary and Henry were joined by two of their surviving children, Philip, freshly returned from the three-year tour around the continent that had followed on the heels of the St Bartholomew's Day Massacre, and the young Mary Sidney, just thirteen, who had joined the court after the death of Ambrosia.[50] The young Mary was a vibrant and cultivated addition to Elizabeth's household. Her education paralleled those of her parents and the queen; she was fluent in French, Italian and Latin, could converse confidently about the Scriptures and classical texts, and was proficient in the arts of rhetoric, music and needlework. She was an excellent adornment for the court, and soon she would make a prize bride. Her elder brother, Philip, now twenty-one, was likewise a shining light, having returned from his tour a polished, educated gentleman. From Paris, Philip had travelled to Frankfurt, Vienna, Pressburg, Venice, Padua, Genoa, Florence, Cracow, Heidelberg and Antwerp, meeting printers, artists, ambassadors, botanists, poets, writers and rulers. He had read books of history and warfare, learned first-hand about political machinations, experienced the bloody clash of religions and seen some of the great artistic wonders of the Renaissance. Standing beside his uncle, Lord Robert, Philip – named for a king and now with a princely air – was the ideal successor in the absence of a Dudley heir.

These and the other guests, including Sir Francis Knollys and his daughter, Lettice, Countess of Essex – whose husband was still in Ireland – enjoyed all the hunting, entertainment, food and drink that Robert could offer.[51] Having spent something in the range of £60,000 on building projects to improve the castle itself – three times the scandalous annual income he was rumoured to have been offered as regent while Elizabeth suffered with smallpox – Robert was now footing the bill for sixteen barrels of wine and forty barrels of beer to be drunk every day by his guests, not to mention the copious food, costumes, fireworks and hunted deer.

Robert and his guests rested on beds of crimson satin, embroidered in silver, gold and the arms of the Earl of Leicester, adorned with plumes of feathers and cushions of velvet, fringed with silk.[52] On the walls hung tapestries portraying scenes of flowers and beasts, hawking and hunting and magnificent verdure. There were also tapestries of biblical and mythical figures, Samson and Hercules, David and Alexander, ranged across the sandstone walls. Of interest to a female spectator, especially a female queen, would be the inclusion of tapestries of two Old Testament figures: Jezebel, the persecutor of God's prophets, and Judith, who violently sawed off the head of a general poised to destroy a Hebrew city.

Also adorning the walls were items from the earl's growing painting collection, gathered from masters around the continent. These included images of courtiers, such as the Dudleys' erstwhile enemy, Henry FitzAlan, the Earl of Arundel, as well as Lettice, Countess of Essex, alongside scintillating images of bare-clad young women, recently martyred Protestant heroes and, of course, various royals, including King Philip II, once the Dudleys' saviour, and Mary, Queen of Scots, once proposed as a Dudley wife.[53] Most important, and created for the festivities at Kenilworth, were two sets of paintings of Robert and his queen, winking at visitors from behind silk and satin curtains. Whereas paired portraits of married couples would show the two facing each other, in these Robert and Elizabeth both faced the same direction, slightly to the left of the viewer with eyes directly trained on them. They were both, nevertheless, undeniably a matched set. In one, Elizabeth wore the white doublet that Robert had gifted her that New Year, her arm resting on a throne; the accompanying portrait of Robert showed him resplendent in a slashed red satin doublet, arm casually placed on a far simpler chair.[54] In the other, the artist had drawn attention to Robert's martial skill, painting him in his armour; juxtaposed with a painting of Elizabeth, standing demure next to symbols of her strength: constancy, fidelity and purity.[55] They were not husband and wife, but the paintings suggested that Robert and his queen were a new sort of powerful couple.[56]

This statement of solidarity between Robert and the queen many had thought he would one day marry was necessary. Both were now in their early forties, the youth that had accompanied the rumours upon Elizabeth's accession long behind them. The portraits showed little sign of this age beyond slightly sunken eyes and the confidence that comes with maturity, but there was no denying that the pair were moving beyond their prime. Although Elizabeth's marriage negotiators confidently asserted her continued fertility, this could not continue much longer, and many were accepting – with resignation – that England would continue to have a maiden on its throne. A virginal queen, however, could still have a dedicated favourite and champion, and Robert was determined that he would hold that place.

Elizabeth was not the only one, however, who lacked a successor of her own blood. Robert had remained unmarried in the fifteen years since the mysterious death of his wife, though he had come close. For at least five years, he had conducted an intermittent affair with the beautiful young widow, Douglass, Baroness Sheffield. At her husband's death, when she was at last free to marry, Robert had told her that he – despite his own widowerhood – was not.[57] Instead, they had become lovers. Recently, however, Douglass had increased the pressure on Robert to at last marry her, causing Robert to lash out at her in frustration. Yes, marrying her was a tempting prospect, as Robert told Douglass, 'my brother you see long married and not like to have children, it resteth so now in my self.'[58] Despite his marriage ten years before, Robert's elder brother had remained childless. However, to marry risked losing the favour of the queen, who guarded Robert like a treasure. It placed him in a difficult position, but he had resolved that retaining the queen's good graces remained a greater priority than marriage, at least to Douglass. 'Is there nothing in the world,' he told Douglass passionately, 'next to that favour that I would not give to be in hope of leaving some children behind me, being now the last of our house.'[59]

Thus, when Douglass Sheffield had brought their son screaming into the world a year before the Kenilworth revels, the child had been born a bastard. Robert Dudley had at last had a son but, despite sharing his father's name, he would not be his heir. Robert had chosen his queen over the continued survival of the Dudley line. The birth of little Robert did change things, however. Before his arrival, after a childless marriage with Amy, there had been little reason for Robert to think that he could produce the much-desired Dudley heir. With Douglass delivered of a healthy and thriving son, and the disappearing possibility of a marriage to the queen, the situation had changed. Perhaps it was time to put the House of Dudley first.

The queen stayed almost three weeks enjoying the revelries at Kenilworth before departing. As she left, Robert ordered one final display: Silvanus, god of the woods, imparted to her the sorrow caused by her departure, before the character of Deep Desire chimed in, speaking from a holly tree: 'I am that wretch Desire,' he declared, 'whom neither death could daunt: / Nor dole decay, nor dread delay,

/ Nor feigned cheer enchant. / Whom neither care could quench, / nor fancy force to change.'

Having implored the queen to remain, Deep Desire burst into song, aided by the sound of nearby musicians:

> Then farewell sweet, for whom I taste such sour
> farewell delight, for whom I dwell in dole:
> Free will, farewell, farewell my fancy's flower,
> farewell content whom cruel cares control.
> Oh farewell life, delightful death farewell,
> I die in heaven, yet live in darksome hell.

The Lady Lettice entered the darkened room. The windows had been hung with black curtains, but the linen was fresh and herbs had been strewn about. The room looked funereal but smelled of brightness and new life.[60] The focus of the room was the bed, dressed with white linen and set in the centre of the chamber, so that there was plenty of room for her attendants to busy themselves around it. The bed needed to be neither too close to the fire as to be overly warm, nor too close to the windows and doors, all covered in arras, as to be subject to draughts. This would be Lettice's world for the next several weeks, attended only by her closest female servants and companions. As dark a scene as it was, Lettice had every reason to feel triumphant. She had accomplished what no other woman had in several decades, though a number had tried: she had married Robert Dudley, Earl of Leicester. What's more, Lettice Dudley, Countess of Leicester, was preparing to give birth to Robert's child: a legitimate heir to the House of Dudley.

Their wedding had taken place two and a half years before, on the Sunday following the three sacred Ember Days in September 1578. These days, taking place on Wednesday, Friday and Saturday, were set aside for fasting and contemplation, marking the beginning of the new season of autumn and harvest, and were thus followed by days of feasting and celebration. Robert had spent the Ember Days with the court, eating meatless tarts and vegetables at various country homes in Essex as the queen completed her summer progress. There was no grand reception at Kenilworth this year; instead, Robert had spent much of the summer at Buxton, in Derbyshire, taking the waters for a swelling in his leg. This time away at Buxton was also an opportunity to reassess his standing. The Kenilworth celebrations, as grand as they had been, had not led to a significant change in his status, and the anxieties he had expressed to Douglass around the continuation of his house had only increased. The bastard son of Robert and Douglass was toddling around the households of Robert's friends and kin, but without a legitimate child to follow him Robert's achievements were nothing. And he knew only too well how rapidly and unexpectedly it could all come crashing down around him, as it had for his father and grandfather. The world was watching him. As he had written to his friend Thomas Wood, a Puritan who had previously served under Ambrose at Le Havre, 'I stand on top of the hill, where I know the smallest slip seemeth a fall.'[61] Any sin or fault Robert exhibited was scrutinized, judged and condemned. He had to walk very carefully indeed.

His sacrifices – years of his life and the possibility of an heir – which he had laid at the queen's feet were joined there by those of his family – Mary's illness, Henry's absences in Ireland, Ambrose's battle injury – and seemed to have been ignored. The queen was growing ever closer to a marriage with the duc d'Anjou, the slightly less attractive younger brother of King Henry III, who had succeeded Charles IX in 1574. Robert and his family were vehemently against such a marriage, not least because matters for Protestants in France had not improved much since the St Bartholomew's Day Massacre, when Robert's nephew had first cultivated his fierce aversion to all the sons of that Catholic Jezebel, Catherine de Medici.

Robert had rejected his lover Douglass, even when she had borne him a son but, as he carved into the glass window at Buxton, '*tempora mutantur et nos mutamur in illis*' – 'the times are changing and we are changing with them' – and '*ogni cosa col tempo*' – 'everything in its time'.[62] The Italian writer Niccolò Machiavelli had warned against those who did not change with the time and seize their occasion. Such men were lost to history, as the Dudley name would be. In order to avoid such a fate, Robert Dudley needed a legitimate son. He needed to marry.

Fortune had provided an opportunity in the person of Lettice

Devereux. Rumours of their flirtation had pestered Lettice and Robert for decades, especially when her husband, Walter Devereux, Earl of Essex, was away in Ireland as he so often was. He had left again in July 1576, joined by Sir Henry Sidney, who had taken his commission to return to Ireland in the weeks following the Kenilworth celebrations. They had not been there long, however, when Walter fell ill.[63] Having dined in his home in Ireland one evening at the end of August, Walter was suddenly seized by intense digestive pain, and he rushed to the privy to expel the contents of his bowels. Walter had enough enemies to suspect he may have been poisoned. Two years before, while wrangling with the Irish lords, he had invited Sir Brian MacPhelim O'Neill, Lord of Clandeboye, to a feast in Belfast. The Irish lord, trusting Walter's invitation and being generally accommodating to the English Crown, brought his wife, brother and an entourage of some two hundred attendants with him for what appeared to be a convivial diplomatic exchange. Midway through the gathering, however, Walter's men had attacked, massacring the men, women and children of MacPhelim's train, and capturing both the lord and his wife, who were executed.[64] If someone had poisoned Walter Devereux, it might not have been much of a shock.

Weeks after Walter had first fallen ill, he still had not recovered, growing weak from dozens of bowel movements a day, bloody and black. Growing desperate, Walter ingested unicorn horn, which promptly caused him to vomit, but did not solve the problem of his intense, tormenting stomach pains. By the end of September, less than a month after he had first felt the painful pangs in his bowels, he had expired in shit and blood, a frail shadow of the man he had been just four weeks before. Immediately, Henry Sidney called for a post-mortem, aware of the suspicions of poisoning. He himself had declared that there was no evidence to support these claims.

Walter Devereux's death had been precisely two years less a day before Lettice's wedding to Robert Dudley. It was not long after she had become a widow that Lettice began spending time with Robert at Kenilworth, in the company of her eldest daughter, Penelope, and Robert's elder brother, Ambrose, but with plenty of opportunity for the two to spend time alone, walking the gardens or praying together in the chapel. While there, she also hunted, sending Kenilworth bucks to friends, a privilege that was usually the purview of the lady of the manor.

She knew her time with her daughters, Penelope and Dorothy, both on the cusp of womanhood, would be brief. Their father's will had laid out that the girls would be sent to the household of Katherine and Henry Hastings, the Countess and Earl of Huntingdon, to be prepared for their entry to court. Though a sadness, this only brought Lettice closer into the Dudley circle, as Katherine Hastings was Robert's younger sister, also childless. Lettice's eldest son, Robert, had already become the ward of William Cecil, Lord Burghley, erstwhile Dudley secretary.

Now, Lettice was carrying another child, to be born nearly two decades after her first. Childbirth, never safe, was even more a danger as she was approaching the age of forty. That being said, she would be made as comfortable as possible between now and her delivery. Lettice was to spend her confinement, labour and delivery at Leicester House, a towering building overlooking the London Thames. Located between the Strand and the river, the house was bordered by the Middle Temple, one of the Inns of Court. Once one of the Templar's properties, and then owned by the Bishops of Exeter, the house had been briefly in the hands of Thomas Howard, Duke of Norfolk, in 1548 before being acquired by William Paget, ally of the Duke of Somerset, whose Somerset House was nearby.[65] Leicester had purchased the building in 1570 from William's son, Thomas, whose Catholic leanings did not make him one of the fashionable Strand set, and quickly renamed it from Paget Place to Leicester House.

On the Strand side, Leicester House had been broken up into smaller tenements, interrupted only by the small gatehouse to the property from the street. Lettice and Robert thus lived within spitting – and smelling – distance of London's less well-heeled residents.[66] There were few reasons to exit the building this way, however; it was far more pleasant to wander through the river-side quadrangle gardens and alight a waiting barge. The centrality of Leicester House also made it a locus of artistic display and exchange. Robert Dudley amassed one of the largest picture collections in the country, displayed in the gallery, hall and chamber of Leicester House.[67] It had also become a meeting ground for young courtly poets, Robert's nephew Philip included. There, Philip conversed with friends Edmund Spenser and Edward Dyer about the rudiments of poetry and art, and scratched out his reflections and creations. Its proximity to Westminster, just a quarter of an hour by boat, made it an ideal London home for the court-bound Robert, though he might not have expected, when he purchased it a decade before, to make it a home for a pregnant wife.

Lettice had been avoiding London in the time since the news of her marriage to Robert had become public. Their secret wedding at Robert's home at Wanstead had only been sprung upon Robert's chaplain the day before and was attended by a very few: the couple, Robert's brother, Lettice's father and brother, and some select friends. This secrecy was essential. The queen had always carefully guarded her Lord Robert, as his rejection of marriage to Douglass Sheffield had shown. Lettice and Robert risked her fearsome and fatal wrath should she find out. Catherine Grey, despite her appeals to Robert for help, had given birth in the Tower of London and died in confinement at only twenty-seven. Lettice was no Catherine Grey, she was not a direct – legitimate – descendant of royal blood, but she was the queen's cousin on the Boleyn side, and it was difficult to deny that she might carry some illegitimate blood of Henry VIII as well. With dark Boleyn eyes and red hair, she could easily be mistaken for the queen herself. It was almost as if she had been crafted by some devil to mock Elizabeth: a younger, prettier version of the queen, with the freedom to marry the man she loved and carry his child. It was imperative that they keep their marriage from Elizabeth.

This level of secrecy was not an easy task. Elizabeth and her court had arrived at Wanstead just two days after the wedding, and Robert busied himself with feasting her and the French ambassador, neither of whom were any the wiser that he was a newlywed. Robert and Lettice kept up the charade for almost a year, despite rumours and the betrayal of Thomas Radclyffe, the Earl of Sussex. Related by blood to Lettice – he was a direct cousin of Mary Boleyn, Lettice's grandmother – and by marriage to Robert – his wife was Henry Sidney's sister – he might have been an ally to their cause, but had long ago counted

Robert as an enemy. Robert had worked against his interests as Lord Lieutenant of Ireland in the early years of Elizabeth's reign, causing him to be recalled in failing health. Radclyffe had, on his return, wholeheartedly backed Elizabeth's marriage to Archduke Charles of Austria, at a time when Robert was still considered a leading candidate for her hand. This had come to naught, but now, twenty years later, he had received information that could serve a cold revenge. Certainly, his wife was in a position to have heard the rumours, and even confirm them, but such close connections were not necessary. Frankly, the queen may have been the only person at court unaware that the man who presented her with love knots that New Year was already married to her attractive cousin.

Whereas Robert had let the queen know directly of the marriage between Catherine Grey and Edward Seymour, Radclyffe instead whispered his clandestine knowledge into the ears of the person who could do the most damage with it: the French ambassador. The ambassador, in turn, dutifully communicated this to the envoy of the duc d'Anjou, Jean de Simier, who had quickly taken a dislike to the Earl of Leicester upon his arrival in January 1579, and for good reason. Robert and his family were not in support of his duc's suit.

Everyone, however, maintained a strategic and steely silence on the matter of Robert and Lettice's marriage. De Simier, too, knew it was best to wait until the opportune moment. This came on 17 July 1579. The queen was enjoying a trip down the Thames on her royal barge towards Greenwich Palace, joined by de Simier – to whom she'd taken an affectionate liking, dubbing him her 'Monkey' – a nickname similar to those of her 'eyes' – Robert Dudley – and 'lids' – Christopher Hatton.[68] As they floated along, a shot rang out from the shore. Panic broke loose. Quickly, moans and cries filled the air: someone had been shot. At last, desperate eyes found the source of the screams. The bargeman had been hit and lay in a growing pool of blood. The queen, along with her favourites, was unscathed. But for whom had the shot been intended?

De Simier decided it had been him, and despite Robert's presence on the barge, was sure the earl had ordered his assassination. Wasting no time – striking before the queen had much time to recover her senses – de Simier fired his own long-carried bullet. He informed the queen that Robert Dudley was not only married, but had been for almost a year, and to Elizabeth's cousin. The queen reacted with all the fury that might be expected. Robert was banished from the court to Wanstead; Lettice left London not long after.

If this was the end of all of Robert's efforts and sacrifices, it was tragic indeed. For generations his family had sought to thrive and survive under England's monarchs. He was alive, and his family name might endure, but he was thrown dramatically from favour. He had traded all the labours of the past for a chance at his family's continuance, as well as some present contentment. But survival in mediocrity was not the Dudley way.

Robert and Lettice's gamble with fortune was rewarded. By Christmas 1580 she was showing all the signs of being pregnant and shortly after took up residence at Leicester House for her lying in. Robert, meanwhile, had finally been welcomed back to the court, though Lettice was not. Her presence in London may have irritated the queen, but there were still greater matters to attend to. Commissioners from the French court had arrived on behalf of the duc d'Anjou to arrange a marriage.[69]

On 27 April, as Lettice entered the final phases of her pregnancy, her husband hosted the commissioners for dinner at Leicester House.[70] The queen, though welcoming the commissioners and allowing them to come and speak to her, remained in the banqueting pavilion outside in the elaborate garden, overlooking the water of the Thames. She did not set foot in the same house as the pregnant Lettice. Of course, she did not have to; the queen's presence was everywhere in Lettice's new home. Robert had even commissioned matching alabaster busts of himself and his mistress to be displayed at Leicester House, though these disappeared not long after Lettice's arrival. The portrait of Douglass Sheffield may have also brought mixed feelings, but it survived Lettice.[71] Rather than a fond remembrance of a past love, perhaps for her husband it served instead as a reminder of a near miss, as did the map showing the murder of Lord Darnley, which also hung in Leicester House.[72]

Regardless of the past loves and courtships (and never mind his first wife, whose presence was not obvious at Leicester House), it was Lettice who was now the lady of the house and the Countess of Leicester. She was carrying Robert Dudley's child, a son they would name for his illustrious father, to be heir to his father's growing holdings and the Dudley name. Robert would not be the ruin of his house, as he so feared. As Lettice Dudley rested her hand on her growing stomach, she and her husband could feel a swell of hope for the future of their family.

18

Ready to take on my journey

Robert Dudley, Earl of Leicester, left Hampton Court in mid-October 1584 under a cloud of scandal and despair that would darken even the sunniest autumn day. He rode through Kingston and north to Syon, where coaches provided by his friend Sir Christopher Hatton waited to carry him west.[1] Robert had departed from Hampton Court following meetings with Sir Francis Walsingham and William Cecil, Lord Burghley, agreeing to drastic steps to muster support for their queen. Dark times called for desperate measures.

The summer had brought shock and heartache, and Robert and the court were still trying to get their collective footing. At the beginning of June, the duc d'Anjou had died suddenly, it seemed of malaria. His death meant that the Protestant Henry of Navarre, whose wedding had precipitated the St Bartholomew's Day Massacre, was now the heir to the French throne. Though good news, perhaps, in the long term for Europe's Protestants, this had significantly raised the stakes in the ongoing wars over the soul of Christendom. A few weeks later saw another troubling death: the assassination of William the Silent, Duke of Orange, shot at close range in his own home after dinner. Leader of the Protestant Dutch uprising against Catholic Habsburg control and persecution, he had become a hero to European Protestants. The outcry at his death had resonated across Europe, and was not sated by the tortuous death of his murderer, who had his hand burned off, his flesh torn off with pincers, his bowels ripped from his body, and his heart thrown in his face.[2]

The news reached England quickly, and the immediate concern was for the threat that Spain now presented, and how such an assassination could embolden Catholic subjects across the continent. This was driven home for many by the execution of Francis Throckmorton, a cousin of one of Elizabeth's ladies-in-waiting. Throckmorton had plotted with the Spanish ambassador to release Mary, Queen of Scots, soon to enter her second decade of English imprisonment, and put her on the throne in place of Elizabeth. Though he had been imprisoned the previous autumn, his execution on the heels of the deaths of the duc d'Anjou and Orange reminded England's defenders how fragile Elizabeth's regime really was.

Though Robert was at the centre of such events, they were soon overshadowed by even greater tragedy much closer to home. On 19 July, while the court at Richmond was still reeling from the shocks of the past few weeks, Robert received a letter. His young son, just three years old, had died at Wanstead. Robert left the court and rushed to Wanstead to be at his grieving wife's side. Not long ago the noble imp, as they affectionately called him, had been running amok in Leicester House, destroying priceless paintings as he left hapless nurses in his wake.[3] And now he was gone. Lettice, unsurprisingly, had taken the death of her son hard, as he did. They would be unable to have another. The condolences from those like George Talbot, Earl of Shrewsbury, that 'God will increase you with many good children, which I wish with all my heart' was cold comfort indeed.[4] 'I do thank you for the care you take for the loss of my young son,' Robert replied, 'which was indeed, my good Lord, great to me for that I have no more and unlikely to have, my growing old.'[5] The dream of a legitimate heir of his own body would be buried along with the noble imp.

He had returned to court after a few weeks spent with his wife. His return, however, was met with a further twisting of the knife. 'This Bearwhelp,' the text circulating the court read, 'turneth all to his own commodity, and for greediness thereof will overturn all if he be not stopped or muzzled in time.'[6] Passed between hands in manuscript as well as clandestine printed copies smuggled into England from France, the book which had acquired the name *Leicester's Commonwealth* was on everyone's lips.[7] Never mind the scurrilous gossip that seeped from its pages about Robert himself – that he had murdered, among others, his first wife and both Lettice's and Douglass's husbands, not to mention killed Sir Nicholas Throckmorton with a salad – the text took aim at his entire family. 'I would not doubt,' its author proclaimed, 'but that if these two his ancestors,' his father and grandfather, 'were found worthy to lose their heads for treason, this man would not be found unworthy to make the third in kindred, whose treacheries do far surpass them both.'[8]

What was worse, in maligning Robert, they had attacked his recently deceased son, suggesting that Robert had been married to Douglass Sheffield, and thus 'my young Lord of Denbigh' was a bastard.[9] 'His young son by the widow of Essex', the author wrote, has 'such a strange calamity of the falling sickness in his infancy as may well be a witness of the parents' sin & wickedness'.[10] Quoting Scripture, the text noted, 'The children of adulterers shall be consumed, and the seed of a wicked bed shall be rooted out, saith God.'[11] Without knowing the child's sad fate, the author had condemned him to death for his parents' wickedness.

Censure from the queen and Council was fierce and decisive. Anyone who did not immediately return their copy, and was caught with one, would face indefinite imprisonment.[12] Interrogations would soon begin of those caught passing on the book or its content. This did not stop its circulation, however, and only gave the suggestion that Robert held the queen 'in the compass of his furious paws' more credence.[13]

On the morning of Monday, 19 October, Robert had met with his fellow Privy Councillors, ratifying a document they called 'the Instrument of Association'. All signatories, beginning with the Council and to be gathered from English subjects far and wide, promised not only to serve, obey and defend the queen, but 'with our whole powers, bodies, lives, lands, and goods, and with our children and servants' to also 'pursue and offend, as well by force of arms as by all other means of revenge, all manner of persons, of whatsoever state they shall be, and their abettors, that shall attempt any act, or counsel or consent to any thing that shall tend to the harm of Her Majesty's royal person; and will never desist from all manner of forcible pursuit against such persons, to the utter extermination of them, their counsellors, aiders and abettors.'[14] They also vowed 'to prosecute such person or persons to death' and 'to act the utmost revenge upon them, that by any means we or any of us can devise or do, or cause to be devised or done for their utter overthrow and extirpation.' Those who broke with the bond, were to be prosecuted by those remaining as 'public enemies to the Queen, and to our native country'. This was the business that Robert saw to before leaving Hampton Court, and he carried it with him on his journey.

He was keen to set off. The next day his son would be interred in St Mary's Church in Warwick, and he sought consolation and distraction. From Colbrook, where Hatton's coaches left him, he continued west to Henley, giving two shillings to the poor and paying for the lodging of his men. He himself could find welcome accommodation at Henley Manor, held by his brother-in-law, Henry Hastings, the Earl of Huntingdon.[15] The next morning, the day of his son's interment, he headed north and west for Oxford via Dorchester, passing pennies to the poor along the way. At last, by evening, he arrived at Woodstock, eight miles north-west of Oxford. A fairly minor Oxfordshire town, Woodstock nevertheless boasted a royal palace, used frequently by the great monarchs of the past, including Henry II and Richard the Lionheart. Both Henry VII and Henry VIII had enjoyed hunting there, instituting improvements and extensions costing thousands of pounds and making the royal lodgings the largest outside of London.[16] Robert's queen had been imprisoned at Woodstock thirty years before, following the rebellion against her sister, which had also resulted in the execution of Robert's brother. According to the history compiled by the Protestant John Foxe and printed by the Dudley friend John Day, while at Woodstock Elizabeth had carved into the window, 'Much suspected by me, Nothing proved can be.'[17]

The manor was now officially in the possession of one of Robert's nephew's poet friends, Edward Dyer, though he had passed the keeping of it to Sir Henry Lee ten years before. Of an age with Robert, Lee had recently become queen's champion and master of the armoury, arranging the annual accession day tilts every November. Lee had also provided elaborate entertainments at Woodstock for the queen on her progresses. Robert's visit was not nearly so extravagant, though it was a pleasant stay, in the company of visitors from nearby Oxford. Two young students took time out of their studies to spend four days at

Woodstock. Thomas Clinton, sixteen, was grandson of the Earl of Lincoln, who had shared command of the queen's armies with Ambrose Dudley a decade before. He was joined by Robert's fifteen-year-old stepson, Walter Devereux. The company were entertained by musicians sent by Robert's cousin, Edmund Sutton, Baron Dudley. Son of the baron known as 'lord quondam', who had lost Dudley Castle to Robert's father, the relations between Edmund and Robert were far more cordial. Edmund had taken as his third wife Margaret Howard, Douglass Sheffield's sister, which had almost made the cousins brothers, and Elizabeth and her court had visited Dudley Castle not long after they had left Kenilworth in 1575.[18] Though Edmund had refused all offers in exchange for Dudley Castle, he did send Robert a piece of it: a chimneypiece for Kenilworth, which Robert may have remembered from his childhood.[19] Robert parted with twenty shillings to reward the musicians sent by Baron Dudley to Woodstock.

So it was that as his late son spent his first nights in his tomb at St Mary's Church thirty-five miles away, Robert at least had company and the consolation of music. The site of his son's interment had been carefully chosen, to demonstrate the Dudleys' link to their Beauchamp predecessors, the ancient earls of Warwick; a line that ended in the body of his young son. As the epitaph on the elaborate tomb read:

> Here resteth the body of the noble imp Robert Dudley, Baron of Denbigh, son of Robert Earl of Leicester, nephew and heir unto Ambrose Dudley Earl of Warwick, brethren, both sons of the most mighty Prince, John, late Duke of Northumberland, herein interred, a child of great parentage but far greater hope and towardness, taken from this transitory world unto everlasting life, in his tender age at Wanstead in Essex on Sunday, 19th of July, in the year of our Lord God 1584 … and in this place laid up among his noble ancestors, in assured hope of the general resurrection.

Robert remained only two days at Woodstock, enjoying the music and the hunt, before moving on to even more familiar ground. To the west lay Wychwood Forest and Langley, which had been held by Robert's father. In his will, he had given the two properties to his daughter-in-law Anne, the wife of his eldest son, John. Anne had remained Countess of Warwick after John's death, marrying Sir Edward Unton, with whom she had seven children. Unfortunately, in recent years Anne had experienced bouts of madness, which by 1582 had proven too much. She had been declared a lunatic, and her interests in Langley and Wychwood passed to Robert. Wychwood Forest offered excellent hunting, and nearby Langley was ideally suited to accommodate royalty and noblemen chasing deer as they rode through Oxfordshire.[20] The medieval manor had come into the hands of the Crown a century before, and Henry VII had turned it into a royal hunting lodge, carving his initials and roses into the stonework. With a two-storey hall, punctuated by bay windows, and royal accommodations, Robert and his men could dine well and enjoy both the quiet and the thrill of the nearby forest.[21]

The next day Robert, travelling south and east, at last arrived at his ultimate destination, another of his Oxfordshire manor houses: Witney. Witney itself was a small market town, known for its woollen blankets, perched on the River Windrush. Witney manor had long been held by the bishops of Winchester, but under Edward VI, it was given instead to Robert's uncle Andrew, who had died in the first year of Elizabeth's reign. Robert had acquired the lease from the queen the year before. Entering from the north through the gatehouse and portcullis, Robert traversed the moat and passed under the curtain wall of Witney. He entered a small courtyard block, edged by farm buildings and stables, the manor house itself before him. The rectangular solar tower and range, built in the twelfth century, had been enlarged to include a chapel, a raised terrace and a garderobe block.[22] It was a comfortable house, though lacking the great medieval hall of Langley.

At Witney, Robert was met by his son. Now ten years old, Robert's illegitimate son with Douglass Sheffield was becoming a young man and would soon be ready for an Oxford education. Robert had taken great care with his son's education and upbringing, entrusting the boy to learned men. While at Witney he paid £5 to Dr John Delabere, formerly of Christ Church College Oxford, who had been elected by the scholars of Gloucester Hall College as Principal three years before.[23] This election had almost certainly been helped by the nomination of

Robert Dudley, Earl of Leicester, who had been Chancellor of the University of Oxford for the past two decades. Robert also paid £3 to the younger Robert's schoolmaster, who would have been expected to teach the young boy everything from Latin to Scripture, rhetoric to mathematics.

They feasted on the does Robert had hunted at Woodstock and were entertained by the singers of the town. Robert was only at Witney one night, however, and not all of it could be spent indulging his young son. In particular, it was incumbent upon him to begin circulating the Bond of Association for those across England to sign. The entire body politic would be engaged to defend its head, and any signatories who later showed evidence of sedition – or abetting sedition – would by force of the Bond be thoroughly eradicated. Robert took leave of his son, passing on five shillings that might go towards the cost of schoolbooks or new clothes for the growing boy, and allocating four times that for the poor of the town. He had already spent five days from Hampton Court – a long time away from a possessive mistress and a court in crisis.

The return journey was quicker. Instead of travelling north through Woodstock and Oxford again, Robert took a more direct route, via Abingdon and very close to Cumnor, where Amy Dudley had died. Twenty shillings were given to the poor at Abingdon, and money was paid out for the costs of his servants' meals as they passed through the town before him, perhaps dining at the same inn that Blount had visited almost twenty-five years before. Robert had not been gone a week by the time he returned to Hampton Court and his queen. As much comfort as his namesake might bring him, bastard sons were not heirs. His heir would once again be his sister's child, the poet. Philip would have to be ready to take on the mantle of the House of Dudley, 'tribe of traitors' though it may be.[24]

*

'I am a Dudley in blood,' Philip Sidney had written with speed and passion; 'I say, that my chiefest honour is to be a Dudley.'[25] And yet, as he stood aboard the nearly five-hundred-ton galleon, smelling the salt air and staring west towards the endless horizon of the sea, his back was turned to his familial duties, including his heavily pregnant

345

wife. The *Elizabeth Bonaventura* was bound for the West Indies, and Philip had ignored missives from his family and the court demanding he not accompany it.[26] He was determined, it appeared, to adventure into the unknown, to a new world, and leave the squabbles of the old one behind.

Leicester's Commonwealth had been an attack on Philip as well, especially now that he was his uncle's heir once again. 'Our house,' he wrote, 'received such an overthrow, and hath none else in England done; so I will not seek to wash away that dishonour with other honourable tears.' Sidney's primary concern was not with the slanders made against his uncle, but with the suggestion that the House of Dudley was not truly and anciently noble. What is intolerable, Philip wrote, is that the author should 'rake up the bones of the dead', by seeking to shame their common ancestors. This would be to cast a pall over Sidney's nobility as well, and though his uncle might live for decades more, eventually Sidney would stand as the defender of the House of Dudley.

Philip, married and about to become a father, was finally in a good position to take on that role. It had taken some time. Several matches had been proposed, and Philip himself had set eyes on a few of the court beauties, including Lettice's daughter with Walter Devereux, Penelope. There had been discussion of a marriage between the two at the death of Penelope's father, but given Devereux's debts, the offer had been rejected. Instead, four years later, Robert and Lettice had married Penelope to the young Robert, Lord Rich, elevating Penelope to the status of an unattainable and thus even more romantic subject to Philip. He had poured out his love for Penelope in a lengthy sonnet sequence he titled *Astrophil and Stella*, in which he was the lover of the star, Astrophil, and the star, Stella, was undoubtedly Lady Penelope Rich:

> Towards Aurora's Court a Nymph doth dwell,
> Rich in all beauties which man's eye can see:
> Beauties so far from reach of worlds, that we
> Abase her praise, saying she doth excel:
> Rich in the treasure of deserv'd renown,

Rich in the riches of a royal heart,
Rich in those gifts which give th'eternal crown;
Who though most rich in these and every part,
Which make the patents of true worldly bliss,
Hath no misfortune, but that Rich she is.

Instead of the elusive Penelope, the summer before little Denbigh's death Philip had been married to young Frances, the daughter of Francis Walsingham. Frances had grown somewhat since when Philip had seen her in Paris, hiding with her father from the horrors of the St Bartholomew's Day Massacre, though was still only fifteen at the time of their wedding. As he wrote the defence of his uncle, he also busied himself with his marital duties, ensuring there would be a further generation to come after him. By the spring of 1585, Frances Sidney was with child.

There was every reason to think that Philip would not be present for the arrival of this new heir. There was talk that he would accompany his uncle to the Low Countries, where the Dutch were in need of leadership in their revolt against the Catholic Spanish Habsburgs. By the end of August, however, this had come to naught. Elizabeth had refused Robert permission to lead forces into the Low Countries, apparently still simmering over his marriage to Lettice. Robert, away from the court and injured after a riding accident, was not near enough to the queen to charm her into changing her mind.

For the restless Philip, however, there was another option. For almost a decade, he had been entranced by the exploration of the new world. English ships had first landed in this new land a hundred years before, under the reign of Henry VII, but there had not been the resources available to do much more than make claims to ownership. Instead, the Spanish and the Portuguese had taken the lead in the colonization and exploitation of this continent of which neither Scripture nor the writings of the ancients had ever made mention. The Spanish had found a font of seemingly endless treasure and wealth in the new world, which had been put to use funding the further development of their fleets. If the English did not follow them into this profitable unknown, they risked being entirely overpowered in

Europe. Along with his friend Edward Dyer and the eccentric polymath Dr John Dee, once in the service of Philip's grandfather the Duke of Northumberland and now an adviser to the queen, Philip had supported English efforts to explore the new world and search for a passage to the wonders and wealth of the East. If he could not go to the Low Countries, perhaps his destiny lay in seizing the opportunity which had been presented by the tantalizing new world.

The *Elizabeth Bonaventura* could take him there. From the deck Philip could see the docks and ports of Plymouth, where he had arrived two weeks before, in the first days of September. On the south coast of Devonshire, across the haven from Cornwall, Plymouth had become a centre for the wool trade, as well as for exploration. The town had become famous five years before, when the first successful English circumnavigation of the globe had set off and landed at Plymouth. Commanded by Francis Drake, who – unlike the Spanish captain Ferdinand Magellan – had managed to return from his circumnavigation, the voyage had come at great human cost but brought home great wealth. Drake now commanded the *Elizabeth Bonaventura*, the ship on which Philip was poised to seek out his adventure. The two men had met some time before, sharing in parliamentary committees, and Philip could not help but be captivated by Drake's exciting life of adventure.

Whereas his ships were sleek and long, built for speed as well as power, Drake himself was short and broad, with impressive strength. His riches were beginning to make him even broader, but there was no denying the fierce passion of the man, outwardly evidenced in his fiery red hair and angry scars. At forty-five, Drake had been commanding ships for almost two decades, most of which had been spent slaving and raiding along the Spanish main. About ten years before, he had made the acquaintance of Philip's father-in-law, Francis Walsingham, who had supported his piracy efforts, alongside Philip's uncle Robert, Christopher Hatton and the queen herself. With this level of support, Drake had attempted his voyage around the world. After an abortive setting off from Plymouth, the five ships had sailed around the western coast of Africa and on to South America. Two ships had to be abandoned before crossing the Straits of Magellan at the southern tip of South America, a third was soon shipwrecked and a fourth forced to return to England. On the final ship, the *Golden Hinde*, Drake and his much-reduced crew continued their journey, raiding as they explored the western coast of America. Finally, they made the treacherous journey across the Pacific Ocean, through the lands of the east, around the southern tip of Africa, and at last to Plymouth once again. The entire trip had taken three years and the lives of some hundred and fifty men, but brought back countless riches, snatched from the hands of the Spanish.

Four years later, Drake was ready again to sail to the Spanish main and assault the ships he found there. Unlike his previous journey, which had involved only five ships and some two hundred men, Philip stood on a ship in the company of two dozen others, holding over two thousand men. His brother-in-law, Christopher Carleill, son of Francis Walsingham's first wife, commanded the military force and the explorer Martin Frobisher served as vice-admiral. Drake commanded the flagship, on which stood Philip. With some forty or fifty guns and room for over two hundred and fifty men, the *Elizabeth Bonaventura* had been purchased in 1567 for £2,230 and rebuilt in 1581 to make it more sleek and powerful.[27]

As the sun rose on 14 September, this massive fleet, the largest to sail from England in a century, was ready to set forth. Philip remained on the *Elizabeth Bonaventura* as anchors were weighed, sails unfurled and orders barked on each of the two dozen ships. Crowds had inevitably gathered on the shore to see this massive fleet embark. Lovers, parents and children waved goodbye and said quiet prayers, hoping that they would see their loved ones return. Heading south, they were bound for the Spanish coast. Drake's fleet would attack the Spanish ships carrying home treasure from the West Indies and steal it for the English Crown. If this attack was unsuccessful, he would go to the source itself, attacking the Spanish Indies. For Philip such a trip would bring action, adventure and the experience of a world few had ever seen.

Although the ships were taking him away from the court and his family, there was every reason to consider travel an essential part of his duty to Crown and country. Young noblemen such as he could bring back not just riches but information to their monarch, who could not risk herself by going abroad. This would be an extension of the education he had embarked upon when he had arrived in Paris twenty years before, and the next step in his service to his queen. His father-in-law and uncle might gripe, but his hand had been forced by the queen's reticence to let him serve in the Low Countries.

As the ships departed, however, a messenger arrived, passing on a message to be delivered to Philip. It contained an offer and a reminder. In Philip's absence, his uncle had at last arrived back at court, and convinced the queen to let him lead forces into the Low Countries, with his nephew at his side. Of course, in order to join him, Philip would have to disembark the ship immediately. This was tempting, but it was the reminder the message contained of Philip's duty of obedience which moved him. He was being commanded, and he ought to obey.

An hour or so after setting sail, as England had begun to disappear into the distance, Philip and his company left the *Elizabeth Bonaventura* and returned to English soil. Philip would profess to his queen that he had never intended to join Drake's voyage, and all would be forgiven. His uncle, however, would remember his impetuosity as they made plans for their expedition to the Low Countries.

*

It was New Year's Day in The Hague. Or rather, it was 10 January in The Hague, but New Year's Day to the Englishmen there under the command of Robert Dudley, Earl of Leicester. The United Provinces of the Netherlands had switched to the new version of the calendar introduced by Pope Gregory XIII, placing them ten days ahead of England, which had resisted such 'Romish computation'. This, however, was not the only factor making Dudley and his men feel especially distanced from their homeland, only some hundred and fifty miles away across the North Sea.

Robert and his fleet had arrived a month before in the Low Countries, on the north-western coast of Europe between France and the Holy Roman Empire. Five years before, after almost twenty years of revolt, these Protestant territories had thrown off Catholic Spanish Habsburg control, declaring themselves independent United Provinces.

With the assassination of William of Orange, however, they had lost a significant leader. The Spanish Governor General, Alexander Farnese, Duke of Parma, was gaining ground, and the Provinces needed aid. Robert Dudley, as Lieutenant General of the English forces, was there to provide it.

Robert had not set foot on the continent in almost thirty years. Then he had been a youth, battling to restore his family name with his brothers and fighting alongside the Spanish, not against them. He had lost young Harry on that trip. Since then, Ambrose had carried the family's military honour; Robert had merely replicated it in tournaments, and he was too old for even that now. Past the age of fifty and in need of spectacles to help his failing eyes, Robert was not the young gallant knight he had once been.[28]

Robert had set off on 8 December with a fleet of fifty vessels and some three thousand soldiers. In his company were his twenty-one-year-old stepson, Robert Devereux, Earl of Essex, and his sixteen-year-old nephew, Thomas Sidney. Thomas's elder brothers, Philip and Robert, had already arrived in the Low Countries almost a month before. Although well wined and dined, both of Robert's nephews had been desperate for their uncle to arrive. Philip had disembarked his ship only to have to walk three miles through freezing cold November mud. 'Your Lordship's coming', he wrote to his uncle four days later, 'is here longed for as Messiah's is for the Jews.'[29] Likewise, his younger brother a week later reiterated that Dutch captains he encountered were at the end of their ropes, and only his uncle's arrival could remedy the situation: 'They all swear they will rather kill themselves than continue their service to the States. And I think nothing keeps them from mutining but the expectation of your Lordship's coming.'[30] It was hard to believe that Philip had been forced to miss the christening of his own daughter, named Elizabeth for her godmother the queen, for this.

The mission had almost not happened at all. It had taken years of convincing Elizabeth – naturally averse to war and the expenses that came with it – to aid their fellow Protestants in the Low Countries. By the end of September, with Robert's return to court and Philip's retrieval from Drake's ship, she had at last seemed persuaded. However, she had continued to fluctuate through September and October, even as Robert made plans and assembled men. In the end, it had been December by the time Robert left Leicester House and proceeded across the North Sea.

It had not been an easy passage and they were lucky to have made it at all. They had travelled by land from Wanstead to Colchester and then Maningtree by land, and from there travelled by boat along the River Stour to Harwich, positioned on the coast of the North Sea.[31] Robert, having been long delayed, was anxious that they take the opportunity of the favourable wind and weather, and wrote to the Admiral of the Fleet, Stephen Burrough, demanding that they set sail the next day for the Low Countries. Having dined in Harwich, Robert boarded the ship the *Amity* and spent the night there, ready to set sail, even as the others slept in secure comfort on land. He was equally determined to arrive into Brill,[32] just south of The Hague, rather than Flushing,[33] where Philip was, some eighty miles south along the coast. Warned by the captains that this was too dangerous a change, Robert insisted, but then at last relented, and so they departed on the afternoon of 9 December, sailing overnight and arriving at Flushing the next morning.

Robert had been right to seize the occasion in this instance. It was an especially bad season in the North Seas and further delays might have meant weeks, perhaps even months of waiting. As it was, Robert arrived into Flushing only a little behind schedule. Making a tour of the towns of the Low Countries, Robert had been impressed at their shows of appreciation and loyalty to him, and through him to Queen Elizabeth. He had arrived at The Hague two days after the English celebrated Christmas. The Hague was a nominal seat of government but, without city walls, a relatively indefensible city. For Robert's arrival, the citizens of The Hague had decorated the streets with ragged staff emblems, which hung like icicles from towering arches lit with torches, and staged ten elaborate pageants, including one in which Robert was compared to King Arthur.[34]

After the celebrations, Robert had had a few days to himself. The States General of the United Provinces, the governing body of the Netherlands made up of representatives from the various provinces, was meeting, and he expected them to finish their consultations on (his) New Year's Day. The States General had initially been set up as a means by which Spain governed and controlled its territories in the Low Countries but, after the rebellion of the Northern provinces, had since become a mechanism for independent rule, replacing Philip II as the absolute authority in the region. No important decisions could be taken without the unanimous approval of the seven provincial states represented in the States General, allowing each province to remain sovereign.

It had been a cold and icy few days and Robert had given twelve pennies to a boy who slipped on ice beneath his window.[35] While he waited for the States General to come to its decision, he took the opportunity to write once again to his contacts in England, William Cecil, Lord Burghley, and Sir Francis Walsingham. Despite having been on the continent nearly a month, he'd not had a word from them since before he left and was anxious to hear how the queen was taking the news he passed on. Surely they had some response to the many letters he had been writing? As New Year's Day dawned, still there was no letter from England.

The entourage from the States General arrived in the morning, as the chill was still fresh on the windows and before Robert was even fully ready to receive them.[36] Hearing word that they awaited him in his great chamber, Robert rushed to meet them. Entering the great chamber, he was greeted by a larger entourage than he might have expected, complete with a herald and trumpeters. Upon his arrival, the chancellor of Gelderland, Elbert de Leeuw, known as Dr Elbertus Leoninus, stepped forward. In his mid-sixties and a professor of canon law, Dr Leoninus did not lack for words. He began a grand oration in praise of the queen. Perhaps noting a small sign of his confusion or boredom evidenced on his face, one of Robert's men standing nearby whispered in his ear: the group had brought a herald and trumpeters with them for a reason; they intended to offer Robert the role of absolute Governor of the United Provinces.

Immediately, Robert stopped the chancellor mid-flow. 'I have heard,' Robert told him, 'that you have some matter rather to deal more privately in, than so openly,' and he invited them to join him in his private chamber instead.

At this, the chancellor turned to the assembly and said in French, 'You hear my lord desires us to withdraw with him into his chamber', and they followed him into the smaller, more private room. This bought Robert some time, as well as taking them out of the more public setting. Hurriedly, he summoned a few of his company to join them.

Once settled in his bedchamber, the chancellor started up again, pontificating on the queen's goodness, the love of the country for her, the trust they had in her above all others in the world, the necessity they had for safety, and other such diplomatic niceties. At last, reaching his point, he explained that since the queen could not take the sovereignty on herself, someone else must be chosen. Given that the queen had put Robert in her trust in the Low Countries and given his many good qualities – which the chancellor proceeded to list at length – they now turned to him.

'We do not know any person,' the chancellor at last drew to his point, 'whom we could desire so much to take this office in hand as your lordship, and, therefore, with one whole consent we do beseech your lord, even for the love her majesty bears us, and for the help of so afflicted a country, that was ever a faithful friend to the Crown of England, your lordship would take the place and name of absolute governor, and general of all our forces and soldiers, with our whole revenues, taxes, compositions, and all manner of benefits that we have, or may have, to be put freely and absolutely into your lord's hands, disposition and order.'

When the oration was at last finished, Robert responded, the ambassador William Davison translating into French as he spoke: 'As this is a matter unlooked for,' he began, 'being further than had passed in the contract with her most excellent majesty heretofore, I am presently very far unprovided to give you answer to this matter. Albeit,' he continued, 'in her majesty's behalf, greatly to thank you for your earnest goodwills and great affection born to her majesty.' He thanked them for himself as well, 'that you conceive so well of me, being but a stranger to you, that you would hazard so great a matter upon me, as all their state, both well and ill doing, should depend thereupon.' He, however, needed more time to consider their offer. Having heard this diplomatic answer, the company departed, not failing to reiterate their request earnestly as they went.

It was not lost on Robert what was being offered. As 'absolute governor', he might rule on behalf of the queen, but he would be taking up sovereignty himself, essentially as a prince of Europe. The Dutch had offered a sovereign position previously both to King Henry III of France and Queen Elizabeth, who had both refused. Now they were offering something similar to Robert Dudley. Robert had not been charged with taking up this role; he was there to lead the troops. On the other hand, no one had expressly instructed him not to.

It was widely acknowledged that the death of William of Orange had left a gaping hole in the leadership of the Netherlands, which left them open to Spanish advances. What was worse, Elizabeth had had to be pressured into intervening in the Dutch affair at all, and there were concerns that she would back out or conclude a peace with Spain. If Robert refused, he could jeopardize the Dutch revolt and all the efforts that the English had already poured into supporting it. He would also lose the offer of payments that the Dutch were promising to make to him; money he desperately needed in the absence of financial support from England. If he agreed, however, Elizabeth was sure to see it as an act of contempt and defiance, and a dangerous one at that.

Less than a fortnight later Robert Dudley made his decision. He had left The Hague two days after New Year's, travelling twelve miles up the coast to Leiden, a town known for its weaving and publishing industries. He was joined by his stepson, the Earl of Essex, now twenty, as well as his brother-in-law through the Countess of Warwick, William Russell. Philip he left in The Hague with Davison to press forward with the negotiations. Robert spent the days gambling with his younger relations and enjoying the entertainments provided by his players, especially the clownish antics of one William Kemp. After a week in Leiden, he was resolved.

Mustering some of his forces, Robert sent a letter to his distant kinsman and comptroller of his household, Thomas Dudley, notifying him that he planned to send William Davison to London, to explain to the queen and the court why he had made the choice that he did, difficult as it was.[37] He called for a day of fasting on 12 January through three of the seven provinces as a demonstration of piety.[38] Two days later, he wrote his letters to London, fully outlining his choice. It had been over a month since he had a single word of guidance from England. He was alone.

'Thus it standeth presently,' he told Cecil, 'as either all must be hazarded and lost, or else I must take it, which, as far as I can see, and all here with me, as the case enforceth it, must needs be best for her majesties service every way.'[39] In order to serve the queen's interests, he had resolved that he must accept the States General's offer. He could not let this advantage slip past; it would not be available again.[40]

By the end of the month, his excellency Robert Dudley, Earl of Leicester and absolute governor of the United Provinces of the Netherlands, was seated beneath his cloth of state, receiving oaths from his councillors, like any prince of Europe.[41] It remained to be seen, however, how those other princes of Europe would react.

*

'If I were you,' Ambrose told his younger brother, 'I would go to the furthest part of Christendom rather than ever come into England again.'[42] It was the third Sunday of Lent in England, but Robert could not be expected to receive the letter Ambrose wrote for weeks, if not months. Robert had left for the Low Countries three months before, and neither Ambrose nor Robert's friends at court had heard much from him since. The passage between the Low Countries and England had been so bad that messengers had been held up for well over a month; at the end of December, William Cecil, Lord Burghley, had received the letters that Robert had written him in the middle of November. What was worse, it was clear none of their letters were getting to him either. Cecil had responded to those letters soon after receiving them the day after Christmas, entrusting them to his son, Thomas, who was travelling to the Low Countries to take up a position in Brill. Three weeks later and his son still hadn't left, however, unable to cross the stormy seas.

It was the end of January before anyone could get a clear picture of what was going on in the Netherlands. When news broke, one hearer in particular was incensed to her core. 'Our mistress's extreme rage doth increase rather than in any way diminish,' Ambrose warned his brother, more than a month after Elizabeth had first heard of Robert's new title, 'and giveth out great threatening words against you, therefore,' he advised him, 'make the best assurance you can for yourself, and trust not her oath, for that her malice is great and unquenchable.' Robert should put his trust in God, 'and let this be a great comfort to you, and so it is likewise to myself and all your assured friends, and that is, you were never so honoured and loved in your life amongst all good people as you are at this day.' Cold comfort that was, however, when Ambrose's overriding advice was to quit England entirely and flee to the furthest corners of Christendom.

'I pray you,' Ambrose ended, 'make me no such stranger as you have done,' Ambrose too felt he had not been the recipient of sufficient correspondence, 'but deal frankly with me, for that that toucheth you toucheth me likewise.'[43] The two brothers had maintained a deep, loving and profitable relationship over the decades, forged at least in part by virtue of being the last two survivors.[44] Had he been well enough to travel, Ambrose would undoubtedly have been with his brother.[45] As it was, however, all he could do was try to advise him from afar, knowing that by the time the letter reached him, it would probably be too late.

Ambrose was not the only one frantically writing warnings to Robert, while staring anxiously across the storm-wracked sea. William Cecil, Lord Burghley, wrote that Sunday in Lent as well, having received some six or more belated letters from Robert, ranging across all of February. Cecil had been one of the first to hear the news and write to the earl in the Low Countries. Though they had once been rivals, Cecil had promised Robert before he embarked that he would protect Robert's honour and reputation while he was away as if he were a Dudley himself.[46] This had not been easy. Cecil had been afflicted with gout and other illnesses that had kept him in his chamber. Nevertheless, he, alongside Francis Walsingham and Christopher Hatton, had fought for Robert against the unabating anger of the queen. Ambrose had informed his brother rightly about his friends at court; however, it did little good.

Upon hearing the news, Elizabeth had dispatched firm instructions to force Robert to publicly renounce the title and have his powers revoked, to be carried out by Sir Thomas Heneage. This was a particularly cutting choice, as the queen had flirted with Heneage twenty years before, in the years following the death of Robert's first wife. Heneage carried a devastating letter from the woman Robert might have once thought to marry. 'How contemptuously we conceive ourself to be used by you,' she began, 'you shall by this bearer understand. We could never have imagined, had we not seen it fall out in experience,' she went on, 'that a man raised up by ourself, and extraordinarily favoured by us above any other subject of this land, would have in so contemptible a sort broken our commandment.'[47] Robert was to do everything Heneage instructed, or else face dire consequences: 'fail you not,' she concluded, 'as you will answer the contrary at your uttermost peril.' No member of the House of Dudley would have to ask precisely what she might mean by that.

Heneage and his letter had been dispatched in the middle of February, just as William Davison arrived in London. Davison had not left The Hague until the beginning of the month, three weeks after Robert had first proposed sending him. Travelling to Brill, he had been further held up almost a week by the fierce winds and weather. Davison too carried letters and instructions, sent to plead his lord's case. This mission was cursed from the start, however; perhaps, as Walsingham suggested to Davison on the day he arrived at Greenwich, due to his various delays.[48] Walsingham brought Davison up to speed on the situation: how the queen had taken Robert's decision to accept the governance of the United Provinces so badly that she had decided to send Heneage to demand he give it up, and that both Philip Sidney and Davison himself had been held as principal persuaders of the plan. Davison was amazed and entirely taken aback. He had not predicted that there would be so little understanding of the reasons why the Earl of Leicester had taken the proffered post. Walsingham, hearing him out, went up to the queen, along with Sir Christopher Hatton. After a time, Davison was fetched to join them. The queen was in her withdrawing chamber along the Thames side of the palace at Greenwich. She wasted no time in attacking the Earl of Leicester for accepting the role, not only without warrant but also against – she was at pains to insist – her express commandment. This was, she stressed, a thing done in contempt of her, as if her consent were worth nothing. She was no less upset at Davison himself, for having not opposed the earl's decision.

'I humbly beseech your majesty,' Davison replied, 'first to retain that gracious opinion of my poor duty as to think, that no particular respect whatsoever could carry me to deal otherwise with your majesty than becomes an honest and dutiful servant. It would please your majesty,' he continued, 'to lend me a patient and favourable ear, which obtained, I doubt not but your highness would conceive more equally both of his lordship's person and proceeding than your majesty presently appears to do.'[49] Hoping that he did indeed have such a favourable ear, Davison began his discourse, detailing the state of the country, the difficulties faced by the Earl of Leicester on arrival, and the need for leadership. He explained in great detail the earl's reluctance to take the post, and the necessities which had driven him to do so.

The queen, however, remained unconvinced, and retorted with the same complaints with which she had begun. Robert Dudley had held her, the queen, in contempt; he respected his greatness more than her honour or service. A further two meetings resulted in little more progress, as did pleas to revoke Heneage, who carried the damning letters to the Earl of Leicester. Although Davison felt that the queen's rage abated with every day, it was not the sea-change that was needed to protect Robert Dudley. Heneage now waited at Kent for the winds to turn, allowing him to cross the North Sea and accomplish the queen's rage. Somewhat defeated, Davison quit the court and instead travelled to visit Lettice, Countess of Leicester, who had been without her husband several months now. He found her deeply troubled by the news from court, and unsurprisingly so. It was said that what had particularly incensed the queen was not just that her former favourite had accepted this position, but that he had intended to bring Lettice over to rule beside him, with a court that rivalled her own. Once again, it seemed, it was the presence of Lettice that threatened danger and dishonour to her husband.

By the time Ambrose was composing the letter to his brother, three weeks after Davison's arrival, little had changed, except that three days earlier, Heneage and his letter had finally reached the shores of the Netherlands, as had the news of the queen's condemnation of Robert's actions. Robert's risk in accepting the title had not paid off, though the fact that he had been discredited as carrying the support and authority of the Queen of England certainly did not help. In the almost two months that had passed between his acceptance of the role of Governor General and Heneage's arrival, he had continued to send letters across the sea, begging for more support and money, little knowing the circumstances in which his letters would arrive.

When at last this was revealed to him, Robert was devastated. He wrote to the Privy Council advising his immediate removal from the Netherlands. 'I have no cause,' he wrote to them, 'to have played the fool this far for myself; first, to have her majesty's displeasure, which no kingdom in the world could make me willingly deserve; next, to undo myself in my later days; to consume all that should have kept me all my life, in one half-year.'[50] Had he indeed lost everything he had worked for his entire life, in just six months?

Writing a letter to Walsingham to accompany his official missive to the Lords of the Privy Council, Robert could be less formal about his feelings: 'being loath to trouble my lords with too long a letter,' he wrote, 'maketh me thus bold to use some addition to you, being not only grieved but wounded to the heart. For it is,' he confessed to his friend, 'more than death unto me, that her majesty should be thus ready to interpret always hardly of my service, specially before it might please her to understand the reasons for that I do.'[51] It was true, the queen tended somewhat to the paranoia of her grandfather, assuming the worst of those around her. Perhaps it could not be helped, living a life teetering above the turbulent and malicious snake-pit of the court. Nevertheless, Robert felt he had done what he thought was best for her service, especially in the absence of any explicit instruction from England. What if he had not taken the role? 'I would fain know,' he ruminated to Walsingham, 'if any other had had it but one wholly her majesty's, whether she had not been disappointed of every part of that she looked for: specially for a good peace for herself and England?' The States General had at one point been considering France for the source of their governor, for instance; where would that have left England? He suspected, however, that it was not just the action which infuriated her so, it was that fact that he, in particular, had taken it. 'I am now sorry that ever I was employed in this service,' he wrote to Walsingham. 'For if any man of a great number else had brought such a matter to pass for her, I am sure he should have had, instead of displeasure, many thanks. But such is now my wretched case,' he lamented, perhaps a little too piteously, 'as for my faithful, true and loving heart to her majesty and my country, I have utterly undone myself: for favour, I have disgrace; and for reward, utter spoil and ruin.'

This ruin, it seemed, would come via the hand of Sir Thomas Heneage, who landed at Flushing on 3 March, greeted by Philip Sidney. Worried for his uncle, Philip met with Heneage to discuss his mission in the Low Countries. Fortunately, it soon became clear that Heneage was not there to destroy the Earl of Leicester, though many others would have jumped at the chance. Philip found him to be considerate of his uncle's cause and honour, and disposed to do what he could for him within the bounds of duty to the queen.[52] Despite their rivalrous beginnings, Dudley and Heneage had become friends, and Heneage was not keen to make the situation any worse for him. He decided he would not act until he received further instruction from the queen, making the delay between the two countries finally work in Robert's favour.

Robert, perhaps in consultation with Heneage, had also decided to find a scapegoat. Abruptly changing his tone, Robert's next letters to the Council displayed far more confidence and a simmering rage. 'It is true,' he admitted, 'that I faulted, because I did not advertise her majesty first or I should take such an authority upon me, but she doth not consider,' he went on with more fire, 'what commodities she hath withall, and herself no way engaged for it, either one way or other, as Mr Davison might have better declared it, if it had pleased him. And I must thank him only,' he continued, 'for my blame, and so he will confess to you, for, I protest before God, no necessity here could have made me leave her majesty unacquainted with the cause before I would have accepted of it, but only his so earnest pressing me.'[53] While William Davison, sick from his journey across the North Sea, sought every way in his power to alleviate the queen's rage against Robert Dudley, the earl himself had quite decidedly thrown him to the salivating wolves. Rather than blame the weather, the demands of the opportune moment, his own readiness to accept or his fear of refusal, Robert was blaming William Davison. He was not ashamed, either, in letting Davison know, unleashing his rage at the unwitting ambassador for not only persuading him, as he reported it, to take the role so speedily, but for his poor handling of his cause in London. Davison objected to it all.

'It hath grieved me a little,' Robert wrote to Davison, 'that by your means, I have fallen into her majesty's so deep displeasure.'[54]

'Denied,' the ambassador responded in the margins of the letter.

'You, also,' Robert continued, 'have so carelessly discharged your part, in the due declaration of all things as they stood in truth.'

'I appeal,' Davison retorted, 'to the testimony of others.'

'For by the letters, and message I have received by Mr Heneage, neither doth her majesty know, how hardly I was drawn to accept this place before I had acquainted her.'

'He' – Thomas Heneage – 'was dispatched the same night I arrived.' It was true, Heneage could not accurately report on the insufficiencies of Davison's report to the queen, as it had taken place after he had left the court. Had Heneage misinformed the earl, or did the earl simply not care?

'I did,' Robert pressed on the matter of the absolute governorship, 'very unwittingly come to the matter.'

'Hereof let the world judge,' was all Davison replied.

'All thus lost; and falls out by your negligent carelessness,' Robert reprimanded him, coming to a close on the question of Davison's mission to England, 'where I many hundred times told you of, that you would both mar the goodness of the matter and breed me her majesty's displeasure.'

'You might doubt it,' Davison retorted, 'but if you had uttered so much, you should have employed some other in the journey, which I had no reason to affect so much, pre-seeing well enough how thankless it would be.'

Davison might have failed to restore Robert's reputation, and paid for it, as the earl vengefully turned on him, but others were craftier. Sir Thomas Shirley arrived in England from the Netherlands as Heneage arrived in Flushing. Shirley adopted a more cunning tactic than had Davison, perhaps suggested by Robert Dudley himself. Approaching the queen as she went for a walk in the garden at Greenwich, Shirley reported to her that her once-beloved Earl of Leicester was in fear of falling into a sickness and that he begged, as a humble suitor, that she send her physician Dr Goodridge[55] to attend on him, as he had once treated him successfully for the same in the past.[56] Moved by fear of losing her favourite to illness, the queen responded that she wished with all her heart to send Dr Goodridge to him, and was sorry that the earl was in need of him. Pushing his luck perhaps a bit, Shirley acknowledged her graciousness in seeking the preservation of the earl's health, though otherwise she was offended by his actions.

'You know my mind,' the queen responded, sensing the game. 'I may not endure that my man should alter my commission, and the authority that I gave him, upon his own fancies, and without me.'[57] With this, she called another attendant on her, ending the conversation with Shirley. It was, however, a positive step forward.

By the end of March, she had authorized money to Leicester's campaign in the Low Countries and on 1 April, wrote to him herself.

> We are persuaded that you, that have so long known us, cannot think, that we could have been drawn to have taken so hard a course herein, had we not been provoked by an extraordinary cause. But for that your grieved and wounded mind hath more need of comfort than reproof, whom we are persuaded, that the act in respect of the contempt can no way be excused, had no other meaning and intent than to advance our service; we think meet to forbear to dwell upon a matter wherein ourselves do find so little comfort, assuring you that whosoever professeth to love you best taketh not more comfort of your well doing, or discomfort of your evil doing, than ourself.[58]

Robert Dudley had been forgiven. Now, he must turn to the reason why he was across the North Sea in the first place, a cause which had not been helped by the long refusal of funds and the damage done to his credit in the preceding months. He needed to win back the Low Countries from the Spanish.

*

The English, having been repelled twice by Spanish musket shot, regrouped for a third charge as the sun moved higher in the sky and the last of the heavy morning mists receded. Roger North, Lord North – who had been one of the few guests at the wedding of Philip's uncle – though injured, was demanding to be returned to his horse so that he could ride out and fight once again. The accomplished soldier Sir William Stanley was in need of a new mount, his having been shot some eight times. One of Stanley's men had been shot in the arm and would surely need it amputated.[59] Philip Sidney prepared his own men for another attack. This assault wasn't supposed to have been this difficult or deadly. It was going downhill for the English, and quickly.

Philip had left for the continent not long after disembarking Drake's ship. Just as Drake assaulted and harassed the Spanish on the seas, the mission to the Low Countries had the potential to prune away at growing Spanish control. For Philip, the journey had another meaning. As his grandfather, John Dudley, had joined his guardian Sir Richard Guildford, and his uncle, Henry, had joined John, so now Philip would join Robert fighting on the continent for England. Philip was older than they had been, but too must learn how the Dudley reputation was earned and re-earned on the battlefield.

The English forces were entrenched and encamped just outside the Dutch town of Zutphen, deep in the heart of Gelderland and some hundred and fifty kilometres east of The Hague. Philip had arrived there almost two weeks before, with his uncle and a significant English force. While the Earl of Leicester set up camp by a hillside to the west of Zutphen, Philip joined the camp of Sir John Norris, recently recovered from a pike-wound in the chest, in Warnsfeld churchyard a mile east of the town.[60]

The summer campaign had begun in earnest some months before, and it could not be said to be going seamlessly for the English. At the beginning of June they had lost the critically positioned town of Grave, about sixty kilometres south of their current position at Zutphen, to the Spanish. The town's governor had yielded so quickly and easily that Philip's uncle had had him court-martialled and executed. Many of the Dutch had seen this as overly harsh and a worrying sign of the way in which this English lord might be inclined to rule.

Success had come at Philip's own hands a month after the disaster at Grave. Thirty kilometres south of Philip's posting at Flushing was the Flemish town of Axel, which had been taken by the Spanish three years before and been besieged by the English for some weeks. Under cover of night, Philip had led his five hundred men across the Schelde river and to within a mile of the town, where he stirred their hearts for battle with a rousing speech. Traversing the last mile of land, some three dozen men silently swam across the moat holding ladders between them, which they used to scale the walls, before silently dispatching the guards and opening the gates to Philip and the rest of his troops. Under a nearly full moon, Philip had entered the city, where his men slaughtered almost every member of the Spanish garrison.

Riding a high from this success, however, Philip had soon after faced military embarrassment at Gravelines, a town on the northern coast of Flanders, not half a day's ride from Calais. Having heard that the commander who held the town was willing to hand it over, Philip had sailed there, to discover if this intelligence was correct.[61] Having sent in men who all assured him that the town was his, but without producing the hostages he had asked for, Philip sent two small troops of sixty-six men between them to advance on the town. He realized on the sound of musket-shot that he had been tricked. His men rushed to get back to the ship but were slaughtered by the town's garrison and ambushed by waiting cavalry. The order was called, and Philip's ship weighed anchor and returned to Flushing, the dying screams of the men they left behind fading into the distance. Philip had been wise to have been cautious, and he had avoided walking into the trap himself, but he had still ordered dozens of men to death on a false hope.

This humiliation was compounded by news of personal tragedy. Philip had already received word at the end of May while he was stationed at Arnhem, just thirty kilometres from Zutphen, of the death of his father Sir Henry Sidney. Henry had died at the age of fifty-seven at Ludlow Castle in Wales, after being refused the peerage he had demanded as a condition for his return to Ireland. Philip requested that he be allowed to return to England on hearing of the death of his father – his mother should not be left to sort out the Sidney family affairs alone – but he was turned down. More saddening news came in August. Philip's mother had died three months after her husband. The eldest daughter of John and Jane Dudley had died, as disappointed in the recompense for her decades of service to the Crown as her husband. With both their parents gone, the Sidney sons were almost as lost on the continent as their uncles had been thirty years before.

By the middle of September, all eyes were on Zutphen. On the east bank of the IJssel river, Zutphen was defended by two seemingly impregnable forts, one on each side of the river. The English forces were split on either side, with a bridge of ships across the river to connect them. Of course, they did not necessarily have to take the town or its invulnerable forts, merely starve them out. Having maintained the siege for some weeks, the English knew that the Duke of Parma, governor general and commander of the Spanish troops, would have to send victuals soon to Zutphen, or risk its surrender. At last, on the evening of 21 September, as the trenches around the town were completed, a messenger was intercepted.[62] He had been sent by Parma and had been tasked to inform the colonel holding the town, Don Francisco Verdugo, that a convoy of some five hundred carts – enough to sustain the town for several months – with an escort of six hundred horsemen was on its way to Zutphen. As it arrived, they would need a further thousand men from Zutphen to come and see it to its destination, given that there were English troops lurking. All was proceeding as planned. Norris and Stanley had combined forces of some five hundred men, and another fifty or sixty crossed the river. The English, ambushing the convoy, would undoubtedly have the upper hand, even if their numbers were only marginally superior. They also had a number of well-trained and well-equipped men of noble and notable families – Robert Devereux, Earl of Essex, Roger North, Lord North, Peregrine Bertie, Lord Willoughby, Sir John Norris, Sir William Russell, Sir William Stanley, Sir Thomas Perrot, and Sir Philip Sidney – perhaps even too many of this better sort to be in one place at the same time.[63]

As day dawned, the forces prepared, and Philip shot off a short missive to his father-in-law. The morning fog was heavy, but the men from the western camp made it over the river and joined the waiting foot- and horsemen under Norris and Stanley. They lay in wait for the convoy to arrive. As the sun pierced the fog, however, they realized they had severely underestimated their enemy. The convoy had arrived earlier than expected, and the forces defending it – some five or six times what they had expected – were already entrenched, waiting for their attack. There was no choice, however; the call rang out and the English horsemen advanced.

Spanish horsemen fell before them as they advanced, hacking and hewing through armour, leather, skin and bone. Breaking through the Spanish cavalry, the English horsemen – Philip among them – forced them back to the line of pikemen behind them. Any feeling of imminent victory was soon quelled, however, as they were repulsed by a line of musket-fire from the Spanish trenches. Muskets had been introduced by the Duke of Alba thirty years prior as a weapon with the power to pierce the armour worn by enemy cavalry.[64] Trenches allowed for the heaviest muskets to be used, propped up by forked rests. They had the power, as Philip and his comrades were all too aware, to devastate an advancing cavalry line, even if they wore heavy plate armour.

The English forces collected themselves in a nearby lane beyond the shot of the muskets for a second charge.[65] Philip's kinsman the Earl of Essex had some success breaking through a line of pikemen but was again forced back by the Spanish guns. In the smoke and screams of the battle, Philip felt the stomach-dropping shock of his horse crumpling beneath him under the volley of Spanish musket shot.[66] He, nevertheless, made it back to the English line, where he was given a fresh mount. The English made a third charge. They rushed the Spanish trenches once again, and once again the Spanish cavalry line broke, but the rain of musket shot was overwhelming. Norris rode to Philip's uncle to beg him to send more men, but he refused; to do so would make them vulnerable in territories they only weakly held elsewhere.[67] As two thousand more men poured out of Zutphen to protect the convoy's entrance, Norris called the retreat.

Turning his new mount to follow Norris back across the river, Philip's unarmoured left leg was struck by a Spanish musket ball. Entering an inch or two above his knee, the almost sixty-gram bullet shattered the lower part of his thigh bone.[68]

It was a serious injury. In retreat and some distance from the trench, such a shot need not have done so much damage. Philip, however, had ridden into battle without his cuisses: the curved single plate of metal that protected the thigh especially from shots from below, such as the thrust of a pikeman or the shot of a musket in a trench. Such heavy armour had gone out of fashion amongst the mounted lords who led soldiers into battle; a fashion much at odds with the increased threat of the Spanish musket.[69] The bullet was thus lodged in Philip's thigh at a depth that would make extraction and the re-forming of bone extremely difficult. At best, Philip would end up like his elder uncle, Ambrose: lamed and unable to serve. At worst, infection would set in that would threaten his leg and his life.

Ferried down the IJssel to Arnhem, Philip was laid in a bed at the home of a judge's widow. His uncle was optimistic, but concerned. 'I pray God save his life,' Robert wrote to Lord Burghley, 'and I care not how lame he be.'[70] Following his first full day after the battle, Philip slept a full four hours and awoke with an appetite. Fever set in two days later, and Philip sank into a feverish half-sleep from which those around him would pray he might wake.

Awake he did and, slipping into a more peaceful slumber for a few hours, he awoke with the fever gone. He even called to be dressed. Attended by the best physicians in the English company, including Dr Goodridge, who the queen had made good on her promise of sending, they checked his wound and saw it was healing as they might hope. His uncle, still encamped at Zutphen, visited again three days later, on 29 September. All the surgeons and physicians assured him, as they undoubtedly had Philip, that the worst was past.[71] Philip was eating and sleeping well, with no ill effects. The wound, though worrying, was healing. Robert was relieved, and passed the news on to Philip's father-in-law, reassuring him that the man they both considered a son would soon be well.[72] Visiting, Robert could let Philip know that many of his companions and contemporaries had been made knights, including William, the son of Christopher Hatton, and Henry Unton, son of Robert's once sister-in-law, Anne Seymour, as well as two of his uncle's namesakes: Philip's brother Robert, and Robert Devereux, Earl of Essex, all for their valour at Zutphen. Philip had been knighted three years before, but his courage was spoken of and celebrated, he could be assured.

The next day, despite the optimism of the surgeons, Philip drew up a new will. Though 'sore wounded in the body', Philip declared himself to be whole in mind.[73] He thought first of his wife Frances, who had arrived in the Low Countries in late June, shortly before Philip had taken Axel, and who was now showing the first signs of pregnancy with their second child. Next, he considered his brothers, allowing his uncle, the Earl of Huntingdon, to assign them lands. His father-in-law was also given rights to sell land in order to pay his debts, many of which had only recently been inherited from his father. He also thought of his infant daughter, Elizabeth, born as he had set off to the Low Countries. She was to receive the total of £4,000 as her dowry. He also considered the child within his wife's womb. If it was the long-awaited male heir, he would get preference, receiving the lands Philip had otherwise assigned to his brother Robert; if it was not, she would simply be awarded an equal portion as her elder sister.

His issue considered, he also remembered his uncle in his will. 'I give,' he wrote, 'to my most honourable good Lord, the Earl of Leicester, one hundred pounds, as a token of my devowed service, and great love, which I have ever borne to him in all duty.'[74] He bestowed the same amount on his uncle, the Earl of Warwick. To his sister he granted his best jewel, set with diamonds, and further jewels were given to each of his three aunts: the countesses of Huntingdon, Warwick and Leicester. Armour went to Sir William Russell and books to friends Edward Dyer and Fulke Greville, who had shared in his aborted maritime adventure. Money and jewels he likewise bequeathed to his father- and mother-in-law to remember him by. Finishing the will with the regnal year, he remembered the queen, and added that a jewel worth a hundred pounds should be given to her majesty the queen in remembrance of his duty to his sovereign, as well as a jewel worth just twenty to be given to Sir Thomas Heneage. With this, the will was sealed.

More than two weeks after his injury, he was still recovering well, chafing only at having to lie in bed so long, for which there was no ready remedy.[75] The hurt that was being done by overlong time in bed was likely to have been physical as well as emotional. Three weeks of being bed-ridden made him particularly susceptible to itchy, painful and odorous bedsores, which themselves had to be treated to avoid infection. Still, this was to be expected, and recovery remained possible.

By the middle of October, however, Philip began once again to feel feverish and weak.[76] The swelling and sores on his body were going far beyond what might be expected of bedsores. Red, swollen and extremely painful, Philip's sores were giving off a smell akin to a corpse. Gangrene had set in.[77] The surgeons could try to bleed him, in the hope of purging the accumulated corrupted blood, but given how long it had remained in his body, by now the gangrene had probably infected other areas of his tissue and bone.[78] It might be possible to try to remove the affected tissue, and perhaps some of the healthy tissue nearby, and cauterize it, but this was risky, especially when it had set in so deeply. Amputation was a last resort, as it was frequently just as lethal as the gangrene itself, but not to be dismissed.[79] If left unchecked, as it had been, the disease would eat away at Philip's body, until there was no heat or vital spirit remaining.[80] Before his eyes gangrene was slowly transforming Philip's young, healthy physique into a corpse.

'My Weyer, come, come,' Philip wrote desperately from his bed four days later, 'I am at risk of my life and wish for you.'[81] Johann Weyer, a Dutch physician who specialized in fever and infection, was the one man in Europe who Philip thought might be able to save him. 'Neither alive nor dead will I be ungrateful,' he assured him. 'I cannot write more,' he ended, 'but earnestly beg you to hurry.' It was a vain hope. Not only – as he had been told – was the septuagenarian Johann Weyer himself unwell and unable to travel, but it would take time for the letter to reach him. Time that Philip almost certainly did not have.

The next day he had more or less resigned himself to his fate. Struggling through the fog of fever and intense physical pain, he added a codicil to his will. He wanted to give signs of his thanks to the physicians who had looked after him in his last illness: Ivert, who set his bones, Mr Marten, his surgeon, and Robert, his apothecary, as well as the surgeons who had served him from the start, including Goodridge.[82] To his uncle, the Earl of Leicester, who had visited, he left his best room hangings and the best piece of plate in his possession. He added to his will the gift of his best sword to his uncle's stepson, the Earl of Essex. Both he and Robert Devereux were sons of a kind to Robert Dudley and had the honour of fighting beside and for him. His best sword was an appropriate bequest.

Though it was wise to keep his pregnant wife, likely to be distressed by his fatal injury, away, Philip was surrounded by his friends and his brothers, Robert and Thomas, as he prepared for his death. They were there to comfort the dying man with assurances of resurrection and to witness his good Christian death. Once he could no longer speak, each lift of Philip's eyes and arms was a sign that he prayed to God and petitioned the Almighty for entry into his Holy Kingdom.[83] At last, at two o'clock on 17 October, Philip, worn away with the weakness of his disease, his body unable to keep the vital heat burning in him any longer, took his last shaky breath, and died.[84]

Thirty-one years before, Philip had come screaming into the world in a room full of women; now he departed silently, watched over by many of the men who were closest to him. At his birth, the Dudley family had been in disgrace; his very name had been an appeal to an unlikely patron to rescue them. In this attempt to gain a defender for the Dudley family, Philip's parents had named him after the king he had eventually died fighting against. Now, the Dudley family was in the ascendant, but in Philip they had lost another promising heir to carry them into the next generation. Philip had declared with flair and passion not two years ago that Dudley blood ran in his veins. Now that blood was cold.

*

'Not doubting but by your concord in the camp and valour in the field, and your obedience to my self and my general,' the queen declared to the troops gathered at West Tilbury, 'we shall shortly have a famous victory over these enemies of my God, and of my kingdom.'[85] Robert Dudley, Earl of Leicester, was once again Elizabeth's

Lieutenant General and commander of the queen's forces, though this time the battleground was to be England itself.

Robert had left the Low Countries for England a month after his nephew's death.[86] Philip's death had, he admitted to Walsingham, devastated him. They had both lost a son, and a man Robert was sure would have been an ornament to both their houses.[87] Remaining with Robert in the Low Countries at Philip's death was his young pregnant widow, Frances Sidney, who had been desperate to get home, but great care would have to be taken to avoid losing the child, a child that Robert would – girl or boy – treat as if she or he were his very own.[88]

Robert had returned to court to find it preoccupied with the matter of the Queen of Scots. Two days before the Battle of Zutphen, seven co-conspirators of a plot to assassinate Elizabeth and replace her with Mary had been hanged, drawn and quartered at St Giles' Field near Holborn. Walsingham had been watching them buzz about with their plots, waiting until they had entangled the imprisoned Queen of Scots in his web as well. This they had done that very summer, when she had written to them authorizing their assassination plan. Robert had heard of the conspiracy while at Zutphen and while Philip was – it seemed – recovering, and had written to Walsingham insisting that the Queen of Scots must die.[89]

Few disagreed. Her trial had taken place at Fotheringhay four days after Robert had penned the letter. She appeared in front of a commission which included most of the peers of the realm, including Ambrose, Earl of Warwick.[90] Mary had defended herself valiantly and impressively, but futilely.[91] Ten days later the commissioners declared that Mary had indeed plotted the death of the queen and thus was sentenced to death. A few weeks later, parliament also agreed. Law and parliament were all well enough, however; the queen also had to be convinced. There was only one person close enough to the queen who might successfully persuade her to execute a fellow anointed sovereign.

Robert had returned to England a month after the sentence against Mary had been given. Welcomed back by the queen, he had soon joined the chorus of councillors encouraging her to act with decisive, lethal justice.[92] Allowing Mary to live only gave England's enemies a figurehead to rally behind, as well as a viable alternative to the rule of

Elizabeth, whose legitimacy had never been without question. Every day wasted was another one that traitors had to plot. To keep the queen safe, and they had all sworn to do so, they must dispatch her enemies: justice as well as policy demanded it.[93]

Still, the queen had temporized. In mid-December she had called for a death warrant to be drawn up.[94] The warrant meant nothing, however, unless she signed it and had it sealed. Just before Christmas, Robert had found the queen in tears over a letter she had received from Mary. 'And since I know,' her cousin had written to her, 'that your heart, more than that of any other, ought to be touched by the honour or dishonour of your own blood, and of a Queen, the daughter of a King, I require you, Madam, for the sake of Jesus, to whose name all persons bow, that after my enemies have satisfied their black thirst for my innocent blood, you will permit my poor disconsolate servants to remove my corpse, that it may be buried in holy ground'.[95] The letter seemed to have found its mark, leaving Elizabeth distraught and Robert concerned it would cause further delay. That was not his only concern that day; Frances Sidney, who he esteemed as his own daughter, had fallen ill, and he was anxious to know how she fared.[96] She improved, but her child by Philip Sidney did not survive.

The matter of the Queen of Scots had reached a crux in January. Alarm bells were rung, and messages carried from one end of the country to the other. Travellers were searched and every man who could nervously took up arms. Councillors' servants were bounding out from Greenwich at all hours to confirm reports and rumours. It was said that the Queen of Scots had escaped her prison and was raising an army, much as Elizabeth's sister had against the Duke of Northumberland and his false queen. Others whispered that the queen had been shot, that many members of the Privy Council had been killed, that entire towns – even London – had been destroyed, burned or taken by the French.[97] One can never tell from whence a rumour first arises, but if some of these had been whispered by agents of Sir Francis Walsingham, it certainly would have served to increase the pressure on his queen to execute the Queen of Scots.

And it was working; Elizabeth was starting to buckle. On the morning of 1 February, Robert Dudley had been in William Cecil's chamber at Greenwich, when the queen's Secretary of State entered, clutching a pile of papers.[98] Sir William Davison, the same man with whom Robert had exchanged fierce words over the cold North Sea not a year before, had been made Secretary of State the previous autumn, and had already felt the weight of his office. Though relations between the two men remained professional, they were not especially warm, especially as Davison also held the warrant Robert and his allies so desperately needed to dispatch the Queen of Scots. On that February morning, however, he was able to present the document to Leicester and Burghley, signed. He had just come from her majesty's presence, he told them, where she had explained why she had at last made the decision to sign it. He was to send it quickly to the commissioners, who would see the execution done at Fotheringhay. She had added as well, that on his way he should show the warrant to Sir Francis Walsingham, sick at his home in London, as the sight of it might just kill him outright. The two men hurried Davison on his task, Cecil offering to take care of business remaining at court for him that afternoon.

Two days later, however, Davison found himself once again with both men in Cecil's chambers, and this time a number of members of the Privy Council had joined them.[99] Just twenty-four hours after Davison had left the queen with the warrant signed, she appeared to have demurred. On being told by Davison that the warrant had been sealed, she asked him why such haste had been taken, and worried about the burden of the act falling upon herself. This had woken Davison to the possibility that he could be blamed for the whole affair, and he was resolute he would not. And so the Privy Council met to decide what to do. Cecil suggested that, given they had a clear commission for the execution, as evidenced by the signed and sealed warrant, they should proceed with sending it to the commissioners. They would not trouble her majesty further with this matter, he advised diplomatically, having done all that she could. Robert and the others agreed. The warrant was dispatched the next day. Two days later, Robert Dudley left the court for Wanstead. He was not there when news arrived at court of the botched but ultimately successful execution of the Queen of Scots, or for the livid reaction of his queen. Neither was he there four days later, when Elizabeth had Davison locked in the Tower for disobeying the queen and misleading the Privy Council.

The execution of Mary, Queen of Scots, had severe consequences, increasing the Catholic condemnation of England's actions. By the summer, Robert had returned to the Netherlands, despite a disinclination to go and his deteriorating health; the queen's commission had first come while he lay indisposed in his bed in Wanstead.[100] On his fifty-fifth birthday, Robert left from Leicester House in London, travelled to Sittingbourne in Kent where he dined, and ended the day in Margate on the coast of the North Sea.[101] Two days later he was in Flushing once again, tasked with sorting out the mess that had erupted since his departure. It seemed half of the people there were desperate for his return and the other half despised him.

Perhaps unsurprisingly, this venture was as unsuccessful as the first. Once again he was forced to defend himself to his queen, writing letters to her himself, despite persistent pains in his hands as he wrote. 'Therefore dispose of me as shall please you,' he had written from Utrecht at the end of September. 'If my life may no way stand you in better stead to be a little prolonged at home, I shall submit myself to God's will and yours, and once perceiving your so little care of your so old and faithful servant, I shall the less care what shall become of me,' signing off: 'your majesty's humble and most faithful servant, too unworthy to be your ▰.'[102] Once again he had been slowly forgiven, and then recalled. He had been back in London by the middle of December, where he formally resigned his posts as Governor General and Lieutenant General.[103]

Now, in August, he was Lieutenant General once again, and his enemy was still the Spanish, but he was facing their attack on English soil. Philip II, once great saviour to the Dudley family – after enduring years of English piracy, English support of the Netherlands, and the execution of the Catholic Queen of Scots – had launched an attack on England itself. It was not the greatest fleet England had ever confronted; Robert's father had faced a much larger invading force at the Battle of the Solent on the days before Robert's thirteenth birthday.

Philip II, however, was confident that the armada would be successful in its invasion, especially if they could coordinate with the Duke of Parma's forces from the Netherlands. In mid-July, Robert had received intelligence that Parma, his foe in the Netherlands, would be making an attempt on London itself.[104]

On the north bank of the Thames, about ten miles from where it flowed into the North Sea, West Tilbury had been strategically selected as the location to gather troops of ground soldiers in preparation for a Spanish invasion along the Thames, with the English Lieutenant General in command. Robert had his doubts about the location and the strategy, but by 25 July 1588, only a day after his renewed title had been ratified, he had four thousand men gathered at the camp at Tilbury.[105] It was not enough, and yet he was struggling to feed them all. Some men arrived with not even a meal's worth of provision with them, leaving Robert to try to locate food – and drink – locally for them. Nevertheless, he found them all to be loyal and willing to fight or starve for the defence of the queen.[106] Having spent months of pessimistic misery in the Netherlands, distant from those who could help or fund him, Robert was cautiously optimistic, seemingly revived by the spirits of those around him.

Inspired, perhaps, by the unwavering loyalty of his men, and always master of display, Robert came to an idea. Writing to his queen, he suggested that she pay a visit to the camps and forts at Tilbury. 'Thus shall you comfort,' Robert advised her from across the river in the camp at Gravesend, 'not only these thousands but many more that shall hear of it'.[107] There would be, he assured her, little danger in it, and she would rest comfortably nearby. 'So will I pray to God,' he ended, 'not only for present victory over all your enemies, but longest life, to see the end of all those who wish you evil, and make me so happy as to do you some service.'

He could not have known that on that very day the Armada was anchored off Calais, waiting to be joined with the forces from the Netherlands that would make them nearly unstoppable in their conquest of England. The Spanish Armada had been sighted off the coast of Cornwall on 19 July, less than a week before Robert had begun to gather his troops at Tilbury. The English fleet was commanded by

Charles Howard, Baron of Effingham, whose uncle had died in such dramatic circumstances on the water against the French seventy-five years before. Second in command was none other than Sir Francis Drake himself. For about a week, they had harassed the Spanish ships off the coast of Plymouth and the Isle of Wight, but there had as yet been no serious engagement.

That had changed the day after Robert wrote his letter to the queen. The Spanish ships were unable to join with those from Parma, and the armada was vulnerable as they waited. This was the moment to be seized. By night, the English sent eight flaming ships full of gunpowder towards the anchored Spanish ships, breaking their formation.[108] The next morning, the English ships attacked the disbanded Spanish fleet near Gravelines, at last halting their assault when they ran out of ammunition. The wind did the rest, sending the Spanish ships first toward the Low Countries and then, faced with the waiting English fleet, towards Scotland. The invasion had not gone as planned, but that did not mean it could not regroup and make a further attempt. There were still some hundred or more enemy ships in British waters, and there remained fears that Parma would attempt to take London.

On the morning of 5 August, in the midst of bad weather and broken bridges, Robert had received secret word that the queen had agreed to come to Tilbury to visit the troops.[109] He hastily wrote a letter expressing his thanks to her, adding the flourish of eyebrows over the 'oo's – their little sign to each other. Robert could also expect his stepson, now twenty-three, to be part of the queen's visit, as Robert Devereux, Earl of Essex, had been given the position that his stepfather had held since the queen's coronation – Master of the Horse – as well as having been made a Knight of the Garter and been given command of the cavalry at Tilbury. Robert had been endorsing his stepson to the queen to great success, and Robert Devereux was now one of the queen's closest companions and favourites, to the anxiety of all others who clamoured for that spot, excepting Robert himself, of course, who had put him there.

Three days later, in the afternoon, Elizabeth I arrived at Tilbury as promised, to the shot of ordinance, drum and celebration. Now almost fifty-five, Elizabeth had lost the flush of the young triumphant queen that Robert had followed through London thirty years before. She retained a fairness of complexion, but the cares of the Crown had added lines to her face. Her nose, always small, now looked almost hooked – a trait she may have inherited from her grandfather, Henry VII, with whom she shared a cautious aversion to haste, war and expense. Her fierce red hair, the sign of her royal heritage and connection with her father, was now replaced by a wig of red curls, upon which she could rest a crown. Dainty and sacred, as Robert described her, she was no less commanding or regal than she had been thirty years before. On that day she also wore a militaristic air.[110] Robert welcomed her to the camp, and she reviewed the assembled troops. That night, as Elizabeth retired to a nearby country house, Robert met with Francis Walsingham in his tent.[111] Walsingham (who had not dropped dead at the sight of the Queen of Scots' death warrant) was aware that the Spanish fleet had been chased north but there was still no knowing what would become of them there. The ultimate question was whether to disarm the queen's troops. No one seemed to have any news of where Parma's ships were. As long as that was the case, the army needed to stand prepared and ready.

The next day, as well as dining with Robert, the queen addressed the assembled troops. As she spoke, nearby servants hurried to record her words, to pass on to those who were not able to hear the queen.[112] As Robert had predicted, that day she would speak to more than those assembled.

'My loyal people,' she told them, 'we have been persuaded by some that are careful of my safety, to take heed how I committed my self to armed multitudes for fear of treachery. But I tell you,' she went on, 'I would not desire to live to distrust my faithful and loving people.

'Being resolved,' she continued, 'in the midst and heat of battle to live and die amongst you all, to lay down for my God and for my kingdom and for my people mine honour and my blood even in the dust. I know,' she told them, 'I have the body but of a weak and feeble woman, but I have the heart and stomach of a king, and of a king of England too.

'My Lieutenant General,' the queen proclaimed, 'shall be in my stead, than whom never Prince commanded a more noble or worthy subject.'

Beauchamp carving, with roses, gillyflowers, oak and honeysuckle surrounding the Dudley crest.

Jane Dudley's brass funeral monument, with five daughters, from a 16th century monument.

marid to sir francis Jobson knight & vrtell
second doughter to Edward Gray viscount Lisley
and sister and one of the heires to the aforesaid
John Gray viscount Lisley was maried vnto
henry Stafford Erle of wiltshere by whom he
had no issue

John duke
of Northomberland
Erle of warwike
viscount Lisley &
Baron Bassett &
Teyes

Jane the
doughter and
heire of Sir
Edward Guldeforde
knight

Family Tree showing the eldest sons of Jane and John Dudley. Robert Dudley has been
added in the margins.

henry dudley
first son died
at the a siege of
Bullen beinge
xiv yeres olde

Thomas
dudley second
son died at the
age of two yeres

John Erle
of warwike third
son died without
issu xviii yeres olde

Lord
Ambrose forth
son Erle of warwik
and Lorde Lisley z
knight of y garter
and one of y privy
cownsaile

Lord Gulde =
ford fift sonne
maried the Lady
Jane and died with
her

Lord
henry seuenth
son slayne at the
a siege of S Qwyn =
tens

Robert Dudley
afterwards erle
of Leycester ys
straungely left
out here so as
with him there
should be 9.
sonns.

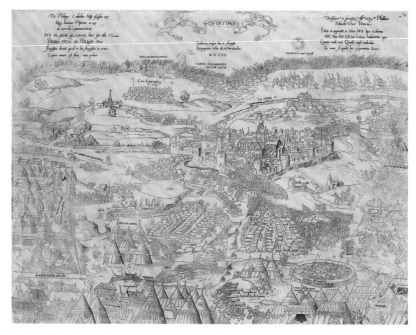

Battle of Saint Quentin, 1557.

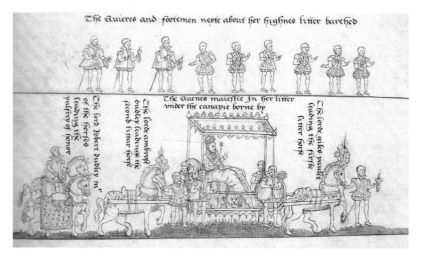

Elizabeth I's coronation procession, 1559. Ambrose Dudley leads the second litter horse and Robert Dudley leads the palfrey of honour, directly behind the queen.

Allegory of the Tudor Succession, *c.*1572. Mary I and Philip II on the left bring in war, Elizabeth I on the right brings in peace and plenty.

Coronation miniature of Elizabeth I, *c.*1600.

Portrait of Mary Sidney, from the mid-16th century.

Two images of Ambrose and Robert Dudley competing in a joust.

Fireplace at Kenilworth, c.1570.

Portrait of Robert Dudley, c.1575, forming a quasi-pair with the portrait of Elizabeth I.

Portrait of Elizabeth I ('the Reading portrait'), c.1575.

Nature and God taking vengeance on the Earl of Leicester.

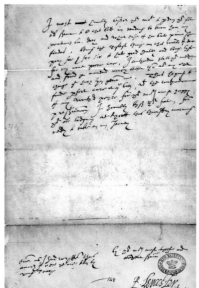

The final letter sent by Robert Dudley to Elizabeth I, on 29 Aug 1588. It has been marked 'his last letter' by the queen.

It was a moment to be remembered for generations, just as Robert had intended. The fierce queen and her noble general, Robert Dudley.

*

Robert rode through the verdant woods of Oxfordshire on his way to Kenilworth. It was the last flush of summer before the leaves turned and fell. Only three weeks after the queen's visit to Tilbury, the Spanish ships were still making their way around Scotland and the coast of Ireland, but the weather was making quicker work of them than any fireships could. Breaking up the camp not long after the queen's visit, Robert had returned to Wanstead, and then by coach to St James's in London where the queen had been reviewing her troops. The young Earl of Essex performed the final review at the end of August, leading dozens of musketeers and harquebusiers, as well as two hundred horse, dressed in orange cloth, white silk and silver trim.[113] Robert had watched his stepson from a window at the queen's side. It was a glorious performance to impress a queen, as well as to make a stepfather proud. He left London the next day, riding west from London, as he had almost four years before, at his son's death.

He had left Rycote that morning, the home of Sir Henry Norris. Norris had been a schoolboy with Robert's elder brother, and was the father of John Norris, a man Robert had fought alongside in the Netherlands. The house at Rycote had been rebuilt in brick in the early sixteenth century and had faint echoes of Hampton Court about its brick-built façade.[114] Before leaving, Robert had penned a letter for his queen. After asking her how she fared, and adding accents over the double 'oo's in 'poor old servant' in the first line, he had thanked her for the medicine she had given him, which was standing him in good stead. Taking the waters, he assured her, would remedy his illness, and he would be back at her side again soon. As he finished the letter, a young servant from the queen arrived with a small token for him, to take on his journey. From there he continued west and north, travelling the twenty-eight miles to his home at Cornbury, where he would retire for the night.

Robert entered the irregular rectangular courtyard, bordered by two-storey ranges of rooms, cut through with mullioned windows. Sharing Wychwood Forest with nearby Langley, Cornbury had been left to

379

Robert's mother by his father. Although it had then reverted to the Crown, Robert had made use of it on several occasions, especially for hunting in nearby Wychwood. He retired that night in a wood-panelled room, decorated with lozenges and dentil cornices, ready to leave again at first light.[115] He awoke feverish and too unwell to continue. He had been ill frequently over the past few years, and always recovered, ready to be at the queen's side once again. This time, however, he seemed to slip further and further away from life. Memory and imaginings mixed in his fevered state as those around him prayed for his soul.

On 4 September 1588, as the sun rose above the trees, bringing the smell of fresh leaves and decaying branches, Robert Dudley, Earl of Leicester, breathed his last and departed this world for the next. With no child to succeed the last of the Dudley sons, the family tree would wither to naught. Yet, having graven their legacy into the very fabric of history, death would never truly overcome the House of Dudley.

> *The longest day, in time resigns to night.*
> *The greatest oak, in time to dust doth turn.*
> *The Raven dies, the Eagle fails of flight.*
> *The Phoenix rare, in time her self doth burn.*
> *The princely stag at length his race doth run.*
> *And all must end, that ever was begun.*[116]

Epilogue

So ill the race of Dudleys could endure

The last surviving son of John and Jane Dudley died in February 1590. At the age of sixty, Ambrose Dudley had been born under the reign of King Henry VIII and Queen Catherine of Aragon, the fourth son to parents of no title and little wealth. He had fought in battles against rebels and foreign enemies, been sentenced to death for treason, mourned the death of children and celebrated victories alongside monarchs. He died Earl of Warwick, the eldest and last son of his line.

When his younger brother had died eighteen months earlier, Ambrose had been the closest thing Robert had to a legitimate heir. Robert left him land and gifts, but most importantly 'as dear an Affection as ever Brother bare to other'.[1] Now that Ambrose was gone, the House of Dudley was at an end. Robert, however, had also left behind him three young men who each bore his name, and all of whom could vie for the position of his successor: his stepson – Robert Devereux, Earl of Essex; his nephew – Robert Sidney; and his illegitimate son – Robert Dudley. And vie they did.

Robert's widow, Lettice, Countess of Leicester, had been named the Executrix of the will the Earl of Leicester had written in the summer of 1587.[2] This made her responsible for the massive debts he had acquired, especially in the years before his death. 'I have lived,' Dudley admitted, 'always above any living I had (for which I am heartily sorry).'[3] The apology was appropriate but perhaps insufficient. Robert had left his widow to dispense with some £50,000 in debts.[4]

For assistance, and perhaps for comfort, Lettice had quickly married again. Ten months after her husband's death, she took as her third husband not another earl, but a member of the household: Sir Christopher Blount, son of the man that Dudley had sent to Cumnor all those years ago. Blount was an odd choice by all reckonings. A dozen or more years her junior, Blount was far below the countess in station and, what's more, was an ardent Catholic.

Six months after his sister-in-law's bewildering wedding, Ambrose died. With Ambrose dead, the bastard Robert Dudley became the primary heir to a number of Robert's estates, including Kenilworth. This did not occur without opposition. The countess and her new husband had to be forced to hand over Kenilworth to the bastard Dudley, and Robert Sidney aligned with her interests against those of his illegitimate cousin. This was in part because Sidney had joined the circle around Lettice's son, Robert Devereux, who had taken his father's place as the glittering favourite of the court, as well as marrying the widow of Robert's brother, Frances.

Just as Philip Sidney had left Devereux his sword (though not, wittingly, his wife), the Earl of Leicester had left his stepson his best armour, along with his Garter, 'in Hope he shall wear it shortly'.[5] After his stepfather's death, Devereux quickly acquired leases for his London homes, including Wanstead and Leicester House. He, however, was not the master of charm and rumour that his stepfather had been and exhibited a restlessness and rebelliousness which pushed the queen's tolerance. Having failed miserably as Lord Lieutenant of Ireland in 1599, and after surprising the undressed queen in her bedchamber at Nonsuch Palace, Devereux was confined to Leicester – now Essex – House. Rather than, as his stepfather had done so frequently, retreating and begging the queen's forgiveness (or sending others to do the begging for him), Robert Devereux responded to the queen's rage by mounting a rebellion. With the support of his new stepfather, in early February 1601 Devereux led some two hundred people from Essex House through the city. He quickly lost followers, however, once it was pointed out that they were committing treason and after his stepfather was beaten to the ground with pikes. Two weeks later Devereux was beheaded on Tower Green and Blount a month after that. Robert Devereux had attempted to follow his stepfather into the queen's good graces, but had instead followed

Robert Dudley's brother, father and grandfather to the block. Devereux left his ten-year-old son, also named Robert, bereft of father and title, just as the Earl of Leicester's father had been almost a century before.

Robert Dudley's nephew, however, was proving more astute. Robert Sidney had distanced himself from Devereux during the failed Ireland campaign, and had rushed to Essex House in February 1601 to quell rather than join the rebellion. Two years later, the final Tudor monarch, Elizabeth I, died; Robert Dudley's last letter written from Ryecote still in a box by her bedside. Despite all the decades of concern over her heir, the crown passed peacefully to the son of the Queen of Scots, James VI of Scotland, now also James I of England. It was James who finally recognized the Sidneys' long service to England, granting Robert first the title Baron Sidney and then Viscount Lisle. Robert, however, considered himself his uncle's heir, and thus deserving of an even greater station. Finally, in 1618, at the age of fifty-five, Robert Sidney was created Earl of Leicester. He died eight years later, passing the title to his son, another Robert, Earl of Leicester.

The bastard Robert Dudley, however, maintained this title was his, along with that of Earl of Warwick. Dudley had spent the last decade of Elizabeth's reign on naval expeditions, sailing on his flagship, the *Bear's Whelp*. Reaching the West Indies, he claimed the island of Trinidad for his queen. His attempt to finance a circumnavigation of the globe in 1601, however, went worse than his kinsman's rebellion: only one man survived.

Shortly after James's accession, Dudley claimed that he was not a bastard after all but that his mother, Douglass Sheffield, had been legally married to the earl his father. There was scant proof, however, and the Countess of Leicester had managed to produce substantial evidence arguing the other side. The Star Chamber rejected his claims.

Three months later, Robert Dudley was on a ship bound for the continent, along with his nineteen-year-old cousin, Elizabeth Southwell. They converted to Catholicism in Lyon and asked the pope to grant them dispensation to marry. They needed it; not only were they cousins, but Robert Dudley was already married to Alice Leigh, whose grandfather had led Elizabeth I's coronation procession. Despite the rulings of the English Star Chamber, from then on Robert Dudley styled himself Earl of Leicester and Warwick. He and his new wife settled in the Renaissance city of Florence, but with the hope that they would one day return home to England, never mind the Catholicism and the bigamy.

For his restoration, Robert placed much of this hope in James I's strong and attractive eldest son, Henry, the Prince of Wales. Selling him Kenilworth for less than half its value, Robert trusted that Henry would see him home and restored to his rightful lands and titles, especially once he became Henry IX. Unfortunately, in the midst of the deal, Prince Henry suddenly died, leaving Robert once again adrift. Six years later Robert, Lord Rich, the former husband of Penelope Devereux (whom he had divorced in 1605 for adultery) was given the title of Earl of Warwick and Robert Sidney that of Earl of Leicester. In Italy, Robert Dudley had little hope of ever regaining these titles, so he pushed even higher. Two years later he convinced the Holy Roman Emperor Ferdinand II to recognize another title he felt was his by blood. In 1620 Robert Dudley became the Duke of Northumberland.

In the same year that Robert Dudley was created Duke of Northumberland in Italy, the final child of the last Dudley to hold that title died. Well over seventy, Katherine Hastings, Countess of Huntingdon, had endured everything that the age could throw at her. Childless, she had raised others' children, including those of her nephew Robert Sidney, Earl of Leicester. She was buried alongside her mother at Chelsea, reunited with her brothers and sisters, gathered around their mother in brass.

*

For over a century, the Dudley family had fought for security through the acquisition of power, perhaps never fully appreciating that the more power they acquired, the less secure they became. As each generation rose on Fortune's wheel, their fall became all the more dramatic and inevitable. Certainly not without flagrant ambition and self-interest, they nonetheless exhibited a fierce commitment to the monarchs they served. A dedication which was not always returned and, when absent, left them entirely unprotected from their enemies.

And enemies they had in abundance. Edmund Dudley had neglected to even attempt making powerful friends. John had not been able to retain those he did cultivate (his penchant for executing his friends and pardoning his enemies did not help). It took three generations, but Robert Dudley, despite attainders, scandals and the enmity of large parts of Christendom, managed to survive to die in his bed, warm in the loving favour of his queen. He had learned, more than likely from his adept mother, not only how to cultivate and keep powerful friends, but to use the pernicious power of rumour in his favour. If there were going to be lies told about the Dudley family, better they be their lies.

For this the women of the Dudley family were its undeniable secret weapon. Forging powerful connections and fuelling advantageous rumour, the wives, daughters and sisters of the House of Dudley were its protection and its continuance. Elizabeth Grey Dudley's marriage to the uncle of the king smoothed the path to John's restoration. On her deathbed, Jane Guildford Dudley, with her last effort and breath, preserved the lives of her sons, suffering under the shadow of the block. Mary Dudley Sidney was the secret maestro of swirling rumour, playing ambassadors for fools in games with the highest stakes in the land.

'*Te stante virebo*' – 'With you standing, I shall flourish'. The fates of the House of Dudley and the House of Tudor were from beginning to end intertwined. The Tudor monarchs depended on the Dudleys for support and sacrificed them for their own gain. The Dudleys served their rulers, but also determinedly crept closer to taking the throne for themselves, succeeding only for the briefest of moments. Had fate, Fortuna, Nemesis or God made only the slightest adjustment to their orchestration of events, the Dudley dynasty might have ruled for generations. As it was, both the House of Dudley and the House of Tudor came to their end, almost in the same moment and for the same reason. The fears of Edmund Dudley and Henry VII were realized in their grandchildren, who died without heirs to carry on their name.

The legacy of the Dudley family, however, through a century of warfare and scheming, love and desire, ambition and greed, ensured that – for good or ill – tongues would continue to tell of their deeds, and eager fingers would forever clutch at books bearing their name.

*

A man approached the executioner's block. Before him was a large crowd, braving the January cold to witness his death. He spoke to them, his final words, but they were lost to the winds. The people knew the way of treacherous favourites who found their way to the block. Nine years ago, as tracts poured out of the London presses about the scheming private advisers seducing the king, the book known as *Leicester's Commonwealth* was reprinted, reminding the London public of the machinations of those malevolent traitors, the Dudleys. The text was accompanied by another tract: *Leicester's Ghost*, in which the Earl of Leicester of old rose from his grave, to counsel any who would listen about the fleeting nature of fame and the permanence of death:

> O, then let not the sovereign monarch trust
> To any one peculiar potentate
> That ruleth, not by reason, but by lust,
> So consequently brings himself in hate,
> And doth endanger his dread prince's state;
> This makes me wish no such, I being dead,
> May of the prince, like me, be favoured.

But it was no Dudley, no favourite, dying that cold January morning. It was a king. Charles I, grandson of Mary, Queen of Scots, would die as she had, by an executioner's blade. His head, mercifully, was off in one stroke. There was no king to replace him; England would do without one, at least for a time.

A thousand miles away, the earl's bastard lay in Florence. He would die the same year as the doomed king. Robert Dudley had been denied the inheritance he had spent his life pursuing, though he had, five years before, at last been recognized as the legitimate son of Robert Dudley, Earl of Leicester. Charles I had corrected his father's decision, declaring that Dudley's had been a lawful birth after all. As recompense – and in the midst of a Civil War he was swiftly losing – he had created the title of Duke of Dudley. He bestowed the title, however, not on Robert, but on the wife he had left behind in England, Alice.

The Duchess Dudley lived another twenty years after the death of the king of England and her estranged husband. She left a world very different from the one she had entered, dying in 1669 at the age of ninety. With her died the dukedom and the memory of an England in which the House of Dudley had walked with kings.

> Now the short springtime of our pomp is past,
> The tedious autumn of our fall is come;
> What thing beneath the moon can ever last?
> The fox, the ass, the ape, possessed our room,
> And triumphed in our dreadful days of doom,
> Yet now the ragged staff, once borne so high,
> Is broken, and in dust the bears do lie.

Notes

PROLOGUE: A TRIBE OF TRAITORS

1 From the French translation which was reported to have appeared in Paris in 1585: *Discours de la vie abominable, ruses, trahisons, meurtres, impostures, empoisonnements, paillardises, atheismes, & autres tres-iniques conversations . . . le my Lorde de Lecestre, machiaveliste . . .* See D. C. Peck, ed., *Leicester's Commonwealth: The Copy of a Letter Written by a Master of Art of Cambridge (1584) and Related Documents* (Athens, OH: Ohio University Press, 1985), 154–67.

2 Peck, ed., *Leicester's Commonwealth*, 53.

3 Peck, ed., *Leicester's Commonwealth*, 127.

1. REMEMBER THAT YOU MUST DIE

1 SP 1/2 fol. 3.

2 Psalm 118:20. See Julian Litten, *The English Way of Death: The Common Funeral Since 1450* (London: Robert Hale Ltd, 2002); Ralph Houlbrooke, *Death, Religion, and the Family in England, 1480–1750* (Oxford: Oxford University Press, 2000); Christopher Daniell, *Death and Burial in Medieval England, 1066–1550* (London; New York: Routledge, 1998). Unless otherwise noted I have used the King James Version English translation, as at the time all elements of the service would have been in Latin.

3 Daniell, *Death and Burial*, 40–1.

4 Daniell, *Death and Burial*, 52–3.

5 Historic England, 'Tortington Augustinian Priory and Ponds, Including Part of Priory Precinct, Arundel – 1021459 | Historic England', accessed 8 March 2018, https://historicengland.org.uk/listing/the-list/

list-entry/1021459. Mary Magdalene is not named as a prostitute in the New Testament, but the medieval cult around her held her as such.

6 Philip Mainwaring Johnston, 'Tortington Church and Priory: Notes on Their History and Architecture', Churches in Sussex, accessed 4 March 2018, http://sussexchurches.co.uk/tortington.htm; Alfred H. Peat and Leslie C. Halsted, *Churches and Other Antiquities of West Sussex: With Architectural and Historical Notes and Thirty-One Illustrations* (Chichester: J. W. Moore, 1912).

7 Printed in Nicholas Harris Nicolas, ed., *Testamenta Vetusta: Being Illustrations from Wills, of Manners, Customs, &c. as Well as of the Descents and Possessions of Many Distinguished Families. From the Reign of Henry the Second to the Accession of Queen Elizabeth* (London, Nichols & Son, 1826), 352–6.

8 There is evidence of a number of land exchanges in which Dudley and Windsor were both involved, see for instance: WSRO Add Ms 4200; TNA E326/4047. Whether any of these had a connection to Dudley's role as a Justice of the Peace in Sussex, or as a commissioner for concealed lands in the county, is impossible to tell; see Derek Wilson, *The Uncrowned Kings of England: The Black Legend of the Dudleys* (London: Robinson, 2015), 14–16. Dudley also appears on records in connection to Reginald Bray; see TNA E 40/3987, and Richard Guildford; see ESRO SAS-G/21/4.

9 PROB/11/12/386.

10 Thessalonians 4:13; Psalm 23:4.

11 Steven Gunn, *Henry VII's New Men and the Making of Tudor England* (Oxford: Oxford University Press, 2016), 124.

12 Gunn, *Henry VII's New Men*, 8. This was the prerogative writ of *quo warranto* ('by what warrant?'): 'a royal writ obliging a person to show by what warrant an office or franchise is held or claimed', *OED*.

13 Litten, *English Way of Death*, 150.

14 Thomas Penn, *Winter King: The Dawn of Tudor England* (London: Penguin, 2012), 96–7; Robert Fabyan, *The Great Chronicle of London*, ed. A. H. Thomas and I. D. Thornley (London: Alan Sutton, 1983), 321–2. My thanks to Thomas Penn for sharing his insights on these chapters.

15 Penn, *Winter King*, 70–71.

16 Penn, *Winter King*, 96, 112.

17 Erin Sullivan, 'A Disease unto Death: Sadness in the Time of Shakespeare', in *Emotions and Health, 1200–1700*, ed. Elena Carrera, 159–83, accessed

2 May 2018. http://www.academia.edu/4885269/A_Disease_unto_ Death_Sadness_in_the_Time_of_Shakespeare.

18 Penn, *Winter King*, 112–13.

19 S. B. Chrimes, *Henry VII* (New Haven: Yale University Press, 1999), 255.

20 Gunn, *Henry VII's New Men*.

21 Penn, *Winter King*, 148.

22 R. Somerville, 'Henry VII's "Council Learned in the Law"', *The English Historical Review* 54, no. 215 (1939): 439.

23 Gunn, *Henry VII's New Men*, 80.

24 Penn, *Winter King*, 152; Gunn, *Henry VII's New Men*, 40.

25 Penn, *Winter King*, 155–6.

26 Samantha Harper, 'The Problem of Access at the Early Tudor Court: Some Case Studies' (Tudor Chamber Books Conference, Winchester, 2018).

27 Penn, *Winter King*, 123.

28 David Loades, *John Dudley, Duke of Northumberland* (Oxford: Oxford University Press, 1996), 2–3. Prerogative: 'The special right or privilege exercised by a monarch over all other persons: 'the prerogative of the British monarch under common law', *OED*.

29 Henry did not, of course, give up the hope of marrying and having more children; in fact he pursued the option actively, almost desperately in the coming years. He was aware, however, of the possibility this would come to naught before his own demise. As Sean Cunningham, 'Loyalty and the Usurper: Recognizances, the Council and Allegiance under Henry VII', *Historical Research* 82, no. 217 (2009): 459–81 shows, this was an increase in scale and scope, but not in kind; Henry had been using such strategies before 1504. My thanks to Sean Cunningham for his assistance with documents related to Henry VII and Edmund Dudley.

30 See Edward Hall, *Chronicle*, 499.

31 Bray was one of the executors of Edmund's father's will, PROB/11/12/386; see Penn, *Winter King*, 159 for Bray's knowledge of Edmund's expertise. See D. M. Brodie, 'Edmund Dudley: Minister of Henry VII', *Transactions of the Royal Historical Society* 15 (January 1932): 134–5 for the connections between Bray and John Dudley. Bray had also been the executor of Edmund's grandfather's will, signed in August 1487; see Nicholas, ed., *Testamenta Vetusta*, 391.

32 David Dean, 'Image and Ritual in Tudor Parliaments', in *Tudor Political Culture*, ed. Dale Hoak (Cambridge: Cambridge University Press, 1992), 243–71.

33 For the rates of attendance of lords and bishops at Henry VII's parliaments see Chrimes, *Henry VII*, 140–1.

34 Paul Cavill, *The English Parliaments of Henry VII, 1485–1504* (Oxford: Oxford University Press, 2009), 220.

35 Michael A. R. Graves, *Tudor Parliaments, The Crown, Lords and Commons, 1485–1603* (Routledge, 2014), 39.

36 Chrimes, *Henry VII*, 144; there were 296 members in total.

37 Pamela Tudor-Craig, 'The Painted Chamber at Westminster', *Archaeological Journal* 114, no. 1 (1957): 92–105. It is possible that the fifteenth-century Trojan tapestries covered these walls during the reign of Henry VII, but it is referred to as 'the Painted Chamber' during the reign of Henry VIII, and 'The Chamber of the Holy Cross' also suggests a connection with the biblical scenes on the walls; see Miss Ivy M. Cooper, 'The Meeting-Places of Parliament in the Ancient Palace of Westminster', *Journal of the British Archaeological Association* 3, no. 1 (1938): 97–138.

38 Paul Binski, *The Painted Chamber at Westminster* (London: Society of Antiquaries of London, 1986).

39 Paul Binski, 'The Painted Chamber at Westminster, the Fall of Tyrants and the English Literary Model of Governance', *Journal of the Warburg and Courtauld Institutes* 74 (2011): 121–54.

40 The contrast was due to the very different styles of rulership of the two kings who had left their artistic marks on this hall. Henry III, the pious son of King John I, was dedicated to reviving the legacy of St Edward the Confessor and was responsible for the more saintly and holy elements of the room. It was his son, Edward I, named for Henry's patron saint, who added the more war-like features, reflective of his very different style of rule. Reeve, 'The Painted Chamber', 191.

41 Chrimes, *Henry VII*, 240; Steven Gunn, 'Edmund Dudley and the Church', *The Journal of Ecclesiastical History* 51 (2000): 515.

42 The portrait of Oct 1505 does not show the strain apparent in his death mask four years later but may have been a flattering portrayal; see Penn, *Winter King*, 197. The Spanish ambassador, in a report of 1498, suggests that the king 'looks old for his years'; Robert Hutchinson, *Young Henry: The Rise of Henry VIII*, UK edition (London: W&N, 2012), 42; *CSPS*, I, no. 210. The description which follows is taken from this portrait, the death mask, Vergil's description in *The English History* and Hall, 504.

43 Timothy Jones Mucklow, 'William Warham: A Political Biography' (Ph.D., United States – West Virginia, West Virginia University, 1982).

44 Mucklow, 'William Warham', 69.

45 Mucklow, 'William Warham', 85.

46 *PRME.*

47 Graves, *Tudor Parliaments*, 20–21.

48 'Chapter House', Westminster Abbey, accessed 11 October 2020, https://www.westminster-abbey.org/about-the-abbey/history/chapter-house.

49 Hawkyard, 'The Tudor Speakers', 22–48; see Gunn, *Henry VII's New Men* for the offices of Treasurer and Comptroller, and who held them at this time.

50 Penn, *Winter King*, 159.

51 It had cost him more than £46 to turn down the post; Wilson, *Uncrowned Kings*, 16.

52 Hawkyard, 'The Tudor Speakers', 22–48.

53 Graves, *Tudor Parliaments*, 21–2.

54 Graves, *Tudor Parliaments*, 48–9; Cavill, *The English Parliaments of Henry VII*, 117–18.

55 *SR*, II, 19 Henry VII, c. 1, 12.

56 Frank Arthur Mumby, ed., *The Youth of Henry VIII: A Narrative in Contemporary Letters* (London: Houghton Mifflin, 1913), 66; 'Picture Reveals Young Henry VIII', *BBC News*, 19 October 2012, sec. Wales, https://www.bbc.com/news/uk-wales-20003806.

57 *SR*, II, 19 Henry VII, c. 26.

58 They clashed on Deptford Bridge, just to the south-east of London; 25,000 of Henry's soldiers against the rebels, who folded under the superior power of the king's army. Cavill, *The English Parliaments of Henry VII*, 191–3.

59 Penn, *Winter King*, 161.

60 *SR*, II, 19 Henry VII, c. 32.

61 Penn, *Winter King*, 160–63.

62 *PRME*, Introduction. In the end, Henry reduced it further to £30,000, perhaps sensing unrest. Andrew Windsor was one of the commissioners named for Middlesex as well as Buckinghamshire; *SR*, II, 19 Henry VII, c. 32.

63 Chrimes, *Henry VII*, 211.

64 *SR*, II, 19 Henry VII, c. 32.

65 William Roper, *The Life of Sir Thomas More*, ed. Gerard Wegemer and Stephen W. Smith (Dallas: Centre for Thomas More Studies, 2003), https://thomasmorestudies.org/docs/Roper.pdf, 4.

66 *LL*, I, 155.

67 Simon Adams, *Leicester and the Court: Essays on Elizabethan Politics* (Manchester University Press, 2002), 316.

68 For the relationship between Edmund Dudley and the prior of Tortington see Gunn, *Henry VII's New Men*, 165–6; Henry A. Harben, 'Sweating's Passage – Sydes (Seint) Lane', in *A Dictionary of London* (London, 1918), *British History Online* http://www.british-history.ac.uk/no-series/dictionary-of-london/sweatings-passage-sydes-lane [accessed 5 March 2018]; A. E. Daniell, *London City Churches* (London: Archibald Constable and Co. Ltd, 1907), 292.

69 C. L. Kingsford, 'On Some London Houses of the Early Tudor Period', *Archaeologia* 71 (1921): 17–54.

70 See David Cressy, *Birth, Marriage, and Death: Ritual, Religion, and the Life-Cycle in Tudor and Stuart England* (Oxford: Oxford University Press, 1997).

71 Catherine French, 'The Material Culture of Childbirth in Late Medieval London and Its Suburbs', *Journal of Women's History* 28, no. 2 (2016): 126–48.

72 Peter Murray Jones and Lea T. Olsan, 'Performative Rituals for Conception and Childbirth in England, 900–1500', *Bulletin of the History of Medicine* 89, no. 3 (2015): 406–33.

73 Monica Helen Green, ed., *The Trotula: A Medieval Compendium of Women's Medicine*, Middle Ages Series (Philadelphia: University of Pennsylvania Press, 2001).

74 Green, ed., *The Trotula*.

2. TWO RAVENING WOLVES

1 Account of the Clopton case from James Ross, '"Contrary to the Ryght and to the Order of the Lawe": New Evidence of Edmund Dudley's Activities on Behalf of Henry VII in 1504', *The English Historical Review* 127, no. 524 (2012): 24–45.

2 Edmund Dudley had become a full-time royal councillor in October 1504, at about the same time the Clopton affair was taking place; Gunn, *Henry VII's New Men*, 8.

3 The 'Galarre next to the Great Chamber', which is almost certainly on the upper floor, is the most likely room into which Edmund Dudley would receive such petitioners. It contained all the necessary furnishings, as well as 'a coffer with bylles and boxis with evidence', further suggesting it was a work-room. It was adjacent to the Great Chamber,

which in turn had a 'Closett' in which was contained the rest of Dudley's papers and purses; NA E 154/2/17, printed in C. L. Kingsford, 'On Some London Houses of the Early Tudor Period', *Archaeologia* 71 (1921): 39-42. See also Lena Cowen Orlin, *Locating Privacy in Tudor London* (Oxford; New York: Oxford University Press, 2007), 227, 235. My thanks to Nicola Clark for this reference.

4 My thanks to Eva Johanna Holmberg for this detail.

5 Penn, *Winter King*, 267.

6 Penn, *Winter King*, 269.

7 W. J. W. Potter and E. J. Winstanley, 'The Coinage of Henry VII', *British Numismatic Journal* 30 (1960), 262.

8 Steve Lee Rappaport, *Worlds within Worlds: Structures of Life in Sixteenth-Century London* (Cambridge: Cambridge University Press, 1989), 128-30.

9 Mark R. Horowitz, 'Henry Tudor's Treasure'. *Historical Research* 82, no. 217 (2009): 562-3; Breverton, 393.

10 Hollie L. S. Morgan, *Beds and Chambers in Late Medieval England: Readings, Representations and Realities* (Woodbridge: Boydell & Brewer, 2017), 140-1; John Lydgate, 'Prohemy of a Mariage Betwixt an Olde Man and a Yonge Wife, and the Counsail', Robbins Library Digital Projects, accessed 4 May 2018, http://d.lib.rochester.edu/teams/text/salisbury-trials-and-joys-prohemy-of-a-mariage-betwixt-an-olde-man-and-a-yonge-wife-and-the-counsail.

11 Martin Ingram, *Carnal Knowledge: Regulating Sex in England, 1470–1600*, Cambridge Studies in Early Modern British History (Cambridge: Cambridge University Press, 2017), 44-6.

12 Conor McCarthy, *Marriage in Medieval England: Law, Literature, and Practice* (Woodbridge: Boydell & Brewer, 2004), 107-9.

13 Morgan, *Beds and Chambers*, 155-6.

14 Jennifer Evans, *Aphrodisiacs, Fertility and Medicine in Early Modern England* (Woodbridge: Boydell & Brewer Ltd, 2014), 78; Thomas Laqueur, 'Orgasm, Generation, and the Politics of Reproductive Biology', *Representations*, no. 14 (1986): 1-41.

15 SP 1/2 fol. 3.

16 Morgan, *Beds and Chambers*, 77, 172-3.

17 James Daybell, *Women Letter-Writers in Tudor England* (Oxford: Oxford University Press, 2006), 13.

18 LA DDCL 298, by kind permission of J. C. Hilton, Lord of the Manor of Lytham.

19 For the description of Richmond see Robert Cowie and John Cloake, 'An Archaeological Survey of Richmond Palace, Surrey', *Post-Medieval Archaeology* 35, no. 1 (2001): 3–52. The royal apartments were those closest to the river: Cowie and Cloake, 'Archaeological Survey', 4.

20 Penn, *Winter King*, 272.

21 Fabyan, 261. Philip of Austria had been shipwrecked off the coast of Dorset on his way to Spain in January 1506. It became an opportunity for the two rulers to meet; Penn, *Winter King*, 215–16.

22 Gunn, *Henry VII's New Men*, 40.

23 Chrimes, *Henry VII*, 103.

24 The case of Thomas Sunnyff is taken from Mark R. Horowitz, '"Agree with the King": Henry VII, Edmund Dudley and the Strange Case of Thomas Sunnyff', *Historical Research* 79, no. 205 (2006): 325–66.

25 It is unclear for what purpose Sunnyff entered into this particular bond, see Horowitz, '"Agree with the King"', 340–1. For more on bonds under Henry VII, see Mark R. Horowitz, 'A Country under Contract: Early-Tudor England and the Growth of a Credit Culture', *Essays in Economic and Business History* 29 (2011): 75–86.

26 Penn, *Winter King*, 153.

27 Empson retaliated by having Cornysh imprisoned, though he was bound by an obligation to the king not to seek physical revenge on Cornysh.

28 justicetyrwhit, 'Babington v Venour (1465): Bankruptcy, Ravishment and the Fleet Prison', *Order of the Coif* (blog), 29 January 2017, https://orderofthecoif.wordpress.com/2017/01/29/babington-v-venour-1465-bankruptcy-ravishment-and-the-fleet-prison/.

29 Camby later placed the blame on one Robert Fenrother, a goldsmith who had entered into an obligation with the king and Edmund Dudley in November 1505, in order to be made a master of the mint; Horowitz, '"Agree with the King"', 332.

30 It is unclear why Camby does not follow through on Dudley's threat of the Tower. Perhaps by keeping Sunnyff in his home and local prisons, he hoped to scrape more off the top if Sunnyff paid, or perhaps at this point both he and Dudley were acting without the king's authorization.

31 Gunn, *Henry VII's New Men*, 239.

32 Gunn, *Henry VII's New Men*, 240.

33 Gunn, *Henry VII's New Men*, 8.

34 Penn, *Winter King*, 334 gives February, Terry Breverton, *Henry VII: The Maligned Tudor King* (Stroud: Amberley Publishing, 2016), 390

records it as January. The former is more probably the case, if Fisher delivered a sermon to him on 25 February at Hanworth.

35 'The King's Tomb Part I – KING HENRY VI', accessed 17 May 2018, http://www.henrysixth.com/?page_id=120.

36 *CSPS*, I, no. 511.

37 *CSPS*, I, no. 398.

38 According to the report made by the ambassador Fuensalida, visiting in 1508; J. J. Scarisbrick, *Henry VIII* (Berkeley: University of California Press, 1968), 6–7.

39 W. R. Lethaby, 'The Romance Tiles of Chertsey Abbey', *The Volume of the Walpole Society* 2 (1912): 69–80.

40 'Tile | V&A Search the Collections', V and A Collections, 17 May 2018, http://collections.vam.ac.uk/item/O129390.

41 Hilary M. Carey, 'Henry VII's Book of Astrology and the Tudor Renaissance', *Renaissance Quarterly* 65, no. 3 (2012): 689.

42 'Pastscape – Detailed Result: HANWORTH MANOR', accessed 22 December 2020, https://www.pastscape.org.uk/hob.aspx?hob_id=398090.

43 Penn, *Winter King*, 307, 333.

44 Michael K. Jones and Malcolm G. Underwood, *The King's Mother: Lady Margaret Beaufort, Countess of Richmond and Derby* (Cambridge: Cambridge University Press, 1993), 92; Penn, *Winter King*, 343; Nicola Tallis, *Uncrowned Queen: The Fateful Life of Margaret Beaufort Tudor Matriarch* (London: Michael O'Mara, 2019), 273.

45 Horowitz, 'The Accession of Henry VIII', 284–5.

46 Horowitz, 'The Accession of Henry VIII', 285.

47 In early 1509, Edmund worked to help the Sussex heiress Elizabeth Lovell escape her marriage to Edward Bray, a young lawyer. Not long after she instead married the younger Windsor brother, Anthony.

48 Kingsford, 'On Some Houses', 40.

49 Penn, *Winter King*, 338–9.

50 *The Will of King Henry VII* (London, 1775). Abridged version printed in Nicolas, ed., *Testamenta Vetusta*, 26–36.

51 *Will of Henry VII*, 2.

52 *Will of Henry VII*, 13.

53 *Will of Henry VII*, 12.

54 Anglicus Gilbertus, *Healing and Society in Medieval England: A Middle English Translation of the Pharmaceutical Writings of Gilbertus Anglicus*, ed. Faye Marie Getz (Univ. of Wisconsin Press, 1991), 101–2.

1 The details of what proceeded directly after the death of Henry VII comes from S. J. Gunn, 'The Accession of Henry VIII', *Historical Research* 64, no. 155 (1991): 278–88.

2 G. Parnell, 'The Rise and Fall of the Tower of London', *History Today* 42, no. 3 (1992): 13.

3 See SP 1/2, fol. 7^r.

4 G. R. Elton, 'Henry VII: Rapacity and Remorse', *The Historical Journal* 1, no. 1 (1958): 37.

5 TNA C 82/335.

6 Taken from Fabyan, 348.

7 *LP*, I, no. 20.

8 *LP*, I, no. 19.

9 BL Arundel 26 fol. 28^r–29^r; *LP*, I, no. 20.

10 Account of the procession from BL Harley 3504 fol. 264^r–267^r; *LP*, I, 20.

11 *LP*, I, 81; Jennifer Loach, 'The Function of Ceremonial in the Reign of Henry VIII', *Past & Present*, no. 142 (1994): 48.

12 *LP*, I, 81, 82.

13 Lauren Johnson, *So Great a Prince: England in 1509* (London: Head of Zeus, 2016), 108.

14 'Coronation Ode of King Henry VIII' http://www.thomasmorestudies. org/docs/Mores_1509_Coronation_Ode.pdf.

15 Account of the trial from Deputy Keeper of the Public Records, 'Appendix II', *Annual Report. V.1–3.* (London: HMSO, 1840), 226–7.

16 *SR*, III, 3 Henry VIII c. 19.

17 *SR*, III, 3 Henry VII c. 34.

18 The timing of these messages, and Edmund Dudley's interaction with them is unclear, and they might have come after his 'petition'; see Horowitz, '"Agree with the King"', 359–63.

19 *SR*, III, 3 Henry VIII c. 19.

20 SP 1/231 fol. 187.

21 Horowitz, '"Agree with the King"', 359.

22 For an analysis and text of the petition see C. J. Harrison, 'The Petition of Edmund Dudley', *The English Historical Review* 87, no. 142 (1972): 82–99.

23 Edmund Dudley, *The Tree of Commonwealth: A Treatise*, ed. D. M. Brodie (Cambridge: Cambridge University Press, 1948), 36.

24 Dudley, *Tree of Commonwealth*, 37.

25 Dudley, *Tree of Commonwealth*, 82.

26 Dudley, *Tree of Commonwealth*, 83.

27 This assumption is based on the fact that no women's or children's clothing is in the Candlewick inventory described below.

28 TNA E 154/2 fol. 17.

29 For John Digby's history with Edmund Dudley, see Harrison, 'Petition', 93 n. 23.

30 Maria Hayward, *Rich Apparel: Clothing and the Law in Henry VIII's England*, 1st edition (Farnham, England; Burlington, VT: Routledge, 2009), 29–31.

31 Gunn, *Henry VII's New Men*, 202–3.

32 *LP*, II, 2, no. 2055.

33 The account of the planned escape is taken from Edmund Dudley's will: TNA SP 1/2 fol. 7ʳ. I have been unable to find records to connect by blood Edmund Dudley and James Beamond. He appears as Dudley's 'servant' in a record from 1507 (see Steven Gunn, 'Edmund Dudley and the Church', *The Journal of Ecclesiastical History* 51 (2000): 518), and appears to be named in pardons in 1511 (*LP*, I, 438; *LP*, I, 804 (23)).

34 *LJ*, I, 7–8.

35 By 24 March the king was looking for officers to oversee Edmund Dudley's lands; TNA E 36/215, fol. 49.

36 LA DDCL 298, by kind permission of J. C. Hilton, Lord of the Manor of Lytham.

37 SP 1/2, fol. 5ʳ. His executors included Richard FitzJames, who had sworn at him about his unjust treatment at the king's hands, John Colet, the humanist who had recently begun the work of establishing a new school in London, John Yonge, the Master of the Rolls, who had been handed Edmund's petition from Fox and Lovell, and of course his brother-in-law, Andrew Windsor.

38 SP 1/2, fol. 7ᵛ.

39 Two manuscripts detailing her dealings with the London fuller William Cawarden place her in London. In the first, on 31 August 1510, she received money and cloth from him (SHC 6729/2/11), the second (SHC LM 345/7) is a quitclaim for all 'actions, divisions, quarrels and debts' on 19 November 1510. Both contain her signature. My thanks to the archivists at the Surrey History Centre for their assistance. It is also probable that Lady Lytton helped Elizabeth and the children at this time, as is indicated by Edmund's will; LA DDCL 298, by kind permission of J. C. Hilton, Lord of the Manor of Lytham.

40 Condon, M. M. 'Empson, Sir Richard (c. 1450–1510)', *ODNB*.

41 The only account of the executions, in Fabyan, is brief; its brevity has here been assumed to indicate that all went according to the usual procedure.

4. MY LORD THE BASTARD

1 Account of the Whitsuntide tournament from CA MS L. 12, fol. 10ʳ–11ʳ. See also Viscount Dillon, 'Barriers and Foot Combats', *Archaeological Journal* 61, no. 1 (1 January 1904): 276–308; Alan Young, *Tudor and Jacobean Tournaments* (Dobbs Ferry, NY: Sheridan House, 1987).

2 John Grey died in 1504, shortly before his daughter's birth. Muriel married again not long after.

3 Gunn, *Charles Brandon*, 18.

4 Edward IV had a number of mistresses, and it is unclear which of them gave birth to Arthur; his father was happy to claim him as his own.

5 Gunn, *Charles Brandon*, 19–20; see *LP*, II, 'The King's Book of Payments, 1510'; *LP*, II, 'The King's Book of Payments, 1514'.

6 *CSPS*, II, no. 44.

7 Charles Isaac Elton, *The Tenures of Kent* (London: Parker and Company, 1867), 374–5, from the *Patent Rolls* of Mary I, 1553. It is possible that the lands were slightly different in 1510.

8 BL Cotton Caligula D/VI fol. 146.

9 Though Edward Guildford was the son of Anne Pympe, Richard Guildford's first wife, not Jane Vaux.

10 Kenneth Charlton, *Women, Religion and Education in Early Modern England* (London: Routledge, 2014), 13–14; Barbara Whitehead, *Women's Education in Early Modern Europe: A History, 1500 to 1800* (New York: Routledge, 1999).

11 Aysha Pollnitz, *Princely Education in Early Modern Britain* (Cambridge: Cambridge University Press, 2015), 203.

12 *LP*, I, no. 1602; D. M. Loades, *John Dudley, Duke of Northumberland, 1504–1553* (Oxford: Clarendon Press, 1996). My thanks to Judith Loades for providing access to David Loades's publications in the Davenant Press. In September 1512, for instance, Edward Guildford received a payment of £120 from revenues of Dudley's land; *LP*, II, no. 4.4.

13 *SR*, III, 41; *LP*, I, no. 1046; Loades, *John Dudley*, 288.

14 Much of the account of the battle taken from: David Childs, *The Warship Mary Rose: The Life & Times of King Henry VIII's Flagship* (Barnsley: Seaforth Publishing, 2014), 105–8.

15 Alfred Spont, *Letters and Papers Relating to the War with France,
1512–1513* (London: Navy Records Society, 1897), xiv.

16 Spont, *Letters and Papers*, xxi–xxii.

17 Spont, *Letters and Papers*, xxv.

18 Spont, *Letters and Papers*, xxvii.

19 Childs, *Mary Rose*, 112.

20 BL Cotton Caligula E/I f.9; Childs, *Mary Rose*, 115. As Childs points
out, this story could be a tactic to win the king's clemency.

21 This account also taken largely from Childs, *Mary Rose*, 116–17.

22 He received £120 in September 1512; *LP*, II, 'King's Book of Payments: 1512'.

23 Gunn, *Charles Brandon*, 20–3.

24 Details of Brandon's marriages and flirtations from Gunn, *Charles
Brandon*.

25 Gunn, *Charles Brandon*, 20.

26 SP 1/3; S. J. Gunn, *The English People at War in the Age of Henry VIII*
(Oxford: Oxford University Press, 2018), 17.

27 George Goodwin, 'Your Guide to the Battle of Flodden 1513', *HistoryExtra*, 2013, https://www.historyextra.com/period/tudor/battle-
flodden-battlefield-scotland-scottish-invasion-guide-facts-dates/.

28 SP 1/7 fol. 134.

5. SOME FIT EXERCISE FOR WAR

1 Much of the description of Calais taken from Susan Rose, *Calais: An
English Town in France, 1347–1558* (Woodbridge: Boydell & Brewer,
2008) and contemporary maps.

2 Theodor Dumitrescu, *The Early Tudor Court and International
Musical Relations* (London: Routledge, 2017), 36.

3 David Grummitt, *The Calais Garrison: War and Military Service in
England, 1436–1558* (Woodbridge: Boydell & Brewer, 2008), 127.

4 Rose, *Calais*, 124.

5 Rose, *Calais*, 112.

6 Rose, *Calais*, 118.

7 Grummitt, *Calais Garrison*, 5.

8 Dumitrescu, *The Early Tudor Court*, 53; Grummitt, *Calais Garrison*, 1.

9 Rose, *Calais*, 140; Grummit, *Calais Garrison*, 5.

10 Rose, *Calais*, 134.

11 Rose, *Calais*, 134.

12 Rose, *Calais*, 115–16.

13 Rose, *Calais*, 141.

14 Rose, *Calais*, 139.

15 Rose, *Calais*, 140.

16 Grummitt, *Calais Garrison*, 1.

17 Grummitt, *Calais Garrison*, 1, 10.

18 Grummitt, *Calais Garrison*, 46, 61–2.

19 Grummitt, *Calais Garrison*, 120.

20 Grummitt, *Calais Garrison*, 122.

21 The conflict was over the clergy's 'benefits': 'immunity from the king's courts when accused of serious crimes'. At a conference in Baynard's Castle in 1515, Warham pointed out to Henry that one of his predecessors (Thomas Becket) had been martyred in defence of clerical liberties (by Henry II). Henry maintained that 'God only' was superior to the king; J. J. Scarisbrick, 'Warham, William (1450?–1532)', *ODNB*. Fox resigned too shortly thereafter; C. S. L. Davies, 'Fox [Foxe], Richard (1447/8–1528)', *ODNB*.

22 Catherine was the second-youngest daughter of Edward IV and Elizabeth Woodville, and had married William Courtenay in 1495.

23 Peter Gwyn, 'Wolsey's Foreign Policy: The Conferences at Calais and Bruges Reconsidered', *The Historical Journal* 23, no. 4 (1980): 755–72.

24 Gwyn, 'Wolsey's Foreign Policy', 761.

25 See Richard Turpyn, *The Chronicle of Calais: In the Reigns of Henry VII and Henry VIII to the Year 1540. Ed. from Mss. in the British Museum* (London: Camden Society, 1846), 94–8; BL MS Harl. 620.

26 Sharon Turner, *The History of the Reign of Henry the Eighth: Comprising the Political History of the Commencement of the English Reformation* (London: Longman, Rees, Orme, Brown and Green, 1828), 299.

27 Hall, 624.

28 An account of the Cardinal's visit is given in Cambridge, Corpus Christi College MS 111, 383–95. My thanks to the Parker Library for providing a digital copy of this MS.

29 Cambridge, Corpus Christi College MS 111, 384.

30 Cambridge, Corpus Christi College MS 111, 390.

31 Peter Gwyn, *The King's Cardinal: The Rise and Fall of Thomas Wolsey* (London: Pimlico, 1992), loc. 5052.

32 *The Prince* circulated in manuscript long before it was printed. Men like Cardinal Giovanni Salviati knew Machiavelli's writings well and were engaged in diplomacy across Europe; Sydney Anglo, *Machiavelli – The First Century: Studies in Enthusiasm, Hostility, and Irrelevance*

(Oxford: Oxford University Press, 2005), 33. Two years after Dudley was in Calais, a 'reworking' of *The Prince* was published in Florence by Agostino Nifo, a protégé of Pope Leo X; Anglo, *Machiavelli*, 42–3. It was, of course, unlikely that John Dudley read the text at this time, and may have never read it, but by the 1520s, its ideas were probably beginning to be discussed. My thanks to Catherine Fletcher for her assistance with this point.

33 Machiavelli, *The Prince*, 20, 62; I have changed 'luck' to 'fortune' to reflect the original '*fortuna*'.

34 Dudley, *Tree of Commonwealth*, 13.

35 Dudley, *Tree of Commonwealth*, 50.

36 S. J. Gunn, *The English People at War in the Age of Henry VIII* (Oxford: Oxford University Press, 2018), 6.

37 Gunn, *The English People at War*, 98.

38 S. J. Gunn, 'The Duke of Suffolk's March on Paris in 1523', *The English Historical Review* 101, no. 400 (1986): 598–9.

39 Gunn, 'The Duke of Suffolk's March', 596.

40 Hall, 655; I have slightly abridged and amended from the original.

41 Hall, 656.

42 Elis Gruffydd, *Suffolk's Expedition to Montdidier 1523*, ed. M. Bryn Davies (Cairo: Fouad I University, 1944), 2.

43 Harry Leonard, 'Knights and Knighthood in Tudor England' (Thesis, Queen Mary, University of London, 1970), 217. This is the ceremony used for dubbing knights banneret, which Leonard maintains (221) would have been the basis for the dubbing of ordinary knights as well.

44 Gruffydd, *Suffolk's Expedition*, 9.

45 SP 1/32 fol. 256.

46 CA M 6 57^v; see also Hall, 688.

47 CA M 6 57^v, slightly abridged.

48 *SR*, III, 41; *LP*, I, no. 1046.

49 Cressy, *Birth, Marriage and Death*, 337.

50 Based on a portrait of John Dudley from the 1540s, housed at Penshurst, Kent.

51 Service from *Sarum Missal*, 144–60.

52 William Carpenter, *Peerage for the People* (London: W. Strange, 1841), 698–9.

53 It is probable that Richard Guildford had suffered wound dehiscence caused by infection and mobility.

54 BL Cotton Vespasian C/III fol. 273^v.

55 SP 1/32 fol. 20^v–21^r.

56 BL Cotton Vitellius B/VI fol.142ᵛ, 153ᵛ–54ʳ.

57 *LP*, IV, no. 1938.

58 BL Cotton Vitellius B/VII fol. 112ʳ; SP 1/37 fol. 17ʳ.

59 *LP*, IV, no. 1925.

60 LP, IV, no. 1583; *LP*, IV, no. 2569.

61 Gunn, *Charles Brandon*, 132.

6. AND THE QUEEN HERSELF SHALL
BE CONDEMNED

1 Account from Hall, 805–6 and *LP*, 6, no. 1111.

2 There appears to have been a gallery that connected the west part of
   the palace to the church. See Historic England, 'Greenwich Palace, Non
   Civil Parish – 1410710l Historic England', accessed 5 August 2018,
   https://historicengland.org.uk/listing/the-list/list-entry/1410710 and
   Hall, *Chronicle*, 805.

3 Simon Thurley, *Houses of Power: The Places That Shaped the Tudor
   World* (London; New York: Bantam Press, 2017), 68.

4 Nicholas Harpsfield, *A Treatise on the Pretended Divorce Between
   Henry VIII and Catherine of Aragon* (London: Camden Society, 1878),
   203. This is a later account, and with its own agenda. Nevertheless, the
   imperial ambassador Chapys also confirms that Henry was given a
   warning that day about letting his affections get the better of him, so
   we can surmise that something controversial was preached.

5 *LP*, V, no. 941; *LP*, XII, no. 952.

6 SP 1/78 fol. 25.

7 Nigel Reynolds, 'Henry VII's Chapel Found at Greenwich', 25 January
   2006, see News, https://www.telegraph.co.uk/news/uknews/1508708/
   Henry-VIIs-chapel-found-at-Greenwich.html.

8 CA M. 6bis, fol. 17ʳ.

9 CA M. 8, fol. 76ᵛ, 85ʳ.

10 Alison Weir, *Henry VIII: King and Court* (London: Random House,
    2011), 107.

11 See James Williams, 'Hunting and the Royal Image of Henry VIII',
    Sport in History 25, no. 1 (2005): 41–59; Glenn Richardson, 'Hunting
    at the Courts of Francis I and Henry VIII', *The Court Historian* 18, no.
    2 (2013): 127–41.

12 Dudley was granted the post on 29 June 1534 and given '12d. a day for
    himself, 6d. a day for a page, and 3d. a day for an under-page, under

him, out of the issues of the port of Cirencester as lately enjoyed by Sir Edward Guildford; and to have all buildings, &c. on the wharf of the Tower and on Tower Hill'; LP, 7, no. 1026 (15). In 1540 he was making about £31/year from the post; *LP*, 15, no. 599(2). The last record of Dudley as master of the armoury is in 1541, presumably superseded once he became Viscount Lisle and Lord Admiral; *LP*, 16, no. 1489.

13 *LL*, 403, 506; SP 3/3, 156.

14 Welbore St Clair Baddeley, *Cotteswold Manor; Being the History of Painswick* (Gloucester: John Bellows, 1907), 143–4.

15 Loades, *John Dudley*, 289.

16 For the path and timings of the progress of 1535 see Sarah Morris and Natalie Grueninger, *In the Footsteps of Anne Boleyn* (Stroud: Amberley Publishing Limited, 2013), 176–270.

17 St Clair Baddeley, *Cotteswold Manor*, 159.

18 Weir, *Henry VIII*, 281.

19 Eric Ives, *The Life and Death of Anne Boleyn: The Most Happy* (Malden, MA: Wiley-Blackwell, 2005), 39–41.

20 Nicolas Bourbon, *Nugarum libri octo*, 1540, 87; Margaret M. Phillips, 'The Paedagogian of Nicholas Bourbon', in *Neo-Latin and the Vernacular in Renaissance Florence*, ed. Terence Cave and Graham Castor (Oxford: Clarendon Press, 1984), 74; Eric Ives, 'A Frenchman at the Court of Anne Boleyn', *History Today* 48, no. 8 (August 1998): 21.

21 Nicolas Bourbon, *Nugarum libri octo*, 1540, 181. Translation my own.

22 Phillips, 'Paedagogian', 74.

23 Phillips, 'Paedagogian', 76.

24 Quoted in Phillips, 'Paedagogian', 76.

25 Phillips, 'Paedagogian', 77.

26 Quoted in James Mearns, 'The Influence of Erasmus's Educational Writings on Nicholas Bourbon's *Paidagogeion*', *Bibliothèque d'humanisme et Renaissance; Travaux et Documents* 72 (1 March 2010): 69.

27 Quoted in Mearns, 'Nicholas Bourbon's *Paidagogeion*', 74.

28 SP 3/3 fol. 21.

29 SP 3/10 fol. 122.

30 Ives, *Anne Boleyn*, 307.

31 *CSPS*, V, ii, no. 43.

32 SP 3/10 fol. 122.

33 Anne's mother was Thomas Howard's sister.

34 Account of the trial from Wriothesley, I, 37–8.

35 Wriothesley, I, 38.

36 Wriothesley, I, 41–2.

37 Description of the funeral procession of Queen Jane from CA M. 6 fol. 1ʳ-12ᵛ. My thanks to Lynsey Darby at the College of Arms for her research assistance.

38 It is unclear whether the 'Lady Dudley' who came to stay with Lady Mary in November 1533 was Jane Dudley or the wife of Baron Dudley; *LP*, 6, no. 1540.

39 BL Royal MS 17B xxviii, fols. 7ʳ, 13ʳ; BL Harley MS 523 fol. 11ʳ; Susan Higginbotham, 'How Old Was Guildford Dudley? (Beats Me.)', *History Refreshed* (blog), 2011, http://www.susanhigginbotham.com/blog/posts/how-old-was-guildford-dudley-beats-me/. Mary and Guildford are the most probable candidates for Mary's godchildren in January and March 1537. See Appendix on the birth dates of the Dudley children.

40 *LP*, 13, no. 1280.

41 Elizabeth Norton, *Anne of Cleves: Henry VIII's Discarded Bride* (Stroud: Amberley Publishing, 2010), Chapter 10.

42 Anne of Cleves was descended from Edward I, as well as being related to the King of France and Charles V. She was reported in 1539 to be of 'lowly [humble] and gentle [noble] conditions'; Norton, *Anne of Cleves*, Chapter 1; Sarah-Beth Watkins, *Anne of Cleves: Henry VIII's Unwanted Wife*, (Winchester: Chronos Books, 2018), Chapter 1. My thanks to Valerie Schutte for her assistance with this section.

43 Norton, *Anne of Cleves*, Chapter 3; for an assessment of Anne's physical appearance and 'beauty', see Norton, *Anne of Cleves*, Chapter 5.

44 Diarmaid MacCulloch, *Thomas Cromwell: A Life* (London: Penguin UK, 2018), 425; Norton, *Anne of Cleves*, Chapter 9.

45 Loades, *John Dudley*, 288–9.

46 MacCulloch, *Thomas Cromwell*, 485.

47 Account of the meeting at Blackheath from CA M. 6bis, fols. 118–27; Hall, 832–6; BL Cotton Vitellius C/XVI fol. 271.

48 Wriothesley, I, 109–10; *CSPS*, VI. i, no. 144.

49 Roger Bigelow Merriman, *Life and Letters of Thomas Cromwell* (Oxford: Clarendon Press, 2000), 270.

7 . A MORTAL BREAKFAST IF HE WERE THE KING'S ENEMY

1 For the description of Dudley Castle, see Harold Brakspear, 'Dudley Castle', *Archaeological Journal* 71, no. 1 (1914): 1–24; W. Douglas

Simpson, 'Dudley Castle: The Renaissance Buildings', *Archaeological Journal* 101, no. 1 (1944): 119–25; 'Exrenda – Dudley Castle C1550 Visualisation', accessed 28 August 2018, http://www.exrenda.com/dudley/dudley.htm.

2 See Loades, *John Dudley*, 289 for this exchange of lands.

3 SP 1/73 fol. 102.

4 SP 1/85 fol. 150.

5 Details of the visit from Dudley's letter to Cromwell: SP 1/58 fol. 65.

6 Felicity Heal, *Hospitality in Early Modern England* (Oxford: Oxford University Press, 1990), 23.

7 Walter Jost and Wendy Olmsted, *A Companion to Rhetoric and Rhetorical Criticism* (Oxford: John Wiley & Sons, 2008), 106–7, from George Puttenham's *The Arte of English Poesie* (1589).

8 Jost and Olmsted, *A Companion*, 107.

9 *LP*, 9, no. 41, no 85; Charles Creighton, *A History of Epidemics in Britain: From A. D. 664 to the Extinction of Plague* (Cambridge: Cambridge University Press, 1891), 298–9.

10 Paul Slack, *The Impact of Plague in Tudor and Stuart England* (Oxford: New York: Oxford University Press, USA, 1991), 65.

11 Heal, *Hospitality*, 192.

12 It is unclear whether John Dudley simply wanted to join the Council or to become President. The office was occupied by a close Cromwell ally, Bishop Rowland Lee, who in May 1539 was ill (Dudley made the request in July); Penry Williams, *The Council in the Marches of Wales under Elizabeth I* (Cardiff, University of Wales Press, 1958), 16.

13 SP 1/152 fol. 132.

14 MacCulloch, *Thomas Cromwell*, 443.

15 The details of the tournament and participants can be found in BL Harley MS. 69 f. 18. More details can be found in Wriothesley, I, 116–19.

16 TNA E 326/12370. I am not convinced that the Andrew Dudley who is a servant of the Duke of Norfolk, and presumably the same who is a customs officer in Kent, is also John Dudley's brother; see SP 1/163 fol. 101; TNA E 122/130/9.

17 Thurley, *Houses of Power*, 132–3.

18 Thurley, *Houses of Power*, 133.

19 Giles Tremlett, *Catherine of Aragon: Henry's Spanish Queen* (Faber & Faber, 2010), 106.

20 *LP*, XV, no. 901.

21 Katherine's mother, Joyce Culpeper, had died some years before; her father died in 1539.

22 *LP*, XV, no. 613.

23 SP 1/98 f.8.

24 SP 3/12 fol. 100.

25 SP 1/161 fol. 81.

26 *LP*, XV, no. 902.

27 SP 1/167 fol. 121. My thanks to Nicola Clark and Bradley J. Irish for their help with this source.

28 Thurley, *Houses of Power*, 171–2.

29 *LP*, XVI, no. 1297.

30 Thurley, *Houses of Power*, 293.

31 Alec Ryrie, 'Lassells [Lascelles], John (d. 1546)', *ODNB*.

32 Gareth Russell, *Young and Damned and Fair: the Life of Catherine Howard, Fifth Wife of King Henry VIII* (Simon & Schuster, 2017), 54.

33 BL Cotton Otho C/X fol. 250.

34 Mannock in the MS.

35 Quoted in Russell, *Young and Damned and Fair*, 303.

36 FitzWilliam had also been involved in Anne Boleyn's fall, breaking up her household on 13 May 1536.

37 He himself would become Earl of Southampton the next year.

38 *LP*, XVI, no. 1339.

39 *LP*, XVI, no. 1332.

40 Loades, *John Dudley*, 47–8 assumes John Dudley was also present at the interview.

41 *OED*.

42 SP 1/167 fol. 123.

43 *CSPV*, VI, no. 884.

44 BL Royal MS 17B xxviii.

45 *HMCR*, 55.

46 *HMCR*, 55.

47 *LP*, XVI, no. 1366.

48 Russell, *Young and Damned and Fair*, 347.

49 Russell, *Young and Damned and Fair*, 356.

50 I can find no evidence for the assertion that John Dudley was Howard's Master of the Horse; see Russell, *Young and Damned and Fair*, 132–3.

51 *CSPS*, VI, i, no. 223.

52 *CSPS*, VI, i, no. 232.

53 Thurley, *Houses of Power*, 132–3 for the description of the chamber at Whitehall.

54 Details of the ceremony from BL Egerton MS 2642, fols. 9–10.

8. ENVIOUS NEMESIS

1 Quoted in Steven G. Ellis, *Tudor Frontiers and Noble Power* (Oxford: Oxford University Press, 1995), 55, 71.

2 BL Add. MS. 32648. fol. 170.

3 SP 1/174 fol. 96 sets out John Dudley's new appointment, taking over from Seymour.

4 William Barclay D. D. Turnbull, *Historic Memorials of Coldstream Abbey, Berwickshire, Collected by a Delver in Antiquity*, London, 1850.

5 Janet E. Burton, and Karen Stöber, *Monasteries and Society in the British Isles in the Later Middle Ages* (Woodbridge: Boydell & Brewer Ltd, 2008), 133–4.

6 Quoted in Howard Pease, *The Lord Wardens of the Marches of England and Scotland* (London: Constable, 1913), 83.

7 D. Hay, 'England, Scotland and Europe: The Problem of the Frontier', *Transactions of the Royal Historical Society* 25 (1975): 79.

8 See Loades, *John Dudley*, 29, 43.

9 *LP*, 17, no. 1002.

10 BL Add MS 32648, fol. 170.

11 N. A. M. Rodger, *The Safeguard of the Sea: A Naval History of Britain 660–1649* (London: Penguin, 2004), 209–11. A proclamation would follow in 1544.

12 BL Add. MS 32648, fol. 170; *LP*, 17, no. 1130.

13 BL Add. MS 32648, fol. 190.

14 Marie de Guise's father had been made a duke in 1528, a position previously only held by members of the monarch's family. Her uncle was a cardinal and close adviser to the King of France.

15 BL Add. MS 32648, fol. 191.

16 BL Add. MS 32648, fol. 238.

17 BL Add. MS 32648, fol. 238.

18 *LP*, XVII, no. 1194.

19 BL Add. MS 32648, fol. 224.

20 M. Merriman, Douglas, 'Sir George, of Pittendriech (1490?–1552)', *ODNB*.

21 BL Add. MS 32648, fol. 207.

22 BL Add. MS 32648, fol. 224; BL Add. MS 32648, 217.

23 BL Add. MS 32648, fol. 220.

24 BL Add. MS 32648, fol. 220.

25 BL Add. MS 32648, fol. 224.

26 BL Add. MS 32648, fol. 234; there was even dispute about who should act as regent: the Earl of Arran, Cardinal Beaton or, of course, Mary's mother.

27 Loades, *John Dudley*, 57.

28 S. James, 'Katherine [Kateryn, Catherine] [née Katherine Parr] (1512–1548)', *ODNB*.

29 Tracy Borman, *Henry VIII and the Men Who Made Him: The Secret History behind the Tudor Throne* (London: Hachette UK, 2018), 375.

30 Elizabeth T. Hurren, 'Cultures of the Body, Medical Regimen, and Physic at the Tudor Court', in *Henry VIII and the Court: Art, Politics and Performance*, ed. Suzannah Lipscomb and Thomas Betteridge (Routledge, 2016).

31 Account from Elis Gruffydd, *Boulogne and Calais: From 1545 to 1550*, ed. M. Bryn Davies (Cairo: Fouad I University, 1950).

32 BL Add. MS. 32654. fol. 189; BL Add. MS. 32654, fol. 198.

33 Samuel Haynes, ed., *A Collection of State Papers, Relating to Affairs in the Reigns of King Henry VIII, King Edward VI, Queen Mary, and Queen Elizabeth, Transcribed from Original letters and Other Authentick Memorials, Left by William Cecill Lord Burghley* (London: Bowyer, 1740), no. 44.

34 Neil Murphy, *The Tudor Occupation of Boulogne: Conquest, Colonisation and Imperial Monarchy, 1544–1550* (Cambridge: Cambridge University Press, 2019), 1.

35 SP 1/190 fol. 96.

36 Phillips, 'Paedagogian', 79.

37 Phillips, 'The Paedagogian', 79.

38 TNA LR 2/119, 10ᵛ; BL Add. MS 32649, fol. 93.

39 John Leland, *Naenia in Mortem Splendidissimi Equitis Henrici Duddelegi Somarigana, Insulani, Verovicani* (London, 1545). My thanks to Francis Young for his assistance with the translation.

40 Leonard, 'Knights and Knighthood', 217.

41 Leonard, 'Knights and Knighthood', 210.

42 *OED*, N. Udall, trans., Erasmus, *Apophthegmes* fol. 329ᵛ.

43 My thanks to Eva Johanna Holmberg for her help with dysentery; see Hieronymus Brunschwig, *A Most Excellent and Perfecte Homish*

Apothecarye or Homely Physik Booke, for All the Grefes and Diseases of the Bodye, trans. John Hollybush (Cologne, 1561), 54ʳ.

44 William B. Robison, ed., 'Incomplete Prescription: Maladies and Medicine in *The Tudors*', in *History, Fiction, and The Tudors: Sex, Politics, Power, and Artistic License in the Showtime Television Series* (New York: Springer, 2017), 337.

45 Murphy, *Tudor Occupation of Boulogne*, 56.

46 SP 1/195 fol. 161; Childs, *Mary Rose*, 159.

47 Geoffrey Moorhouse, *Great Harry's Navy: How Henry VIII Gave England Sea Power* (London: Phoenix Press, 2005), 237.

48 Childs, *Mary Rose*, 162.

49 *HMCSP*, V, iv, 390.

50 Rodger, *Safeguard*, 183.

51 'About the Mary Rose', The Mary Rose, accessed 26 July 2021, https://maryrose.org/about-the-mary-rose/; Childs, *Mary Rose*, 27.

52 SP 1/205 fol. 46.

53 Moorhouse, *Great Harry's Navy*, 253–4.

54 Childs, *Mary Rose*, 166.

55 From Haynes, 2018.

56 Childs, *Mary Rose*, 190.

57 Miranda Kaufmann, *Black Tudors: The Untold Story* (London: Oneworld Publications, 2017), 37.

9. FLESH, BLOOD AND BONE

1 TNA E 328/358.

2 PROB 11/30/443.

3 *CSPS*, VIII, no. 174.

4 Andrew Windsor did not live long enough to make it to Ambrose's wedding. He had fallen ill in 1543 while John Dudley was in the borderlands and died at seventy-six, just a month shy of seeing John take up a place on the Privy Council and installed as a Knight of the Garter. Andrew's third son had been named Edmund, just as Edmund had named one of his sons Andrew. In his will, Andrew Windsor tasked him specifically with ensuring that the responsibilities given to Andrew in Edmund Dudley's will continued to be fulfilled. Even on his deathbed, Andrew had not forgotten his old friend and brother (PROB/11/29, fol. 23ᵛ).

5 S. T. Bindoff, *The House of Commons, 1509-1558* (Woodbridge: Boydell & Brewer, 1982), 445.

6 John Dudley, for instance, claimed not to understand Italian (SP 68/10 fol. 125) or Latin (SP 10/18 fol. 7). Thomas Wilson dedicated his *Art of Rhetoric* (1553) to John Dudley, then Duke of Northumberland; Thomas Wilson, *The Arte of Rhetorique* (London, 1553). He later dedicated his *Discourse upon Usury* (1572) to Robert Dudley, then Earl of Leicester, writing 'the bolder I am to deal thus with your honour before others, because I have known you, and that noble race of your brethren, even from their young years. And with your honour, and [John], and your noble brother, [Ambrose], I have had more familiar conference, than with the rest: and especially with your honour (I do thank you most humbly therefore) I have had sufficient proof of your careful mind, even in reading not only of the Latin, but also of the Italian good & and sound writers'; Thomas Wilson, *A Discourse Vppon Vsurye* (London, 1572), C2, i^r. Roger Ascham wrote to Robert Dudley in 1564, chiding him for preferring mathematics over rhetoric in his studies; Rev Giles, ed., *The Whole Works of Roger Ascham*, vol. 2 (London: John Russell Smith, 1864), 103–4. For John Dee's association with the Dudley family, see Peter J. French, *John Dee: The World of the Elizabethan Magus* (New York: Routledge, 2013), 32–3.

7 Alan Stewart, *Philip Sidney: A Double Life* (London: Random House, 2011), loc. 814.

8 Suzannah Lipscomb, *The King Is Dead: The Last Will and Testament of Henry VIII* (London: Head of Zeus, 2015), 44.

9 Lipscomb, *The King Is Dead,* 70.

10 Elaine V. Beilin, ed., *The Examinations of Anne Askew*, (Oxford: Oxford University Press, 1996), xvii.

11 Also known as the Treaty of Ardres. See Murphy, *Tudor Occupation of Boulogne*, 74.

12 Anne Askew, *The Lattre Examinacyon of Anne Askewe* (1547), 18^r. Original 'that it was great shame for them to counsell contrarye to their knowlege', I have taken the account of Anne's interrogation and torture from her *Examinations*.

13 Virginia Rounding, *The Burning Time: The Story of the Smithfield Martyrs* (Pan Macmillan, 2017).

14 *LP*, XXI, no. 1207.

15 *CSPS*, VIII, no. 291.

16 SP 1/220 fol. 35.

17 *LP*, XXI, no. 1219.

18 SP 1/221 fol. 187.

19 Accounts from BL Vespasian C/XIV., Pt. I., 67; Wriothesley, 173; Hall, 867. Hall suggests 2,000 men with the Prince, Wriothesley 1,000. The manuscript source is closest to this number at just under 800.

20 BL Harley MS 5087, no. 17.

21 Murphy, *Tudor Occupation of Boulogne*, 74–5; Charles Howard Carter, *The Secret Diplomacy of the Habsburgs: 1598–1625* (Columbia University Press, 1964), 62.

22 SP 1/223 fol. 190.

23 SP 1/221 fol. 200.

24 Hall, 867.

25 BL Vespasian C/XIV, Pt. I, fol. 67.

26 SP 1/225 fol. 6.

27 SP 1/223 fol. 34.

28 *LP*, XXII, no. 533.

29 SP 1/227 fol. 76.

30 SP 1/221 fol. 181.

31 SP 1/227 fol. 109ʳ.

32 *CSPS*, VIII, no. 208, 210.

33 *CSPS*, VIII, no. 325; *CSPS*, VIII, no. 365.

34 *CSPS*, VIII, no. 370.

35 *CSPS*, VIII, no. 386.

36 *LP*, XXII, no. 696.

37 *SC,* 146–7.

38 *SC,* 147.

39 *LP*, XXI, no. 697.

40 Stanford E. Lehmberg, *The Later Parliaments of Henry VIII: 1536–1547* (Cambridge: Cambridge University Press, 1977), 235.

10. THE BEAR AND RAGGED STAFF

1 Account of the coronation from CA I.18, fols. 69–102; SP 10/1 fol. 5, TNA LC 2/3/1, TNA LC 2/3/2.

2 This is given as '*Deus humilium*' in SP 10/1 fol. 25a and may have still been recited in Latin, despite the rest of the ceremony being performed in English. I have rendered it in English for the ease of the reader.

3 This is of course the traditional coronation chair, though the description given by the heralds does not seem to exactly match the appearance of the chair extant today; TNA LC 2/3/1 fol. 33.

4 TNA LC 2/3/1, fol. 33; see also TNA LC 2/3/2.

5 Alice Hunt, *The Drama of Coronation: Medieval Ceremony in Early Modern England* (Cambridge: Cambridge University Press, 2008), 90.

6 TNA LC 2/3/1, fol. 53.

7 Hunt, *The Drama of Coronation*, 89.

8 TNA LC 2/3/1, fol. 53.

9 TNA LC 2/3/1, fol. 26.

10 In the description of the service this says gold; in the description of the apparel it says crimson.

11 TNA LC 2/2, fol. 5^v.

12 TNA LC 2/2, fol. 6^v.

13 TNA LC 2/2, fol. 7^r, 9^r.

14 TNA LC 2/2, fol. 9^v.

15 TNA LC 2/2, fol. 9^v.

16 TNA LC 2/3/1, fol. 33.

17 Hunt, *The Drama of Coronation*, 94–5.

18 This may have been done as part of a group of two, or as a large crowd; the sources conflict on this. Dudley's position was high-ranking enough that he may have paid homage before the decision was made, for time, to have the remaining nobles pay homage as a group.

19 Description of the forces, terrain and battle from Alexander Hodgkins, 'Reconstructing Rebellion: Digital Terrain Analysis of the Battle of Dussindale (1549)', *Internet Archaeology*, no. 38 (2015), http://intarch.ac.uk.ezproxy.sussex.ac.uk/journal/issue38/hodgkins_toc.html and from the primary sources recorded in Frederic William Russell, *Kett's Rebellion in Norfolk: Being a History of the Great Civil Commotion That Occurred at the Time of the Reformation, in the Reign of Edward VI.* (London: Longmans, Brown, Green, Longmans and Roberts, and William Panny, 1859). See also Alexander Hodgkins, '"A Great Company of Country Clowns": Guerilla Warfare in the East Anglian and Western Rebellions (1549)', in *Unconventional Warfare from Antiquity to the Present Day*, ed. Brian Hughes and Fergus Robson (Cham: Palgrave Macmillan, 2017), 177–95.

20 Anthony Fletcher and Diarmaid MacCulloch, *Tudor Rebellions* (New York: Routledge, 2015).

21 John Guy, *Gresham's Law: The Life and World of Queen Elizabeth I's Banker* (London: Profile Books, 2019), 27.

22 Guy, *Gresham's Law*, 46.

23 W. K Jordan, ed., *The Chronicle and Political Papers of King Edward VI* (Ithaca, NY: Cornell University Press, 1966), 6.

24 Loades, *John Dudley*, 115.

25 Quoted in Loades, *John Dudley*, 115.

26 Loades, *John Dudley*, 119.

27 SP 10/9 fol. 3.

28 SP 10/9 fol.11.

29 For the description of Richmond/Sheen see Thurley, *Houses of Power*, 48–53. I have assumed that Edward VI instituted the same changes at Sheen as he did in his other chapels, see *Houses of Power*, 295–6. My thanks to Elizabeth Velluet at the Richmond Local History Society for her assistance with this text.

30 There are no details of Edward VI's building works at Sheen, though there were some, see John Cloake, *Richmond Palace: Its History and Its Plan* (Richmond: Richmond Local History Society, 2001), 92–3. I have used the previously existing description of Sheen.

31 For their marriage settlement see TNA E 355/204.

32 From BL Add. MS 48126, fol. 16ʳ, printed in Ian W. Archer, ed., *Religion, Politics, and Society in Sixteenth-Century England* (Cambridge: Cambridge University Press, 2003), 136; see Loades, *John Dudley*, 145, n. 76, who disputes whether the episode would have been so 'dramatic' as is described, but certainly would have been no less 'decisive'.

33 Wriothesley, II, 33.

34 The imperial ambassador Van der Delft suggests this meeting was at John Dudley's home; the Privy Council records place it at the home of Sir John York, Sheriff of London; *CSPS*, X, pp. 21–32; *APC*, II, 383. John Dudley had been staying with John York periodically throughout this period.

35 *CSPS*, X, Mar 1550, 1–15

36 Loades, *John Dudley*, 154.

37 Archer, ed., *Religion, Politics, and Society*, 52, transcription of BL Add. MS 48023, fol. 350.

38 For the wedding ceremony see *The Booke of the Common Praier and Administracion of the Sacramentes: And Other Rites and Ceremonies of the Churche: After the Use of the Churche of Englande* (London, 1549), 'Of Matrimony'; Cressy, *Birth, Marriage and Death*, Chapter 15.

39 Derek Wilson, *Sweet Robin: A Biography of Robert Dudley, Earl of Leicester 1533–1588* (London: Allison & Busby, 1981), 45–6.

40 Anna Whitelock, *Mary Tudor: England's First Queen* (London: Bloomsbury Paperbacks, 2010), 291.

41 Whitelock, *Mary Tudor*, 296; Loades, *John Dudley*, 158; Jordan, ed., *Chronicle*, 40.

1   Jordan, ed., *Chronicle*, 86–100 for the conspiracy and trial of Edward Seymour, Duke of Somerset.

2   SP 10/10 fol. 21.

3   Loades, *John Dudley*, 160–1.

4   Jordan, ed., *Chronicle*, 88.

5   Margaret Scard, *Edward Seymour: Lord Protector: Tudor King in All But Name* (Stroud: The History Press, 2016), loc. 4648.

6   *CSPS*, X, Nov. 1551.

7   Thurley, *Houses of Power*, 131.

8   Thurley, *Houses of Power*, 16, 337.

9   'Early History', UK Parliament, accessed 8 July 2019, https://www. parliament.uk/about/living-heritage/building/palace/westminsterhall/ architecture/early-history/.

10 Loades, *John Dudley*, 186.

11 See Loades, *John Dudley*, 187–8; by the terms of the Act under which he was being tried, the unlawful assembly needed to be told to disperse, and it was not. For this reason, they could not convict him.

12 *CSPS*, X, Dec. 1551, 1–15.

13 Edward VI, *Chronicle*, 99.

14 Jordan, ed., *Chronicle*, 103–5.

15 BL Cotton MS Vespasian F/XIII, fol. 273; 'Off With His Head – Medieval Manuscripts Blog', accessed 9 July 2019, https://blogs.bl.uk/ digitisedmanuscripts/2016/07/off-with-his-head.html.

16 Edward VI, *Chronicle*, 87.

17 TNA PC 2/4 fol. 476.

18 These reflections are contained in two letters to William Cecil during this time: SP 10/15 fol. 137 and SP 10/18 fol. 3. For Chelsea, see Loades, *John Dudley*, 179.

19 SP 10/15 fol. 137.

20 TNA LR 119, 10^r.

21 Loades, *John Dudley*, 183.

22 SP 10/15 fol. 137.

23 Edward VI, *Chronicle*, 100.

24 Loades, *John Dudley*, 193.

25 Loades, *John Dudley*, 196–7.

26 Henry Ellis, *Original Letters, Illustrative of English History* (London: Harding, Triphook, and Lepard, 1824), 66.

27 Niccolò Machiavelli, *Nicholas Machiavel's Prince*, trans. Edward Dacres (London, 1640), 118.

28 William Thomas, *The Works of William Thomas*, ed. Abraham D'Aubant (London: J. Almon, 1774), 170.

29 SP 10/18 f.3

30 SP 10/14, fol. 85; SP 10/14 f.87

31 SP 10/15 fol. 137.

32 SP 10/15 fol. 137.

33 John 5:24.

34 For accounts of Edward VI's illness see *CSPS*, XI, April 1553; *CSPS*, XI, May 1553; *CSPS*, XI, June 1553, 1–15; *CSPS*, XI, June 1553, 16–30.

35 *CSPS*, XI, May 1553.

36 *CSPS*, XI, June 1553, 1–15.

37 *CSPS*, XI, June 1553, 1–15.

38 *CSPS*, XI, May 1553; *CSPS*, XI, June 1553, 1–15.

39 *CSPS*, XI, March 1553; *CSPS*, XI, April 1553; *CSPS*, XI, May 1553.

40 *CSPS*, XI, February 1553.

41 *CSPS*, XI, February 1553.

42 *CSPS*, XI, May 1553.

43 *CSPS*, XI, June 1553, 1–15.

44 *CSPS*, XI, June 1553, 1–15.

45 R. W. Hoyle, ed., *Letters of the Cliffords, Lords Clifford and Earls of Cumberland, c. 1500–c. 1565* (Cambridge: Cambridge University Press, 1992), 21.

46 Lipscomb, *The King is Dead*; thank you to Nicola Tallis for this important point.

47 Nicholas Pocock, ed., *Records of the Reformation* (Oxford: Clarendon, 1870), 386.

48 SP 10/18 fol. 11.

49 New College MS 328, my thanks to Nicola Tallis for her help with the manuscripts relating to Jane and Guildford.

50 SHC 6729/2/11 fol. 113.

51 *CSPS, XI,* June 1553, 16–30.

52 CSPS, XI, June 1553, 16–30; Loades, *John Dudley*, 255.

53 *CSPS*, XI, June 1553, 1–15.

54 Loades, *John Dudley*, 241.

55 S. C. Lomas, ed., *Report on the Manuscripts of Lord Montagu of Beaulieu* (London: H.M. Stationery Office, 1900), 6.

1 *CSPS*, XI, July 1553, 16–20; Commendone, *The Accession, Coronation and Marriage of Mary Tudor*, trans C. V. Malfatti (Barcelona, 1956) 45. For the legitimacy of this source see Eric Ives, *Lady Jane Grey: A Tudor Mystery* (Chichester: John Wiley & Sons, 2011), 18.

2 Juan Luis Vives, *The Education of a Christian Woman: A Sixteenth-Century Manual*, ed. Charles Fantazzi (Chicago: University of Chicago Press, 2000), 177.

3 Commendone, *The Accession*, 45.

4 Description from the inventory in TNA LR 119, fol. 39ʳ; see 'Heston and Isleworth: Syon House', in *A History of the County of Middlesex: Volume 3*, ed. Susan Reynolds (London, 1962), pp. 97–100. *British History Online* http://www.british-history.ac.uk/vch/middx/vol3/pp97-100 [accessed 12 July 2019].

5 TNA LR 119, fol. 40ʳ; TNA LR 2/120, fol. 7ᵇ.

6 It is difficult to determine if this is her younger sister Margaret, or her sister-in-law Margaret, wife of Harry Dudley. The crossed-out reference to 'the tyme of her mariage' would suggest the former, but confuses the issue of which daughter died in 1552.

7 TNA LR 2/120, fol. 3ᵇ.

8 TNA LR 119, fol. 80ᵛ.

9 Commendone, *The Accession, Coronation and Marriage of Mary Tudor*, 46–7.

10 TNA LR 2/120, fol. 3ᵃ⁻ᵇ.

11 TNA LR 2/118, fol. 118ʳ⁻ᵛ lists the clothes taken with him to Cambridge. Aside from a scarlet cloak, a gown of purple velvet and russet nightgown, everything listed was black; *CSPS*, XI, July 1553, 16–20.

12 TNA LR 119, fols. 1–25; TNA LR 2/120, 21ᵇ–78ᵃ.

13 See John Gough Nichols, *The Chronicle of Queen Jane* (London: Camden Society, 1801), 7–8; *CSPS* XI, July 1553, 11–15.

14 *DHM*, 34–50. My thanks to Valerie Schutte for bringing 'Poor Pratte' to my attention.

15 John Edwards, *Mary I: England's Catholic Queen* (New Haven: Yale University Press, 2011), 96.

16 *CSPS*, XI, July 1553, 11–15.

17 Haynes, 156. Edwards, *Mary I*, 97–8 notes that these rewards are the same as those issued in the Bedingfield proclamation, and suspects collusion between Mary's council at Framlingham and the London

Council. Equally likely was that these were later claimed as the actions of the Privy Council, when Mary was recognized as queen.

18 Edwards, *Mary I*, 97.

19 See BL Lansdowne MS Vol/3 fol. 50.

20 Paul H. Hughes and James L. Larkin, *Tudor Royal Proclamations* (New Haven: Yale University Press, 1964), vol. 2, 3.

21 TNA LR 2/118, fol. 118ʳ.

22 TNA LR 2/120.

23 TNA PRO 31/9/67. My thanks to Benjamin MacLean for his help with this translation.

24 Haynes, 160.

25 *CSPS*, XI, July 1553, 21–31.

26 James Daybell, ed., *Women and Politics in Early Modern England, 1450–1700* (Aldershot: Routledge, 2004); Catherine Medici-Thiemann, "'She Governs the Queen": Jane Dudley, Mary Dudley Sidney, and Catherine Dudley Hastings' Political Actions, Agency, and Networks in Tudor England' (Thesis, University of Nebraska, 2016).

27 S. J. Gunn, 'A Letter of Jane, Duchess of Northumberland, in 1553', *The English Historical Review* 114, no. 459 (1999): 1267–71.

28 TNA PC 2/4 fol. 564.

29 TNA PC 2/4 fol. 538.

30 Jane's assertion that she 'doe nott so meche care fore theme [her children] as fore there fathere' seems cold to a modern reader, but in this context 'care' more likely means 'to be troubled, uneasy, or anxious', *OED*.

31 *The Copie of a Pistel or Letter Sent to Gilbard Potter in the Tyme When He Was in Prison* (London, 1553), A, ii ᵛ. The pamphlet was published 1 August 1553.

32 TNA E 154/2/39, fol. 31ʳ.

33 TNA LR 119, 42ʳ.

34 TNA LR 119, 40ʳ.

35 TNA LR 119, fol. 10ᵛ, 19ʳ, 22ʳ.

36 *CSPS*, XI, August 1553, 26–31.

37 TNA LR 119, fol. 22ʳ; TNA LR 2/118, fol. 118ʳ.

38 TNA LR 119, fol. 25ʳ; TNA LR 2/120, fol. 42ᵇ.

39 SP 11/1 fol. 16.

40 'CHAPEL OF ST PETER AD VINCULA, Tower Hamlets – 1357540 | Historic England', accessed 25 July 2019, https://historicengland.org.uk/listing/the-list/list-entry/1357540.

41 BL Harley MS 284 fol. 129; Wriothesley, 100; Nichols, *Chronicle of Queen Jane*, 17–18.

42 I have taken BL Harl MS 284, fol. 127 as the script of his scaffold speech. See W. K. Jordan and M. R. Gleason, 'The Saying of John Late Duke of Northumberland upon the Scaffold, 1553', *Harvard Bulletin* 23, no. 3 (1975): 324–5 for a discussion of this manuscript and its relationship to the later printed text.

43 *CSPS*, XI, September 1553, 1–5.

44 Jordan and Gleason, 'The Saying of John Late Duke of Northumberland', 325.

45 'sparcle' in the original.

46 Original: 'betime' for 'in good time', *OED*.

13. THE RAGGED STAFF AND FIREBRAND

1 *CSPS*, XI, July 1553, 21–31.

2 BL Harley MS 523 fol. 12^r.

3 Nichols, *Chronicle of Queen Jane*, 32.

4 My sincerest thanks to Nicola Tallis for sharing her transcription and translation of the trial documents, TNA KB8/23.

5 'Parishes: Dudley', in *A History of the County of Worcester: Volume 3* (London, 1913), pp. 90–105. *British History Online* http://www.british-history.ac.uk/vch/worcs/vol3/pp90-105 [accessed 7 August 2019].

6 I have paraphrased slightly, removing the specifications 'each of them should so be dragged', etc.

7 Edwards, *Mary I*, 170–1.

8 Quoted in Andrew Strycharski, 'Some Verses of Henry and Mary Dudley Sidney and Prince Edward's "Little School"', *ANQ: A Quarterly Journal of Short Articles, Notes and Reviews*, 24, no. 4 (2011): 249–54. My thanks to Tamise Hills on help isolating material which made claims about the 'school' of Edward VI.

9 See Cressy, *Birth, Marriage, and Death*, Chapter 1; Ingram, *Carnal Knowledge*, 47–8.

10 He adds this as a note to a letter written to Walsingham in 1583: 'My going to Spain for the liberty of Warwick and his brethren'; John Sherren Brewer and William Bullen, eds., *Calendar of the Carew Manuscripts: 1515–1574* (Longmans, Green, Reader & Dyer, 1867), 359; see Adams, *Leicester and the Court*, 157.

11 SP 69/4 fol. 27.

12 SP 69/4.

13 SP 69/4.

14 SP 69/4 fol. 87.

15 Edwards, *Mary I*, 180.

16 Erika Spivakovsky, *Son of the Alhambra: Don Diego Hurtado de Mendoza, 1504–1575* (Austin: University of Texas Press, 1970), 334 is unsure whether or not he was in attendance on Philip, but his appearance in Jane Dudley's will (see below) would seem to confirm it.

17 Edwards, *Mary I*, 181.

18 Henry Kamen, *Philip of Spain* (Yale University Press, 1997), 56.

19 Edwards, *Mary I*, 184, 186.

20 Eucharius Roeslin, *The Byrth of Mankynde*, trans. Thomas Raynald, 1540, fol. C,xliia^r.

21 Cathy McClive, 'The Hidden Truths of the Belly: The Uncertainties of Pregnancy in Early Modern Europe', *The Society for the Social History of Medicine* 15, no. 2 (2002): 209–27.

22 Roeslin, *Byrth*, fol. C,i^r.

23 Roeslin, *Byrth*, fol. C,i^v.

24 SP 69/3 fol. 111.

25 SP 69/4 fol. 122.

26 SP 69/4 fol. 122.

27 *The Byble in Englyshe* (London, 1540), fol. L.lxxxi^v. For similar examples of allusions to Scripture in Tower graffiti, see Ruth Ahnert, *The Rise of Prison Literature in the Sixteenth Century* (Cambridge: Cambridge University Press, 2013), 35–8.

28 Quoted in Loades, *John Dudley*, 224.

29 Haynes, 155.

30 Rivkah Zim, *English Metrical Psalms: Poetry as Praise and Prayer, 1535–1601* (Cambridge: Cambridge : Cambridge University Press, 1987), 104–11.

31 Ruth Hughey, ed., *The Arundel Harington Manuscript of Tudor Poetry*, Vol. 1 (Columbus: Ohio University Press, 1960), 338–9.

32 Hughey, ed., *Arundel Harington Manuscript*, Vol. 1, 340–1.

33 Adams, *Leicester and the Court*, 157; along with Robert and Harry. Ambrose had, no doubt, been held behind as the eldest Dudley son, should John die; his wife Elizabeth went to work to secure his release as well, petitioning Philip; Roger Ascham, *The Whole Works of Roger Ascham: Life and letters*, ed. Edward Grant (London: J. R. Smith, 1865), 419–20.

34 Cressy, *Birth, Death, and Marriage*, Chapter 2.

35 Cressy, *Birth, Death, and Marriage*, Chapter 1.

36 Cressy, *Birth, Death, and Marriage*, Chapter 3.

37 Alan Stewart, *Philip Sidney: A Double Life* (London: Random House, 2011), 14.

38 PROB 11/37/342.

39 'Landownership: Chelsea Manor,' in *A History of the County of Middlesex: Volume 12, Chelsea*, ed. Patricia E. C. Croot (London: Victoria County History, 2004), 108–115. *British History Online*, accessed 13 August 2017, http://www.british-history.ac.uk/vch/middx/vol12/pp108-115.

40 *CSPS*, XIII, no. 37.

41 Henry's date of birth is often given as 1531, which would mean that for six years Jane and John had two sons named 'Henry' (as the elder Henry was born in 1526). Sibling name-sharing was very uncommon in the Tudor period. When it did occur, the death of the elder often preceded the Christening of the younger; Scott Smith-Bannister, *Names and Naming Patterns in England 1538–1700* (Oxford; New York: OUP Oxford, 1997), ebook.

42 John Strype, *Ecclesiastical Memorials* (Oxford: Clarendon Press, 1822).

14. RESTORED IN BLOOD

1 *DHM*, pp. 79–90. Machyn gives 'Westminster', but this is probably a reference to Whitehall as the 'King's Palace at Westminster', as it was often known.

2 From the account of a 1501 tournament: '[there] was nothing to the eye but only visages and faces without appearances of their bodyes'; quoted in Young, *Tudor and Jacobean Tournaments*, 74.

3 Description from Young, *Tudor and Jacobean Tournaments*, 118–22.

4 From John Wadell's *Journey Through England* of 1584, quoted in 'The Holbein Gate and the Tiltyard Gallery', in *Survey of London: Volume 14, St Margaret, Westminster, Part III: Whitehall II*, ed. Montagu H. Cox and G. Topham Forrest (London, 1931), pp. 10–22. *British History Online* http://www.british-history.ac.uk/survey-london/vol14/pt3/pp10-22 [accessed 13 August 2017]. This particular portrait may not have been in the gallery in 1555.

5 Young, *Tudor and Jacobean Tournaments*, 22.

6 Description below from Richard C. McCoy, 'From the Tower to the Tiltyard: Robert Dudley's Return to Glory', *The Historical Journal* 27, no. 2 (1984): 425–35.

7 *CSPS*, XIII, no. 60.

8 *CSPS*, XIII, no. 72.

9 *CSPS*, XIII, no. 72.

10 See McCoy, 'From the Tower'.

11 *DHM*, pp. 79–90.

12 McCoy, 'From the Tower', 432.

13 *CSPV*, VI, no. 37.

14 See Young, *Tudor and Jacobean Tournaments*, 30–2.

15 See Anthony John Harper and Ingrid Höpel, *The German-Language Emblem in Its European Context: Exchange and Transmission* (Librairie Droz, 2000), 160; Young, *Tudor and Jacobean Tournaments*, 125–7; though Young gives the date of the tournament as 1559 or 1560, this is corrected in McCoy, 'From the Tower'.

16 AMRE *Correspondence Politique, Angleterre*, ix, fol. 449. My thanks to Simon Adams for providing this reference.

17 Holinshed, IV, 82.

18 Kamen, *Philip*, 68.

19 Alexander Samson, *Mary and Philip: The Marriage of Tudor England and Habsburg Spain* (Manchester: Manchester University Press, 2020).

20 *DHM*, pp. 123–141.

21 Adams, *Leicester and the Court*, 158.

22 Holinshed, IV, 87; SP 11/11 fol. 12.

23 BL Harley MS 4712, fol. 275; Chris Skidmore, *Death and the Virgin* (London: Weidenfeld & Nicolson, 2010), 50–4.

24 Adams, *Leicester and the Court*, 160.

25 Charles Oman, *A History of the Art of War in the Sixteenth Century* (Abingdon: Routledge, 1937), 254–66.

26 Ambroise Paré, *Life and Times of Ambroise Pare 1510–1590 with a New Translation of His Apology and an Account of His Journeys in Divers Places*, ed. Francis R. (Francis Randolph) Packard (New York: P. B. Hoeber, 1921).

27 Kamen, *Philip*, 70.

28 ShP MSS/696; Holinshed, IV, 89. It is Stow who suggests that Henry was one of 'the first that aduanced banner on the wall'; John Stow, *The Annales, or Generall Chronicle of England* (London, 1615), 631. My thanks to Steph Eeles at Lambeth Palace Archives for her assistance.

29 Holinshed, IV, 89.

30 He recalled this moment almost twenty years later in a letter; AGR, *papiers d'état et de l'audience* 361, fol. 156ᵛ.

31 'for my part, I have not seen the like in all my life. The *sault* was soon won, and with the loss of no great number; but the slaughter was in the town about the spoil ... [The German mercenaries] have now showed such cruelty, as the like hath not been seen for greediness: the town by them was set a-fire, and a great piece of it burnt; divers were brent [burnt] in cellars, and were killed immediately; women and children gave such pitiful cries, that it would grieve any Christian heart.'; Patrick Fraser Tytler, ed., *England Under the Reigns of Edward VI and Mary: With the Contemporary History of Europe* (R. Bentley, 1839), 493.

32 Account from *DHM*, pp. 169–84.

33 V. C. Medvei, 'The Illness and Death of Mary Tudor', *Journal of the Royal Society of Medicine* 80, no. 12 (1987): 766–70.

34 David Loades, *Elizabeth I: The Golden Reign of Gloriana* (London: Hambledon and London, 2003), 122.

35 SP 12/1 fol. 4; BL Cotton Titus C/X.

36 BL Cotton Caligula E/V fol. 56.

37 Skidmore, *Death and the Virgin*, 2.

15. CARNAL MARRIAGES

1 *CSPS(S)*, I, no. 60; see also Victor Von Klarwill, ed., *Queen Elizabeth And Some Foreigners* (London: Bodley Head, 1928), 127–33.

2 Tracy Borman, *Elizabeth's Women: The Hidden Story of the Virgin Queen* (London: Jonathan Cape, 2009), 191.

3 Charlotte Isabelle Merton, 'Women Who Served Queen Mary and Queen Elizabeth: Ladies, Gentlewomen and Maids of the Privy Chamber, 1553–1603.' (Thesis, University of Cambridge, 1992), 68, 165.

4 Merton, 'Women Who Served', 120–1.

5 Borman, *Elizabeth's Women*, 190.

6 Ciaran Brady, *A Viceroy's Vindication?: Sir Henry Sidney's Memoir of Service in Ireland, 1556–1578* (Cork: Cork University Press, 2002), 4.

7 Nicholas Patrick Canny, 'Glory and Gain: Sir Henry Sidney and the Government of Ireland, 1558–1578' (Thesis, University of Pennsylvania, 1971), 1–2, 15–16.

8 Canny, 'Glory and Gain', 46–7.

9 Merton, 'Women Who Served', 91.

10 *HMCB*, II, 143–4; DPL, I/42.

11 *CSPS(S)*, II, no. 27.

12 Simon Adams, ed., *Household Accounts and Disbursement Books of Robert Dudley, Earl of Leicester* (Cambridge: Cambridge University Press, 1995), 62–3.

13 *CSPS(S)*, I, no. 67; *CSPV*, VII, no. 71.

14 Adams, ed., *Household Accounts*, 61, 96.

15 Von Klarwill, ed., *Queen Elizabeth*, 113–15.

16 SP 12/6/7; *DHM*, pp. 202-; Reavley Gair, *The Children of Paul's: The Story of a Theatre Company, 1553–1608* (Cambridge: Cambridge University Press, 1982), 76.

17 Thurley, *Houses of Power*, 264–5.

18 Thurley, *Houses of Power*, 268.

19 SP 12/6 fol. 76.

20 Von Klarwill, ed., *Queen Elizabeth*, 113.

21 Von Klarwill, ed., *Queen Elizabeth*, 120.

22 *CSPS(S)*, I, no. 62; BL Add. MS 26056a.

23 Sidney spoke to the imperial ambassador, Caspar Breuner, as well; Von Klarwill, ed., *Queen Elizabeth*, 123–6.

24 *CSPS(S)*, I, no. 60; BL MS Add. 26056a.

25 DPL 1/140.

26 Thurley, *Houses of Power*, 381.

27 Thurley, *Houses of Power*, 142.

28 Thurley, *Houses of Power*, 143.

29 Kervyn de Lettenhove, ed., *Relations politiques des Pays-Bas et de l'Angleterre, sous le règne de Philippe II*, vol. 2 (Brussels: L'académie Royal, 1883), 304; see Marion E. Colthorpe, 'The Elizabethan Court', Folgerpedia, accessed 1 April 2020, https://folgerpedia.folger.edu/The_Elizabethan_Court_Day_by_Day#The_Elizabethan_Court_Day_by_Day.

30 Skidmore, *Death and the Virgin*, 160; Adams, ed., *Household Accounts*, 151.

31 *DHM*, pp. 202–21.

32 Von Klarwill, ed., *Queen Elizabeth*, 120.

33 Adams, ed., *Household Accounts*, 162–3.

34 Von Klarwill, ed., *Queen Elizabeth*, 157–8.

35 DPL 1/140.

36 See DPL 1/64, 1/68, 1/70 among others.

37 Adams, ed., *Household Accounts*, 164.

38 Klarwill, ed., *Queen Elizabeth*, 157–8.

39 Jacqueline Smith and John Carter, *Inns and Alehouses of Abingdon, 1550–1978* (J. Smith and J. Carter, 1989).

40 From a letter transcribed in Skidmore, *Death and the Virgin*, 380–3, original Magdalen College, Cambridge, Pepys MS 2503 (Letters of State II) fols. 705^r–6^r.

41 Adams, ed., *Accounts*, 464.

42 From the same letter as above, Skidmore, *Death and the Virgin*, 381.

43 As above, Skidmore, *Death and the Virgin*, 379–80.

44 J. A. Sharpe, 'Domestic Homicide in Early Modern England', *The Historical Journal* 24, no. 1 (1981): 32–3; Malcolm Gaskill, *Crime and Mentalities in Early Modern England* (Cambridge University Press, 2003), 246.

45 Sharpe, 'Domestic Homicide', 40.

46 'Parishes: Cumnor', in *A History of the County of Berkshire: Volume 4*, ed. William Page and P. H. Ditchfield (London, 1924), pp. 398–405. *British History Online* http://www.british-history.ac.uk/vch/berks/vol4/pp398-405 [accessed 24 January 2020].

47 Peggy Inman, 'Amy Robsart and Cumnor Place', Cumnor History Society, accessed 24 January 2020, http://users.ox.ac.uk/~djp/cumnor/articles/inman-robsart.htm.

48 Letter transcribed in Skidmore, *Death and the Virgin*, 382.

49 Alexander Murray, *Suicide in the Middle Ages: The Violent against Themselves* (Oxford: Oxford University Press, 1998), 28.

50 Michael MacDonald, Terence R. Murphy, *Sleepless Souls: Suicide in Early Modern England* (Oxford: Clarendon Press, 1990), 15.

51 Sheldon Brammall, *English Aeneid: Translations of Virgil, 1555–1646* (Edinburgh: University Press, 2015).

52 *The Seuen First Bookes of the Eneidos of Virgill, Conuerted in Englishe Meter by Thomas Phaer Esquier, Sollicitour to the King and Quenes Maiesties, Attending Their Honorable Counsaile in the Marchies of Wales by Virgil* (1558), L, iii^r.

53 Murray, *Suicide*, 178.

54 Murray, *Suicide*, 404–5.

55 From Skidmore, *Death and the Virgin*, 198–9 and Lettenhove, *Relations Politiques*, II, 529–33.

56 See *CSPS(S)*, I, no. 119, where 'y por oltimo me dixo que pensavan hazer morir a su muger de Roberto y que agora publicamente estava mala' has been translated (incorrectly) as 'He ended by saying that Robert was thinking of killing his wife, who was publicly announced to be ill.' The verb 'pensavan' is third person plural and therefore is unlikely to refer to Robert. For this reason I have used Skidmore's translation.

57 Skidmore, *Death and the Virgin*, 238–9.

58 'Milor Roberto estaria mejor en parayso que aqui', Lettenhove, *Relations Politiques*, II, 531.

59 Canon Jackson, 'Charles, Lord Stourton, and the Murder of the Hartgills', *The Wiltshire Archaeological and Natural History Magazine* 8, no. 24 (1864): 242–336.

60 K. J. Kesselring, *Making Murder Public: Homicide in Early Modern England, 1480–1680* (Oxford: Oxford University Press, 2019), 4.

61 Kesselring, *Making Murder Public*, 15.

62 Skidmore, *Death and the Virgin*, 210; TNA, 'Coroner's Report into the Death of Amy Robsart, August 1561 (KB 9/1073/f.80)', text, *The National Archives* (blog), accessed 7 February 2020, https://www.nationalarchives.gov.uk/education/resources/elizabeth-monarchy/coroners-report/.

63 Kesselring, *Making Murder Public*, 45.

64 Letters transcribed in Skidmore, *Death and the Virgin*, 383–4.

65 Letter transcribed in Skidmore, *Death and the Virgin*, 384–5.

66 Skidmore, *Death and the Virgin*, 208–9.

67 TNA, 'Coroner's Report', https://www.nationalarchives.gov.uk/education/resources/elizabeth-monarchy/coroners-report/.

68 Gaskill, *Crime and Mentalities*, 254.

69 Kesselring, *Making Murder Public*, 50.

70 Susanne Groom and Lee Prosser, *Kew Palace: The Official Illustrated History* (London: Merrell Publishers Ltd, 2006), 14–16.

71 She would give birth before 10 October, by which time she had delivered a daughter, apparently christened by the queen; SP 70/19 fol. 46. See Adams, *Household Accounts*, 142–3.

72 DPL vol. IV/6, fol. 23.

73 Adams, *Household Accounts*, 143.

74 Haynes, I, no. 1740.

75 Letter transcribed in Skidmore, *Death and the Virgin*, 384–5.

76 SP 70/19 fol. 132.

77 SP 70/20 fol. 38.

78 *CSPS(S)*, I, no. 122.

79 *CSPS(S)*, I, no. 121.

80 Von Klarwill, ed., *Queen Elizabeth*, 152.

81 *CSPS(S)*, I, no. 123.

82 *CSPS(S)*, I, no. 124.

1   BL MS Add. 37749, fol. 43.

2   Leanda de Lisle, *The Sisters Who Would Be Queen: Mary, Catherine, and Lady Jane Grey: A Tudor Tragedy* (London: Harper Press, 2009), 213–14.

3   de Lisle, *The Sisters*, 212–14.

4   G. R. Clarke, *The History and Description of the Town and Borough of Ipswich* (London: Hurst, Chance & Co., 1830), 328.

5   Greg Walker, *The Politics of Performance in Early Renaissance Drama* (Cambridge: Cambridge University Press, 1998), 208.

6   BL MS Add. 37749, fol. 43.

7   See SP 52/5 fol. 59.

8   DPL 1/58, fol. 183.

9   Alice Hunt, 'Dumb Politics in Gorboduc', in *The Oxford Handbook of Tudor Drama*, ed. Thomas Betteridge and Greg Walker (Oxford: Oxford University Press, 2012), 547–65.

10 Marie Axton, 'Robert Dudley and the Inner Temple Revels', *The Historical Journal* 13, no. 3 (1970): 365–78.

11 *DHM*, 262–74.

12 TP, fol. 409.

13 DPL I/207; see Adams, *Leicester and the Court*, 165.

14 Hunt, 'Dumb Politics', 552.

15 It is unclear how much was actually performed as planned, see Axton, 'Robert Dudley', 371.

16 Mike Pincombe, 'Robert Dudley, Gorboduc, and "The Masque of Beauty and Desire": A Reconsideration of the Evidence for Political Intervention'. *Parergon* 20, no. 1 (2003), 19–44 suggests that the masque was not performed, or at least was not performed before the queen. I think we might assume it was a part of the Christmas celebrations at the Inner Temple 1561–2, however.

17 From Gerard Legh, *The Accedens of Armory* (London, 1576), fols. 207^r-211^v.

18 Legh, *The Accedens*, fol. 213^{r-v}.

19 Legh, *The Accedens*, fols. 203^r-232^v.

20 Legh, *The Accedens*, fol. 216^r.

21 Legh, *The Accedens*, fol. 218^v, foldout.

22 Legh, *The Accedens*, fol. 224^v.

23 Hunt, 'Dumb Politics', 557.

24 Thomas Norton and Thomas Sackville, *The Tragedie of Gorboduc* (London, 1565), E, ii^v.

25 Norton and Sackville, *Gorboduc*, E, iii^v.

26 Norton and Sackville, *Gorboduc*, E, iiiv-E, iv^r.

27 There is some debate about the message of the play in performance at the Inner Temple and subsequently (on 18 January) at Westminster. Whereas at the Inner Temple there appears to have been some reference to the marriage question, this may have been removed in the later performance, leading some scholars to wonder why it would not have been stressed in front of the audience of one who needed to hear it. If we remember, however, the centrality of counsel to the play, and the presence of Elizabeth's councillors at the Inner Temple performance, we might conclude that the arguments about her marriage were not so much intended for her as for her councillors, who were seen as partakers in her rule by the Inner Temple. See Axton, 'Robert Dudley', 365–78; Walker, *The Politics of Performance*, 196–221; Pincombe, 'Robert Dudley, Gorboduc', 19–44.

28 Norton and Sackville, *Gorboduc*, B, iii^{r-v}; BL MS Add. 48023 transcribed in Walker, *The Politics of Performance*, 210–11.

29 *CSPS(S)*, I, no. 170, BL MS Add. 26056a; see Colthorpe, 'The Elizabethan Court'.

30 See Anna Whitelock, *Elizabeth's Bedfellows: An Intimate History of the Queen's Court* (London: A&C Black, 2013), 66–70; *CSPS(S)*, I, no. 190.

31 Translation from John Hungerford Pollen, ed., *A Letter from Mary Queen of Scots to the Duke of Guise* (Edinburgh: Edinburgh University Press, 1904), 75–7. Original: SP 52/7 fol. 84.

32 SP 12/23 fol. 121.

33 Haynes, 391.

34 SP 70/38 fol. 67.

35 *CSPF*, V, no. 132, 134, 135.

36 Lettenhove, *Relations Politiques*, 9–12.

37 *CSPF*, V, no. 380.

38 *CSPF*, V, no. 438.

39 Olga Krylova and David J. D. Earn, 'Patterns of Smallpox Mortality in London, England, over Three Centuries', *BioRxiv*, 2019, online preprint.

40 Lettenhove, *Relations Politiques*, 164–5; *CSPS(S)*, I, no. 187.

41 SP 70/43 fol. 135.

42 *CSPS(S)*, I, no. 190.

43 *CSPS(S)*, I, no. 188, 189, 190.

44 *CSPS(S)*, I, no. 190; The National Archives, 'Sir Thomas Gresham to Elizabeth I, 25 February 1560 (SP 70/11 fol. 78)', text, *The National*

Archives (blog), accessed 13 March 2020, https://www.national-archives.gov.uk/education/resources/elizabeth-monarchy/sir-thomas-gresham-to-elizabeth-i/.

45 *CSPS(S)*, I, no. 190.

17. BEING NOW THE LAST OF OUR HOUSE

1 Thurley, *Houses of Power*, 381.

2 Account of the wedding from John Leland, *Antiquarii de Rebus Britannicis Collectanea*, vol. 1, Pt 2 (London: Impensis Gul. & Jo. Richardson, 1770), 666–9.

3 Kate Williams, *Rival Queens: The Betrayal of Mary, Queen of Scots* (London: Arrow, 2018), 139–42.

4 SP 12/29 fol. 122. The fact that both Ambrose and Robert may have been exposed to plague made matters worse.

5 Church of England, *The Book of Common Prayer: Commonly Called the First Book of Queen Elizabeth*, Printed by Grafton, 1559 (London: W. Pickering, 1844), fol. 96^r–99^v.

6 Thurley, *Houses of Power*, 289.

7 Accounts from Alan Stewart, *Philip Sidney: A Double Life* (London: Random House, 2011) and Anna Waymack, 'Paradoxes, Pibrac and Phalaris: Reading beyond Sidney's Silence on the St. Bartholomew's Day Massacre', *Sidney Journal* 36, no. 2 (2018): 29–49.

8 Historians have often incorrectly placed Walsingham's embassy at Faubourg Saint-Germain. I am grateful to John Cooper for the correction and assistance; see John Cooper, *The Queen's Agent: Francis Walsingham at the Court of Elizabeth I* (London: Faber and Faber, 2011), 62, 332, fn. 15. This is based on the account of the ambassador Tomasso Sassetti; see Tomasso Sassetti, '"Account of the St. Bartholomew's Day Massacre" (from the "Brieve Raccontamento Del Gran Macello Fatto Nella Città Di Parigi Il Viggesimo Quarto Giorno d'agosto d'ordine Di Carlo Nono Re Di Francia")', trans. Steven Baker, accessed 14 April 2020, https://www.academia.edu/7599166/Tomasso_Sassetti_Account_of_the_St._Bartholomews_Day_Massacre_from_the_Brieve_raccontamento_del_gran_macello_fatto_nella_citt%C3%Ao_di_Parigi_il_viggesimo_quarto_giorno_dagosto_dordine_di_Carlo_Nono_re_di_Francia_; John Tedeschi, 'Tomasso Sassetti's Account of the St. Bartholomew's Day Massacre', in *The Massacre of St Bartholomew: Reappraisals and Documents*, ed. Alfred Soman, Archives

Internationales D'histoire Des Idees / International Archives of the History of Ideas (Dordrecht: Springer Netherlands, 1974), 99–154.

9 Francis Walsingham, *Journal of Sir Francis Walsingham, from Dec. 1570 to April 1583*, ed. Charles Trice Martin (London: Camden Society, 1870), 2.

10 SP 70/124 fol. 35.

11 BL MS Harleian 260 fol. 251.

12 From Roger Kuin, ed., *The Correspondence of Sir Philip Sidney* (Oxford, New York: Oxford University Press, 2012), 3–5.

13 Colthorpe, 'The Elizabethan Court'.

14 Stewart, *Philip Sidney*, loc. 1017.

15 Stewart, *Philip Sidney*, loc. 1548.

16 Jean-Noël Biraben and Didier Blanchet, 'Essay on the Population of Paris and its Vicinity Since the Sixteenth Century', *Population* 11, no. 1 (1999): 155–88.

17 SP 70/124 fol. 9.

18 For the arrival and reception of Lincoln and his train, see Cotton Vespasian F/V fols. 97–100.

19 BL MS Harleian 260 f.263, 278, 282.

20 Natalie Zemon Davis, 'The Rites of Violence: Religious Riot in Sixteenth-Century France', *Past & Present*, no. 59 (1973): 83.

21 BL MS Harleian 260 fol. 292

22 BL MS Harleian 260 fol. 252; SP 70/124 fol. 31.

23 BL MS Harleian 260 f.257

24 Stewart, *Philip Sidney*, loc. 1613.

25 Stewart, *Philip Sidney*, loc. 1684.

26 Geoffrey Treasure, *The Huguenots* (New Haven: Yale University Press, 2013), 171.

27 Donald R. Kelley, 'Martyrs, Myths, and the Massacre: The Background of St. Bartholomew', *The American Historical Review* 77, no. 5 (1972): 1338.

28 Zemon Davis, 'The Rites of Violence', 51–91; Mack P. Holt, *The French Wars of Religion, 1562–1629* (Cambridge: Cambridge University Press, 2005), 88; Treasure, *The Huguenots*, 173.

29 Catherine Duncan-Jones and Jan van Dorsten, eds., *Miscellaneous Prose of Sir Philip Sidney* (Oxford: Oxford University Press, 1973), 48.

30 G. Blakemore Evans, ed., 'Robert Laneham's *Letter*', *Elizabethan-Jacobean Drama: The Theatre in Its Time* (New York: New Amsterdam Books, 1998), 170.

31 Account of the events at Kenilworth from Robert Laneham, *A Letter: Whearin, Part of the Entertainmnet Untoo the Queens Maiesty, at Kill-ingworth Castl, in Warwick Sheer* (1575?); George Gascoigne, *The Whole Woorkes of George Gascoigne Esquire* (London, 1587), A1ʳ-D1ʳ; and Colthorpe, 'The Elizabethan Court'.

32 Elizabeth Goldring, 'The Earl of Leicester's Inventory of Kenilworth Castle, *c.*1578', *English Heritage Historical Review* 2, no. 1 (1 June 2007): 38; my thanks to Elizabeth Goldring for her assistance. My thanks to Cathryn Enis for pointing out the uniqueness of this shared heraldic device.

33 Jim Ellis, 'Kenilworth, King Arthur, and the Memory of Empire', *English Literary Renaissance* 43, no. 1 (2013): 21–2.

34 Gascoigne, *Whole Woorkes*, A1ʳ-A1ᵛ.

35 Elizabeth was at Kenilworth 18–22 August 1572.

36 Gascoigne, *Whole Woorkes*, Aiiᵛ-Aiiiʳ.

37 For the layout and building works at Kenilworth see Richard K. Mor-ris, '"I Was Never More in Love with an Olde Howse nor Never Newe Worke Coulde Be Better Bestowed": The Earl of Leicester's Remodel-ling of Kenilworth Castle for Queen Elizabeth I', *The Antiquaries Journal* 89 (September 2009): 241–305. This account of the fireworks comes from Laneham's description of the Sunday evening, but one might have expected a similar show on the night of the queen's arrival; Laneham, *Letter*, 16.

38 Laneham, *Letter*, 4.

39 This description of the hunt from Laneham, *Letter*, 17.

40 David Jacques, 'The Place of Kenilworth in Garden History', in *The Elizabethan Garden at Kenilworth Castle*, ed. Anna Keay and John Watkins (London: English Heritage, 2013), 14; Laneham, *Letter*, 68.

41 David Jacques, 'The Form and Structure of the Garden', in *The Eliza-bethan Garden*, ed. Keay and Watkins, 93–102.

42 Laneham, *Letter*, 67.

43 Jacques, 'Form and Structure', 100.

44 Laneham, *Letter*, 68.

45 Richard K. Morris and Anna Keay, 'The Aviary', in *The Elizabethan Garden*, ed. Keay and Watkin, 139–48.

46 Laneham, *Letter*, 70.

47 Laneham, *Letter*, 71; the ambiguity of Laneham's 'boll' has generally been resolved as 'ball' rather than 'bowl', though either is possible; see Esther Godfrey, 'Sources for the New Fountain and the Stories Around It', in *The Elizabethan Garden*, ed. Keay and Watkins, 110–13.

48 Laneham, *Letter*, 84.

49 Stewart, *Philip Sidney*, loc. 2873.

50 Stewart, *Philip Sidney*, loc. 2865.

51 Colthorpe, 'The Elizabethan Court'; The list of stags killed in the chase at Richmond Walk, Kenilworth in 1575 mentions 'Lady Essex'.

52 Goldring, 'Inventory', 42–3.

53 Elizabeth Goldring, *Robert Dudley, Earl of Leicester, and the World of Elizabethan Art: Painting and Patronage at the Court of Elizabeth I* (New Haven: Yale University Press, 2014), 256–63. See also Goldring, 'Inventory', 36–59.

54 Goldring, *Robert Dudley*, 100–1.

55 Goldring, *Robert Dudley*, 106–7.

56 Laneham, *Letter*, 76.

57 Conyers Read, 'A Letter from Robert, Earl of Leicester, to a Lady', *The Huntingdon Library Bulletin*, no. 9 (1936): 15–26.

58 Read, 'A Letter', 25.

59 Read, 'A Letter', 25.

60 Cressy, *Birth, Marriage, and Death*, 50–2.

61 Patrick Collinson, *Godly People: Essays On English Protestantism and Puritanism* (London: Bloomsbury Publishing, 1983), 48, 96.

62 *Calendar of the Manuscripts of the Marquis of Bath, Preserved at Longleat, Wiltshire*, vol. 2, 1–3 vols (London: H.M. Stationery office, 1904), 22.

63 Nicola Tallis, *Elizabeth's Rival: The Tumultuous Tale of Lettice Knollys, Countess of Leicester* (London: Michael O'Mara, 2017), 145–6.

64 Tallis, *Elizabeth's Rival*, 126.

65 Nicholas Cooper, 'A Building Project for William, Lord Paget, at Burton-on-Trent', *The Antiquaries Journal* 93 (September 2013): 250; Goldring, *Robert Dudley*, 211.

66 Goldring, *Robert Dudley*, 212.

67 See Golding, *Robert Dudley*, Chapter 7.

68 Whitelock, *Elizabeth's Bedfellows*, 150.

69 Susan Doran, *Monarchy and Matrimony: The Courtships of Elizabeth I* (New York: Routledge, 2002).

70 Colthorpe, 'The Elizabethan Court'.

71 Goldring, *Robert Dudley*, 121, 304.

72 Goldring, *Robert Dudley*, 307.

18. READY TO TAKE ON MY JOURNEY

1 Details of his travel, moneys paid and those encountered on the journey from Adams, *Accounts*, 186–90; Simon Townley, ed. *A History of the County of Oxford*, vol. 16 (Woodbridge: Boydell & Brewer, 2011), https://www.british-history.ac.uk/vch/oxon/vol16/, 73–8.

2 Jan Frans van Dijkhuizen and Karl A. E. Enenkel, *The Sense of Suffering: Constructions of Physical Pain in Early Modern Culture* (Leiden: Brill, 2009), 77.

3 Goldring, *Robert Dudley*, 209.

4 Edmund Lodge, ed., *Illustrations of British History*, vol. 2 (London: John Chidley, 1838), 243.

5 Ellis, *Original Letters*, I/137.

6 Peck, ed., *Leicester's Commonwealth*, 53.

7 D. C. Peck, 'Government Suppression of Elizabethan Catholic Books: The Case of "Leicester's Commonwealth"', *The Library Quarterly* 47, no. 2 (1 April 1977): 163–77.

8 Peck, ed., *Leicester's Commonwealth*, 54.

9 Peck, ed., *Leicester's Commonwealth*, 57.

10 Peck, ed., *Leicester's Commonwealth*, 62.

11 Peck, ed., *Leicester's Commonwealth*, 132.

12 Peck, 'Government Suppression', 170.

13 Peck, ed., *Leicester's Commonwealth*, 92.

14 David Cressy and Delloyd J. Guth, 'Binding the Nation: The Bonds of Association, 1584 and 1696', in *Tudor Rule and Revolution: Essays for G. R. Elton from His American Friends* (Cambridge: Cambridge University Press, 2009), 218–19; SP 12/173/1 fol. 132.

15 Townley, ed., *County of Oxford*, vol. 16, 73–8.

16 Thurley, *Houses of Power*, 310.

17 John Foxe, *Actes and Monuments of Matters Most Speciall and Memorable, Happenyng in the Church* (London: John Day, 1583), 2096.

18 S. Adams, Sutton [Dudley], Edward, fourth Baron Dudley (c. 1515–1586), *ODNB*.

19 Goldring, *Robert Dudley*, 172.

20 'Site of Langley Palace Royal Hunting Lodge, an Associated Enclosure and Later Garden Earthworks at Langley Farm, Leafield – 1008495 | Historic England', accessed 7 May 2020, https://historicengland.org.uk/listing/the-list/list-entry/1008495.

21 'Site of Langley Palace'.

22 T. G. Allen and Jonathan Hiller, *The Excavation of a Medieval Manor House of the Bishops of Winchester at Mount House, Witney, Oxford-shire, 1984–92* (Oxford: Oxford Archaeological Unit, 2002); Simon Townley, ed., *A History of the County of Oxford*, vol. 14 (Woodbridge: Boydell & Brewer, 2004), https://www.british-history.ac.uk/vch/oxon/vol14/, 68–73.

23 H. E. Salter and Mary D. Lobel, *A History of the County of Oxford*, vol. 3 (London: Boydell & Brewer, n.d.), http://www.british-history.ac.uk/vch/oxon/vol3/, 298–309.

24 Peck, ed., *Leicester's Commonwealth*, 53.

25 Philip Sidney, 'Defence of Leicester', in *Miscellaneous Prose of Sir Philip Sidney*, ed. Katherine Duncan-Jones and Jan van Dorsten (Oxford: Oxford University Press, 1973), 123–4, 134.

26 For this episode in Sidney's life, see Stewart, *Philip Sidney*, Chapter 10; SP 84/3, 73; *CSPS(S)*, III, no. 411.

27 Rif Winfield, *British Warships in the Age of Sail 1603–1714: Design, Construction, Careers and Fates* (Barnsley: Seaforth Publishing, 2010), 16; C. S. Knighton and David Loades, *The Navy of Edward VI and Mary I* (Farnham: Ashgate Publishing, Ltd., 2013), 476.

28 Adams, ed., *Accounts*, 287, 342, 373.

29 Kuin, ed., *Correspondence of Sir Philip Sidney*, 1129.

30 SP 84/5 fol. 69.

31 Account from John Bruce, ed., *Correspondence of Robert Dudley, Earl of Leycester: During His Government of the Low Countries, in the Years 1585 and 1586* (London: Camden Society, 1844), 461–6.

32 Brielle.

33 Vlissingen.

34 Goldring, *Robert Dudley*, 139.

35 Adams, ed., *Accounts*, 370.

36 Account from Bruce, *Correspondence*, 57–63; I have adjusted some of the report to fit with spoken dialogue.

37 Bruce, ed., *Correspondence*, 111.

38 Stewart, *Philip Sidney*, loc. 5713.

39 Bruce, ed., *Correspondence*, 63.

40 Bruce, ed., *Correspondence*, 98.

41 SP 84/6 fol. 116.

42 Bruce, ed., *Correspondence*, 151.

43 Bruce, ed., *Correspondence*, 151.

44 My thanks to Cathryn Enis for sharing her work on the relationship between Ambrose and Robert.

45 Bruce, ed., *Correspondence*, 355.

46 Bruce, ed., *Correspondence*, 24.

47 Bruce, ed., *Correspondence*, 110.

48 Account of Davison's time at Richmond from Bruce, ed., *Correspondence*, 117–26.

49 I have adjusted some of the report to fit with spoken dialogue.

50 Bruce, ed., *Correspondence*, 97.

51 Bruce, ed., *Correspondence*, 99–101.

52 Kuin, ed., *Correspondence of Sir Philip Sidney*, 1193.

53 Bruce, ed., *Correspondence*, 165.

54 Bruce, ed., *Correspondence*, 168–171. Davison underlined passages in Leicester's letter and responded to them in the margins.

55 Goodrowse in the MS.

56 Bruce, ed., *Correspondence*, 174. My thanks to Kurosh Meshkat.

57 Bruce, ed., *Correspondence*, 175.

58 Bruce, ed., *Correspondence*, 209.

59 SP 84/17 fol. 61.

60 Stewart, *Philip Sidney*, loc. 6197.

61 Stewart, *Philip Sidney*, loc. 6099.

62 *Calendar of the Manuscripts of the Most Hon. the Marquis of Salisbury, Preserved at Hatfield House, Hertfordshire. Vol. 3: 1583–1589*, 189.

63 SP 84/10/1 fol. 58.

64 Geoffrey Parker, *The Cambridge Illustrated History of Warfare* (Cambridge: Cambridge University Press, 2000), 154.

65 *Calendar ... Salisbury*, 3, 190.

66 Stewart, *Philip Sidney*, loc. 6245.

67 Stewart, *Philip Sidney*, loc. 6232.

68 SP 84/10/1 fol. 58; Gábor Ágoston, *Guns for the Sultan: Military Power and the Weapons Industry in the Ottoman Empire* (Cambridge: Cambridge University Press, 2005), 89.

69 Stewart, *Philip Sidney*, loc. 6245.

70 SP 84/10/1 fol. 58.

71 Bruce, ed., *Correspondence*, 422.

72 Bruce, ed., *Correspondence*, 415.

73 Arthur Collins, ed., *Letters and Memorials of State* (London: F. Osborne, 1746), 109.

74 Collins, ed., *Letters*, 111.

75 Bruce, ed., *Correspondence*, 429.

76 Kuin, ed., *Correspondence*, 1320–1.

77 Lindsay J. Starkey, 'Gangrene or Cancer? Sixteenth-Century Medical Texts and the Decay of the Body of the Church in Jean Calvin's Exegesis of 2 Timothy 2:17', *Renaissance and Reformation/Renaissance et Réforme* 39, no. 3 (2016): 119.

78 Starkey, 'Gangrene', 120.

79 Starkey, 'Gangrene', 120–1. It was reported that Philip 'would not have [his leg] cut off', *CSPF*, XXI, Appendix: November 1586.

80 A disease known as *syderatio* or St Anthony's Fire; see Starkey, 'Gangrene', 121.

81 SP 84/10/1. Translation my own, guided by Stewart, *Philip Sidney*, loc. 6361.

82 Collins, ed., *Letters*, 112.

83 Cressy, *Birth, Marriage, and Death*, 390; Stewart, *Philip Sidney*, loc. 6402.

84 Stewart, *Philip Sidney*, loc. 6402.

85 BL Harleian 6798, fol. 87, available online: http://www.bl.uk/learning/timeline/item102878.html. See also Leigh S. Marcus, Janel Meuller, and Mary Beth Rose, eds., *Elizabeth I: Collected Works* (Chicago: University of Chicago Press, 2002), 325–6. For a discussion of the authenticity of Leonel Sharpe's account of the Tilbury speech, see Janet M. Green, '"I My Self": Queen Elizabeth I's Oration at Tilbury Camp', *The Sixteenth Century Journal* 28, no. 2 (1997): 421–45; Estelle Paranque, *Elizabeth I of England through Valois Eyes: Power, Representation, and Diplomacy in the Reign of the Queen, 1558–1588* (Cham: Palgrave Macmillan, 2018), 42–3.

86 SP 84/10/1 fol. 194; SP 12/195 fol. 7.

87 Bruce, ed., *Correspondence*, 445.

88 Bruce, ed., *Correspondence*, 446.

89 Bruce, ed., *Correspondence*, 431.

90 Thomas Wright, *Queen Elizabeth and Her Times* (London: H. Colburn, 1838), 314.

91 See Williams, *Rival Queens*, 311–17.

92 SP 84/11 f.56; SP 84/11 f.51.

93 Bruce, ed., *Correspondence*, 431.

94 *CSPS(S)*, IV, no. 28; *CSPV*, VIII, no. 483; see also BL MS Harleian 290 fol. 222.

95 Agnes Strickland, ed., *Lives of the Queens of Scotland and English Princesses: Connected with the Regal Succession of Great Britain*, vol. 7 (Edinburgh and London: W. Blackwood, 1858), 458.

96 BL Harleian 285 fol. 268.

97 From the compilation of sources by William Davison in Colthorpe, 'The Elizabethan Court', 1587: 7–8. See also PC 2/14 fol. 266.

98 Account from BL Harleian 285 fol. 268 and Colthorpe, 'The Elizabethan Court', 1587: 7–8.

99 See PC 2/14 fol. 268 for the formal account of the Privy Council meeting that day, at which Robert Dudley was present.

100 SP 84/16 fol. 18; SP 84/16 fol. 78; SP 84/17 fol. 215.

101 SP 84/15 fol. 149.

102 SP 84/18 fol. 211.

103 SP 84/19 fol. 171.

104 Colthorpe, 'The Elizabethan Court', 1588: 29.

105 SP 12/213 fol. 22, 51. Printed in John Knox Laughton, ed., *State Papers Relating to the Defeat of the Spanish Armada, Anno 1588* (London: Navy Records Society, 1894), 305–9.

106 SP 12/213 fol. 64. Printed in Laughton, ed., *State Papers*, 318–21.

107 SP 12/213 fol. 79. Printed in Agnes Strickland, ed. *Lives of the Queens of England: From the Norman Conquest.* Vol. 2. (London: H. Colburn, 1851), 577–8.

108 Colin Martin and Geoffrey Parker, *The Spanish Armada* (Manchester: Manchester University Press, 2002) 172.

109 Laughton, ed., *State Papers*, 305; SP 12/214 fol. 86. Printed in Robert Pierce Cruden, ed., *The History of the Town of Gravesend in the County of Kent, and of the Port of London* (London: W. Pickering, 1843), 248.

110 SP 12/213 fol. 79; see Green, 'Elizabeth I's Tilbury Camp Oration', 426–7.

111 Laughton, *State Papers*, ii, 69.

112 Laughton, *State Papers*, ii, 82; Green, 'Elizabeth I's Tilbury Camp Oration', 440.

113 Colthorpe, 'The Elizabethan Court', 1588: 43.

114 Simon Townley, ed., *A History of the County of Oxford*, vol. 18 (Woodbridge: Boydell & Brewer, 2016), https://www.british-history.ac.uk/vch/oxon/vol18/, 235–74.

115 'CORNBURY HOUSE, Cornbury and Wychwood – 1053113 | Historic England', accessed 24 May 2020, https://historicengland.org.uk/listing/the-list/list-entry/1053113.

116 Geffrey Whitney, *Choice of Emblemes* (Chester: Lovell Reeve, 1866), 230.

EPILOGUE: SO ILL THE RACE
OF DUDLEYS COULD ENDURE

1 Arthur Collins, ed., *Letters and Memorials of State*, vol. 1 (London: F. Osborne, 1746), 75.

2 Collins, ed., *Letters and Memorials*, 71.

3 Collins, ed., *Letters and Memorials*, 70.

4 Tallis, *Elizabeth's Rival*, 246.

5 Collins, ed., *Letters and Memorials*, 75.

Glossary of Names

Anne of Cleves, Queen of England (1515–1557)
Queen consort of England for six months from January 1540, Anne of Cleves was born in Düsseldorf to John III of the House of La Marck and his wife Maria of Jülich-Berg. Anne's marriage to **Henry VIII** was a failed one, but she remained a part of the English court for the rest of her life. **John Dudley (1504–1553)** and **Jane Dudley (1508/9–1555)** both served her during her short reign as queen.

Ascham, Roger (*c*.1515–1568)
An English scholar and writer, Roger Ascham spent time in the household of **John Dudley (1504–1553)** and **Jane Dudley (1508/9–1555)** before becoming tutor to the future queen **Elizabeth I**.

Ashley (née Champernowne), Kat (*c*.1502–1565)
Governess and friend to **Elizabeth I**, Kat Ashley was vehemently opposed to the queen marrying **Robert Dudley (1532–88)**.

Askew, Anne (1521–1546)
Writer, poet and martyr, Anne Askew was tried and executed for her denial of transubstantiation and other Catholic doctrine. During her interrogation, she implied **John Dudley (1504–1553)** shared her beliefs, but even under torture she refused to give up any names of women in the court who supported her, which might have included **Jane Dudley (1508/9–1555)**. Her brother, Sir Francis Askew, was knighted alongside **Henry Dudley (1525–1544)** in France.

Beaufort, Margaret, Countess of Richmond and Derby (1443–1509)
Mother of Henry VII, Margaret Beaufort played an essential role in the

Wars of the Roses and the eventual triumph of her son. She remained a powerful figure in her son's court, and was likely one of those who stood opposed to the actions and influence of **Edmund Dudley**.

Blount, Christopher (1555/56–1601)
Son of **Thomas Blount**, Christopher Blount was raised a Catholic but nevertheless followed his father into the service of **Robert Dudley** (1532–1588). Following Dudley's death, Blount married **Lettice Dudley**, the earl's widow. He supported his stepson, **Robert Devereux**, in his rebellion against **Elizabeth I** and was beheaded in 1601.

Blount, Thomas (d. 1568)
A servant and kinsman of **John Dudley** (1504–1553), Thomas Blount went on to serve **Robert Dudley**, including investigating the death of Robert's wife, **Amy Dudley**. His son was **Christopher Blount**.

Boleyn, Anne, Queen of England (c.1501–1536)
Daughter of the French ambassador **Thomas Boleyn**, Anne Boleyn became the second wife and queen to **Henry VIII** after a long courtship. Marrying her required annulling his marriage to his first wife, **Catherine of Aragon**, which could not be done within the confines of the Roman Catholic Church. Boleyn gave birth to one surviving daughter, **Elizabeth I**, but no sons. She was accused of adultery and treason, and she was executed in 1536.

Boleyn (née Howard), Elizabeth, Countess of Wiltshire (c.1480–1538)
Eldest daughter of **Thomas Howard** (1443–1524), Elizabeth Boleyn married **Thomas Boleyn** and was the mother of **Anne Boleyn**, **George Boleyn** and **Mary Carey**. Through her, the Boleyns had connections to the powerful Howard family, including her brothers **Thomas Howard** (1473–1554), **Edward Howard** and **Edmund Howard**.

Boleyn, George, Viscount Rochford (c.1503–1536)
Brother of **Anne Boleyn**, George Boleyn rose high in her court, before being executed for adultery with the queen in 1536.

Boleyn (née Parker), Jane, Lady Rochford (c.1505–1542)
Wife of **George Boleyn**, Jane Boleyn survived her husband's fall to serve as lady-in-waiting to queens **Jane Seymour**, **Anne of Cleves** and **Katherine Howard**. Under Katherine, she played a role in facilitating the queen's meetings with **Thomas Culpeper**, and she was executed in 1542.

Boleyn, Thomas, Earl of Wiltshire and Ormond (1476/7–1539)
Thomas Boleyn rose to prominence as an ambassador early in the reign of Henry VIII. Father of **Anne Boleyn**, he played a less significant role in the court following the execution of his son and daughter.

Bourbon, Nicholas (1503 or 1505–after 1550)
A French poet and writer, Nicholas Bourbon travelled to England under the protection of **Anne Boleyn** and was also patronized by the Dudley family, tutoring **Henry Dudley (1525–1544)**.

Brandon, Charles, 1st Duke of Suffolk (c.1484–1545)
Raised in the court of **Henry VIII**, Charles Brandon became the king's friend and companion, despite marrying the king's sister, **Mary Tudor**, without his permission. Through her, his daughter **Francis Grey** carried royal blood and entered the royal succession. Brandon knighted **John Dudley (1504–1553)** in 1523 and they fought together in France in 1544. Brandon's granddaughter, **Jane Dudley (1537–1554)**, and John's son, **Guildford Dudley**, married in 1553.

Bray, Reginald (c.1440–1503)
A servant of **Margaret Beaufort**, Reginald Bray entered the service and administration of her son **Henry VII**, including leading the Council Learned in the Law. One of the executors of the will of **John Sutton (c.1427–1504)**, it is probable that he recommended Dudley's son, **Edmund Dudley**, to the king.

Carew, George (c.1504–1545)
Vice-admiral to **John Dudley (1504–1553)** as Lord Admiral, George Carew was killed in command of the *Mary Rose* during the Battle of the Solent in 1545.

Carey, Henry (1526–1596), 1st Baron Hunsdon
Son of **Mary Carey**, it was speculated that Henry Carey may have been an illegitimate son of **Henry VIII**, given his mother's affair with the king. He was tutored alongside **Henry Dudley (1525–1544)** by **Nicholas Bourbon**.

Carey (née Boleyn, later Stafford), Mary (c.1499–1543)
Daughter of **Thomas Boleyn** and **Elizabeth Boleyn**, Mary Carey had an affair with **Henry VIII** while married to her husband, William Carey, which led to the speculation that her children, **Catherine Knollys** and **Henry Carey**, were illegitimate children of the king.

Catherine de Medici, Queen of France (1519–89)

Wife of **Henry II** of France, Catherine de Medici was the mother of three successive kings of France: **Francis II**, **Charles IX** and **Henry III**. She was thought by many, including **Philip Sidney**, to have been responsible for the massacre of French Protestants during the St Bartholomew's Day Massacre of 1572.

Catherine of Aragon, Queen of England (1485–1536)

Daughter of Isabella I of Castille and Ferdinand II of Aragon, Catherine of Aragon was first married to the eldest son of **Henry VII**, **Arthur Tudor**, though was widowed soon after their marriage. After the accession of his younger brother, **Henry VIII**, they were married. She gave birth to one surviving daughter, **Mary I**. Her marriage to Henry VIII was annulled in 1533 in order to allow the king to marry **Anne Boleyn**.

Cecil, William, 1st Baron Burghley (1520/1–1598)

A secretary of **Edward Seymour** (1500–1552), William Cecil served **John Dudley** (1504–1553) after Seymour's fall, but was part of the campaign against him and Dudley's daughter-in-law, **Jane Dudley** (1537–1554), switching his allegiance to **Mary I**. An administrator of **Elizabeth I**'s estate, he became one of her most trusted councillors and ministers.

Charles V, Holy Roman Emperor (1500–1558)

Heir to a series of titles, which included King of Spain, and elected Holy Roman Emperor in 1519, Charles V was one of the most powerful rulers in Europe. His conflict with **Francis I** resulted in a series of wars during which England varied its alliances, at times helped and hindered by **Henry VIII**'s marriage to Charles's aunt, **Catherine of Aragon**. He abdicated his role in 1555, bestowing his Spanish lands and titles upon his son, **Philip II**.

Charles IX, King of France (1550–1574)

Son of **Henry II** and **Catherine de Medici**, Charles IX came to the throne at the age of only nine, following the death of his elder brother **Francis II**. Following the marriage of his sister, **Marguerite de Valois** to the future **Henry IV** (then Henry of Navarre) in 1572, Charles ordered the massacre of French Protestants, who had been welcomed to Paris to celebrate the wedding.

Courtenay (née Grey), Elizabeth, Viscountess Lisle (1505–1519)

Only child of John Grey and Muriel Grey (née Howard), Elizabeth Courtenay was orphaned in 1512 after the death of her mother and stepfather,

Thomas Knyvet. She became the ward of **Charles Brandon** and the two were betrothed, granting him the title Viscount Lisle, but he married **Mary Tudor** instead in 1515. Elizabeth was married to Henry Courtenay before dying young. Her title passed to her aunt, **Elizabeth Dudley** (*c*.1482/84–*c*.1525/26), then wife of **Arthur Plantagenet** and mother of **John Dudley** (1504–1553).

Cranmer, Thomas, Archbishop of Canterbury (1489–1556)

Thomas Cranmer provided theological support for **Henry VIII**'s annulment of his marriage to **Catherine of Aragon** and break from the Roman Catholic Church. He received support from the king and his new queen **Anne Boleyn**, and served Henry throughout his reign, including informing him of the previous sexual experiences of **Katherine Howard**. He was essential to the continued Reformation under **Edward VI**, but was executed by the Catholic monarch **Mary I**, having been tried alongside **Guildford Dudley** and **Jane Dudley** (1537–1554) following Wyatt's Rebellion.

Cromwell, Thomas, Earl of Essex (*c*.1485–1540)

Essential to the annulment of the marriage between **Henry VIII** and **Catherine of Aragon**, Cromwell later played a pivotal role in the trial and execution of **Anne Boleyn**. He was also seen as responsible for the marriage between the king and **Anne of Cleves** and was executed for treason following the annulment of this union.

Culpeper, Thomas (1514–1541)

A servant of **Arthur Plantagenet** and his wife **Honor Plantagenet**, Thomas Culpeper became a gentleman of the King's Privy Chamber. During the reign of **Katherine Howard**, the two met frequently in secret. When this was discovered, both were executed.

d'Annebault, Claude, Admiral of France (1495–1552)

The French counterpart to **John Dudley** (1504–1553) as Lord Admiral, Claude d'Annebault led the French in the Battle of the Solent, successfully invading the Isle of Wight. He and Dudley later agreed the Treaty of Camp in 1546, and he travelled to England later that summer.

Davison, William (*c*.1541–1608)

Cousin (by **Jane Dudley** (1508/09–1555)) of **Robert Dudley** (1532–1588), William Davison served as ambassador during Dudley's mission to the Netherlands in 1584. When Dudley accepted the role of Governor General,

Davison was required to defend this action to **Elizabeth I** and Dudley quickly blamed him for the substantial political misstep. Nevertheless, Davison was promoted to Secretary of State, which made him central to the trial of **Mary, Queen of Scots**, including being in possession of the warrant for her execution, which the queen had signed. Elizabeth I later claimed that she had not wished it to be carried out and Davison was put on trial and imprisoned, but he was released soon after.

de la Quadra, Álvaro (d.1564)
Bishop of Aquila, Álvaro de la Quadra was imperial ambassador during the early years of the reign of **Elizabeth I**.

Devereux, Robert, Earl of Essex (1565–1601)
The eldest son of **Walter Devereux** and **Lettice Devereux**, Robert Devereux was named for his future stepfather, **Robert Dudley** (1532–1588), and followed him into battle in the Netherlands. He married his friend and cousin, **Philip Sidney**'s, widow, **Frances Sidney**. In 1601 he mounted a rebellion against the queen, supported by his new stepfather, **Christopher Blount**, and was executed.

Devereux, Walter, Earl of Essex (1541–1576)
First husband of **Lettice Dudley** and father of **Robert Devereux**, Walter Devereux served as Earl Marshal of Ireland under **Elizabeth I**. He fell ill in 1576 and died. Despite a post-mortem to the contrary, rumours that he was poisoned, either by his enemies in Ireland or by **Robert Dudley** (1532–1588), who not long after married his widow, persisted.

Dudley (née Leigh), Alice, Duchess Dudley (1579–1669)
Wife of **Robert Dudley** (1574–1649), Alice Dudley gave birth to seven daughters, five of whom survived into adulthood (Alice, Douglass, Katherine, Frances and Anne). She was abandoned by Dudley, who fled England with his cousin, **Elizabeth Dudley** (1584–1631), whom he married in Italy. In 1644 King Charles I created her Duchess of Dudley for the duration of her life.

Dudley, Ambrose, Earl of Warwick (c.1531–1590)
Born the fourth son of **Jane Dudley** (1508/09–1555) and **John Dudley** (1504–1553), Ambrose Dudley first took to the field under his father's command during Kett's Rebellion and then later in defending the claim of his sister-in-law, **Jane Dudley** (1537–1554). He was imprisoned, attainted and

condemned to death, but was released following the death of his father, mother and elder brother, **John Dudley** (*c.*1530–1554). Along with his two remaining brothers, **Robert Dudley** (1532–1588) and **Henry Dudley** (**d.**1557), Dudley travelled to France to fight alongside **Philip II**; Henry was killed in battle. Under **Elizabeth I**, Dudley was made Earl of Warwick and gained a reputation as an impressive military commander. He married three times but had no surviving children.

Dudley (née Robsart), Amy (1532–1560)
Daughter of a Norfolk gentleman with substantial land holdings, Amy Dudley married **Robert Dudley** (1532–1588) when they were both just shy of eighteen. She died in mysterious circumstances, generating rumours that she had been murdered on the orders of her husband, to clear the way for his marriage to **Elizabeth I**.

Dudley, Andrew (*c.*1507–1559)
The younger son of **Elizabeth Dudley** (*c.*1482/84–*c.*1525/26) and **Edmund Dudley**, Andrew Dudley entered court life as officer of the exchequer before serving in the royal navy and taking on a variety of significant appointments under **Edward VI**, including ambassador to **Charles V**. He joined his brother, **John Dudley** (1504–1553) and nephews in defending the claim of **Jane Dudley** (1537–1554), and shared in their imprisonment. He was released and pardoned in 1555, dying four years later.

Dudley (née Russell), Anne, Countess of Warwick (1548/49–1604)
The third wife of **Ambrose Dudley**, they married in an elaborate ceremony at Whitehall Palace. This marriage, like Ambrose's earlier unions, was childless. Anne Dudley went on to serve **Elizabeth I**, including at her death.

Dudley (née Seymour, later Unton), Anne, Countess of Warwick (1538–1588)
The eldest daughter of **Edward Seymour** (1500–52), Anne Dudley married **John Dudley** (*c.*1530–1554) as the sign of a union between their respective fathers. This did not last, however; her father was executed two years after her wedding and her father-in-law took control of the Council. She remarried but was declared insane and placed in the custody of her son, Henry Unton.

Dudley (née Whorewood), Anne (**d.**1552)
Ward of **John Dudley** (1504–1553), she became the first wife of **Ambrose Dudley**. Her father had been the Attorney General, **William Whorewood**. The pair married in about 1549 and had no surviving children.

Dudley (née Windsor), Anne (d. by 1503)
First wife of **Edmund Dudley** and sister of **Andrew Windsor**, Anne Dudley gave birth to a daughter, **Elizabeth Stourton**. She was buried at Tortington Church, Sussex.

Dudley, Edmund (c.1462–1510)
Son of **John Sutton** (c.1427–1503) and educated as a lawyer, Edmund Dudley was an expert in the king's prerogative. He was chosen as Speaker of the House of Commons in 1504 and soon after began working for **Henry VII**, collecting money owed to the king. This made him highly unpopular and when Henry VII died, Edmund was arrested and imprisoned in the Tower of London. He was executed in 1510, leaving his wife, **Elizabeth Dudley** (1482/84–1525/26), and three sons: **John Dudley** (1504–1553), **Jerome Dudley** and **Andrew Dudley**.

**Dudley, (née Grey, later Plantagenet) Elizabeth, Viscountess Lisle (c.1482/
84–c.1525/26)**
Daughter of Edward Grey, Viscount Lisle, Elizabeth Dudley married **Edmund Dudley** between 1500–1503 and bore him three sons: **John Dudley** (1504–1553), **Jerome Dudley** and **Andrew Dudley**. After Edmund's execution, she married **Arthur Plantagenet**, an illegitimate son of Edward IV, and they had three daughters. She succeeded to the title of Viscountess of Lisle in 1523, which passed on her death first to her second husband, and then on his death to her eldest son.

Dudley (née Southwell), Elizabeth (1584–1631)
A descendant of the Howard family, Elizabeth was a maid of honour to **Elizabeth I** and Anne of Denmark before leaving England with her cousin **Robert Dudley** (1574–1649). The pair married in Lyon, despite Dudley's pre-existing marriage to **Alice Dudley**, before settling in Florence. They had at least eleven children (Carlo, Ambrogio, Ferdinando, Teresa, Cosimo, Maria Christina, Maria Magdalena, Antonio, Enrico, Anna and Giovanni).

Dudley (née Tailboys), Elizabeth, Baroness Tailboys (c.1520–1563)
Daughter of one of the mistresses of **Henry VIII**, Elizabeth Blount, Elizabeth was half-sister to the king's illegitimate son (and may have been his illegitimate daughter as well). Her second husband was **Ambrose Dudley**. She worked to secure his freedom after the abortive reign of **Jane Dudley** (1537–1554), but was later abandoned by her husband and appears to have suffered a phantom pregnancy.

Dudley, Guildford (c.1537–1554)

Born the sixth son of **Jane Dudley** (1508/09–1555) and **John Dudley** (1504–1553), Guilford Dudley was probably the Dudley son baptised with **Mary I** as godmother in 1537 and confirmed a year later with the Spanish diplomat Diego Hurtado de Mendoza as godfather. He was married to **Jane Dudley** (1537–1554) at Durham Place in 1553. Later that year Jane was promoted as heir to the throne of England, despite the more established claims of Mary. The coup was ultimately unsuccessful, and Dudley was imprisoned, along with his father and four brothers: **John Dudley** (c.1530–1554), **Ambrose Dudley**, **Robert Dudley** (1532–1588) and **Henry** (d. 1557). He was tried and executed for treason following Wyatt's Rebellion in 1554.

Dudley, Henry (1525–1544)

The first son born to **Jane Dudley** (1508/09–1555) and **John Dudley** (1504–1553), Henry Dudley was educated by **Nicholas Bourbon** as a child. He was knighted following the taking of Boulogne in 1544, but died soon after, probably of dysentery. There was a poem written and published to commemorate Henry's death by John Leland: *Naenia in mortem splendidissimi equitis Henrici Duddelegi*: 'An elegy in praise of Sir Henry Dudley' (1545).

Dudley, Henry (d. 1557)

The seventh son born to **Jane Dudley** (1508/09–1555) and **John Dudley** (1504–1553), Henry Dudley shared his name with his elder brother who died in 1544. This makes it possible that he was born after his elder brother's death, but he likewise could have been born any time after 1538. He married **Margaret Dudley** in 1553, when she was only thirteen. He was imprisoned with his older brothers following the overthrow of his sister-in-law **Jane Dudley** (1537–1554) and journeyed to France in 1557 to fight in the siege of Saint-Quentin. He was killed while scaling the walls.

Dudley (née Grey), Jane (1537–1554)

The granddaughter of **Charles Brandon** and **Mary Tudor** by their daughter **Frances Grey**, Jane Dudley carried a claim to the throne. This claim should have sat behind the stronger claims of her cousins **Mary I** and **Elizabeth I**; however, nearing the end of his life, **Edward VI** skipped over his half-siblings to award the crown to her. This may have been thanks to the influence of the Lord President of the Council, **John Dudley** (1504–1553), who was now her father-in-law, as she had married his son, **Guildford Dudley**, earlier that year. Likewise, Edward may have been searching for the quickest route to a male (Protestant) heir; as a recently married woman, Dudley was more likely to be carrying a son than her unmarried cousins. Her regime was quickly overthrown by Mary I and her supporters, and she and her Dudley supporters were imprisoned. She was tried and executed for treason following the failure of Wyatt's Rebellion in 1554.

Dudley (née Guildford), Jane (1508/09–1555)
Jane Dudley, daughter of **Edward Guildford**, married her father's ward, **John Dudley (1504–1553)** at the age of sixteen. Over the following decades they had thirteen children (sons: **Henry Dudley (1525–1544)**, Thomas, **John Dudley (c.1530–1554)**, **Ambrose Dudley**, **Robert Dudley (1532–88)**, **Guildford Dudley**, **Henry Dudley (d.1557)**, Charles; daughters: **Mary Sidney (c.1535–86)**, Margaret, **Katherine Hastings**, Temperance and Catherine). Dudley was part of the funeral procession for **Jane Seymour**, served **Anne of Cleves** and was a friend of **Catherine Parr**. She was probably one of the women who supported **Anne Askew**. Following the arrest of her husband and sons in 1553, Dudley, alongside her daughters and daughters-in-law, campaigned for their release. It was probably her death in 1555 which prompted **Mary I** to release and restore the remaining Dudley sons.

Dudley, Jerome (c.1504–1510–after 1555)
A younger son of **Elizabeth Dudley (c.1482/84–c.1525/26)** and **Edmund Dudley**, Jerome Dudley was probably their second son following **John Dudley (1504–1553)**. Edmund's will suggests a role in the church for him, and later documents suggest some incapacity that required others to care for him. Unlike his brothers he does not appear to have held any court posts and is not implicated in the **Jane Dudley (1537–1554)** affair.

Dudley, John, Duke of Northumberland (1504–1553)
The eldest son of **Elizabeth Dudley (c.1482/84–c.1525/26)** and **Edmund Dudley**, John Dudley became a ward of **Edward Guildford** after his father's attainder and execution. He travelled to the continent in the company of **Thomas Wolsey** as a young man and was knighted by **Charles Brandon** in 1523. Shortly thereafter, he married the daughter of his guardian, **Jane Dudley (1508/09–1555)** and over the next decades they had thirteen children (sons: **Henry Dudley (1525–1544)**, Thomas, **John Dudley (c.1530–1554)**, **Ambrose Dudley**, **Robert Dudley (1532–1588)**, **Guildford Dudley (c.1537–1554)**, **Henry Dudley (d.1557)**, Charles; daughters: **Mary Sidney (c.1535–1586)**, Margaret, **Katherine Hastings**, Temperance and Catherine). The pair rose under queens **Anne Boleyn**, **Jane Seymour** and **Anne of Cleves**,

and Dudley played an important role in the downfall of **Katherine Howard**. As Lord Admiral, Dudley significantly improved the English Navy and commanded the fleet during the Battle of the Solent. After the death of **Henry VIII**, Dudley was one of the members of the Regency Council of **Edward VI**, and orchestrated the removal, rehabilitation and eventual execution of his rival, the Lord Protector, **Edward Seymour (1500–1552)**. As Lord President of the Council, Dudley was in a position to influence the young king, and may have encouraged him to leave the throne to his daughter-in-law, **Jane Dudley (1537–1554)**, who had recently married his son, Guildford. He supported Jane's claim, but was outmanoeuvred by **Mary I**, arrested and executed.

Dudley, John, Earl of Warwick (c.1530–54)
The third son born to **Jane Dudley (1508/09–1555)** and **John Dudley (1504–1553)**, John Dudley was married to the eldest daughter of **Edward Seymour (1500–1552)**, **Anne Dudley (1538–1588)**, as part of the (brief) reconciliation between the two men. John seems to have had scholarly interests and did not accompany his father on military expeditions like his elder brother **Henry Dudley (1525–1544)** or his younger brothers **Ambrose Dudley** and **Robert Dudley (1532–1588)**. Despite this he was arrested with his father and brothers after the overthrow of **Jane Dudley (1537–1554)**. He sickened while imprisoned and was released to the care of his sister **Mary Sidney (c.1535–1586)** at Penshurst but died soon after.

Dudley (née Knollys – also Devereux and later Blount), Lettice, Countess of Essex and Leicester (1543–1634)
The granddaughter of **Mary Carey**, and daughter of **Catherine Knollys (c. 1524–1569)** and **Francis Knollys**, Lettice Dudley was a cousin of **Elizabeth I**, and may have also been the granddaughter of Elizabeth's father, **Henry VIII**. She first married **Walter Devereux** and they named their eldest son, **Robert Devereux**, after **Robert Dudley (1532–1588)**. When Devereux died, she married Robert in secret; the revelation of their marriage to the queen caused their removal from court, though he was welcomed back some time after. The couple had one child, **Robert Dudley (1581–1584)**, who died young. Six months after her second husband's death, she married a third time, to **Christopher Blount**.

Dudley (née Audley, later Howard), Margaret (1540–1564)
Margaret married **Henry Dudley (d.1557)** at a young age. After his death she married **Thomas Howard (1536–1572)**.

Dudley, Robert, Earl of Leicester (1532–1588)

Born the fifth son of **Jane Dudley** (1508/09–1555) and **John Dudley** (1504–1553), Robert Dudley married **Amy Dudley** a day after his elder brother John's (*c.*1530–1554) elaborate wedding to **Anne Dudley** (1538–1588). During the **Jane Dudley** (1537–1554) affair, Robert was sent to capture **Mary I**, but was arrested instead at King's Lynn and convicted of treason. He was imprisoned along with his brothers, John Dudley, **Ambrose Dudley** and **Henry Dudley** (d.1557). After their release he fought in the siege of Saint-Quentin, where his younger brother Henry was killed. On the accession of **Elizabeth I**, Dudley became Master of the Horse and was rumoured to be a marriage prospect for the young queen, especially after the death of his wife in mysterious circumstances in 1560. The suggestion that he may have been involved in his wife's death, however, seriously damaged his chances. He was given the title of Earl of Leicester in 1564 and remained the queen's favourite through most of her reign, despite his secret marriage to her cousin, **Lettice Dudley**. His expedition to the Netherlands and acceptance of the position of Governor General was a significant misstep, but one from which he recovered in time to oversee the preparations for the Spanish Armada in 1588. He died a short while after. He left an illegitimate son, **Robert Dudley** (1574–1649), a stepson, **Robert Devereux**, and a nephew, **Robert Sidney**, his only legitimate son, **Robert Dudley** (1581–1584), having predeceased him.

Dudley, Robert (1574–1649)

The son of **Douglass Sheffield** and **Robert Dudley** (1532–1588), Robert Dudley repeatedly made the case for his legitimacy, despite lacking strong evidence for his parents' marriage. His father always acknowledged him as his son, however, even taking him to Tilbury during the preparations for the Spanish Armada. After his father's death, Dudley went on several naval expeditions, including to the Caribbean. In 1605 he left England with his cousin, **Elizabeth Dudley** (1584–1631), whom he married in Lyon, before they settled in Florence, despite his already being married to **Alice Dudley**. He and Elizabeth had eleven children (in addition to the six he had with Alice) and they never returned to England.

Dudley, Robert, Lord Denbigh (1581–1584)

The only child of the marriage between **Lettice Dudley** and **Robert Dudley** (1532–1588), Robert Dudley was known affectionately as 'the little imp' but died at the age of three. He was given an elaborate tomb in Warwick which immortalized the great 'hope' that his parents had had for him.

Edward VI, King of England (1537–1553)

The only son of **Jane Seymour** and **Henry VIII**, Edward VI was the long-awaited male heir to Henry's throne. Educated and guided by evangelicals, on his accession in 1547 Edward furthered the Reformation. A minor for the whole of his reign, Edward's protectorship was awarded to his uncle, **Edward Seymour** (1500–1552), despite the instructions for a regency council outlined in his father's will. After Seymour's fall from power and execution, **John Dudley** (1504–1553) was selected as Lord President of the Council, though he did not take the position of Lord Protector, probably beginning the process of transitioning Edward into taking up rule himself. Edward, however, fell ill before reaching the age of majority, and instead of leaving the throne to his half-sister, **Mary I**, who was unmarried and a Catholic, or his other half-sister, **Elizabeth I**, who was unmarried and Protestant, he left it to his cousin, **Jane Dudley** (1537–1554), who was Protestant and recently married to **Guildford Dudley**, son of John Dudley, causing the Succession Crisis of 1553.

Elizabeth I, Queen of England (1533–1603)

The only surviving child of **Anne Boleyn** and **Henry VIII**, Elizabeth I was stripped of her title of princess and declared a bastard when her parents' marriage was annulled in advance of her mother's execution in 1536. Nevertheless, she received an impressive (Protestant) education and was restored to the succession, as set out by her father's will. She was imprisoned under the reign of her half-sister, **Mary I**, but released and peacefully ascended to the throne on her sister's death in 1558. From the beginning of her reign, her closeness to and preference for **Robert Dudley** (1532–1588) was clear, causing many to suspect that they would soon marry. This marriage did not take place, but he remained dear to her throughout his life. After Robert's death her affection for his stepson, **Robert Devereux**, was short-lived, especially after his attempted rebellion in 1601, for which he was executed. She died in 1603, and was succeeded by **James VI/I**, son of **Mary, Queen of Scots**.

Elizabeth of York, Queen of England (1466–1503)

Daughter of King **Edward IV**, the Yorkist king during the Wars of the Roses, Elizabeth of York was also sister to a king, **Edward V**, and niece to a king, **Richard III**, who supplanted her brother. After the overthrow of Richard III by **Henry VII**, a marriage to Elizabeth was expedient to unite the warring factions and bolster Henry's weak claim to the throne. They had four surviving children, **Arthur Tudor**, **Margaret Tudor**, **Henry VIII** and **Mary Tudor**, though Arthur died a year before his mother. The combined deaths of Arthur and Elizabeth, alongside two infant children, provided context for the miserly paranoia of Henry VII's later years, and the employment of men like **Edmund Dudley** to shore up the Crown's finances.

Empson, Richard (*c.*1450–1510)

High Steward of the Duchy of Lancaster, Richard Empson became associated with **Edmund Dudley** in their roles of collecting money for **Henry VII**. He was arrested and executed alongside Dudley.

Erik XIV, King of Sweden (1533–1577)

Erik XIV was a suitor of **Elizabeth I** early in her reign, at a time when there were also rumours she might marry **Robert Dudley** (1532–1588).

Farnese, Alexander, Duke of Parma (1545–1592)

A grandson of **Charles V** (by his illegitimate daughter), Alexander Farnese was appointed as Governor General of the Spanish Netherlands under **Philip II**, returning cities in the United Provinces to Catholic Spanish control.

Fisher, John (1469–1535)

A former chaplain to **Margaret Beaufort**, John Fisher later refused to agree to Henry VIII's Oath of Supremacy and was executed.

FitzAlan, Henry, 12th Earl of Arundel (1512–1580)

A long-serving member of the court of **Henry VIII**, Henry FitzAlan was one of the twelve members of the Regency Council in the reign of **Edward VI**. A religious conservative, he opposed the rule of the Lord Protector, **Edward Seymour** (1500–1552) and worked with **Thomas Wriothesley** and **John Dudley** (1504–1553) to bring him down. Once Dudley assumed control, however, he arrested and fined FitzAlan and Wriothesley, who then allied with Seymour against him. Imprisoned, fined and released once again, FitzAlan initially supported the claim of **Jane Dudley** (1537–1554), but quickly turned on Dudley. He served **Mary I** in a variety of offices. After her death, it was rumoured he sought the hand of her successor, **Elizabeth I**, though this may have just been a joke or an attempt to play up the attractiveness of **Robert Dudley** (1532–1588) as an alternative suitor (or both). Certainly FitzAlan strongly opposed Dudley's suit. He was implicated in Catholic plots in the 1570s, but ironically was supported by Dudley (who may have been doing so just to irk **William Cecil**). He died of natural causes, having served and survived four Tudor monarchs.

Fox, Richard (*c.*1448–1528)

One of **Henry VII's** 'new men', Richard Fox came from obscure beginnings and received an extensive education at Oxford and Cambridge. He joined the service of Henry VII while the future king was in exile in France and was rewarded when Henry VII overthrew **Richard III**. When Henry VII died, Fox oversaw the transition of power and was probably responsible for the scapegoating and arrest of **Richard Empson** and **Edmund Dudley**. He held a powerful position in the early court of **Henry VIII** until the rise of his protégé **Thomas Wolsey**.

Francis I, King of France (1494–1547)

Successor to Louis XII, who left as his widow the young **Mary Tudor**, Francis I was the sworn enemy of **Charles V**, with whom he had an intense rivalry. **Henry VIII** often acted as the balance between these two much more substantial powers, and England and France found themselves at war several times throughout their overlapping reigns. He died, leaving the throne to his son, **Henry II**.

Francis, duc d'Anjou (formerly duc d'Alençon) (1555–1584)

The youngest son of **Henry II** and **Catherine de Medici**, Francis followed his elder brother in courting **Elizabeth I**, despite an age difference of over twenty years. He was the only one of her foreign suitors to press his suit in person. This marriage, supported by **William Cecil**, was strongly opposed by members of her court, including **Robert Dudley (1532–1588)** and **Francis Walsingham**. Heir to his brother, **Henry III**, his death led to the accession of **Henry IV** in France.

Gardiner, Stephen, Bishop of Winchester (1483–1555)

A servant of **Thomas Wolsey**, Stephen Gardiner was employed on a variety of diplomatic missions in the 1520s and 1530s. A conservative, he opposed evangelical reforms, but remained active in the court, nonetheless. He was imprisoned under **Edward VI** and freed by **Mary I**, who appointed him Lord Chancellor.

Grey (née Brandon, later Stokes), Frances, Duchess of Suffolk (1517–1559)

The daughter of **Charles Brandon** and **Mary Tudor**, she married **Henry Grey** in 1533 and had three daughters, **Jane Dudley (1537–1554)**, **Catherine Seymour** and Mary Grey. On the accession of her daughter Jane in 1553, Frances became queen mother. When Jane was deposed, Henry Grey, now Duke of Suffolk, was arrested. Frances pleaded for her husband to **Mary I** and was successful, securing his release. However, after Grey's involvement in Wyatt's Rebellion both he and Jane were executed. She later married her Master of the Horse, Adrian Stokes.

Grey, Henry, Duke of Suffolk (1517–1554)

Henry Grey married the daughter of **Charles Brandon** and **Mary Tudor**, **Frances Grey**, in 1533 and they had three daughters, **Jane Dudley** (1537–1554), **Catherine Seymour** and Mary Grey. He was arrested following the short-lived accession and then deposition of his daughter but released thanks to the intervention of his wife. He was a participant, however, in Wyatt's Rebellion against **Mary I** and was executed eleven days after his daughter.

Guildford, Edward (c.1474–1534)

Son of **Richard Guildford** (c.1450–1506), Edward Guildford inherited his father's position of Master of the Armoury, overseeing the weapons provisions for **Henry VIII**'s invasion of France in 1513. He was awarded the wardship of **John Dudley** (1504–1553) and raised him alongside his two children, **Richard Guildford** (d.1526) and **Jane Dudley** (1508/09–1555), the latter of whom married Dudley when they were both of age.

Guildford, Richard (c.1450–1506)

A close servant of **Reginald Bray**, Richard Guildford was an integral part of the court of **Henry VII** from the outset and awarded the position of Master of the Armoury. In 1506 he made his will and began a pilgrimage to the Holy Land. Forced to spend a night in a cave, Guildford soon after fell ill, and he died a day after arriving in Jerusalem.

Guildford, Richard (d.1526)

The son of **Edward Guildford** and brother of **Jane Dudley** (1508/09–1555), Richard Guildford was raised alongside his father's ward, **John Dudley** (1504–1553). He was sent to the continent following his education to serve the brother of **Charles V**, Ferdinand, before entering the service of the Prince of Orange, Philibert of Chalon. He was injured in a naval battle in 1524 and died in Granada two years later.

Hastings (née Dudley), Katherine, Lady Huntingdon (c.1545–1620)

Born the third daughter of **Jane Dudley** (1508/09–1555) and **John Dudley** (1504–1553), Katherine Hastings was probably the daughter baptized in 1545 with **Mary I** and Katherine, Duchess of Suffolk (widow of **Charles**

Brandon) as godmothers, the latter of whom was her namesake. She was betrothed in 1553 to **Henry Hastings**, at the same time as the marriage of her brother **Guildford Dudley** to **Jane Dudley** (1537–1554), but was too young for the marriage to be solemnized. Katherine had no children, but helped to raise and educate other young women, including the daughters of her brother's second wife, **Lettice Dudley**. After her husband's death, she became a close friend of **Elizabeth I**. She was the only one of her siblings to survive into the reign of **James VI/I**.

Hastings, Henry, Earl of Huntingdon (c.1535–1595)

Hastings married **Katherine Hastings** in 1553, though she was too young to consummate the union. He was briefly imprisoned after the accession and deposition of his sister-in-law **Jane Dudley** (c.1536–1554), but his kinship to **Mary I**'s former governess, Margaret, Countess of Salisbury, and her son, the queen's trusted councillor Reginal Pole, helped secure his speedy release. A descendant of the Plantagenets through **George, Duke of Clarence**, Hastings was a potential claimant for the throne, and especially attractive as one of the few Protestant, male candidates following the death of **Edward VI**.

Heneage, Thomas (c.1532–1595)

A member of the court of **Elizabeth I**, it was rumoured that she had flirted with Thomas Heneage to make **Robert Dudley** (1532–1588) jealous. He was chosen to deliver the queen's disapproval to Dudley when the earl became Governor General of the Netherlands.

Henry II, King of France (1519–1559)

The second son of **Francis I**, Henry II inherited the throne from his father in 1547. With his wife **Catherine de Medici** he had nine children, including three monarchs, **Francis II**, **Charles IX** and **Henry III**, none of whom produced heirs of their own. He died unexpectedly following a jousting accident, at which point his eldest son, Francis II and his wife, **Mary, Queen of Scots**, became monarchs of France.

Henry III, King of France (formerly duc d'Anjou) (1551–1589)

The fourth son of **Francis II** and **Catherine de Medici**, as duc d'Anjou, Henry III was briefly suggested as a suitor for **Elizabeth I**. He came to the throne after the untimely death of his brother **Charles IX** but was assassinated fifteen years into his reign, leading to the accession of the Protestant **Henry IV**.

Henry IV, King of France (1553–1610)

Henry IV ascended to the throne of Navarre, a small Protestant nation on the border of Spain and France, in 1572. That same year he travelled to Paris to marry the sister of **Charles IX**, Marguerite de Valois. Following the wedding and celebrations, thousands of French Protestants were massacred by official royal forces and Catholic mobs. Following the assassination of **Henry III**, he became King of France. He converted to Catholicism in 1593.

Henry VII, King of England (1547–1509)

Son of **Margaret Beaufort** and Edmund Tudor, a half-brother of Henry VI, Henry VII remained in exile in Brittany during the Wars of the Roses. He invaded England in 1485 and defeated **Richard III** at the Battle of Bosworth. He married the daughter of Edward IV, **Elizabeth of York**, and they had four surviving children: **Arthur Tudor**, **Margaret Tudor**, **Henry VIII** and **Mary Tudor**. He lost two infant children, his eldest son and his wife in the space of a few years, however, causing him to become paranoid about the security of his throne for his remaining son, Henry VIII, still a minor, employing men like **Edmund Dudley** to collect money for the Crown. He died close enough to his son's age of majority to ensure a peaceful transition of power and avoid a regency.

Henry VIII, King of England (1491–1547)

Second son of **Elizabeth of York** and **Henry VII**, **Henry VIII** became heir to the throne on the death of his brother **Arthur Tudor**. On his accession Henry VIII had two of his father's most hated ministers, **Richard Empson** and **Edmund Dudley**, arrested. They were executed the next year. He also quickly married his elder brother's widow, **Catherine of Aragon**, securing a dispensation from the pope to do so. His early reign was marked by his campaign in France, led by himself and one of his closest friends, **Charles Brandon**, who remained his friend even after he secretly married the king's sister, **Mary Tudor**. The king's own marriage was proving unsuccessful, as despite repeated pregnancies, Catherine and Henry had only one living child, **Mary I**. The pope, a prisoner of the queen's nephew **Charles V**, refused to grant an annulment so that the king could marry **Anne Boleyn**. Henry, supported by ministers such as **Thomas Cromwell** and **Thomas Cranmer**, instead established an independent English Church. This second marriage, however, also only produced one daughter, **Elizabeth I**, and Henry had Boleyn executed for adultery and treason. His third marriage, to **Jane Seymour**, produced the long-awaited male heir, **Edward VI**, but Seymour died soon after the birth. Marriages to **Anne of Cleves** and **Katherine Howard** did not last long and did not produce any further children. His last wife, **Catherine Parr**, was decidedly evangelical, and fostered a circle of like-minded women, which included **Jane Dudley** (1508/09–1555), whose husband was rising in the king's court. On Henry's death, **John Dudley** (1504–1553) was included on the Regency Council for his young son and heir, along with the new king's uncle, **Edward Seymour** (1500–1552).

Hepburn, James, 4th Earl of Bothwell (1534/5–1578)
A Scottish nobleman, James Hepburn was accused of the murder of **Mary, Queen of Scots'** second husband, **Henry Stuart**. Shortly thereafter he abducted and married the queen. Their twin children died in infancy. He died in exile.

Howard, Edmund (c.1478–1539)
The third son of **Thomas Howard** (1443–1524), Edmund Howard was an uncle of **Anne Boleyn** and the father of **Katherine Howard**.

Howard, Edward (1476/77–1513)
The second son of **Thomas Howard** (1443–1524), Edward Howard gained a military reputation at a young age. He was appointed admiral of the fleet during the war with France in 1512, and then Lord Admiral in 1513. He died at sea.

Howard, Henry, Earl of Surrey (1516/17–1547)
Eldest son of **Thomas Howard** (1473–1554), Henry was a cousin of both **Anne Boleyn** and **Katherine Howard**. Fiercely opposed to those of lower birth powerful in the court, such as **John Dudley** (1504–1553), he was arrested along with his father in the final months of the reign of **Henry VIII** and beheaded just two weeks before the king's death.

Howard, Katherine, Queen of England (c.1523–1542)
The daughter of **Edmund Howard**, Katherine Howard was the cousin of **Anne Boleyn**. She came to court as part of the household of **Anne of Cleves** and married **Henry VIII** within three weeks of the annulment of that marriage. Information about previous physical relationships came to light, however, as well as an ongoing liaison with **Thomas Culpeper**, for which she was executed.

Howard, Thomas, 2nd Duke of Norfolk (1443–1524)
Knighted for service to Edward IV, Thomas Howard supported **Richard III**

against **Henry VII**, leading to his imprisonment following the Battle of Bosworth. Refusing an opportunity to escape, Howard was restored by Henry VII and soon became a member of the king's Privy Council, working closely with **Richard Fox** and **William Warham**, including during the transition of power to **Henry VIII**, which saw the arrest of **Richard Empson** and **Edmund Dudley**. The success at Flodden Field in 1514 led to Thomas's elevation as Duke of Norfolk. He had some sixteen children, including **Thomas Howard** (1473–1554), **Edward Howard**, **Edmund Howard**, and **Elizabeth Boleyn**.

Howard, Thomas, 3rd Duke of Norfolk (1473–1554)
Eldest son of **Thomas Howard** (1443–1524), Thomas Howard gained a military reputation at a young age, helping to restore his family's name after they supported **Richard III** against **Henry VII** during the Wars of the Roses. He became a companion of the new king **Henry VIII** early in his reign and was appointed Lord Admiral after the death of his brother **Edward Howard** in 1513. The uncle of **Anne Boleyn**, her rise to power helped Howard oversee and benefit from the downfall of **Thomas Wolsey**. He later presided over his niece's trial and announced her sentence. He likewise played a central role in the fall of **Thomas Cromwell** and benefitted from the marriage of a second niece, **Katherine Howard**, to Henry VIII. His standing was barely impacted by her disgrace and execution. In the final months of the king's reign, however, both Howard and his eldest son, **Henry Howard**, were arrested, having fallen foul of the evangelicals at court, led by the king's final wife, **Catherine Parr**. Both were sentenced to death, but the king died before his sentence could be carried out. He was released by **Mary I** and presided over the trial of his former enemy, **John Dudley** (1504–1553), in 1553.

James V, King of Scots (1512–1542)
Son of James IV of Scotland and **Margaret Tudor**, James V became king at less than two years old, when his father was killed at the Battle of Flodden in 1513. War with England broke out again in 1542, and James fell ill, dying six days after the birth of his daughter, **Mary, Queen of Scots**.

James VI/I, King of Scotland, England and Ireland (1566–1625)
Son of **Mary, Queen of Scots** and Henry Stuart, James was the great-great-grandson of **Henry VII** by his daughter, **Margaret Tudor**, mother of **James V**. He became King of Scotland in 1567, following the forced abdication of his mother. At the death of **Elizabeth I** he was also recognized as heir to the throne of England.

Kingston, William, Constable of the Tower (c.1476–1540)
After joining the army of **Charles Brandon** in France in 1523, alongside **John Dudley** (1504–1553), William Kingston became Constable of the Tower in 1524, overseeing the executions of **Thomas More, Anne Boleyn** and others. He was also a neighbour of the property owned by the Dudley family at Painswick.

Knollys (later FitzGerald and Butler), Catherine (1559–1620)
Daughter of **Catherine Knollys** (c.1524–1569) and **Francis Knollys**, and sister of **Lettice Dudley**, Catherine Knollys was present at the wedding of **Anne Dudley** (1548/49–1604) and **Ambrose Dudley**. She went on to marry twice: Gerald FitzGerald, Earl of Kildare and Phillip Butler.

Knollys (née Carey), Catherine (c.1524–1569)
Daughter of **Mary Carey**, Catherine Knollys may have been an illegitimate daughter of **Henry VIII** and was a cousin of **Elizabeth I**. She joined the household of **Anne of Cleves** and **Katherine Howard**. She married **Francis Knollys** and they had some fourteen children, including **Lettice Dudley** and **Catherine Knollys** (1559–1620). Their last child, born in 1562, was named Dudley, acknowledging a relationship between the two families.

Knollys, Francis (1511/14–1596)
A long-serving member of the Tudor court, Francis Knollys had various dealings with the Dudley and Sidney families. He married **Catherine Knollys** (c.1524–1569) and they had some fourteen children, including **Lettice Dudley** and **Catherine Knollys** (1559–1620). He was responsible for the imprisonment of **Mary, Queen of Scots** at Carlisle Castle.

Knyvet, Thomas (c.1485–1512)
Stepfather of **Elizabeth Courtenay** and son-in-law of **Thomas Howard** (1443–1524), Knyvet was given command of the flagship the *Regent*, which went down in 1512.

Lassells, John (d.1546)
A servant of **Thomas Cromwell**, John Lassells was an ardent evangelical and opposed to the conservatives at court, including **Stephen Gardiner** and **Thomas Howard** (1473–1554). He gained information from his sister, Mary, about the previous sexual relationships of **Katherine Howard**, which he passed on to **Thomas Cranmer**, leading to the downfall of the queen. He was later arrested for heresy and burned alongside **Anne Askew**.

Luther, Martin (1483–1546)

Instigator of the religious schism known as the Reformation, which led to the establishment of various 'Protestant' churches, Martin Luther published his *95 Theses* in 1517, which prompted other critics of the Catholic Church to join him in seeking not reform of the Church, but the establishment of one truer to Christian Scripture. His followers were persecuted in England under **Henry VIII** and **Mary I**. Under **Edward VI** and **Elizabeth I** Catholics were persecuted as heretics.

Machiavelli, Niccolò (1469–1527)

A political writer from Florence, Niccolò Machiavelli's writings advocated moral flexibility in politics and were associated with immorality, atheism and the pursuit of naked self-interest. These doctrines became associated with the Dudley family.

Mary, Queen of Scots (1542–1587)

The daughter of **James V** and a great-granddaughter of **Henry VII**, Mary, Queen of Scots, was born six days after her father's death. She married **Francis II** and was Queen of France for just over a year. When he died, she returned to Scotland, where she married first **Henry Stuart** and then, following his murder, **James Hepburn**. She was forced to abdicate in favour of her son with Stuart, **James VI/I**, in 1567 and fled to England where she was imprisoned for two decades. A possible rival candidate for the throne of England, due to her Tudor blood and Catholic religion, she was executed in 1587 for her involvement in schemes to overthrow her cousin, **Elizabeth I**.

Mary I, Queen of England (1516–1558)

The daughter of **Catherine of Aragon** and **Henry VIII**, Mary I was the only surviving child of their marriage. She was stripped of her royal titles following the annulment of her parents' marriage but re-entered the succession and was heir to her half-brother **Edward VI** according to her father's will. Upon his death, however, Edward left the throne to their cousin **Jane Dudley** (1537–1554) and Mary was forced to win it back. She did this easily and supplanted Jane and her supporters, executing **John Dudley (1504–1553)**. Mary married **Philip II**, who supported the restoration of the remaining Dudleys, but had no children. The crown passed to her half-sister, **Elizabeth I**, on her death.

More, Thomas (1478–1535)

Son of a London lawyer, Thomas More was associated with opposition to

Edmund Dudley late in the reign of **Henry VII**. He later went on to become Lord Chancellor under **Henry VIII** but was executed for opposing Henry VIII's break with Rome.

Norris, Henry (*c.*1482–1536)
Groom of the Stool to **Henry VIII**, Henry Norris was executed for adultery with **Anne Boleyn**. His son was educated alongside **Henry Dudley** (1525–1544).

Paget, William, 1st Baron Paget (1505/6–1563)
Appointed to the Council of **Edward VI**, William Paget originally supported **Edward Seymour** (1500–1552), being imprisoned with him in 1551, but was later restored and supported the accession of **Jane Dudley** (1537–1554). With the rest of the Council, he welcomed **Mary I** but retired under **Elizabeth I**.

Parr, Catherine, Queen of England (1512–1548)
Daughter of **Thomas Parr**, Catherine Parr was the sixth and final woman to marry **Henry VIII**. A supporter of the evangelical cause, Catherine was unpopular with the conservatives at court, elevating religious reformers instead, such as **Jane Dudley** (1508/09–1555) and **John Dudley** (1504–53). When Henry died, she married **Thomas Seymour** but died in childbirth.

Parr, Thomas (*c.*1483–1517)
A courtier under **Henry VIII**, his wife served **Catherine of Aragon**, and they undoubtedly named their daughter, **Catherine Parr**, after this queen.

Parr, William, Marquess of Northampton (1513–1571)
Son of **Thomas Parr** and brother of **Catherine Parr**, William Parr was well liked by **Edward VI** and rose to prominence alongside **John Dudley** (1504–1553). He was convicted of treason for supporting **Jane Dudley** (1537–1554) but was released and restored under **Elizabeth I**.

Philip II, King of Spain (1527–1598)
The eldest son of **Charles V**, Philip II inherited the Spanish Empire on the abdication of his father. Despite opposition, he married **Mary I** and became king consort of England. Requiring support in England, he supported the restoration of those imprisoned following the fall of **Jane Dudley** (1537–1554), including the sons of **John Dudley** (1504–1553), who also supported his continental wars. Philip spent little time in England and the couple had

no children. On Mary's death, Philip proposed a marriage to her sister and successor, **Elizabeth I**, which was refused. Relations soured between the two monarchs, and the execution of the Catholic **Mary, Queen of Scots,** spurred the attack of the Spanish Armada in 1588, which was defeated.

Plantagenet, Arthur, Viscount Lisle (d.1542)
An illegitimate son of Edward IV, Arthur Plantagenet became a close companion of his nephew **Henry VIII**. He married **Elizabeth Dudley** (*c.*1482/84–*c.*1525/26) the widow of **Edmund Dudley**, but was not given the wardship of their son, **John Dudley** (1504–1553). As Constable of Calais, he became an enemy of **Thomas Cromwell** and was arrested and imprisoned. He was released two years later but died after hearing the news of his restoration.

Plantagenet (née Grenville), Honor, Lady Lisle (*c.*1493/95–1566)
Second wife of **Arthur Plantagenet**, Honor joined him in Calais. One of her servants, whom she was favourable towards, was **Thomas Culpeper.**

Rich (née Devereux, later Blount), Penelope, Lady Rich (1563–1607)
Daughter of **Lettice Dudley** and her first husband **Walter Devereux**, Penelope Rich was raised in the household of **Katherine Hastings**. She was considered as a wife for **Philip Sidney** but married **Robert Rich**. She later had a lengthy affair and she and her husband divorced. She was not permitted to marry her lover, but a private ceremony was carried out in defiance of canon law.

Rich, Robert, 3rd Baron Rich (later Earl of Warwick) (1559–1619)
Grandson of Richard Rich, the servant of **Henry VIII** involved in the trial against **Thomas More** and the torture of **Anne Askew**, Robert Rich married **Penelope Rich** in 1581. He became Earl of Warwick in 1618.

Richard III, King of England (1452–1485)
The brother of Edward IV, Richard III fought alongside the Yorkists in the Wars of the Roses. On his elder brother's death and the accession of his nephew, Edward V, he became Lord Protector, but quickly seized power for himself. He was defeated and killed at the Battle of Bosworth by the forces of **Henry VII**.

Russell, Francis, 2nd Earl of Bedford (1526/7–1585)
A religious reformer, Francis Russell was imprisoned during the early reign of

Mary I. Like the sons of **John Dudley** (1504–1553), he was released in time to fight for **Philip II** at the Battle of Saint-Quentin. On the accession of **Elizabeth I** he became a privy councillor and held various diplomatic posts. His eldest daughter, **Anne Dudley** (1548/49–1604), married **Ambrose Dudley**.

Scheyfve, Jean (c.1515–1581)
Imperial ambassador to the English court from 1550–1553, Scheyfve was in England during the accession and overthrow of **Jane Dudley** (1537–1554).

Seymour (née Stanhope), Anne, Duchess of Somerset (c.1510–1587)
Wife of **Edward Seymour** (1500–1552) and sister-in-law of **Jane Seymour**, Anne held powerful roles in the courts of **Henry VIII and Edward VI**. Like **Jane Dudley** (1508/09–1555), she was a friend of **Catherine Parr** and likely supported **Anne Askew**. When her husband fell from power under **Edward VI** and was executed, she was arrested and imprisoned. She was freed after the accession of **Mary I**. Her children included **Edward Seymour** (1539–1621) and **Anne Dudley** (1538–1588).

Seymour (née Grey), Catherine (1540–1568)
The daughter of **Frances Grey** and sister of **Jane Dudley** (1537–1554), Catherine Seymour was a descendant of **Henry VII** and therefore in the line of succession. This made her secret marriage to **Edward Seymour** (1539–1621) dangerous and illegal. After Seymour's departure for the continent, she was left pregnant with their child, and appealed to her brother-in-law **Robert Dudley** (1532–1588), who reported her marriage and pregnancy to **Elizabeth I**. Seymour was imprisoned, along with her husband. They had two more children while in the Tower, despite their imprisonment and the annulment of their marriage. She was eventually removed from the Tower and died a short while later.

Seymour, Edward, Duke of Somerset (1500–1552)
Brother of **Jane Seymour**, Edward Seymour served in the army of **Charles Brandon** in France in 1523, alongside **John Dudley** (1504–1553), with whom he continued to ally over the coming decades. He rose to prominence after his sister's marriage to **Henry VIII** and the birth of their son **Edward VI**. After the death of Henry, Edward was named to the Regency Council meant to oversee the rule of the young king, but soon after was made Lord Protector. A series of unpopular moves, however, including the execution of his own brother, **Thomas Seymour**, led to his removal and imprisonment and the rise of John Dudley as President of the Council. He re-entered the

court and Council but was arrested and executed for treason. He and his second wife, **Anne Seymour,** had some ten children, including **Edward Seymour (1539–1621)** and **Anne Dudley (1538–1588).**

Seymour, Edward, 1st Earl of Hertford (1539–1621)
Son of **Anne Seymour** and **Edward Seymour (1500–1552),** Edward Seymour was stripped of his titles following his father's execution. He was restored under **Mary I,** and created Earl of Hertford under **Elizabeth I.** He married **Catherine Seymour,** a descendant of **Henry VII,** in secret before leaving for the continent. When the marriage – and her pregnancy – were revealed by **Robert Dudley (1532–1588),** both were imprisoned. After the death of his first wife, he married Frances Howard, sister of **Douglass Sheffield.** This too was a secret marriage, and he was once again arrested. A final clandestine marriage took place in 1601.

Seymour, Jane, Queen of England (c.1508–1537)
Sister to **Edward Seymour (1500–1552)** and **Thomas Seymour,** Jane Seymour was one of the ladies who served **Anne Boleyn.** As the queen fell from the king's favour, however, **Henry VIII** began to direct his affections towards Jane and the pair were betrothed the day after Anne's execution. They married ten days later. She gave birth to their son, **Edward VI,** in October 1537, dying twelve days later.

Seymour, Thomas, Baron Sudeley (c.1509–1549)
Brother of **Jane Seymour** and **Edward Seymour (1500–1552),** Thomas Seymour rose quickly under the reign of his sister. After the death of **Henry VIII,** he resented the rise of his brother as Lord Protector, especially as he had also married the king's widow, **Catherine Parr.** He made plans to overthrow his brother and perhaps kidnap the king, and he was arrested and executed.

Sheffield (née Howard), Douglass, Lady Sheffield (1542/3–1608)
Following the death of her husband, Douglass Sheffield began an affair with **Robert Dudley (1532–1588),** which produced a son, **Robert Dudley (1574–1649).** She would later claim that the two had married, making her son Dudley's legitimate heir.

Sidney, Ambrosia (1564–1575)
The fourth daughter of **Mary Sidney (c.1535–1586)** and **Henry Sidney,** Ambrosia Sidney was named for her uncle, **Ambrose Dudley.** She died at the age of nine.

Sidney (later Manners), Elizabeth (1585–1612)

The daughter of **Frances Sidney** and **Philip Sidney**, Elizabeth Sidney's father died when she was a child. She went on to marry Roger Manners, Earl of Rutland.

Sidney (née Walsingham, later Devereux and Burke), Frances, Countess of Essex (1567–1633)

Daughter of **Francis Walsingham**, Frances Sidney first met her future husband **Philip Sidney** while in Paris in 1572. They married when she was sixteen and she gave birth to their daughter, **Elizabeth Sidney**, while her husband was with his uncle, **Robert Dudley** (1532–1588), in the Netherlands. Pregnant again, she travelled to be with her husband a year later, but he died following injuries at the battle of Zutphen just three months later and she miscarried their child. She went on to marry one of Philip's close friends, **Robert Devereux**. They had three children. Her second husband was executed for rebellion against the queen in 1601. She married for a third time in 1603.

Sidney, Henry (1529–1586)

Husband of **Mary Sidney** (c.1535–1586), Henry Sidney was quickly pardoned by **Mary I** after the overthrow of **Jane Dudley** (1537–1554) and was sent to the court of **Philip II** to obtain his signature on the marriage treaty. He may have used this opportunity to also gain the new consort's support for his imprisoned brothers-in-law. Henry spent much of his time in Ireland, where he worked closely with **Walter Devereux**. Together he and his wife had some seven children, though only three lived into adulthood, **Philip Sidney**, **Mary Sidney** (1561–1621) and **Robert Sidney**. Towards the end of their lives, he and his wife became frustrated with the lack of reward from **Elizabeth I**, whom they had both served. They died the same year.

Sidney (née Dudley), Mary (c.1535–1586)

Eldest daughter of **Jane Dudley** (1508/09–1555) and **John Dudley** (1504–1553), Mary Sidney may have been the daughter confirmed in January 1537 with **Mary I** as godmother. She married **Henry Sidney** at the age of sixteen and they had some seven children, though only three survived into adulthood, **Philip Sidney**, **Mary Sidney** (1561–1621) and **Robert Sidney**. Thanks to her husband's connections, Mary suffered little after the overthrow of **Jane Dudley** (1537–1554), though she was initially attainted. Her eldest son was named for the new king consort, **Philip II**, perhaps in a bid to curry favour with him and restore her imprisoned brothers. On the accession of

Elizabeth I she became one of the queen's gentlewomen and companions, though she also frequently joined her husband in Ireland. She died three months after her husband.

Sidney (later Herbert), Mary, Countess of Pembroke (1561–1621)

Third daughter of **Mary Sidney** (*c.*1535–1586) and **Henry Sidney**, Mary Sidney married Henry Herbert, Earl of Pembroke, who had briefly been married to **Catherine Seymour** (though the marriage had been annulled following the downfall of her sister, **Jane Dudley** (1537–1554) They had four children. She became known as a writer and patron.

Sidney, Philip (1554–1586)

The eldest son of **Mary Sidney** (*c.*1535–1586) and **Henry Sidney**, Philip Sidney had been named for **Philip II**, who helped restore his mother's family after the overthrow of **Jane Dudley** (1537–1554). Philip was taught the importance of his Dudley ancestry as a young man, especially under the mentorship of his uncle, **Robert Dudley** (1532–1588). After finishing his education, he travelled Europe, including finding himself in Paris at the house of **Francis Walsingham** during the St Bartholomew's Day Massacre, where he also met his future wife, **Frances Sidney**. Before his marriage to Frances, there was talk of his marrying **Penelope Rich**, but this fell through. When Frances was sixteen, the pair married and he left for the Netherlands while she was pregnant with their child, **Elizabeth Sidney**. He was injured at the battle of Zutphen and died soon after.

Sidney, Robert (later 1st Earl of Leicester) (1563–1626)

The second son of **Mary Sidney** (*c.*1535–1586) and **Henry Sidney**, Robert Sidney was named for his uncle, **Robert Dudley** (1532–1588). Like his brother, **Philip Sidney**, he received a gentleman's education, travelled the continent and served in the Netherlands, where Philip was killed. Alongside **Robert Devereux** and **Robert Dudley**, Sidney was one of his uncle's namesakes who was a candidate for his heir, and in 1605 received the Dudley title, Viscount Lisle. He became Earl of Leicester in 1618.

Stourton, Charles (1520–1557)

Eldest son of **Elizabeth Stourton** and **William Stourton**, Charles Stourton avoided supporting either **Jane Dudley** (1537–1554) or **Mary I** in the succession crisis of 1553, despite his kinship with the Dudley family; **John Dudley** (1504–1553) was his uncle, and he sat on his uncle's trial jury. He was executed in 1557 for the murder of two of his neighbours.

Stourton (née Dudley), Elizabeth, Lady Stourton (*c.*1500–1560)
Only child of **Anne Dudley** (d. by 1503) and **Edmund Dudley**, her mother died while she was young. As per her father's will, she married **William Stourton** and they had two daughters and seven sons, including **Charles Stourton**. Her husband had a prolonged affair, however, living with his mistress and claiming to have married her. She died three years after her son's execution.

Stourton, William, Baron Stourton (*c.*1505–1548)
Husband to **Elizabeth Stourton** and father of **Charles Stourton**, William conducted a prolonged affair with Agnes ap Rhys, with whom he lived until his death.

Stuart, Henry, Duke of Albany (known as Lord Darnley) (1545/6–1567)
Grandson of **Margaret Tudor** and her second husband (following the death of **James V**), Henry Stuart had a claim to the English throne, as well as a claim to the Scottish throne through James II, King of Scots. He married **Mary, Queen of Scots** in 1565, and she gave birth to their son, **James VI/I** in 1566, but their marriage was unsuccessful. Mary was rumoured to have played a part in his mysterious murder in 1567.

Sutton, Edmund (1425–*c.*1485)
Eldest son of **John Sutton** (1400–1487), Edmund Sutton predeceased his father by two years. He was the father of **Edward Sutton** (*c.*1460–1531).

Sutton, Edward, 2nd Baron Dudley (*c.*1460–1531)
The son of **Edmund Sutton**, Edward Sutton inherited the title of Baron Dudley from his grandfather, **John Sutton** (1400–1487). His son was **John Sutton** (1494–1553).

Sutton, Edward, 4th Baron Dudley (*c.*1515–1586)
Eldest son of **John Sutton** (1494–1553), Edward Sutton was able to reclaim Dudley Castle following the execution of his cousin **John Dudley** (1504–1553).

Sutton, John, 1st Baron Dudley (1400–1487)
Councillor of Henry VI, John Sutton was the father of **Edmund Sutton**, **John Sutton** (*c.*1427–1503) and William Dudley, Bishop of Durham. He was created Baron Dudley in 1440. John Dudley's eldest son, **Edmund Sutton** (*c.* 1460–1531), carried the title of Baron Dudley. His second son, John, was the father of **Edmund Dudley**.

Sutton, John (c.1427–1503)
Younger son of **John Sutton** (1400–1487), John Sutton married Elizabeth Bramshot and had at least five children, including their eldest son, **Edmund Dudley**. His will was proved in 1500 and contained gifts for his daughter-in-law **Anne Dudley** (d. by 1503) and granddaughter **Elizabeth Stourton**.

Sutton, John, 3rd Baron Dudley (1494–1553)
Son of **Edward Sutton** (c.1460–1531), John Sutton became Baron Dudley in 1532. He sold most of his estates, including Dudley Castle, which went to his cousin **John Dudley** (1504–1553), earning him the nickname 'Lord Quondam'.

Tudor, Arthur, Prince of Wales (1486–1502)
The eldest son of **Elizabeth of York** and **Henry VII**, Arthur Tudor married **Catherine of Aragon** in 1501, but died soon after.

Tudor, Margaret, Queen of Scots (1489–1541)
The eldest daughter of **Elizabeth of York** and **Henry VII**, Margaret Tudor married James IV of Scotland and was mother to **James V**. She was grandmother to both **Mary, Queen of Scots**, and **Henry Stuart**.

Tudor, Mary, Queen of France (1496–1533)
Younger daughter of **Elizabeth of York** and **Henry VII**, she married Louis XII, King of France, who died not long after. She married **Charles Brandon** quickly thereafter. She was the mother of **Frances Grey** and grandmother of **Jane Dudley** (1537–1554).

Van der Delft, François (c.1500–1550)
Imperial ambassador to England in the final years of the reign of **Henry VIII** and the first three years of the reign of **Edward VI**, François Van der Delft was replaced by **Jean Scheyfve**.

Walsingham, Francis (c.1532–1590)
From a well-connected family, Francis Walsingham fled England under the reign of the Catholic **Mary I**, returning on the accession of **Elizabeth I**. He worked closely with **William Cecil** to uncover Catholic plots against the queen, including those involving **Mary, Queen of Scots**, and advocated for her execution. He was present in Paris during the Saint-Bartholomew's Day Massacre, housing **Philip Sidney** during the attacks, who later became his son-in-law after his marriage to **Frances Sidney**. He became Elizabeth's Secretary of State and was instrumental in developing an international intelligence network.

Warham, William (c.1450–1532)
One of the 'new men' promoted under **Henry VII**, William Warham was employed on various diplomatic missions, including helping to arrange the marriage between **Arthur Tudor** and **Catherine of Aragon**. In the final years of the reign, he rose very quickly, becoming Lord Chancellor and Archbishop of Canterbury in 1504. He resigned as Chancellor in 1515 and was succeeded by **Thomas Wolsey**. He was succeeded after his death as Archbishop of Canterbury by **Thomas Cranmer**.

William, Prince of Orange (1533–1584)
Leader of the Dutch Revolt against the Habsburgs, William's assassination in 1584 left a power vacuum in the Netherlands.

Windsor, Andrew, 1st Baron Windsor (1467–1543)
Brother of **Anne Dudley (d. by 1503)**, Andrew Windsor succeeded his stepfather as Keeper of the King's Wardrobe, responsible for the finances of the King's household. Despite the fall of his brother-in-law **Edmund Dudley**, Andrew was made a Knight of the Bath at the coronation of **Henry VIII**. He remained an essential member of the king's entourage throughout his life.

Wolsey, Thomas (c.1473–1530)
Appointed royal chaplain by **Henry VII**, Thomas Wolsey entered the service of **Richard Fox** who appointed him to a variety of tasks. On the accession of **Henry VIII**, he broke with Fox and **William Warham** by advocating for the French war. Wolsey was appointed to the position of Lord Chancellor following Warham's resignation in 1515. Wolsey was seen as an *alter rex* and trusted to negotiate on behalf of the king, which he did in seeking to balance the powers of **Francis I** and **Charles V**, with Henry VIII between them. He struggled, however, to grant Henry the annulment of his marriage to **Catherine of Aragon**, giving his enemies the opportunity to bring him down. He died following his arrest.

Wriothesley, Thomas, 1st Earl of Southampton (1505–1550)
Son of a herald, Thomas Wriothesley entered the service of **Thomas Cromwell**, but betrayed his former master in 1540, leading to Cromwell's downfall and death. He supported the persecution of Lutheran ideas, and along with Richard Rich, he tortured **Anne Askew**. On the death of **Henry VIII** he was named to the Regency Council of **Edward VI**. He opposed, however, the rise and power of **Edward Seymour (1500–1552)** and was dismissed.

Glossary of Terms

Advent
The Christian season which begins the fourth Sunday before Christmas (25 December).

Agate
An ornamental stone also referred to as 'jet'.

Alb
A white liturgical vestment covering the whole body.

Alderman
A senior civil officer in the City of London.

Attainder
The forfeiture of estate and corruption of blood associated with being 'attainted', frequently for treason.

Auld Alliance
The historic alliance between France and Scotland, reaching back to the thirteenth century.

Bishopped
To be confirmed in the Church.

Book of Common Prayer
The English-language prayer books used in the English Church from 1549 until the death of Edward VI and then again after the accession of Elizabeth I.

Borderlands
The area of land near the border between England and Scotland, also termed the **Marches**.

Breech
A short garment covering the loin and thighs.

Catholic
A member of the Roman Catholic Church with the pope at its head. This was the dominant religion in Europe until the Reformation.

Chancery
The court of the **Lord Chancellor**.

Chase
An unenclosed hunting ground.

Chief Mourner
The stand-in for the closest relative at the funeral of a high-standing individual, often a woman.

Cloth of Gold
A fabric interwoven with gold.

Coif
A white cap.

Council Learned in the Law
A tribunal established under Henry VII and led first by Reginald Bray and then Edmund Dudley to deal with the collection of money owed to the king.

Cuisses
Armour protecting the front of the thighs.

Dowry
Money or property transferred with the wife as part of a marriage contract.

Dysentery
A disease usually brought about by poor sanitation, affecting the intestines, and which can lead to diarrhoea, dehydration and death.

Easter
The most significant holy day in the Christian calendar, commemorating the resurrection of Jesus Christ.

Ember Days
Days of fasting, abstinence and prayer as part of the Christian calendar.

Ermine
Referring to both the animal and its fur, often used for trimming garments, ermine is also known as a stoat.

Escutcheons
Shields upon which a coat-of-arms is depicted.

Evangelical
A term for religious reformers dedicated especially to the teachings of the **Gospel** over the **Catholic** Church in the early decades of what became known as the Reformation. Later known as **Protestants**.

Ewery
A room for ewers of water, table linens and towels.

Exchequer
An office for the collection and administration of royal revenues.

Fighting at barriers
A martial exercise frequently associated with tournaments, in which two opponents face each other over a waist- or chest-high barrier.

Flux
An illness associated with the overflowing of bodily fluids or humours, often associated with **dysentery**.

Gangrene
Death of tissue in the body, usually associated with infection.

Garter King at Arms
Senior-most officer at arms, responsible for heraldry and genealogical records, as well as involved in ceremonial roles.

Girdle
A belt worn around the waist, often decorative or used to carry small items.

Good Friday
A solemn Christian holy day taking place the Friday before **Easter**, which marks the death of Jesus Christ.

Gospel
The four books of the New Testament which detail the life and words of Jesus Christ: Matthew, Mark, Luke and John.

Guild
An association formed for the mutual aid and governance of a community, frequently of merchants or artisans.

Habsburg
The royal house associated with the rule of several European countries and duchies, including Spain, Austria and the Low Countries.

Harquebus
A portable firearm.

Herald
An officer responsible for royal proclamations and messages between royals.

Heresy
A belief or doctrine contrary to orthodoxy.

Holy Roman Empire
A complex of territories in Europe centred around present-day Germany and Austria, ruled by the Holy Roman Emperor.

Hood
A covering for the head and neck, often decorated.

Hose
Clothing covering the legs and sometimes the feet.

Informer
Someone who informs against others, frequently to the Crown or its agents; also known as a 'promoter'.

Inns of Court
The four London legal societies (the Inner Temple, the Middle Temple, Lincoln's Inn and Gray's Inn).

Knight Banneret
A title conferred for deeds done on the field of battle in the king's presence.

Knights of the Bath
Those knighted in a ceremony associated with major occasions including coronations.

Knights of the Garter
The most senior order of chivalry, founded in the fourteenth century, and associated with **St George's Day** on 23 April.

Lady Day
The Feast of the Annunciation in the Christian calendar, marking the date when the angel Gabriel told the Virgin Mary that she would carry the son of God. Falling on 25 March, it was also New Year's Day in the old calendar.

Lent
The period of forty days before **Easter** in the Christian calendar, marked by fasting, abstinence and prayer.

Loggia
An open-sided gallery or arcade in the Italian style.

Lollard
A member of the heretical sect following the teachings of John Wyclif known as Lollardy.

Lord Chancellor
The highest-ranking officer of state responsible for the Great Seal and an adviser in both spiritual and temporal matters.

Lord Chamberlain
One of the three principal officers of the Royal Household (with Lord Steward and **Master of the Horse**), responsible for the workings of the chamber, including personnel, ceremonies, the wardrobe and the Chapel Royal.

Lord High Admiral
The head of the Royal Navy.

Lord Privy Seal
Responsible for the personal (privy) seal of the monarch, which would be attached to documents from the Crown.

Lord Protector
A position of regency over a monarch unable to rule, either through minority or incapacity.

Low Countries
Coastal lowland now making up the Netherlands, Belgium and Luxembourg.

Machiavel
A figure thought to embody the tenets of Machiavellianism, including moral flexibility, self-interest and atheism.

Marches
The **borderlands** between England and Wales, and England and Scotland.

Master of the Horse
An officer of the Royal Household responsible for the monarch's horses, as well as transport and hunting animals more generally, frequently on attendance.

Masque
Courtly entertainment involving elaborate costumes, dancing and symbolism.

May Day
A secular festival day associated with a celebration of springtime held on 1 May.

Minever
Fur, usually white, used for trimming garments, particularly those used for ceremonies.

Moor
A term used to describe Muslim North Africans, as well as more broadly anyone with dark skin.

Nemesis
The goddess of retribution in classical mythology, often associated with the reversal of excessive good fortune.

Norman Conquest
The invasion and occupation of England in the eleventh century by William the Conqueror.

Pall
Rich cloth, often associated with robes.

Paly
A heraldic term referring to vertical stripes of alternating colours.

Palm Sunday
The Sunday before **Easter** in the Christian calendar, which marks the entry of Jesus Christ into Jerusalem before his betrayal and execution (on **Good Friday**).

Pentecost
The seventh Sunday after **Easter** in the Christian calendar, when the disciples received the gifts of the Holy Spirit.

Phantom pregnancy
The condition whereby a woman's body manifests all the symptoms of pregnancy without conception having taken place.

Privy Council
The official body providing advice to the monarch, as well as having administrative and judicial roles.

Protestant
The term for the schismatic confessions arising after what is now known as the Reformation, including Lutheranism, Calvinism, etc. The term was not in common use before the latter half of the sixteenth century, which is why the term **evangelical** is often more appropriate before that date.

Purgatory
The place between Heaven and Hell of the **Catholic** belief system, where souls were cleansed of their earthly sins. The doctrine of Purgatory was rejected by the **evangelicals** as it was not mentioned in the **Gospels**.

Quickening
The stage of pregnancy when the foetus begins to move and kick, ruling out a **phantom pregnancy**.

St George's Day
The festival day of the patron saint of England, taking place on 23 April.

Sacrament
The seven ceremonies of the Catholic Church (baptism, confession, confirmation, Holy Communion, Holy Orders, matrimony and Last Rites), which were reduced to three by the **evangelicals** (baptism, communion and matrimony), as the others were not present in the **Gospel**. Also as 'the Sacrament' can refer to Holy Communion, commemorating the Last Supper before the execution of Jesus Christ.

Sappers
Soldiers responsible for building fortifications and executing field works, such as tunnels.

Smallpox
An infectious disease marked by the appearance of pustules and a high fever.

Shrove Sunday
The Sunday before the beginning of **Lent**, often celebrated with the consumption of meat and other luxuries not allowed during Lent.

Star Chamber
The court designed to prosecute the powerful for their crimes.

Stole
A clerical vestment consisting of a narrow strip of fabric worn over the shoulder.

Surcoat
An outer coat worn by those of rank and typically made of rich cloth.

Tabards
A short **surcoat**, often worn over armour.

Tapestry
A textile fabric typically used for wall hangings, embroidered with designs or scenes.

Transubstantiation
The Catholic doctrine that the bread and wine of the **Sacrament** literally become the body and blood of Jesus Christ. This was opposed by the **evangelicals**.

Unction
The act of anointing with holy oil.

Ward
A minor under the guardianship of another, often after being orphaned.

Whitsuntide
The season of **Pentecost**.

CURRENCY

Gold Coins

Sovereign (pound coin) = 20 shillings
Angel = (half-mark) 6 shillings 8 pence
Crown = 5 shillings

Silver Coins

Shilling = 12 pennies
Sixpence = 6 pennies
Groat = 4 pennies
Twopenny (or half-groat) = 2 pennies
Penny

Other measures

Pound = 20 shillings
Mark = $^2/_3$ of a pound (13 shillings and 4 pence)

Note: these values could and did fluctuate. There were other coins that were occasionally minted, including the halfpenny (½ penny) and farthing (¼ penny).

Duke: The highest noble title, frequently and originally given to the sons of the monarch. The female form is duchess.

Marquess: Originally associated with lands in proximity to the marches, ranked below a duke. The female form is marchioness (excepting Anne Boleyn, who was created Marquess of Pembroke in her own right in 1532).

Earl: Ranked below a marquess. The female form is countess.

Viscount: Ranked below an earl. The female form is viscountess.

Baron: The lowest rank of the peerage, below a viscount. The female form is baroness.

Note: the ordinal numbers given before titles (for example, 3rd Duke of Norfolk) are used to distinguish between holders of the same noble title within the same creation. I have used them in the glossary, but not in the text, as they were not in standardized use in the sixteenth century.

Timeline of Events

	Charles Brandon becomes Viscount Lisle (May)
	Henry VIII leads expedition into France (summer)
1515	Charles Brandon and Mary Tudor marry (March)
1516	Mary I born (Feb)
1519	Elizabeth Grey dies, Arthur Plantagenet becomes Viscount Lisle (May)
1521	John Dudley travels to Calais (summer)
1523	Charles Brandon leads expedition into France, John Dudley knighted (autumn)
1525	John Dudley and Jane Guildford marry
	Henry Dudley born
1525–26	Elizabeth Plantagenet (née Grey, also Dudley) dies
1526	Richard Guildford dies
1527	c. Thomas Dudley born
1529	c. Thomas Dudley dies
	Thomas Wolsey arrested, dies (Nov)
1530	John Dudley (younger) born
1531	c. Ambrose Dudley born
1532	Robert Dudley born (June)
1533	Henry VIII and Anne Boleyn marry (Jan)
	Anne Boleyn crowned Queen of England (June)
	Elizabeth I born (Sept)
1535	c. Mary Sidney (née Dudley) born
1536	Anne Boleyn executed (May)
	Henry VIII and Jane Seymour marry (May)
1537	c. Guildford Dudley born
	Edward VI born (Oct)
	Jane Seymour dies (Oct)
1540	Henry VIII and Anne of Cleves marry (Jan)
	Henry VIII and Anne of Cleves's marriage annulled (July)
	Thomas Cromwell executed (July)
	Henry VIII and Katherine Howard marry (July)
1541	Katherine Howard stripped of her title of Queen (Nov)
1542	Katherine Howard executed (Feb)
	Arthur Plantagenet dies (March)
	John Dudley becomes Viscount Lisle (March)
	Mary, Queen of Scots, born (Dec)
1543	Henry VIII and Catherine Parr marry (July)
1544	Henry VIII leads expedition into France (summer)
	Henry Dudley dies (Sept)

1545	*c.* Katherine Hastings (née Dudley) born
	Battle of the Solent (July)
1546	Ambrose Dudley and Anne Whorwood marry
	Anne Askew executed (July)

PART THREE

1547–1555

1547	Henry VIII dies, Edward VI becomes King (Jan)
	John Dudley becomes Earl of Warwick
	Edward VI crowned King of England (Feb)
1549	Thomas Seymour executed (March)
	Kett's Rebellion (summer)
1550	John Dudley (younger) and Anne Seymour marry (June)
	Robert Dudley and Amy Robsart marry (June)
1551	Mary Dudley and Henry Sidney marry (March)
	John Dudley becomes Duke of Northumberland (Oct)
1552	Edward Seymour executed (Jan)
1553	Ambrose Dudley and Elizabeth Tailboys marry
	Guildford Dudley and Jane Grey (May) marry
	Katherine Dudley and Henry Hastings (May) marry
	Edward VI dies, Jane Dudley (née Grey) declared Queen (July)
	Mary I declared Queen, John Dudley and his sons arrested (July)
	John Dudley executed (Aug)
1554	Jane Dudley (née Grey) and Guildford Dudley executed (Feb)
	Mary I and Philip II marry (July)
	John Dudley (younger) dies (Oct)
	Philip Sidney born (Nov)
1555	Jane Dudley (née Guildford) dies (Jan)

PART FOUR

1555–1588

1557	Siege of Saint-Quentin, Henry Dudley (younger) dies (Aug)
1558	Mary I dies, Elizabeth I becomes Queen (Nov)
1560	Amy Dudley (née Robsart) dies (Sept)

1563	Elizabeth Dudley (née Tailboys) dies
	Robert Sidney born (Nov)
1565	Ambrose Dudley and Anne Russell marry (Nov)
1572	St Bartholomew's Day Massacre (Aug)
1574	Robert Dudley (younger) born (Aug)
1575	Robert Dudley entertains the court at Kenilworth (July)
1578	Robert Dudley and Lettice Devereux (née Knollys) secretly marry (Sept)
1581	Robert Dudley, Lord Denbigh, born (June)
1584	*Leicester's Commonwealth* circulates the court
	Robert Dudley, Lord Denbigh, dies (July)
1586	Robert Dudley becomes Governor General of the United Provinces (Jan)
	Henry Sidney dies (May)
	Mary Sidney dies (Aug)
	Philip Sidney dies (Oct)
1587	Mary, Queen of Scots, executed (Feb)
1588	Defeat of the Spanish Armada (July)
	Robert Dudley dies (Sept)

EPILOGUE

1590	Ambrose Dudley dies (Feb)
1601	Robert Devereux executed (Feb)
1603	Elizabeth I dies, James VI/I becomes King (March)
1605	Robert Dudley (younger) leaves England with Elizabeth Southwell (July)
1618	Robert Sidney created Earl of Leicester
1620	Robert Dudley (younger) named Duke of Northumberland by Emperor Ferdinand II (March)
	Katherine Hastings (née Dudley) dies (Aug)
1625	James VI/I dies, Charles I becomes King (March)
1626	Robert Sidney dies
1644	Alice Dudley (née Leigh) becomes Duchess of Dudley
1649	Charles I executed (Jan)
	Robert Dudley (younger) dies (Sept)
1669	Alice Dudley (née Leigh) dies

Note on the Birth Dates of the Children of Jane and John Dudley

There are a number of pedigrees produced in the latter half of the sixteenth century that help shed light on the birth dates of Jane and John Dudley's thirteen children, including CA Muniment 13/1 and UPenn Codex 1070, which were primarily used in the writing of this book.* These list the ages of sons and daughters separately, making it difficult to establish an order between them. Based on these and other available sources, I have established their dates of birth as below:

Sons

Henry

Both pedigrees state that Henry died at the siege of Boulogne (1544) at the age of nineteen years. This places his date of birth in late 1525 or early 1526.

Thomas

Both pedigrees state that Thomas died at the age of two years (though CA L.15 says four years). Presuming he was named for Cardinal Thomas Wolsey, and placing his date of birth between his elder and younger brothers, he was probably born between 1526 and 1529, and died between 1528 and 1531.

John

Both pedigrees state that John died at the age of twenty-three years. He died in Oct 1554, so he was born in late 1530 or early 1531.

* I also consulted CA Muniment 16/5 but it is not as legible.

Ambrose

Neither pedigree gives indications of Ambrose's date of birth, but they do list him as the fourth son, putting his date of birth between those of his elder and younger brothers, so sometime around 1531 or 1532.

Robert

Neither pedigree gives indications of Robert's date of birth, but this is well established as 24 June 1532/3 (with 1532 as the more likely).*

Guildford

Neither pedigree gives indications of Guildford's date of birth; however, it seems likely that Guildford is the child bishopped by Diego Hurtado de Mendoza, who was in England in 1537.† This would also mean he is probably the baby baptized with the Lady Mary as godmother in March 1537 (BL Royal MS 17 Bxxviii). Guildford is named for his mother's natal family; Edward Guildford died in 1534, suggesting a possible earlier date of birth for Guildford.

Henry (the younger)

Both pedigrees note that Henry died at the siege of Saint-Quentin (1557), though neither gives his age. It is possible, as I note, that he was born after the death of the elder Henry Dudley, but this is conjectural and would make him only thirteen at his death.

Charles

The pedigrees disagree about the age of Charles at his death, either four (CA Muniment 13/1) or eight years (UPenn Codex 1070). There is no indication of his date of birth, but presumably he was named for Charles Brandon, who died in 1545.

* See the *ODNB* entry by Simon Adams.
† See Susan Higginbotham, 'How Old Was Guildford Dudley? (Beats Me.)', *History Refreshed* (blog), 2011. http://www.susanhigginbotham.com//blog/posts/how-old-was-guildford-dudley-beats-me/.

Daughters

Mary

Neither pedigree gives indications of Mary's date of birth; however, Mary's marriage was solemnized in May 1551, meaning she was probably sixteen by this date. This would place her birth between those of her brothers Robert and Guildford in about 1535.

Margaret

The pedigrees disagree about the age of Margaret at her death, either ten (CA Muniment 13/1) or four years (UPenn Codex 1070). If the former, she may have been the daughter who died in 1552, placing her date of birth in 1542.

Katherine

Neither pedigree gives indications of Katherine's date of birth; however, a letter in November 1545 notes that a daughter of John Dudley was baptized with Lady Mary and Katherine, Duchess of Suffolk (*CSPS*, VIII, no. 174). It was common for children to be named for their godparents, so this may have been Katherine.

Temperance

Both pedigrees state that Temperance died at the age of one year. No further information is available.

Catherine

Both pedigrees state that Catherine died at the age of seven years. She may have been the Catherine baptized in 1545, making her the daughter who died in 1552. This does mean that Margaret, Katherine and Temperance would all have had to have been born between 1535 and 1545, along with Guildford and Henry, before Catherine's birth in 1545.

Further Reading

In addition to using primary sources, described in 'A Note on the Sources', I have also depended on the work of other scholars. Where these have been especially helpful and might provide the reader with means to further explore this incredible family and the fascinating world they inhabited, I have described them below. This is not an exhaustive list.

THE DUDLEY FAMILY

Simon Adams, *Leicester and the Court: Essays on Elizabethan Politics* (Manchester: Manchester University Press, 2002).

Ciaran Brady, *A Viceroy's Vindication?: Sir Henry Sidney's Memoir of Service in Ireland, 1556–1578* (Cork: Cork University Press, 2002).

Michael G. Brennan, *The Sidneys of Penshurst and the Monarchy, 1500–1700* (New York: Routledge, 2017).

Elizabeth Goldring, *Robert Dudley, Earl of Leicester, and the World of Elizabethan Art: Painting and Patronage at the Court of Elizabeth I* (New Haven: Yale University Press, 2014).

Sarah Gristwood, *Elizabeth & Leicester* (London: Bantam Press, 2007).

Eric Ives, *Lady Jane Grey: A Tudor Mystery* (Chichester: John Wiley & Sons, 2011).

Eric Ives, *The Life and Death of Anne Boleyn: The Most Happy* (Malden, MA: Wiley-Blackwell, 2005).

D. M. Loades, *John Dudley, Duke of Northumberland, 1504–1553* (Oxford: Clarendon Press, 1996).

Glyn Parry and Cathryn Enis, *Shakespeare Before Shakespeare: Stratford-upon-Avon, Warwickshire, and the Elizabethan State* (Oxford; New York: OUP Oxford, 2020).

Chris Skidmore, *Death and the Virgin* (London: Weidenfeld & Nicolson, 2010).

Alan Stewart, *Philip Sidney: A Double Life* (London: Random House, 2011).

Nicola Tallis, *Crown of Blood: The Deadly Inheritance of Lady Jane Grey* (London: Michael O'Mara, 2016).

Nicola Tallis, *Elizabeth's Rival: The Tumultuous Tale of Lettice Knollys, Countess of Leicester* (London: Michael O'Mara, 2017).

Derek Wilson, *Sweet Robin: A Biography of Robert Dudley, Earl of Leicester 1533–1588* (London: Allison & Busby, 1981).

Derek Wilson, *The Uncrowned Kings of England: The Black Legend of the Dudleys*, UK ed. (Constable, 2013).

TUDOR MONARCHS AND THE TUDOR COURT

S. B. Chrimes, *Henry VII* (Yale University Press, 1999).

Susan Doran, *Monarchy and Matrimony: The Courtships of Elizabeth I* (New York: Routledge, 2002).

Steven Gunn, *Charles Brandon: Henry VIII's Closest Friend* (Stroud: Amberley Publishing Limited, 2015).

Steven Gunn, *Henry VII's New Men and the Making of Tudor England* (Oxford: Oxford University Press, 2016).

Mark R. Horowitz, '"Agree with the King": Henry VII, Edmund Dudley and the Strange Case of Thomas Sunnyff', *Historical Research* 79, no. 205 (2006): 325–66.

Suzannah Lipscomb, *The King Is Dead: The Last Will and Testament of Henry VIII* (London: Head of Zeus, 2015).

Diarmaid MacCulloch, *Thomas Cromwell: A Life* (London: Penguin UK, 2018).

Elizabeth Norton, *Jane Seymour: Henry VIII's True Love* (Stroud: Amberley Publishing, 2009).

Thomas Penn, *Winter King: The Dawn of Tudor England* (London: Penguin, 2012).

Gareth Russell, *Young and Damned and Fair: The Life of Catherine Howard, Fifth Wife of King Henry VIII* (New York: Simon and Schuster, 2017).

Margaret Scard, *Edward Seymour: Lord Protector* (Stroud: The History Press, 2016).

J. J. Scarisbrick, *Henry VIII* (Berkeley: University of California Press, 1968).

Chris Skidmore, *Edward VI: The Lost King of England* (London: Hachette UK, 2011).

Giles Tremlett, *Catherine of Aragon: Henry's Spanish Queen* (London: Faber & Faber, 2010).

Anna Whitelock, *Elizabeth's Bedfellows: An Intimate History of the Queen's Court* (London: A&C Black, 2013).

Anna Whitelock, *Mary Tudor: England's First Queen* (London: Bloomsbury Paperbacks, 2010).

Kate Williams, *Rival Queens: The Betrayal of Mary, Queen of Scots* (London: Arrow, 2018).

THE TUDOR PERIOD

David Cressy, *Birth, Marriage, and Death: Ritual, Religion, and the Life-Cycle in Tudor and Stuart England* (Oxford: Oxford University Press, 1997).

James Daybell, ed., *Women and Politics in Early Modern England, 1450–1700* (Aldershot: Routledge, 2004).

S. J. Gunn, *The English People at War in the Age of Henry VIII* (Oxford: Oxford University Press, 2018).

Vanessa Harding and Caroline M. Barron, eds, *A Map of Tudor London: England's Capital City in 1520* (London: The Historic Towns Trust, 2018).

Ralph Houlbrooke, *Death, Religion, and the Family in England, 1480–1750* (Oxford: Oxford University Press, 2000).

Miranda Kaufmann, *Black Tudors: The Untold Story* (London: Oneworld Publications, 2017).

N. A. M. Rodger, *The Safeguard of the Sea: A Naval History of Britain 660–1649* (London: Penguin, 2004).

Simon Thurley, *Houses of Power: The Places That Shaped the Tudor World* (London; New York: Bantam Press, 2017).

Alan Young, *Tudor and Jacobean Tournaments* (Dobbs Ferry, NY: Sheridan House, 1987).

OTHER RESOURCES

British History Online
https://www.british-history.ac.uk/
Oxford Dictionary of National Biography
http://www.oxforddnb.com/

Marion E. Colthorpe, 'The Elizabethan Court Day by Day', Folgerpedia,
   https://folgerpedia.folger.edu/The_Elizabethan_Court_Day_by_Day#
   The_Elizabethan_Court_Day_by_Day
The Agas Map
https://mapoflondon.uvic.ca/agas.htm

A Note on the Sources

I have had two aims in writing this book: to tell a good story and to write a good history. In general, I believe these aims to be complementary, even mutually supportive, but in accomplishing one I have occasionally had to make choices not normally consistent with the other.

Writing a good history means sticking closely to the sources as we have them. There is an important difference between history and the past. The past is what happened; history is our attempt to understand the past. The further back one goes, generally speaking, the fewer sources one has, the harder they are to corroborate, and the less one understands the assumptions that are being made by the creators of those sources. In other words, we venture further into that foreign country known as the past, and need more help understanding the language, customs and culture of those that reside there. Usually, it is the historian's task to think critically about the sources they use and to communicate that analysis to their readers. The historian must assess the extent to which the source describes the past as it really happened.

This is where telling a good story and writing a good history have the potential to diverge. The narrative structure of this book means that there is little space to critically engage with the sources, and yet I still must use them. Where possible, I have tried to weave scepticism regarding the validity of sources into the narrative. Where I think it is especially pertinent to mark their issues, I have done so in my notes. Otherwise, I have presented an analysis of some of the most common sources I use below, so that you, the reader, can form your own judgements about how much like the past the history contained in this book truly is.

ADMINISTRATIVE AND LEGAL DOCUMENTS

For the most part these have been gathered from The National Archive (London), though other archives have also been consulted. There is a fuller list in the Bibliography below.

Contracts, Wills and Inventories

Wills have been particularly useful in establishing family connections and providing information about property, especially material belongings. In this, the fact that the Dudleys were so frequently attainted, and thus had their properties inventoried on at least two occasions, has also been useful. These sources are generally reliable for the uses detailed, though, as we might expect, contracts and bequeathments did not always proceed as set out in the documents in front of us (whether little Elizabeth Dudley ever received the gold set out for her in her grandfather's will, for instance, is unknown to us).

Two wills are especially interesting for providing even further detail. These are the wills of Edmund Dudley and Jane Dudley, Duchess of Northumberland. Edmund's will is available in two versions: SP 1/2 fo. 3–7 and LA DDCL 298, the first of which has been badly damaged, the second of which is a complete copy. It is this second version which details his aborted escape from the Tower of London. There are few conceivable reasons why Edmund would not be largely truthful about his escape plan at this stage, so close to death. Jane Dudley's will (PROB/11/37/342) is also a fascinating document and has been digitized by the National Archives for download. Her gifts to various, especially Spanish, courtiers demonstrate the connections she had been cultivating over the previous few years in seeking to restore her family and save the lives of her sons.

Financial Accounts

Account books, detailing money spent, given and received, can help establish links between individuals, determine their geographical location and often contain the names of servants and other figures left out of other documents. A copy of Edmund Dudley's account book for the king is available in the British Library (Lansdowne 127) and details the vast wealth he accumulated on behalf of the Crown and those he took it from. Especially useful to this book were Robert Dudley's accounts (published by Simon Adams, *Household Accounts*), which provide information about meetings with the queen, dinners with his brother and his journey through Oxfordshire in 1584.

BOOKS AND PAMPHLETS

Most of these texts were published in print, and thus available through the digitization of early modern English texts (Early English Books Online) and through modern editions. Others were circulated in manuscript and only later printed.

Educational and Rhetorical Treatises

In attempting to recover a sense of the educational training of the figures in this book, I have used various published educational treatises, for instance the work of Juan Luis Vives (*Education of a Christian Woman*) and Nicholas Bourbon (*Nugarum libri octo, Paidagogeion*). These are especially useful because Vives' text was written specifically for the use of the Princess Mary, later Mary I, and we know that Bourbon was a tutor of the young Henry Dudley (c.1525–1544). As with all prescriptive texts, however, we cannot be sure that what these writers suggest *ought* to be done in the instruction of children was what actually took place in the classroom.

Medical

There were a number of widely read medical texts in circulation in the sixteenth century, and I have used them here in order to reconstruct a contemporary understanding of the body, as well as its proper and improper functioning, and treatments and remedies. In very few cases do we have records about the progress of a medical event – whether pregnancy and childbirth or infection and illness – or know what specific treatments were used. We can, however, also use these texts to get a sense of what sorts of treatments were recommended. More importantly, we can get a sense of how those events were understood. As scholars have shown, of course, generally accepted understandings of the body are often different from published medical understandings, and I've used other sources to try to recover that sense as well (see, for instance, Ulinka Rublack, 'Pregnancy, Childbirth and the Female Body in Early Modern Germany', *Past & Present* no. 150 (1996): 84–110).

Plays and Performances

Plays and performances were often published, either as what we might recognize today as scripts and stage directions, or as descriptions of the event, or as a hybrid of both. Work has been done to demonstrate that there was often a substantial difference between what was performed and what was published, but we usually only have access to detailed knowledge of the latter. As such, I have typically taken the words published to be the words spoken, and even used these as an opportunity to generate direct quotations, but it must be noted that this is not necessarily the case.

Political Texts

As well as those works of politics directly referenced in the text (*Tree of Commonwealth*, *The Prince*, etc.), I have attempted to furnish the politics of the Tudor court with an awareness of the expectations and standards evidenced in political writings of the time. These include the importance of political counsel, but also the difficulties faced by the counsellor – what has become known as 'the problem of counsel'. Likewise, the move towards formalization and institutionalization from a more informal and personal monarchy, in many ways facilitated by the need to erect 'scaffolding' around the 'weaknesses' of the late Tudor monarchs (Edward VI, Mary I and Elizabeth I). Finally, shifts in the aims and expectations of political deliberation and action, from a more moralistic framework to one defined by 'political interests' and 'reason of state'. Again, we cannot be sure that such political texts accurately reflect contemporary political culture – there is ample evidence, for instance, that political actors were engaging in 'Machiavellian' reasoning long before Machiavelli – but the language and legitimations that they set out are essential for understanding the parameters in which our historical actors were expected to act.

One further political text is worth mentioning here, given how essential it is to the Dudley story, and that is the text now commonly referred to as *Leicester's Commonwealth*. When we put it in the context of the *annus horribilis* that Robert Dudley was experiencing in 1584 it takes on a more personal resonance. Similarly, the response it prompted in Philip Sidney tells us a great deal about Sidney's attachment to his maternal family and his desire to project those connections, which are backed up by what we know about his upbringing and the letters sent to him as a child by his parents.

Scriptural and Liturgical

The importance of adherence to Scriptural and Liturgical texts, and the emphasis placed on the particularities of translation and transmission, make these some of the most reliable sources for describing religious events and ceremonies in the sixteenth century, which is why I have used them frequently for generating direct quotations. The period was, of course, also one of frequent and dramatic religious change, so there are a number of different sources to which one has to turn. Before the Break with Rome the most common liturgical text was the Sarum Missal. Lacking authorized translations of Scripture for this period, I used the King James Bible. After the introduction of the Book of Common Prayer this was the mandated text to use in every church across the country, and I have generally assumed this to be the case in the scenes I describe.

CHRONICLES AND HISTORIES

Ceremonial

Accounts of various court ceremonies, such as coronations, funerals, the bestowing of noble titles and so on were frequently kept by members of the College of Arms, such as the Garter King of Arms, and can still be found at the College of Arms today. These sources can be corroborated with State Papers related to the planning of these events and chronicles written by those present to shape an understanding of what took place. Sometimes these three types of sources do differ, but generally they paint a consistent and thus largely reliable picture.

Chronicles

There are a number of contemporary chronicles that cover the period of the sixteenth century in England, including *The Great Chronicle of London* (attributed to Robert Fabyan), *The Chronicle of Calais* (by Richard Turpyn), *Wriothesley's Chronicle* (by Charles Wriothesley, officer of arms),

Holinshed's Chronicle (by Raphael Holinshed), *Hall's Chronicle* (by Edward Hall) and others. Each of these was written in a particular context for a particular purpose, and one needs to be cautious in taking them as straightforward accounts of what took place, though as chronological listings of events and those in attendance they can be very useful.

'Ego-documents': Diaries, Journals and Autobiographies

These are documents in which we might expect to see the author represented in the first person (I'm excepting letters for the moment, which I will address in the next section). This is an emerging genre in the period, and we see significant overlap with the category of chronicles. For instance, the text known as *The Diary of Henry Machyn* recounts events more than reflects on them, though from his descriptions we can tell something of the allegiances of the author. For these reasons, it is often referred to as a 'chronicle' rather than a 'diary'. The same can be said of the writings of Elis Gruffydd, from which we have such a detailed account of the 1523 French campaign, though he does speak more commonly in the first person, placing himself explicitly in the events he details. Astoundingly, we also have the diary written by Edward VI himself; this too is perhaps more like a chronicle and Edward refers to himself in the third person.

LETTERS AND REPORTS

Diplomatic

Where it is possible to work from an original letter, I have done so, and many of these are collected in The National Archives and available via State Papers Online. However, in other cases, I have been forced to work from the calendar entry. These calendars, such as *Calendar of State Papers Relating to English Affairs in the Archives of Venice* or *Calendar of State Papers, Spain* contain only short summaries of the letters with infrequent direct quotations from the text. They are still useful, of course, as summaries of correspondence in the absence of access to the original.

The letters and reports of ambassadors must be approached very cautiously, and I have tried to represent their tenuous link to the reality of past events in the text. As sources of what the ambassadors thought and their impressions of events, they can probably be considered as largely accurate.

However, perhaps more than any other written source, they are very obviously laden with bias. I have largely taken the actions of the ambassadors reported in their letters as broadly accurate, for instance the interactions of Álvaro de la Quadra, Bishop of Aquila, with the Sidneys (which are also corroborated by the letters of the imperial ambassador, Caspar Breuner). I have also used their reporting of rumours to represent those that might have been circulating the court, even if they were the ones who started those rumours. Especially when we reach the Elizabethan court, and thanks in large part to the manipulations of Robert Dudley and his faction, rumour is easier to reconstruct than truth. Diplomatic letters report these, even if their attempts to report on and predict events wildly diverge from other sources.

Personal

A wide range of letters have been used for this book, coming from a variety of sources. Many of them are contained in the State Papers Online archive, replicating material housed in The National Archive in London. Others, including some of these, were published in the nineteenth century in collections such as Henry Ellis's *Original Letters, Illustrative of English History*. There are also more modern collections, such as Roger Kuin's publication of *The Correspondence of Philip Sidney* and online databases, such as those of the letters of Bess of Hardwick (www.bessofhardwick.org).

These letters range from short snippets of information to prolonged and emotional reflections. Perhaps the most useful of this latter category are the letters sent by John Dudley to William Cecil (SP 10/15 f.137 and SP 10/18 f.3) in winter 1552. There is, of course, an awareness with most of these letters that others will read them, and one must be attentive to the author's need to 'self-fashion' in various ways. John seems to be at least aware of this; his son, Robert, is a master. It doesn't change the fact that, at least in most cases, these were historical 'utterances' by the authors of the letters, which is why I have, in some cases, translated them to direct speech. In particular, the letter sent by Robert Dudley to William Davison, on which the latter has written marginal retorts, I transformed into a two-way conversation (Bruce, ed., *Correspondence*, 168–71).

State

The line between personal and political correspondence is a thin one in the sixteenth century. However, letters of instruction from the monarch or their Council, or reports from their officers and courtiers, do seem to fit comfortably in this category. On these, we can be aware of significant exaggerations conventionally at play. Monarchs frequently write in a way that we would read as deeply emotional, especially to other monarchs but also to their servants. This is reflected in the obvious sycophancy of their lower-status correspondents. Likewise, letters from those away from the court are often filled with woeful accounts of the lack of provisions and financial support. There is often some truth to this, but it is also largely conventional.

PHYSICAL AND MATERIAL SOURCES

Architectural Sources

Many of the settings for this book no longer exist; the work of historians such as Simon Thurley (*Houses of Power*) is invaluable for reconstructing, for instance, the Tudor palace of Whitehall (destroyed by fire in 1698). Other buildings exist in ruins, such as Kenilworth, and there has been much work done to reconstruct its building and gardens (including an English Heritage Project, available online, which used Minecraft to rebuild the castle). Still others exist almost untouched since the sixteenth century, and although my ability to visit some of these locations was limited at the time of writing, travelling to nearby Tortington Church, for instance, was one of the few ways I was able to describe it in the book. Supported by scholarship on its history and fabric, I was able to distinguish those parts of the church that would have existed in the sixteenth century, allowing a full description of a little-known historic building.

Material Sources

In some very rare cases, I have been able to consult material sources, which have survived from the period to today, or at least long enough for a photograph to have been taken. These are very few and far between and in almost every case I have explored these via photograph, rather than viewing or handling the artifact myself. The effect of the ravages of time as well as alterations since the sixteenth century must be taken into account, but where these are available, they are invaluable.

VISUAL SOURCES

Although the majority of sources used in this book are written, I have also made use of a wide variety of visual sources, most of which are available online, but some of which are still only available through archives or printed reproductions. One has to be just as careful, if not more so, using visual sources, considering the purpose and audience of the images, as well as their proximity to what is being represented.

Family Trees

Along with the accounts of various ceremonies (including some illustrations, see below) and coats of arms, the College of Arms also has manuscripts containing family trees, compiled in the sixteenth century. For the Dudley family, these were put together in the latter half of the sixteenth century, to demonstrate Robert Dudley's connection to the earls of Warwick of old and legitimize his nobility (and perhaps legitimacy as royal suitor). As we are lacking firm details about the birth dates of many of the Dudley children, these are our best guides for determining their relative ages.

Illustrations

Manuscript illustrations of buildings, armour, towns, battlegrounds and ceremonies have also provided information essential to this book. Some are more detailed and are created with an eye to accuracy, others not. The visual depiction of the entry of Elizabeth I into London on her coronation, for instance, is one of the few images we have of Ambrose Dudley, positioned as leading one of the litter horses, next to his brother as Master of Horse. Their shared proximity to the queen on such an important occasion speaks more to the restoration of the Dudley family, than our knowledge that Robert alone rode so close to her.

Maps

The sixteenth century saw an increase in maps and cartographical techniques. I have used these extensively to generate a sense of the historical environment. In particular, the Agas Map of London (first printed c.1561, https://mapoflondon.uvic.ca/agas.htm), and Speed's atlas (early seventeenth century).

Portraits

There are very few written descriptions of the appearance of historical figures in the sixteenth century. Ambassadors will sometimes describe a monarch or their consort, but rarely anyone else in the court, and we must be attentive to the biases at work in diplomatic texts outlined above. As such, portraits can help furnish an understanding of their appearance and are also useful for their symbolic and emblematic meanings.

Bibliography

ABBREVIATIONS

AGR: Archives Générales du Royaume, Brussels

AMRE: Archives du Ministère des Relations Etrangères

APC: Acts of the Privy Council of England, ed. John Roche Dasent (London: University of London & History of Parliament Trust, 1890–1895).

BL: British Library

CA: College of Arms

CSPF: Calendar of State Papers Foreign, ed. Joseph Stevenson, et al. (London, 1863–1950).

CSPS: Calendar of State Papers, Spanish, ed. G. A. Bergenroth et al. (London, 1862–1954).

CSPS(S): Calendar of State Papers, Spain (Simancas), ed. Martin A. S. Hume (London, 1892–1899)

CSPV: Calendar of State Papers Relating to English Affairs in the Archives of Venice, ed. Rawdon Brown, et al. (London, 1864–1947)

DHM: The Diary of Henry Machyn, ed. J. G. Nichols (London: Camden Society, 1848)

DPL: Dudley Papers held by Longleat House, available by microfilm

ESRO: East Sussex Record Office

Fabyan: Robert Fabyan, *Great Chronicle of London*, ed. A. H. Thomas and I. D. Thornley (London: Alan Sutton, 1983)

Hall: Edward Hall, *The Union of the Two Noble and Illustre Families of Lancastre and Yorke [Hall's Chronicle]* (London, 1548)

Haynes: Samuel Haynes, ed., *A Collection of State Papers, Relating to Affairs in the Reigns of King Henry VIII, King Edward VI, Queen Mary, and Queen Elizabeth, Transcribed from Original letters and Other Authentick Memorials, Left by William Cecill Lord Burghley* (London, 1740)

HMCB: *Calendar of the Manuscripts of the Marquis of Bath, Preserved at Longleat, Wiltshire*, 9 volumes, (London: H.M. Stationery Office, 1904–1980)

HMCR: HMC: *Twelfth report, appendix, part iv. The Manuscripts of his Grace the Duke of Rutland, preserved at Belvoir Castle* (London: Eyre & Spottiswoode, 1888)

HMCSP: *State Papers Published under the Authority of his Majesty's Commission: King Henry the Eighth* (London, 1830–1852)

Holinshed: Raphael Holinshed, *Chronicles of England, Scotland and Ireland* (London: Johnson, 1808)

LA: Lancashire Archives

LJ: *Journals of the House of Lords*

LL: *The Lisle Letters*, ed. Muriel St Clare Byrne (Chicago: University of Chicago Press, 1981)

LP: *Letters and Papers, Foreign and Domestic, Henry VIII*, ed. J. S. Brewer

ODNB: *Oxford Dictionary of National Biography*

OED: *Oxford English Dictionary*

PRME: *Parliament Roles of Medieval England*, ed. Chris Given-Wilson, Paul Brand, Seymour Phillips, Mark Ormrod, Geoffrey Martin, Anne Curry and Rosemary Horrox (Woodbridge, 2005)

PRO: Public Record Office

SC: *'Spanish Chronicle'*; Martin Hume, ed., *Chronicle of King Henry VIII* (London: George Bell & Sons, 1889)

SHC: Surrey History Centre

ShP: Shrewsbury Papers, Lambeth Palace Library

SP: State Papers

SR: *The Statutes of the Realm*, 9 Volumes, ed. John Raithby (London, 1810–1825)

TP: Talbot Papers, MS 3206, Vol 15, 1499–1580, Lambeth Palace Library

TNA: National Archives

UPenn: University of Pennsylvania

Wriothesley: Charles Wriothesley, *A Chronicle of England during the Reigns of the Tudors, from A.D. 1485 to 1559* ed. William Douglas Hamilton, 2 Volumes (London: Camden Society, 1875–1877).

WSRO: West Sussex Record Office

Manuscript Sources

British Library, London

Additional: 26056a, 32648, 32649, 32654, 37749, 48023, 48126
Arundel: 26
Cottonian: Caligula D/VI E/I; Titus C/X; Vespasian C/III, C/XIV, F/XIII;
   Vitellius B/VI, B/VII, C/XVI
Egerton: 2642
Harleian: 69, 260, 284, 285, 290, 523, 620, 3504, 4712, 5087, 6798
Lansdowne: 127
Royal: 17B xxviii

College of Arms, London

I.18: Coronation Ceremonials
L.15: Pedigrees
M.1bis: Pedigrees
M.6: Ceremonials and Precedents
M.6bis: Ceremonials and Miscellany
M.8: Ceremonial. Time of Henry VIII
Muniment Room 13/1
Muniment Room 16/5

Corpus Christi College, Cambridge

MS 111: The Bath Cartulary and related items. Antiquarian Transcripts of
   Charters

East Sussex and Brighton and Hove Record Office

SAS-G/21/4: Archive of the Gage family of Firle, Viscounts Gage;
   Settlements

Institute of Historical Research, London

Dudley Papers, Longleat House, microfilm
1/64, 68, 70, 140, 207

Lancashire Archives, Preston

DDCL 298: Clifton of Lytham; Wills

Chancery:
Warrants for the Great Seal C 82/335

Exchequer:
The King's Book of Payments E 36/215
Treasury of Receipt: Ancient Deeds, A E 40/3987
King's Remembrancer: Particulars of Customs Accounts E 122/130/9
King's Remembrancer: Inventories E 154/2/39
Augmentation Office: Ancient Deeds, B E 326/4047, /12370
E 326/12370
Augmentation Office: Ancient Deeds, BB E 328/358

King's Bench:
Baga de Secretis KB 8/23
King's Bench Term Indictments Files KB 9/1073

Lord Chamberlain:
Records of Special Events LC 2/2, /3/1, /3/2

Land Revenue:
Inventories LR 2/118, /119, /120

Privy Council:
Registers PC 2/4, /14

Records of the Prerogative Court of Canterbury:
Will Registers PROB/11/12/386, /29, /30/443, /37/342

Public Record Office:
Rome PRO 31/9/67

State Paper Office:
Henry VIII, Letters and Papers SP 1/2, /3, /7, /32, /58, /73, /78, /85, /98, /152, /161, /163, /167, /174, /195, /205, /220, /221, /223, /225, /227, /231
Henry VIII, Letters to Lord Lisle SP 3/3, /10, /12
Edward VI, Letters and Papers SP 10/1, /9, /15, /18
Mary I, Letters and Papers SP 11/1
Elizabeth I, Letters and Papers SP 12/1, /6, 6/7, /23, /29, /213, /214

Scotland; Elizabeth I SP 52/5
Foreign; Edward VI SP 68/10
Foreign; Mary I SP 69/3, /4
Foreign; Elizabeth I SP 70/11, /19
Foreign; Elizabeth I SP 70/20, /43, /124
Foreign; Holland SP 84/3, /5, /10, /10/1, /17, /11, /15, /16, /17, /18, /19

New College, Oxford

MS 328

University of Pennsylvania, Philadelphia

Codex 1070   Cooke, Robert, 1592 – Genelogies of the Erles of Lecestre and Chester

Surrey History Centre, Woking

6729/2/11
LM 345/7

West Sussex Record Office

Add. 4200

PRINTED PRIMARY SOURCES

Archer, Ian W., ed. *Religion, Politics, and Society in Sixteenth-Century England* Cambridge: Cambridge University Press, 2003.

Archives, The National. 'Sir Thomas Gresham to Elizabeth I, 25 February 1560 (SP 70/11 f.78)'. Text. *The National Archives* (blog). The National Archives. Accessed 13 March 2020. https://www.nationalarchives.gov.uk/education/resources/elizabeth-monarchy/sir-thomas-gresham-to-elizabeth-i/.

Ascham, Roger. *The Whole Works of Roger Ascham: Life and letters*. Edited by Edward Grant. London: J. R. Smith, 1865.

Askew, Anne. *The Lattre Examinacyon of Anne Askewe*. 1547.

Brammall, Sheldon. *English Aeneid: Translations of Virgil, 1555–1646*. Edinburgh Critical Studies in Literary Translation. Edinburgh: University Press, 2015.

Brewer, John Sherren, and William Bullen, eds. *Calendar of the Carew Manuscripts: 1515–1574*. Longmans, Green, Reader & Dyer, 1867.

Bourbon, Nicolas. *Nugarum libri octo.* 1540.

Brown, Rawdon Lubbock. *Calendar of State Papers and Manuscripts, Relating to English Affairs: Existing in the Archives and Collections of Venice, and in Other Libraries of Northern Italy.* Cambridge: Cambridge University Press, 2013.

Bruce, John, ed. *Correspondence of Robert Dudley, Earl of Leycester: During His Government of the Low Countries, in the Years 1585 and 1586.* London: Camden Society, 1844.

Brunschwig, Hieronymus. *A Most Excellent and Perfecte Homish Apothecarye or Homely Physik Booke, for All the Grefes and Diseases of the Bodye. Translated out the Almaine Speche into English by Ihon Hollybush.* Translated by John Hollybush. Cologne, 1561.

Byrne, Muriel St Clare. *The Lisle Letters.* Chicago: University of Chicago Press, 1981.

Calendar of Letters, Despatches and State Papers Relating to the Negotiations between England and Spain Preserved in the Archives of Simancas and Elsewhere. Edited by Martin A. S. Hume. London, 1892–1899.

Calendar of the Manuscripts of the Marquis of Bath, Preserved at Longleat, Wiltshire. 3 Volumes. London: H.M. Stationery Office, 1904.

Calendar of the Manuscripts of the Most Hon. the Marquis of Salisbury, Preserved at Hatfield House, Hertfordshire. Vol. 3: 1583–1589. London: Forgotten Books, 2018.

Carmelianus, Petrus, and James Gairdner. *'The Spousells' of the Princess Mary, Daughter of Henry VII, to Charles Prince of Castile, A.D. 1508.* [Westminster] The Camden Society, 1893.

Collins, Arthur, ed. *Letters and Memorials of State.* London: F. Osborne, 1746.

Cromwell, Thomas. *Thomas Cromwell on Church and Commonwealth: Selected Letters, 1523–1540.* Edited by Arthur J. Slavin. Harper and Row, 1969.

Dasent, John Roche, ed. *Acts of the Privy Council of England Volume 3, 1550–1552.* London: University of London & History of Parliament Trust, 1891.

Deputy Keeper of the Public Records. *Annual Report. V.1-3.* London: HMSO, 1840.

Dudley, Edmund. *The Tree of Commonwealth: A Treatise.* Edited by D. M. Brodie. Cambridge: Cambridge University Press, 1948.

Duncan-Jones, Katherine, and Jan van Dorsten, eds. *Miscellaneous Prose of Sir Philip Sidney.* Oxford: Oxford University Press, 1973.

Ellis, Henry. *Original Letters, Illustrative of English History*. London: Harding, Triphook, and Lepard, 1824.

Fabyan, Robert. *The Great Chronicle of London*. Edited by A. H. Thomas and I. D. Thornley. London: Alan Sutton, 1983.

Fortescue, John. *A Learned Commendation of the Politique Lawes of Englande*. London, 1567.

Foxe, John. *Actes and Monuments of Matters Most Speciall and Memorable, Happenyng in the Church*. London: John Day, 1583.

Gascoigne, George. *The Whole Woorkes of George Gascoigne Esquire*. London, 1587.

Gilbertus, Anglicus. *Healing and Society in Medieval England: A Middle English Translation of the Pharmaceutical Writings of Gilbertus Anglicus*. Edited by Faye Marie Getz. Univ of Wisconsin Press, 1991.

Giles, Rev., ed. *The Whole Works of Roger Ascham*. Vol. 2. London: John Russell Smith, 1864.

Great Britain. Office of the Revels, and Albert Feuillerat. *Documents Relating to the Revels at Court in the Time of King Edward VI and Queen Mary (the Loseley Manuscripts) Edited with Notes and Indexes*. Louvain A. Uystpruyst, 1914.

Great Britain. Royal Commission on Historical Manuscripts. *Report of the Royal Commission on Historical Manuscripts*. London: [HMSO], 1870.

Green, Monica Helen, ed. *The Trotula: A Medieval Compendium of Women's Medicine*. Middle Ages Series. Philadelphia: University of Pennsylvania Press, 2001.

Gruffydd, Elis. *Boulogne and Calais: From 1545 to 1550*. Edited by M. Bryn Davies. Cairo: Fouad I University, 1950.

———. *Suffolk's Expedition to Montdidier 1523*. Edited by M. Bryn Davies. Cairo: Fouad I University, 1944.

Hall, Edward. *The Union of the Two Noble and Illustre Families of Lancastre and Yorke [Hall's Chronicle]*. London, 1548.

Haynes, Samuel, ed. *A Collection of State Papers: Relating to Affairs In the Reigns of King Henry VIII, King Edward VI, Queen Mary and Queen Elizabeth: From the Year 1542 to 1570*. London: Bowyer, 1740.

Holinshed, Raphael. *Chronicles of England, Scotland and Ireland*. Vol. 4. London: Johnson, 1808.

Hoyle, R. W., ed. *Letters of the Cliffords, Lords Clifford and Earls of Cumberland, c. 1500–c. 1565*. Cambridge: Cambridge University Press, 1992.

Hughes, Paul H., and James L. Larkin. *Tudor Royal Proclamations*. New Haven: Yale University Press, 1964.

Hughey, Ruth, ed. *The Arundel Harington Manuscript of Tudor Poetry*, Vol. I. Columbus: Ohio University Press, 1960.

Hume, Martin, ed. *Chronicle of King Henry VIII of England: Being a Contemporary Record of Some of the Principal ...* London: George Bell & Sons, 1889.

Kuin, Roger, ed. *The Correspondence of Sir Philip Sidney*. Oxford, New York: Oxford University Press, 2012.

Laneham, Robert. *A Letter: Whearin, Part of the Entertainment Untoo the Queens Maiesty, at Killingworth Castl, in Warwick Sheer*, 1575.

Laughton, John Knox, ed. *State Papers Relating to the Defeat of the Spanish Armada, Anno 1588*; London: Navy Records Society, 1894.

Legh, Gerard. *The Accedens of Armory*. London, 1576.

Leland, John. *Antiquarii de Rebus Britannicis Collectanea*. Vol. 1 Pt 2. London: Impensis Gul. & Jo. Richardson, 1770.

———. *Naenia in Mortem Splendidissimi Equitis Henrici Duddelegi Somarigana, Insulani, Verovicani*. London, 1545.

de Lettenhove, Kervyn, ed. *Relations politiques des Pays-Bas et de l'Angleterre, sous le règne de Philippe II*. Vol. 2. Brussels: L'académie Royal, 1883.

Lodge, Edmund, ed. *Illustrations of British History*. Vol. 2. London: John Chidley, 1838.

Lomas, S. C., ed. *Report on the Manuscripts of Lord Montagu of Beaulieu*. London: H.M. Stationery Office, 1900.

Lydgate, John. 'Prohemy of a Mariage Betwixt an Olde Man and a Yonge Wife, and the Counsail'. Robbins Library Digital Projects, https://d.lib.rochester.edu/teams/text/salisbury-trials-and-joys-prohemy-of-a-mariage-betwixt-an-olde-man-and-a-yonge-wife-and-the-counsail.

Niccolò Machiavelli, *Nicholas Machiavel's Prince*, trans. Edward Dacres. London, 1640.

Marcus, Leigh S., Janel Mueller, and Mary Beth Rose, eds. *Elizabeth I: Collected Works*. Chicago: University of Chicago Press, 2002.

Merriman, Roger Bigelow. *Life and Letters of Thomas Cromwell*. Oxford: Clarendon Press, 2000.

Mumby, Frank Arthur, ed. *The Youth of Henry VIII: A Narrative in Contemporary Letters*. London: Houghton Mifflin, 1913.

Nichols, John Gough. *The Chronicle of Queen Jane*. London: Camden Society, 1801.

Nichols, J. G. *The Diary of Henry Machyn, Citizen and Merchant-Taylor of London*, 1550-1563. London, 1848.

Nicolas, Nicholas Harris, ed. *Testamenta Vetusta: Being Illustrations from Wills, of Manners, Customs, &c. as Well as of the Descents and*

Possessions of Many Distinguished Families. From the Reign of Henry the Second to the Accession of Queen Elizabeth; London, Nichols & Son, 1826.

Norton, Thomas, and Thomas Sackville. *The Tragedie of Gorboduc.* London, 1565.

Paré, Ambroise. *Life and Times of Ambroise Pare 1510–1590 with a New Translation of His Apology and an Account of His Journeys in Divers Places.* Edited by Francis R. (Francis Randolph) Packard. New York: P. B. Hoeber, 1921.

Peck, D. C., ed. *Leicester's Commonwealth: The Copy of a Letter Written by a Master of Art of Cambridge (1584) and Related Documents.* Athens, OH: Ohio University Press, 1985.

Pickering, Danby, ed. *The Statutes at Large.* Vol. 5. Cambridge, 1763.

Pocock, Nicholas, ed. *Records of the Reformation.* Oxford: Clarendon, 1870.

Pollen, John Hungerford, ed. *A Letter from Mary Queen of Scots to the Duke of Guise.* Edinburgh: Edinburgh University Press, 1904.

Raithby, John, ed. *The Statutes of the Realm.* Vol. 2. London, 1816.

———, ed. *The Statutes of the Realm.* Vol. 3. London, 1817.

Read, Conyers. 'A Letter from Robert, Earl of Leicester, to a Lady'. *The Huntingdon Library Bulletin,* no. 9 (1936): 15–26.

Roeslin, Eucharius. *The Byrth of Mankynde.* Thomas Raynald, 1540.

Roper, William. *The Life of Sir Thomas More.* Edited by Gerard Wegemer and Stephen W. Smith. Dallas: Centre for Thomas More Studies, 2003.

Russell, Frederic William, ed. *Kett's Rebellion in Norfolk: Being a History of the Great Civil Commotion That Occurred at the Time of the Reformation, in the Reign of Edward VI.* London: Longmans, Brown, Green, Longmans and Roberts, and William Panny, 1859.

Sassetti, Tomasso. ' "Account of the St Bartholomew's Day Massacre" (from the "Brieve Raccontamento Del Gran Macello Fatto Nella Città Di Parigi Il Viggesimo Quarto Giorno d'agosto d'ordine Di Carlo Nono Re Di Francia")'. Translated by Steven Baker. Accessed 14 April 2020.

Sidney, Philip. 'Defence of Leicester'. In *Miscellaneous Prose of Sir Philip Sidney,* edited by Katherine Duncan-Jones and Jan van Dorsten, 129–41. Oxford: Oxford University Press, 1973.

Sir Harris Nicolas, ed. *Proceedings and Ordinances of the Privy Council of England.* Vol. 7, n.d.

Spont, Alfred. *Letters and Papers Relating to the War with France, 1512–1513.* London: Navy Records Society, 1897.

Stow, John. *The Annales, or Generall Chronicle of England.* London, 1615.

Strickland, Agnes, ed. *Lives of the Queens of England: From the Norman Conquest*. Vol. 2. London: H. Colburn, 1851.

———, ed. *Lives of the Queens of Scotland and English Princesses: Connected with the Regal Succession of Great Britain*. Vol. 7. Edinburgh and London: W. Blackwood, 1858.

Strype, John. *Ecclesiastical Memorials, Volume 3, Part 1*. Oxford: Clarendon Press, 1822.

Tedeschi, John. 'Tomasso Sassetti's Account of the St Bartholomew's Day Massacre'. In *The Massacre of St Bartholomew: Reappraisals and Documents*, edited by Alfred Soman, 99–154. Archives Internationales D'histoire Des Idees/International Archives of the History of Ideas. Dordrecht: Springer Netherlands, 1974.

The Booke of Common Prayer, and Adminystracion of the Sacramentes, and Other Rytes, and Ceremonies in the Churche of Englande. London, 1552.

The Booke of the Common Praier and Administracion of the Sacramentes: And Other Rites and Ceremonies of the Churche: After the Use of the Churche of Englande. London, 1549.

The Book of Common Prayer: Commonly Called the First Book of Queen Elizabeth, Printed by Grafton, 1559. London: W. Pickering, 1844.

The Copie of a Pistel or Letter Sent to Gilbard Potter in the Tyme When He Was in Prison. London, 1553.

'The Diversion of BEAR-BAITING, in the Reign of Queen Elizabeth, Graphically Described by Stow.' *Weekly Miscellany: Or, Instructive Entertainer, Oct. 4, 1773–Dec. 30, 1782; Sherborne* 12, no. 293 (10 May 1779): 135–5.

The Manuscripts of His Grace the Duke of Rutland: Preserved at Belvoir Castle. Vol. 1. London: Eyre & Spottiswoode, 1888.

'The Seuen First Bookes of the Eneidos of Virgill, Conuerted in Englishe Meter by Thomas Phaer Esquier, Sollicitour to the King and Quenes Maiesties, Attending Their Honorable Counsaile in the Marchies of Wales by Virgil.' London, 1558.

The Will of King Henry VII, 1775.

Thomas, William. *The Works of William Thomas*. Edited by Abraham D'Aubant. London: J. Almon, 1774.

Turner, Sharon. *The History of the Reign of Henry the Eighth: Comprising the Political History of the Commencement of the English Reformation*. London: Longman, Rees, Orme, Brown and Green, 1828.

Turpyn, Richard. *The Chronicle of Calais: In the Reigns of Henry VII and Henry VIII to the Year 1540. Ed. from Mss. in the British Museum*. London: Camden Society, 1846.

Vives, Juan Luis. *The Education of a Christian Woman: A Sixteenth-Century Manual.* Edited by Charles Fantazzi. Chicago: University of Chicago Press, 2000.

Von Klarwill, Victor, ed. *Queen Elizabeth And Some Foreigners.* London: Bodley Head, 1928.

Walsingham, Francis. *Journal of Sir Francis Walsingham, from Dec. 1570 to April 1583.* Edited by Charles Trice Martin. London: Camden Society, 1870.

Warner, George F., ed. *The Voyage of Robert Dudley, Afterwards Styled Earl of Warwick and Leicester and Duke of Northumberland, to the West Indies, 1594–1595.* London: Hakluyt Society, 1899.

Warren, F. E. (Frederick Edward), trans. *The Sarum Missal In English, Part 2.* London: A.R. Mowbray, 1913.

Whitney, Geffrey. *Choice of Emblemes.* Chester: Lovell Reeve, 1866.

Wilson, Thomas. *A Discourse Vppon Vsurye.* London, 1572.

———. *The Arte of Rhetorique.* London, 1553.

Wright, Thomas. *Queen Elizabeth and Her Times.* London: H. Colburn, 1838.

Wriothesley, Charles. *A Chronicle of England during the Reigns of the Tudors, from A.D. 1485 to 1559 Volume 1.* Edited by William Douglas Hamilton. Vol. 1. London: Camden Society, 1875.

———. *A Chronicle of England During the Reigns of the Tudors, from A.D. 1485 to 1559.* Edited by William Douglas Hamilton. Vol. 2. London: Camden Society, 1877.

SECONDARY SOURCES

Adams, Simon, ed. *Household Accounts and Disbursement Books of Robert Dudley, Earl of Leicester.* Cambridge: Cambridge University Press, 1995.

———. *Leicester and the Court: Essays on Elizabethan Politics.* Manchester: Manchester University Press, 2002.

Ágoston, Gábor. *Guns for the Sultan: Military Power and the Weapons Industry in the Ottoman Empire.* Cambridge: Cambridge University Press, 2005.

Ahnert, Ruth. *The Rise of Prison Literature in the Sixteenth Century.* Cambridge: Cambridge University Press, 2013.

Allen, T. G., and Jonathan Hiller. *The Excavation of a Medieval Manor House of the Bishops of Winchester at Mount House, Witney, Oxfordshire, 1984–92.* Oxford: Oxford Archaeological Unit, 2002.

Anglo, Sydney. *Machiavelli – The First Century: Studies in Enthusiasm, Hostility, and Irrelevance*. Oxford: Oxford University Press, 2005.

———. 'The Court Festivals of Henry VII: A Study Based upon the Account Books of John Heron, Treasurer of the Chamber'. *Bulletin of the John Rylands Library* 43, no. 1 (1960): 12–45.

Axton, Marie. 'Robert Dudley and the Inner Temple Revels'. *The Historical Journal* 13, no. 3 (1970): 365–78.

Baddeley, Welbore St Clair. *Cotteswold Manor; Being the History of Painswick*. Gloucester: John Bellows, 1907.

Beilin, Elaine V. *The Examinations of Anne Askew*. Oxford: Oxford University Press, 1996.

Bindoff, S. T. *The House of Commons, 1509–1558*. Woodbridge: Boydell & Brewer, 1982.

Binski, Paul. *The Painted Chamber at Westminster*. London: Society of Antiquaries of London, 1986.

———. 'The Painted Chamber at Westminster, the Fall of Tyrants and the English Literary Model of Governance'. *Journal of the Warburg and Courtauld Institutes* 74 (2011): 121–54.

Biraben, Jean-Noël, and Didier Blanchet. 'Essay on the Population of Paris and its Vicinity Since the Sixteenth Century'. *Population* 11, no. 1 (1999): 155–88.

Borman, Tracy. *Elizabeth's Women: The Hidden Story of the Virgin Queen*. London: Jonathan Cape, 2009.

———. *Henry VIII and the Men Who Made Him: The Secret History behind the Tudor Throne*. London: Hachette UK, 2018.

Brady, Ciaran. *A Viceroy's Vindication?: Sir Henry Sidney's Memoir of Service in Ireland, 1556–1578*. Cork: Cork University Press, 2002.

Brakspear, Harold. 'Dudley Castle'. *Archaeological Journal* 71, no. 1 (1914): 1–24.

Brennan, Michael G. *The Sidneys of Penshurst and the Monarchy, 1500–1700*. New York: Routledge, 2017.

Breverton, Terry. *Henry VII: The Maligned Tudor King*. Stroud: Amberley Publishing, 2016.

Brigden, Susan. *Thomas Wyatt: The Heart's Forest*. London: Faber & Faber, 2014.

Brodie, D. M. 'Edmund Dudley: Minister of Henry VII'. *Transactions of the Royal Historical Society* 15 (1932): 133–61.

Burton, Janet E., and Karen Stöber. *Monasteries and Society in the British Isles in the Later Middle Ages*. Woodbridge: Boydell & Brewer Ltd, 2008.

Canny, Nicholas Patrick. 'Glory and Gain: Sir Henry Sidney and the Government of Ireland, 1558–1578'. Thesis, University of Pennsylvania, 1971.

Carey, Hilary M. 'Henry VII's Book of Astrology and the Tudor Renaissance'. *Renaissance Quarterly* 65, no. 3 (2012): 661–710.

Carpenter, William. *Peerage for the People*. London: W. Strange, 1841.

Carter, Charles Howard. *The Secret Diplomacy of the Habsburgs: 1598–1625*. New York: Columbia University Press, 1964.

Cavill, Paul. *The English Parliaments of Henry VII, 1485–1504*. Oxford: Oxford University Press, 2009.

Champion, Matthew. 'Kett's Rebellion 1549: A Dussindale Eyewitness?' *Norfolk Archaeology* 43, no. 4 (2001): 642–44.

'CHAPEL OF ST PETER AD VINCULA, Tower Hamlets – 1357540 | Historic England'. Accessed 25 July 2019. https://historicengland.org.uk/listing/the-list/list-entry/1357540.

'Chapter House'. Westminster Abbey. Accessed 11 October 2020. https://www.westminster-abbey.org/about-the-abbey/history/chapter-house.

Charlton, Kenneth. *Women, Religion and Education in Early Modern England*. London: Routledge, 2014.

Childs, David. *The Warship Mary Rose: The Life & Times of King Henry VIII's Flagship*. Barnsley: Seaforth Publishing, 2014.

Chrimes, S. B. *Henry VII*. New Haven: Yale University Press, 1999.

Clarke, G. R. *The History and Description of the Town and Borough of Ipswich*. London: Hurst, Chance & Co., 1830.

Cloake, John. *Richmond Palace: Its History and Its Plan*. Richmond: Richmond Local History Society, 2001.

Collinson, Patrick. *Godly People: Essays On English Protestantism and Puritanism*. London: Bloomsbury Publishing, 1983.

Colthorpe, Marion E. 'The Elizabethan Court Day by Day'. Folgerpedia. Accessed 1 April 2020. https://folgerpedia.folger.edu/The_Elizabethan_Court_Day_by_Day#The_Elizabethan_Court_Day_by_Day.

Commendone. *The Accession, Coronation and Marriage of Mary Tudor*. Translated by C. V. Malfatti. Barcelona: self-published, 1956.

Cooper, Ivy M. 'The Meeting-Places of Parliament in the Ancient Palace of Westminster'. *Journal of the British Archaeological Association* 3, no. 1 (1938): 97–138.

Cooper, John. *The Queen's Agent: Francis Walsingham at the Court of Elizabeth I*. London: Faber and Faber, 2011.

Cooper, Nicholas. 'A Building Project for William, Lord Paget, at Burton-on-Trent'. *The Antiquaries Journal* 93 (September 2013): 249–86.

'CORNBURY HOUSE, Cornbury and Wychwood – 1053113 | Historic England'. Accessed 24 May 2020. https://historicengland.org.uk/listing/the-list/list-entry/1053113.

Cowie, Robert, and John Cloake. 'An Archaeological Survey of Richmond Palace, Surrey'. *Post-Medieval Archaeology* 35, no. 1 (2001): 3–52.

Creighton, Charles. *A History of Epidemics in Britain: From A. D. 664 to the Extinction of Plague.* Cambridge: Cambridge University Press, 1891.

Cressy, David. *Birth, Marriage, and Death: Ritual, Religion, and the Life-Cycle in Tudor and Stuart England.* Oxford: Oxford University Press, 1997.

Cressy, David, and Delloyd J. Guth. 'Binding the Nation: The Bonds of Association, 1584 and 1696'. In *Tudor Rule and Revolution: Essays for G. R. Elton from His American Friends,* 217–35. Cambridge: Cambridge University Press, 2009.

Croot, Patricia E. C. ed. *A History of the County of Middlesex: Volume 12, Chelsea.* London: Victoria County History, 2004.

Cruden, Robert Pierce, ed. *The History of the Town of Gravesend in the County of Kent, and of the Port of London.* W. Pickering, 1843.

Cunningham, Sean. 'Loyalty and the Usurper: Recognizances, the Council and Allegiance under Henry VII'. *Historical Research* 82, no. 217 (2009): 459–81.

Daniell, A. E. *London City Churches.* London: Archibald Constable & Co. Ltd, 1907.

Daniell, Christopher. *Death and Burial in Medieval England, 1066–1550.* London; New York: Routledge, 1998.

Davis, Natalie Zemon. 'The Rites of Violence: Religious Riot in Sixteenth-Century France'. *Past & Present,* no. 59 (1973): 51–91.

Daybell, James, ed. *Women and Politics in Early Modern England, 1450–1700.* Aldershot: Routledge, 2004.

———. *Women Letter-Writers in Tudor England.* Oxford: Oxford University Press, 2006.

Dean, David. 'Image and Ritual in Tudor Parliaments'. In *Tudor Political Culture,* edited by Dale Hoak, 243–71. Cambridge: Cambridge University Press, 1992.

Dijkhuizen, Jan Frans van, and Karl A. E. Enenkel. *The Sense of Suffering: Constructions of Physical Pain in Early Modern Culture.* Leiden: Brill, 2009.

Dillon, Viscount. 'Barriers and Foot Combats'. *Archaeological Journal* 61, no. 1 (1904): 276–308.

Doran, Susan. *Monarchy and Matrimony: The Courtships of Elizabeth I.* New York: Routledge, 2002.

Douglas Simpson, W. 'Dudley Castle: The Renaissance Buildings'. *Archaeological Journal* 101, no. 1 (1944): 119–25.

Dumitrescu, Theodor. *The Early Tudor Court and International Musical Relations*. London: Routledge, 2017.

'Early History'. UK Parliament. Accessed 8 July 2019. https://www.parliament.uk/about/living-heritage/building/palace/westminsterhall/architecture/early-history/.

Edwards, John. *Mary I: England's Catholic Queen*. New Haven: Yale University Press, 2011.

Ellis, Jim. 'Kenilworth, King Arthur, and the Memory of Empire'. *English Literary Renaissance* 43, no. 1 (2013): 3–29.

Ellis, Steven G. *Tudor Frontiers and Noble Power*. Oxford: Oxford University Press, 1995.

Elton, Charles Isaac. *The Tenures of Kent*. London: Parker and Company, 1867.

Elton, G. R. 'Henry VII: Rapacity And Remorse'. *The Historical Journal* 1, no. 1 (1958): 21–39.

———. 'I. Henry VII: A Restatement'. *The Historical Journal* 4, no. 1 (1961): 1–29.

England, Historic. 'Chertsey Abbey: A Benedictine Monastery on the Banks of Abbey River, Runnymede – 1008524| Historic England'. Accessed 17 May 2018. https://historicengland.org.uk/listing/the-list/list-entry/1008524.

———. 'Greenwich Palace, Non Civil Parish – 1410710| Historic England'. Accessed 5 August 2018. https://historicengland.org.uk/listing/the-list/list-entry/1410710.

———. 'Tortington Augustinian Priory and Ponds, Including Part of Priory Precinct, Arundel – 1021459| Historic England'. Accessed 8 March 2018. https://historicengland.org.uk/listing/the-list/list-entry/1021459.

Evans, G. Blakemore, ed. *Elizabethan-Jacobean Drama: The Theatre in Its Time*. New York: New Amsterdam Books, 1998.

Evans, Jennifer. *Aphrodisiacs, Fertility and Medicine in Early Modern England*. Woodbridge: Boydell & Brewer Ltd, 2014.

'Exrenda – Dudley Castle C1550 Visualisation'. Accessed 28 August 2018. http://www.exrenda.com/dudley/dudley.htm.

Fletcher, Anthony, and Diarmaid MacCulloch. *Tudor Rebellions*. New York: Routledge, 2015.

French, Katherine. 'The Material Culture of Childbirth in Late Medieval London and Its Suburbs'. *Journal of Women's History* 28, no. 2 (2016): 126–48.

French, Peter J. *John Dee: The World of the Elizabethan Magus*. New York: Routledge, 2013.

Frye, Susan. 'The Myth of Elizabeth at Tilbury'. *The Sixteenth Century Journal* 23, no. 1 (1992): 95–114.

Gair, Reavley. *The Children of Paul's: The Story of a Theatre Company, 1553–1608*. Cambridge: Cambridge University Press, 1982.

Gaskill, Malcolm. *Crime and Mentalities in Early Modern England*. Cambridge: Cambridge University Press, 2003.

Godfrey, Esther. 'Sources for the New Fountain and the Stories Around It'. In *The Elizabethan Garden at Kenilworth Castle*, edited by Anna Keay and John Watkins, 103–28. London: English Heritage, 2013.

Goldring, Elizabeth. '"A Mercer Ye Wot Az We Be": The Authorship of the Kenilworth "Letter" Reconsidered'. *English Literary Renaissance* 38, no. 2 (2008): 245–69.

———. 'Gascoigne and Kenilworth: The Production, Reception, and Afterlife of The Princely Pleasures'. *English Literary Renaissance* 44, no. 3 (2014): 363–87.

———. *Robert Dudley, Earl of Leicester, and the World of Elizabethan Art: Painting and Patronage at the Court of Elizabeth I*. New Haven: Yale University Press, 2014.

———. '"So Lively a Portraiture of His Miseries": Melancholy, Mourning and the Elizabethan Malady'. *The British Art Journal* 6, no. 2 (2005): 12–22.

———. 'The Earl of Leicester's Inventory of Kenilworth Castle, c.1578'. *English Heritage Historical Review* 2, no. 1 (2007): 36–59.

Goodwin, George. 'Your Guide to the Battle of Flodden 1513'. HistoryExtra, 2013 https://www.historyextra.com/period/tudor/battle-flodden-battlefield-scotland-scottish-invasion-guide-facts-dates/.

Graves, Michael A. R. *Tudor Parliaments, The Crown, Lords and Commons, 1485–1603*. New York: Routledge, 2014.

Green, Janet M. '"I My Self": Queen Elizabeth I's Oration at Tilbury Camp'. *The Sixteenth Century Journal* 28, no. 2 (1997): 421–45.

Gristwood, Sarah. *Elizabeth & Leicester*. London: Bantam Press, 2007.

Groom, Susanne, and Lee Prosser. *Kew Palace: The Official Illustrated History*. London: Merrell Publishers Ltd, 2006.

Grummitt, David. 'Household, Politics and Political Morality in the Reign of Henry VII'. *Historical Research* 82, no. 217 (2009): 393–411.

———. *The Calais Garrison: War and Military Service in England, 1436–1558*. Woodbridge: Boydell & Brewer, 2008.

Guasco, Michael. *Slaves and Englishmen: Human Bondage in the Early Modern Atlantic World*. Philadelphia: University of Pennsylvania Press, 2014.

Gunn, S. J. 'A Letter of Jane, Duchess of Northumberland, in 1553'. *The English Historical Review* 114, no. 459 (1999): 1267–71.

———. *Charles Brandon: Henry VIII's Closest Friend*. Stroud: Amberley Publishing Limited, 2015.

———. 'Edmund Dudley and the Church'. *The Journal of Ecclesiastical History* 51 (2000): 509–26.

———. *Henry VII's New Men and the Making of Tudor England*. Oxford: Oxford University Press, 2016.

———. 'The Accession of Henry VIII'. *Historical Research* 64, no. 155 (1991): 278–88.

———. 'The Duke of Suffolk's March on Paris in 1523'. *The English Historical Review* 101, no. 400 (1986): 596–634.

———. *The English People at War in the Age of Henry VIII*. Oxford: Oxford University Press, 2018.

Guy, John. *Gresham's Law: The Life and World of Queen Elizabeth I's Banker*. London: Profile Books, 2019.

Gwyn, Peter. *The King's Cardinal: The Rise and Fall of Thomas Wolsey*. London: Pimlico, 1992.

———. 'Wolsey's Foreign Policy: The Conferences at Calais and Bruges Reconsidered'. *The Historical Journal* 23, no. 4 (1980): 755–72.

Halliday, F. E. 'Queen Elizabeth and Dr Burcot'. *History Today* 5, no. 8 (1955): 542–44.

Harding, Vanessa, and Caroline M. Barron, eds. *A Map of Tudor London: England's Capital City in 1520*. London: The Historic Towns Trust, 2018.

Harper, Anthony John, and Ingrid Höpel. *The German-Language Emblem in Its European Context: Exchange and Transmission*. Paris: Librairie Droz, 2000.

Harper, Samantha. 'The Problem of Access at the Early Tudor Court: Some Case Studies'. Tudor Chamber Books Conference, Winchester, 2018.

Harpsfield, Nicholas. *A Treatise on the Pretended Divorce Between Henry VIII and Catherine of Aragon*. London: Camden Society, 1878.

Harrison, C. J. 'The Petition of Edmund Dudley'. *The English Historical Review* LXXXVII, no. CCCXLII (1 January 1972): 82–99.

Hartweg, Christine. 'Daughter Or Daughter-In-Law?' *All Things Robert Dudley* (blog), 25 February 2012. https://allthingsrobertdudley.wordpress.com/2012/02/25/daughter-or-daughter-in-law/.

———. *John Dudley: The Life of Lady Jane Grey's Father-in-Law*. Create-Space Independent Publishing Platform, 2016.

Hawkyard, Alasdair. 'The Tudor Speakers 1485–1601: Choosing, Status, Work'. *Parliamentary History* 29, no. 1 (2010): 22–48.

Hay, D. 'England, Scotland and Europe: The Problem of the Frontier'. *Transactions of the Royal Historical Society* 25 (1975): 77–91.

Hayward, Maria. *Rich Apparel: Clothing and the Law in Henry VIII's England*. Farnham, England; Burlington, VT: Routledge, 2009.

Heal, Felicity. *Hospitality in Early Modern England*. Oxford: Oxford University Press, 1990.

Higginbotham, Susan. 'How Old Was Guildford Dudley? (Beats Me.)'. *History Refreshed* (blog), 2011. http://www.susanhigginbotham.com/blog/posts/how-old-was-guildford-dudley-beats-me/.

Hodgkins, Alexander. '"A Great Company of Country Clowns": Guerilla Warfare in the East Anglian and Western Rebellions (1549)'. In *Unconventional Warfare from Antiquity to the Present Day*, edited by Brian Hughes and Fergus Robson, 177–95. Cham: Palgrave Macmillan, 2017.

———. 'Reconstructing Rebellion: Digital Terrain Analysis of the Battle of Dussindale (1549)'. *Internet Archaeology*, no. 38 (2015). http://intarch.ac.uk.ezproxy.sussex.ac.uk/journal/issue38/hodgkins_toc.html.

Holt, Mack P. *The French Wars of Religion, 1562–1629*. Cambridge: Cambridge University Press, 2005.

Horowitz, Mark R. 'A Country under Contract: Early-Tudor England and the Growth of a Credit Culture'. *Essays in Economic and Business History* 29 (2011): 75–86.

———. '"Agree with the King": Henry VII, Edmund Dudley and the Strange Case of Thomas Sunnyff'. *Historical Research* 79, no. 205 (2006): 325–66.

———. 'Henry Tudor's Treasure'. *Historical Research* 82, no. 217 (2009): 560–79.

Houlbrooke, Ralph. *Death, Religion, and the Family in England, 1480–1750*. Oxford: Oxford University Press, 2000.

Hunt, Alice. 'Dumb Politics in Gorboduc'. In *The Oxford Handbook of Tudor Drama*, edited by Thomas Betteridge and Greg Walker, 547–65. Oxford: Oxford University Press, 2012.

———. *The Drama of Coronation: Medieval Ceremony in Early Modern England*. Cambridge: Cambridge University Press, 2008.

Hurren, Elizabeth T. 'Cultures of the Body, Medical Regimen, and Physic at the Tudor Court'. In *Henry VIII and the Court: Art, Politics and*

Performance, edited by Suzannah Lipscomb and Thomas Betteridge. London: Routledge, 2016.

Hutchinson, Robert. *Young Henry: The Rise of Henry VIII*. London: W&N, 2012.

Ingram, Martin. *Carnal Knowledge: Regulating Sex in England, 1470–1600*. Cambridge Studies in Early Modern British History. Cambridge: Cambridge University Press, 2017.

Inman, Peggy. 'AMY ROBSART AND CUMNOR PLACE'. Cumnor History Society. Accessed 24 January 2020. http://users.ox.ac.uk/~djp/cumnor/articles/inman-robsart.htm.

Ives, Eric. 'A Frenchman at the Court of Anne Boleyn'. *History Today* 48, no. 8 (August 1998): 21.

———. *Lady Jane Grey: A Tudor Mystery*. Chichester: John Wiley & Sons, 2011.

———. *The Life and Death of Anne Boleyn: The Most Happy*. Malden, MA.: Wiley-Blackwell, 2005.

Jack, Sybil. 'Shedding the Earthly Crown Imperial for a Heavenly Crown: Henry VII, Dead and Buried'. *Literature & Aesthetics* 25, no. 1 (2015).

Jackson, Canon. 'Charles, Lord Stourton, and the Murder of the Hartgills'. *The Wiltshire Archaeological and Natural History Magazine* 8, no. 24 (1864): 242–336.

Jacques, David. 'The Form and Structure of the Garden'. In *The Elizabethan Garden at Kenilworth Castle*, edited by Anna Keay and John Watkins, 93–102. London: English Heritage, 2013.

———. 'The Place of Kenilworth in Garden History'. In *The Elizabethan Garden at Kenilworth Castle*, edited by Anna Keay and John Watkins, 9–20. London: English Heritage, 2013.

Johnson, Lauren. *So Great a Prince: England in 1509*. London: Head of Zeus, 2016.

Johnston, Philip Mainwaring. 'Tortington Church and Priory: Notes on Their History and Architecture'. Churches in Sussex. Accessed 4 March 2018. http://sussexchurches.co.uk/tortington.htm.

Jones, Michael K., and Malcolm G. Underwood. *The King's Mother: Lady Margaret Beaufort, Countess of Richmond and Derby*. Cambridge: Cambridge University Press, 1993.

Jones, Peter Murray, and Lea T. Olsan. 'Performative Rituals for Conception and Childbirth in England, 900–1500'. *Bulletin of the History of Medicine* 89, no. 3 (2015): 406–33.

Jordan, W. K., ed. *The Chronicle and Political Papers of King Edward VI*. Ithaca, NY: Cornell University Press, 1966.

Jordan, W. K, and M. R. Gleason. 'The Saying of John Late Duke of Northumberland upon the Scaffold, 1553'. *Harvard Bulletin* 23, no. 3 (1975): 324–55.

Jost, Walter, and Wendy Olmsted. *A Companion to Rhetoric and Rhetorical Criticism*. Oxford: John Wiley & Sons, 2008.

justicetyrwhit. 'Babington v Venour (1465): Bankruptcy, Ravishment and the Fleet Prison'. *Order of the Coif* (blog), 29 January 2017. https://orderofthecoif.wordpress.com/2017/01/29/babington-v-venour-1465-bankruptcy-ravishment-and-the-fleet-prison/.

Kamen, Henry. *Philip of Spain*. New Haven: Yale University Press, 1997.

Kaufmann, Miranda. *Black Tudors: The Untold Story*. London: Oneworld Publications, 2017.

Keay, Anna, and John Watkins, eds. *The Elizabethan Garden at Kenilworth Castle*. London: English Heritage, 2013.

Kelley, Donald R. 'Martyrs, Myths, and the Massacre: The Background of St Bartholomew'. *The American Historical Review* 77, no. 5 (1972): 1323–42.

Kesselring, K. J. *Making Murder Public: Homicide in Early Modern England, 1480–1680*. Oxford: Oxford University Press, 2019.

Kingsford, C. L. 'On Some London Houses of the Early Tudor Period'. *Archaeologia* 71 (1921): 17–54.

Knighton, C. S., and David Loades. *The Navy of Edward VI and Mary I*. Farnham: Ashgate Publishing, Ltd, 2013.

Krylova, Olga, and David J. D. Earn. 'Patterns of Smallpox Mortality in London, England, over Three Centuries'. *BioRxiv*, 16 September 2019, online preprint.

Laqueur, Thomas. 'Orgasm, Generation, and the Politics of Reproductive Biology'. *Representations*, no. 14 (1986): 1–41.

Lehmberg, Stanford E. *The Later Parliaments of Henry VIII: 1536–1547*. Cambridge: Cambridge University Press, 1977.

Leonard, Harry. 'Knights and Knighthood in Tudor England'. Thesis, Queen Mary, University of London, 1970.

Lethaby, W. R. 'The Romance Tiles of Chertsey Abbey'. *The Volume of the Walpole Society* 2 (1912): 69–80.

Liedl, Janice. 'Introduction'. In *The Tree of Commonwealth*, 3–9. Sudbury, ON: Laurentian University, 2012.

Lipscomb, Suzannah. *The King Is Dead: The Last Will and Testament of Henry VIII*. London: Head of Zeus, 2015.

Lisle, Leanda de. *The Sisters Who Would Be Queen: Mary, Katherine, and Lady Jane Grey: A Tudor Tragedy*. London: Harper Press, 2009.

Litten, Julian. *The English Way of Death: The Common Funeral Since 1450.* London: Robert Hale Ltd, 2002.

Loach, Jennifer. 'The Function of Ceremonial in the Reign of Henry VIII'. *Past & Present*, no. 142 (1994): 43–68.

Loades, D. M. *Elizabeth I: The Golden Reign of Gloriana*. London: Hambledon and London, 2003.

———. *John Dudley, Duke of Northumberland, 1504–1553*. Oxford: Clarendon Press, 1996.

Lockyer, Roger, and Andrew Thrush. *Henry VII*. London; New York: Routledge, 2014.

Lowe, E. J. *Natural Phenomena and Chronology of the Seasons*. London: Bell & Daldy, 1870.

MacCulloch, Diarmaid. *Thomas Cromwell: A Life*. London: Penguin UK, 2018.

MacDonald, Michael, and Terence R. Murphy. *Sleepless Souls: Suicide in Early Modern England*. Oxford: Clarendon Press, 1990.

Martin, Colin, and Geoffrey Parker. *The Spanish Armada*. Manchester: Manchester University Press, 2002.

McCarthy, Conor. *Marriage in Medieval England: Law, Literature, and Practice*. Woodbridge: Boydell & Brewer, 2004.

McClive, Cathy. 'The Hidden Truths of the Belly: The Uncertainties of Pregnancy in Early Modern Europe'. *The Society for the Social History of Medicine* 15, no. 2 (2002): 209–27.

McCoy, Richard C. 'From the Tower to the Tiltyard: Robert Dudley's Return to Glory'. *The Historical Journal* 27, no. 2 (1984): 425–35.

Mearns, James. 'The Influence of Erasmus's Educational Writings on Nicholas Bourbon's *Paidagogeion*'. *Bibliothèque d'humanisme et Renaissance; Travaux et Documents* 72 (2010): 65–81.

Mears, Natalie. 'Courts, Courtiers, and Culture in Tudor England'. *The Historical Journal* 46, no. 3 (2003): 703–22.

Medici-Thiemann, Catherine. '"She Governs the Queen": Jane Dudley, Mary Dudley Sidney, and Katherine Dudley Hastings' Political Actions, Agency, and Networks in Tudor England'. Thesis, University of Nebraska, 2016.

Medvei, V. C. 'The Illness and Death of Mary Tudor'. *Journal of the Royal Society of Medicine* 80, no. 12 (1987): 766–70.

Merton, Charlotte Isabelle. 'Women Who Served Queen Mary and Queen Elizabeth: Ladies, Gentlewomen and Maids of the Privy Chamber, 1553–1603.' Thesis, University of Cambridge, 1992.

Moorhouse, Geoffrey. *Great Harry's Navy: How Henry VIII Gave England Sea Power*. London: Phoenix Press, 2005.

Morgan, Hollie L. S. *Beds and Chambers in Late Medieval England: Readings, Representations and Realities*. Woodbridge: Boydell & Brewer, 2017.

Morris, Richard K. '"I Was Never More in Love with an Olde Howse nor Never Newe Worke Coulde Be Better Bestowed": The Earl of Leicester's Remodelling of Kenilworth Castle for Queen Elizabeth I'. *The Antiquaries Journal* 89 (2009): 241–305.

Morris, Richard K., and Anna Keay. 'The Aviary'. In *The Elizabethan Garden at Kenilworth Castle*, edited by Anna Keay and John Watkins, 139–48. London: English Heritage, 2013.

Morris, Sarah, and Natalie Grueninger. *In the Footsteps of Anne Boleyn*. Stroud: Amberley Publishing Limited, 2013.

Mowbray, Charles Botolph Joseph. *The History of the Noble House of Stourton, of Stourton, in the County of Wilts*. London: E. Stock, 1899.

Mucklow, Timothy Jones. 'William Warham: A Political Biography'. Thesis, West Virginia University, 1982.

Murphy, Neil. *The Tudor Occupation of Boulogne: Conquest, Colonisation and Imperial Monarchy, 1544–1550*. Cambridge: Cambridge University Press, 2019.

Murray, Alexander. *Suicide in the Middle Ages: The Violent against Themselves*. Oxford: Oxford University Press, 1998.

'Nonsuch Palace, Its Formal Gardens and Associated Remains, and Cuddington Medieval Settlement, Epsom and Ewell – 1017998 | Historic England'. Accessed 27 August 2019. https://historicengland.org.uk/listing/the-list/list-entry/1017998.

Norton, Elizabeth. *Anne of Cleves: Henry VIII's Discarded Bride*. Stroud: Amberley Publishing, 2010.

———. *Bessie Blount: Mistress to Henry VIII*. Stroud: Amberley Publishing, 2011.

———. *Jane Seymour: Henry VIII's True Love*. Stroud: Amberley Publishing, 2009.

'Off With His Head – Medieval Manuscripts Blog'. Accessed 9 July 2019. https://blogs.bl.uk/digitisedmanuscripts/2016/07/off-with-his-head.html.

Oman, Charles. *A History of the Art of War in the Sixteenth Century*. Abingdon: Routledge, 1937.

Orlin, Lena Cowen. *Locating Privacy in Tudor London*. Oxford; New York: Oxford University Press, 2007.

Page, William, and P. H. Ditchfield. 'Parishes: Cumnor', in *A History of the County of Berkshire: Volume 4*. London, 1924.

Paranque, Estelle. *Elizabeth I of England through Valois Eyes: Power, Representation, and Diplomacy in the Reign of the Queen, 1558–1588.* Cham: Palgrave Macmillan, 2018.

Parker, Geoffrey. *Emperor: A New Life of Charles V.* New Haven: Yale University Press, 2019.

———. *The Cambridge Illustrated History of Warfare.* Cambridge: Cambridge University Press, 2000.

Parnell, G. 'The Rise and Fall of the Tower of London'. *History Today* 42, no. 3 (1992): 13.

Parry, Glyn, and Cathryn Enis. *Shakespeare Before Shakespeare: Stratford-upon-Avon, Warwickshire, and the Elizabethan State.* Oxford; New York: Oxford University Press, 2020.

'Pastscape – Detailed Result: HANWORTH MANOR'. Accessed 22 December 2020. https://www.pastscape.org.uk/hob.aspx?hob_id=398090.

Pease, Howard. *The Lord Wardens of the Marches of England and Scotland.* London: Constable, 1913.

Peat, Alfred H., and Leslie C. Halsted. *Churches and Other Antiquities of West Sussex: With Architectural and Historical Notes and Thirty-One Illustrations.* Chichester: J. W. Moore, 1912.

Peck, D. C. 'Government Suppression of Elizabethan Catholic Books: The Case of "Leicester's Commonwealth"'. *The Library Quarterly* 47, no. 2 (1977): 163–77.

Penn, Thomas. *Winter King: The Dawn of Tudor England.* London: Penguin, 2012.

Phillips, Margaret M. 'The Paedagogian of Nicholas Bourbon'. In *Neo-Latin and the Vernacular in Renaissance France,* edited by Terence Cave and Graham Castor, 71–82. Oxford: Clarendon Press, 1984.

'Picture Reveals Young Henry VIII'. *BBC News,* 19 October 2012, sec. Wales. https://www.bbc.com/news/uk-wales-20003806.

Pincombe, Mike. 'Robert Dudley, Gorboduc, and "The Masque of Beauty and Desire": A Reconsideration of the Evidence for Political Intervention'. *Parergon* 20, no. 1 (2003): 19–44.

Pollnitz, Aysha. *Princely Education in Early Modern Britain.* Cambridge: Cambridge University Press, 2015.

Pollock, Linda A. 'Embarking on a Rough Passage: The Experience of Pregnancy in Early-Modern Society'. In *Women as Mothers in Pre-Industrial England,* edited by Valerie Fildes, 39–67. Abingdon: Routledge, 2012.

Potter, W. J. W., and E. J. Winstanley. 'The Coinage of Henry VII'. *British Numismatic Journal* 30–32 (62 1960).

Rappaport, Steve. *Worlds within Worlds: Structures of Life in Sixteenth-Century London*. Cambridge: Cambridge University Press, 1989.

Reynolds, Nigel. 'Henry VII's Chapel Found at Greenwich', 25 January 2006, sec. News. https://www.telegraph.co.uk/news/uknews/1508708/Henry-VIIs-chapel-found-at-Greenwich.html.

Reynolds, Susan, ed. 'Heston and Isleworth: Syon House'. In *A History of the County of Middlesex: Volume 3, Shepperton, Staines, Stanwell, Sunbury, Teddington, Heston and Isleworth, Twickenham, Cowley, Cranford, West Drayton, Greenford, Hanwell, Harefield and Harlington*. London, 1962.

Richardson, Glenn. 'Hunting at the Courts of Francis I and Henry VIII'. *The Court Historian* 18, no. 2 (2013): 127–41.

Robison, William B., ed. 'Incomplete Prescription: Maladies and Medicine in *The Tudors*'. In *History, Fiction, and The Tudors: Sex, Politics, Power, and Artistic License in the Showtime Television Series*, 329–42. New York: Springer, 2017.

Rodger, N. A. M. *The Safeguard of the Sea: A Naval History of Britain 660–1649*. London: Penguin, 2004.

Rose, Susan. *Calais: An English Town in France, 1347–1558*. Woodbridge: Boydell & Brewer, 2008.

Ross, James. '"Contrary to the Ryght and to the Order of the Lawe": New Evidence of Edmund Dudley's Activities on Behalf of Henry VII in 1504'. *The English Historical Review* 127, no. 524 (2012): 24–45.

Rounding, Virginia. *The Burning Time: The Story of the Smithfield Martyrs*. New York: Pan Macmillan, 2017.

Rublack, Ulinka. 'Pregnancy, Childbirth and the Female Body in Early Modern Germany'. *Past & Present* no. 150 (1996): 84–110.

Russell, Gareth. *Young and Damned and Fair: The Life of Catherine Howard, Fifth Wife of King Henry VIII*. New York: Simon and Schuster, 2017.

Russell, Joycelyne G. 'The Search for Universal Peace: The Conferences at Calais and Bruges in 1521'. *Historical Research* 44, no. 110 (1971): 162–93.

Salter, H. E., and Mary D. Lobel. *A History of the County of Oxford*. Vol. 3. London: Boydell & Brewer, n.d. http://www.british-history.ac.uk/vch/oxon/vol3/.

Samson, Alexander. *Mary and Philip: The Marriage of Tudor England and Habsburg Spain*. Manchester: Manchester University Press, 2020.

Saul, N. 'The Cuckoo in the Nest: A Dallingridge Tomb in the Fitzalan Chapel at Arundel'. *Sussex Archaeological Collections*, no. 147 (2009): 125–33.

Scard, Margaret. *Edward Seymour: Lord Protector: Tudor King in All But Name*. Stroud: The History Press, 2016.

Scarisbrick, J. J. *Henry VIII*. Berkeley: University of California Press, 1968.

Schofield, John. 'Saxon and Medieval Parish Churches in the City of London: A Review'. *Transactions of the London and Middlesex Archaeological Society* 45 (1994): 23–146.

Sharpe, J. A. 'Domestic Homicide in Early Modern England'. *The Historical Journal* 24, no. 1 (1981): 29–48.

'Site of Langley Palace Royal Hunting Lodge, an Associated Enclosure and Later Garden Earthworks at Langley Farm, Leafield – 1008495 | Historic England'. Accessed 7 May 2020. https://historicengland.org.uk/listing/the-list/list-entry/1008495.

Skidmore, Chris. *Death and the Virgin*. London: Weidenfeld & Nicolson, 2010.

———. *Edward VI: The Lost King of England*. London: Hachette UK, 2011.

Slack, Paul. *The Impact of Plague in Tudor and Stuart England*. Oxford; New York: Oxford University Press, 1991.

Smith, Jacqueline, and John Carter. *Inns and Alehouses of Abingdon, 1550–1978*. J. Smith and J. Carter, 1989.

Smith-Bannister, Scott. *Names and Naming Patterns in England 1538–1700*. Oxford; New York: Oxford University Press, 1997.

Society, Ex Libris. *The Journal of the Ex Libris Society*. London: Ex Libris Society, 1970.

Somerville, R. 'Henry VII's "Council Learned in the Law"'. *The English Historical Review* 54, no. 215 (1939): 427–42.

Spivakovsky, Erika. *Son of the Alhambra: Don Diego Hurtado de Mendoza, 1504–1575*. Austin: University of Texas Press, 1970.

Stabler, Arthur Phillips. 'The "Histoires Tragiques" of Francois De Belleforest, a General Critique with Special Attention to the Non-Bandello Group'. Thesis, University of Virginia, 1959.

Starkey, Lindsay J. 'Gangrene or Cancer? Sixteenth-Century Medical Texts and the Decay of the Body of the Church in Jean Calvin's Exegesis of 2 Timothy 2:17'. *Renaissance and Reformation/Renaissance et Réforme* 39, no. 3 (2016): 111–32.

Stewart, Alan. *Philip Sidney: A Double Life*. London: Random House, 2011.

Stillman, Robert E. 'Philip Sidney and the Catholics: The Turn from Confessionalism in Early Modern Studies'. *Modern Philology* 112, no. 1 (2014): 97–129.

Strycharski, Andrew. 'Some Verses of Henry and Mary Dudley Sidney and Prince Edward's "Little School"'. *ANQ: A Quarterly Journal of Short Articles, Notes and Reviews,* 24, no. 4 (2011): 249–54.

Sullivan, Erin. 'A Disease unto Death: Sadness in the Time of Shakespeare'. In *Emotions and Health, 1200–1700,* edited by Elena Carrera. Leiden: Brill, 2013, 159–83.

Tallis, Nicola. *Crown of Blood: The Deadly Inheritance of Lady Jane Grey.* London: Michael O'Mara, 2016.

———. *Elizabeth's Rival: The Tumultuous Tale of Lettice Knollys, Countess of Leicester.* London: Michael O'Mara, 2017.

———. *Uncrowned Queen: The Fateful Life of Margaret Beaufort Tudor Matriarch.* London: Michael O'Mara, 2019.

The Gentleman's Magazine. F. Jefferies, 1832.

'The King's Tomb Part I – KING HENRY VI'. Accessed 17 May 2018. http://www.henrysixth.com/?page_id=120.

The Mary Rose. 'About the Mary Rose'. Accessed 26 July 2021. https://maryrose.org/about-the-mary-rose/.

Thurley, Simon. *Houses of Power: The Places That Shaped the Tudor World.* London; New York: Bantam Press, 2017.

Townley, Simon, ed. *A History of the County of Oxford.* Vol. 14. Woodbridge: Boydell & Brewer, 2004. http://www.british-history.ac.uk/vch/oxon/vol14/pp68-73 http://www.british-history.ac.uk/vch/oxon/vol14/.

Townley, Simon, ed. *A History of the County of Oxford.* Vol. 16. Woodbridge: Boydell & Brewer, 2011. https://www.british-history.ac.uk/vch/oxon/vol16/.

Townley, Simon, ed. *A History of the County of Oxford.* Vol. 18. Woodbridge: Boydell & Brewer, 2016. https://www.british-history.ac.uk/vch/oxon/vol18/.

Treasure, Geoffrey. *The Huguenots.* New Haven: Yale University Press, 2013.

Tremlett, Giles. *Catherine of Aragon: Henry's Spanish Queen.* London: Faber & Faber, 2010.

Tudor-Craig, Pamela. 'The Painted Chamber at Westminster'. *Archaeological Journal* 114, no. 1 (1957): 92–105.

Turnbull, William Barclay D. D. *Historic Memorials of Coldstream Abbey, Berwickshire, Collected by a Delver in Antiquity,* 1850.

Tytler, Patrick Fraser. *England Under the Reigns of Edward VI and Mary: With the Contemporary History of Europe.* R. Bentley, 1839.

Westminster Abbey. 'Henry VII and Elizabeth of York'. Accessed 20 July 2021. https://www.westminster-abbey.org/abbey-commemorations/royals/henry-vii-and-elizabeth-of-york.

Wadell, John. *Journey Through England*. 1584. Quoted in Montagu H. Cox and G. Topham Forrest, eds. 'The Holbein Gate and the Tiltyard Gallery'. In *Survey of London 14. St Margaret, Westminster, Part III: Whitehall II*. London, 1931.

Wagner, John A., and Susan Walters Schmid. *Encyclopedia of Tudor England*. Santa Barbara: ABC-CLIO, 2012.

Walker, Greg. 'The "Expulsion of the Minions" of 1519 Reconsidered'. *The Historical Journal* 32, no. 1 (1989): 1–16.

———. *The Politics of Performance in Early Renaissance Drama*. Cambridge: Cambridge University Press, 1998.

Wallis, Patrick, and Cliff Webb. 'The Education and Training of Gentry Sons in Early Modern England'. *Social History* 36, no. 1 (2011): 36–53.

Watkins, Sarah-Beth. *Anne of Cleves: Henry VIII's Unwanted Wife*. Winchester: Chronos Books, 2018.

Waymack, Anna. 'Paradoxes, Pibrac and Phalaris: Reading beyond Sidney's Silence on the St Bartholomew's Day Massacre'. *Sidney Journal* 36, no. 2 (2018): 29–49.

Weir, Alison. *Henry VIII: King and Court*. London: Random House, 2011.

Wessex Archaeology. 'Syon House, Syon Park: An Archaeological Evaluation of a Bridgettine Abbey and an Assessment of the Results', October 2003. https://www.wessexarch.co.uk/our-work/syon-house-syon-park.

Westminster Abbey. 'Henry VII and Elizabeth of York'. Accessed 20 July 2021. https://www.westminster-abbey.org/abbey-commemorations/royals/henry-vii-and-elizabeth-of-york.

Whitehead, Barbara. *Women's Education in Early Modern Europe: A History, 1500 to 1800*. New York: Routledge, 1999.

Whitelock, Anna. *Elizabeth's Bedfellows: An Intimate History of the Queen's Court*. London: A&C Black, 2013.

———. *Mary Tudor: England's First Queen*. Bloomsbury Paperbacks, 2010.

Williams, James. 'Hunting and the Royal Image of Henry VIII'. *Sport in History* 25, no. 1 (2005): 41–59.

Williams, Kate. *Rival Queens: The Betrayal of Mary, Queen of Scots*. London: Arrow, 2018.

Williams, Penry. *The Council in the Marches of Wales under Elizabeth I*. Cardiff: University of Wales Press, 1958.

Wilson, Derek. *Sweet Robin: A Biography of Robert Dudley, Earl of Leicester 1533–1588*. London: Allison & Busby, 1981.

———. *The Uncrowned Kings of England: The Black Legend of the Dudleys*. London: Robinson, 2015.

Winfield, Rif. *British Warships in the Age of Sail 1603–1714: Design, Construction, Careers and Fates*. Barnsley: Seaforth Publishing, 2010.

Young, Alan. *Tudor and Jacobean Tournaments*. Dobbs Ferry, NY: Sheridan House, 1987.

Zim, Rivkah. *English Metrical Psalms: Poetry as Praise and Prayer, 1535–1601*. Cambridge: Cambridge University Press, 1987.

Acknowledgements

I started writing this book at a difficult time in my life, and it is coming out during one of the happiest. Just as it is nearly impossible to disentangle myself from the book, so it is difficult to draw the line between those who offered their love and care to me in the last five years from those who read and supported the development of the manuscript. If you are not named in the below, it is because of these blurry boundaries and for lack of space, not for lack of gratitude and love, which are in abundance.

I must begin with those who had most direct influence on the initial conception of the book, as well as who saw it through its final production. My thanks therefore to my agent, Adam Gauntlett, who read an article of mine in BBC History Magazine and wondered if I had a trade book in me. That article would have never existed without some very kind emails sent by Suzannah Lipscomb over a lunch in Bloomsbury, suggesting to editors that I had something to say about Thomas More. Copious thanks are also owed, of course, to my formidable and deeply passionate editor, Jillian Taylor, who has offered such faith in me and this book that I've been quite overwhelmed, in the best possible way. My thanks to everyone at Peters, Fraser and Dunlop and Michael Joseph who have played a part in the production of this book.

I have had so many readers at various stages that I cannot hope to thank them all here, but many are noted in the endnotes to the text. For reading the entire lengthy text in draft I especially thank my very patient copyeditors, readers and indexers, along with Rachel Dempsey, Jaqueline MacLean and Nicola Tallis, the last of whom I must also acknowledge for her unfailing generosity of time and resources. I must thank the students of the 'Voices in the Archives' class, along with their tutor, Bethan Stevens, who helpfully reminded me of the importance of narrative voice. I also asked many people a lot of questions, many of them very silly indeed, and again I cannot list them all for lack of space, but I am extremely grateful for all who generously gave of their time and expertise. For assistance with research, transcription and translation, I am grateful to Courtney Herber, Benjamin MacLean, Katie McKeogh, Janet Pennington and Francis Young. A very early morning chance meeting at the Tower of London gave me one of the most essential elements of this book – its narrative structure – thanks to the wise advice of Dan Jones, who told me to read some books on screenwriting.

I had the good fortune, at least at the outset of this book, to visit many historic sites and archives, many of which are listed in the text and notes, a privilege that became even more apparent when this was no longer available to me. Other archivists and experts corresponded with me via email, and graciously sent information and digitised resources when I could not visit in person. I have also been supported by kind colleagues and inspired by passionate students at the University of Sussex.

I end where I began: I cannot possibly thank everyone who offered me their support and encouragement, largely as this book is already much longer than it was originally supposed to be. It is, nevertheless, worth mentioning those who bore the brunt of it, which brings me to the families of my dedication. I benefit from a makeshift but caring family united by a love for history, who support each other in group chats, Twitter encounters, book clubs and over goblets of gin. I cannot overstate how important this family has been to me and to this book, and I must name (not exhaustively) Helen Carr, Nicola Clark, Lindsey Fitzharris, Greg Jenner, Suzannah Lipscomb, Estelle Paranque, Rebecca Rideal, Hallie Rubenhold, Nicola Tallis and Kate Williams, amongst a host of others. By the time this book comes out, I will (legally) be part a new family, who for many years have already felt like home, and I am grateful to them for taking in a wayward Canadian and cooking her Sunday lunches and listening to her blathering on about history; I'm so honoured to be your sister- and daughter-in-law. Though I am an ocean apart from my own family, I know their love is always with me. They have constantly encouraged my passion for history and writing, which began when my parents read *The Chronicles of Narnia* to me as a child.

My final thanks must go to my kind, generous, loving partner, James Darrall, who by the time this book comes out will be my husband. I can think of nothing that brings me more joy than to build a family with you.

Index

He just wanted a decent book to read ...

Not too much to ask, is it? It was in 1935 when Allen Lane, Managing Director of Bodley Head Publishers, stood on a platform at Exeter railway station looking for something good to read on his journey back to London. His choice was limited to popular magazines and poor-quality paperbacks – the same choice faced every day by the vast majority of readers, few of whom could afford hardbacks. Lane's disappointment and subsequent anger at the range of books generally available led him to found a company – and change the world.

'We believed in the existence in this country of a vast reading public for intelligent books at a low price, and staked everything on it'
Sir Allen Lane, 1902–1970, founder of Penguin Books

The quality paperback had arrived – and not just in bookshops. Lane was adamant that his Penguins should appear in chain stores and tobacconists, and should cost no more than a packet of cigarettes.

Reading habits (and cigarette prices) have changed since 1935, but Penguin still believes in publishing the best books for everybody to enjoy. We still believe that good design costs no more than bad design, and we still believe that quality books published passionately and responsibly make the world a better place.

So wherever you see the little bird – whether it's on a piece of prize-winning literary fiction or a celebrity autobiography, political tour de force or historical masterpiece, a serial-killer thriller, reference book, world classic or a piece of pure escapism – you can bet that it represents the very best that the genre has to offer.

Whatever you like to read – trust Penguin.